KING JAMES
VERSION

NEW REVISED
STANDARD
VERSION

2008 | 2009

Eighty-eighth Edition

TOWNSEND**PRESS** Sunday School

Commentary

Based on the International Lesson Series

An Instructional Aid for Persons Involved in the Ministry of Christian Education

Sunday School Publishing Board
National Baptist Convention, USA, Inc.

Writers: Dr. Geoffrey V. Guns; Dr. Riggins R. Earl, Jr.; Dr. L. Ronald Durham; *Editors:* Dr. Gideon Olaleye; Rev. Michael Woolridge.; *Copy Editors:* Yalemzewd Worku, Tanae McKnight, Lucinda Anderson; *Layout Designer:* Royetta Davis.

ISBN: 1-932972-81-1

CONTENTS

Three-year Cycle v
List of Printed Texts vi
Preface vii
Acknowledgements viii
Know Your Writers ix

Fall Quarter, 2008—*The New Testament Community*

General Introduction 1

September: UNIT I—*The Birth of a New Community*
7 A New Community (Mark 1:1-8; Matthew 3:1-3) 3
14 The Birth of a New Community (Matthew 1:18-25; 2:13-15) 10
21 Core Values of the New Community (Matthew 5:1-16) 17
28 Creating a Community of Servants (Matthew 20:17-28) 24

October: UNIT II—*The Development and Work of the New Community*
5 Empowered to Be a Community (Acts 2:1-17a) 31
12 Expansion of the Community (Acts 6:1-5, 8-15) 38
19 Transformed to Witness to the Community (Acts 9:1-11, 16-19a) 45
26 Commissioned by the Community (Acts 13:1-12) 52

November: UNIT III—*The New Community Faces Growth Pains*
2 Fitting into the Community (Ephesians 4:1-16) 59
9 Conflict in the Community (Galatians 2:11-21) 66
16 Communion with God in the Midst of Struggle (Philippians 3:17-21; 4:1-9) 73
23 Witness of the Community (2 Timothy 2:1-3; 4:1-5) 80
30 Persecution Within the Community (2 Corinthians 11:16-18, 21-30; 12:9-10) 86

Winter Quarter, 2008–2009—*Human Commitment*

General Introduction 93

December: UNIT I—*Commitment to the Messiah*
7 Mary's Commitment (Luke 1:46-55) 95
14 Elizabeth's Commitment (Luke 1:39-45) 102
21 Shepherds Glorify God (Luke 2:8-20) 109
28 John the Baptist Proclaims God's Message (Luke 3:7-18) 116

January: UNIT II—*Old Testament People of Commitment*
4 Midwives Serve God (Exodus 1:8-21) 123
11 Rahab Helps Israel (Joshua 2:1-4, 12-14; 6:22-25) 130
18 Joshua Leads Israel (Joshua 3:1-13) 137
25 Samson's Mother Prepares for His Birth (Judges 13:1-7, 8-13, 24) 144

February: UNIT II—*Old Testament People of Commitment*
1 A Shunammite Woman Helps (2 Kings 4:8-17) 151

8 Nathan Challenges David (2 Samuel 12:1-7, 13-15) 158
15 Esther Risks Her Life (Esther 4:1-3, 9-17) 165
22 Isaiah Answers God's Call (Isaiah 6:1-8) 172

Spring Quarter, 2009—*New Creation in Christ*

General Introduction 179

March: UNIT I—*The Promise of New Life*
1 A New Spirit (Ezekiel 11:14-21) 181
8 New Leadership (Ezekiel 34:23-31) 188
15 God's People Restored Again (Ezekiel 36:22-32) 195
22 Prophesying New Life (Ezekiel 37:1-14) 202
29 Envisioning New Life (Ezekiel 47:1-12) 209

April: UNIT II—*The Path to New Life*
5 Suffering unto Death (Luke 23:32-46) 216
12 Resurrected unto New Life (Luke 24:1-12) 223
19 Witnesses to New Life (Luke 24:44-53) 230
26 Bringing New Life to Those in Need (Acts 9:32-43) 237

May: UNIT III—*The Way of New Life*
3 New Family in Christ (Ephesians 1:3-14) 244
10 New Life in Christ (Ephesians 2:1-10) 250
17 New Revelation in Christ (Ephesians 3:1-13) 256
24 New Life in the Home (Ephesians 5:21-33; 6:1-4) 263
31 Equipped for New Life (Ephesians 6:10-18) 270

Summer Quarter, 2009—*Call Sealed with Promise*

General Introduction 277

June: UNIT I—*Called Out of Egypt*
7 God Calls Moses (Exodus 3:1-12) 279
14 Moses and Aaron Respond (Exodus 4:10-16, 27-31) 286
21 Pharaoh Ignores God's Call (Exodus 5:1-9, 22-23; 6:1) 293
28 God Calls the People Out of Egypt (Exodus 14:15-25, 30) 301

July: UNIT II—*Called to Be God's People*
5 God Calls People to Covenant (Deuteronomy 5:1-9, 11-13, 16-21) 309
12 God Calls People to Remember (Deuteronomy 16:1-8) 317
19 God Calls People to Special Service (Leviticus 8:1-13) 324
26 God Calls People to Jubilee (Leviticus 25:8-21, 23-24) 331

August: UNIT III—*Called to Choose Life*
2 People Grumble (Numbers 11:1-6, 10-15) 339
9 People Rebel (Numbers 14:1-12) 346
16 Moses Disobeys (Numbers 20:1-13) 353
23 God Calls for Obedience (Deuteronomy 6:1-9, 20-24) 361
30 God Calls for Decision (Deuteronomy 30:1-10) 368

CYCLE OF 2007-2010

Arrangement of Quarters According to the Church School Year,
September Through August

	Fall	Winter	Spring	Summer
2007– 2008	God Created a People (Genesis)	God's Call to the Christian Community (Luke)	God, the People, and the Covenant (1 and 2 Chronicles, Daniel, Haggai, Nehemiah)	Images of Christ (Hebrews, Gospels)
	Theme: Creation	Theme: Call	Theme: Covenant	Theme: Christ
2008– 2009	New Testament Survey	Human Commitment (Luke, Old Testament)	Christ and Creation (Ezekiel, Luke, Acts, Ephesians)	Call of God's Covenant Community (Exodus, Leviticus, Numbers, Deuteronomy)
	Theme: Community	Theme: Commitment	Theme: Creation	Theme: Call
2009– 2010	Covenant Communities (Joshua, Judges, Ezra, Nehemiah, Mark, 1 and 2 Peter)	Christ the Fulfillment (Matthew)	Teachings on Community (John, Ruth, New Testament)	Christian Commitment in Today's World (1 and 2 Thessalonians, Philippians)
	Theme: Covenant	Theme: Christ	Theme: Community	Theme: Commitment

LIST OF PRINTED TEXTS—2008-2009

The Printed Scriptural Texts used in the *2008-2009 Townsend Press Sunday School Commentary* are arranged here in the order in which they appear in the Bible. Opposite each reference is the page number on which Scriptures appear in this edition of the *Commentary.*

Reference	Page	Reference	Page
Exodus 1:8-21	123	Matthew 3:1-3	3
Exodus 3:1-12	279	Matthew 5:1-16	17
Exodus 4:10-16, 27-31	286	Matthew 20:17-28	24
Exodus 5:1-9, 22-23	293	Mark 1:1-8	3
Exodus 6:1	294	Luke 1:39-45	102
Exodus 14:15-25, 30	301	Luke 1:46-55	95
Leviticus 8:1-13	324	Luke 2:8-20	109
Leviticus 25:8-21, 23-24	331	Luke 3:7-18	116
Numbers 11:1-6, 10-15	339	Luke 23:32-46	216
Numbers 14:1-12	346	Luke 24:1-12	223
Numbers 20:1-13	353	Luke 24:44-53	230
Deuteronomy 5:1-9, 11-13, 16-21	309	Acts 2:1-17a	31
Deuteronomy 6:1-9, 20-24	361	Acts 6:1-5, 8-15	38
Deuteronomy 16:1-8	317	Acts 9:1-11, 16-19a	45
Deuteronomy 30:1-10	368	Acts 9:32-43	237
Joshua 2:1-4, 12-14	130	Acts 13:1-12	52
Joshua 3:1-13	137	2 Corinthians 11:16-18, 21-30	86
Joshua 6:22-25	130	2 Corinthians 12:9-10	86
Judges 13:1-7, 8-13, 24	144	Galatians 2:11-21	66
2 Samuel 12:1-7, 13-15	158	Ephesians 1:3-14	244
2 Kings 4:8-17	151	Ephesians 2:1-10	250
Esther 4:1-3, 9-17	165	Ephesians 3:1-13	256
Isaiah 6:1-8	172	Ephesians 4:1-16	59
Ezekiel 11:14-21	181	Ephesians 5:21-33	263
Ezekiel 34:23-31	188	Ephesians 6:1-4	263
Ezekiel 36:22-32	195	Ephesians 6:10-18	270
Ezekiel 37:1-14	202	Philippians 3:17-21	73
Ezekiel 47:1-12	209	Philippians 4:1-9	73
Matthew 1:18-25	10	2 Timothy 2:1-3	80
Matthew 2:13-15	10	2 Timothy 4:1-5	80

PREFACE

The *Townsend Press Sunday School Commentary,* based on the International Lesson Series, is a production of the Sunday School Publishing Board, National Baptist Convention, USA, Incorporated. These lessons were developed consistent with the curriculum guidelines of the Committee on the Uniform Series, Education Leadership Ministries Commission, National Council of the Churches of Christ in the United States of America. Selected Christian scholars and theologians—who themselves embrace the precepts, doctrines, and positions on biblical interpretation that we have come to believe—are contributors to this publication. By participating in Scripture selection and the development of the matrices for the Guidelines for Lesson Development with the Committee on the Uniform Series, this presentation reflects the historic faith that we share within a rich heritage of worship and witness.

The format of the *Townsend Press Sunday School Commentary* lessons consists of: the Unit Title, the general subject with age-level topics, Printed Text from the *King James* and the *New Revised Standard Versions* of the Bible, Objectives of the Lesson, Unifying Lesson Principle, Points to Be Emphasized, Topical Outline of the Lesson—with the Biblical Background of the Lesson, Exposition and Application of the Scripture, and Concluding Reflection (designed to focus on the salient points of the lesson), Word Power, and the Home Daily Bible Readings. Each lesson concludes with a prayer.

The *Townsend Press Sunday School Commentary* is designed as an instructional aid for persons involved in the ministry of Christian education. While the autonomy of the individual soul before God is affirmed, we believe that biblical truths find their highest expression within the community of believers whose corporate experiences serve as monitors to preserve the integrity of the Christian faith. As such, the Word of God must not only be understood, but it must also be embodied in the concrete realities of daily life. This serves to allow the Word of God to intersect in a meaningful way with those realities of life.

The presentation of the lessons anticipates the fact that some concepts and Scripture references do not lend themselves to meaningful comprehension by children. Hence, when this occurs, alternative passages of Scripture are used, along with appropriate content emphases, that are designed to assist children in their spiritual growth. There will, however, remain a consistent connection between the children, youth, and adult lessons through the Unifying Principle developed for each session.

We stand firm in our commitment to Christian growth, to the end that lives will become transformed through personal and group interaction with the Word of God. The challenge issued by the apostle Paul continues to find relevance for our faith journey: "Do your best to present yourself to God as one approved by him, a worker who has no need to be ashamed, rightly explaining the word of truth" (2 Timothy 2:15, NRSV). May we all commit ourselves to the affirmation expressed by the psalmist, "Your word is a lamp to my feet and a light to my path" (Psalm 119:105).

ACKNOWLEDGEMENTS

The *Townsend Press Sunday School Commentary* is recognized as the centerpiece of a family of church school literature designed especially to assist teachers in their presentation of the lessons as well as to broaden the knowledge base of students from the biblical perspective. Our mission has been and will always be to provide religious educational experiences and spiritual resources for our constituency throughout this nation as well as many foreign countries. To achieve this end, the collaborative efforts of many people provide the needed expertise in the various areas of the production process. Although under the employ of the Sunday School Publishing Board, personnel too numerous to list approach their respective tasks with the dedication and devotion of those who serve God by serving His people. This *Commentary* is presented with gratitude to God for all those who desire a more comprehensive treatment of the selected Scriptures than is provided in the church school quarterlies, and it is intended to be a complementary resource thereto.

We acknowledge the new Executive Director of the Sunday School Publishing Board in the person of Dr. Kelly M. Smith, Jr., who has given a charge to the publishing family to focus on QTC—Quality, Timeliness, and Customer care—in our interaction with our constituency. Special appreciation is appropriately accorded to Dr. Smith, for his continued insightful and inspiring leadership and motivation. While Dr. Smith's tenure at the Sunday School Publishing Board has been brief, the SSPB continues to prosper. It continues as the publisher and printer for the National Baptist Convention, USA, Inc. and its constituent components. There is a greater emphasis on addressing issues germane to the local, national, and international communities, utilizing the latest technologies to promote and distribute our materials—and doing all this based on Christian principles for the advancement of the kingdom of Jesus Christ.

The Sunday School Publishing Board consists of employees with expertise in their assigned areas whose self-understanding is that of "workers together with God," and partners with those who labor in the vineyard of teaching the Word of God in order to make disciples and nurture others toward a mature faith.

Our gratitude is hereby expressed to Dr. Geoffrey V. Guns, expositor for the Fall Quarter, to Dr. Riggins R. Earl, Jr., expositor for the Winter Quarter, and to Dr. L. Ronald Durham, expositor for the Spring and Summer Quarters—for their devotion in the development of the respective lessons. These three writers bring diversity and a broad spectrum of ministerial and educational experience to bear on the exposition and application of the Scripture.

Appreciation is also expressed to Mrs. Kathy Pillow, Associate Director, and Dr. Sherman Tribble, Director of Publishing, for their ongoing leadership. It is a credit to their leadership that the employees have embraced the mission of the Sunday School Publishing Board with a self-perspective that enhances their personal commitment to the cause of Christ as they interact with one another and intersect with the greater community of faith.

The task in which we are all involved would be meaningless and fruitless were it not for the many readers for whom this publication has been so diligently prepared. The faithfulness of our constituency has been enduring for over a century, and we consider ourselves blessed to be their servants in the ministry of the printed Word exalting the living Word, our Lord and Savior Jesus Christ. We pray that God's grace will complement our efforts so that lives will be transformed within and beyond the confines of classroom interaction as the Spirit of God manifests Himself through the intersection of teaching and learning. It is our prayer that God may grant each of us the power to live for Him and be witnesses to the saving grace of the One who died for us, even Jesus Christ, our Lord and Savior.

Wellington A. Johnson, Sr.
Managing Editor

Dr. Geoffrey V. Guns ▼
Fall Quarter

Dr. Geoffrey V. Guns is a native of Newport, Rhode Island. He is the son of a retired Baptist pastor and co-pastor. Dr. Guns received his elementary and secondary education in the Norfolk public school system. He earned his B.S. degree in Business Administration from Norfolk State University in 1972.

In 1981, he earned his Master of Divinity degree from the School of Theology, Virginia Union University, graduating *summa cum laude.* He earned his Doctor of Ministry degree from the School of Religion, Howard University in Washington, D.C. in 1985.

Dr. Guns is the senior pastor of the Second Calvary Baptist Church in Norfolk, Virginia, where he has served for the past twenty-three years. He is active in his denomination, the National Baptist Convention, USA, Inc. Dr. Guns served as the president of the Virginia Baptist State Convention (VBSC) from 1997 to 2001 and is currently the moderator for the Tidewater Peninsula Baptist Association (TPBA).

He has written articles for the *Christian Education Informer* of the Department of Christian Education of the Sunday School Publishing Board. Dr. Guns also serves as vice chairman of the Council of Christian Education for the Department of Christian Education of the Sunday School Publishing Board of the NBC. He works with the Home Mission Board of the NBC and serves as the regional representative for the Southeast region.

Dr. Guns is the author of two books: *Church Financial Management* (1997), which is published by Providence House Publishers; and *Spiritual Leadership: A Practical Guide to Developing Spiritual Leaders in the Church* (2000), published by Orman Press, Inc.

He is married to the former Rosetta Harding of Richmond, Virginia. Mrs. Guns is a licensed social worker and works as a school social worker for the City of Chesapeake public schools. They are the parents of two daughters, Kimberly Michelle Cummings and Nicole Patrice. Dr. and Mrs. Guns have one granddaughter, Kennedy Nicole Cummings.

Dr. Riggins R. Earl, Jr. ▼
Winter Quarter

Dr. Riggins R. Earl, Jr. is a professor of Ethics and Theology at the Interdenominational Theological Center of the Atlanta University Center. He holds the Ph.D. degree from Vanderbilt University in Social Ethics. He has done post-doctoral studies at Harvard and Boston universities respectively. Dr. Earl has done research at the London Institute for African Studies.

Besides his numerous articles in print, Dr. Earl has published two major volumes on the subject of black religion and ethics: *Dark Symbols, Obscure Signs: God, Self, and Community in the Slave Mind* in 1993; *Dark Salutations: Greetings, Ritual, and God in Black America* in 2001. Dr. Earl's work has earned him several national research awards, such as the Lilly Professor Research Fellowship for the academic year 2001-2002 (sponsored through the American Theological Association).

Dr. Earl is actively involved in building bridges of communication with African leaders of churches and universities on such troublesome issues as slavery, genocide, and AIDS. Dr. Earl's major concern is that of encouraging black church leadership in America about the urgent need of being directly involved in critical ways with the leadership of Africa. He thinks that the need for working out an ethics of communication between black leaders of Africa and America must take top priority.

Dr. Earl is a versatile speaker who is in great demand nationally by the academy, the church, and civic groups. An ordained member of the Christian clergy, Dr. Earl knows how to communicate about the contemporary issues of religion and culture in both the popular vernacular of the masses as well as the formal speech of academia.

Dr. Riggins Earl is the proud father of two sons and one daughter, and the grandfather of two grandsons.

Dr. L. Ronald Durham ▼
Spring and Summer Quarters

Dr. L. Ronald Durham is the senior pastor of Greater Friendship Missionary Baptist Church in Daytona Beach, Florida. He has served as the moderator of the North Jersey District Missionary Baptist Association. Dr. Durham has been a teacher for our National Baptist Congress of Christian Education for over fifteen years. He is the president of the Daytona Beach Black Clergy Alliance and sits on the Halifax Hospital Board of Associates, the Daytona Beach Mayor's Kitchen Cabinet, and the Bethune Cookman University Board of Counselors.

Dr. L. Ronald Durham began his ministry at the age of sixteen, was licensed by Rev. T. H. Alexander of Union Baptist Church in Passaic, New Jersey, and was accepted on full scholarship to Shaw University in Raleigh, North Carolina. He completed his graduate and doctoral work at Evangel Christian University in Monroe, Louisiana and holds an honorary Doctor of Divinity degree from Bethune Cookman University in Daytona Beach, Florida.

Dr. Durham pastored First Baptist Church of Anderson, New Jersey for sixteen years and First Mt. Zion Baptist Church for eleven years, and is presently the pastor of Greater Friendship Baptist Church of Daytona Beach, Florida.

Dr. Durham is a prolific writer, a published author, and a teacher for the National Baptist Congress of Christian Education, USA, Inc. He published *The Secret Power of Prayer*, a guidebook for understanding the power of sincere prayer. He is also a writer for the Sunday School Publishing Board—having written the *Baptist Layman* for five years. He has served as one of the writers for the *Townsend Press Sunday School Commentary* and also as one of the writers of the *Baptist Teacher*. Additionally, he has contributed numerous articles for the *The Christian Education Informer*. Dr. Durham is the founder of <u>Blacksermons.com</u>, the premier online ministry for pastors around the world.

The New Testament Community

GENERAL INTRODUCTION

During the fall quarter, we will survey the New Testament. Our general theme for the quarter challenges us to see the New Testament through the lens of community.

We begin our study by first looking at the four gospels and the birth of a new community; then, we move to an exploration of the development and work of this new community with a study of the book of Acts; and we conclude with the growing pains the new community experienced through conflict, struggle, and persecution as described in the epistles.

Unit I, *The Birth of a New Community,* is an exploration (in four lessons) of the beginnings of the Christian community. The first lesson is an examination of John the Baptist as the forerunner to Jesus. John preached a message that hinted at the core values of the new community. The lessons continue with Jesus and His pioneering of the Christian community. We discuss the core values and teachings of this new community and conclude with a focus on a community of servants.

Unit II, *The Development and Work of the New Community,* is a continued exploration of the work and ministry of this new community through four lessons. The study sheds light on the empowerment of the Christian community, the expansion of this community, some key witnesses in the community, and their commission for ministry.

Unit III, *The New Community Faces Growth Pains,* is a focus on the early struggles of the Christian community. This unit has five lessons and deals with the work of the Christian community and the hurdles it faced in its ministry. This study is an exploration of how the community members were equipped for ministry, how they handled conflict, their witness in the world, and the persecution they faced because of their witness.

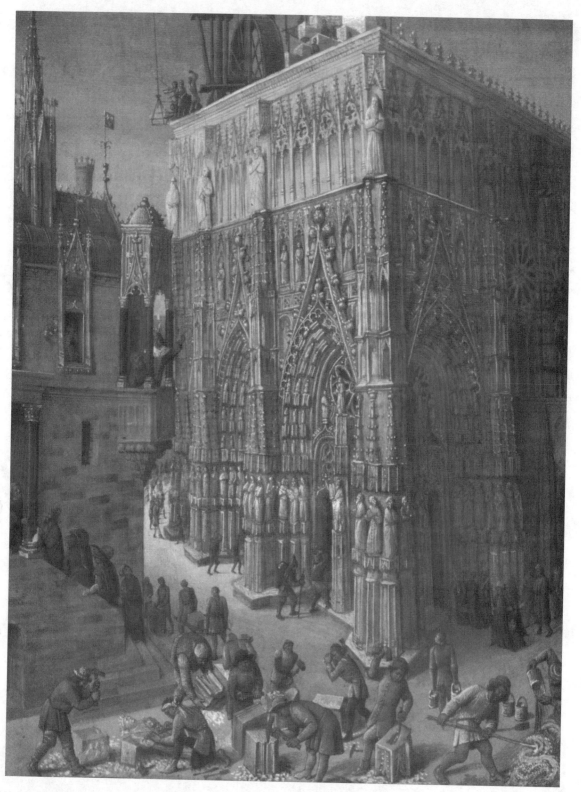

LESSON 1   September 7, 2008

A NEW COMMUNITY

DEVOTIONAL READING: **1 Peter 2:1-10**
PRINT PASSAGE: **Mark 1:1-8; Matthew 3:1-3**
KEY VERSE: **Matthew 3:2**

BACKGROUND SCRIPTURE: **Mark 1:1-8; Matthew 3:1-12**

Mark 1:1-8; Matthew 3:1-3—KJV

THE BEGINNING of the gospel of Jesus Christ, the Son of God;

2 As it is written in the prophets, Behold, I send my messenger before thy face, which shall prepare thy way before thee.

3 The voice of one crying in the wilderness, Prepare ye the way of the Lord, make his paths straight.

4 John did baptize in the wilderness, and preach the baptism of repentance for the remission of sins.

5 And there went out unto him all the land of Judaea, and they of Jerusalem, and were all baptized of him in the river of Jordan, confessing their sins.

6 And John was clothed with camel's hair, and with a girdle of a skin about his loins; and he did eat locusts and wild honey;

7 And preached, saying, There cometh one mightier than I after me, the latchet of whose shoes I am not worthy to stoop down and unloose.

8 I indeed have baptized you with water: but he shall baptize you with the Holy Ghost.

. . . . .

IN THOSE days came John the Baptist, preaching in the wilderness of Judaea,

2 And saying, Repent ye: for the kingdom of heaven is at hand.

3 For this is he that was spoken of by the prophet Esaias, saying, The voice of one crying in the wilderness, Prepare ye the way of the Lord, make his paths straight.

Mark 1:1-8; Matthew 3:1-3—NRSV

THE BEGINNING of the good news of Jesus Christ, the Son of God.

2 As it is written in the prophet Isaiah, "See, I am sending my messenger ahead of you, who will prepare your way;

3 the voice of one crying out in the wilderness: 'Prepare the way of the Lord, make his paths straight,'"

4 John the baptizer appeared in the wilderness, proclaiming a baptism of repentance for the forgiveness of sins.

5 And people from the whole Judean countryside and all the people of Jerusalem were going out to him, and were baptized by him in the river Jordan, confessing their sins.

6 Now John was clothed with camel's hair, with a leather belt around his waist, and he ate locusts and wild honey.

7 He proclaimed, "The one who is more powerful than I is coming after me; I am not worthy to stoop down and untie the thong of his sandals.

8 I have baptized you with water; but he will baptize you with the Holy Spirit."

. . . . .

IN THOSE days John the Baptist appeared in the wilderness of Judea, proclaiming,

2 "Repent, for the kingdom of heaven has come near."

3 This is the one of whom the prophet Isaiah spoke when he said, "The voice of one crying out in the wilderness: 'Prepare the way of the Lord, make his paths straight.'"

BIBLE FACT

There was a period when no prophet prophesied called "the inter-testamental period," after which John the Baptist appeared on the scene to announce the coming of the Messiah—the Son of God.

UNIFYING LESSON PRINCIPLE

People look for a place where they can belong. What kind of community fosters a sense of belonging? The new community, about which John talked, to which Jesus called people was a community of love, acceptance, repentance, and forgiveness.

TOPICAL OUTLINE OF THE LESSON

I. Introduction
  A. The Biblical Concept of Community
  B. Biblical Background

II. Exposition and Application of the Scripture
  A. The Beginning of the Gospel (Mark 1:1)
  B. The Fulfillment of Prophecy (Mark 1:2-3; Matthew 3:2-3)
  C. The Ministry of John in the Wilderness (Mark 1:4-5; Matthew 3:1)
  D. The Preaching of John About Jesus Christ (Mark 1:6-8)

III. Concluding Reflection

LESSON OBJECTIVES

Upon completion of this lesson, the students will know that:

1. Mark gave an accurate and dependable account of Jesus' actions and achievements;
2. The prophecies about Jesus were fulfilled without any shadow of doubt; and,
3. John the Baptist was truly a humble forerunner of Jesus.

POINTS TO BE EMPHASIZED

ADULT/YOUTH

Adult Topic: Repentance Leads to Community
Youth Topic: Turn Around Now!
Adult Key Verse: Matthew 3:2
Youth Key Verse: Mark 1:5
Print Passage: Mark 1:1-8; Matthew 3:1-3

—Mark's prologue includes four major parts: the preaching of John, the baptism of Jesus, the temptation of Jesus, and the Gospel Jesus preached.
—The baptism of Jesus indicates the importance of baptism in the life of the faith community.
—According to Matthew and Mark, John the Baptist not only announced Jesus' coming but also prepared his listeners for the "baptism with the Holy Spirit."
—John the Baptist echoes the message of hope, forgiveness, and healing for the nation Isaiah prophesied hundreds of years earlier (Isaiah 40).
—John's baptism of "repentance" was part of his ministry to prepare the people for the coming of the Lord.
—John proclaimed that repentance was essential for the forgiveness of sins.

CHILDREN

Children Topic: Preparing for the New Community
Key Verses: Matthew 3:5-6
Print Passage: Matthew 3:1-8, 11

—Similar to the prophet Isaiah, John the Baptist urged the people to prepare for the coming Kingdom.
—John preached that the first step in becoming citizens of the kingdom of heaven is to repent of one's sins.
—Neither our heritage, gender, status, nor class will qualify us for membership in God's kingdom.
—John baptized repentant sinners with water, but Jesus would baptize them with the Holy Spirit.
—Repentant sinners who are baptized by the Holy Spirit will belong to the new community.

I. INTRODUCTION

A. The Biblical Concept of Community

In today's lesson we are introduced to the theological concept of "community." The early Hebrews and Christians thought of themselves as one interrelated people who were bound to God and each other by covenant (see Exodus 19:1-7; 24:7). What is a community? First, we think of community as the place where we live. Second, we may think of *community* as a group of people who share a common interest or profession—for example, the medical community or social-work community. Third, we think of community as a group of people who share a common belief system. Christians form a single community of faith, regardless of where they live in the world. This global community of faith crosses all geographical and ethnic backgrounds.

While visiting Israel, a modern group gathered in the place that is venerated as the Upper Room where Jesus instituted the Lord's Supper. After praying and sharing from the Scriptures, the group began to sing "Blessed Assurance." There was another group from the African nation of Cameroon that joined in with the first group, singing in their native tongue. At that very moment they were a single community of faith, rejoicing together over the greatness of God.

B. Biblical Background

The gospel of Mark is the earliest of the three Synoptic Gospels. The word *Synoptic* means "to see with the same or similar eye." The books of Matthew, Mark, and Luke are the Synoptic Gospels. Mark's gospel was written some time around A.D. 70 by John Mark, who was a companion of Paul and Barnabas during their first missionary journey (Acts 12:5; 13:5, 13; 15:36-39). The Holy Spirit used each of the Gospel writers to record a specific aspect of the ministry of Jesus Christ. Mark presented Jesus as the personification of the power of God on the earth. He performed many mighty miracles and turned the hearts of the people from darkness to light.

The first fifteen verses are the prologue of Mark's gospel—and it consists of four major parts: the preaching of John, the baptism of Jesus, the temptation of Jesus, and the Gospel Jesus preached. Baptism is an important part of the Christian community because it identifies all Christians with Jesus Christ.

John the Baptist was the forerunner of the Messiah. His ministry had been foretold by the prophet Isaiah hundreds of years before his birth. He came to prepare the way of the Lord by preaching a message of repentance and the need to return to God. Both Jesus and John preached a message that revolved around the need for repentance as the means by which one would be included into the new community of faith.

II. EXPOSITION AND APPLICATION OF THE SCRIPTURE

A. The Beginning of the Gospel
(Mark 1:1)

THE BEGINNING of the gospel of Jesus Christ, the Son of God.

The writers of the four gospels were used by the Holy Spirit to fulfill a unique purpose by recording their accounts of the life and ministry of Jesus Christ. Each of them wrote for a particular Christian community when they wrote their individual gospels. They all wrote to highlight a unique theological point of view.

Matthew made the connection between Jesus and the historical Hebrew and Jewish faiths (see Matthew 1:1-17). He made it known that Jesus was a descendant of Abraham (see Genesis 12:1-4).

Luke connected Jesus to God's plan for saving the whole world. Luke pointed out how he had thoroughly researched all of the pertinent information about Jesus from credible witnesses and recorded it for Theophilus (see Luke 1:1-4).

John painted a lofty picture of Jesus as God who became a human being to redeem the world from sin and death (see John 1:14; 2 Corinthians 8:9).

The opening verse of the gospel of Mark reveals a great deal of insight into his purpose. The prologue to Mark is a focus on three primary reasons for his writing. First, Mark wanted it known that his writing was the message of God about His Son Jesus Christ. It was the "beginning" of the Gospel, and what would follow in the writing was the unfolding drama of God's defeat of the demonic powers of darkness. Second, Mark wanted to provide written details about the plan and purpose of God to save the world from sin and eternal damnation.

The revelation of this salvation was brought to pass in the life, crucifixion, resurrection, and ascension of Jesus Christ (see Acts 2:16-24). The good news is that in Jesus we see the power of God that is able to save (see Romans 1:16-17). Third, Mark wrote to prove that Jesus Christ is the Son of God. The title "Son of God" was an important theological theme for Mark. He began with the title and we see the title used at the end of Jesus' ministry by the Roman centurion during the Crucifixion (see Mark 15:39).

Mark's gospel was not intended to be a day-by-day historical record of everything that Jesus did and taught. It was a written reflection of the oral tradition that included the accounts of miracles and confrontations with Jewish authorities and demons—and it eventually culminated with the passion of Jesus Christ. It is this story that Christians everywhere are called upon to share with the unbelievers (see Matthew 28:19-20; Acts 1:5-8).

B. The Fulfillment of Prophecy
(Mark 1:2-3; Matthew 3:2-3)

As it is written in the prophets, Behold, I send my messenger before thy face, which shall prepare thy way before thee. The voice of one crying in the wilderness, Prepare ye the way of the Lord, make his paths straight.....And saying, Repent ye: for the kingdom of heaven is at hand. For this is he that was spoken of by the prophet Esaias, saying, The voice of one crying in the wilderness, Prepare ye the way of the Lord, make his paths straight.

Mark quoted two of Israel's most revered prophets—Malachi and Isaiah. The combined quotes come from the Post-Exilic (ca. 523-400 B.C.) prophetic period when the Jews were returning from Babylonian captivity. The first quote comes from Malachi, who was the last of the Old Testament prophetic voices. During the days of his preaching, the Jews who returned from exile in Babylon rebuilt the Temple (Ezra 1-4) and the walls around Jerusalem (Nehemiah 1-6). However, the spiritual life of the nation went into serious free fall and God raised up a prophet to speak to the hearts of the people to prepare them for the "day of the Lord" (Malachi 4:5). The "day of the Lord" was used by the prophets to refer to a time when God would intervene in the affairs of Israel or the world to bring about His salvation.

The second quote comes from Isaiah 40:3, in which is spoken words of comfort and is provided reassurance to the Jews returning from Babylon that God had forgiven them of their rebellion and unfaithfulness (see Isaiah 40:1-2). This is one of many references to Isaiah in the New Testament. The prophet Isaiah is quoted in the New Testament more than any other Old Testament-era prophet.

Mark wrote in such a fashion that his words demanded an immediate response. The Gospel summoned men and women to get ready to receive the Messiah of God. "Behold" is a word that says, "Stop what you are doing; look and listen to what I am about to say." God is sending a messenger who will prepare the way for the coming of the Lord. The sole purpose of the messenger was to lay the groundwork and make ready the hearts and spirits of the people to receive the message of salvation. The messenger would come forth as a "voice crying in the wilderness." The word for *crying* literally means "to speak with a strong voice." The messenger was John the Baptist who preached in the Judean Wilderness, calling the nation of Judah to repentance by turning away from their sins and turning back to God. John's purpose was to pave the way for the preaching and teaching of Jesus Christ.

The place where John the Baptist preached was a lonely, solitary place. The wilderness was in the Jordan River valley not far from the ancient city of Jericho. This area is extremely dry and arid. There was very little wildlife or human life in the area. Why would John spend time alone away from civilization? Several reasons have been given. First, John spent time alone so that he could hear God's voice more clearly without outside distractions. Second, John did this to fulfill Old Testament prophecies that said he would be "The voice of him that crieth in the wilderness" (Isaiah 40:3).

There are periods in the life of every believer when one must retreat to a solitary place to hear the voice of God. Just think for a moment how deep and more intense your walk with the Savior would be if you were to immerse yourself in God's Word. When we retreat to the inner closet, God is able to sow in our hearts and minds the deeper revelations of His truths that propel us to new heights of mission and service.

C. The Ministry of John in the Wilderness (Mark 1:4-5; Matthew 3:1)

John did baptize in the wilderness, and preach the baptism of repentance for the remission of sins. And there went out unto him all the land of Judaea, and they of Jerusalem, and were all baptized of him in the river of Jordan, confessing their sins.....IN THOSE days came John the Baptist, preaching in the wilderness of Judaea.

The preaching ministry of John the Baptist sparked a national religious revival. During the days of John's ministry there was an aura of expectation concerning the coming of the Jewish Messiah. John's ministry laid the foundation for the culmination of the period of waiting. The coming of the Messiah would mark the beginning of the last days when God's Spirit would be poured out upon all flesh (see Joel

2:28-32). The preaching of John drew crowds that cut across every economic and political boundary. People came from across Judea to hear his message and to be baptized by him in the Jordan River (see Matthew 3:4-6).

Revivals today are more like calendar events versus being a time of serious religious renewal and spiritual cleansing. They have become a time in the life of most congregations when we call for the preacher with the greatest reputation and name to come and fill the church house so that we can say we had a "great revival." However, Spirit-filled preaching ought to bring about serious change in the life of the people of God.

The ministry of John consisted of two things: baptizing and preaching. The Greek word *baptize* means "to dip or immerse in water for the purpose making clean"; it is an outward sign of an inward change (see Romans 6:1-12). Mark used language that suggests that when the people started to come to be baptized they kept coming from across the region. People were turning away from their sins and seeking God for forgiveness and healing. What was the meaning of John's baptism? And where did he pick up this ritual? First, John may have acquired this rite from the members of the Qumran community. These were a group of very devout Jews who lived in the Jordan River valley near the Dead Sea in a place called Qumran. These deeply devout Jews separated themselves from Jerusalem and the Temple religion. Second, some scholars think John may have been a part of the sect and therefore he gained insight from them and then adapted it to his purposes. Third, others believe that John may have gotten this idea from the ritual baths of the ancient Old Testament priests who would cleanse themselves prior to engaging in Temple activities.

John's baptism was an outward symbol of change and the washing away of the sins of the former life (see Ephesians 4:22-24). Christian baptism is the point of entry and inclusion into the body of Christ (see Acts 2:38, 41). Baptism does not save us. Instead, it points to something spiritually dynamic having taken place within the heart of a man or woman.

D. The Preaching of John About Jesus Christ (Mark 1:6-8)

And John was clothed with camel's hair, and with a girdle of a skin about his loins; and he did eat locusts and wild honey; And preached, saying, There cometh one mightier than I after me, the latchet of whose shoes I am not worthy to stoop down and unloose. I indeed have baptized you with water: but he shall baptize you with the Holy Ghost.

John looked, acted, and lived like a prophet. His garments were the traditional clothes worn by prophets (see Zechariah 13:4). His clothes were made of camel's hair and he wore a leather belt. There was nothing extravagant about his attire or residence. He ate locusts and wild honey (Leviticus 11:21-22). John was humble.

John preached that Jesus was the one coming after him who was so much mightier that he was not even worthy to stoop down and untie His shoes. The baptism of Jesus was a baptism with the fire of the Holy Spirit. Fire symbolizes purification. The Holy Spirit's baptism would purify the hearts and minds of the people, making them fit to be partners with God.

The teachings about the baptism of the Holy Spirit have not been without deep theological controversy in the body of Christ. Some believe that the Holy Spirit's baptism is an experience of God's grace that comes about after conversion and that is evidenced by speaking in tongues with greater spiritual awareness and discernment. Those who hold this position believe that one must diligently seek this experience of grace. Then there are Christians who hold an opposing perspective. As Baptists, we believe that the Holy Spirit baptizes us into the body of Christ, giving each of us gifts for ministry (see Romans 12:3-8; 1 Corinthians 12:4-11; 1 Peter 4:10-11).

III. CONCLUDING REFLECTION

From this session we learned several important lessons. First, the Gospel is the message of Jesus Christ. It is Good News to the lost and downtrodden. Second, God's plan for the salvation of the world was a deliberate and intentional plan that was announced by the ancient Hebrew prophets hundreds of years before it came to pass. Third, Christians are all called to a ministry of preparation. We are sent to prepare the world for the coming of Jesus Christ. John prepared men and women for the first coming; we are tasked to prepare them for the Second Coming.

PRAYER

Heavenly Father, we confess our sins repenting of every evil deed, idle word, and failure in our service to You. Forgive us of the things that we have done that have brought shame to Your name and grant us Thy peace. In Jesus' name we pray. Amen.

WORD POWER

Repent *(metanoeite [me-ta-no-ei-te])*—the word *repent,* as we have it in our Bible, means "to be sorry again." There is no English word that reproduces exactly the meaning of repentance as it is used in Greek. The Greek word for "sorry" is *metamelomai,* where we get our English word *repent.* This is used to describe Judas's behavior when he had sold Christ. John used the word *metanoeite,* which means "to change mental attitude, a change of one's conduct, or a virtuous alteration of the mind."

HOME DAILY BIBLE READINGS
(September 1-7, 2008)

A New Community

MONDAY, September 1: "God's Coming Messenger" (Malachi 3:1-5)

TUESDAY, September 2: "Preparing the Way" (Isaiah 40:1-5)

WEDNESDAY, September 3: "A Voice Crying Out" (Isaiah 40:6-11)

THURSDAY, September 4: "Proclaiming Good News" (Matthew 3:4-10)

FRIDAY, September 5: "Pointing to Christ" (Matthew 3:11-19)

SATURDAY, September 6: "You Are God's People" (1 Peter 2:1-10)

SUNDAY, September 7: "John Prepares the Way" (Mark 1:1-8; Matthew 3:1-3)

LESSON 2   September 14, 2008

THE BIRTH OF A NEW COMMUNITY

DEVOTIONAL READING: **Hosea 11:1-4**
PRINT PASSAGE: **Matthew 1:18-25; 2:13-15**

BACKGROUND SCRIPTURE: **Matthew 1:18–2:23**
KEY VERSE: **Matthew 2:6**

Matthew 1:18-25; 2:13-15—KJV

18 Now the birth of Jesus Christ was on this wise: When as his mother Mary was espoused to Joseph, before they came together, she was found with child of the Holy Ghost.

19 Then Joseph her husband, being a just man, and not willing to make her a publick example, was minded to put her away privily.

20 But while he thought on these things, behold, the angel of the Lord appeared unto him in a dream, saying, Joseph, thou son of David, fear not to take unto thee Mary thy wife: for that which is conceived in her is of the Holy Ghost.

21 And she shall bring forth a son, and thou shalt call his name Jesus: for he shall save his people from their sins.

22 Now all this was done, that it might be fulfilled which was spoken of the Lord by the prophet, saying,

23 Behold, a virgin shall be with child, and shall bring forth a son, and they shall call his name Emmanuel, which being interpreted is, God with us.

24 Then Joseph being raised from sleep did as the angel of the Lord had bidden him, and took unto him his wife:

25 And knew her not till she had brought forth her firstborn son: and he called his name Jesus.

.....

13 And when they were departed, behold, the angel of the Lord appeareth to Joseph in a dream, saying, Arise, and take the young child and his mother, and flee into Egypt, and be thou there until I bring thee word: for Herod will seek the young child to destroy him.

14 When he arose, he took the young child and his mother by night, and departed into Egypt:

15 And was there until the death of Herod: that it might be fulfilled which was spoken of the Lord by the prophet, saying, Out of Egypt have I called my son.

Matthew 1:18-25; 2:13-15—NRSV

18 Now the birth of Jesus the Messiah took place in this way. When his mother Mary had been engaged to Joseph, but before they lived together, she was found to be with child from the Holy Spirit.

19 Her husband Joseph, being a righteous man and unwilling to expose her to public disgrace, planned to dismiss her quietly.

20 But just when he had resolved to do this, an angel of the Lord appeared to him in a dream and said, "Joseph, son of David, do not be afraid to take Mary as your wife, for the child conceived in her is from the Holy Spirit.

21 She will bear a son, and you are to name him Jesus, for he will save his people from their sins."

22 All this took place to fulfill what had been spoken by the Lord through the prophet:

23 "Look, the virgin shall conceive and bear a son, and they shall name him Emmanuel," which means, "God is with us."

24 When Joseph awoke from sleep, he did as the angel of the Lord commanded him; he took her as his wife,

25 but had no marital relations with her until she had borne a son; and he named him Jesus.

.....

13 Now after they had left, an angel of the Lord appeared to Joseph in a dream and said, "Get up, take the child and his mother, and flee to Egypt, and remain there until I tell you; for Herod is about to search for the child, to destroy him."

14 Then Joseph got up, took the child and his mother by night, and went to Egypt,

15 and remained there until the death of Herod. This was to fulfill what had been spoken by the Lord through the prophet, "Out of Egypt I have called my son."

UNIFYING LESSON PRINCIPLE

Regardless of the nature of our humble beginnings, we want to know that life has significance and value. What community offers value and significance to those who, in the world's eyes, may seem insignificant? The new community, as exemplified in Jesus, provides a place where all people have value and significance.

TOPICAL OUTLINE OF THE LESSON

I. Introduction
A. Early Beginnings
B. Biblical Background

II. Exposition and Application of the Scripture
A. The Miraculous Conception and Joseph's Dilemma (Matthew 1:18-21)
B. God's Messenger of Hope (Matthew 1:22-25)
C. The Warning and Flight to Egypt (Matthew 2:13-15)

III. Concluding Reflection

LESSON OBJECTIVES

Upon completion of this lesson, the students will know that:

1. The miraculous conception of Jesus is good news to the world;
2. God used and is still using angels to send hope to His people; and,
3. The life of Jesus was threatened when He was an infant.

POINTS TO BE EMPHASIZED

ADULT/YOUTH

Adult Topic: A Humble Beginning

Youth Topic: From Christ to Christianity

Adult Key Verse: Matthew 2:6

Youth Key Verse: Matthew 1:21

Print Passage: Matthew 1:18-25; 2:13-15

—Matthew emphasized that Joseph's role in the story has to do with his Davidic descent. He also reminds us that the miraculous conception announced to Joseph has to do with Jesus' messiahship.

—The name *Jesus* is the Greek rendering for the Hebrew name "Joshua," a derivative of the verb meaning "to save."

—The theme of Emmanuel ("God with us") is central to Matthew's entire Gospel.

—Christians view the conception and birth of Jesus as the fulfillment of the hope for the Messiah.

—Joseph experienced conflict and doubts but sought to be faithful to God.

—Joseph accepted the angel's assurance of Mary's faithfulness and that Jesus' birth was part of the divine plan for God's people.

CHILDREN

Children Topic: A New Community Is Born

Key Verses: Luke 4:14, 15

Print Passage: Luke 3:21-23; 4:1-9, 12-15

—The baptism of Jesus was the first public declaration of His ministry.

—As Jesus prayed, the Holy Spirit descended on Him and a voice from heaven confirmed that Jesus was the beloved Son of God.

—Jesus was thought to be the son of Joseph; His human background was humble.

—Jesus, armed with the Word of God, faced temptation.

—Jesus used the Word of God to successfully defeat all of Satan's attempts to get Him to disobey God.

—Jesus returned to Galilee in the power of the Spirit and began teaching in the synagogues.

I. INTRODUCTION

A. Early Beginnings

John H. Johnson has been called the "most influential African-American publisher in American history." He was born on January 19, 1918 to Leroy and Gertrude Johnson in Arkansas City, Arkansas. When he graduated from the University of Chicago in 1942, he took out a $500 loan on his mother's furniture and raised another $6,000 through charter subscriptions and began publishing *Negro Digest,* which later became *Black World.* Three years later he began publishing *Ebony Magazine.* He went on to create *Jet Magazine,* and founded Fashion Fair Cosmetics and Supreme Beauty Products.

In this lesson, we see the start of another empire that has spanned nearly two thousand years and has millions of followers. This is not a financial or industrial empire, but a spiritual kingdom which has God as its Supreme Head and salvation of the world as its ultimate aim.

B. Biblical Background

Today's lesson is Matthew's account of the early beginnings of Jesus' earthly life. Of the four canonical gospels, only Luke and Matthew have birth narratives. These authors had different theological perspectives about the birth of Jesus. Luke emphasized the birth of Jesus from the perspective of Mary's family, while Matthew presented us Joseph's perspective. Luke stressed that the birth of Jesus was a part of the plan of God to save the entire world, beginning with Adam (see Luke 3:23-38). Matthew showed us who Jesus Christ was in relation to His Hebrew roots. In verses 1-17, Matthew laid out the Hebrew genealogy of Jesus beginning with Abraham and concluding with Joseph in verse 16. Jesus was son and heir of both Abraham and King David (see Matthew 1:1).

II. EXPOSITION AND APPLICATION OF THE SCRIPTURE

A. The Miraculous Conception and Joseph's Dilemma (Matthew 1:18-21)

Now the birth of Jesus Christ was on this wise: When as his mother Mary was espoused to Joseph, before they came together, she was found with child of the Holy Ghost. Then Joseph her husband, being a just man, and not willing to make her a publick example, was minded to put her away privily. But while he thought on these things, behold, the angel of the Lord appeared unto him in a dream, saying, Joseph, thou son of David, fear not to take unto thee Mary thy wife: for that which is conceived in her is of the Holy Ghost. And she shall bring forth a son, and thou shalt call his name Jesus: for he shall save his people from their sins.

Verse 18 is a resumption of the genealogy of Jesus Christ that began at Matthew 1:1.

The intent was to show that the birth of Jesus Christ was supernatural in origin. His conception was the result of the Holy Spirit impregnating Mary. We are not told how this was done. God does many things that defy human understanding (see Isaiah 55:8-9). At some time, Joseph became aware that Mary was pregnant. He did not know that the child was of the Holy Spirit.

Mary and Joseph were engaged to be married when Joseph discovered that his future wife was pregnant. Betrothal or engagement was a very serious matter in first-century Israel. The engagement itself was considered to be just as formal as the marriage because it was legally binding and could only be officially terminated by either divorce, the commission of adultery, or death (see Deuteronomy 22:13-30). In first-century Israel a marriage consisted of two stages. In the first stage the father usually arranged the marriage of his daughter with someone in the local community or immediate family (see Genesis 24:1-4). The second stage of the marriage occurred when the groom would come and take his wife to his home, usually the home of his parents, where they would live for an undetermined number of years (see Genesis 24:62-67).

The supernatural conception of Jesus Christ is shrouded in divine mystery and will never be known by us. It is a fact we accept by faith (see Hebrews 11:6).

We do not know how Joseph came to know or discover that Mary was expecting. She could have told him, or he may have observed the physical changes in her appearance. We can only imagine the shock and dismay that filled his heart when the reality came to light. His first reaction must have been that Mary had engaged in an adulterous relationship and defiled the marriage bed (see Hebrews 13:4). Conversely, Mary was faced with the dilemma of explaining this unbelievable set of circumstances to Joseph and to her own parents. We can only imagine what may have happened since there is no actual record of her conversation with either of them.

Joseph is described as a just, righteous man. This means that he observed and obeyed the Law of Moses. His discovery of Mary's pregnancy put him in a difficult situation, given all of the possible outcomes. What was he to do about this matter? According to the Law, he could bring Mary before the local elders and formally accuse her of adultery, which was punishable by stoning (see Deuteronomy 22:21). This would bring public humiliation upon the whole house of Mary's parents. Acts of premarital sex were not tolerated because they were a reflection on the girl's father and a violation of the moral laws of Israel. Should such an accusation prove to be true, a man's daughter would be called a harlot or a whore. Joseph wanted to spare Mary and her family this public embarrassment. His willingness to quietly terminate their relationship pointed to his true love and compassion for Mary.

B. God's Messenger of Hope
(Matthew 1:22-25)

Now all this was done, that it might be fulfilled which was spoken of the Lord by the prophet, saying, Behold, a virgin shall be with child, and shall bring forth a son, and they shall call his name Emmanuel, which being interpreted is, God with us. Then Joseph being raised from sleep did as the angel of the Lord had bidden him, and took unto him his wife: And knew her not till she had brought forth her firstborn son: and he called his name Jesus.

Joseph is described as being contemplative and deliberate. He spent time thinking about how to handle difficult circumstances. We are not told how long he spent reflecting and mulling over how to respond to his situation. But while he thought about these matters, the angel of the Lord appeared to him in a dream and reassured him that Mary had done nothing amiss nor had she acted unfaithfully toward him. The angel of the Lord appeared to him in a dream to lift the spirit of fear and uncertainty that had gripped his heart. In the Bible, we read of God communicating His plans and purposes through dreams (see Genesis 20:3, 6; 37:5; 41:7-32; 1 Kings 3:5). Joseph needed heavenly guidance and wisdom about what to do and God sent it through His angel.

God sent an angel to reassure Joseph that what was happening was not a fluke or act of infidelity. Rather, it was all within His divine will for the salvation of the human race. We do not know who this angel was because not all angels are named in the Bible (see Revelation 5:11). There are two angels named in the Bible, Gabriel and Michael, both of whom are archangels (see Daniel 8:15-26; Revelation 12:7-8). The word from the angel was "fear not to take unto thee Mary thy wife" (verse 20). God often sends His messengers to encourage His people when they are faced with overwhelming odds (see Exodus 14:13; Proverbs 3:25; Isaiah 41:10; Luke 1:30; Revelation 1:17). Mary had not acted unfaithfully like Hosea's wife, but had been completely loyal. Joseph would certainly face criticism, but that possibility was not to enter into his thinking about proceeding with his future marriage to Mary.

In verse 20, we have a second reference to Jesus' miraculous birth and conception—"for that which is conceived in her is of the Holy Ghost." His name was going to be Jesus because His mission was to save His people from their sins. Jesus came into the world to deliver His people from their rebellion and transgression against God. In verse 22, the chain of events unfolding before the very eyes of Joseph were all within the predetermined will and plan of God (see Isaiah 7:14).

Emmanuel is a very important theological name for God. It literally means that "God is with us." Jesus Christ was the visible manifestation of the invisible God (see John 1:14; 2).

Joseph was completely obedient to the words of the messenger of God. This statement further affirms his commitment to being righteous. He was faithful to the word that the Lord God sent. He did three things that pointed to his obedience. First, he overcame any fears he may have had about marrying Mary. Second, he had no sexual relations with her until after she had given birth to Jesus. Third, he gave Jesus the name told him by the angel. Mary and Joseph went on to have a happy and normal marriage that produced several other children (see Matthew 13:55-56).

C. The Warning and Flight to Egypt (Matthew 2:13-15)

And when they were departed, behold, the angel of the Lord appeareth to Joseph in a dream, saying, Arise, and take the young child and his mother, and flee into Egypt, and be thou there until I bring thee word: for Herod will seek the young child to destroy him. When he arose, he took the young child and his mother by night, and departed into Egypt: And was there until the death of Herod: that it might be fulfilled which was spoken of the Lord by the prophet, saying, Out of Egypt have I called my son.

The news of the birth of Jesus generated a tremendous uproar and groundswell of excitement in Jerusalem. Wise men from the east had come seeking the child so that they might worship Him (see Matthew 2:1-2). Herod was troubled and began to plot how he might destroy the child (see Matthew 2:3ff.). It had been foretold by the prophets that the Messiah would be born in Bethlehem (see Micah 5:2). The wise men found the house where the child was living and went in and worshiped Him. When they left, the angel of the Lord warned Joseph in another dream that he must take the child and go to Egypt until he received word that it would be safe to return. The angel of the Lord told Joseph that Herod wanted to destroy the child.

The Herod mentioned in Matthew 2 was Herod the Great. Historians note that he was quite successful as a builder of public works. This helped to solidify his political presence. However, Herod was not a full Jew. He came from the region of Idumea which included the traditional territory of the Edomites. Thus, he would be extremely threatened by mention of a Jewish king because this king would have a more legitimate right to be the monarch of the land even though it was under Roman rule. The Romans would work with local leaders as long as they paid proper respect to Roman domination. Homegrown leadership could be very useful in quashing rebellions. Thus, the birth of a so-called Jewish king worried Herod greatly and he was willing to do whatever it took to eliminate the competitor.

Joseph took the child and his mother and fled to Egypt under the cover of darkness so as not to be noticed. Herod had already issued his orders that every male child two years old and under was to be slain. Joseph, Mary, and Jesus were in Egypt until Herod died. The coming of family out of Egypt fulfilled the words of the prophets that out of Egypt God had called His Son (see Numbers 24:8; Hosea 11:1). Matthew included this story to help his readers see the connection between the horror of Herod's actions and God's preeminent protection for God's Son that had been foretold centuries before it happened (see Jeremiah 31:15). God was not surprised by the actions of Herod. Thus, He had resources in place to combat the plan of evil. That is what the birth, life, death, and resurrection of Jesus signals. It signifies that God has planned to defeat evil and has already done so through His Son. Evil may plot, but God has already planned His good. God's ultimate plans will be fulfilled.

III. CONCLUDING REFLECTION

Joseph teaches us how to have compassion on others and the need to be sensitive to their hurts and pains. Rather than gossip and find fault, which it would have been easy to do, he considered Mary and her family. Is there a lesson to be learned? We can take from this story the need to be prudent and thoughtful in all matters before we jump to a conclusion about the guilt or innocence of another person. Difficult-to-understand circumstances may well signal that God is doing a new or different thing.

Matthew's gospel makes it crystal clear that the birth of Jesus Christ was the fulfillment of every promise God made to Abraham and David. God promised Abraham that out of his loins a great nation would rise and that through him all of the families of the earth would be blessed (see Genesis 12:1-3). Through the prophet Nathan God promised David that his throne would be a perpetual throne from which would come a King who would rule forever and there would be no end to His kingdom (see 2 Samuel 7:12-14). Both of these promises have been fulfilled in the birth, life, ministry, death, resurrection, and ascension of Jesus Christ.

Additionally, Matthew made it clear that Jesus Christ was the very Son of God. In that regard, he joined the other gospel writers in boldly declaring that Jesus of Nazareth was not just another prophet whose life ended in death in Jerusalem—He was the Son of God who came into the world to save sinners—specifically Jews (according to Matthew). The genealogy of Jesus Christ shows God's intention to save the world in His own way, in His own time.

Jesus Christ marched through the corridors of time, wrapped Himself in human flesh, and was born in a small, insignificant place called Bethlehem. The Church of the Nativity in Manger Square, which is located in the City of Bethlehem, is the second holiest place in the world for Christians. Each year, thousands of Christian pilgrims make their way to the place venerated as the place of the birth of Jesus Christ. Something powerful and inexplicable happens in the hearts of men and women who come to this lowly place for the first time. Their hearts are filled with abundant joy and excitement as they stand and kneel in absolute reverence at the place where the Christ was born. In Bethlehem, the tradition of the birth of the Messiah still lives.

PRAYER

Heavenly Father, may the joy of the Savior's birth radiate in our hearts as we contemplate the great salvation that He brought to us. May we be reminded each day of His coming and His sacrifice for our sins. In Jesus' name we pray. Amen.

WORD POWER

Betrothed *(Greek: mne-es-tu-thei-sees)*—this word is the same as "espoused." A betrothed or espoused woman was considered and treated as if she were actually married. The parents were heavily involved in the deal. The union could be dissolved only by regular divorce. This was the reason why Joseph was disturbed and planning a secret divorce upon hearing the news of Mary's pregnancy. This kind of breach would have been considered as adultery and was punishable by death (see Deuteronomy 22:23-24).

HOME DAILY BIBLE READINGS
(September 8-14, 2008)

The Birth of a New Community

MONDAY, September 8: "God's Care for God's People" (Hosea 11:1-7)
TUESDAY, September 9: "To All Who Receive Christ" (John 1:10-14)
WEDNESDAY, September 10: "Consider Your Call" (1 Corinthians 1:26-31)
THURSDAY, September 11: "Gifted by God's Spirit" (1 Corinthians 12:4-13)
FRIDAY, September 12: "Members of the Body" (1 Corinthians 12:14-27)
SATURDAY, September 13: "The Kingdom of God's Son" (Colossians 1:9-14)
SUNDAY, September 14: "God Is with Us" (Matthew 1:18-25; 2:13-15)

LESSON 3   September 21, 2008

CORE VALUES OF THE NEW COMMUNITY

DEVOTIONAL READING: **Numbers 6:22-27**
PRINT PASSAGE: **Matthew 5:1-16**

BACKGROUND SCRIPTURE: **Matthew 5:1–7:28**
KEY VERSE: **Matthew 6:33**

Matthew 5:1-16—KJV

AND SEEING the multitudes, he went up into a mountain: and when he was set, his disciples came unto him:

2 And he opened his mouth, and taught them, saying,

3 Blessed are the poor in spirit: for theirs is the kingdom of heaven.

4 Blessed are they that mourn: for they shall be comforted.

5 Blessed are the meek: for they shall inherit the earth.

6 Blessed are they which do hunger and thirst after righteousness: for they shall be filled.

7 Blessed are the merciful: for they shall obtain mercy.

8 Blessed are the pure in heart: for they shall see God.

9 Blessed are the peacemakers: for they shall be called the children of God.

10 Blessed are they which are persecuted for righteousness' sake: for theirs is the kingdom of heaven.

11 Blessed are ye, when men shall revile you, and persecute you, and shall say all manner of evil against you falsely, for my sake.

12 Rejoice, and be exceeding glad: for great is your reward in heaven: for so persecuted they the prophets which were before you.

13 Ye are the salt of the earth: but if the salt have lost his savour, wherewith shall it be salted? it is thenceforth good for nothing, but to be cast out, and to be trodden under foot of men.

14 Ye are the light of the world. A city that is set on an hill cannot be hid.

Matthew 5:1-16—NRSV

WHEN JESUS saw the crowds, he went up the mountain; and after he sat down, his disciples came to him.

2 Then he began to speak, and taught them, saying:

3 "Blessed are the poor in spirit, for theirs is the kingdom of heaven.

4 "Blessed are those who mourn, for they will be comforted.

5 "Blessed are the meek, for they will inherit the earth.

6 "Blessed are those who hunger and thirst for righteousness, for they will be filled.

7 "Blessed are the merciful, for they will receive mercy.

8 "Blessed are the pure in heart, for they will see God.

9 "Blessed are the peacemakers, for they will be called children of God.

10 "Blessed are those who are persecuted for righteousness' sake, for theirs is the kingdom of heaven.

11 "Blessed are you when people revile you and persecute you and utter all kinds of evil against you falsely on my account.

12 Rejoice and be glad, for your reward is great in heaven, for in the same way they persecuted the prophets who were before you.

13 "You are the salt of the earth; but if salt has lost its taste, how can its saltiness be restored? It is no longer good for anything, but is thrown out and trampled under foot.

14 "You are the light of the world. A city built on a hill cannot be hid.

People search for happiness in many places, but they often find the opposite due to their wrong choices. Who teaches us to know true and lasting happiness? Through His teachings, Jesus described how to find true happiness.

15 Neither do men light a candle, and put it under a bushel, but on a candlestick; and it giveth light unto all that are in the house.
16 Let your light so shine before men, that they may see your good works, and glorify your Father which is in heaven.

15 No one after lighting a lamp puts it under the bushel basket, but on the lampstand, and it gives light to all in the house.
16 In the same way, let your light shine before others, so that they may see your good works and give glory to your Father in heaven."

TOPICAL OUTLINE OF THE LESSON

I. Introduction
  A. Happiness
  B. Biblical Background

II. Exposition and Application of the Scripture
  A. Jesus the Teacher (Matthew 5:1-2)
  B. The Beatitudes (Matthew 5:3-12)
  C. Salt of the Earth (Matthew 5:13)
  D. Light of the World (Matthew 5:14-16)

III. Concluding Reflection

LESSON OBJECTIVES

Upon completion of this lesson, the students will know that:

1. Jesus told us the ways to true happiness;
2. Following Jesus' prescribed ways will lead to true happiness; and,
3. The choices we make in life are crucial.

POINTS TO BE EMPHASIZED

ADULT/YOUTH
Adult Topic: Finding True Happiness
Youth Topic: What Matters Most
Adult Key Verse: Matthew 6:33
Youth Key Verse: Matthew 6:21
Print Passage: Matthew 5:1-16

—Jesus' words "Blessed are those . . . " have to do with a deep and abiding sense of spiritual well-being that grows out of one's way of living.
—"You" is corporate and plural. The instruction to be salt and light is given to a community, not to an individual person.
—Jesus challenges His followers to radical devotion to and dependence on God.
—The word *blessed,* also rendered "happy," denotes an inward experience rather than an outward motivation.
—Seven of the nine beatitudes relate to character, or internal circumstances. The final two are concerned with certain external circumstances, which lead to blessings.
—Salt was a valuable and essential food preservative during ancient times.

CHILDREN
Children Topic: The Community Is like Salt and Light
Key Verse: Matthew 5:16
Print Passage: Matthew 5:1-2, 13-16
—Jesus took His disciples away from the crowds and used a hillside as a classroom as He taught them how to find true happiness.

—Followers of Jesus are like salt because they help in their communities.

—Followers of Jesus are like bright lights that bring cheer and comfort wherever they go.

—Jesus teaches His disciples that heartfelt love and obedience to God will bring true joy.

I. INTRODUCTION

A. Happiness

The quest for happiness is one of the great journeys of life. People everywhere want to be happy. *Happiness* is the "state of having or experiencing great joy or excitement." Happiness can be produced by a number of factors or circumstances that are favorable to our well-being. Happiness can result from having fulfilled some lifelong dream or ambition. We want to know that our lives have counted for something and that we have achieved some measure of personal success. Where does happiness come from? Happiness has to come from within. Ultimate happiness cannot be derived from material possessions, fame, fortune, or the accumulation of power. All of these are temporary and will bring no real, lasting happiness. True happiness comes from knowing and confessing the Lord Jesus Christ as our Savior.

B. Biblical Background

The Sermon on the Mount is unique to the gospel of Matthew. It is the first of five major discourses that are found in Matthew (see Matthew 5:1–7:27; 10:1-2; 13:1-52; 18:1–19:2; 23:1– 25:46). Verses 3-12 are called the *Beatitudes* (Latin) and they form the introduction to the Sermon on the Mount. *Beatitude* is a pronouncement of blessing, phrased in a formula that begins with the term "blessed." The wording of these Beatitudes (5:3-12) is unique to Matthew. Luke does list a series of Beatitudes in Luke 6:20-26, but the theme is entirely different and they are followed by a list of woes.

When someone pronounces a blessing upon one's life, utilizing the language of Scripture, he or she is in fact declaring a reality that is yet to be realized but that is already in existence. When it is expressed, God is going to bless our lives to the extent that we are faithful and obedient to His will and Word. It is being said that the potential exists within an individual to know these blessings and to walk in the very favor of God. To have God's favor upon one's life means that life should be abundantly blessed in everything that is done.

The Sermon on the Mount is one of the most profound messages ever delivered. It is the very first recorded sermon of Jesus. He taught these lessons to impress upon them the truth that God called them to a higher standard of conduct and living.

II. EXPOSITION AND APPLICATION OF THE SCRIPTURE

A. Jesus the Teacher
(Matthew 5:1-2)

AND SEEING the multitudes, he went up into a mountain: and when he was set, his disciples came unto him: And he opened his mouth, and taught them, saying.

The Gospels make it quite clear that Jesus spent a great deal of time teaching; He is called "teacher" more than forty-five times in the Gospels, while the more original title of "rabbi" is used roughly fourteen times. Jesus was not just another rabbinic teacher in Israel trying to gather a following. There was something unusually powerful and provocative about His teaching. He taught with authority and not as the scribes and Pharisees (see Matthew 7:29).

In the early days of His ministry, Jesus was followed by large crowds of people in Galilee. The Galileans were very conservative in their thinking but were quite open to the message of Jesus. The first major discourse of Jesus took place on the side of a mountain near the northern shore of the Sea of Galilee. Today, this site is called the Mount of the Beatitudes, is perfectly situated near the sea, and is the site of many of the miracles of Jesus. He went to a particular place, sat down, and began to teach the people the Word of God.

B. The Beatitudes
(Matthew 5:3-12)

Blessed are the poor in spirit: for theirs is the kingdom of heaven. Blessed are they that mourn: for they shall be comforted. Blessed are the meek: for they shall inherit the earth. Blessed are they which do hunger and thirst after righteousness: for they shall be filled. Blessed are the merciful: for they shall obtain mercy. Blessed are the pure in heart: for they shall see God. Blessed are the peacemakers: for they shall be called the children of God. Blessed are they which are persecuted for righteousness'
sake: for theirs is the kingdom of heaven. Blessed are ye, when men shall revile you, and persecute you, and shall say all manner of evil against you falsely, for my sake. Rejoice, and be exceeding glad: for great is your reward in heaven: for so persecuted they the prophets which were before you.

There are nine beatitudes and each one begins with the word "blessed." Who are the blessed, and why did Jesus call them "blessed?" *The poor in spirit* are blessed because they recognize that without God their lives are empty and devoid of true power (verse 3; see also Psalm 41:1-2). *Poor* (Greek: *ptochos*) means "to be destitute of wealth, influence, power, and position." Jesus was not referring to earthly wealth, but poverty as it relates to the things of God. Those who are poor in spirit are the exact opposite of the Pharisees of Jesus' day who were often filled with pride and religious arrogance (see Luke 18:9-14).

Those that *mourn* (Greek: *penthountes*), meaning "to experience deep, heart-wrenching grief," will one day be comforted, meaning that God will come alongside of them. Jesus spoke to the hearts of His hearers who grieved over the current state of affairs in Israel, which was under Roman occupation. In Isaiah 61:1-11, on which the beatitudes are based, the community lamented the desolation of the holy city. This is the community that does not resign itself to the present condition of the world as final, but laments the fact that God's kingdom has not yet come and that God's will is not yet done.

The *meek* (gentle or soft-spirited) are not those who are doormats for the world; rather, they are the ones who display a gentle spirit which is the manifestation of great strength. Leon Morris, a leading New Testament scholar, wrote, "True meekness may be a quality of the strong, those who assert themselves but choose not to do so." In Numbers 12:3, Moses is described as being meek in spirit (see Psalm 22:26; Isaiah 11:4).

Jesus stated that those who *hunger,* meaning "to deeply desire or to crave incessantly and thirst and long for the things that only God could give," particularly for righteousness, would be filled. In the narrowest sense, *righteousness* referred to the practice of justice and fairness. It was the one thing that God required if one wanted to meet the standards for being righteous in the Old Testament (see Micah 6:6-8). In the apostolic writings of Paul, *righteousness* is "the state of being in a right relationship with the Father" and is the result of what God has done through the cross of Jesus Christ (see Romans 1:16-17).

The *merciful* are those whose lifestyles are governed by showing deep compassion for the least of the earth (verse 7). They will be the recipients of mercy when the time comes (see Psalm 41:1-4). One of God's most notable attributes is His mercy. He delights in mercy and showing compassion (see Micah 7:19-20).

The *pure,* meaning the clean in heart, are not those who simply avoid impure thoughts, but those whose whole orientation in life is bent toward serving God faithfully. There are more than 830 references to the heart in the Bible. This indicates the importance that is placed upon the source of the human will. The heart is often referred to metaphorically in the Scriptures as the seat and center of the human will, the source of our appetites, ambitions, passions, thoughts, and motivations. An evil heart will produce evil fruit (see Genesis 6:5). Out of the heart flows the essence of who we are (see Matthew 12:35).

Jesus pronounced blessings upon the *peacemakers.* Peace with God is one of the results of reconciliation and the grace of God (see Romans 5:1-8). Believers are encouraged to live in peace with each other, which is a reflection of the very nature of God (see Romans 12:18; 14:14).

In the Sermon on the Mount, Jesus gave instructions and warned that His disciples would face persecution (Greek: *dioko*—to harass with the intention of doing harm). They would be persecuted for the sake of righteousness, not because they had committed some crime or broken some laws. This would be suffering at a different level and for a different purpose (see 1 Peter 4:15-19).

Christians in the first century lived with the constant threat of persecution by other Jews and the Romans. The Jews were the earliest persecutors of the disciples of Jesus. They were arrested for preaching, forbidden to preach in the name of Jesus, tortured, stoned, killed, and sometimes hounded from city to city (see Acts 4:1-3). Eventually, the Romans began to persecute the Christians because of their unwillingness to give devotion to Caesar and worship him as Lord. The book of Revelation tells of a time when Christians in the latter days of the first century faced unparalleled persecution by the Romans.

The last of the nine beatitudes continued the theme of persecution with a different twist. Christians must be prepared for a time when men and women would *revile* them, meaning "to speak words of condemnation and scorn." They would be *falsely accused* (Greek: *pseudomai*), meaning "to deliberately speak against." Jesus did not want His disciples to feel rejected and despondent because of the ill treatment—rather, they were to rejoice.

This joy would come from knowing that one had received a great reward for one's faithful commitment to Jesus and the Kingdom. This reward was waiting for them in heaven (see 1 Peter 1:3-5).

C. Salt of the Earth
(Matthew 5:13)

Ye are the salt of the earth: but if the salt have lost his savour, wherewith shall it be salted? it is thenceforth good for nothing, but to be cast out, and to be trodden under foot of men.

The next two statements by Jesus were metaphors, or words that are used to act in the place of something else. "You are the salt of the earth" was addressed specifically to the disciples of Jesus and to other Christians as well. The statement was expressed in the imperative tense, meaning that the disciples had no options in this matter. The *Interpreters Bible* offers this explanation about salt. The saying is evocative and has multiple layers of meaning, since salt had many connotations in Matthew's tradition and context—including sacrifice (Leviticus 2:13; Ezekiel 43:24), loyalty, and covenantal fidelity (Numbers 18:19; Ezra 4:14); eating together was called "sharing salt" and expressed a binding relationship. The disciples of Jesus were not to confine their preaching and teaching efforts to just Jerusalem and Israel, but were to be the salt of the entire earth. Their field of labor was wherever people lived. If they failed to carry out their work, they would be considered useless like salt that had been diluted and no longer retained its unique character. It would be thrown out and cast under the feet of humankind. Salt was a major staple and was plentiful; it came from the Dead Sea or "Great Salt Sea," as it was sometimes called.

D. Light of the World
(Matthew 5:14-16)

Ye are the light of the world. A city that is set on an hill cannot be hid. Neither do men light a candle, and put it under a bushel, but on a candlestick; and it giveth light unto all that are in the house. Let your light so shine before men, that they may see your good works, and glorify your Father which is in heaven.

The second metaphor declared that the disciples of Jesus were the light of the world. Here again "You" is emphatic, meaning that it referred exclusively to those who were the true followers of Jesus. Unlike the Pharisees whose only purpose was to be a religious show for others, Jesus' disciples were charged to illuminate the whole world with the message of salvation and reconciliation.

The reference to a city sitting on a hill is quite illustrative because from the Sea of Galilee one could see the lights flickering from the many small towns and villages perched upon the hills of Judea and Galilee. The lights made the locations of these cities very prominent and visible from great distances. Jesus offered a second analogy by saying the lights were not placed under bushels or buckets; rather, they were left in the open so that they might give illumination to all. Lights serve a very distinct purpose, which is to provide illumination during periods of darkness.

The purpose of the disciple is not to bring attention to oneself but to God. Let your lights shine in such a way that men see you but recognize that what they see is a reflection of God. One of the ways that the light of the disciple would shine would be by doing good works or acts of service (see Matthew 25:31-46; Ephesians 2:8-10). Good works are an indication of a life that is governed by God because they are a reflection of the very nature and character of God.

III. CONCLUDING REFLECTION

The Sermon on the Mount and the Beatitudes in particular were spoken by Jesus for a threefold purpose. They were meant first to instill the fact that as disciples of Christ we must focus on developing the type of character that reflects our relationship with Him. Second, the Beatitudes infuse us with a deep, driving commitment to the cause of the Kingdom. Third, they promote growth, courage, and confidence, especially when faced with persecution and rejection. We are to never lose hope because God is always with us, and when one takes a stand for Jesus, one can expect the world to react negatively. However, we are not to run away because our presence in the world keeps the world from collapsing into complete corruption from the presence of Satan. We are the lights which enable the world to see God through our actions that reflect His character and nature.

PRAYER

Heavenly Father, empower us to live in such a way that the world will be drawn to know You as their Lord and Savior. In Jesus' name we pray. Amen.

WORD POWER

First (Greek: *proton [pro-ton]*)—Matthew 6:33 in the original language reads "Seek, but first his kingdom seek." The word *proton* is used adverbially in this text and it means "first in time, place, or order of importance." Jesus, in this verse and in the Beatitudes, draws a picture of the person with a new heart. If we truly have new hearts, then we must "seek ye first the kingdom of God, and his righteousness; and all these things shall be added unto you."

HOME DAILY BIBLE READINGS
(September 15-21, 2008)

Core Values of the New Community

MONDAY, September 15: "Asking for God's Blessing" (Numbers 6:22-27)

TUESDAY, September 16: "Blessed by the Father" (Matthew 25:31-40)

WEDNESDAY, September 17: "Acting on Jesus' Words" (Matthew 7:24-29)

THURSDAY, September 18: "Returning Evil with Good" (Romans 12:9-13)

FRIDAY, September 19: "Living in Harmony with Others" (Romans 12:14-21)

SATURDAY, September 20: "Inheriting a Blessing" (1 Peter 3:8-15)

SUNDAY, September 21: "Blessing for God's People" (Matthew 5:1-16)

CREATING A COMMUNITY OF SERVANTS

DEVOTIONAL READING: **Philippians 2:1-11**
PRINT PASSAGE: **Matthew 20:17-28**
KEY VERSE: **Matthew 20:28**

BACKGROUND SCRIPTURE: **Matthew 20:1-28;
Mark 10:35-45**

Matthew 20:17-28—KJV

17 And Jesus going up to Jerusalem took the twelve disciples apart in the way, and said unto them,
18 Behold, we go up to Jerusalem; and the Son of man shall be betrayed unto the chief priests and unto the scribes, and they shall condemn him to death,
19 And shall deliver him to the Gentiles to mock, and to scourge, and to crucify him: and the third day he shall rise again.
20 Then came to him the mother of Zebedee's children with her sons, worshipping him, and desiring a certain thing of him.
21 And he said unto her, What wilt thou? She saith unto him, Grant that these my two sons may sit, the one on thy right hand, and the other on the left, in thy kingdom.
22 But Jesus answered and said, Ye know not what ye ask. Are ye able to drink of the cup that I shall drink of, and to be baptized with the baptism that I am baptized with? They say unto him, We are able.
23 And he saith unto them, Ye shall drink indeed of my cup, and be baptized with the baptism that I am baptized with: but to sit on my right hand, and on my left, is not mine to give, but it shall be given to them for whom it is prepared of my Father.
24 And when the ten heard it, they were moved with indignation against the two brethren.
25 But Jesus called them unto him, and said, Ye know that the princes of the Gentiles exercise dominion over them, and they that are great exercise authority upon them.
26 But it shall not be so among you: but whosoever will be great among you, let him be your minister;
27 And whosoever will be chief among you, let him be your servant:
28 Even as the Son of man came not to be ministered unto, but to minister, and to give his life a ransom for many.

Matthew 20:17-28—NRSV

17 While Jesus was going up to Jerusalem, he took the twelve disciples aside by themselves, and said to them on the way,
18 "See, we are going up to Jerusalem, and the Son of Man will be handed over to the chief priests and scribes, and they will condemn him to death;
19 then they will hand him over to the Gentiles to be mocked and flogged and crucified; and on the third day he will be raised."
20 Then the mother of the sons of Zebedee came to him with her sons, and kneeling before him, she asked a favor of him.
21 And he said to her, "What do you want?" She said to him, "Declare that these two sons of mine will sit, one at your right hand and one at your left, in your kingdom."
22 But Jesus answered, "You do not know what you are asking. Are you able to drink the cup that I am about to drink?" They said to him, "We are able."
23 He said to them, "You will indeed drink my cup, but to sit at my right hand and at my left, this is not mine to grant, but it is for those for whom it has been prepared by my Father."
24 When the ten heard it, they were angry with the two brothers.
25 But Jesus called them to him and said, "You know that the rulers of the Gentiles lord it over them, and their great ones are tyrants over them.
26 It will not be so among you; but whoever wishes to be great among you must be your servant,
27 and whoever wishes to be first among you must be your slave;
28 just as the Son of Man came not to be served but to serve, and to give his life a ransom for many."

Everyone yearns to be recognized as important in the eyes of others. How does one achieve greatness? Jesus taught that if we wish to be great we must become servants and follow His example of service to others.

TOPICAL OUTLINE OF THE LESSON

I. Introduction
A. The Biblical Concept of Serving
B. Biblical Background

II. Exposition and Application of the Scripture
A. Passion Revealed (Matthew 20:17-19)
B. A Mother's Request (Matthew 20:20-21)
C. Jesus' Response (Matthew 20:22-23)
D. Conflict and Resolution (Matthew 20:24-28)

III. Concluding Reflection

LESSON OBJECTIVES

Upon completion of this lesson, the students will know that:

1. Jesus Christ gave the best example of servant-hood;
2. We are duty-bound to follow the example of Jesus in our daily activities; and,
3. The Bible is the authoritative book on godly servant-hood.

POINTS TO BE EMPHASIZED

ADULT/YOUTH

Adult Topic: Serving Others
Youth Topic: Created to Serve
Adult Key Verse: Matthew 20:28
Youth Key Verse: Matthew 20:26
Print Passage: Matthew 20:17-28

—In asking Jesus to give her sons important positions in Jesus' kingdom, the mother of James and John tried to turn favor into privilege.

—Until their dreams of a worldly kingdom were crushed by Jesus' execution on the Cross, Jesus' followers expected that they would play some prominent role in the Messiah's new government.

—Jesus' disciples seemed unable to understand that His words about suffering were literal and not merely figurative.

—In the new community that Jesus established, greatness is measured in terms of service.

—Jesus tried to prepare His disciples for His passion by sharing some of the particulars of His suffering.

—The request of James and John's mother revealed a general lack of understanding of Jesus' purpose and mission.

CHILDREN

Children Topic: The Community Learns to Be Servants
Key Verse: Matthew 20:26
Print Passage: Matthew 20:20-28

—The mother of James and John asked Jesus for a favor.

—The mother wanted her sons to help Jesus rule His kingdom.

—The other disciples became very angry with James and John.

—Jesus taught that greatness in His kingdom is the result of serving others.

I. INTRODUCTION

A. The Biblical Concept of Serving

The biblical concept of service or serving is rich with a depth of meaning. At the very core of what we find in the Bible is the practice of master-servant relationships. The master is the one of superior rank who has persons working for him or her either voluntarily or involuntarily. In the Old Testament, the pinnacle of success in the eyes of God was to be accorded the title "servant of the Lord" (see Numbers 12:7). The New Testament concept has two basic meanings. The first is expressed by the Greek word *doulous,* and it can mean "one who serves or is a slave" (see Luke 15:29). The other commonly used word in the New Testament is the Greek word *diakonia,* which means "deacon" (see Acts 6:2). Both of these words point to someone who works for the benefit of someone else. Their lives are characterized by obedience, humility, and submission.

B. Biblical Background

The text today speaks to us about how to achieve true greatness. This was the third time that Jesus taught His disciples about humility (see Matthew 18:3-4; 19:13-14). In this story, Jesus was just a few days from entering Jerusalem for the final time. He and His disciples were among the thousands of pilgrims who were headed to Jerusalem for the annual Passover celebration. This incident may have happened near or in the city of Jericho. According to Matthew 20:17, they were about to go up to Jerusalem. Matthew 20:29 notes their departure from Jericho.

At some point, the mother of James and John approached Jesus and requested that her two sons be given chief seats in His kingdom. She wanted one to sit on the right and the other on the left. Jesus turned down her request telling her that she had no idea what she was requesting. Those seats of honor had been reserved by the Father. The cup that He would have to drink from was too bitter for them. They simply could not take it then, but in time they would rise to that level. When the other ten disciples heard this, they became indignant, or were very displeased by the brothers' request. Jesus turned to the Twelve and gave them this lesson on true greatness.

Jesus said that greatness as it is understood by the world is far different than Kingdom greatness. In the world's model of greatness, the leaders lorded it over the people and dictated what was to be. However, in the kingdom of God, greatness is defined by altruistic love, service, humility, and sacrifice. Whoever wishes to become great in God's eyes must first be willing to become a servant of others. Jesus would say that you are not to consider yourselves as tyrants, big wheels, or shot callers who will power over the little people. You are to labor tirelessly and diligently in this Kingdom, giving of yourself until the Father rewards you for your faithfulness. He used Himself as the model. He said, "Even as the Son of man came not to be ministered unto, but to minister, and to give his life a ransom for many." Here is the Christ-centered model of true greatness–service and sacrifice. God's will is that we all become great disciples of the Lord Jesus Christ. Consider the marks of service as sacrifice.

II. EXPOSITION AND APPLICATION OF THE SCRIPTURE

A. Passion Revealed
(Matthew 20:17-19)

And Jesus going up to Jerusalem took the twelve disciples apart in the way, and said unto them, Behold, we go up to Jerusalem; and the Son of man shall be betrayed unto the chief priests and unto the scribes, and they shall condemn him to death, And shall deliver him to the Gentiles to mock, and to scourge, and to crucify him: and the third day he shall rise again.

Jesus' ministry in Galilee had come to an end. He and the disciples were going to Jerusalem for the annual observance of the Jewish Passover feast. Jesus began to say to them for the third time that He was going to face condemnation and death in Jerusalem (see Matthew 16:21). Jesus described more of the details of His passion at this point. He was going to be delivered or handed over to the chief priests and scribes who would condemn Him to death. They would hand Him over to the Gentiles, meaning the Roman authorities who reserved the right to carry out capital punishment for crimes committed against Rome. The Romans would mock Jesus, whip Him, and eventually crucify Him.

However, He also emphasized His resurrection after being in the grave for three days. The link between Cross and Resurrection is critical because it reveals the whole point of the Crucifixion. The Crucifixion and suffering would be pointless unless there was a point of triumph. Jesus was passionate about His work because He knew that humanity would benefit eternally. His resurrection signaled the beginning of that everlasting victory.

B. A Mother's Request
(Matthew 20:20-21)

Then came to him the mother of Zebedee's children with her sons, worshipping him, and desiring a certain thing of him. And he said unto her, What wilt thou? She saith unto him, Grant that these my two sons may sit, the one on thy right hand, and the other on the left, in thy kingdom.

Jesus was approached by the mother of two of His disciples almost immediately after speaking about His pending crucifixion in Jerusalem. The use of the adverb "then" at the beginning of Matthew 20:20 denotes that the events described in verses 20-28 occurred during the journey to Jerusalem, but we are not told the exact time when they occurred. The woman is identified as the mother of the children of Zebedee, who came to Jesus along with her two sons, James and John. She came and worshiped at the feet of Jesus. The Greek word for *worship (Proskunousa)* is used here and literally means "to bow before in an act of respect and humility."

In verse 21, the mother asked that her two sons be given the privilege of sitting one on His right, and the other on His left when Jesus established His kingdom. The seats on either side of the king were the most prominent and indicated a high place within the hierarchy of leadership. That the disciples of Jesus were in full expectation of the establishment of the kingdom in Jerusalem was obvious from this request and from what is said in Luke 19:11. There is no indication that either the brothers or their mother knew what this Kingdom entailed. It may be that they were recalling the large crowds of admirers and supporters of Jesus during His Galilean ministry. Or they may have been looking at the throng that was with them in Jericho. Whatever may have been the case, they felt that maybe this would be the final death blow to Roman rule and they would be right in the middle of being able to play significant roles in this new world order. What they revealed by their actions were attitudes of selfishness and self-seeking pride which are endemic to human nature. Men and women seek positions as a means for self-elevation and self-enrichment. They may not seek positions to be of service to the people, but to serve their own ends.

Here we have a practice that appears common among Christians, even to this day. It is the belief that we can approach God to seek favor, positions, power, or personal wealth for our own benefit. This is the essence of much contemporary preaching and teaching that promotes prosperity and self-empowerment to the neglect of Christian piety, social justice, and Christian service (see James 2:15-17; 4:13). There are many preachers today who are seeking power and prosperity for themselves. This overt practice has been described by Marvin McMickle as a "royal consciousness" on the part of many preachers who believe that the church exists to support their extravagant lifestyles.

C. Jesus' Response
(Matthew 20:22-23)

But Jesus answered and said, Ye know not what ye ask.
Are ye able to drink of the cup that I shall drink of, and to be baptized with the baptism that I am baptized with? They say unto him, We are able. And he saith unto them, Ye shall drink indeed of my cup, and be baptized with the baptism that I am baptized with: but to sit on my right hand, and on my left, is not mine to give, but it shall be given to them for whom it is prepared of my Father.

These men had no idea what they were asking (see verse 22). The tone of the statement by Jesus indicated that they were completely clueless about the consequences of such high and lofty places in the Kingdom. These were not cheap seats. Instead, there was tremendous cost to be paid by the ones who sat in these places. Jesus asked the brothers if they were able to endure the scorn, shame, and suffering of the cup and be baptized with the baptism which He would face. Jesus did not explain what He meant by the cup or this baptism. Leon Morris noted that "the cup is used in the Old Testament with associations with suffering sometimes of the wrath of God (see Psalm 75:8; Isaiah 51:17, 22). Without hesitation they responded that they were fully capable of drinking from the cup and receiving the same baptism with which Jesus would be baptized.

Jesus told James and John that they indeed would face the agony which He faced. They had no way of knowing how prophetic the words of Jesus were because within a matter of months they would face the wrath of Jewish religious leaders who were opposed to the spread of Christianity. Jesus also told them it was not His place to grant their requests for chief seats in the Kingdom. The Father had already prepared these privileged seats for persons of His own choosing. Who could possibly be worthy of such a high and lofty honor?

Clearly, there are positions of leadership to which only God can qualify the saints. As the time drew near for Moses to step down from the helm of leadership, he asked God to choose a man to lead His people (see Numbers 27:15-23).

D. Conflict and Resolution
(Matthew 20:24-28)

And when the ten heard it, they were moved with indignation against the two brethren. But Jesus called them unto him, and said, Ye know that the princes of the Gentiles exercise dominion over them, and they that are great exercise authority upon them. But it shall not be so among you: but whosoever will be great among you, let him be your minister; And whosoever will be chief among you, let him be your servant: Even as the Son of man came not to be ministered unto, but to minister, and to give his life a ransom for many.

The request by the mother of James and John did not go unnoticed. The other ten disciples of Jesus witnessed the conversation. They were moved to indignation, meaning that they became very displeased by their actions. The Greek word used *(ee-ganak-tee-sa)* is a very strong word for "angry resentment." The other ten disciples felt cheated because James and John had taken advantage of their relationship to Jesus. After all, what would qualify just the two of them for such a high and lofty honor? There was no backlash against their mother because it is possible that the disciples felt that James and John initiated her raising the question with Jesus.

Jesus took the opportunity at this point to redefine and clarify the vast difference between leadership in the kingdom of God and worldly leadership as practiced most notably by the Romans. The Romans ruled with an iron fist and did not tolerate insubordination or insurrection regardless of how small it may have been. They exercised great authority and dominion over the Jewish people.

In contrast to their form of leadership, Jesus stated that among those of the Kingdom this would not be the case. Greatness in the Kingdom would not be defined by position, but by one's posture as a minister. The Greek word used for "minister" is *diakonos,* which gives us the word *deacon* or *deaconess.* The diakonos was one who served tables and waited on another. This was not a lofty position but was one that involved humility and submission to the will of one's master.

Jesus connected Himself to this form of leadership. He did not come to be served, but to serve and to give Himself as a *ransom* (Greek: *Lutron),* meaning "redemption price." Jesus came and paid the price for the sin of the whole world. He did not state how this was to be done; one concludes that it was through His death and suffering on the cross. The declaration that His life was a ransom was a clear allusion to Isaiah 53, where the servant of the Lord is depicted as one who suffers on behalf of others. The model of leadership that Jesus described is sacrificial and servant-oriented.

III. CONCLUDING REFLECTION

Is there a crisis of leadership in the African-American Christian church today? Some would shout a resounding "Yes!" The writer agrees that the church today faces a critical shortage of men and women who are willing to divest themselves of their own interests for the broader interests of God's kingdom on the earth. Some Christian leaders today are much more interested in the trappings of prosperity and view these as a sign that they have performed outstanding miracles of leadership within their respective congregations. One may also see this distorted view of leadership and ineffective criterion of performance even on the continent of Africa. Some of the emerging nations have been severely compromised by selfish and inept leadership. The political, social, economic, and even religious infrastructure of these countries cannot be solidified because of misplaced ambitions. The notion that God rewards us with perks is foreign to the teachings of Jesus Christ and even reeks of blasphemy. The model of leadership that is needed today is one that points to servant-hood.

Jesus teaches us, as He taught His disciples, that we must not be too quick to seek positions of power because they come with a high price tag. Not everyone is suited for such high levels of responsibility because of the self-sacrifices that must be made.

The question we must ask ourselves is: "What is the motive of my being active in the church?" As pastors, why are we seeking high and lofty positions in the church? Many are not satisfied with the name *pastor*. They want to be ordained as "bishop." Some bishops still feel that they must outrank other bishops and, therefore, have become prelates.

In the final analysis, the reward of the servant of God is not based upon whether or not one has built massive ministries and presided over multiple congregational settings; rather, it will be based upon our service and commitment to the "least of these my brethren." As ministers of the Most High, whether we serve as deacon or pastor, let us serve as those who will one day give account to God.

PRAYER

Heavenly Father, teach us how to serve You faithfully and in deep humility. May the pattern and model of our elder brother Jesus Christ be ours as well. Forgive us of selfishness and pride that gets in the way of our service to Thee. In Jesus' name we pray. Amen.

WORD POWER

A Ransom *(lutron [lut-ron])*—the letter "a" that precedes *ransom* means "one atonement" instead of many prescribed in the Jewish law. The word *ransom* literally is "a price paid for the redemption of captives." In Christian understanding, it means that God had declared that sinners would die and suffer hell eternally, but God sent His Son to die in their place. Jesus Christ laid down His life as a ransom for our lives and souls.

HOME DAILY BIBLE READINGS
(September 22-28, 2008)

Creating a Community of Servants

MONDAY, September 22: "The Humility of Christ" (Philippians 2:1-11)
TUESDAY, September 23: "The Greatest in the Kingdom" (Matthew 18:1-5)
WEDNESDAY, September 24: "Serving and Following Jesus" (John 12:20-26)
THURSDAY, September 25: "Serving Fearlessly" (Matthew 10:24-33)
FRIDAY, September 26: "Serving in God's Strength" (1 Peter 4:7-11)
SATURDAY, September 27: "The Last Will Be First" (Matthew 20:1-16)
SUNDAY, September 28: "The Serving Son of Man" (Matthew 20:17-28)

LESSON 5   October 5, 2008

EMPOWERED TO BE A COMMUNITY

DEVOTIONAL READING: **Ephesians 2:11-22**
PRINT PASSAGE: **Acts 2:1-17a**

BACKGROUND SCRIPTURE: **Acts 2:1-47**
KEY VERSE: **Acts 2:4**

Acts 2:1-17a—KJV

AND WHEN the day of Pentecost was fully come, they were all with one accord in one place.

2 And suddenly there came a sound from heaven as of a rushing mighty wind, and it filled all the house where they were sitting.

3 And there appeared unto them cloven tongues like as of fire, and it sat upon each of them.

4 And they were all filled with the Holy Ghost, and began to speak with other tongues, as the Spirit gave them utterance.

5 And there were dwelling at Jerusalem Jews, devout men, out of every nation under heaven.

6 Now when this was noised abroad, the multitude came together, and were confounded, because that every man heard them speak in his own language.

7 And they were all amazed and marvelled, saying one to another, Behold, are not all these which speak Galilaeans?

8 And how hear we every man in our own tongue, wherein we were born?

9 Parthians, and Medes, and Elamites, and the dwellers in Mesopotamia, and in Judaea, and Cappadocia, in Pontus, and Asia,

10 Phrygia, and Pamphylia, in Egypt, and in the parts of Libya about Cyrene, and strangers of Rome, Jews and proselytes,

11 Cretes and Arabians, we do hear them speak in our tongues the wonderful works of God.

12 And they were all amazed, and were in doubt, saying one to another, What meaneth this?

13 Others mocking said, These men are full of new wine.

14 But Peter, standing up with the eleven, lifted up his voice, and said unto them, Ye men of Judaea, and all ye that dwell at Jerusalem, be this known unto you, and hearken to my words:

15 For these are not drunken, as ye suppose, seeing it is but the third hour of the day.

16 But this is that which was spoken by the prophet Joel;

17 And it shall come to pass in the last days, saith God, I will pour out of my Spirit upon all flesh.

Acts 2:1-17a—NRSV

WHEN THE day of Pentecost had come, they were all together in one place.

2 And suddenly from heaven there came a sound like the rush of a violent wind, and it filled the entire house where they were sitting.

3 Divided tongues, as of fire, appeared among them, and a tongue rested on each of them.

4 All of them were filled with the Holy Spirit and began to speak in other languages, as the Spirit gave them ability.

5 Now there were devout Jews from every nation under heaven living in Jerusalem.

6 And at this sound the crowd gathered and was bewildered, because each one heard them speaking in the native language of each.

7 Amazed and astonished, they asked, "Are not all these who are speaking Galileans?

8 And how is it that we hear, each of us, in our own native language?

9 Parthians, Medes, Elamites, and residents of Mesopotamia, Judea and Cappadocia, Pontus and Asia,

10 Phrygia and Pamphylia, Egypt and the parts of Libya belonging to Cyrene, and visitors from Rome, both Jews and proselytes,

11 Cretans and Arabs—in our own languages we hear them speaking about God's deeds of power."

12 All were amazed and perplexed, saying to one another, "What does this mean?"

13 But others sneered and said, "They are filled with new wine."

14 But Peter, standing with the eleven, raised his voice and addressed them, "Men of Judea and all who live in Jerusalem, let this be known to you, and listen to what I say.

15 Indeed, these are not drunk, as you suppose, for it is only nine o'clock in the morning.

16 No, this is what was spoken through the prophet Joel:

17 'In the last days it will be, God declares, that I will pour out my Spirit upon all flesh.'"

UNIFYING LESSON PRINCIPLE

In our individualistic society, many people long for a sense of community. Where can we find resources to develop such community? At Pentecost, God provided spiritual power that brings together life's disjointed elements and bridges the gaps that divide people.

TOPICAL OUTLINE OF THE LESSON

I. **Introduction**
   A. The Pentecost
   B. Biblical Background

II. **Exposition and Application of the Scripture**
   A. The Mighty Wind of the Spirit
      (Acts 2:1-4)
   B. The Powerful Witness to the Nations
      (Acts 2:5-13)
   C. The Convicting Word Delivered
      (Acts 2:14-17a)

III. **Concluding Reflection**

LESSON OBJECTIVES

Upon completion of this lesson, the students will know that:

1. Pentecost was an actual historical phenomenon;
2. The disciples were baptized with the Holy Spirit; and,
3. The disciples were endued with uncommon power to witness for Christ.

POINTS TO BE EMPHASIZED
ADULT/YOUTH

Adult Topic: **United by the Spirit**
Youth Topic: **The Power of the Faithful**
Adult/Youth Key Verse: **Acts 2:4**
Print Passage: **Acts 2:1-17a**

—Pentecost was originally an Old Testament festival that occurred fifty days after Passover. Jewish tradition held that the Law was given on this day.
—The Spirit's coming at Pentecost is often understood as the reversal of the Tower of Babel story.
—This story affirms the close relationship between baptism and the Spirit's gifts.
—The coming of the Holy Spirit was the fulfillment of a promise Jesus had made to His disciples (John 15:26; Acts 1:8).
—The presence of the Holy Spirit was symbolized by the tongue-shaped, flame-like appearances emerging from a common source, and resting on the 120 believers gathered there.
—The believers present began speaking in languages that could be understood in their own tongues.

CHILDREN

Children Topic: **The Power of Togetherness**
Key Verse: **Acts 2:4**
Print Passage: **Acts 2:1-8, 11-12, 14, 38-42**

—The believers were together when God's Spirit filled them.
—When the Galileans spoke in other languages, it caught the crowd's attention and amazed them.
—Jews from every nation heard the Gospel preached in their native tongues.
—Peter addressed the crowd about salvation.
—Three thousand persons received Peter's message and became believers.

I. INTRODUCTION

A. The Pentecost

Pentecost was one of the most important days in the lives of the first disciples of Jesus Christ. It was important then and it is equally important now for several reasons. First, it marked the end of the era of the earthly mission and ministry of Jesus, and the beginning of the end-time ministry of the Holy Spirit. God is at work in the world today through the Holy Spirit. Second, it marked the fulfillment of God's promise that He would pour out His Spirit upon all flesh, which had been made hundreds of years before the birth of Jesus during the prophetic ministry of Joel (see Proverbs 1:23; and Joel 2:28).

Third, Pentecost marked the beginning of the new age of the Spirit-filled and Spirit-led church. The new messianic community of faith came into existence with mighty signs and supernatural wonders. Jesus had promised His disciples that He would send them another Comforter, who would be the Holy Spirit (see John 14:16). Luke recorded the events that led up to the coming of the Holy Spirit in Acts 1:4, 8, where we read the command of Jesus to His disciples to remain in Jerusalem until they had received the promise of the Father, followed by the command to go and preach the Gospel everywhere. "And, being assembled together with them, commanded them that they should not depart from Jerusalem, but wait for the promise of the Father, which, saith he, ye have heard of me" (Acts 1:4). "But ye shall receive power, after that the Holy Ghost is come upon you: and ye shall be witnesses unto me both in Jerusalem, and in all Judaea, and in Samaria, and unto the uttermost part of the earth" (Acts 1:8).

The final reason Pentecost was and is important is that it was the day that God filled the church with spiritual power so that they could continue the mission of Jesus, which was to preach the Gospel to a lost and dying world—beginning in Jerusalem and eventually going into the entire world.

B. Biblical Background

The Old Testament name for *Pentecost* is "the Feast of Weeks." The Feast of Weeks was one of the three major festivals that required every male to "appear before the Lord" (see Exodus 23:16-17; Deuteronomy 16:16). The others were Passover and the Feast of Booths. No one was to appear "empty-handed." According to ancient Jewish historian Josephus, the Feast of Weeks came to be called *Pentecost* about 200 years before the birth of Christ. The Hebrew celebration of the Feast of Weeks is the foundation for the Christian celebration of Pentecost. The Christian celebration of then *Feast of Weeks* h an entirely different purpose, which will be discussed later in the lesson. Our pur to understand Pentecost, or the Feast of Weeks, as it was originally given by Hebrew people.

The word *Pentecost* literally means "fifty," which is where the feast gets its name. The Feast of Weeks was to be celebrated at the end of seven complete Sabbaths following Passover and Unleavened Bread. Accordingly, it was celebrated on the day following the seventh Sabbath, which marked the fiftieth day. It was a feast that celebrated the completion of the grain and barley harvests. The Feast of Weeks usually falls in the early summer between May and June. First fruits celebrated the pending harvest while Pentecost celebrated the results of the actual harvest.

The Feast of Weeks was observed on the fiftieth day. The number "fifty" is used to express (in symbolic terms) liberty, freedom, and deliverance. In Leviticus 25:8-17, *fifty* represented the Year of Jubilee in which freedom was proclaimed throughout the land. Debts were cancelled, slaves were set free, and families were reunited during the Jubilee celebration. Fifty was also the mandatory retirement age for the Levites. After the age of fifty they were released from service in the Tabernacle and Temple (see Numbers 4:1-3). The Feast of Weeks was characterized by the giving of five major offerings—a new grain offering and wave, burnt, sin, and peace offerings. More was given by the individual during this feast than any other feast. The feast consisted of a bread offering, baked from fine flour and leaven. This is the only feast where the bread offerings use leaven or yeast. The feast was proclaimed a holy convocation or sacred gathering. God told Moses that the celebration was to be treated as a Sabbath, wherein no work was to be done.

II. EXPOSITION AND APPLICATION OF THE SCRIPTURE

A. The Mighty Wind of the Spirit
(Acts 2:1-4)

AND WHEN the day of Pentecost was fully come, they were all with one accord in one place. And suddenly there came a sound from heaven as of a rushing mighty wind, and it filled all the house where they were sitting. And there appeared unto them cloven tongues like as of fire, and it sat upon each of them. And they were all filled with the Holy Ghost, and began to speak with other tongues, as the Spirit gave them utterance.

Luke recorded that the coming of the Holy Spirit occurred on the Day of Pentecost. It was Luke's practice to give as precise a date and time as possible for the events that he recorded (see Luke 2:1). The disciples of Jesus were all gathered together in Jerusalem awaiting the promise of the Father (see Acts 1:4-5). The Greek word for "one accord" is *homo-thu-*. It literally means "to have to be of one mind, one passion, or to do something in unison." They were in complete agreement about where they were supposed to be, what they were supposed to be doing, and what they were expecting. We are not sure where in Jerusalem they were waiting, and it is not that critical to the events described.

The coming of the Holy Spirit was a sudden occurrence that began without any prior notice. There was the sound from heaven that was as a mighty rushing wind. The house was filled and there appeared something like tongues of fire which rested upon each of them. Everyone in the place was filled with the Holy Spirit and began to speak in languages that they had never spoken before. The fact that these men began to speak in other languages is critical to understanding the import of the text. First, the Spirit empowered them to do something beyond their natural abilities. They did not speak in these tongues or languages based on their desire, but on the desire of the Spirit. Secondly, this heavenly communication occurred to help unbelievers understand the Gospel. There is a popular but unrealistic teaching which suggests that "speaking in tongues" helps believers to draw closer to God. However, this instance of tongues or languages was to help the unbelievers hear the Gospel in languages that they could understand. This only happened as the Spirit empowered them to do it.

One of the things that characterized this day for the disciples was the spirit of expectancy. The disciples remained in Jerusalem because they were told to wait for the Father's promise. Thus, they were expecting something great to happen. They had a sense that something would happen, but they were not sure what it would be. When the Spirit descended upon the disciples on the Day of Pentecost, they were expecting God to do something great. They had no idea what this would be. The Holy Spirit exceeded their expectations of what would happen. They had no idea that God would come in such a miraculous and powerful way. The best Luke could say was, "It was the sound of a mighty rushing wind and there appeared things like cloven tongues like fire and rested over each one of the disciples' heads" (see verses 2-3). God came with signs and wonders.

There are two important lessons for post-modern Christians to learn. The first one is to have the unity and oneness among them. The body of Christ will become much more effective when the spirit of division is truly eradicated. Unity is something that we must work at and promote. Second, believers need to learn how to expect God to do great things in their lives, through their lives, and with their lives. Jesus said, "Truly, truly, I say to you, he who believes in Me, the works that I do, he will do also; and greater works than these he will do; because I go to the Father. Whatever you ask in My name, that will I do, so that the Father may be glorified in the Son" (John 14:12-13, NASB). Jesus promised us that we would be able to do things that He did not do.

B. The Powerful Witness to the Nations (Acts 2:5-13)

And there were dwelling at Jerusalem Jews, devout men, out of every nation under heaven. Now when this was noised abroad, the multitude came together, and were confounded, because that every man heard them speak in his own language. And they were all amazed and marvelled, saying one to another, Behold, are not all these which speak Galilaeans? And how hear we every man in our own tongue, wherein we were born? Parthians, and Medes, and Elamites, and the dwellers in Mesopotamia, and in Judaea, and Cappadocia, in Pontus, and Asia, Phrygia, and Pamphylia, in Egypt, and in the parts of Libya about Cyrene, and strangers of Rome, Jews and proselytes, Cretes and Arabians, we do hear them speak in our tongues the wonderful works of God. And they were all amazed, and were in doubt, saying one to another, What meaneth this? Others mocking said, These men are full of new wine.

Jews had come to Jerusalem from all over the Roman Empire for the annual Feast of Weeks celebration. The sounds coming from Jesus' disciples were so loud that they aroused a deep curiosity among the visitors in the city. They rushed to the place to see if they could discover from where the noise and commotion were emerging. Then amazement gripped them because they were hearing and understanding in their own language. They knew that the speakers were Galileans, but they could not understand how they spoke fluently in a manner that the visitors understood.

These verses have been among the most

hotly debated and contested in the Christian faith. They have served as the framework for the establishment of entire denominations (for example, the Church of God in Christ and the Assemblies of God). Essentially, Luke recorded that the coming of the Holy Spirit was evidenced by the disciples as being given a gift to speak the Word of God at that moment in a way that everyone could understand. How do we understand speaking in tongues? We must understand that they were not speaking in unknown or unintelligible languages or in ecstatic speech, which was the case in Corinth. There is but one plausible explanation that fits the context of the text. They spoke in such a way that the Holy Spirit empowered everyone present to hear and understand what was being said. It was the Holy Spirit doing the work and not the disciples. They were merely the instruments through whom God was working. Men and women understood in the language of their birth and country. How someone could speak in a Galilean dialect and be understood by someone speaking in the language of the Medes is inexplicable. This event took place on the Day of Pentecost, and it heralded the birth of the Christian church and beginning of the spread of the Gospel to all nations (see Matthew 28:19-20; Acts 1:8). There was another such occasion in Acts 10:44-46.

There were three reactions from the crowds of people who witnessed what was happening. The first was amazement. They had never seen nor heard anything like this before. Second, some people were in doubt about what they were witnessing. Third, others mocked and thought that the disciples were drunk. Often, the disciples of Jesus face varying responses to the power and presence of the Holy Spirit.

The church of the Lord Jesus Christ has been sent into the world to be a witness of God's saving grace and mercy. The lack of presence and commitment to global evangelism and missions is the biggest shortcoming of the African-American Christian church. While we have been actively engaged in social ministry in America, we have been virtually absent in Africa, South America, and the Caribbean. Christians have been empowered to speak for God through the presence and power of the Holy Spirit. Pentecost revealed that the Word of God breaks across all barriers and speaks to men and women in their own languages and experiences. The most incredible thing about Pentecost was its impact: it reached the entire Jewish nation at one time on one day. God had honored His Word that Israel would be brought together and would receive a new power of prophetic speech and the gift of salvation (see Joel 2:28-32).

C. The Convicting Word Delivered (Acts 2:14-17a)

But Peter, standing up with the eleven, lifted up his voice, and said unto them, Ye men of Judaea, and all ye that dwell at Jerusalem, be this known unto you, and hearken to my words: For these are not drunken, as ye suppose, seeing it is but the third hour of the day. But this is that which was spoken by the prophet Joel; And it shall come to pass in the last days, saith God, I will pour out of my Spirit upon all flesh.

Peter stood and began to speak to the crowd that had gathered at the place where the disciples were gathered. He declared that they were not drunk as some people thought, but they were walking and talking in the power of the Holy Spirit. Peter stated that what was occurring had already been prophesied by the prophet Joel. The book of the Acts of the Apostles provides us with a view of the earliest Christian preaching. We know that the earliest Christian writings were done by the apostle Paul—for example, 1 Thessalonians. C. H. Dodd, the New Testament scholar, identified the kernel of apostolic preaching. He noted that there were six basic elements of apostolic preaching: (1) the age of fulfillment had dawned–"This is that…"; (2) this had all taken place through the death and resurrection of Jesus; (3) by virtue of His resurrection Jesus has been exalted to the right hand of God, as messianic Head of the New Israel, the church; (4) the Holy Spirit in the church is the sign of God's presence in power and glory; (5) the Messianic Age will shortly reach its consummation in the return of Christ; and (6) the *kerygma* (apostolic proclamation of salvation through Jesus Christ) always closes with an appeal to repent and the promise of salvation in this life and the age to come.

III. CONCLUDING REFLECTION

The postmodern Christian church can learn a great deal from the saints of the first century about obedience to Jesus Christ, commitment to the Great Commission, and perseverance under pressure. Pentecost teaches us that God continues to save and redeem the world through the power of the Holy Spirit. It speaks to us about God's creative genius and ability to fashion new beginnings.

Through the power and presence of the Holy Spirit, each believer gains the power and authority to achieve the great purpose of God in the world.

PRAYER

Heavenly Father, we thank You for the power of the Holy Spirit that enables us to achieve Your purpose in the world. In Jesus' name we pray. Amen.

WORD POWER

Filled (Greek: *eplesthesan [ep-le-sthe-san]*)—**this means they were all filled. Grammatically, it is cast in a passive statement which means they have nothing to do with the filling. An outside agent (Holy Spirit) came with a visible sign upon each of them, and they were entirely under His sacred influence and power.** *To be filled* **denotes that all the faculties were pervaded by it and engaged in it.**

HOME DAILY BIBLE READINGS
(September 29–October 5, 2008)

Empowered to Be a Community

MONDAY, September 29: "Fellowship with God and Jesus" (1 John 1:1-4)

TUESDAY, September 30: "Living in Hope" (Acts 2:22-35)

WEDNESDAY, October 1: "Living in Fellowship" (Acts 2:37-47)

THURSDAY, October 2: "Receive the Holy Spirit" (John 20:19-23)

FRIDAY, October 3: "One Body in Christ" (Romans 12:3-8)

SATURDAY, October 4: "The Coming of the Holy Spirit" (Acts 2:1-13)

SUNDAY, October 5: "Living in the Last Days" (Acts 2:1-21)

LESSON 6

October 12, 2008

EXPANSION OF THE COMMUNITY

DEVOTIONAL READING: **Acts 1:3-11**
PRINT PASSAGE: **Acts 6:1-5, 8-15**

BACKGROUND SCRIPTURE: **Acts 6:1-15; 8:1-8**
KEY VERSE: **Acts 6:7**

Acts 6:1-5, 8-15—KJV

AND IN those days, when the number of the disciples was multiplied, there arose a murmuring of the Grecians against the Hebrews, because their widows were neglected in the daily ministration.

2 Then the twelve called the multitude of the disciples unto them, and said, It is not reason that we should leave the word of God, and serve tables.

3 Wherefore, brethren, look ye out among you seven men of honest report, full of the Holy Ghost and wisdom, whom we may appoint over this business.

4 But we will give ourselves continually to prayer, and to the ministry of the word.

5 And the saying pleased the whole multitude: and they chose Stephen, a man full of faith and of the Holy Ghost, and Philip, and Prochorus, and Nicanor, and Timon, and Parmenas, and Nicolas a proselyte of Antioch.

…..

8 And Stephen, full of faith and power, did great wonders and miracles among the people.

9 Then there arose certain of the synagogue, which is called the synagogue of the Libertines, and Cyrenians, and Alexandrians, and of them of Cilicia and of Asia, disputing with Stephen.

10 And they were not able to resist the wisdom and the spirit by which he spake.

11 Then they suborned men, which said, We have heard him speak blasphemous words against Moses, and against God.

12 And they stirred up the people, and the elders, and the scribes, and came upon him, and caught him, and brought him to the council,

13 And set up false witnesses, which said, This man ceaseth not to speak blasphemous words against this holy place, and the law:

14 For we have heard him say, that this Jesus of Nazareth shall destroy this place, and shall change the customs which Moses delivered us.

15 And all that sat in the council, looking stedfastly on him, saw his face as it had been the face of an angel.

Acts 6:1-5, 8-15—NRSV

NOW DURING those days, when the disciples were increasing in number, the Hellenists complained against the Hebrews because their widows were being neglected in the daily distribution of food.

2 And the twelve called together the whole community of the disciples and said, "It is not right that we should neglect the word of God in order to wait on tables.

3 Therefore, friends, select from among yourselves seven men of good standing, full of the Spirit and of wisdom, whom we may appoint to this task,

4 while we, for our part, will devote ourselves to prayer and to serving the word."

5 What they said pleased the whole community, and they chose Stephen, a man full of faith and the Holy Spirit, together with Philip, Prochorus, Nicanor, Timon, Parmenas, and Nicolaus, a proselyte of Antioch.

…..

8 Stephen, full of grace and power, did great wonders and signs among the people.

9 Then some of those who belonged to the synagogue of the Freedmen (as it was called), Cyrenians, Alexandrians, and others of those from Cilicia and Asia, stood up and argued with Stephen.

10 But they could not withstand the wisdom and the Spirit with which he spoke.

11 Then they secretly instigated some men to say, "We have heard him speak blasphemous words against Moses and God."

12 They stirred up the people as well as the elders and the scribes; then they suddenly confronted him, seized him, and brought him before the council.

13 They set up false witnesses who said, "This man never stops saying things against this holy place and the law;

14 for we have heard him say that this Jesus of Nazareth will destroy this place and will change the customs that Moses handed on to us."

15 And all who sat in the council looked intently at him, and they saw that his face was like the face of an angel.

TOPICAL OUTLINE OF THE LESSON

I. **Introduction**
   A. Christian Leadership
   B. Biblical Background

II. **Exposition and Application of the Scripture**
   A. Church Growth Produces Conflict
      (Acts 6:1-3)
   B. The Apostles Established Priorities
      (Acts 6:4-5)
   C. Stephen's Ministry in Jerusalem
      (Acts 6:8-15)

III. **Concluding Reflection**

LESSON OBJECTIVES

Upon completion of this lesson, the students will know that:

1. Growth in the apostolic church gave rise to the choosing of deacons;
2. Leaders are chosen on the basis of need; and,
3. Because of his ability to preach, Deacon Stephen became the first Christian martyr.

POINTS TO BE EMPHASIZED

ADULT/YOUTH

Adult Topic: **Discerning Gifts for Leadership**
Youth Topic: **Get More Help**
Adult/Youth Key Verse: **Acts 6:7**
Print Passage: **Acts 6:1-5, 8-15**

—There was a long-standing tradition of care of the poor within the synagogue, and Christians continued this practice. The Hellenists, Greek-speaking Jews of the diaspora, felt that their widows were being neglected in the daily distribution of goods.
—The apostles took decisive action to select seven deacons so that the necessary service of the table fellowship could be assured.
—The Spirit played a vital role in choosing Stephen.
—Bringing Stephen before the Sanhedrin Council indicated the significant growth and impact of the Christian community.
—The Christian community had grown larger than the apostles could handle alone.
—By appointing deacons, the apostles instituted a model of shared leadership in the community of faith.

CHILDREN

Children Topic: **Choosing Helpers for the Work**
Key Verse: **Acts 6:3**
Print Passage: **Acts 6:1-8**

—The believing community addressed the complaint of the Hellenists.
—The apostles established high qualifications for serving the widows.
—Seven men were chosen and commissioned for their task.
—The apostles were able to continue with their work.
—The Word of God spread and the believers increased.

I. INTRODUCTION

A. Christian Leadership

Over the past twenty years the subject of Christian leadership has probably been more widely discussed, debated, and written about. Our bookstores are filled with books on leadership. Many congregations around the world are looking for men and women who will embody the spirit of Jesus and make a difference in the life of their local church and community. Why has so much attention been given to Christian leadership? The answers vary and are as numerous as the people who would offer an explanation. There are two possible reasons. First, there are numerous counterfeit models in the church today that have virtually crippled the body of Christ.

Second, the decline in traditional denominations has given rise to independent churches and leaders who feel that they embody the true church of Jesus Christ.

B. Biblical Background

The rapid growth of the Christian faith prompted the apostles to recruit and ordain additional people who could help with the ministry to the widows and orphans. According to Acts 6:1-6, the members of the congregation recommended seven men. The criterion for choosing these men were that they be full of the Holy Spirit, possess wisdom, and have good reputations. They brought these men to the apostles and they laid their hands on them and appointed them the task of distributing the daily bread to the widows.

Traditionally, this passage has been interpreted as the biblical foundation for the establishment of the office of deacon. But it is obvious that they did much more than make sure that the widows received daily rations of food. They did evangelistic work and in some cases performed miraculous signs and wonders (see Acts 8:1-8, 46).

II. EXPOSITION AND APPLICATION OF THE SCRIPTURE

A. Church Growth Produces Conflict
(Acts 6:1-3)

AND IN those days, when the number of the disciples was multiplied, there arose a murmuring of the Grecians against the Hebrews, because their widows were neglected in the daily ministration. Then the twelve called the multitude of the disciples unto them, and said, It is not reason that we should leave the word of God, and serve tables. Wherefore, brethren, look ye out among you seven men of honest report, full of the Holy Ghost and wisdom, whom we may appoint over this business.

After Pentecost, the Christian church grew very rapidly in and around Jerusalem (see Acts 2:41; 4:4; 5:14). As the church grew, it took on a multicultural flavor consisting of Hellenistic (Greek-speaking) and Hebrew-speaking members. Rapid growth gave rise to a new set of challenges for the apostles who were not only giving leadership, teaching, and preaching, but also tending to the needs of the widows and the helpless among them. These actions were in line with the ancient Hebrew tradition of taking care of the widows, orphans, and strangers in their midst (see Leviticus 19:15; Deuteronomy 15:11; Malachi 3:5). Soon conflict erupted between the Greek-speaking and Hebrew-speaking members over how the church's resources were being distributed among the widows in the church. Early on, the apostles made sure that there was no one among them in need of the basic necessities of life (see Acts 2:46; 4:34-35). The Greek-speaking believers began to *murmur* (Greek: *gongusmos*), which means "to debate in secret, or secret displeasure about a matter." We are not sure how their discontent reached the ears of the apostles. However, within any congregation it is difficult to keep widespread displeasure and disagreement hidden. Eventually, these feelings begin to manifest themselves in overt ways that indicate a problem.

The apostles called a meeting of the entire congregation to consider the nature of the conflict and to look for ways of peacefully resolving it. Prior to calling the meeting they must have come together as leaders, prayed for guidance from the Holy Spirit, and considered the matter in great detail. They informed the congregation that it was unrealistic for them to devote so much time to serving tables and doing work that others surely could do. The wording of verse 2 gives the impression that they had discussed among themselves what should be their first priority—being ministers of the Word of God and prayer.

They appealed to the congregation to look out among themselves and find seven men with good reputations, who were full of the Holy Spirit and wisdom. *Seven* is the number of perfection and completion and very well-attested to in the Scriptures. The congregation was instructed to bring the names or the persons

before the apostles and they would be formally commissioned to take on the responsibility of looking after the widows in the daily administration of the food.

Verse 3 is one of the most important passages in the New Testament when it comes to giving clear and discernible direction regarding the selection and appointment of persons to responsible leadership positions in the church. One of the earliest examples of this process is found in the life of Moses (see Exodus 18:13-27). During the Exodus, Jethro, Moses's father-in-law, offered him some wise counsel regarding the selection of a group of leaders who could assist him with his work (see Exodus 18:13-27). The lessons learned and applied from this event in the history of the Christian church would save a lot of congregations from experiencing grief at a later time.

First, the leaders were selected based upon their spiritual maturity, not a kinship or relationships within the body. They were to look out among them, which implied a diligent searching and examination of all of the possible choices in their midst. In the New Testament, those who were spiritual and mature were always charged with helping the young to grow in grace (see Galatians 6:1; 1 Timothy 3:6; 5:22; 1 Peter 5:5).

Second, the leaders were chosen based upon a specific set of selection criteria. The disciples were given three areas upon which to base their recommendations: (1) the person had to be full of the Holy Spirit; (2) the individual must have a good reputation; and (3) this person must possess wisdom. How do we know if someone is full of the Holy Spirit? They manifest the fruit of the Spirit according to Galatians 5:22-23, and they are bold in their witness (see Acts 5:31). A good reputation is the result of living a righteous life in the community. Our lifestyles become readily available to those who live around us (see Acts 16:1-2). The candidate must possess wisdom, which is the capacity to make good, sound decisions. Spiritual leaders could not be self-made nor could (or can) the congregation produce them. They come from being born-again and filled with the power and presence of the Holy Spirit. Thus, they reflect the visible and manifest presence of the power of the Holy Spirit at work in their lives and ministries.

B. The Apostles Established Priorities
(Acts 6:4-5)

But we will give ourselves continually to prayer, and to the ministry of the word. And the saying pleased the whole multitude: and they chose Stephen, a man full of faith and of the Holy Ghost, and Philip, and Prochorus, and Nicanor, and Timon, and Parmenas, and Nicolas a proselyte of Antioch.

The apostles announced that it was not right for them to neglect their primary duties—which were preaching, teaching, and prayer—in order to serve widows and orphans. This did not lessen the importance of the church's responsibility. Rather, it forced them to think clearly about their primary function as spiritual leaders. Every pastor knows the challenge of being consumed with a vast array of busy tasks that rob him or her of precious time that could be spent in the preparation for ministry of the Word of God. Busyness must never be equated with doing ministry. We can certainly be busy about the wrong things and have our priorities misplaced from God's true purpose for our ministries (see 1 Kings 20:39-40). Many congregations are busy with a host of activities, but activity is not a sign that ministry and mission are a priority in the church.

The apostles were going to give themselves to prayer continually. The Greek word that is used is *proskatereo* and it means "to continue steadfastly, to be earnest toward a thing, or to be completely consumed with a thing." Prayer and ministry of the Word of God are the central responsibilities of the apostles and should be the responsibility of pastors.

The recommendation of the apostles pleased the entire congregation. There was agreement with the recommendation coming to the apostles. They selected seven men who met the qualifications outlined by the apostles. We are not told how they went about doing this. However, the Jews had a history of organizing themselves by tribes, clans, or families (see Exodus 13:18; 18:13-27; Numbers 2:1-34). It would not be surprising to find the same sort of structure in the church of Jerusalem.

All of the seven men had Greek names, indicating that they were Hellenists. Their selection pointed out that the people were more interested in choosing the right people than simply selecting someone who was from their clan. Stephen was named first and was described as a man full of faith and of the Holy Spirit. This is not to say that the others were not full of faith or of the Holy Spirit. Stephen demonstrated his commitment and faith to Jesus Christ by his willingness to face martyrdom at the hands of Jewish religious leaders.

C. Stephen's Ministry in Jerusalem
(Acts 6:8-15)

And Stephen, full of faith and power, did great wonders and miracles among the people. Then there arose certain of the synagogue, which is called the synagogue of the Libertines, and Cyrenians, and Alexandrians, and of

them of Cilicia and of Asia, disputing with Stephen. And they were not able to resist the wisdom and the spirit by which he spake. Then they suborned men, which said, We have heard him speak blasphemous words against Moses, and against God. And they stirred up the people, and the elders, and the scribes, and came upon him, and caught him, and brought him to the council, And set up false witnesses, which said, This man ceaseth not to speak blasphemous words against this holy place, and the law: For we have heard him say, that this Jesus of Nazareth shall destroy this place, and shall change the customs which Moses delivered us. And all that sat in the council, looking stedfastly on him, saw his face as it had been the face of an angel.

We do not know anything about Stephen's family background or his social history. All we know is what we read in Acts 6 and 7. Here is what we do know about Stephen.

- He was highly respected and regarded by the members of the Jerusalem church.
- He had a very active preaching and healing ministry around Jerusalem.
- He performed great signs and wonders among the people.
- He was a skilled orator and was well-versed in the Scriptures.
- He was bold and relentless in the face of stiff opposition. He was not a weak man.
- He was tried by a court of outraged religious leaders who eventually incited a mob to stone him outside the city walls of Jerusalem.
- He is remembered as the first martyr of the Christian faith.

The Jewish religious leaders became the first antagonists of the church (see Acts 4:1-19; 5:17-29). In addition to the apostles, opposition arose against the seven, particularly Stephen, which was a direct result of the effectiveness of his ministry (verse 8). "Then there arose certain of the synagogue, which is called the synagogue of the Libertines, and Cyrenians, and Alexandrians, and them of Cilicia and of Asia, disputing with Stephen" (verse 9). These Jewish religious leaders were very influential in their religious circles and they were adamantly opposed to the spread of Christianity.

Stephen confounded the Jewish religious leaders through his words (verse 10). The message of Jesus Christ was a real threat to them and their traditions. They were ready to defend their traditions at all costs. They gathered false witnesses and instigated hostility against Stephen (verse 11). The leaders accused Stephen of speaking blasphemous words against the Law of Moses, defaming the Temple, and seeking to change the customs that had been handed down to them by Moses (verses 11, 13-14).

Stephen was up against deeply entrenched religious traditions and customs that the religious leaders embraced. There were a number of factors at work against Stephen. For one thing, he was interacting with a group of people who were jealous about the successes of the apostles. People were being saved, filled with the Holy Spirit, delivered from demonic possession, edified, healed—and lives were being changed. Another obstacle Stephen faced stemmed from the fabricated half-truths of the Jewish religious leaders who were highly regarded in the city. The scribes and elders of the people were saying that this Jesus was going to destroy the Temple (verse 14). Who could be more credible than them? Stephen was arrested and brought before the Sanhedrin to face the charges against him. When the leaders looked into his face, it was as though they had seen the face of an angel (verse 15).

III. CONCLUDING REFLECTION

This study has taught us several important lessons that every congregation would do well to heed. First, numerical growth and spiritual growth are not the same thing. When leaders do not pay attention to the internal spiritual life of the church, conflict can and usually does erupt. Second, leaders must be selected based upon clear spiritual standards. We should not appoint leaders based on social standing. We should not appoint leaders based on connections. When congregations appoint unspiritual leaders, they set themselves up for a host of problems. Third, congregations must see the relationship between congregational growth and the spiritual growth of the leader. When pastors are free to give unfettered time to study and prayer, it can only be a positive thing for the church. Finally, ingrained traditions and customs can be a powerful deterrent to congregational growth and change.

Our churches will be stronger spiritually if we look at the method by which the apostles selected the first seven deacons. First, there was a need. They recognized the need and they told the congregation about it. It is a common saying that "an idle hand is the workshop of Satan." When there is no definitive role for deacons, they will easily foment troubles. Second, they did not have hand in the selection of the men. Today, pastors should stay away from pushing anybody for the office of deacon. Third, based on the criterion stipulated by the apostles, the congregation fulfilled their mission and they presented them before the apostles for laying on of hands.

PRAYER

Heavenly Father, thank You for loving us and calling us to the ministry of the Word. Give us the boldness that characterized the life and ministry of Stephen, so that we will be willing to take a strong stand for You. In Jesus' name we pray. Amen.

WORD POWER

Increased (Greek: *eeuxanen [ee-ok-sa-nen]*) —**means "the word of God kept on growing all the more." The increase is attributed to the coming down of the Holy Spirit upon the disciples and the newly chosen deacons. God will continue to multiply and increase His Word, when ministered by those whom He has qualified to proclaim it. In the words of Charles Spurgeon, "There are ministers sailing in false colors."**

HOME DAILY BIBLE READINGS
(October 6-12, 2008)

Expansion of the Community

MONDAY, October 6: "No Other Name" (Acts 4:1-12)
TUESDAY, October 7: "What We Have Seen and Heard" (Acts 4:13-22)
WEDNESDAY, October 8: "Speaking the Word Boldly" (Acts 4:23-31)
THURSDAY, October 9: "Breaking Community Trust" (Acts 5:1-11)
FRIDAY, October 10: "Obeying God" (Acts 5:27-39)
SATURDAY, October 11: "Scattered but Proclaiming" (Acts 8:1-8)
SUNDAY, October 12: "Full of the Spirit and Wisdom" (Acts 6:1-15)

LESSON 7   October 19, 2008

TRANSFORMED TO WITNESS
TO THE COMMUNITY

DEVOTIONAL READING: **Galatians 1:11-24**
PRINT PASSAGE: **Acts 9:1-11, 16-19a**

BACKGROUND SCRIPTURE: **Acts 9:1-31**
KEY VERSE: **Acts 9:17b**

Acts 9:1-11, 16-19a—KJV

AND SAUL, yet breathing out threatenings and slaughter against the disciples of the Lord, went unto the high priest,

2 And desired of him letters to Damascus to the synagogues, that if he found any of this way, whether they were men or women, he might bring them bound unto Jerusalem.

3 And as he journeyed, he came near Damascus: and suddenly there shined round about him a light from heaven:

4 And he fell to the earth, and heard a voice saying unto him, Saul, Saul, why persecutest thou me?

5 And he said, Who art thou, Lord? And the Lord said, I am Jesus whom thou persecutest: it is hard for thee to kick against the pricks.

6 And he trembling and astonished said, Lord, what wilt thou have me to do? And the Lord said unto him, Arise, and go into the city, and it shall be told thee what thou must do.

7 And the men which journeyed with him stood speechless, hearing a voice, but seeing no man.

8 And Saul arose from the earth; and when his eyes were opened, he saw no man: but they led him by the hand, and brought him into Damascus.

9 And he was three days without sight, and neither did eat nor drink.

10 And there was a certain disciple at Damascus, named Ananias; and to him said the Lord in a vision, Ananias. And he said, Behold, I am here, Lord.

11 And the Lord said unto him, Arise, and go into the street which is called Straight, and enquire in the house of Judas for one called Saul, of Tarsus: for, behold, he prayeth.

.....

16 For I will shew him how great things he must suffer for my name's sake.

17 And Ananias went his way, and entered into the

Acts 9:1-11, 16-19a—NRSV

MEANWHILE SAUL, still breathing threats and murder against the disciples of the Lord, went to the high priest

2 and asked him for letters to the synagogues at Damascus, so that if he found any who belonged to the Way, men or women, he might bring them bound to Jerusalem.

3 Now as he was going along and approaching Damascus, suddenly a light from heaven flashed around him.

4 He fell to the ground and heard a voice saying to him, "Saul, Saul, why do you persecute me?"

5 He asked, "Who are you, Lord?" The reply came, "I am Jesus, whom you are persecuting.

6 But get up and enter the city, and you will be told what you are to do."

7 The men who were traveling with him stood speechless because they heard the voice but saw no one.

8 Saul got up from the ground, and though his eyes were open, he could see nothing; so they led him by the hand and brought him into Damascus.

9 For three days he was without sight, and neither ate nor drank.

10 Now there was a disciple in Damascus named Ananias. The Lord said to him in a vision, "Ananias." He answered, "Here I am, Lord."

11 The Lord said to him, "Get up and go to the street called Straight, and at the house of Judas look for a man of Tarsus named Saul. At this moment he is praying.

.....

16 "I myself will show him how much he must suffer for the sake of my name."

17 So Ananias went and entered the house. He laid

house; and putting his hands on him said, Brother Saul, the Lord, even Jesus, that appeared unto thee in the way as thou camest, hath sent me, that thou mightest receive thy sight, and be filled with the Holy Ghost.

18 And immediately there fell from his eyes as it had been scales: and he received sight forthwith, and arose, and was baptized.

19 And when he had received meat, he was strengthened.

his hands on Saul and said, "Brother Saul, the Lord Jesus, who appeared to you on your way here, has sent me so that you may regain your sight and be filled with the Holy Spirit."

18 And immediately something like scales fell from his eyes, and his sight was restored. Then he got up and was baptized,

19 and after taking some food, he regained his strength.

TOPICAL OUTLINE OF THE LESSON

I. **Introduction**
   A. Saul's Conversion
   B. Biblical Background

II. **Exposition and Application of the Scripture**
   A. Vendetta Against the Disciples (Acts 9:1-2)
   B. Vision of the Son of God (Acts 9:3-9)
   C. Visitation by the Servant of God (Acts 9:10-11, 16-19a)

III. **Concluding Reflection**

LESSON OBJECTIVES

Upon completion of this lesson, the students will know that:

1. After Saul's conversion, he became a world-renowned evangelist;
2. No one is too sinful to be used after a conversion experience; and,
3. No earthly power can stop the work of God from advancing.

POINTS TO BE EMPHASIZED

ADULT/YOUTH

Adult Topic: New Vision
Youth Topic: I'm Not the Same
Adult Key Verse: Acts 9:17b
Youth Key Verse: Acts 9:15
Print Passage: Acts 9:1-11, 16-19a

—"The Way" (verse 2) was one of the earliest names for Christianity.

—This story describes a powerful and immediate experience of the presence of Christ for Paul.

—The calling of Saul is identified with the mission to the Gentiles and ministry that involves suffering.

—The question "Why do you persecute me?" accentuates the close relationship between the risen Christ and the disciples. The voice moves from accusation to commission, indicating that this story is not simply about conversion but also about vocation—a call.

—Saul was a Roman citizen, a Pharisee, and a student of the legendary Gamaliel, and was notoriously zealous in his efforts to annihilate the followers of Jesus.

—Saul perceived those who followed Jesus Christ as a threat to Judaism, and as possibly violating the first commandment (see Exodus 20:3).

—The Lord prepared Ananias's heart to receive Saul as a brother in Christ.

CHILDREN

Children Topic: A Changed Life

Key Verse: Acts 9:15

Print Passage: Acts 9:3-11, 13-15, 17-19

—Saul's wrong actions were stopped by a personal encounter with Jesus Christ.

—A determined Saul started out on the road to Damascus—and a helpless Saul was led into the city.

—Ananias was not eager to go to a man who was considered evil.

—Ananias was obedient to God and went to Saul.

—Saul began to see both physically and spiritually.

—Saul changed from an opponent of Jesus to a follower.

INTRODUCTION

A. Saul's Conversion

The conversion of Saul (popularly known as Paul) on the road to Damascus is the account of one of the most renowned personal transformations in history. Saul's personal experience of the risen Lord led him to channel his energy and intellect into preaching and teaching the Gospel across the Roman Empire. The remainder of the book of Acts will devote considerable attention and space to Saul's work among the Gentiles (see Acts 13:1ff). Saul would come to think of himself as the "Apostle to the Gentiles" (see Galatians 2:2, 8; Ephesians 3:8). How could a man turn from persecutor of Christians into a proclaimer of the Gospel so dramatically and completely? The dictionary of biblical images reads, "Saul's experience was so dramatic that it is a metaphor for cataclysmic change in a person's life." Saul's conversion was full and complete. Conversion is, by definition, a complete change in one's life. It is our willing response to the Gospel call in which we sincerely repent of our sins and place our complete trust in Jesus Christ for salvation.

B. Biblical Background

We first meet Saul in Acts 7:58 at the stoning of Stephen. Saul was a young Pharisee from the Roman province of Cilicia in Asia Minor. Early on, Saul became convinced that Christianity was a serious challenge to the orthodox teachings of Judaism. In his mind it needed to be wiped out. Shortly after the stoning of Stephen, Christians experienced a tidal wave of persecution. We are told, in Acts 8:1, that about that time a great persecution broke out against the church in Jerusalem. All of the Christians left Jerusalem except the apostles. Some went to Samaria, others may have gone to Egypt, while others headed north to Antioch and as far north as Damascus, Syria (which was 135 miles north of Jerusalem). Saul gained influence among the religious leaders of Jerusalem for his zeal for the Law of Moses and the tradition of the elders. Somehow Saul found out that there was a thriving community of Christians living in Damascus. He determined that he must go there to put an end to their work. The high priest regarded him highly enough to honor his request for letters to go as far as Damascus to arrest any persons he found following this new teaching.

II. EXPOSITION AND APPLICATION OF THE SCRIPTURE

A. Vendetta Against the Disciples
(Acts 9:1-2)

AND SAUL, yet breathing out threatenings and slaughter against the disciples of the Lord, went unto the high priest, And desired of him letters to Damascus to the synagogues, that if he found any of this way, whether they were men or women, he might bring them bound unto Jerusalem.

Saul vehemently opposed the spread of Christianity. In verse 1, we are told that "Saul was breathing out threatenings…." In other words, Saul was still restless in his zeal to defend his Jewish faith from the new faith. He was bent on final annihilation of Christianity. The persecution that was unleashed with the stoning of Stephen further heightened his determination to stamp out the movement altogether. Saul had such hatred for Christians that his very persona breathed out anger and resentment. He was not just opposed to individuals, but these were the disciples of the Lord Jesus Christ. Paul confessed his sins to the church in Philippi. This is Paul in his own words: "Concerning zeal, persecuting the church; touching the righteousness which is in the law, blameless" (Philippians 3:6).

Saul was not satisfied with what he had done. Acts 8:3 reads: "As for Saul, he made havock of the church, entering into every house, and haling men and women committed them to prison." Saul's emotions moved from anger to rage. The combination of these two emotions is human dynamite in the soul—only God can defuse it. The word "yet" in verse 1 indicates that the stoning death of Stephen increased Saul's popularity as persecutor per excellence. The phrase "Breathing out threatenings" is cast in present active participle, which means that Saul was consumed with unparalleled zeal to end Christianity. Saul breathed like a warhorse that sniffed the smell of battle. The excessive rage drove him to request permission to pursue the disciples as far as Damascus. When he found some of them—whether they were male or female—he wanted to arrest them. He would bring them back to Jerusalem bound in chains or cords like animals to stand trial for blasphemy. Saul requested and received authorization to go into the synagogues and arrest any whom he found following "the Way." The name "the Way" was used early on to identify the first disciples of Jesus who adhered to His teachings (see Acts 19:9, 23; 22:4; 24:14).

B. Vision of the Son of God
(Acts 9:3-9)

And as he journeyed, he came near Damascus: and suddenly there shined round about him a light from heaven: And he fell to the earth, and heard a voice saying unto him, Saul, Saul, why persecutest thou me? And he said, Who art thou, Lord? And the Lord said, I am Jesus whom thou persecutest: it is hard for thee to kick against the pricks. And he trembling and astonished said, Lord, what wilt thou have me to do? And the Lord said unto him, Arise, and go into the city, and it shall be told thee what thou must do. And the men which journeyed with him stood speechless, hearing a voice, but seeing no man. And Saul arose from the earth; and when his eyes were opened, he saw no man: but they led him by the hand, and brought him into Damascus. And he was three days without sight, and neither did eat nor drink.

Saul's encounter with the living Lord Jesus Christ was an unforgettable experience that he told several times (see Acts 22:6-18; 26:12-18). As he and his followers journeyed to Damascus, a light suddenly appeared from heaven completely surrounding him (verse 3). When he told his experience to King Agrippa,

Paul noted that the light was brighter than the noon-day sun (see Acts 26:13). We are told that Saul, along with two other companions set out for Damascus on the ancient highway known as "the Way of the Sea." Tradition has it that when they neared the ridge that offers the first view of the ancient city something amazing happened.

Acts 9:3 reads: "And as he journeyed, he came near Damascus: and suddenly there shined round about him a light from heaven." We refer to this as a *theophany,* which means "an appearance of the Lord." In the Scriptures, when God was going to commission someone to go and do a great work there were these dramatic appearances (see Exodus 3:1ff; 19:16; Ezekiel 1:4). Saul fell to the ground and heard a voice saying, "Saul, Saul why are you persecuting me?" What Saul did to the disciples he was doing also to Jesus, for the persecuted ones were "the least of these" (see Matthew 25:40). Not sure about the light or the voice, Saul wanted to know who was speaking: "Who are you Lord?" The reply was, "I am Jesus whom thou persecutest: it is hard for thee to kick against the pricks." At this very dramatic moment, Saul came to the realization that Jesus was the Christ, and that He had been raised from the dead. He was fighting against a cause to which he could never defeat. "Kicking against the pricks" was a metaphor for senseless resistance. Saul was told that he must get up and go into the city of Damascus and he would be told there what he must do. What of the men who were with him? This was Saul's moment of truth and calling. Whenever God is moving in the life of an individual, others who are present are not addressed nor do they play any role in the event. God's call to service is a personal and private matter, although it can occur in the midst of a public place with others present. None can say how God will call anyone to the ministry. But it becomes visible when the one called responds to the powerful invisible voice.

In verse 6, Saul's reactions are noted in two ways. First, he was so overwhelmed by fear that he trembled or literally shook with fear (see Genesis 27:33; Exodus 19:16; 1 Samuel 4:13). Second, he was astonished, which literally means "to be amazed." At that very moment Saul submitted his life to the will of God. He said, "Lord, what wilt thou have me to do?" He was no longer in control of his life or destiny. His obedience to the command of Jesus was evidenced by his willingness to get up and go into the city, being led by others.

The men who were with him heard a voice, but there is no evidence that they heard the exact conversation between Jesus and Saul. They were astounded to the point that they were speechless. When Saul arose from the ground, his eyes were opened, but he could not see. The men who were with him took him and led him into the city of Damascus. As he entered Damascus, he was completely helpless and blind.

C. Visitation by the Servant of God (Acts 9:10-11, 16-19a)

And there was a certain disciple at Damascus, named Ananias; and to him said the Lord in a vision, Ananias. And he said, Behold, I am here, Lord. And the Lord said unto him, Arise, and go into the street which is called Straight, and enquire in the house of Judas for one called Saul, of Tarsus: for, behold, he prayeth.....For I will shew him how great things he must suffer for my name's sake. And Ananias went his way, and entered into the house; and putting his hands on him said, Brother Saul, the Lord, even Jesus, that appeared unto thee in the way as thou camest, hath sent me, that thou mightest receive thy sight, and be filled with the Holy Ghost. And immediately

there fell from his eyes as it had been scales: and he received sight forthwith, and arose, and was baptized. And when he had received meat, he was strengthened.

Through a vision Jesus touched a disciple living in Damascus named Ananias—whom He sent to Saul—who was in the home of a man named Judas. Jesus also told Ananias what Saul's new assignment would be and what Saul would go through for the cause of Jesus Christ (verse 11; see also 2 Corinthians 11:23-33). Jesus had to change the thinking of Ananias about who could be used for the sake of the Gospel (see verse 13). Once his mind had been changed, Ananias went his way and did as the Lord Jesus told him to do (verse 17).

God confirmed Saul's call to the work through the visit of Ananias. Ananias was told where to meet Saul. This meeting was divinely appointed. Straight Street was and still is one of the main thoroughfares of Damascus. Ananias was directed to the street and to the house of a man called Judas (not Iscariot). The Lord gave specific instructions to His ambassador about where to go and what to look for. The Lord told Saul ahead of time to expect Ananias. God will always confirm His call to service. There were at least three acts of confirmation of Saul's experience. First, when Ananias arrived, he relayed to Saul how the Lord Jesus Christ had sent him. Second, he related how he had been sent so that Saul would receive his sight. Third, he was sent so that Saul might be filled with the Holy Spirit—who would reveal the purpose of God for his life. Ananias, in obedience to Jesus, went and laid hands on Saul. Immediately, something fell from Saul's eyes that looked like scales. He arose and was baptized.

Saul was righteous and committed to God. Saul, Ananias, Peter, and Cornelius were all lovers and followers of God. But God had something more for them to do, and their lives and thinking had to be changed in order to move to that level of commitment. If you want to move to the next level of service, then let God change your thinking about where you are right now and in your life.

It is this radical commitment to Jesus Christ that is often misunderstood by many postmodern Christians who want the label of "Christian" but not the responsibility. Jesus Christ must become the very air of commitment that we breathe. What makes a Christian different is not the church to which one belongs but the radical change that has occurred in one's life.

III. CONCLUDING REFLECTION

In the experience of Saul, we see a man who was not a heathen, idol worshiper, atheist, or pagan. He was a very religious man who had a deep commitment to God. He was trained under Gamaliel, one of the legal luminaries in rabbinical and Jewish laws. He was very well-trained in the Scriptures and had met all of the qualifications for being a Pharisee. According to the customs of that day, he was a very righteous man. His religious credentials were impeccable. In Philippians 3:4-11, he wrote of his own credentials.

A cursory look at Psalm 2:1 reveals the inordinate ambition of earthly powers. They ganged up against the Lord and His anointed, but their gathering was an effort in futility. Saul, before he became the instrument of God's grace to the world, threatened to exterminate Christianity. However, Psalm 2:4 reads, "He who sits in the heavens shall laugh." There is no power to halt or stop the plan of God for His church.

The purpose of our lives may be revealed to us in many ways, such as: responding to the altar call, in a dramatic way, with gentle promptings of the Holy Spirit, or with a deep sense of urgency to fulfill a need in the community. These are some ways through which we may realize the calling of God to the ministry. God is incomprehensible; He works in different ways to accomplish His purposes through us. We must be willing to yield to Him when He calls us.

There are many lessons from this passage that speak to believers of every age. First, we note that no life is beyond the power of Jesus Christ. When men and women receive a vision of the resurrected Christ, their lives will change. Second, God has a plan and purpose for everyone's life. Saul's earliest training as a Pharisee would become very useful throughout the days of his ministry. Third, the church of the Lord Jesus Christ cannot be overthrown regardless of how determined the opponents of the Gospel may be. Fourth, when Jesus calls us, our first response should always be, "Yes, Lord, here am I. Send me."

PRAYER

Father, help us to know that Your church is indestructible by the forces of evil. Help us to love Your church and do what is required of us to keep her chaste until You come to take her unto Yourself. In Jesus' name we pray. Amen.

WORD POWER

Appeared (Greek: *oftheis [of-theis]*)—means "to gaze with wide-open eyes at something remarkable." It is different from *blepo,* which denotes simply voluntary observation. There are people who believed that Paul saw a vision that was not real, or concrete. The Greek word that is used to describe his experience helps us to know that Paul was not hallucinating. Jesus appeared vividly to Saul. Saul, a Greek scholar, could have used other words to describe his encounter with Jesus, but he used *oftheis.*

HOME DAILY BIBLE READINGS
(October 13-19, 2008)

Transformed to Witness to the Community

MONDAY, October 13: "A Revelation of Jesus Christ" (Galatians 1:11-17)

TUESDAY, October 14: "Persecutor Now Proclaimer" (Galatians 1:18-24)

WEDNESDAY, October 15: "The Surpassing Value of Christ" (Philippians 3:2-11)

THURSDAY, October 16: "Befriended by Barnabas" (Acts 9:22-31)

FRIDAY, October 17: "Content in All Circumstances" (Philippians 4:10-20)

SATURDAY, October 18: "A Light from Heaven" (Acts 9:1-9)

SUNDAY, October 19: "God's Chosen Instrument" (Acts 9:10-21)

LESSON 8

October 26, 2008

COMMISSIONED BY THE COMMUNITY

DEVOTIONAL READING: **Matthew 28:16-20**
PRINT PASSAGE: **Acts 13:1-12**

BACKGROUND SCRIPTURE: **Acts 13**
KEY VERSE: **Acts 13:3**

Acts 13:1-12—KJV

NOW THERE were in the church that was at Antioch certain prophets and teachers; as Barnabas, and Simeon that was called Niger, and Lucius of Cyrene, and Manaen, which had been brought up with Herod the tetrarch, and Saul.

2 As they ministered to the Lord, and fasted, the Holy Ghost said, Separate me Barnabas and Saul for the work whereunto I have called them.

3 And when they had fasted and prayed, and laid their hands on them, they sent them away.

4 So they, being sent forth by the Holy Ghost, departed unto Seleucia; and from thence they sailed to Cyprus.

5 And when they were at Salamis, they preached the word of God in the synagogues of the Jews: and they had also John to their minister.

6 And when they had gone through the isle unto Paphos, they found a certain sorcerer, a false prophet, a Jew, whose name was Bar-jesus:

7 Which was with the deputy of the country, Sergius Paulus, a prudent man; who called for Barnabas and Saul, and desired to hear the word of God.

8 But Elymas the sorcerer (for so is his name by interpretation) withstood them, seeking to turn away the deputy from the faith.

9 Then Saul, (who also is called Paul,) filled with the Holy Ghost, set his eyes on him,

10 And said, O full of all subtilty and all mischief, thou child of the devil, thou enemy of all righteousness, wilt thou not cease to pervert the right ways of the Lord?

11 And now, behold, the hand of the Lord is upon thee, and thou shalt be blind, not seeing the sun for a season. And immediately there fell on him a mist and a darkness; and he went about seeking some to lead him by the hand.

12 Then the deputy, when he saw what was done, believed, being astonished at the doctrine of the Lord.

Acts 13:1-12—NRSV

NOW IN the church at Antioch there were prophets and teachers: Barnabas, Simeon who was called Niger, Lucius of Cyrene, Manaen a member of the court of Herod the ruler, and Saul.

2 While they were worshiping the Lord and fasting, the Holy Spirit said, "Set apart for me Barnabas and Saul for the work to which I have called them."

3 Then after fasting and praying they laid their hands on them and sent them off.

4 So, being sent out by the Holy Spirit, they went down to Seleucia; and from there they sailed to Cyprus.

5 When they arrived at Salamis, they proclaimed the word of God in the synagogues of the Jews. And they had John also to assist them.

6 When they had gone through the whole island as far as Paphos, they met a certain magician, a Jewish false prophet, named Bar-Jesus.

7 He was with the proconsul, Sergius Paulus, an intelligent man, who summoned Barnabas and Saul and wanted to hear the word of God.

8 But the magician Elymas (for that is the translation of his name) opposed them and tried to turn the proconsul away from the faith.

9 But Saul, also known as Paul, filled with the Holy Spirit, looked intently at him

10 and said, "You son of the devil, you enemy of all righteousness, full of all deceit and villainy, will you not stop making crooked the straight paths of the Lord?

11 And now listen—the hand of the Lord is against you, and you will be blind for a while, unable to see the sun." Immediately mist and darkness came over him, and he went about groping for someone to lead him by the hand.

12 When the proconsul saw what had happened, he believed, for he was astonished at the teaching about the Lord.

TOPICAL OUTLINE OF THE LESSON

I. Introduction
A. Paul's Mission Work Begins
B. Biblical Background

II. Exposition and Application of the Scripture
A. The Church in Antioch (Acts 13:1)
B. Saul and Barnabas Commissioned (Acts 13:2-3)
C. Saul and Barnabas in Cyprus (Acts 13:4-12)

III. Concluding Reflection

LESSON OBJECTIVES

Upon completion of this lesson, the students will know that:

1. The early Christians took the Word of Jesus seriously by appointing Paul and Barnabas as missionaries;
2. Paul and Barnabas depended on the Holy Spirit's directives; and,
3. The Holy Spirit is still working to advance the kingdom of Christ.

POINTS TO BE EMPHASIZED

ADULT/YOUTH

Adult Topic: **Set Apart to Work**
Youth Topic: **We're on a Mission!**
Adult Key Verse: **Acts 13:3**
Youth Key Verse: **Acts 13:2**
Print Passage: **Acts 13:1-12**

—With the commissioning of Barnabas and Saul, the Christian community spread primarily among Gentiles.
—The church in Antioch served as a major center for the early Christian church.
—Leaders in the church were identified as prophets and teachers. Some opponents were identified as magicians.
—Beginning with 13:9, Saul is known as Paul. Saul did not become known as Paul simply because of the conversion experience.
—The faith community laid hands on Paul and Barnabas and set them apart, as directed by God, for service to the Lord.

CHILDREN

Children Topic: **Going Out to Serve**
Key Verse: **Acts 13:3**
Print Passage: **Acts 13:1-12**

—While the church was worshiping together, the Holy Spirit spoke.
—Barnabas and Saul were called by the Holy Spirit to serve.
—Barnabas and Saul were sent to Cyprus to preach.
—A magician who opposed Barnabas and Saul became physically blind.
—The first time Saul was referred to as Paul is in this passage.

I. INTRODUCTION

A. Paul's Mission Work Begins

The conversion of Saul of Tarsus to the Christian faith was a high water mark in early Christianity. His conversion gave to the church one of her most prolific thinkers and writers. His background and training as a Pharisee gave him the depth of knowledge that helped shape his interpretation of the Law and its applicability to the Gospel. He and his missionary companions were the primary reasons why the Christian faith exploded and took root in the Roman Empire. Their relentless determination to preach the Gospel and establish Christian congregations was a direct result of the power of the Holy Spirit at work in their lives.

In this lesson, we have the beginning of the first of three missionary journeys of Paul and his companions (see Acts 13:4–14:28; 15:40–18:22; 18:2–21:7). In chapter 13, we are given a glimpse of the organizational structure of the early Gentile churches and shown something of the internal spiritual climate of the congregation in Antioch. There were at least two types of leaders in the church of Antioch—teachers and prophets. Acts 13:1 reads, "Now there were in the church that was at Antioch certain prophets and teachers; as Barnabas, and Simeon that was called Niger, and Lucius of Cyrene, and Manaen, which had been brought up with Herod the tetrarch, and Saul." Furthermore, the church in Antioch was a congregation that devoted time to fasting and prayer.

B. Biblical Background

The events described in Acts 13:1-4 took place in the ancient city of Antioch of Syria. Antioch was located about 300 miles north of Jerusalem and was the third most important city in the Roman Empire. It was second only to Jerusalem as a major center of early Christianity. It was situated in northern Syria on the Orontes River, about twenty miles inland from the Mediterranean Sea. Antioch was founded sometime around 300 B.C. by Seleucus I, who was one of the generals of Alexander the Great.

The city was home to a large Jewish population, as well as a sizeable population of Romans and Greeks. It was the commercial capital of the Roman province of Syria. Today, Antioch is located in southeastern Turkey near the border with Syria and is still a relatively large and thriving city. In this cosmopolitan city, Judaism, Christianity, and the mystery religions all thrived and grew.

In this chapter, we are shown how the Gospel took root and spread among Gentiles living throughout the Roman Empire. Before we proceed to our main focus, let us review some pertinent questions. How did Christianity spread north from Israel to Syrian Antioch? During the period of the great persecution, many Christians in Israel migrated to Antioch to find peace. Acts 11:19 reads, "Now they which were scattered abroad upon the persecution that arose about Stephen travelled as far as Phenice, and Cyprus, and Antioch, preaching the word to none but unto the Jews only."

In addition to the Jewish Christians who came and preached, another group came from Cyprus and Cyrene and preached to Gentiles living in the city. How did Paul and Barnabas come to settle in Antioch? Barnabas was initially sent to the city to investigate the news regarding the establishment of a new congregation of believers in the city (see Acts 11:22). What brought Saul of Tarsus to Antioch? Barnabas went to Tarsus, found Saul, and brought him to Antioch to assist him in the teaching of the new disciples (see Acts 11:25-26). Paul and Barnabas spent an entire year teaching the disciples the Word of God. It was in Antioch that the name "Christian" was first used to identify the followers of Jesus (see Acts 11:26).

II. EXPOSITION AND APPLICATION OF THE SCRIPTURE

A. The Church in Antioch
(Acts 13:1)

NOW THERE were in the church that was at Antioch certain prophets and teachers; as Barnabas, and Simeon that was called Niger, and Lucius of Cyrene, and Manaen, which had been brought up with Herod the tetrarch, and Saul.

We have no record of how much time passed between the time that the Gospel was first preached in Antioch and the period we have covered in Acts 13. It must have been several years; however, by the time of the text, the church in Antioch had become a full-fledged church (Greek: *ekklesia,* meaning "called-out ones"). There is nothing that is known about the size of the congregation or where they met within the city. There is a traditional cave site which overlooks the city that is revered as the site of the first Christian gatherings, but there is no way of knowing for certain. The church in Antioch had a rudimentary leadership structure which consisted of prophets and teachers. A *prophet* literally means "someone who speaks for God under the power of the Holy Spirit." A *teacher* on the other hand is "someone who explains and interprets the Word of God under the power of the Holy Spirit."

Barnabas must have been the chief leader of the church, given that his name is mentioned first in the hierarchy and the role that he played in the early history of the church in Antioch (see Acts 4:36-37 for a biographical sketch of his life). Simeon, who was called Niger, was more than likely an African proselyte (a convert from one religious belief to another) who migrated from northern Africa to Israel and eventually Antioch. The name *Niger* indicates that he was someone with a dark complexion. It is thought that this Simeon was the same one who helped Jesus carry the cross in Luke 23:26. Lucius of Cyrene may have been one of the earliest missionaries to come to Antioch (see Acts 11:20). Manaen was brought up with Herod the tetrarch, probably a reference to Herod Antipas who ruled Galilee during the time of Jesus' ministry. Manaen was one of the prophets and teachers in the Gentile church of Antioch. Finally, there was Saul, whose place on the list indicated that he was the lowest of the ranked leaders in the church. Eventually, he would become the central figure in the spread of the Gospel.

B. Saul and Barnabas Commissioned
(Acts 13:2-3)

As they ministered to the Lord, and fasted, the Holy Ghost said, Separate me Barnabas and Saul for the work

whereunto I have called them. And when they had fasted and prayed, and laid their hands on them, they sent them away.

While they were ministering to the Lord and fasting, the Holy Spirit said, "Separate for me Barnabas and Saul for the work to which I have called them." *Ministering* refers to worship and service. While in worship and in fasting, the Holy Spirit spoke. We are not told who received the message or how it was transmitted. There were prophets in the church who often received messages from God for the church; therefore, it may have come through them.

Nearly ten years after his conversion on the Road to Damascus, Saul was released by the Holy Spirit to fulfill his calling. Barnabas and Saul had been specifically chosen by the Holy Spirit to begin the process by which Christianity would grow into the largest religion in the world. One cannot be effective in ministry until the Lord releases one to serve His purpose.

Why Barnabas and Saul? First and foremost, the Lord saw them fit as vessels of honor. Second, they had already demonstrated a tenacious drive and a courageous commitment to the cause of Jesus Christ. Third, they had proven that they could work together for long stretches of time. Fourth, they had demonstrated that their personal egos would never override the greater purpose of God. Fifth, they were committed to preaching and teaching the Gospel. Ministry is not a vacation—it is work, and it is a good work which demands total commitment. These two men received a high calling to be envoys of the Lord Jesus Christ.

In verse 3, the church officially recognized their call and commissioned them to go forth. They laid hands on Barnabas and Saul, which indicated that they were conferring upon them authority to act and speak for Jesus. It was the church's way of identifying with and affirming the mission to which God had called a particular person. It was not ordination, but recognition of what the Holy Spirit had already decided. The most remarkable thing is that the church sent its two best teachers forth to serve the greater interests of Jesus Christ.

C. Saul and Barnabas in Cyprus (Acts 13:4-12)

So they, being sent forth by the Holy Ghost, departed unto Seleucia; and from thence they sailed to Cyprus. And when they were at Salamis, they preached the word of God in the synagogues of the Jews: and they had also John to their minister. And when they had gone through the isle unto Paphos, they found a certain sorcerer, a false prophet, a Jew, whose name was Bar-jesus: Which was with the deputy of the country, Sergius Paulus, a prudent man; who called for Barnabas and Saul, and desired to hear the word of God. But Elymas the sorcerer (for so is his name by interpretation) withstood them, seeking to turn away the deputy from the faith. Then Saul, (who also is called Paul,) filled with the Holy Ghost, set his eyes on him, And said, O full of all subtilty and all mischief, thou child of the devil, thou enemy of all righteousness, wilt thou not cease to pervert the right ways of the Lord? And now, behold, the hand of the Lord is upon thee, and thou shalt be blind, not seeing the sun for a season. And immediately there fell on him a mist and a darkness; and he went about seeking some to lead him by the hand. Then the deputy, when he saw what was done, believed, being astonished at the doctrine of the Lord.

Barnabas and Saul traveled west to the port city of Seleucia, where they boarded a ship and sailed to Cyprus. Cyprus is situated about sixty miles off the coast of Syria and is about 140 miles long and 60 miles wide. The terrain is very rugged in places. The missionaries landed at Salamis and began to preach in the synagogues of the Jews (verse 5). There must have been a relatively sizeable Jewish population living on the island, given the reference to multiple synagogues. There was an openness and readiness to receive the preached Word of God because there is no record of opposition coming from the synagogue leaders, as would be the case in Asia (see Acts 13:45; 14:3-4). God will always prepare the hearts of people to receive the Word.

They preached across the island and eventually made their way to Paphos, the largest city on the west coast of Cyprus (verse 6). Here they met a Jew whose name was Bar-jesus (son of Joshua). In verse 8, he is referred to as Elymas. He was a sorcerer and a false prophet and was a confidant of Sergius Paulus, who served as the Roman governor. Sergius heard of the two missionaries and the impact of their ministry. He called for Barnabas and Saul to meet with him because he wanted to hear the Gospel personally from them (verse 7). However, Elymas sought to keep Sergius from hearing the message because he knew firsthand the impact that it was having (verse 8). He feared that he might lose influence with Sergius if committed to Jesus Christ.

In verse 9, Saul is called Paul for the first time. Paul was filled with the Holy Spirit at that moment and confronted Elymas (see Acts 4:8). God will always empower His servants for decisive moments of service. Paul called Elymas a "child of the devil" who was full of deceit and mischief. He was not a Jew because he was opposed to the righteousness of God, thus he was an enemy of God (compare verse 10 with Genesis 32:11; Proverbs 10:9; Jeremiah 5:27; and Hosea 14:10). The hand of the Lord was against him, meaning that he had no chance of stopping what God was doing (verse 11). Paul not only preached with power, but also he demonstrated it by pronouncing God's judgment in the form of blindness that afflicted Elymas. Acts 13:11 reads, "And immediately there fell on him a mist and a darkness; and he went about seeking some to lead him by the hand." When Sergius saw the manifestation of God's power and heard the preaching of the Gospel, we believe he became a disciple of the Lord Jesus Christ (verse 12).

III. CONCLUDING REFLECTION

Acts 13 is significant for several reasons. First, we have a congregation of Christians who took seriously the mandate to make disciples and preach the Gospel to the ends of the earth (see Matthew 28:19-20; Acts 1:8). This passage is important to us historically because it affirms the church's call and commitment to missions and evangelism. Missions must be the central focus of every congregation of baptized believers in the Lord Jesus Christ. Without a serious commitment to cross-cultural missions, we are nothing more than tinkling cymbals and sounding brass.

Second, it teaches us the importance of having leaders who are open to the work of the Holy Spirit in the life of the congregation. They ministered, prayed, and fasted. Third, we see that God calls individuals to service in congregations that are devoted to Him. Your own calling to ministry is one that will be affirmed by the congregation. Fourth, we see a courageous commitment to Jesus Christ. Often, pastors and lay leaders lack courage when it comes to doing the work of missions cross-culturally, especially in Africa. No one can give you the courageous commitment to Christ. The call of God is a divine summons to become involved in the work of ministry and missions.

Our calling is not a call to just sit in a church house and sing, pray, preach, teach, and shout to His glory, but to become involved in the world where men and women are living under the tyranny of evil and destruction.

The church can still experience the power of the Holy Spirit in operation. How? The answer is found in today's text. In Acts 13:1, the church was praying fervently. The early church believed in the command of the Lord Jesus Christ, who told them to pray often. Today, prayer has become official. There is a segment in our bulletin every Sunday designated as "Pastoral Prayer." This was not the practice in the early church. Everybody was engaged in prayer. In some denominations today, prayers are written for different occasions. There is no more inspired prayer. A few years ago in a Bible college in the south, a woman was asked to lead prayer during the commencement exercise. The woman was part of the ordained clergy. When she got up to pray, she said, "In our denomination, prayers are written and not supposed to be done extemporaneously." If we are going to experience the power of the Holy Spirit among us, the church must return to the apostolic spirit, in prayer and evangelism.

God has placed you in this generation to serve His purpose. Begin to see your work environment as your mission field and claim for the Lord Jesus Christ one person at a time.

PRAYER

Heavenly Father, grant that Your servants may live in the power of Your Holy Spirit and serve you with boldness and courage. Take away any fears that we have of being witnesses for Jesus Christ. In Jesus' name we pray. Amen.

WORD POWER

Fast, Fasting, Fasted *(neesteusantes [nees-teu-san-tes])*—means "to abstain from food for religious purposes." There are other forms of fasting in the Bible. But in this context the apostles realized the magnitude of the work ahead of the new missionaries; hence, they abstained from physical food. Fasting could be practiced in times of distress (see 2 Samuel 1:2) and in times of grief (see 1 Chronicles 10:12). Jesus fasted for forty days and forty nights (see Matthew 4:2).

HOME DAILY BIBLE READINGS
(October 20-26, 2008)

Commissioned by the Community

MONDAY, October 20: "Filling a Vacancy" (Acts 1:15-26)

TUESDAY, October 21: "Go, Proclaim the Good News" (Matthew 10:1-15)

WEDNESDAY, October 22: "Persevere in Persecution" (Matthew 10:16-25)

THURSDAY, October 23: "Finding Life" (Matthew 10:32-39)

FRIDAY, October 24: "The Gift that Is in You" (1 Timothy 4:6-16)

SATURDAY, October 25: "Salvation Sent to the Gentiles" (Acts 28:25-31)

SUNDAY, October 26: "Set Apart for God's Work" (Acts 13:1-12, 42-43)

FITTING INTO THE COMMUNITY

DEVOTIONAL READING: **1 Corinthians 12:4-20**
PRINT PASSAGE: **Ephesians 4:1-16**
KEY VERSE: **Ephesians 4:7**

BACKGROUND SCRIPTURE: **1 Corinthians 12:3-21; Ephesians 4:1-16**

Ephesians 4:1-16—KJV

I THEREFORE, the prisoner of the Lord, beseech you that ye walk worthy of the vocation wherewith ye are called,

2 With all lowliness and meekness, with longsuffering, forbearing one another in love;

3 Endeavouring to keep the unity of the Spirit in the bond of peace.

4 There is one body, and one Spirit, even as ye are called in one hope of your calling;

5 One Lord, one faith, one baptism,

6 One God and Father of all, who is above all, and through all, and in you all.

7 But unto every one of us is given grace according to the measure of the gift of Christ.

8 Wherefore he saith, When he ascended up on high, he led captivity captive, and gave gifts unto men.

9 (Now that he ascended, what is it but that he also descended first into the lower parts of the earth?

10 He that descended is the same also that ascended up far above all heavens, that he might fill all things.)

11 And he gave some, apostles; and some, prophets; and some, evangelists; and some, pastors and teachers;

12 For the perfecting of the saints, for the work of the ministry, for the edifying of the body of Christ:

13 Till we all come in the unity of the faith, and of the knowledge of the Son of God, unto a perfect man, unto the measure of the stature of the fulness of Christ:

14 That we henceforth be no more children, tossed to and fro, and carried about with every wind of doctrine, by the sleight of men, and cunning craftiness, whereby they lie in wait to deceive;

15 But speaking the truth in love, may grow up into him in all things, which is the head, even Christ:

Ephesians 4:1-16—NRSV

I THEREFORE, the prisoner in the Lord, beg you to lead a life worthy of the calling to which you have been called,

2 with all humility and gentleness, with patience, bearing with one another in love,

3 making every effort to maintain the unity of the Spirit in the bond of peace.

4 There is one body and one Spirit, just as you were called to the one hope of your calling,

5 one Lord, one faith, one baptism,

6 one God and Father of all, who is above all and through all and in all.

7 But each of us was given grace according to the measure of Christ's gift.

8 Therefore it is said, "When he ascended on high he made captivity itself a captive; he gave gifts to his people."

9 (When it says, "He ascended," what does it mean but that he had also descended into the lower parts of the earth?

10 He who descended is the same one who ascended far above all the heavens, so that he might fill all things.)

11 The gifts he gave were that some would be apostles, some prophets, some evangelists, some pastors and teachers,

12 to equip the saints for the work of ministry, for building up the body of Christ,

13 until all of us come to the unity of the faith and of the knowledge of the Son of God, to maturity, to the measure of the full stature of Christ.

14 We must no longer be children, tossed to and fro and blown about by every wind of doctrine, by people's trickery, by their craftiness in deceitful scheming.

15 But speaking the truth in love, we must grow up in every way into him who is the head, into Christ,

Diversity is a reality in every human community. In what ways is diversity important to the unity of the church? Paul's letter to the church in Ephesus and his encounter with the jailer in Philippi challenge us to use our diverse identities and gifts to build up the Christian community.

16 From whom the whole body fitly joined together and compacted by that which every joint supplieth, according to the effectual working in the measure of every part, maketh increase of the body unto the edifying of itself in love.

16 from whom the whole body, joined and knit together by every ligament with which it is equipped, as each part is working properly, promotes the body's growth in building itself up in love.

TOPICAL OUTLINE OF THE LESSON

I. Introduction
  A. Unity in the Body
  B. Biblical Background

II. Exposition and Application of the Scripture
  A. Greatness of the Body (Ephesians 4:1-6)
  B. Gifts to the Body (Ephesians 4:7-12)
  C. Growth of the Body (Ephesians 4:13-16)

III. Concluding Reflection

LESSON OBJECTIVES

Upon completion of this lesson, the students will know that:

1. God created us and gave different gifts to each of us;
2. Using our gifts gives glory to God and builds up the body of Christ; and,
3. Failure to use our gifts is a betrayal of God.

POINTS TO BE EMPHASIZED

ADULT/YOUTH

Adult Topic: **Embracing Diversity**
Youth Topic: **Fitting In**
Adult Key Verse: **Ephesians 4:7**
Youth Key Verse: **Ephesians 4:13**
Print Passage: **Ephesians 4:1-16**

—The Spirit gives diverse gifts to bring about unity in the church community.

—In verses 4-6, Paul names seven elements of unity, all preceded by the word *one*: body, spirit, hope, leader, faith, baptism, God.

—In verse 11, Paul named diverse gifts of ministry that Christ gives to the church: apostles, prophets, evangelists, pastors, and teachers.

—Spiritual gifts are given to equip the whole church for ministry and to strengthen the community of faith.

—Paul appealed to the believers in Ephesus to conform their lives to the high command given to the church by its Head.

—Paul taught the qualities that characterize the lives of believers if we are to be worthy of the work God has called us to do.

CHILDREN

Children Topic: **Uniting in Christ**
Key Verse: **Acts 16:31**
Print Passage: **Acts 16:25-34**

—While imprisoned, Paul and Silas were praying and singing hymns.

—Our unconditional love of everyone can motivate others to accept Jesus as their Savior.
—The salvation and baptism of the jailer and his household was reason to celebrate God's love.

—Paul's and Silas's personal faith helped motivate others to love God.
—With Christ, we can experience unparalleled freedom in our personal lives.

I. INTRODUCTION

A. Unity in the Body

Paul's letter to the church in Ephesus was written to strengthen the bond of unity and commitment to Jesus Christ among the believers. The letter is one of the most important New Testament writings because of the nature of its context and the uniqueness of its message. Paul wrote that God's purpose in Jesus Christ was to create one unified body of believers who would fulfill His purpose in the world. The death of Jesus Christ upon the cross abolished the wall of separation between Jews and Gentiles and created one unified people (see Ephesians 2:11-16). In Jesus Christ, the revelation of the mystery of God was made manifest for the whole world to see.

B. Biblical Background

Paul visited Ephesus at least two times. His first visit was a brief stay, at which point he left Aquila and Priscilla (see Acts 18:18-21). Paul's third missionary journey began in Acts 18:23. We know that he went through several different cities eventually arriving in the city of Ephesus (Acts 19:1ff.). He found some disciples and these more than likely became the nucleus of the church in that city.

Ephesus was located in a Roman province in Asia, near the mouth of the Cayster River. It was the chief commercial and religious center of the region. Ephesus was the center for the worship of Artemis (Diana). Like Corinth, it was a city that was noted for its high rates of religious prostitution, which was a part of their worship. Some of the most impressive ruins to be found anywhere in the world are in Ephesus.

II. EXPOSITION AND APPLICATION OF THE SCRIPTURE

A. Greatness of the Body

(Ephesians 4:1-6)

I THEREFORE, the prisoner of the Lord, beseech you that ye walk worthy of the vocation wherewith ye are called, With all lowliness and meekness, with longsuffering, forbearing one another in love; Endeavouring to keep the unity of the Spirit in the bond of peace. There is one body, and one Spirit, even as ye are called in one hope of your calling; One Lord, one faith, one baptism, One God and Father of all, who is above all, and through all, and in you all.

The key that unlocks the letter's intention is Ephesians 4:1, in which Paul appealed for the Ephesians to "walk worthy of the vocation wherewith they had been called." Paul used "therefore" to show that the first three chapters and the last three chapters have a connection. The word *walk* is a key word in the second half of his epistle; it is used in the New Testament to describe the direction of one's life. In the New Testament, it signifies the ways and activities that characterize the Christian's lifestyle. In Ephesians 2:10 we are told to walk in good works and in Ephesians 5:2 to walk in love. In the second half of Ephesians, the word *walk* appears in 4:1, 17; 5:2, 8 and 15.

The believer walks worthy by manifesting five graces listed by Paul: the first is *lowliness* (Greek: *tapeinophrosune)*, which means "having a humble opinion of oneself." In the ancient world in which Paul lived, humility was a virtue that was to be avoided. The Greeks considered it a cringing, servile, ignoble, and despised quality to have, but Jesus exalted humility to the highest level (see Matthew 18:4; 23:12). It means having a proper self-estimate based upon the life of Christ.

The second of these graces is *meekness* (Greek: *praotes)*, which means "gentleness of spirit." Meekness is power under control. Aristotle referred to the meek person as the person who lived between excessive anger and complete passivity. This is the person who gets angry, but at the right times for the right reasons. In this sense, it refers to being controlled by God at all times (see 2 Corinthians 10:1).

The third grace is *long-suffering* (Greek: *makrothumia)*, which means "steadfastness or slow to seek revenge." *Long-suffering* is that quality of self-restraint that the believer displays in the face of provocation. *Long-suffering* is frequently used in the Bible to describe the attitude of God toward the world of sinful men and women (see Romans 2:4; 9:22; 12:17-21).

The fourth grace is *love* (Greek: *agape)*, which means "selfless love for others." The expression of Christian love among believers during the time of Jesus and in the early church was so new that a word had to be invented to describe it. That word was *agape*. This is the kind of love that always seeks the highest good of others (see Matthew 5:43-48; 1 Corinthians 13).

The final grace in the list is *peace* (Greek: *eirene)* and it means "tranquility or the absence of havoc." The word *peace* as used here means "harmonious relationship between individuals, particularly among believers" (see Ephesians 2:14-15; 1 Thessalonians 5:13).

B. Gifts to the Body
(Ephesians 4:7-12)

But unto every one of us is given grace according to the measure of the gift of Christ. Wherefore he saith, When he ascended up on high, he led captivity captive, and gave gifts unto men. (Now that he ascended, what is it but that he also descended first into the lower parts of the earth? He that descended is the same also that ascended up far above all heavens, that he might fill all things.) And he gave some, apostles; and some, prophets; and some, evangelists; and some, pastors and teachers; For the perfecting of the saints, for the work of the ministry, for the edifying of the body of Christ.

The church is strong because of its diversity of gifts. Everyone has received a gift of grace from Jesus Christ (see Romans 12:3-8; 1 Corinthians 12:7-11). Verses 8-10 have been interpreted to paint the picture of a king who goes off to war and, after returning victorious, distributes the spoils of war to all of his subjects. Jesus has gained the great victory over the powers of Satan and in His victory He has distributed gifts to His followers so that they can continue the work He began. Among these gifts is the gift of various leaders to the body for the purpose of building up the body.

The first of these leadership gifts is *apostles* (Greek: *apostolos),* which literally means "one who is sent forth with a message." The word is used in the Gospels to describe the original twelve disciples of Jesus (see Matthew 10:5; Luke 6:13; 9:10). According to Acts 1:21-26, there are two essential qualifications for one to be an apostle: (1) one must be an eyewitness of the resurrection of Jesus, and (2) one must have seen Jesus during His earthly ministry. Because of these qualifications, Paul was always on the defensive concerning his apostleship (see 1 Corinthians 9:1; 15:8). There were others who were listed as apostles in the New Testament (see Acts 14:14; Romans 16:7; 2 Corinthians 8:23; Philippians 2:25). They were confined largely to Jerusalem. The apostles were the foundation of the early church (see Ephesians 2:20). Their principal tasks were teaching, preaching, and leadership of the church. The apostles and prophets were the foundation of the church because they pointed to and witnessed to Jesus.

The second of these gifts is the *prophets* (Greek: *prophetes),* which denote those who speak the Word of God. Biblically, the prophet was one upon whom the Spirit of God rested (see Numbers 11:17-29) and one through whom God spoke (see Numbers 12:2; Amos 3:7-8). There were numerous prophets in the early church (see Acts 13:1; 15:32; 21:10). Some were considered to be false prophets (pseudo-prophets). In 1 John 4:1 it is said, "Beloved, believe not every spirit, but try the spirits whether they are of God: because many false prophets are gone out into the world." Jesus Christ warns about false prophets (see Matthew 7:15; 24:11; Acts 13:6). The prophets were not just foretellers of the future, but proclaimers of the will of God and the consequences of disobedience to that will.

The third leadership gift is the *evangelist* (Greek: *euangelistas),* which denotes one who is a proclaimer of Good News. Like the prophets, the evangelists were wanderers, but with a distinct difference: they were called to preach the Gospel in areas where churches had not been established. They were the rank-and-file missionaries (see Acts 8:6-40; 21:8). Paul said in 2 Timothy 4:5, "But watch thou in all things, endure afflictions, do the work of an evangelist, make full proof of thy ministry."

The last of these leadership gifts are the offices of *pastor* and *teacher.* The use of the article "the" before these offices describes one person with a dual function. The Greek words used are *poimen* (pastor) and *didaskalos* (teacher). The word *pastor* denotes one who is the shepherd of the flock. As the shepherd of the flock, the pastor is the church's chief teacher and leader. This does not mean that others in the congregation do not have the gift of teaching; it merely denotes the office of the chief leader who is responsible for what is taught in the church. The definition further describes the role of pastor as congregational leader. The pastor/teacher was the settled leader of a local congregation, whose work was largely confined to his congregation. His job was to lead and feed the flock the spiritual food necessary to live for Christ and to protect the church from error. See the following passages for a description of Jesus Christ as shepherd: John 10:11, 14; Hebrews 13:20; 1 Peter 2:25; 5:4. Jesus Christ has called men and women to lead His flock (see 1 Peter

5:2; Acts 21:15; 20:28). Every pastor must be able to teach according to 1 Timothy 3:2; Paul (in Titus 1:9) said, "Holding fast the faithful word as he hath been taught, that he may be able by sound doctrine both to exhort and to convince the gainsayers."

These various leaders were given to the body of Jesus Christ for the purpose of building up the saints so that they could do the work of the ministry. What is this work of the ministry? It is living out the words of Jesus in Matthew 25:31-46 and 28:19-20, the Great Commandment and the Great Commission.

C. Growth of the Body
(Ephesians 4:13-16)

Till we all come in the unity of the faith, and of the knowledge of the Son of God, unto a perfect man, unto the measure of the stature of the fulness of Christ. That we henceforth be no more children, tossed to and fro, and carried about with every wind of doctrine, by the sleight of men, and cunning craftiness, whereby they lie in wait to deceive; But speaking the truth in love, may grow up into him in all things, which is the head, even Christ: From whom the whole body fitly joined together and compacted by that which every joint supplieth, according to the effectual working in the measure of every part, maketh increase of the body unto the edifying of itself in love.

In verses 13-16, Paul laid out for the Ephesians the goal of the church's ministry, which is growth in Jesus Christ. The overall objective of the ministry of the church is to build up (edify) the body of Christ. In order to achieve the objective of building up the church, there are several goals that we must strive to reach. It is important to remember that numerical growth is not the ultimate goal—it is spiritual growth; numerical growth is a natural by-product of our spiritual growth. Before we try to interpret the verses we need

to understand their grammatical construction. The word in verse 13, *till*, is a conjunction and shows a relationship between verses 12 and 13. *Till* indicates how long the work of building up is to go on. It goes on until we all come to full maturity; there is no time limit placed on the process. Next, notice the word *in*. This word is a preposition and indicates the desired goal we are trying to reach. That is to say, "till we all come in the unity of the faith." Thus, the verse has the idea that building up the body of Christ is to go on until we all arrive at the same spiritual level together. The work of spiritual growth goes on from generation to generation until the coming of the Lord Jesus Christ. This is all the more reason we need to equip our youth to grow into Christlike adults.

What did Paul mean here by the *unity of the faith*? If we take out the phrase "and of the knowledge..." we will be able to follow the thought better. One would read, "till we all come into the unity of the faith of the Son of God." Here the emphasis is not on saving faith, nor even the exercise of faith in Jesus Christ. Rather, it is on the content of our faith—that is to say, the content of what we believe about Jesus Christ. Therefore, the teaching ministry of the church has as its goal increasing the corporate content of our faith in Jesus Christ. What that means is that we will grow when each believer has a fully developed understanding of who Jesus Christ was, is, and will be.

When we reach that decisive point, several important things will take place in the church. First, we will no longer be children (see Hebrews 5:11–6:2). Second, we will not be tossed about like feathers subject to the winds. Third, we will recognize deceitful and distorted teaching (verse 14). When we are spiritually mature, we will be able to speak the truth to each other with no fear of reprisal of conflict erupting. Second, the body will grow in love. Third, every part of the body will grow and mature and continue to mature in what builds the whole body in love (verse 16). Finally such spiritual maturity will give God the glory.

III. CONCLUDING REFLECTION

The whole focus of the passage we were considering revolves around the importance and maintenance of unity among the members of the church. Unity is not something that happens automatically, but must be worked at diligently among believers—hence the idea of endeavoring. We are to endeavor to work for the unity of the church. Such endeavoring gives glory to God and it exalts the name of Christ, the Head of the body. As a spiritual reality, unity is present within the church; it simply must be kept.

All of the virtues that were discussed have their basis in right relationships among believers. The Christian life is a relational life—that is to say, not only must we be concerned about our relationship to God, but also our relationship to others. The problem with unity in the church is evident by the view of people in society which is clearly focused on itself. When we are more concerned about ourselves, our needs, our feelings, our points of view, our ideas, our position, our families, our jobs, and our titles, there will not and cannot be any unity. However, when self dies and Christ is raised to the level of first place, then the unity envisioned in the Bible will become a reality in the church.

PRAYER

Lord God, almighty Father, grant that Your servants may know the peace that surpasses knowledge in our fellowship. May we love without pretense and hypocrisy. Forgive us of any act of jealousy or hypocrisy. In Jesus' name we pray. Amen.

WORD POWER

Grace *(charis [cha-ris])*—this is the root word for "charisma." Every child of God is given grace (charis) to use for the glory of God (see Ephesians 4:7). It is a gross misunderstanding of the word when we say that a man or woman is charismatic. Every child of God who knows his or her gift and uses it effectively is charismatic.

HOME DAILY BIBLE READINGS
(October 27–November 2, 2008)

Fitting into the Community

MONDAY, October 27: "Drawn by God's Power" (Acts 8:12-25)
TUESDAY, October 28: "Drawn from a Distant Land" (Acts 8:26-38)
WEDNESDAY, October 29: "Drawn from Other Nations" (Acts 22:3-16)
THURSDAY, October 30: "Drawn to Be Christians" (Acts 11:19-26)
FRIDAY, October 31: "Seekers Among All People" (Acts 17:22-28)
SATURDAY, November 1: "A Worthy Calling" (Ephesians 4:1-6)
SUNDAY, November 2: "Joined and Knit Together" (Ephesians 4:7-16)

LESSON 10

November 9, 2008

CONFLICT IN THE COMMUNITY

DEVOTIONAL READING: **Romans 10:5-17**
PRINT PASSAGE: **Galatians 2:11-21**

BACKGROUND SCRIPTURE: **Galatians 2:11–3:29**
KEY VERSE: **Galatians 3:28**

Galatians 2:11-21—KJV

11 But when Peter was come to Antioch, I withstood him to the face, because he was to be blamed.

12 For before that certain came from James, he did eat with the Gentiles: but when they were come, he withdrew and separated himself, fearing them which were of the circumcision.

13 And the other Jews dissembled likewise with him; insomuch that Barnabas also was carried away with their dissimulation.

14 But when I saw that they walked not uprightly according to the truth of the gospel, I said unto Peter before them all, If thou, being a Jew, livest after the manner of Gentiles, and not as do the Jews, why compellest thou the Gentiles to live as do the Jews?

15 We who are Jews by nature, and not sinners of the Gentiles,

16 Knowing that a man is not justified by the works of the law, but by the faith of Jesus Christ, even we have believed in Jesus Christ, that we might be justified by the faith of Christ, and not by the works of the law: for by the works of the law shall no flesh be justified.

17 But if, while we seek to be justified by Christ, we ourselves also are found sinners, is therefore Christ the minister of sin? God forbid.

18 For if I build again the things which I destroyed, I make myself a transgressor.

19 For I through the law am dead to the law, that I might live unto God.

20 I am crucified with Christ: nevertheless I live; yet not I, but Christ liveth in me: and the life which I now live in the flesh I live by the faith of the Son of God, who loved me, and gave himself for me.

21 I do not frustrate the grace of God: for if righteousness come by the law, then Christ is dead in vain.

Galatians 2:11-21—NRSV

11 But when Cephas came to Antioch, I opposed him to his face, because he stood self-condemned;

12 for until certain people came from James, he used to eat with the Gentiles. But after they came, he drew back and kept himself separate for fear of the circumcision faction.

13 And the other Jews joined him in this hypocrisy, so that even Barnabas was led astray by their hypocrisy.

14 But when I saw that they were not acting consistently with the truth of the gospel, I said to Cephas before them all, "If you, though a Jew, live like a Gentile and not like a Jew, how can you compel the Gentiles to live like Jews?"

15 We ourselves are Jews by birth and not Gentile sinners;

16 yet we know that a person is justified not by the works of the law but through faith in Jesus Christ. And we have come to believe in Christ Jesus, so that we might be justified by faith in Christ, and not by doing the works of the law, because no one will be justified by the works of the law.

17 But if, in our effort to be justified in Christ, we ourselves have been found to be sinners, is Christ then a servant of sin? Certainly not!

18 But if I build up again the very things that I once tore down, then I demonstrate that I am a transgressor.

19 For through the law I died to the law, so that I might live to God. I have been crucified with Christ;

20 and it is no longer I who live, but it is Christ who lives in me. And the life I now live in the flesh I live by faith in the Son of God, who loved me and gave himself for me.

21 I do not nullify the grace of God; for if justification comes through the law, then Christ died for nothing.

TOPICAL OUTLINE OF THE LESSON

I. Introduction
   A. Dealing with Conflicts
   B. Biblical Background

II. Exposition and Application of the Scripture
   A. Peter's Hypocrisy
      (Galatians 2:11-13)
   B. Paul Corrects Peter's Hypocrisy
      (Galatians 2:14)
   C. Paul Expatiates on Doctrine of Justification
      (Galatians 2:15-19)
   D. Paul's Declaration
      (Galatians 2:20-21)

III. Concluding Reflection

LESSON OBJECTIVES

Upon completion of this lesson, the students will know that:

1. Conflict is part of human experience, but there are godly ways to resolve it;
2. Leaders in the church are saddled with the responsibility of resolving conflicts; and,
3. Conflict should be resolved with impartiality.

POINTS TO BE EMPHASIZED

ADULT/YOUTH

Adult Topic: Confronting Opposition
Youth Topic: Growing Pains
Adult/Youth Key Verse: Galatians 3:28
Print Passage: Galatians 2:11-21

—This passage illustrates the divisions in the early church between Jewish and Gentile Christians.
—"Christ living in me" is a strong metaphor for how Paul and others in the early church experienced the resurrected Christ.
—The link between Christ's dying and rising and the believer's own death and resurrection is also strongly expressed in Romans 6.
—Paul's revelation of the Gospel had come directly from Christ, not secondhand from the other apostles.
—Paul's team (Barnabas and Titus) was a living example of the new freedom in Christ for Jews and Gentiles to build close relationships.

CHILDREN

Children Topic: Learning to Work Together
Key Verse: Acts 15:9
Print Passage: Acts 15:6-14, 19

—The council held on to traditions and practices that were not validated by the Gospel message.
—The council demonstrated that differences can be resolved when all parties are committed to a peaceful resolution.
—Some believers are reluctant to follow God's Word.
—Believers may engage in differing traditions and practices that do not conflict with the Gospel message.
—Salvation comes by grace through faith.

I. INTRODUCTION

A. Dealing with Conflicts

The high-minded Baptist church was an affluent congregation in a mid-sized city. The pastor was very charismatic and was a very gifted preacher and teacher. The church had a strong reputation for community service. The church drew members from many different social and economic backgrounds. During its annual business meeting, Sister Sue Ellen Jones was nominated to serve as a deaconess. When her name was presented by the nominating committee, there was strong opposition from Sister Betty F. Socialite. Her opposition centered on the fact that five years ago, Sister Jones had been convicted of welfare fraud and served six months in jail. Upon her release, she apologized to the congregation and received forgiveness for her error. She was welcomed back into the fellowship with all of her rights of membership restored. Since returning Sister Jones has been a faithful and committed disciple of Christ and a strong supporter of the church's ministry.

During the meeting, Sister Socialite objected, stating that the high-minded church could not have a woman serving as a deaconess who had been convicted of a felony. Her passionate speech before the congregation persuaded several influential members to go along with her, and Sister Jones's nomination was defeated. This created the impression among many of the less affluent members that the only people welcome to serve in leadership positions were the highly educated and those who were financially well-off. The church was thrust into bitter turmoil and conflict over the issue, and it took nearly a generation before the matter subsided.

Conflict can erupt in a congregation over just about anything. Sometimes the smallest, most insignificant matter can start a major fire (see James 3:2-3). During times of congregational stress, the leaders of the church must be Spirit-led and focused. They must be willing to address the real issues that face the church and not allow personal preferences to dictate decision making. In today's lesson, we will examine one of the most hotly debated issues that faced the Christian church of the first century—which was the inclusion of Gentiles into the fellowship. The conflict reached a boiling point between two of the leading apostles of the church: Peter and Paul.

B. Biblical Background

The Jewish people lived in every major city in the Roman Empire. It was during the periods of the Assyrian and Babylonian Empires when Jews began to be moved away from Israel by their captors (see 2 Kings 17, 24-25). This continued right through the time of the rise and fall of Alexander the Great's Empire, where we see the rise of Hellenism among the Jews in Judea. Everett Ferguson wrote, in his book *Backgrounds of Early Christianity*, "Judaism enjoyed a privileged position in the Roman Empire. The Jews were an ancient people with a traditional religion, had been allied with Rome during the Maccabean age, and had rendered important assistance to Roman leaders such as Julius Caesar." Jews of the first century had a very good relationship with the Romans dating back to the time of Herod the Great. In particular, the aristocratic and wealthy segments of Jewish society had a good relationship with the Romans. Therefore, Jews who lived in Greco-Roman cities enjoyed a high quality of life and lived in peace with their Gentile neighbors. This all began to change with the rise of the Christian faith.

The conversion and inclusion of Gentiles into the Christian church was the beginning of a period of real internal conflict for the first Christian leaders. Christianity initially began as a part of the Jewish faith. All of the original twelve apostles were Jews, as were the earliest converts. In that regard they all shared a common ethnic and religious heritage which linked them to the historical Jewish faith and traditions. Additionally, even Jesus linked Himself to the historical faith of their ancestors and accepted and followed several customs mandated by the Law (see Matthew 8:4; Luke 2:39-42; 22:14ff; John 5:1; 6:4). The apostles continued to follow many of the Jewish religious customs and practices even after Pentecost (see Acts 2–4).

The churches of Galatia were established during the first and second missionary journeys of Paul and Barnabas.

II. EXPOSITION AND APPLICATION OF THE SCRIPTURE

A. Peter's Hypocrisy
(Galatians 2:11-13)

But when Peter was come to Antioch, I withstood him to the face, because he was to be blamed. For before that certain came from James, he did eat with the Gentiles: but when they were come, he withdrew and separated himself, fearing them which were of the circumcision. And the other Jews dissembled likewise with him; insomuch that Barnabas also was carried away with their dissimulation.

Paul was extremely upset that the Galatians had been drawn away from the simple truth of the Gospel by the Jewish legalists (see Galatians 3:1). We are not sure when the events he wrote about occurred within the church. They may have taken place shortly after the first apostolic conference mentioned in Acts 15. There are several things we learn about the confrontation between Paul and Peter (verse 11). First, it took place in Syrian Antioch. Second, it was a face-to-face confrontation. Third, Peter was one of the primary reasons that confusion was rising in the churches.

Everything in the church was fine until one day certain leaders arrived from Jerusalem with a message from James. Prior to their arrival, Peter had regular fellowship and contact with the brethren, eating and sharing in their homes. Peter was socializing with them with a free mind. However, when the brethren from Jerusalem arrived, he did two things: first, he withdrew—that is, he stopped associating with the Gentiles; second, he separated himself (verse 12). He drew boundaries that clearly indicated that he was no longer going to have contact as he had done previously. Paul remarked that he did these things out of fear of the brethren and what they would think and report back to the church in Jerusalem. Peter's unwillingness to associate with the believers from Galatia was followed by the other Jews who had come from Jerusalem. This was such a huge slap in the face to the saints in Antioch that even Barnabas was appalled by their behavior.

"During a July 2007 short-term mission trip to Kenya, I and two other missionaries spent the day with the Massai people in the Great Rift Valley. At the end of our day, they invited us to share a meal of potatoes and goat meat. They were surprised that we ate with them. As we sat at the simple table prepared, the children began to sing a song about what they saw. They were all surprised because when the white missionaries would come, they would preach and teach but would never remain to eat with the people."

Peter's example was so decisive that the rest of the Jews in the church of Antioch, including Barnabas, followed suit. Sometimes our actions can say more about our true feelings than the best sermons we preach or the lessons we teach.

B. Paul Corrects Peter's Hypocrisy (Galatians 2:14)

But when I saw that they walked not uprightly according to the truth of the gospel, I said unto Peter before them all, If thou, being a Jew, livest after the manner of Gentiles, and not as do the Jews, why compellest thou the Gentiles to live as do the Jews?

Paul could not possibly allow this sort of behavior to go unchallenged. He spoke to Peter publicly before everyone present. He wanted to know why they were not walking "uprightly" (Greek: *ouk orthopodousin*—literally means "to not be straight-footed, walking inconsistently"; in the Christian context, it means "unable to walk the talk," and "unable to live uprightly"). Peter and the other Jews preached one thing, but their actions told an entirely different story. Paul rebuked them in the open so that all of the saints would know that he was not afraid to confront the leader of the apostles. Why would Peter compel the Gentiles to live as Jews when he had been very willing to live like a Gentile at one point? Paul viewed Peter's action as inconsistent. Paul opposed Peter (2:11) because he (Peter) lived inconsistently with the Gospel—which meant that Peter was not following the truth. Peter's action was done in the open and Paul corrected him in the open as well.

We learn some valuable lessons about Paul and Peter. First, Peter was humble about the situation and never responded. He never mentioned the incident in his letters (see 1 and 2 Peter). He knew that Paul was right and that he had stepped over the line. Therefore, he graciously accepted the rebuke. Second, we see the willingness of Paul to confront behavior that was the opposite of what Christians should do and be. How often will we dismiss bad behavior as just "a person's ways"? We can do more harm than good by ignoring bad behavior among believers.

C. Paul Expatiates on Doctrine of Justification (Galatians 2:15-19)

We who are Jews by nature, and not sinners of the Gentiles, Knowing that a man is not justified by the works of the law, but by the faith of Jesus Christ, even we have believed in Jesus Christ, that we might be justified by the faith of Christ, and not by the works of the law: for by the works of the law shall no flesh be justified. But if, while we seek to be justified by Christ, we ourselves also are found sinners, is therefore Christ the minister of sin? God forbid. For if I build again the things which I destroyed, I make myself a transgressor. For I through the law am dead to the law, that I might live unto God.

In verses 15-19 is formed the essential theological framework for Paul's teaching and preaching about the finished work of Jesus Christ. We refer to this teaching as the "Doctrine of Justification by Faith." Paul may have been inspired by the prophetic writings of Habakkuk 2:4 or Psalm 143:2. The Greek word "justified" is *diakaioo,* and it means "to render or pronounce that someone is righteous or acceptable." It was a word that was used in the Greek legal system to denote that someone was being declared free of all of the charges brought against him or her. The word *justified* appears four times in verse 16-17. These verses have been among some of the most difficult to interpret because of the construction of the sentences and how Paul had a way of having multiple streams of thought flowing through his mind. We will opt for a literal rendering that will best capture the essence of Paul's critically important belief about justification by faith.

Paul reported that he told Peter that he and the other brethren were Jews by birth which afforded a special and unique relationship with God. They were not like the Gentiles whom Jews considered to be sinners (see Ephesians 2:1-4). Paul argued that no man or woman is made or declared to be righteous before God because of what they do or because of their works (see Ephesians 2:8-10). It is faith in the sacrificial death of Jesus Christ that makes us righteous before God (see Romans 5:8-10). God is the only one who can turn a sinner into a saint. Even if it were possible to do the right thing all the time and follow everything that the Law prescribed, we would still be sinners. Paul told Peter that even Jews, who obeyed the Law with its rich traditions, had believed in Jesus Christ (verse 16).

Verse 17 is very obscure and has posed very difficult challenges for biblical interpreters as to exactly what Paul meant. Paul argued that if the Gentiles (who did not keep the Law) were sinners, then he and the other Jews who had been eating and fellowshiping with the Gentiles were considered to be sinners as well. Therefore, because Jesus never considered dietary laws as a prerequisite for salvation, then they had made Jesus into an accomplice of their sins. Paul answered by declaring that such a thought was beyond reality. He emphatically declared, "May it never be!"

How could he return to a life that he had abandoned and had been freed from by the death of Jesus Christ on the cross? Freedom in Jesus Christ meant freedom from the burden of the Law and its rigorous demands (verse 18). When he accepted Jesus Christ as Lord, every confidence that he had put in the rituals and ceremonies of Judaism had died. He now lived unto God (verse 19).

D. Paul's Declaration
(Galatians 2:20-21)

I am crucified with Christ: nevertheless I live; yet not I, but Christ liveth in me: and the life which I now live in the flesh I live by the faith of the Son of God, who loved me, and gave himself for me. I do not frustrate the grace of God: for if righteousness come by the law, then Christ is dead in vain.

These words are among the most quoted of Paul's writings, and they reflect his thinking about what it meant to him and means to us to live in a mystical spiritual union with Jesus Christ. Crucifixion was the cruelest form of human execution. Paul took the scandal of the cross of Christ and pronounced that the death of the "old man" was nothing less than crucifixion. The old man was crucified when he accepted Jesus Christ as Lord (see Romans 6:6).

It was the power of the resurrected Christ who lived in the heart and life of Paul that changed his values, his worldview, and his ultimate purpose in life (see Philippians 3:4-10). For Paul, that crucifixion of Jesus was not just an event that occurred in the past, it was one that was a present reality for him each and every day.

It is the preaching of the Cross that is the source of the believer's power and the means by which salvation is realized (see Romans 1:16-17; 1 Corinthians 1:18; 2:5). The Cross was a transformative event that had changed the world and incorporated Paul—along with all who receive the Gospel—into a new sphere of power. Paul was crucified with Christ, and it was not him who lived, but Christ living and manifesting Himself through Paul's life (verse 20a). Paul's life of faith was under a new authority—not the law, but Jesus Christ who had died for him (verse 20). Paul had no intention of nullifying what God had done through Jesus at Calvary. To return to a form of righteousness based purely upon keeping the Law would mean that Jesus died for nothing.

III. CONCLUDING REFLECTION

What would have happened in the high-minded Baptist church if the congregation had been more focused on living according to their faith? Rituals, traditions, and religious customs and practices all have their place, but this lesson has taught that they are not the basis on which we can base our relationship with Jesus Christ. We have been saved, not because of what we do, but because of the shed blood of Jesus Christ. God has made us righteous through His death and resurrection.

The Gospel of Jesus Christ cannot be compromised. If we feel we have to change our Christian beliefs to match those of our companions, we are on dangerous ground.

PRAYER

Lord God, may we walk in the newness of life and joy of Your salvation. Help us to praise You for all that You have done in our lives through the cross of Your dear Son, Jesus Christ. Thank You for loving us and forgiving us. In Jesus' name we pray. Amen.

WORD POWER

One (Greek: *heni [he-ni]*)—this is an important word in our Key Verse. God is not concerned about whether you are Greek or Jew, white or black—there is only one moral personality. The point is, in Jesus Christ (note the word *in*), race, nationality, or gender distinction disappears. Robertson, in his book *Word Pictures in the New Testament*, admits, "Candor compels one to confess that this goal has not yet been fully attained."

HOME DAILY BIBLE READINGS

(November 3-9, 2008)

Conflict in the Community

MONDAY, November 3: "Dissension and Debate" (Acts 15:1-5)
TUESDAY, November 4: "Evidence of God's Work" (Acts 15:6-11)
WEDNESDAY, November 5: "The Basis for Unity" (Acts 15:12-21)
THURSDAY, November 6: "The Confession that Saves" (Romans 10:5-9)
FRIDAY, November 7: "Everyone May Be Saved" (Romans 10:10-17)
SATURDAY, November 8: "Not Running in Vain" (Galatians 2:1-10)
SUNDAY, November 9: "Living by Law or Faith" (Galatians 2:11-21)

LESSON 11   November 16, 2008

COMMUNION WITH GOD IN THE MIDST OF STRUGGLE

DEVOTIONAL READING: **Psalm 46**
PRINT PASSAGE: **Philippians 3:17-21; 4:1-9**

BACKGROUND SCRIPTURE: **Philippians 3:3–4:9**
KEY VERSE: **Philippians 4:7**

Philippians 3:17-21; 4:1-9—KJV

17 Brethren, be followers together of me, and mark them which walk so as ye have us for an ensample.
18 (For many walk, of whom I have told you often, and now tell you even weeping, that they are the enemies of the cross of Christ:
19 Whose end is destruction, whose God is their belly, and whose glory is in their shame, who mind earthly things.)
20 For our conversation is in heaven; from whence also we look for the Saviour, the Lord Jesus Christ:
21 Who shall change our vile body, that it may be fashioned like unto his glorious body, according to the working whereby he is able even to subdue all things unto himself.

    …..

THEREFORE, MY brethren dearly beloved and longed for, my joy and crown, so stand fast in the Lord, my dearly beloved.
2 I beseech Euodias, and beseech Syntyche, that they be of the same mind in the Lord.
3 And I intreat thee also, true yokefellow, help those women which laboured with me in the gospel, with Clement also, and with other my fellowlabourers, whose names are in the book of life.
4 Rejoice in the Lord alway: and again I say, Rejoice.
5 Let your moderation be known unto all men. The Lord is at hand.
6 Be careful for nothing; but in every thing by prayer and supplication with thanksgiving let your requests be made known unto God.
7 And the peace of God, which passeth all understanding, shall keep your hearts and minds through Christ Jesus.
8 Finally, brethren, whatsoever things are true, whatsoever things are honest, whatsoever things are

Philippians 3:17-21; 4:1-9—NRSV

17 Brothers and sisters, join in imitating me, and observe those who live according to the example you have in us.
18 For many live as enemies of the cross of Christ; I have often told you of them, and now I tell you even with tears.
19 Their end is destruction; their god is the belly; and their glory is in their shame; their minds are set on earthly things.
20 But our citizenship is in heaven, and it is from there that we are expecting a Savior, the Lord Jesus Christ.
21 He will transform the body of our humiliation that it may be conformed to the body of his glory, by the power that also enables him to make all things subject to himself.

    …..

THEREFORE, MY brothers and sisters, whom I love and long for, my joy and crown, stand firm in the Lord in this way, my beloved.
2 I urge Euodia and I urge Syntyche to be of the same mind in the Lord.
3 Yes, and I ask you also, my loyal companion, help these women, for they have struggled beside me in the work of the gospel, together with Clement and the rest of my co-workers, whose names are in the book of life.
4 Rejoice in the Lord always; again I will say, Rejoice.
5 Let your gentleness be known to everyone. The Lord is near.
6 Do not worry about anything, but in everything by prayer and supplication with thanksgiving let your requests be made known to God.
7 And the peace of God, which surpasses all understanding, will guard your hearts and your minds in Christ Jesus.
8 Finally, beloved, whatever is true, whatever is honorable, whatever is just, whatever is pure, whatever

During difficult times, people in community support one another and find reasons to give thanks. How do people in community come together in the midst of struggle? Paul exhorted the Philippians to follow examples of those who worked together for the common good and to rejoice together.

just, whatsoever things are pure, whatsoever things are lovely, whatsoever things are of good report; if there be any virtue, and if there be any praise, think on these things.

9 Those things, which ye have both learned, and received, and heard, and seen in me, do: and the God of peace shall be with you.

is pleasing, whatever is commendable, if there is any excellence and if there is anything worthy of praise, think about these things.

9 Keep on doing the things that you have learned and received and heard and seen in me, and the God of peace will be with you.

TOPICAL OUTLINE OF THE LESSON

I. Introduction
   A. Effective Church Ministry
   B. Biblical Background

II. Exposition and Application of the Scripture
   A. The Christian and His Brethren (Philippians 3:17-21)
   B. The Christian's Birthright (Philippians 4:1-7)
   C. The Christian and His Thoughts (Philippians 4:8-9)

III. Concluding Reflection

LESSON OBJECTIVES

Upon completion of this lesson, the students will know that:

1. Difficult times often present opportunities for a community to come together;
2. Members in the community are capable of working together for the common good; and,
3. Difficult times bring out the good side of humankind.

POINTS TO BE EMPHASIZED

ADULT/YOUTH
Adult Topic: Mutual Support
Youth Topic: We're in This Together
Adult Key Verse: Philippians 4:7
Youth Key Verse: Philippians 3:17
Print Passage: Philippians 3:17-21; 4:1-9

—Euodia and Syntyche were two women in the church in Philippi who had been disagreeing.
—The "whatever" statements in verse 8 suggest a series of attitudes for living that can help a community face difficulty well.
—In this passage, Paul addressed false doctrines that threatened the unity of the Philippian church.
—Paul described the fate of those spreading false doctrines and leading the faithful astray.
—The false teachers took pleasure in what believers were taught to eschew (e.g., pride, arrogance, and immorality).
—Paul cautioned against preoccupation with earthly things, telling believers to focus on the return of Christ.

CHILDREN
Children Topic: Praise God
Key Verse: Philippians 4:4
Print Passage: Acts 16:11-15; Philippians 4:4-7

—God worked through Paul and others to spread the Gospel message.
—The powerful Gospel message changed the hearts of Lydia and her household.

—Some people are called to deliver the Gospel message in unfamiliar places.

—Paul and his companions sought out women by the riverbank who appeared ready to receive the Gospel message.

—God rewards us with peace of mind when we make our requests known to God.

—Sometimes we must make sacrifices to fulfill our roles as God's servants.

I. INTRODUCTION

A. Effective Church Ministry

How should we measure the healthiness and effectiveness of a church's ministry? Many times we measure the effectiveness of a church by the size of the membership, the annual church budget, the number and variety of ministries in place, and a host of other factors that may not give a real indication of the spiritual health of the church's members. What are the marks of a healthy church? Mark Dever, Senior Pastor of Capitol Hill Baptist Church in Washington, D.C., wrote: "We need churches that are self-consciously distinct from the culture… churches in which the key indicator …is persevering biblical faithfulness."

B. Biblical Background

Paul's love and affection for the church in Philippi was unmistakable. The members were his joy and crown. The church in Philippi was established during Paul's second missionary journey. In Acts 16:6-7, Paul and his companions passed through the provinces of Phrygia and Galatia with the intention of going north to Bithynia. However, they were forbidden by the Holy Spirit and instead went through Mysia and came to the port city of Alexandra Troas (see Acts 16:8). During the night, Paul had a vision of man in Macedonia exhorting him, "Come over into Macedonia and help us." He concluded that this was God's call for him to carry the Gospel to Europe. Within a few days they boarded a commercial vessel bound for the port city of Neapolis, which is in Macedonia. After arriving in Neapolis, Paul and his companions (Silas, Timothy, and Luke) walked the ten to twelve miles along the Via Egnatia to the city of Philippi (see Acts 16:12).

II. EXPOSITION AND APPLICATION OF THE SCRIPTURE

A. The Christian and His Brethren
(Philippians 3:17-21)

Brethren, be followers together of me, and mark them which walk so as ye have us for an ensample. (For many walk, of whom I have told you often, and now tell you even weeping, that they are the enemies of the cross of Christ: Whose end is destruction, whose God is their belly, and whose glory is in their shame, who mind earthly things.) For our conversation is in heaven; from whence also we look for the Saviour, the Lord Jesus Christ: Who shall change our vile body, that it may be fashioned like unto his glorious body, according to the working whereby he is able even to subdue all things unto himself.

Who could be a more fitting example for the young Philippian converts than Paul? He encouraged the brethren to use him—and others who were also worthy of emulation—as their example (see 1 Corinthians 4:16; 1 Thessalonians 1:6). On the surface this looks and sounds like a man who was full of self-conceit, but this was not the case. One must keep this verse in context with the larger discussion that preceded it in verses 4-16, where Paul described all of the credentials that he had once put great confidence in (verses 4-6). However, when Jesus Christ arrested him and changed the course of his life, he knew that all of the things that he had previously considered important no longer mattered (verse 7). What really mattered for Paul was the excellence of the knowledge that he gained in Jesus Christ (see verse 8). Therefore, if anyone was to be followed, Paul wanted them to follow him. Moreover, they were to "mark" the others in their fellowship who lived in the same manner as the apostle.

Contrary to him there were others who were enemies of the Cross (verse 18). Paul had warned the saints in Philippi of the very destructive nature of these men who would come among the young churches and wreak havoc on them (see Acts 15:1-3; 2 Corinthians 11:3-4; Galatians 1:7). Paul was more than likely referring to the Judaizers, missionaries who wanted the Gentile converts to keep the laws and customs of Moses. These were the men for whom Paul was crying tears of deep sorrow day and night. He gave several reasons for his deep sorrow. First, their practices would eventually lead them to destruction. Second, they were ruled by their bellies, "whose glory is in their shame." Verse 19 is quite revealing: the Jews and some Christians satisfy their own desires, before even thinking about the needs of others.

B. The Christian's Birthright
(Philippians 4:1-7)

THEREFORE, MY brethren dearly beloved and longed for, my joy and crown, so stand fast in the Lord, my dearly beloved. I beseech Euodias, and beseech Syntyche, that they be of the same mind in the Lord. And I intreat thee also, true yokefellow, help those women which laboured with me in the gospel, with Clement also, and with other my fellowlabourers, whose names are in the book of life. Rejoice in the Lord alway: and again I say, Rejoice. Let your moderation be known unto all men. The Lord is at hand. Be careful for nothing; but in every thing by prayer and supplication with thanksgiving let your requests be made known unto God. And the peace of God, which passeth all understanding, shall keep your hearts and minds through Christ Jesus.

The word *therefore* forms the concluding thought to everything that the apostle had written about up to this point. In light of all that had been said, he wanted them to "stand fast." He loved them and wanted to see them complete their journey of faith successfully. In verse 1, Paul stated why he felt such a deep love for the Philippians. He referred to them as his "brothers," a term of endearment. Paul dearly loved them and longed to see them. They were his joy and crown. At the coming of the Lord, Paul intimated that the Philippians will be "his wreath of victory," hence the reference to the crown. They were not just anybody to him nor did he think of them in the same way he thought of the Corinthians, who caused him considerable pain (see 2 Corinthians 12:14-15, 19-21).

Yet, as in any congregation, all was not well. Paul strongly urged Euodias and Syntyche to work together in the church. This is the second appeal to unity (see Philippians 1:27–2:4). We do not know the nature of the conflict, nor how long it had persisted. However, it is apparent that for Paul to mention these two women by name was an indication that everyone in the church knew of their differences. They had labored with him in the Gospel along with Clement and many others whose names were written in the Book of Life. Women were very instrumental in the ministry of Paul (see Acts 16:11-15; Romans 16:1, 3, 6). Paul did not minimize the contribution of the women in the work of ministry. Paul appealed to someone else whom he called a "true yokefellow" to help the women reach some agreement. In mission work in Nigeria and Kenya, women are playing leading roles.

The apostle wrote in verse 4: "Rejoice in the Lord always: and again I say rejoice." This is a command, which means that just as we must eat to survive, the believer must rejoice to endure trials, pain, despair, and tribulation. This kind of rejoicing is not circumstantial happiness, or situational peace, or even occasional delight. Rather, it is constant attitude, which is grounded in our relationship with Jesus Christ. The act of rejoicing is an expression of an overwhelming, enthusiastic, boundless joy in the Lord. No one except God can give it, and nothing can take it away.

Our joy is found in Jesus Christ. He is the source of our joy. In Him we live, move, and have our being. In Jesus Christ, we have a Friend and Elder Brother, who has gone down the road of suffering and death, who shows us that we have nothing to fear. In Jesus we have someone who meets us at the point of our struggle and helps us through the darkness of the night. Life is filled with suffering, trials, tribulations, death, pain, disappointments, and evil and sinister people who are being used by Satan to try to rob us of the joy of our relationship with Jesus Christ. Paul was keenly aware of the extremes of life on the mission field (see 2 Corinthians 11:23-32).

The paragraph closes with Paul's appeal a second time to let their "moderation be known unto all men." This phrase is better translated by the idea of *gentleness*. Gentleness is a noun which identifies a person who manifests calmness and fairness of spirit. The Lord Jesus Christ could come at any moment; therefore, Paul urged the congregation to work at promoting peace among themselves.

Paul encouraged the saints in Philippi not to be anxious or overly concerned about anything (see Matthew 6:25-34). They were to give all of their concerns to God in prayer with supplication and thanksgiving. Once they had made their requests known to God they must leave them at His feet.

The words in verse 7 are so precious that they have remained virtually unchanged from one English translation of the Bible to the next: "And the peace of God, which surpasses all comprehension, will guard your hearts and your minds in Christ Jesus" (NASB). Let us first define what is meant by the words "the peace of God." One of the ways that we come to understand the Bible's meaning is by understanding the relationship of words and how they are structured in the biblical text.

First, the word *the* is a definite article and points not just to peace, but to a specific kind of peace—the peace of God. *Peace* means "the absence of turmoil, strife, tension, anxiety, and hostility." It is the presence of external and internal harmony. The word *of* is a preposition and it points to a relationship between what came before it and what follows. In the New Testament, *of* is always used to indicate the point of origin—that is to say, the Bible speaks of the Word of God, the church of God, and the Spirit of God, all of which indicate that God is the point of origin. It is not just a word, but it is the Word of God that is holy, divine, and spiritual.

When we speak of *the peace of God*, we are speaking of a particular peace that has its origin in God; it is not just peace from God, but it is God's peace. It is the tranquility that is in and emanates from God's own eternal being. It is the peace which God Himself has. It is the calm serenity that characterizes the very nature of God. It is absolute freedom from frustration and anxiety. It is mental and emotional heaven here on earth. The only way that we can have the peace of God is to have peace with God. Paul wrote about this peace in Romans 5:1 (NKJV): "Therefore having been justified by faith, we have peace with God through our Lord Jesus Christ." When we give our lives to Jesus Christ we receive God's peace.

C. The Christian and His Thoughts (Philippians 4:8-9)

Finally, brethren, whatsoever things are true, whatsoever things are honest, whatsoever things are just, whatsoever things are pure, whatsoever things are lovely, whatsoever things are of good report; if there be any virtue, and if there be any praise, think on these things. Those things, which ye have both learned, and received, and heard, and seen in me, do: and the God of peace shall be with you.

Paul had arrived at the end of all that he wanted to tell the Philippians what to guard against. He concluded by reminding them of the importance of their thoughts. They must constantly think good thoughts. The apostle listed several noteworthy qualities that the Philippians should cultivate: truth, honesty, justice, purity, and loveliness. These were all virtues admired in the ancient world.

Thoughts originate in the brain, which is the center of all of our thinking processes.

In the brain, we possess the cognitive ability to think and reason, as we form perceptions about life and those with whom we come in contact. The mind is the place where all of our actions—past, present, and future—find their point of origin. Paul wanted them to spend time thinking about the things that promote spiritual well-being. It is easy to allow the enemy to attack our minds and capture our thoughts. Believers are encouraged and warned against giving the devil a free hand in their thoughts (see 2 Corinthians 10:3-5). Thoughts must be brought into obedience to Christ, meaning that our thoughts must be held captive by us to see whether or not they honor God.

The apostle wanted the Philippians to fill their minds with thoughts that promoted healthy spiritual growth. Paul knew that we become what we think (see Proverbs 23:7). He had sought to model the kind of life that they would find worthy of emulation. Paul reminded them to do the things that they had received and learned through his teachings. It is not enough that we say the right things, but Christianity is also about doing good works (see Ephesians 2:10; James 1:27). He would say to them, "Do these things and the God of peace shall be with you." God not only gives peace—He is the God of peace.

III. CONCLUDING REFLECTION

We are living in some of the most mentally anguishing days in human history. Our nation is bogged down in a global war against Islamic extremism and terror in two countries. The displaced residents of New Orleans and the Gulf Coast are still trying to recover from Hurricane Katrina. There is anxiety worldwide. Around the world people are mangled and mauled by the massive array of perplexing problems and sticky situations. We find ourselves asking these questions: "How am I supposed to feel good with all of this pressure? How am I supposed to be inspired with all of these financial problems? How am I supposed to feel motivated when there are people I cannot stand to be around? How can I feel good about being a Christian when my [husband/wife/child] ridicules the faith I stand on? How am I supposed to get pumped up with all of these problems in my life? How am I supposed to be at peace when I can hardly sleep at night?"

There is a simple explanation that answers each one of those questions: maybe you have not started to enjoy the peace that God has given you in His Son (Jesus Christ). This sounds so simple that it is almost hard to believe, accept, or comprehend. The way you get this peace is not some mystery that is beyond human comprehension. There is no six-step process for getting and enjoying the peace of God. You do not have to go to a conference on peace in order to know God's peace. You do not have to pass an IQ test and score 1600 on the SAT to get His peace. God's peace is free and available to all believers who will yield themselves to Him and learn to live free of anxiety.

The two women mentioned in Philippians 4:2 were Christians, but there was disagreement between the two of them. Paul appealed to them to reconcile, so that the work of God would not be hindered.

Is there anyone you need to reconcile with today? Do it in the name of the Lord.

PRAYER

Lord, teach us to trust You completely and fully in everything and in every situation. Thank You for giving us peace in the midst of our trials. In Jesus' name we pray. Amen.

WORD POWER

Peace *(eireenee [ei-ree-nee])*—this is the very peace of God. Paul did not say peace *from* God, but peace *of* God. This peace harmonizes all passions and appetites which are produced by the Holy Spirit. This peace arises from a sense of pardon and the favor of God. In contrast, the peace of man is limited and conditional, but God's peace is unlimited and it covers our lives from the day we receive pardon from Him.

HOME DAILY BIBLE READINGS
(November 10-16, 2008)

Communion with God in the Midst of Struggle

MONDAY, November 10: "God Is Our Refuge" (Psalm 46)
TUESDAY, November 11: "Sharing God's Grace" (Philippians 1:3-11)
WEDNESDAY, November 12: "Rejoice! Christ Is Proclaimed" (Philippians 1:12-18)
THURSDAY, November 13: "The Help of the Spirit" (Philippians 1:19-26)
FRIDAY, November 14: "Striving Side by Side" (Philippians 1:27-30)
SATURDAY, November 15: "Stand Firm in the Lord" (Philippians 3:17–4:1)
SUNDAY, November 16: "The Peace that Guards" (Philippians 4:2-9)

LESSON 12   November 23, 2008

WITNESS OF THE COMMUNITY

DEVOTIONAL READING: **Acts 4:13-20**
PRINT PASSAGE: **2 Timothy 2:1-3; 4:1-5**

BACKGROUND SCRIPTURE: **2 Timothy 2:1-3; 4:1-5**
KEY VERSE: **2 Timothy 2:2**

2 Timothy 2:1-3; 4:1-5—KJV

THOU THEREFORE, my son, be strong in the grace that is in Christ Jesus.

2 And the things that thou hast heard of me among many witnesses, the same commit thou to faithful men, who shall be able to teach others also.

3 Thou therefore endure hardness, as a good soldier of Jesus Christ.

.....

I CHARGE thee therefore before God, and the Lord Jesus Christ, who shall judge the quick and the dead at his appearing and his kingdom;

2 Preach the word; be instant in season, out of season; reprove, rebuke, exhort with all longsuffering and doctrine.

3 For the time will come when they will not endure sound doctrine; but after their own lusts shall they heap to themselves teachers, having itching ears;

4 And they shall turn away their ears from the truth, and shall be turned unto fables.

5 But watch thou in all things, endure afflictions, do the work of an evangelist, make full proof of thy ministry.

2 Timothy 2:1-3; 4:1-5—NRSV

YOU THEN, my child, be strong in the grace that is in Christ Jesus;

2 and what you have heard from me through many witnesses entrust to faithful people who will be able to teach others as well.

3 Share in suffering like a good soldier of Christ Jesus.

.....

IN THE presence of God and of Christ Jesus, who is to judge the living and the dead, and in view of his appearing and his kingdom, I solemnly urge you:

2 proclaim the message; be persistent whether the time is favorable or unfavorable; convince, rebuke, and encourage, with the utmost patience in teaching.

3 For the time is coming when people will not put up with sound doctrine, but having itching ears, they will accumulate for themselves teachers to suit their own desires,

4 and will turn away from listening to the truth and wander away to myths.

5 As for you, always be sober, endure suffering, do the work of an evangelist, carry out your ministry fully.

BIBLE FACT

Paul and Timothy: Timothy stood shoulder-to-shoulder with Paul's companions and fellow laborers. He was Paul's own convert. Timothy's parents were Hellenists (Greek). In Paul's second visit to Derbe and Lystra, Paul was impressed with Timothy's unfeigned faith. Paul referred to him as a son in the Lord and always admonished him not to neglect the gift of God in him. Paul became a mentor to Timothy in spiritual matters. According to Eusebius, Timothy was the first bishop of Ephesus.

Through constructive living, people have a positive influence on and set a good example for others in their community. What characterizes a good example? Paul wrote that living as Jesus did was a strong witness for others to follow in good times and bad and that this message should be shared with all who would listen.

TOPICAL OUTLINE OF THE LESSON

I. **Introduction**
  A. Timothy—A Model for Christians
  B. Biblical Background

II. **Exposition and Application of the Scripture**
  A. Be Strong (2 Timothy 2:1-2)
  B. Endure Hardness (2 Timothy 2:3)
  C. Preach the Truth (2 Timothy 4:1-5)

III. **Concluding Reflection**

LESSON OBJECTIVES

Upon completion of this lesson, the students will know that:

1. Timothy led an exemplary Christian life;
2. Paul poured his life into Timothy's mind; and,
3. As Christians, our lives are open books.

POINTS TO BE EMPHASIZED

ADULT/YOUTH

Adult Topic: **A Good Example**
Youth Topic: **Watch Yourself**
Adult Key Verse: **2 Timothy 2:2**
Youth Key Verse: **2 Timothy 4:5**
Print Passage: **2 Timothy 2:1-3; 4:1-5**

—The illustration of the soldier is the first of three such illustrations in the verses that follow: soldier, athlete, and farmer.
—Paul gave Timothy godly advice, as a father would give to a son.
—Paul admonished Timothy to prepare others, just as Paul had prepared him for discipleship, ministry, and service.
—Paul's appeal was given with the anticipation of Christ's return coming quickly; however, his godly directive is still valid for servants of the Lord today.

CHILDREN

Children Topic: **Let's Tell Others About Jesus**
Key Verse: **Acts 15:35**
Print Passage: **Acts 15:22-23a, 30-35; 2 Timothy 2:1-2**
—When Paul and Barnabas returned to Antioch, the leaders of the Jerusalem Council selected Judas (called Barsabbas) and Silas to accompany them.
—A letter was sent to the Antioch church, which declared the Jerusalem Council's recommendations for personal piety.
—Judas and Silas encouraged and strengthened the Antioch church.
—Sometimes people will treat an old message as new when a newcomer delivers the message.
—Training and proclaiming the Word of God to others is a never-ending process.

I. INTRODUCTION

A. Timothy—A Model for Christians

Timothy was one of the most well-known young Christians in the early church. We know a great deal about his life. According to Acts 16:1-3, Paul met the young man during his second missionary journey (see Acts 16:1-2).

Paul was so impressed by the young man's commitment to Jesus Christ that he requested that Timothy join their mission team. Before departing he circumcised Timothy to quiet the Jews in the region. Timothy had not been circumcised because his father was Greek. However, to make Timothy acceptable to the Jews, he was circumcised. Why was there such a close relationship between Paul and Timothy? One reason was because Timothy shared the unquenchable spirit ministry of Paul. Timothy was a trustworthy Christian. In his letter to the church in Philippi, Paul shared with the believers his plans to send Timothy to see them (see Philippians 2:19-20). Timothy cared about the saints and wanted to see them grow in Christ. Therefore, when Paul sent Timothy it was like going himself.

B. Biblical Background

Today's lesson comes from Paul's second letter to Timothy. It was written during the latter days of Paul's life, just prior to his execution in Rome (see 2 Timothy 4:6-7). Paul wanted Timothy to know how he was faring and he wanted to tell him of his suffering (see 2:9). These words must have been both a source of encouragement and heart-wrenching grief. Timothy knew that he would not see Paul again.

Paul knew that Timothy would face challenging days ahead. Our study today uses the illustration of a faithful teacher and a battle-hardened soldier to teach believers lessons about courage, patience, and discipline (2:1-3). Timothy was charged to preach the Word of God without fear. He must be prepared to endure afflictions and the hardships that came with devotion to full-time ministry. Every believer can benefit from the words of this seasoned saint.

II. EXPOSITION AND APPLICATION OF THE SCRIPTURE

A. Be Strong
(2 Timothy 2:1-2)

THOU THEREFORE, my son, be strong in the grace that is in Christ Jesus. And the things that thou hast heard of me among many witnesses, the same commit thou to faithful men, who shall be able to teach others also.

In verse 1, Paul affectionately addressed Timothy as "my son." Why did Paul say that?

First, he wanted Timothy to be strong, given all of the trials that he had personally faced and been forced to endure because of his apostolic calling. Second, he said "My son, be strong…" because in 2 Timothy 1:15 we read, "This thou knowest, that all they which are in Asia be turned away from me; of whom are Phygellus and Hermogenes." In this verse, there was a defection. Therefore, Paul exhorted Timothy to remain faithful and loyal.

In verse 2, we are made privy to a second source of Timothy's strength—the things that he had heard and learned from Paul. Timothy had been an eyewitness and participant in the greatest ministry outside of the life of Jesus Christ. He had seen Paul overcome near-impossible situations and had heard his preaching—which converted thousands to Christianity—and watched him teach with such skill that even the most astute Jewish rabbi was astounded. The words "among many witnesses" referred to the many people who could bear witness that God had sent Paul to be an apostle. They were his crown in the Lord (see Philippians 4:1).

Timothy must recruit, train, and commit to faithful men the things that he had learned. Two thoughts are critical in this verse. The first had to do with what Paul meant by "commit" (Greek: *paratithemi*—literally means "to keep alongside"). One can think of a safe deposit box where we keep our most important documents and papers safe from damage, theft, or loss. Timothy was to take what he had learned and deposit it into others, who would be able to teach others. Paul was reminding Timothy that his faith in Christ, and the example he (Paul) had laid down, must be taught along with the Gospel. This means that the life of a believer in Christ is intricately woven together with the Gospel. If we fail to live up to what we teach, we are hypocrites. Faithful people are those whose very characters denote unswerving commitment to Jesus Christ.

B. Endure Hardness
(2 Timothy 2:3)

Thou therefore endure hardness, as a good soldier of Jesus Christ.

The first illustration that Paul presented to his son in ministry was that of a soldier, with which would be an image that he would be all too familiar. Timothy had seen firsthand the discipline, skill, and courage of the Roman soldiers.

In 1972, there was a soldier who was commissioned as an Infantry Second Lieutenant in the U.S. Army. After the basic course and airborne school, he went to Ranger School in the dead of winter. This training tested his resolve and commitment to complete the training and get the coveted Ranger patch. This soldier learned to endure some of the harshest training conditions that the army could devise. At the end of the eight-week course, he had earned the right to be called Army Ranger. Persons who accept Jesus Christ as Lord and would call themselves true disciples must earn this honor on the battlefield of life.

C. Preach the Truth
(2 Timothy 4:1-5)

I CHARGE thee therefore before God, and the Lord Jesus Christ, who shall judge the quick and the dead at his appearing and his kingdom; Preach the word; be instant in season, out of season; reprove, rebuke, exhort with all longsuffering and doctrine. For the time will come when they will not endure sound doctrine; but after their own lusts shall they heap to themselves teachers, having itching ears; And they shall turn away their ears from the truth, and shall be turned unto fables. But watch thou in all things, endure afflictions, do the work of an evangelist, make full proof of thy ministry.

Paul's final charge to Timothy is often used during the occasion of either an ordination or licensure of a minister to preach the Gospel. He reminded Timothy that his preaching must be measured against the backdrop of the coming of the Lord Jesus Christ who would judge the living and the dead at His appearing. From the Greek word we get the word *epiphany*, which is often used to denote the season of the church year that commemorates the first appearance of Jesus at the start of His public ministry. One day Jesus Christ will appear in the heavens unannounced and the Son of Man will come in the clouds with the holy angels to take His people back to heaven. The implication was that those who preach the Gospel should expect to receive the harshest judgment for failing to preach the truth.

Timothy was charged to preach (Greek: *kerruso*—meaning "the act of proclamation or to act as a herald"). The content of his preaching must be the Word (see Mark 1:15-16; Romans 1:15; 1 Corinthians 2:1-5; 1 Timothy 4:5; 2 Timothy 2:9). In the New Testament, there is a distinct difference between the act of preaching and the content of what is preached. One can engage in proclamation, but the preaching may not be the Word. The Word is the Gospel about Jesus Christ (see Acts 3:20; 8:5; Romans 15:19; 1 Corinthians 15:12; 2 Corinthians 1:9; Philippians 1:18). Timothy needed to be ready at every opportune moment to preach Jesus Christ.

Timothy bore a major responsibility because his preaching needed to expose sin and explain how to live free of sin's dominion (see Romans 6:12-14). He needed to *reprove* (Greek: *elegxon,* meaning "to refute or expose of the faults of something"), *rebuke* (Greek: *epitimao,* meaning "to sharply censure or reprove), and *exhort* (Greek: *parakaleo,* meaning "to comfort, encourage, or stand beside")—and do so with *patience* (Greek: *makrothume,* meaning "to suffer long") and doctrine. Why was this necessary? There may be many of the members of the church who could be stuck in their ways and resistant to the preaching and teaching of the Word.

In verse 3, Paul pointed out why there was a clear need for this kind of preaching and teaching. Paul envisioned a time when false teachers would arise and draw people after themselves (see Acts 20:28-30). He said that there would come a time when people would not endure or put up with listening to preaching that convicted. Instead, they would seek out teachers who would satisfy their curiosity. The image of "itching ears" denotes listening to a message that informs but does not lead to any conformation to the truth. They would find fables more appealing than the truth.

Paul concluded by encouraging Timothy to be watchful, endure afflictions, do the work of an evangelist, and make full proof of his ministry. What did Paul mean by "make full proof of your ministry"? It refers to being faithful without wavering and carrying out every responsibility that God has called one to. Sometimes we want to make excuses for not wanting to be held accountable for our service and ministry. However, he or she who strives to make full proof will never offer an excuse for failing to do the will of the Father.

III. CONCLUDING REFLECTION

One of the greatest needs of the body of Christ is for pastoral leaders who are deeply spiritual and committed to building up the body of Christ. One of the biggest scourges in the church today is the presence of a theology that proclaims that God's sole purpose is to make each of us rich and famous. This proclamation of prosperity has hurt, hindered, and hemmed the church into a corner of apathy and complacency. Why are there so many weak, troubled, spiritually anemic churches today? The answer lies with their leadership. Wherever you find weak, unspiritual leaders, the congregation can be no more. The way out of this morass of emptiness is to return to the basic fundamental truths of the Gospel that Jesus Christ is the power of God to all who believe, offer themselves as living sacrifices, and are committed to Kingdom expansion.

Paul told Timothy to commit what he had learned to other faithful believers. The times in which we now live call for strong pastors and leaders in our congregations. A presiding bishop Katharine Jefferts Shori was asked by *Time* if belief in Jesus is the only way to get to heaven. She replied, "We who practice the Christian tradition understand Him (Jesus) as our vehicle to the Divine. But for us to assume that God could not act in other ways is, I think, to put God in an awfully small box. That is not the faith that I received" (*Time*: 7/10/06, or *The Tennessean*: 1/15/08). We need strong pastors who will stand on the truth without wavering.

Timothy epitomized a true spirit of contentment. He was a dependable companion of Paul. Dependability is uncommon in our day. Many associate ministers have a private ambition of derailing the senior pastor. In many churches, deacons have become so powerful that they rule the church of God. Many auxiliary leaders are carving unbiblical authority for themselves. The combination of all of this has rendered the church of God impotent. Timothy was an example of true humility.

Are there followers like Timothy in your congregation?

PRAYER

Lord, teach us to trust You in the dry places of ministry. May we learn to persist and be faithful even when it looks dark and the road has been washed away. Thank You for the example of Jesus Christ, who shows us how to serve and not grow weary. In Jesus' name we pray. Amen.

WORD POWER

Witness *(matureo [ma-tu-reo])*—A witness is one who attests to his or her belief in the Gospel with personal suffering. The words *martyr* and *witness* have the same form in Greek. In the context of this lesson, Paul was telling Timothy to remember that there were many witnesses to his ordination to the ministry; therefore, Timothy could not afford to fail.

HOME DAILY BIBLE READINGS
(November 17-23, 2008)

Witness of the Community

MONDAY, November 17: "Power, Love, Self-discipline" (2 Timothy 1:3-7)

TUESDAY, November 18: "I Am Not Ashamed" (2 Timothy 1:8-14)

WEDNESDAY, November 19: "The Power of the Gospel" (Romans 1:8-17)

THURSDAY, November 20: "The Unchained Word of God" (2 Timothy 2:8-13)

FRIDAY, November 21: "An Approved Worker" (2 Timothy 2:14-19)

SATURDAY, November 22: "Continue in What You Learned" (2 Timothy 3:14-17)

SUNDAY, November 23: "Proclaim the Message!" (2 Timothy 2:1-3; 4:1-5)

PERSECUTION WITHIN THE COMMUNITY

DEVOTIONAL READING: **1 Corinthians 1:18-25**
PRINT PASSAGE: **2 Corinthians 11:16-18, 21-30; 12:9-10**

BACKGROUND SCRIPTURE: **2 Corinthians 11:16–12:10**
KEY VERSE: **2 Corinthians 12:10**

2 Corinthians 11:16-18, 21-30; 12:9-10—KJV

16 I say again, Let no man think me a fool; if otherwise, yet as a fool receive me, that I may boast myself a little.

17 That which I speak, I speak it not after the Lord, but as it were foolishly, in this confidence of boasting.

18 Seeing that many glory after the flesh, I will glory also.

.....

21 Howbeit whereinsoever any is bold, (I speak foolishly,) I am bold also.

22 Are they Hebrews? so am I. Are they Israelites? so am I. Are they the seed of Abraham? so am I.

23 Are they ministers of Christ? (I speak as a fool) I am more; in labours more abundant, in stripes above measure, in prisons more frequent, in deaths oft.

24 Of the Jews five times received I forty stripes save one.

25 Thrice was I beaten with rods, once was I stoned, thrice I suffered shipwreck, a night and a day I have been in the deep;

26 In journeyings often, in perils of waters, in perils of robbers, in perils by mine own countrymen, in perils by the heathen, in perils in the city, in perils in the wilderness, in perils in the sea, in perils among false brethren;

27 In weariness and painfulness, in watchings often, in hunger and thirst, in fastings often, in cold and nakedness.

28 Beside those things that are without, that which cometh upon me daily, the care of all the churches.

29 Who is weak, and I am not weak? who is offended, and I burn not?

30 If I must needs glory, I will glory of the things which concern mine infirmities.

2 Corinthians 11:16-18, 21-30; 12:9-10—NRSV

16 I repeat, let no one think that I am a fool; but if you do, then accept me as a fool, so that I too may boast a little.

17 What I am saying in regard to this boastful confidence, I am saying not with the Lord's authority, but as a fool;

18 since many boast according to human standards, I will also boast.

.....

21 But whatever anyone dares to boast of—I am speaking as a fool—I also dare to boast of that.

22 Are they Hebrews? So am I. Are they Israelites? So am I. Are they descendants of Abraham? So am I.

23 Are they ministers of Christ? I am talking like a madman—I am a better one: with far greater labors, far more imprisonments, with countless floggings, and often near death.

24 Five times I have received from the Jews the forty lashes minus one.

25 Three times I was beaten with rods. Once I received a stoning. Three times I was shipwrecked; for a night and a day I was adrift at sea;

26 on frequent journeys, in danger from rivers, danger from bandits, danger from my own people, danger from Gentiles, danger in the city, danger in the wilderness, danger at sea, danger from false brothers and sisters;

27 in toil and hardship, through many a sleepless night, hungry and thirsty, often without food, cold and naked.

28 And, besides other things, I am under daily pressure because of my anxiety for all the churches.

29 Who is weak, and I am not weak? Who is made to stumble, and I am not indignant?

30 If I must boast, I will boast of the things that show my weakness.

UNIFYING LESSON PRINCIPLE

People will face many trials in life from friend and foe, as well as from expected and unexpected sources. How can one overcome such hardships? Paul said that through his weaknesses he found strength in the grace of God.

.....

9 And he said unto me, My grace is sufficient for thee: for my strength is made perfect in weakness. Most gladly therefore will I rather glory in my infirmities, that the power of Christ may rest upon me.

10 Therefore I take pleasure in infirmities, in reproaches, in necessities, in persecutions, in distresses for Christ's sake: for when I am weak, then am I strong.

.....

9 but he said to me, "My grace is sufficient for you, for power is made perfect in weakness." So, I will boast all the more gladly of my weaknesses, so that the power of Christ may dwell in me.

10 Therefore I am content with weaknesses, insults, hardships, persecutions, and calamities for the sake of Christ; for whenever I am weak, then I am strong.

TOPICAL OUTLINE OF THE LESSON

I. Introduction
   A. Suffering for Christ's Sake
   B. Biblical Background

II. Exposition and Application of the Scripture
   A. Reluctant Boasting (2 Corinthians 11:16-18, 21)
   B. Facing Hardships for Christ (2 Corinthians 11:22-30)
   C. Paul's Boast of His Power in Christ (2 Corinthians 12:9-10)

III. Concluding Reflection

LESSON OBJECTIVES

Upon completion of this lesson, the students will know that:

1. Suffering for Christ's sake is noble;
2. God promised His presence at all times; and,
3. Our suffering is limited.

POINTS TO BE EMPHASIZED

ADULT/YOUTH

Adult Topic: **Grace in Times of Trouble**
Youth Topic: **No Pain, No Gain**
Adult/Youth Key Verse: **2 Corinthians 12:10**
Print Passage: **2 Corinthians 11:16-18, 21-30; 12:9-10**

—Paul's boasts about ministry were prompted by challenges from others in the Corinthian church who thought they had it rough. Paul said their complaints were no match for the suffering he had known.

—Paul's boasts are examples of irony.

—Despite his great contributions to laying the groundwork of the early church, Paul faced great opposition and many detractors.

—Paul had given of himself to the Corinthian church and had accepted no monetary offerings from them, yet some tried to twist his motives for doing so in a negative light.

—Paul had suffered greatly for the work of the Kingdom, yet despite his sacrifices, the Corinthians had allowed themselves to be duped by false apostles who made light of Paul's great sacrifice.

—This second letter to the Corinthians expresses Paul's obvious hurt as a result of their actions.

CHILDREN

Children Topic: **Power for Living**
Key Verse: **2 Corinthians 12:9**
Print Passage: **2 Corinthians 11:24-29, 32-33; 12:9-10**

—God's people suffer because of their choice to follow Jesus Christ.

—God gives believers the stamina to withstand hardships encountered as they seek to honor God's call on their lives.

—Although Paul suffered through beatings, a stoning, and imprisonment and experienced shipwrecks and danger from bandits and fellow Jews, he continued to expound faithfully the cause of Jesus Christ.

—Paul escaped imprisonment in Damascus because he was let down in a basket through a window in a wall, and yet, he saw all he did as weakness.

—Paul declared that his times of weakness and suffering were opportunities to demonstrate the power of God's grace.

—The power of Christ in believers will allow them to experience victory in times of great distress.

I. INTRODUCTION

A. Suffering for Christ's Sake

What does it mean to suffer for the cause of Jesus Christ? Many times we are prone to think that if we are talked about and conspired against, this is the worst form of persecution and suffering. What have we lost in the process? We must remember that there are missionaries and believers around the world who have paid and will pay the ultimate price for preaching and teaching Jesus Christ. There are Christians today who are being persecuted and killed because of their faith in Christ. Early this year, violence erupted in Kenya because the ruling party manipulated the general election. The angry mob burnt three churches. It is disheartening that fifty women and children were burnt in the Assembly of God Church. There is a missionary who often travels to Muslim nations training indigenous believers to witness to people of the Islamic faith. It is extremely dangerous work and requires the utmost courage. If he were arrested in one of those countries he could be tried, convicted, and executed. This is the case with many missionaries who share their faith in the Lord Jesus Christ. In the Sudan, many Christians are being persecuted. In the northern part of Nigeria, many Christians are living under fear of persecution.

Throughout the history of the Christian faith believers have suffered some of the worst indignities known for the cause of Christ. Stephen, one of the first deacons, was stoned by an angry mob (see Acts 7:54-58). James, the brother of John, was killed by Herod (see Acts 12:2). Christian tradition holds that Peter was crucified upside-down. Bishop Polycarp of Smyrna was burned at the stake for not bowing to Caesar. The apostle John was exiled to the Isle of Patmos for preaching Jesus Christ in Asia. Martin Luther was put out of the Roman Catholic Church for challenging papal authority. Savonarola of Florence was hanged and his body burned by the city government. Martin Luther King, Jr. was assassinated in Memphis, Tennessee for his standing with garbage workers on strike in Memphis and for his stance against the war in Vietnam. Indeed, many have given their lives for Christ.

B. Biblical Background

We have more details about the suffering of the apostle Paul than any other New Testament personality. He suffered some of the worst human indignities for Christ. Sprinkled throughout his letters are chronicled litanies of his sufferings (see 2 Corinthians 6:4-10; 11:23-30; Philippians 1:13; 4:16; 2 Timothy 1:12; see also Acts 14:19-20; 16:22-24). In his letter to the Corinthians, he wrote how he had been in prison more frequently, been whipped severely, and been exposed to death again and again. Five times he was whipped with thirty-nine lashes, three times beaten with rods, stoned once, shipwrecked three times, spent a day and night in the open sea, been in danger from rivers, bandits, his own countrymen, hunger, and had often gone without food, and had been cold and naked. In spite of all these things, he never gave up preaching the Gospel.

The high moment for him came when he had a spiritual experience that words could not describe (12:1-7). However, to keep him humble and from becoming overly confident in his personal experiences, a thorn in the flesh was given to buffet him. In this experience, he found that when he was at his weakest point, the power of God made him strong.

II. EXPOSITION AND APPLICATION OF THE SCRIPTURE

A. Reluctant Boasting
(2 Corinthians 11:16-18, 21)

I say again, Let no man think me a fool; if otherwise, yet as a fool receive me, that I may boast myself a little. That which I speak, I speak it not after the Lord, but as it were foolishly, in this confidence of boasting. Seeing that many glory after the flesh, I will glory also....Howbeit wherein-soever any is bold, (I speak foolishly,) I am bold also.

Boasting of one's personal achievements or about what one possesses is clearly not a way of the Christian faith. In this section, Paul told the Corinthians that he was *boasting* (Greek: *Kaukseomai*, pronounced Ka-uk-se-o-mai)—which means "to exalt, brag about, or glory in." He was not bragging about himself. Paul would never want anyone to think that his bragging here was sanctioned by the Lord—"That which I speak, I speak it not after the Lord...." Paul was faced with a dire situation that threatened to derail the hard work that had gone into evangelizing and establishing the church in Corinth. There were opponents who had come into the church and wreaked havoc. We have very little information about them or what they did. What is known is that they were obviously Jewish, and relished debating and bragging about themselves and their achievements. They had also taken advantage of the Corinthians who were not at all bothered by their tactics (verses 18-20). Paul wanted the Corinthians to think of him as they would any other *foolish person* (Greek: *aphrosune*)—meaning "a reckless, thoughtless, and senseless individual." A fool is someone who acts recklessly and without thought. The Prodigal Son is a good example of a fool (see Luke 15:13-14; also there are more than fifty references to the words *fool* or *foolish* in Proverbs). Paul wanted them to bear with his foolishness since they had already shown their willingness to put up with others (verse 19). He admitted that, unlike his opponents who had come to Corinth and taken advantage of the church, he was actually too weak to do such a thing (verse 21). However, he was bold enough to speak about his sufferings for the cause of Jesus Christ, which would put his Corinthian opponents to shame.

B. Facing Hardships for Christ
(2 Corinthians 11:22-30)

Are they Hebrews? so am I. Are they Israelites? so am I. Are they the seed of Abraham? so am I. Are they ministers

of Christ? (I speak as a fool) I am more; in labours more abundant, in stripes above measure, in prisons more frequent, in deaths oft. Of the Jews five times received I forty stripes save one. Thrice was I beaten with rods, once was I stoned, thrice I suffered shipwreck, a night and a day I have been in the deep; In journeyings often, in perils of waters, in perils of robbers, in perils by mine own countrymen, in perils by the heathen, in perils in the city, in perils in the wilderness, in perils in the sea, in perils among false brethren; In weariness and painfulness, in watchings often, in hunger and thirst, in fastings often, in cold and nakedness. Beside those things that are without, that which cometh upon me daily, the care of all the churches. Who is weak, and I am not weak? who is offended, and I burn not? If I must needs glory, I will glory of the things which concern mine infirmities.

Anyone seeking to faithfully serve Jesus Christ must be prepared for hardship (see 2 Timothy 2:1). In this section, we learn something about what may have been the nature of the opposition's attacks against Paul by looking at the things he addressed. First, he addressed his Jewish heritage. "Are they Hebrews?" He answered for himself, "so am I." This phrase, "So am I," indicates that his adversaries were Jews and apparently felt that this made them superior not only to the Gentiles but also to the Greeks. Paul boasted that he was just as Jewish as they were.

He was not a Jew with a Hellenistic or Greek background such as Timothy (see Acts 16:1). Paul was not converted to the Christian faith and incorporated into the body of Christ, as were other Gentile believers (see Ephesians 2:1-10). He was not a proselyte, someone who converted from Judaism and then became a Christian. He was born a Hebrew and met all of the ethnic qualifications to be called a Jew (see Romans 11:1; Philippians 3:5). He traced his lineage back to the patriarchs, declaring that he was born of the seed of Abraham (verse 22). Paul made three statements about his

ethnicity—he was a Hebrew, an Israelite, and of the seed of Abraham.

Second, he continued to dispute the claims of his opponents by stating that it was foolish for him to speak in this regard. The phrase "I speak as a fool" means that Paul was hesitant to boast about his spiritual accomplishments. Paul knew very well that he was an instrument, and God was the only One who deserved the glory. His boast was in the Lord. But if his opponents had rendered great service as apostles, his was extraordinary by comparison. He asked a rhetorical question whose answer would be supplied by the following description of his labors and trials in the church externally and internally: "Are they ministers of Christ?" He asserted three times in verse 23 that he was more (Greek: huper, meaning "to go beyond") of a servant of Christ than his opponents. Once again, Paul's ministry is ironically best measured by the difficulties, adversities, afflictions, and setbacks he had encountered and surmounted in his presentation of the Gospel (see also 1:3-11; 4:7-10; 6:4-10).

Paul pointed out that he had been involved in more suffering than all of the others—in more labor, in more prisons, beaten more, and near death more than the others (verse 23). He stated that he had been physically beaten by the Jews five times, receiving thirty-nine lashes, an almost intolerable number to think of enduring (verse 24; see also Deuteronomy 25:3). Three times he was beaten with rods (verse 25; see also Acts 16:22-23). He indicated that he was stoned once (see Acts 14:19).

Next, Paul described a list of perils or dangers that he had faced over the years. He spent a lot of time traveling, which opened him up to the possibility of facing a wide range of different types of trouble. He had faced weariness, pain, hunger, thirst, cold, and nakedness (verse 27). On top of all the external things he had to endure, there was the constant struggle of dealing with the various internal issues that faced the churches (verse 28). We know that Paul faced numerous challenges in trying to get the church he established to grow and develop. Corinth was plagued by one vexing situation after another (see 1 Corinthians 1-12). The situation in Galatia was so grievous that Paul wrote to ask if he had become their enemy because he told them the truth (see Galatians 4:16). When anyone of them fell into sin, it grieved him to the point of burning within (verse 29). This was a reference to the passion that Paul had for the saints in the churches. He cared. The bottom line in this long list of trials was to show that he was not the weakest of the apostles. In fact, the record of his service would say that he was great, especially among those who troubled the saints in Corinth.

The dangers from the journeys, water perils, robbers, his own countrymen (perhaps a reference to the Jews), false brethren, weariness, pain, hunger, and thirsting had all added to his years of toil in the ministry. Yet, he would not boast, unless he boasted of his infirmities or weaknesses. Paul did boast at times of his work and how those whom he had led to saving faith in the Lord Jesus Christ were the ground for his boasting (see 1 Thessalonians 2:19). Earlier, he wrote to the Corinthians that he wanted them to back up his boasting about them and their readiness to give the offering for the saints in Jerusalem (see 2 Corinthians 8:24).

I have traveled through Turkey and Greece on several occasions and, therefore, have a great appreciation for the range of dangers Paul talked of facing. The terrain is extremely mountainous and the temperature can be extremely hot or cold. The Great Plateau upon which the cities of Galatia were located was subjected to extremely dry conditions in the summer and harsh cold in the winter.

C. Paul's Boast of His Power in Christ (2 Corinthians 12:9-10)

And he said unto me, My grace is sufficient for thee: for my strength is made perfect in weakness. Most gladly therefore will I rather glory in my infirmities, that the power of Christ may rest upon me. Therefore I take pleasure in infirmities, in reproaches, in necessities, in persecutions, in distresses for Christ's sake: for when I am weak, then am I strong.

The final section of the lesson deals with Paul's declaration of a powerful spiritual experience that has been the subject of much debate and very little agreement among biblical scholars. No one knows what this thorn in the flesh was and any statement of assurance as to what it was would be mere speculation. In the opening verses of the section, verses 1-6, Paul discussed an extraordinary spiritual revelation and experience that rivaled anything known by those who sought to discredit his apostleship. This too has been the subject of many books, debates, and discussions. We are not sure of exactly what Paul was making reference to because he never made mention of this experience in any of his other writings. At any rate, Paul remarked how the Lord had given him a thorn in the flesh to keep him from becoming puffed up within himself. In his desire to be free of this spiritual or physical malady, he sought God three times. He received an answer that was not what he wanted to hear, but which nonetheless encouraged him to take comfort in the grace or gift of eternal life in Jesus Christ. God's grace was sufficient (Greek: *arkeo*—meaning "to be possessed with unfailing strength, or a barrier to ward off danger").

In the moments when we feel that we cannot go on, God will carry us and His power will fortify our spirits against despair. Although Paul may have appeared weak in the eyes of his opponents, yet he was strong because of the power of God.

III. CONCLUDING REFLECTION

Whenever believers come together for conventions, workshops, or associational meetings there is bound to be some boasting about what they are doing in their congregations. Generally, our boasting is going to be about the number of new members joining each week, the enormous financial windfalls from our giving, and the multiple programs that dot our weekly schedules. Rarely do we hear or delight in discussing the things that are near to the heart of God—missions, ministry to the powerless of the earth, prayer, fasting, and the things that promote spiritual growth among the members. Paul showed us that our greatest strength is not our perceived weakness. Rather, the greater the trials we face for the cause of Jesus Christ, the greater are the manifestations of God's power in our lives. If we are to boast at all, let it be of Him.

PRAYER

Heavenly Father, teach us to trust You in our moments of weakness. May we learn to lean with confidence upon Your strong arm of protection. Thank You for keeping us in the hour of our trials. In Jesus' name we pray. Amen.

WORD POWER

Pleasure *(eudokeo [yu-do-keo])*—means "it seems good to one, is one's good pleasure." In the Christian experience, so many benefits result from trials. This is the reason why Paul rejoiced in affliction. Paul was not looking at things as they appeared to the physical eyes. Paul, in the midst of his tribulation, had a joy above all that the wealth and honor of this world could afford.

HOME DAILY BIBLE READINGS
(November 24-30, 2008)

Persecution Within the Community

MONDAY, November 24: "Persecution in the World" (John 16:25-33)

TUESDAY, November 25: "Suffering in Similar Ways" (1 Thessalonians 2:13-16)

WEDNESDAY, November 26: "Present Suffering, Future Glory" (Romans 8:18-25)

THURSDAY, November 27: "Through Many Persecutions" (Acts 14:21-23)

FRIDAY, November 28: "Sharing Christ's Sufferings" (1 Peter 4:12-19)

SATURDAY, November 29: "Come to Our Help!" (Psalm 44:17-26)

SUNDAY, November 30: "Made Perfect in Weakness" (2 Corinthians 11:16-18, 21-30; 12:9-10)

Human Commitment

GENERAL INTRODUCTION

This study is a focus on humankind's response to God's call. Commitment of a specific person or persons is examined in each of the twelve lessons.

Unit I, *Commitment to the Messiah,* is drawn from four passages in Luke. The first lesson is a look at the commitment of Mary, the mother of Jesus. In lesson 2, the subject turns to Elizabeth and her commitment as mother of John the Baptist. In lesson 3, the Christmas story is approached through the shepherds who glorify God at the birth of Jesus. Finally, lesson 4 is an examination of the commitment of John the Baptist to prepare the way for the Messiah.

In **Unit II,** *Old Testament People of Commitment,* the commitment of several Old Testament personalities is explored. Lesson 5 is about the midwives who kept the Hebrew male babies alive. In lesson 6, the focus will be on Rahab, the Jericho harlot who cooperated with the Hebrew spies. Next, in lesson 7, is a look at Joshua's commitment as the successor to Moses; and then in the following lesson (8) is an examination of the role of Samson's mother in preparing for his birth. In lesson 9, we will study the Shunammite woman who assisted Elisha. In lesson 10, Nathan confronts King David. Lesson 11 is a glimpse at the story of Esther, and lesson 12 is a consideration of the response of Isaiah to God's call.

Note: For lesson 10 (February 8), the children will study the story of Elijah and Elisha rather than Nathan's challenge of David.

LESSON 1   December 7, 2008

MARY'S COMMITMENT

DEVOTIONAL READING: **1 Samuel 2:1-10**
PRINT PASSAGE: **Luke 1:46-55**

BACKGROUND SCRIPTURE: **Luke 1:26-38, 46-55**
KEY VERSES: **Luke 1:46-47**

Luke 1:46-55—KJV

46 And Mary said, My soul doth magnify the Lord,
47 And my spirit hath rejoiced in God my Saviour.
48 For he hath regarded the low estate of his handmaiden: for, behold, from henceforth all generations shall call me blessed.
49 For he that is mighty hath done to me great things; and holy is his name.
50 And his mercy is on them that fear him from generation to generation.
51 He hath shewed strength with his arm; he hath scattered the proud in the imagination of their hearts.
52 He hath put down the mighty from their seats, and exalted them of low degree.
53 He hath filled the hungry with good things; and the rich he hath sent empty away.
54 He hath holpen his servant Israel, in remembrance of his mercy;
55 As he spake to our fathers, to Abraham, and to his seed for ever.

Luke 1:46-55—NRSV

46 And Mary said, "My soul magnifies the Lord,
47 and my spirit rejoices in God my Savior,
48 for he has looked with favor on the lowliness of his servant. Surely, from now on all generations will call me blessed;
49 for the Mighty One has done great things for me, and holy is his name.
50 His mercy is for those who fear him from generation to generation.
51 He has shown strength with his arm; he has scattered the proud in the thoughts of their hearts.
52 He has brought down the powerful from their thrones, and lifted up the lowly;
53 he has filled the hungry with good things, and sent the rich away empty.
54 He has helped his servant Israel, in remembrance of his mercy,
55 according to the promise he made to our ancestors, to Abraham and to his descendants forever."

BIBLE FACT

We hold our goals as important and significant and give our all to their completion. God requires of us a commitment that reveres God's goals as more important and significant than our own—a total commitment of mind, body, and soul. Mary exemplified this in her hymn. She gave herself over completely to the work of God. Mary did this with a spirit of gladness that we should seek to emulate every chance we get, remembering that God's delight in using us is a great thing, indeed!

UNIFYING LESSON PRINCIPLE

Many people have encountered someone or something so charismatic and powerful that has demanded their complete commitment. Who or what is able to command such a commitment? Mary recognized the glory of God and gave her total commitment to God.

TOPICAL OUTLINE OF THE LESSON

I. Introduction
   A. Complete Commitment
   B. Biblical Background

II. Exposition and Application of the Scripture
   A. Mary's Song (Luke 1:46-47)
   B. Mary's Rejoicing Commitment (Luke 1:48)
   C. God's Goodness (Luke 1:49-55)

III. Concluding Reflection

LESSON OBJECTIVES

Upon completion of this lesson, the students are expected to:

1. Become familiar with Mary's "hymn of commitment" to God;
2. Consider the characteristics of others that may lead them to similar acts of commitment; and,
3. Strategize ways of being totally faithful to their commitments to others and to God.

POINTS TO BE EMPHASIZED

ADULT/YOUTH

Adult Topic: Making Total Commitment
Youth Topic: A Song of the Heart
Adult/Youth Key Verses: Luke 1:46-47
Print Passage: Luke 1:46-55

—Mary's song indicates that she was moved to heights of joy because God chose her for such greatness in spite of her low economic and social status.

—This song of Mary's utterance of prayer is known as the "Magnificat" (from Latin "magnifies") and is Mary's response to her calling to be the mother of the Messiah.

—Gabriel's appearance to Mary and her song of praise indicate the place of honor that God gives to women.

—The verbs in the song (*looked, scattered, brought down, lifted, filled, helped*) indicate God's active relationship with human beings.

—Jesus is the fulfillment of God's promise to Abraham and his descendants (see Genesis 12:1-3). The Messiah is the Redeemer and shows God's love for all people.

—Mary celebrated God's faithfulness to His people and His concern for the humble.

CHILDREN

Children Topic: Mary Chooses God
Key Verse: Luke 1:38
Print Passage: Luke 1:26-38, 46-48

—God uses angels to deliver divine messages.

—Mary was concerned about the meaning of the angel's greeting to her.

—The angel calmed Mary's fears by letting her know that God had looked with favor upon her and had chosen her for a special task.

—The angel explained to Mary that things impossible for humans are possible with God.

—Mary was told that a miracle had occurred in the life of her cousin Elizabeth.

—Mary rejoiced and praised God for the miracle in her life.

I. INTRODUCTION

A. Complete Commitment

Weight loss, buying a home, rearing children, creating wealth, getting married, and earning a degree are among many sought-after "goals." Has any of these ever been so powerfully dynamic in your life that it demanded your total commitment—mind, body, and soul? Sometimes, we assume total commitment is based on "putting your money where your mouth is." But has this financial focus ever healed a relationship? Sometimes we think total commitment is purely intellectual, focusing solely on how much thought we give to a particular issue. Has thinking about poverty and homelessness brought an end to these social ills? Total commitment is a holistic commitment. It is a commitment centered on body, soul (mind), and spirit. Is there any one thing, event, person, or being that can or should command your total commitment? For Mary, the answer was unequivocally "yes," and this commitment was God. God could command, and by some standards demand, her unwavering commitment.

Today's lesson helps us see God's desire for our unwavering and complete commitment.

B. Biblical Background

Chapter 1 of Luke's gospel opens with an effort to convince the reader, Theophilus, of the certainty of the teachings of and about Jesus. He begins his Gospel account by telling of Jesus' forerunner, John the Baptist. Luke's rendering of the foretelling of Jesus' birth locates this event in relation to John the Baptist's foretold birth announcement. From Luke 1:26-38, Luke told of the events preceding Jesus' birth.

Luke's presentation of the Virgin Mary as a key figure in this account is consistent with his prominent portrayal of women in the Christ events. Throughout Luke's gospel, and in more than any other Gospel account, women are featured as significant to Jesus' life and ministry. For example, Mary, the recipient of the angelic revelation of what God was going to do in her life, shared importance with the women of the Hebrew texts who were also recipients of angelic news (Sarah, for example). This varies with the foretelling of John the Baptist's birth, where Zechariah witnessed the angel's revelation, as well as Matthew's account of Joseph being told of Jesus' impending birth.

Mary's hymn in verses 46-55 is also known as the "Song of Mary" or the "Magnificat." It is said to be based loosely on Hannah's prayer in 1 Samuel 2:1-10. These signature verses were Mary's way of magnifying or declaring God's greatness in her life experience. These words spoken by the mother of Jesus are among the lengthiest attributed to any woman in the New Testament. Mary's hymn is a part of her experience while staying with Elizabeth for three months. This passage signifies the depth of Mary's adoration of and commitment to God.

II. EXPOSITION AND APPLICATION OF THE SCRIPTURE

A. Mary's Song
(Luke 1:46-47)

And Mary said, My soul doth magnify the Lord, And my spirit hath rejoiced in God my Saviour.

Since the culture that Mary lived in dictated that women be betrothed to marry and be virgins upon marriage, it was important that Luke established God's favor with Mary. This was especially necessary because Mary was impregnated before marriage. If Mary had been less favored in God's eyes, she certainly would have been far less favored by her community, and Joseph in particular. Joseph would no longer have been obliged to marry Mary, thus leaving her an unwed mother. This would have left her without the protections afforded her by marriage—protection and resources that were expected to be provided by a man (father, brother, or husband). None of these possible male providers would have associated with an unwed but pregnant Mary. She would likely have been banished from her family. Thankfully, in our current social context, these repercussions are highly unlikely for a young unmarried woman about to give birth. For Mary, the risks were especially high.

In spite of the high risks, Mary chose to believe the angelic report that she would bear the Son of God and that she need not be afraid. Her choosing is critical in helping us understand commitment to God. We, too, choose daily whether we will live in fear of social repercussions based on how we commit ourselves to God. In the face of potential ridicule and ostracizing, we must consider ourselves favored, since we are created in the image and likeness of God. Our greatest challenge may simply be found in our willingness to acknowledge God as Christians in a pluralistic society that tolerates many faith traditions. Further, we may discover ourselves alienated from certain groups that strive to accommodate everyone, thus excluding any hearty recognition of your particular faith. From declaring "Happy Holidays" instead of "Merry Christmas" to avoiding saying "God bless you" when someone sneezes, the changes we are willing to make—the sacrifices to which we are willing to yield—often very clearly reflect the difficulty we experience in our day-to-day opportunities to show our commitment to God.

Mary declared to the angel, in Luke 1:38 (NIV), "I am the Lord's servant, …May it be to me as you have said." This declaration was a firm pronouncement of Mary's commitment. This type of pronouncement needs to be a mainstay in our Christian vocabularies. Mary exercised her faith by stretching her realm of belief that she, as a virgin, could be impregnated by the Holy Spirit, and committed to what could have been a socially and economically detrimental situation. She engendered a total commitment of body, soul (mind), and spirit. How far can we stretch our realm of belief?

Mary was tasked to stretch beyond just believing about herself becoming pregnant as a virgin. She was also led to believe that her aged cousin, Elizabeth, was also pregnant with a son. Sometimes it seems just enough in our lives to believe what God says for and about us. It can be a stretch to believe for our wayward spouses and/or children, or to believe for our unsaved loved ones. Yet, God requires this of us. Some of us are afraid of being seen as "fanatics" or "over-the-top Christians" when we speak and act on the unlikely or unbelievable acts of

God in our lives or the lives of our loved ones. Stories of people relocating without a job or acting on an "unlikely" call to ministry are but a couple of examples of holistic commitment. Seen throughout the Old and New Testaments, body, soul (mind), and spirit commitments to the unlikely or unbelievable are a deep sign of abiding faith and trust in God. Mary exemplified this not only in her "song," but also in her faith-filled actions. It was clearly a leap of faith in commitment that led Mary to travel—alone, unwed, and pregnant, to visit an aging cousin and her husband—Elizabeth and Zacharias.

In her affirmed commitment, Mary moved forward and visited her cousin Elizabeth to find all that the angel had said was true. Elizabeth encouraged Mary's exuberant state of faith and commitment. Her words of encouragement, as will be explained further in another lesson, help us see the value of being positive reinforcers of God's good in our lives and in the lives of others. It was from this state of being encouraged that Mary began her hymn/song. In a state of delight and rapturous glee, Mary said, "My soul glorifies the Lord and my spirit rejoices in God my Savior, for he has been mindful of the humble state of his servant. From now on all generations will call me blessed, for the Mighty one has done great things for me—holy is his name" (verses 46-49, NIV). Mary first recognized that her body had indeed been given to God and was being used for the purpose that the angel of the Lord said it would be used for with Elizabeth's earlier proclamation that "blessed is she that believed: for there shall be a performance of those things which were told her from the Lord" (verse 45). Additionally, she stated in her hymn the holistic aspect of her awareness and gladness—in her conveyance of a soul and spirit dynamic expression.

"And Mary said, My soul doth magnify the Lord, and my spirit hath rejoiced in God my Saviour" (verses 46-47). The focus on the body, soul (mind), and spirit connections is critical to a fully expressed commitment to God.

B. Mary's Rejoicing Commitment (Luke 1:48)

For he hath regarded the low estate of his handmaiden: for, behold, from henceforth all generations shall call me blessed.

Mary's rejoicing commitment models for us the excitement and willingness of "spirit" we too should bring to our commitments to God and the Messiah. Nothing short of a holistic body, soul, and spirit commitment should be offered. A singular commitment in presenting our bodies only is limited and shortsighted. A "holy" body sanctified or set apart with a reprobate mind is an anomaly. In fact, how can the one be separate and distinct from the other? A devout and clear mind "stayed on Jesus" with a spirit that is loathsome to the spirit of God and all that matters to God is irreverent. Further, how can the one be separate and distinct from the other? We are to be wholly holy as Christians and live our lives in such a way that reflects a holistic wholeness and abiding commitment as such to God, in our movements forward and upward toward the promises of God.

Mary maintained this spirit and holistic approach as she readied herself and hurried out of the area to visit one who had received similar news from the angelic messenger. She eagerly moved forward toward the promise. Her swift forward movement toward one who could affirm and further encourage her level of faith and commitment showed this young virgin's early wisdom. She wisely sought out the company of another who would support and encourage her commitment.

It is a sad experience of many newly committed, as well as well-seasoned Christians that they remain surrounded by those who do not bolster and support their new commitment to the faith. Mary's relationship with Elizabeth served as a major support in her commitment. It is wise to eagerly seek communication and relationships with those who can be positive and affirming in their support of your commitment to God. We are not privileged to know whether Mary wavered in her commitment, but from the account we are given we do know that she had a support network. This network of support is key to maintaining the early zest and fervor individuals experience as new converts in their holistic commitments to God. In an old spiritual, the words suggest that this desire has been lost by seasoned Christians in their requests for God to "Take me, take me back dear Lord, to the place where I first received You. Take me back, take me back dear Lord, where I first believed." The place of first belief is often the place where our deepest, most heartfelt intent to commit is present. The retention of a strong support network helps keep this heartfelt intent alive.

In addition to her support network in Elizabeth, Mary seemed to have had an unquenchable desire to recognize God at the core of her commitment. Indeed her commitment was centered on God's purpose and plan. So too our lives should reflect an unyielding recognition of God at the core of our commitment to a Christian life as a part of God's purpose and plan for human creation. Mary sang of the mindfulness of God in recognizing her, for the things God did for her and others. This attitude of gratitude is a key characteristic of those who would be committed to God.

C. God's Goodness
(Luke 1:49-55)

For he that is mighty hath done to me great things; and holy is his name. And his mercy is on them that fear him from generation to generation. He hath shewed strength with his arm; he hath scattered the proud in the imagination of their hearts. He hath put down the mighty from their seats, and exalted them of low degree. He hath filled the hungry with good things; and the rich he hath sent empty away. He hath holpen his servant Israel, in remembrance of his mercy; As he spake to our fathers, to Abraham, and to his seed for ever.

The irresistible nature of God's goodness provokes one to deep and abiding commitment. It is hard not to be gracious and desirous of committing to One who has been so good and done so much good in one's life. Mary did not acquire an experience or knowledge of God at the point of her interaction with the angel. Her hymn indicates (see verses 49-55) that she had a prior knowledge of God's mighty deeds. She said, "For he that is mighty hath done to me great things; and holy is his name" (verse 49). This awareness helped Mary establish and maintain her commitment. Having a core set of "faith files" is a way to ground our commitments as Christians. Simply remembering the feats of God in our everyday-lived experience should bring us back to a place of recognizing God's goodness in our lives, and this should spur us onward toward continued and greater commitments. Further, acknowledging God's holiness displaces any possibility for irreverent gloating of our unworthy efforts to do well in doing God's bidding. Mary further fondly recalled God's mercy and strength. She said, "And his mercy is on them that fear him from generation to generation. He hath shewed strength with his arm" (verses 50-51a). God's mercy and strength were a major point of remembrance among the people of the Jewish faith tradition. Recalling the many exploits of God toward the people of Israel strengthened Mary's resolve to be wholly committed. As Christians we can recall God's mercy and strength in our collective and individual lives. Just like those of ancient Jewish faith groups, we can recall God's mercy in delivering us from horrid situations, as well as God's strong arm in aiding us through a variety of struggles.

III. CONCLUDING REFLECTION

As we reflect on Mary's commitment, we must consider the implications of making a total commitment to God. Noting Mary's high risks, we should be reminded of the possibility of stigmatization and ridicule for being totally committed to God. Knowing that we always have a choice, we, as Christians, should aim to make the best choice. Mary's choice to believe the angelic testimony shows that we too are always faced with a choice to believe and act on our beliefs. While we may speculate that it was not easy for Mary to make this choice, we know nonetheless that she did. We should be duly inspired to risk the possible alienation and ostracizing that may come with acknowledging the sometimes hard-to-believe truth of God's action in our lives and in the lives of our loved ones. Mary's hymn, or the "Magnificat," helps us see beyond just the voice of our faith, as we realize she was speaking in the company of her aged cousin Elizabeth. This means that Mary had to move beyond speaking to *action*. It is a risk for many Christians to stretch their realms of belief, but we know with strong support networks we can boldly proclaim and act on our holistic commitments to God. We learned in Mary's hymn that her commitment extended beyond the use of her body for God's purpose, but that her holistic self, soul and spirit, were instrumental in her maintained and stable commitment to God.

PRAYER

God, we humbly and gratefully thank You for Jesus. Our souls rejoice in the gift of Your Son, Jesus the Christ. We acknowledge with great joy Your commitment to us. Help us, God, in our commitment to You and each other. May Your Holy Spirit govern and guide all of our commitment interactions. In Jesus' name we pray. Amen.

WORD POWER

Magnify (*gadhal; μ, megaluno*)—**means to "make great," "extol," "celebrate in praise"—used especially in exaltation of the name, mercy, and other attributes of God.**

HOME DAILY BIBLE READINGS
(December 1-7, 2008)

Mary's Commitment

MONDAY, December 1: "The Prayer of Hannah" (1 Samuel 2:1-10)
TUESDAY, December 2: "Gabriel's Announcement" (Luke 1:26-33)
WEDNESDAY, December 3: "Mary's 'Let It Be'" (Luke 1:34-38)
THURSDAY, December 4: "Simeon and Mary" (Luke 2:25-35)
FRIDAY, December 5: "Do What He Tells You" (John 2:1-11)
SATURDAY, December 6: "Praying with the Disciples" (Acts 1:6-14)
SUNDAY, December 7: "Praise for God's Mercy" (Luke 1:46-55)

ELIZABETH'S COMMITMENT

DEVOTIONAL READING: **Isaiah 7:10-14**
PRINT PASSAGE: **Luke 1:39-45**

BACKGROUND SCRIPTURE: **Luke 1:5-24, 39-45**
KEY VERSES: **Luke 1:41b-42**

Luke 1:39-45—KJV

39 And Mary arose in those days, and went into the hill country with haste, into a city of Juda;
40 And entered into the house of Zacharias, and saluted Elisabeth.
41 And it came to pass, that, when Elisabeth heard the salutation of Mary, the babe leaped in her womb; and Elisabeth was filled with the Holy Ghost:
42 And she spake out with a loud voice, and said, Blessed art thou among women, and blessed is the fruit of thy womb.
43 And whence is this to me, that the mother of my Lord should come to me?
44 For, lo, as soon as the voice of thy salutation sounded in mine ears, the babe leaped in my womb for joy.
45 And blessed is she that believed: for there shall be a performance of those things which were told her from the Lord.

Luke 1:39-45—NRSV

39 In those days Mary set out and went with haste to a Judean town in the hill country,
40 where she entered the house of Zechariah and greeted Elizabeth.
41 When Elizabeth heard Mary's greeting, the child leaped in her womb. And Elizabeth was filled with the Holy Spirit
42 and exclaimed with a loud cry, "Blessed are you among women, and blessed is the fruit of your womb.
43 And why has this happened to me, that the mother of my Lord comes to me?
44 For as soon as I heard the sound of your greeting, the child in my womb leaped for joy.
45 And blessed is she who believed that there would be a fulfillment of what was spoken to her by the Lord."

BIBLE FACT

While performing regular day-to-day duties, Zechariah received notification of a major life change. As is indicated here and in other biblical accounts, God will seek you out and put you on notice of your latest major life change, often while you are in the midst of your day-to-day routines. Zechariah, as a priest, was performing his regular priestly duties, lighting incense, sending forth prayers, and so forth when the angel of the Lord appeared at the right side of the altar of incense with the news that Zechariah and his wife would have a son, who would be the forerunner for the Messiah.

UNIFYING LESSON PRINCIPLE

Sometimes a commitment varies in its degree of complexity. How can a person make multiple commitments? Elizabeth remembered God's promise to her and to Zechariah, recognized the fulfillment of God's promise to Mary, and committed herself to the Messiah.

TOPICAL OUTLINE OF THE LESSON

I. Introduction
A. Multiple Commitments
B. Biblical Background

II. Exposition and Application of the Scripture
A. Mary's Surprising Visit (Luke 1:39-40)
B. Elizabeth Enabled by the Holy Spirit (Luke 1:41-42)
C. Confirmation of the Messiah's Birth (Luke 1:43-45)

III. Concluding Reflection

LESSON OBJECTIVES

Upon completion of this lesson, the students are expected to:

1. Examine Elizabeth's response to God's action in Mary's life;
2. Evaluate the challenges of new and "unbelievable" commitments; and,
3. Consider ways they may be encouraged and encourage others to go forth gladly in their commitments to God.

POINTS TO BE EMPHASIZED

ADULT/YOUTH
Adult Topic: Coping with Multiple Commitments
Youth Topic: A Little Encouragement Goes a Long Way
Adult Key Verses: Luke 1:41b-42
Youth Key Verse: Luke 1:45
Print Passage: Luke 1:39-45

—God's power can be seen manifested through the miracle of birth in an aged and barren couple.
—Elizabeth was overjoyed at Mary's visit as the mother of the Messiah.
—Mary visited her relative Elizabeth, who was pregnant with John the Baptist.
—Verses 41-44 indicate that Elizabeth, through the power of the Holy Spirit acting through her unborn child, was able to identify Mary's baby as the Messiah.
—Elizabeth encouraged Mary's acceptance of the Lord's message to her.
—Elizabeth had the privilege to be a spokesperson for God.

CHILDREN
Children Topic: Elizabeth Believes God
Key Verse: Luke 1:25
Print Passage: Luke 1:39-45

—In response to the angel's message to her, Mary went to visit her cousin Elizabeth in the hill country.
—Elizabeth and her unborn baby rejoiced when they heard Mary's voice and greeting.
—Elizabeth recognized the actions of God in the life of her cousin Mary.
—Elizabeth recognized that she was blessed to have received a visit from Mary, who would be the mother of Jesus.
—A mark of true faith is to believe what God has promised and to be willing to be part of bringing those promises into reality.

I. INTRODUCTION

A. Multiple Commitments

"This is the last one. I'm tired of doing this. I quit. I don't get paid enough for all of this. How much more? Whew, I hope they don't send anymore this way. The people want too much from me. When do I get a break?" These are statements and questions spoken by those who experience what the writer calls MCS (multiple commitment syndrome). These timeless responses to doing more than you imagined commonly show up in every generation. Less common is a querying of our arrival at having multiple commitments and developing coping strategies for them.

Elizabeth, the mother of John, presented a sterling example of coping with multiple commitments. She was the wife of a well-known priest, who was also an old priest. She was "getting on up in age" herself. She and her husband lived righteous lives, living blameless before God. Yet, they had no children, though Zechariah had been praying for children. They finally got an answer—they would have a baby, at a late stage of their lives. Did Zechariah show fear and doubt, questioning the possibility to the angel of the Lord? Yes, he did, and was duly silenced. Did Elizabeth have multiple commitments with which she must cope? Of course—she had an old, doubting priest for a husband, who was now mute, as she was experiencing pregnancy for the first time. Yet, she provided for us modern-day men and women a model for how we too might cope with our multiple commitments that frequently pop up in our lives.

B. Biblical Background

Luke's gospel, the third of the four main Gospels, is socially oriented as he richly detailed the experiences of women and other marginalized groups like none of the other Gospels. Luke's texts are attributed to a physician, Luke, said to be a friend of Paul. While Luke's account is not an eyewitness account, it does provide significantly more details about the social realities of the more common citizen, not focusing specifically on Jews and the elite in society. Luke is said by some scholars to be a Gentile convert. The exact chronological placement of this Gospel's writing is unknown, but is said to have been penned near the latter portion of the first century.

Luke's account of John the Baptist's birth socially and politically locates Zechariah and his wife Elizabeth. Luke emphasized this couple's relationship and status with God by saying that they were model Jews. Zechariah was a priest from a prominent priestly division, and his wife was a descendant of Aaron. Yet, their lives were incomplete, because of what was considered, for the time, a tragic flaw for married women—barrenness.

Luke introduced this element early in the Gospel, to begin expanding the readers' field of vision for the miraculous. This account of the prediction of Elizabeth's pregnancy serves as a foreshadowing of an even more unbelievable pregnancy. While also foretelling of the role this first "miracle" would play in the coming of a greater gift, Luke was preparing the reader for the accounts of the lives of John and Jesus.

II. EXPOSITION AND APPLICATION OF THE SCRIPTURE

A. Mary's Surprising Visit
(Luke 1:39-40)

And Mary arose in those days, and went into the hill country with haste, into a city of Juda; And entered into the house of Zacharias, and saluted Elisabeth.

In the previous verses, the angel Gabriel visited Mary and gave her an unusual message. The message was full of messianic promises (see Luke 1:31-33). Later on Mary made a surprising visit to a village in Judah where Elizabeth resided. Luke did not mention the name of the city. However, some commentators believe the place to be Hebron. Mary went to this city to share the good news with her cousin, Elizabeth. What happened to Mary had never happened to anybody in history, and the news was too good to hold to herself, hence the trip to Zechariah's city. The phrase "In those days" means in a day or two after the angel had visited her. She took some time to process the strange visitation and the uncommon message which the angel brought to her. Mary went to the right place, the priest house, where she could get spiritual help from the family of a priest. The Greek word used to describe the preparation for her trip—*meta-spoudes*—means "with care, diligence, expedition, and sense of urgency." In other words, she went to Zechariah with expectation of receiving support. Some people fail to seek spiritual support when they receive unsolicited help from God. Some unfortunately attribute it to luck or their own astuteness.

Mary arrived at Elizabeth's house. Elizabeth had also been providentially visited by the same angel. God visited a woman who had passed child-bearing age, and He also visited a teenager who had never experienced conjugal love. In both instances, God is a miracle-working God. We Christians should celebrate the love of God which passes human understanding. If we surrender our will completely to Him and let Him have His ways in our lives, we will experience His divine favor that will blow our minds and which will in turn give Him the glory.

B. Elizabeth Enabled by the Holy Spirit
(Luke 1:41-42)

And it came to pass, that, when Elisabeth heard the salutation of Mary, the babe leaped in her womb; and Elisabeth was filled with the Holy Ghost. And she spake out with a loud voice, and said, Blessed art thou among women, and blessed is the fruit of thy womb.

No sooner had Mary entered her cousin's house than Elizabeth experienced an unusual push in her womb. Even though Elizabeth had been pregnant for six months, she had not experienced anything of the kind which she felt when Mary stepped in. At that moment, the Holy Spirit filled Elizabeth. This filling of the Holy Spirit enabled her to burst into prophetic utterance. She was enabled to have advance knowledge of the character of the child that would be borne by Mary. It is amazing that the Holy Spirit made everything known to her, even though there was no visible evidence that Mary was pregnant at the time of her visitation.

The phrase *spake out, or aneefooneese* in Greek, is often used to signify persons who burst into poetic or prophetic exclamations. There is no human explanation for the experience of Elizabeth, other than to attribute it to power from heaven. She exclaimed, "Blessed art thou among women" (Luke 1:42). Here we see Elizabeth echoing the same message of the angel that brought the news to Mary (see Luke 1:28).

Elizabeth, in her gladness that she would bear a son who would be the forerunner to the Messiah, encouraged an excited and perhaps somewhat apprehensive Mary. This was another commitment for Elizabeth. How did she acquire these commitments? She did not call for Mary, nor did she encourage her husband to speak with doubt while he was at work. She was just like many of us—living out her life every day, while life continued to do what it does—manifest swift transitional changes. Many things were changing all around Elizabeth, from her husband, to her body and hormones, to her social status, even to her distant cousin Mary; yet, she coped with these multiple realities.

C. Confirmation of the Messiah's Birth (Luke 1:43-45)

And whence is this to me, that the mother of my Lord should come to me? For, lo, as soon as the voice of thy salutation sounded in mine ears, the babe leaped in my womb for joy. And blessed is she that believed: for there shall be a performance of those things which were told her from the Lord.

Mary, who eagerly sought her out, was well-received by Elizabeth. This may be one of the first clues as to how Elizabeth coped so well with multiple commitments. She knew the value of being hospitable and welcoming to guests. This required any good host or hostess to have a warm, inviting, friendly spirit that welcomed all in the name of the Lord. Even in the throes of our deepest and sometimes most challenging commitments, we can still receive others well. Short-tempered, irritated responses have no place in the lives of those committed to Christ. We may be having a bad day, but must we take it out on the unsuspecting loved one, co-worker, or nearby pet? Our coping

strategies should never leave us on the frazzled end of an interpersonal exchange. While our communications will certainly bear the marks of human imperfection, we should find within our Christian hearts a godly space that can look in the face of someone we do not like and offer a genuine smile. Elizabeth welcomed Mary, while living out the multiple responsibilities of an older woman carrying her own child, and managed also for three months to provide support to her cousin Mary, who would bring forth the Messiah.

Elizabeth had already considered the wondrous ways of God to "take away her reproach" and allow her to bear a son. This was significant at the time because a woman's worth was associated with her ability to bring forth offspring, especially boys. She could have been selfish and told Mary that Mary was young and a pregnancy at her age was not unexpected, but instead she allowed Mary's joy to be contagious, even with Mary's personal major life change. During her last three months of pregnancy, Elizabeth committed not only to her own wellness, but also to the well-being of someone else. Mary slipped away from her home and kindred for three months. She might likely, even in her acceptance of her pregnancy, have been experiencing some emotional challenges. Elizabeth took the time to affirm what Mary had been told, pronounced her blessed among women, called the child she was carrying *blessed,* and said Mary was further blessed because she believed that what she had been told would come to pass. Elizabeth was a seasoned woman. She had lived long enough to know how to do things rightly and wisely. We may excuse ourselves for falling short of Elizabeth's dynamic example, but lest we forget, Elizabeth was a devout woman of God, who lived blameless according to the commandments of God. This should be our starting point. We may feel that we are a good distance behind the starting block, but take heart—God is faithful and knows our hearts' desires to be pleasing. In developing and/or maintaining our ability to cope with multiple commitments, keeping God first is central to our best coping strategies.

Elizabeth knew this and clearly exemplified it as she committed to an unseen, unknown Messiah and with gladness maintained her commitment. Like the shepherds in a later study, Elizabeth acknowledged Jesus as the Messiah before she saw Him. Regardless of the difficulties and complexities of her own experience (being older and pregnant, with a mute husband), Elizabeth unquestionably recognized the move of God's presence in another woman's life and was glad for her. Taking the time to be good to someone else who gets what you want before you do is a sure sign of maturity in Christ. Acknowledging God's goodness to another when you feel left out and behind shows more than your ability to put on a good "face"; it also shows your authentic commitment to Christ, which shines through you so brightly that the unsuspecting eye will see. Elizabeth bolstered Mary's faith, even when in the first five months of her pregnancy she had no one to bolster her own faith. This takes immense commitment to God, the Messiah, and a fierce set of coping strategies that help one balance all commitments in an authentic spirit of faith-filled joy. It is likely, as is the case with many of us, that if Elizabeth had exhibited one shred of insincerity, Mary would have known it. It is important to be authentic as we manage our multiple commitments. Our gladness should be real. In the words of an old familiar hymn, "Just let it be real, real, real. Let it be real, real, real. Whatever you do for the Lord, let it be real, real, real."

Many people with hectic lives and multiple commitments face struggles when they do not have words of encouragement from anyone. Sometimes, these people are Christians who would rather see someone else struggle with the same experience, just because *they* struggled without support. The thought "I went through it alone and struggling, so they should too" was not Elizabeth's idea and should not be exemplified by any committed Christian. In coping with our multiple commitments, let us be inspired by Elizabeth's model of going forth gladly while we commit to our own wellness and that of others—all through our greatest commitment to the Messiah.

III. CONCLUDING REFLECTION

We can conclude the following from this lesson: multiple commitments are inextricably tied to our daily life experiences. Life indeed is filled with swift transitions and it frequently happens in the course of our lives that we experience major life changes. Zechariah, while performing his priestly duties, was approached by the angel of the Lord. His strong attitude of disbelief reminds us of the importance of the golden quality of silence. Sometimes the best response to the unbelievable is silence. The prayer of two devout elderly persons to have a child was fulfilled at a time in their lives when they least expected it. Zechariah's disbelief led him to be muted by the angel until after his baby was born. Elizabeth's commitment to managing multiple commitments meant that she started her management strategies by taking some time to herself first. This likely helped to keep her grounded as she confronted and managed her multiple commitments. She extended an ongoing spirit of warmth and welcome to her distant cousin Mary, who was pregnant with the Messiah. Elizabeth's generous hospitality amid her several commitments models for us a way to manage our multiple commitments—keep the authenticity of God's spirit front and center in our everyday-lived experience. Indeed it is hard to draw water from a dry well. Mary came obviously with a need for emotional support. She stayed away from her home and kindred for three months and Elizabeth, thank God, had something to give her. Elizabeth's experience further helps us see that we take nothing from ourselves when we can authentically revel in someone else's good thing that God is doing in their lives. Our deepest expression of our ability to manage multiple commitments is when we manage these said commitments with sincere gladness.

PRAYER

God, most magnificent Creator, we graciously thank You for Your Son, Jesus Christ. In our busyness and hectic lifestyles, we appreciate Your many gifts in our lives. Our commitment to You is renewed as the morning comes. Strengthen our hearts that we may commit our daily works to You. Help us in our struggles to honor our commitments to You in glad faith. We humbly submit this prayer. In Jesus' name we pray. Amen.

WORD POWER

Leaped *(eskirteesen [es-ka-tee-sen])*—means "to leap," and is found in Luke 1:41,44 and 6:23, there translated "leap for joy"; (in 1:44 the words "for joy" are expressed separately). This was a common-enough incident with unborn children (see Genesis 25:22), but Elizabeth was filled with the Holy Spirit to understand what had happened to Mary.

HOME DAILY BIBLE READINGS
(December 8-14, 2008)

Elizabeth's Commitment

MONDAY, December 8: "Do Not Pass by Your Servant" (Genesis 18:1-8)

TUESDAY, December 9: "Hope for the Barren" (Genesis 18:9-14)

WEDNESDAY, December 10: "Righteous and Blameless" (Luke 1:5-11)

THURSDAY, December 11: "The Promise of a Son" (Luke 1:12-20)

FRIDAY, December 12: "The Lord's Favor" (Luke 1:21-25)

SATURDAY, December 13: "Faith in God's Promises" (Luke 1:39-45)

SUNDAY, December 14: "He Is to Be Called John" (Luke 1:57-63)

LESSON 3   December 21, 2008

GOD FRANKEN SENSE   MER.

SHEPHERDS GLORIFY GOD   *ISAIH 9:6   MATT 6:24,25*

DEVOTIONAL READING: **Psalm 107:1-15**
PRINT PASSAGE: **Luke 2:8-20**   *GO TIME TESTIH*

BACKGROUND SCRIPTURE: **Luke 2:1-20**
KEY VERSE: **Luke 2:20**

Luke 2:8-20—KJV

8 And there were in the same country shepherds abiding in the field, keeping watch over their flock by night.

9 And, lo, the angel of the Lord came upon them, and the glory of the Lord shone round about them: and they were sore afraid.

10 And the angel said unto them, Fear not: for, behold, I bring you good tidings of great joy, which shall be to all people.

11 For unto you is born this day in the city of David a Saviour, which is Christ the Lord.

12 And this shall be a sign unto you; Ye shall find the babe wrapped in swaddling clothes, lying in a manger.

13 And suddenly there was with the angel a multitude of the heavenly host praising God, and saying,

14 Glory to God in the highest, and on earth peace, good will toward men.

15 And it came to pass, as the angels were gone away from them into heaven, the shepherds said one to another, Let us now go even unto Bethlehem, and see this thing which is come to pass, which the Lord hath made known unto us.

16 And they came with haste, and found Mary, and Joseph, and the babe lying in a manger.

17 And when they had seen it, they made known abroad the saying which was told them concerning this child.

18 And all they that heard it wondered at those things which were told them by the shepherds.

19 But Mary kept all these things, and pondered them in her heart.

20 And the shepherds returned, glorifying and praising God for all the things that they had heard and seen, as it was told unto them.

Luke 2:8-20—NRSV

8 In that region there were shepherds living in the fields, keeping watch over their flock by night.

9 Then an angel of the Lord stood before them, and the glory of the Lord shone around them, and they were terrified.

10 But the angel said to them, "Do not be afraid; for see—I am bringing you good news of great joy for all the people:

11 to you is born this day in the city of David a Savior, who is the Messiah, the Lord.

12 This will be a sign for you: you will find a child wrapped in bands of cloth and lying in a manger."

13 And suddenly there was with the angel a multitude of the heavenly host, praising God and saying,

14 "Glory to God in the highest heaven, and on earth peace among those whom he favors!"

15 When the angels had left them and gone into heaven, the shepherds said to one another, "Let us go now to Bethlehem and see this thing that has taken place, which the Lord has made known to us."

16 So they went with haste and found Mary and Joseph, and the child lying in the manger.

17 When they saw this, they made known what had been told them about this child;

18 and all who heard it were amazed at what the shepherds told them.

19 But Mary treasured all these words and pondered them in her heart.

20 The shepherds returned, glorifying and praising God for all they had heard and seen, as it had been told them.

UNIFYING LESSON PRINCIPLE

People yearn to hear the good news of the fulfillment of promises. What results from our appreciation for promises that are kept? The shepherds glorified and praised God for the gift of the long-awaited Messiah and told others the Good News.

TOPICAL OUTLINE OF THE LESSON

I. **Introduction**
   A. Shepherds Glorify God
   B. Biblical Background

II. **Exposition and Application of the Scripture**
   A. Shepherds Receive an Angelic Announcement (Luke 2:8-12)
   B. An Angelic Response to the Good News (Luke 2:13-14)
   C. Shepherds Respond and Are Eager to Share (Luke 2:15-20)

III. **Concluding Reflection**

LESSON OBJECTIVES

Upon completion of this lesson, the students are expected to:

1. Become familiar with the angels' and shepherds' interaction;
2. Explore the issues of proclamation, promises, and commitment; and,
3. Develop demonstrative acts of praise in their commitment to God.

POINTS TO BE EMPHASIZED

ADULT/YOUTH

Adult Topic: The Gift of Kept Promises
Youth Topic: Good News of the Ultimate Shepherd
Adult Key Verse: Luke 2:20
Youth Key Verse: Luke 2:11
Print Passage: Luke 2:8-20

—The world into which Jesus the Messiah (Christ) was born, much like ours, had people from all levels of society (for example, from emperor to shepherds).
—God sent angels to announce the birth of Jesus as the fulfillment of the promised Messiah, long-awaited by the Jews.
—Shepherds were a despised and outcast group of the very young and very old who could not do any other type of work.
—That Jesus was born to and announced to people of low standing means that Jesus is the Savior of all people.
—Even the most humble people understand the Gospel.
—The expression "praising God" appears more frequently in Luke than in all the remainder of the New Testament books combined.

CHILDREN

Children Topic: The Shepherds Rejoice
Key Verse: Luke 2:20
Print Passage: Luke 2:4-20

—The shepherds were watching their sheep when an angel appeared and they saw the Lord's glory.
—While in Bethlehem, Mary gave birth to her Son and laid Him in a manger, because there was no place for them in the inn.
—Shepherds in the area were the first to receive the Good News concerning the birth of Jesus.
—Shepherds went into Bethlehem to determine if the message of the angels was true.
—From this passage we learn the importance of being obedient to the revelations God gives us.
—The shepherds understood the significance of Jesus' birth and helped to spread the Good News.

I. INTRODUCTION

A. Shepherds Glorify God

In the black church tradition of testifying, a common phrase is used in reflecting on the goodness of God in the testifiers' lives: "I said I wasn't gonna tell nobody, but I just couldn't keep it to myself." Encountering the fulfillment of a promise engenders in us a desire to thank God and to share, to tell it "everywhere we go." Good news (and sometimes bad news) travels fast.

The angelic interaction with the shepherds set the stage for an exciting expectation for the declared promise. As the angels proclaimed the Good News, the shepherds received it and eagerly desired to share it with others. They made haste in verifying the promise before they shared it with others. It was a marvelous testimony to them and their commitment to the baby Christ. God used these shepherds—everyday, ordinary shepherds—to share the Good News of Jesus' arrival and to encourage others to praise God. The shepherds in this text glorified God and proclaimed appreciation for God's promise, setting a marvelous example of the gift of a kept promise—with magnificent praise, ultimately glorifying the goodness of God.

B. Biblical Background

The writing of Luke's gospel is attributed to the physician Luke, who was also a great friend to Paul. It is positioned as the third of four Gospel accounts of the life and ministry of Jesus. Luke's recount richly chronicles the experiences of Jesus' birth narrative and arrival stories. His Gospel has a much more socially oriented focus and features prominently those relegated to the margins in many other biblical texts—namely women and Gentiles. Luke's gospel brings a non-eyewitness account to Jesus' ministry, as told in a gifted literary style.

This lesson's text is opened with a historical and geographical placement of Jesus' birth. The political climate and events of the time are brought to the fore, emphasizing the historical reality of Jesus' arrival, and to give time and place to the shepherds' experience. The opening verses, specifically verses 1-8, also trace Joseph's ancestry and place Jesus' paternal ancestry in the city and lineage of David. This is significant, as the writer seeks throughout the text to situate Jesus clearly in the "house of David," as well as among the common and the elite, the Jew and the Gentile. Further, Jesus' birth narrative (as well as John the Baptist's), unique to Luke's account, emphasizes God's key role in the manifestation of an earlier promise. This promise, kept thematically, is an illustration of God's concern for the oppressed in society. Most specifically, God's use of the ordinary person in society, in this lesson the shepherds specifically, further emphasizes God's concern for everyone in society, not just the elite and the Jews.

II. EXPOSITION AND APPLICATION OF THE SCRIPTURE

A. Shepherds Receive an Angelic Announcement (Luke 2:8-12)

And there were in the same country shepherds abiding in the field, keeping watch over their flock by night. And, lo, the angel of the Lord came upon them, and the glory of the Lord shone round about them: and they were sore afraid. And the angel said unto them, Fear not: for, behold, I bring you good tidings of great joy, which shall be to all people. For unto you is born this day in the city of David a Saviour, which is Christ the Lord. And this shall be a sign unto you; Ye shall find the babe wrapped in swaddling clothes, lying in a manger.

Shepherds working at night watching their flocks received an angelic visitation. God's presence filled the environment and the shepherds were scared. Most people would be frightened by the appearance of a spirit or an angel. So it was necessary for the angel to speak these next words. The angel spoke to them, as was done with Mary earlier, saying "Do not be afraid." In some cases, this may be easier said than done. God still works and reaches out to people in these ways. We as believers should be receptive to those who claim God speaks through angelic apparitions of which they are not afraid.

The overwhelming fear of the shepherds was assuaged because as the angel had declared, the Good News was being delivered. The news of Jesus' arrival was told without mentioning His name. However, He was identified immediately as "Saviour," "Christ," and "the Lord." These significant immediate identifications and proclamations of Jesus as the Christ served as a seal to the angel's message in preparation for the shepherds' journey to see and meet the Baby Jesus. Jesus looked like a commonly clad baby of that day (wrapped in swaddling clothes). While babies in that period were known to be wrapped in cloths, called "swaddling clothes," holding the baby "close together," it was much less common for babies to be born in a manger or stable. Yet, once these identifying factors were in place and this Good News was told, even the angels could not refrain from rejoicing.

In a way that was like Zechariah's experience, the shepherds were engaged in the regular activity of their lives when the angel of the Lord visited them. This theme is one of many illustrations given by Luke of God's interaction with the common individual. God will meet you where you are currently located—no special circumstances or locations are required. This is also a theme found in Old Testament texts. For example, there is the vivid account of God finding Gideon while he (Gideon) was in the wine press threshing wheat to prevent enemies from stealing it (see Judges 6). God will find us in some of the most unlikely and/or exceptionally common places of our lives. We need not be living fancy lives or having some uncommon experience for God to find and use us. God is content to find us where we are and how we are and use us just as we are. This is one of Luke's major themes throughout his gospel. Unlike Zechariah and Gideon, the shepherds expressed no doubt about what they were told. However, they were very scared. Like Mary, the shepherds' fear ruled the earliest moments of the angelic visitation. Similar to Mary, they had to be told not to be afraid. Yet, once they pushed past the fear of the unknown, this startled response to the angelic visitation was smoothed over.

B. An Angelic Response to the Good News (Luke 2:13-14)

And suddenly there was with the angel a multitude of the heavenly host praising God, and saying, Glory to God in the highest, and on earth peace, good will toward men.

The angelic message was one of great appeal not only to the listening shepherds, but also to everyone else. The announcement that Jesus had been born was more than a general birth announcement. Notification was being given that a promise had been kept, an immediate one that the shepherds were not privy to—a promise to Mary, Elizabeth, and Zechariah. However, while the shepherds were not privy to the promise told to Mary, Elizabeth, and Zechariah, they might very well have been aware of the significance of this promise to the Jews (though this is not mentioned in Luke's account). Sometimes, God makes unique promises to us that no one else is privy to. The news of your "good thing" to someone else by way of God's special messengers can be exhilarating, but limited when they do not know the full scope of God's promise to you. This also works when we hear just a portion of someone else's good news. Yet, we should all be filled with an exuberantly joyful response to the goodness God brings into someone else's life. A baby born in a manger may not seem like much, unless one knows the rest of the story.

The news was so exhilarating that some of the angelic host appeared with the angel of the Lord and began to rejoice. How seriously exciting must it have been to be among a host of rejoicing angels in the company of an angel of the Lord? Good news frequently serves as a catalyst for celebration. Think about the last time you got really outstanding news: you were given a raise far greater than you anticipated— you probably celebrated. You got married! Yes, there was a party. Hmm, perhaps you graduated at the top of your class—didn't you celebrate just a little bit? Of course you did.

It was no accident that all who heard the Good News of Jesus that was told to the shepherds began praising God with a refrain magnifying God and affirming peace among those who found favor with God. It is hard not to celebrate good news. The omission of testifying (sharing good news of God's greatness in the life of a person) from many mainline black churches has in many cases diminished the immediate relevancy of the celebratory praise. We sing praise songs and observe praise dancers, yet we miss out on the real-life individual stories of people's good news in the church. Good news encourages us. We are inspired by good news. God intends this, hence the Gospel—Good News of Jesus Christ. We like to celebrate, but it is hard to celebrate what we have no knowledge or awareness of occurring in the life of the people in faith communities. It is imperative that the church restore this arm of service, as it blesses and affirms God's purpose in bringing forth the Good News in people's everyday lives.

C. Shepherds Respond and Are Eager to Share (Luke 2:15-20)

And it came to pass, as the angels were gone away from them into heaven, the shepherds said one to another, Let us now go even unto Bethlehem, and see this thing which is come to pass, which the Lord hath made known unto us. And they came with haste, and found Mary, and Joseph, and the babe lying in a manger. And when they had seen it, they made known abroad the saying which was told them concerning this child. And all they that heard it wondered at those things which were told them by the shepherds. But Mary kept all these things, and pondered them in her heart. And the shepherds returned, glorifying and praising God for all the things that they had heard and seen, as it was told unto them.

Once the angels left the shepherds, the shepherds discussed leaving the area to go and see what God had made known to them. They did not delay in their quest to lay sight on the child of promise. So often we lose our zest, our excited nature, because we drag out the process, thinking about whether we should really believe what God has spoken into our experience. We may talk about it with some other people who were not there to feel and hear the excitement of the message, and then wonder why they are not urging us to go onward and receive the viewing or the gift of the promise. Stop waiting on somebody to get glad with you who is not already glad.

The shepherds wasted no time. They hurriedly found Mary, Joseph, and the Baby in the manger. Upon sight of the Baby in the manger, they knew what the angel of the Lord had declared was true. They also did what any excited "I-just-got-good-news" person would do—they decided to spread the Word. The shepherds all experienced the revelatory news flash. So they traveled together and shared the news with people near and far. The people who got the news were amazed and gave serious consideration to what the shepherds were saying about the Child. Mary, meanwhile, a quiet mother, listened, but spoke little of the matters that were told by the shepherds. Mary pondered these things in her heart about who her Son was to be, but she let the others speak His praises while He was a baby.

The shepherds were the average citizens tasked by God to do a marvelous work— spreading the Good News of Christ's arrival. They returned to their flocks deeply grateful to God for the fulfillment of the promise of which they had now heard and seen, just like it was told to them. Often, we too return to our everyday routines all the more grateful for our rich "God experience." It may be miniscule in the eyes of some, but you, as the individual to whom God revealed a great inspiration, know the fullness of the gift you received. Sometimes, we receive gifts from our children or other loved ones that do not appear to be much to the outside observer because those persons simply do not and cannot recognize the fullness of what you have received, or know what it means to you.

The shepherds were eager to share their Good News. We are all the more eager, as were the shepherds, when the experience is what was promised to us. They shared the news of what they had heard and seen not just for their own benefit, but to encourage others as well. They moved beyond an inner circle of shepherds' conversation and spread the news. This too is one way for us to be used by God. Sharing the goodness of God in our lives—from the mundane to the elaborate—makes us available vessels through whom God can reach someone else. Our messages and testimonies of how we believed God's promise for this or that, and it was fulfilled, can and often does turn other people's lives completely around. They are more encouraged than they can often express and this is what God intends. The shepherds' message was directed at them but was also an encouragement to other Jews, as well as Gentiles. The angelic message reflected a great joy that would be for all people; so, too, our everyday messages from God can be an encouragement to everyone with whom we make contact.

The angel of the Lord encouraged the shepherds directly, and the shepherds encouraged the others to whom the news was spread. We often act as "shepherds" in this regard, when we share with others the goodness of what God has done in our lives. We become the "middle person," bridging the divide to guide someone else into a posture of praise. God is not limited in how people are used to elicit a rejoicing and glorifying God response to the events in the world of everyday living. This event was important enough that it was identified early as being Good News of great joy to benefit all people.

III. CONCLUDING REFLECTION

We can conclude from this lesson that our faithful commitment to the Messiah maintains at its core a rich and viable willingness to articulate with great joy God's gifts of kept promises. These are our moments to testify. We (in our expressed commitment) must declare God's goodness in our lives, especially in the keeping of promises. At a time when promises are easily made and just as easily broken, it is refreshing to hear an encouraging word that says God makes promises that God also keeps. This function of encouragement is also central to the life of the believer who is committed to the Messiah. We are tasked to encourage others by sharing the Good News. The shepherds in our lesson exemplified this aim as they traveled and shared the Good News of the angelic hosts' announcement of Jesus' arrival. It is difficult to hold in exceptionally good news, and this is as God intends: hence, we have the Gospels. Telling the Good News is not to promote a gloating or boastful spirit about how deserving you are of God's goodness and certainly not to promote your somehow "favored" status. God is too big for that. Telling the Good News of God's goodness in your life and in the lives of others around you is free promotion for God.

PRAYER

God, we proclaim Your goodness and righteousness. We are grateful for Your many kept promises. We humbly beseech the presence of Your Spirit to guide us out of our comfort zones, so that we may boldly tell others of Your goodness in our lives. Let Your light so shine in us that men and women, boys and girls, will see You in us and desire You. In Jesus' name we pray. Amen.

WORD POWER

Glorify (*doxazo [dok-sad-so]*)—primarily denotes "to suppose" (from *doxa*, "an opinion"); in the NT "to magnify, extol, praise" especially of "glorifying"; God, for example: ascribing honor to Him, acknowledging Him as to His being, attributes, and acts.

HOME DAILY BIBLE READINGS
(December 15-21, 2008)

Shepherds Glorify God

MONDAY, December 15: "God's Plan Fulfilled" (Isaiah 46:8-13)
TUESDAY, December 16: "The King of Glory" (Psalm 24)
WEDNESDAY, December 17: "Who Is like the Lord?" (Psalm 113)
THURSDAY, December 18: "Praise the Lord" (Psalm 148)
FRIDAY, December 19: "Glory Forever" (Romans 16:25-27)
SATURDAY, December 20: "Mary's First Baby" (Luke 2:1-7)
SUNDAY, December 21: "Glory to God!" (Luke 2:8-20)

JOHN THE BAPTIST PROCLAIMS GOD'S MESSAGE

DEVOTIONAL READING: **Psalm 51:10-19**
PRINT PASSAGE: **Luke 3:7-18**

BACKGROUND SCRIPTURE: **Luke 3:1-20**
KEY VERSE: **Luke 3:8a**

Luke 3:7-18—KJV

7 Then said he to the multitude that came forth to be baptized of him, O generation of vipers, who hath warned you to flee from the wrath to come?

8 Bring forth therefore fruits worthy of repentance, and begin not to say within yourselves, We have Abraham to our father: for I say unto you, That God is able of these stones to raise up children unto Abraham.

9 And now also the axe is laid unto the root of the trees: every tree therefore which bringeth not forth good fruit is hewn down, and cast into the fire.

10 And the people asked him, saying, What shall we do then?

11 He answereth and saith unto them, He that hath two coats, let him impart to him that hath none; and he that hath meat, let him do likewise.

12 Then came also publicans to be baptized, and said unto him, Master, what shall we do?

13 And he said unto them, Exact no more than that which is appointed you.

14 And the soldiers likewise demanded of him, saying, And what shall we do? And he said unto them, Do violence to no man, neither accuse any falsely; and be content with your wages.

15 And as the people were in expectation, and all men mused in their hearts of John, whether he were the Christ, or not;

16 John answered, saying unto them all, I indeed baptize you with water; but one mightier than I cometh, the latchet of whose shoes I am not worthy to unloose: he shall baptize you with the Holy Ghost and with fire:

17 Whose fan is in his hand, and he will throughly purge his floor, and will gather the wheat into his garner; but the chaff he will burn with fire unquenchable.

18 And many other things in his exhortation preached he unto the people.

Luke 3:7-18—NRSV

7 John said to the crowds that came out to be baptized by him, "You brood of vipers! Who warned you to flee from the wrath to come?

8 Bear fruits worthy of repentance. Do not begin to say to yourselves, 'We have Abraham as our ancestor'; for I tell you, God is able from these stones to raise up children to Abraham.

9 Even now the ax is lying at the root of the trees; every tree therefore that does not bear good fruit is cut down and thrown into the fire."

10 And the crowds asked him, "What then should we do?"

11 In reply he said to them, "Whoever has two coats must share with anyone who has none; and whoever has food must do likewise."

12 Even tax collectors came to be baptized, and they asked him, "Teacher, what should we do?"

13 He said to them, "Collect no more than the amount prescribed for you."

14 Soldiers also asked him, "And we, what should we do?" He said to them, "Do not extort money from anyone by threats or false accusation, and be satisfied with your wages."

15 As the people were filled with expectation, and all were questioning in their hearts concerning John, whether he might be the Messiah,

16 John answered all of them by saying, "I baptize you with water; but one who is more powerful than I is coming; I am not worthy to untie the thong of his sandals. He will baptize you with the Holy Spirit and fire.

17 His winnowing fork is in his hand, to clear his threshing floor and to gather the wheat into his granary; but the chaff he will burn with unquenchable fire."

18 So, with many other exhortations, he proclaimed the good news to the people.

Making a commitment requires action to accompany verbal assent. What actions may be required to fulfill a commitment? When John took the message to the people about the coming of the Messiah, he challenged them to respond.

TOPICAL OUTLINE OF THE LESSON

I. Introduction
A. Acting on One's Commitments
B. Biblical Background

II. Exposition and Application of the Scripture
A. John Proclaims God's Message (Luke 3:7-9)
B. "What Do We Have to Do?" (Luke 3:10-14)
C. John Clarifies His Role (Luke 3:15-18)

III. Concluding Reflection

LESSON OBJECTIVES

Upon completion of this lesson, the students are expected to:

1. Review John's commitment in calling people to repentance in preparation for the Messiah;
2. Consider the general requirements of any commitment; and,
3. Evaluate actions associated with their commitment(s) to God.

POINTS TO BE EMPHASIZED

ADULT/YOUTH

Adult Topic: **Acting on One's Commitments**
Youth Topic: **Called to Prepare**
Adult Key Verse: **Luke 3:8a**
Youth Key Verse: **Luke 3:16**
Print Passage: **Luke 3:7-18**

—John's witness to the Gospel was powerful in that many responded to his call and warning, including soldiers and tax collectors.
—Many people expected the Messiah to come in the time of John the Baptist, and some persons thought John the Baptist was the Messiah.
—The message of John the Baptist was for people to turn from sin to a life of sharing, honesty, and using power rightly.
—John was chosen by God to be the forerunner of the Messiah.
—When the people began to ask if John was the Messiah, he was quick to say "no" and point to Jesus as the Messiah, who would baptize them with the Holy Spirit.

CHILDREN

Children Topic: **John Speaks for God**
Key Verse: **Luke 3:18**
Print Passage: **Luke 3:7-8, 10-16, 18-20**

—John spoke in strong language to the people who gathered to hear him.
—What lesson is taught in this passage about God's desire for people to have a right relationship with Him?
—John instructed the people to do those things that would show their willingness to follow God's laws.
—John recognized his role as a "forerunner" to Jesus Christ, the Messiah.
—John was committed to calling people from a life of disobedience to one of obedience to God.
—John challenged the people to make a commitment to God.

I. INTRODUCTION

A. Acting on One's Commitments

Actions speak louder than words. This familiar aphorism illuminates the lesson focus. A verbal claim to do something that is not followed by the appropriate corresponding action is hardly worthy of being called a commitment. When we are hired to work and actually go on the job and perform the designated task(s) we have acted on our commitment. When we propose marriage and received an affirmative response and actually marry the person we have acted on our commitment. When we agree to deliver a sermon, teach a class, support our youth, and we follow through, we have acted on our commitment. Commitment is a void check if there is not a corresponding action as resource to deliver the payout.

John fulfilled his commitment to proclaim God's message and challenged others to act on their commitments. His faithfulness to acting on his commitments paved the way for many to receive the coming Christ, to whom he was the forerunner. John's direct challenge to the multitude to bring forth fruits worthy of repentance will ground the lesson's aim that we focus our commitment not only on words but also deeds. Further, we are tasked to go beyond those actions that are self-serving to an individually focused self, and to reach beyond the expected behaviors and offer more in the way of God's goodness to the unsuspecting. Finally, John clarifies any confusion in the minds of those who would hear him speak that he was not the one to be worshiped, but he was the messenger proclaiming the One who was to come.

B. Biblical Background

Luke's account of John's active commitment is central to the developing story of the coming Christ. Hebrew accounts of the coming Messiah are texts that this gospel writer had at his disposal because of the people's familiarity with those texts. This account, like the earlier birth narratives, is aimed at historically and socially locating John's activity. This association also helps the reader identify Jesus' location at this time period. In this sense, Luke wrote as a historian, although some scholars have debated the historical accuracy of the writing. Luke positioned John as a widespread prognosticator of the Good News, speaking to people from every walk of life (the crowd, tax collectors, military personnel, and so forth). This element of John's presentation is consistent with the emphasis this Gospel account places on the vast reach of God's work in humanity, not limiting it to a specific group of people.

II. EXPOSITION AND APPLICATION OF THE SCRIPTURE

A. John Proclaims God's Message (Luke 3:7-9)

Then said he to the multitude that came forth to be baptized of him, O generation of vipers, who hath warned you to flee from the wrath to come? Bring forth therefore fruits worthy of repentance, and begin not to say within yourselves, We have Abraham to our father: for I say unto you, That God is able of these stones to raise up children unto Abraham. And now also the axe is laid unto the root of the trees: every tree therefore which bringeth not forth good fruit is hewn down, and cast into the fire.

John began his proclamation with a defaming assessment of the group being addressed. He called them a group of vipers. This was a poisonous snake common to the area. John's characterization was not a friendly gesture, to be sure. While we seek models and examples in the biblical text, it is noteworthy to remind readers that John the Baptist was a bit of a renegade. Those who would be harsh toward the people they serve, take caution. The people to whom John was speaking had come to him to be baptized. The people would have been familiar with baptism as a result of their Judaic heritage, which emphasized baptism as a purification rite. John's baptism was a bit more expansive and drew a broader crowd. His baptism focused on repentance for the forgiveness of sins. Repentance in this context is significant as it points to a major concept in Luke's Gospel account—a changed perspective/focus. Of significant import for our lesson is the key to repentance. Repentance is suggestive of a turning back and away from. Repentance literally conveys a reestablishing of penance—a way of atoning "again" for one's unrighteous living. The Old Testament model for atonement was disappearing with the onset of John's ministry, which set the stage for Jesus' ministry.

John admonished the people to produce results that reflect changed minds. This is the new covenant focus of repentance or atonement. There is an overall atonement for the human condition of sin, by way of Jesus' salvation work. Yet there is also repentant work that must be done in the hearts and minds of each individual that leads the person to a changed life. This is John's focus and intent in his message of repentance. He reminded the people not to rest on their laurels—being part of the Abrahamic tradition—because God could raise up stones as children of Abraham. People could call on their genealogical foundations as a claim to excuse their unrighteous behavior, while calling themselves righteous. John was encouraging the people to move past this rudimentary understanding of righteousness and to instead produce action-based outcomes reflecting their esteemed lineage.

This admonition is critical to our modern context, since many proclaim Christianity yet do not show Christianity in their lives. As the saying goes, "many can talk the talk, but do not walk the walk." The imperative to produce underscores the importance of "bearing fruit" that reveal a changed perspective. This imperative requires action. It is hard to produce or bear fruit, when you have not tilled the soil, planted any seeds, fertilized the planted seeds, watered the seeds, pruned the outgrowth, and protected the growth against harsh weather conditions. Failure to act in ways that are appropriate to bearing good fruit leads to fruitlessness. An unproductive tree, one that is not useful, will be cut down. While Christians may not literally face annihilation through a failure to act, their productivity will not be what God desires. Christ came that we might have life and have it more abundantly. The bearing of good fruit is a sign of this abundant life. Individuals and communities of faith can joyously live out this admonition that requires follow-through action. Many, sadly, remain unfulfilled because of their failure to act on their commitments to Christ.

B. "What Do We Have to Do?"
(Luke 3:10-14)

And the people asked him, saying, What shall we do then? He answereth and saith unto them, He that hath two coats, let him impart to him that hath none; and he that hath meat, let him do likewise. Then came also publicans to be baptized, and said unto him, Master, what shall we do? And he said unto them, Exact no more than that which is appointed you. And the soldiers likewise demanded of him, saying, And what shall we do? And he said unto them, Do violence to no man, neither accuse any falsely; and be content with your wages.

Rightly, the people queried John about what needed to be done to produce such fruit. John suggested to the crowd that they give from their abundance. If one has more than one needs, one should give to people who are in need. This applies to clothing, food, or any resource. Most specifically, John was referring to giving beyond expectations. Some people expect certain behaviors and gifts from people who profess Christ. Letting go of our reluctance to give because we will only have "one" left is what John is seeking to move us beyond. Generally, we should express our commitment to Christ in our giving liberally to those who are without.

We frequently attempt these efforts at major holidays, as though this is the only time we experience personal abundance. Our giving can and should be any time of the year to any person or group of people who stand in need. Children in foster care, the elderly in nursing homes, persons living in poverty in the United States and abroad, and a host of other communities of people could benefit from our giving. It is noteworthy that John did not tell his audience that they needed to pray first thing in the morning, or fast three days a week prior to giving or as a substitute for giving. While

these actions were important, John, instead, simply pointed the people to the act of giving, specifically to those who did not have, as a way of producing outcomes that reflected a changed mind/perspective. The importance of giving of whatever one has in abundance is at the core of John's reply—and this could be giving of one's smile in the morning to an office of people who are grumpy before noon, giving an extra dose of attention to your loved ones, or sharing whatever one has more of than one needs or can genuinely use.

Our positions can and do frequently influence the realm and scope of our giving. We know that if we are earning over six figures annually, our giving can and should be different from that of someone who barely brings in minimum wage. Further, if we own our own businesses and control the resources within it, then our giving can and should be different from that of someone who works for a franchise, where they have to go through a multitude of channels to encourage a donation of any kind. Naturally, specific groups within the crowd came to John and asked what *they* should be doing. Their response to John provides a good example of what we can and should be doing—asking what we could be doing or what else we can do. Beyond the general populace, some of us may be in positions of privilege and thereby able to take additional measures to relieve the oppressed in society. In many cases, we know what we can and should be doing, but we are just not doing it.

In John's time (and ours too, in certain regards), tax collectors had a certain privilege and access to gain from the citizenry. They could "fix" the books, change the rules, and demand more than was legally required. It appears that this may have been a common practice, according to John. He said to tax collectors not to charge people more than they knew they were required to collect. To the soldiers, who enforced the law and had power to be oppressive in their responsibilities, John said not to abuse their authority by forcefully or illegally taking money from people or accusing them of some deed falsely (another way to get them to pay for their "freedom" from repercussions of the false accusation).

It stands to reason that Christians in positions of power and authority have greater obligation to avoid oppressive behaviors and produce results that show a Christian mindset as central to all of their actions. Refraining from the abuse of power should always be key to those in powerful positions. Whether in the forefront of everyone's view or in the background, in power or subjugated to other's power, all Christians should create a well-paved path for others to be exposed to Christ. This was central to John's life purpose. He was indeed, literally, preparing the way for Jesus as the Christ. Many had no concept of what it meant for him to be preparing people to receive Christ, because so many confused him with the Christ. They assumed because of his fervor in preaching repentance and his baptismal practices that he was the one come to redeem them. It is hard for some of us to be recognized as *Christian,* let alone be perceived as the returning Christ. So our preparation of others for Christ, while not literal in an embodied sense, should nonetheless be just as critically engaging for us as it was for John the Baptist. Our actions in our commitment to Christ should reflect a meaningful existence that prepares someone else to meet Him.

C. John Clarifies His Role
(Luke 3:15-18)

And as the people were in expectation, and all men mused in their hearts of John, whether he were the Christ, or not; John answered, saying unto them all, I indeed baptize you with water; but one mightier than I cometh, the latchet of whose shoes I am not worthy to unloose: he shall baptize you with the Holy Ghost and with fire: Whose fan is in his hand, and he will throughly purge his floor, and will gather the wheat into his garner; but the chaff he will burn with fire unquenchable. And many other things in his exhortation preached he unto the people.

John served as a preparation for people's exposure to Christ. The people, who were Jews, had been expecting the fulfillment of the Hebrew account of the coming Messiah. They eagerly began to wonder if John might have been the fulfillment of that promise. His actions through preaching and baptizing were so impressive to the listeners that they thought he might have been the Christ. John took a moment to assure them that he was not Christ and was hardly worthy to be considered the Christ. Further, the coming Christ would baptize them again in a different way. This was central to John's preparatory message to the people. His baptism was a purification rite similar to their Judaic tradition of baptism in that it "cleansed" them in preparation for a baptism of the Holy Spirit and of fire. This baptism that would come from the Christ pushed the listeners beyond the cleansing element of baptism to a conversion experience of baptism. Not only would they be cleansed, but they would indeed be changed. From this perspective of preparation, John continued to admonish and encourage the people, while preaching the Good News of Christ's coming.

III. CONCLUDING REFLECTION

We can conclude from this lesson that

true repentance is the cornerstone to acting on one's commitment to Christ. John the Baptist's message in our lesson gave a critical assessment of the common people of the day who proclaimed themselves to be God's people. John's admonition to them to bear fruit is a salient admonition to modern followers of Christ who may from time to time tend to want to rest on their experience of a rich historical family faith tradition or cultural church tradition. John reminded us that these things are not enough in laying claim to being children of God. He wisely suggested that our lives must reflect something of God's activity manifested in our activity. It is a truism that "you can't beat God giving, no matter how you try." Yet, this is the direction to which John pointed the querying ones of the group. He told them to give out of their abundance, as a sign of bearing fruit. More specifically, he advised them to do that which went beyond the expected to the good of the unsuspecting one. Finally, John modeled what should be a central aim of the Christian life. John served as an emissary, or one who goes before and declares the message of the one to come. John's mission in life was indeed to get the people ready for Jesus. It should also be our goal as Christians to conduct our lives in ways that prepare the way for someone else to see and come to Christ. This is centrally acting on our commitments to Christ.

PRAYER

God, You are holy. We hold Your name in high esteem. May it be that You find us here on earth carrying out Your purpose. Since we are subject to error, we ask You to cleanse us and renew us, so that we may better serve You. We know our best efforts are feeble before You, yet we humbly seek to do Your bidding. Help us to give freely as You have blessed us to give. Encourage us that we might encourage others in the faith. We submit this prayer in gratitude. In Jesus' name we pray. Amen.

WORD POWER

Repent, Repentance *(metanoia [met-an'-oy-ah])*—means "afterthought, change of mind, repentance," and corresponds in meaning to *metanoeo* (NT:3340), lit., "to perceive afterwards" (*meta*, "after," implying "change"; *noeo*, "to perceive"; *nous*, "the mind, the seat of moral reflection"), and is used of "repentance" from sin or evil.

HOME DAILY BIBLE READINGS
(December 22-28, 2008)

John the Baptist Proclaims God's Message
MONDAY, December 22: "More than a Prophet" (Luke 7:24-29)
TUESDAY, December 23: "A Witness to the Light" (John 1:6-9)
WEDNESDAY, December 24: "A Voice in the Wilderness" (John 1:19-27)
THURSDAY, December 25: "John's Testimony" (John 1:29-34)
FRIDAY, December 26: "A Shining Lamp" (John 5:30-35)
SATURDAY, December 27: "I Must Decrease" (John 3:22-30)
SUNDAY, December 28: "Call to Repentance" (Luke 3:7-18)

LESSON 5

January 4, 2009

MIDWIVES SERVE GOD

DEVOTIONAL READING: **Proverbs 16:1-7**
PRINT PASSAGE: **Exodus 1:8-21**

BACKGROUND SCRIPTURE: **Exodus 1:8-21**
KEY VERSE: **Exodus 1:17**

Exodus 1:8-21—KJV

8 Now there arose up a new king over Egypt, which knew not Joseph.

9 And he said unto his people, Behold, the people of the children of Israel are more and mightier than we:

10 Come on, let us deal wisely with them; lest they multiply, and it come to pass, that, when there falleth out any war, they join also unto our enemies, and fight against us, and so get them up out of the land.

11 Therefore they did set over them taskmasters to afflict them with their burdens. And they built for Pharaoh treasure cities, Pithom and Raamses.

12 But the more they afflicted them, the more they multiplied and grew. And they were grieved because of the children of Israel.

13 And the Egyptians made the children of Israel to serve with rigour:

14 And they made their lives bitter with hard bondage, in morter, and in brick, and in all manner of service in the field: all their service, wherein they made them serve, was with rigour.

15 And the king of Egypt spake to the Hebrew midwives, of which the name of the one was Shiphrah, and the name of the other Puah:

16 And he said, When ye do the office of a midwife to the Hebrew women, and see them upon the stools; if it be a son, then ye shall kill him: but if it be a daughter, then she shall live.

17 But the midwives feared God, and did not as the king of Egypt commanded them, but saved the men children alive.

18 And the king of Egypt called for the midwives, and said unto them, Why have ye done this thing, and have saved the men children alive?

19 And the midwives said unto Pharaoh, Because the Hebrew women are not as the Egyptian women; for they are lively, and are delivered ere the midwives come in unto them.

20 Therefore God dealt well with the midwives: and the people multiplied, and waxed very mighty.

Exodus 1:8-21—NRSV

8 Now a new king arose over Egypt, who did not know Joseph.

9 He said to his people, "Look, the Israelite people are more numerous and more powerful than we.

10 Come, let us deal shrewdly with them, or they will increase and, in the event of war, join our enemies and fight against us and escape from the land."

11 Therefore they set taskmasters over them to oppress them with forced labor. They built supply cities, Pithom and Rameses, for Pharaoh.

12 But the more they were oppressed, the more they multiplied and spread, so that the Egyptians came to dread the Israelites.

13 The Egyptians became ruthless in imposing tasks on the Israelites,

14 and made their lives bitter with hard service in mortar and brick and in every kind of field labor. They were ruthless in all the tasks that they imposed on them.

15 The king of Egypt said to the Hebrew midwives, one of whom was named Shiphrah and the other Puah,

16 "When you act as midwives to the Hebrew women, and see them on the birthstool, if it is a boy, kill him; but if it is a girl, she shall live."

17 But the midwives feared God; they did not do as the king of Egypt commanded them, but they let the boys live.

18 So the king of Egypt summoned the midwives and said to them, "Why have you done this, and allowed the boys to live?"

19 The midwives said to Pharaoh, "Because the Hebrew women are not like the Egyptian women; for they are vigorous and give birth before the midwife comes to them."

20 So God dealt well with the midwives; and the people multiplied and became very strong.

21 And it came to pass, because the midwives feared God, that he made them houses.

21 And because the midwives feared God, he gave them families.

TOPICAL OUTLINE OF THE LESSON

I. **Introduction**
   A. Midwives Serve God
   B. Biblical Background

II. **Exposition and Application of the Scripture**
   A. Change of the Guard (Exodus 1:8-10)
   B. Oppressive Conditions (Exodus 1:11-14)
   C. Midwives Disobeyed Pharaoh's Edict (Exodus 1:15-17)
   D. Received God's Reward (Exodus 1:18-21)

III. **Concluding Reflection**

LESSON OBJECTIVES

Upon completion of this lesson, the students are expected to:

1. Discuss the midwives' civil disobedience to Pharaoh;
2. Consider how competing demands influenced their willingness to establish commitments and whether God being on "their" side was a dominant factor; and,
3. Evaluate possibilities for ordering commitments around their primary loyalty to God and their faith community.

POINTS TO BE EMPHASIZED

ADULT/YOUTH

Adult Topic: Choosing Among Commitments
Youth Topic: Just Say "NO"
Adult/Youth Key Verse: Exodus 1:17
Print Passage: Exodus 1:8-21

—The Egyptians saw the Israelites as a threat because they had surpassed the Egyptian population.
—The Egyptians subjected the Israelites to a cruel enslavement.
—The king of Egypt sought to curb the growth of the Israelite population by ordering that all male Hebrew babies be killed.
—God was still with the Israelites in their hardships and troubles.
—The Hebrews lived in Egypt for 430 years (see Exodus 12:40) and went from being welcomed guests to the level of a feared and oppressed foreign element.
—The Hebrews continued to increase in population and became "numerous."
—The Hebrews lived in the part of the Nile Delta called "Goshen," which was a "doorway" for foreign armies to enter to conquer. Thus, the Hebrews were seen as a threat to Egypt's national security because they could join with Egypt's invading enemies.

CHILDREN

Children Topic: Midwives Help Their People
Key Verse: Exodus 1:17
Print Passage: Exodus 1:8-21

—The new king feared the Hebrews but not their God.
—The midwives feared God more than they feared the king.
—The king sought to keep the Hebrews subservient, weak, and fewer in numbers by killing the male babies.
—God blessed the Hebrews through the intervention of the midwives.

I. INTRODUCTION

A. Midwives Serve God

Demands on our time and our resources abound. How do we decide among competing commitments? An example, often used in courses that discuss moral issues and ethics, describes a parent driving a child to a necessary doctor's appointment. The parent encounters an accident where a child has been injured and they are a long distance from medical support. The parent is also a nurse who can provide immediate care for the child in the accident. This scenario presents a competing claim on the parent's time and resources. To whom does the parent owe the primary obligation? How does this parent taking her child to a necessary doctor's appointment decide whether to forestall her own child's medical visit or provide as much immediate assistance that only she can provide for the child in the car wreck? Faithfulness to family needs, faithfulness to one's profession, and faithfulness to the care of others in society all factor into the parent's decision.

While this example may be easily resolved for some, for others it represents peculiar complexities depending on how they understand the nature of their commitments. The Hebrew midwives in this lesson faced challenging competing claims but were ultimately governed in their decision by their faithfulness to God and their people. The midwives were situated in a social and political snafu that required them to make a decision that went against the grain of the social and political order. Their decision between competing claims was difficult, but one that they faithfully made and for which their loyalty was rewarded.

B. Biblical Background

In the book of Exodus are the details of one of the signature experiences in the lives of the people of Israel—namely, the exodus from Egypt. Its writings are attributed to Moses, as it is situated second among the remaining four books of the Pentateuch or Torah. These first five books include Genesis, Exodus, Leviticus, Numbers, and Deuteronomy. The critical exodus experience figures prominently at the core of the Judaic and Christian faith traditions. Moses stood singularly as the arbiter of God's move toward liberating God's people—Israel. His life is chronicled throughout these first five books. He is the key figure, apart from God, in the exodus and the obtaining of the laws that were revealed at Mt. Sinai—The Ten Commandments.

This lesson's text is at the beginning of the first half of the Exodus account. It is a part of the Pharaoh's ruling traditions that details the plight of the children of Israel. The earliest portions of the Israelites' Egyptian experience were pleasant and positive, due to Joseph's (Jacob's son—see Genesis) prominent status and relationship with the king of Egypt. In this state of grace, experiencing a peaceful existence, the Israelite population greatly increased in Egypt, while they expected a fulfillment of the promise to leave Egypt and go to the land promised to Abraham (see Genesis). At the point of our text, Pharaoh did not know Joseph's history in Egypt and had no mercy on the Israelite people. He placed them under extremely harsh slavery conditions to oppress them and suppress in them any potential spirit of rebellion.

II. EXPOSITION AND APPLICATION OF THE SCRIPTURE

A. Change of the Guard
(Exodus 1:8-10)

Now there arose up a new king over Egypt, which knew not Joseph. And he said unto his people, Behold, the people of the children of Israel are more and mightier than we: Come on, let us deal wisely with them; lest they multiply, and it come to pass, that, when there falleth out any war, they join also unto our enemies, and fight against us, and so get them up out of the land.

A new king who did not know Joseph's history came into power while the children of Israel were enjoying relative peace and growth as a people. A shift in power can often change the course of any political or social process. The history of life in America is testament to this dynamic. Whether the political climate shifts from Republican rule to Democratic, or the economic shift moves in the stock market from a Bull market to a Bear market, the effects are generally felt by the masses. This experience was the experience of the ancient Israelites. The shift in political leadership created a wave of pain in their lives. They were "snatched" from their relatively peaceful prior experience in the land of Egypt as a result of the new pharaoh, who was unfamiliar with Joseph's history with the land and its leaders. The new leader of Egypt felt no obligation to the Israelites, and this attitude would prove extremely traumatic for them.

The new king observed the incongruence of the population and strength of the Egyptians versus the population and strength of the Israelites. This prompted fear in the mind of the king that the Israelites would continue to increase and in the event of war might even partner with Egypt's enemies and fight against the Egyptians. We can see glimpses of this dynamic in American history in the enslavement of African people and their high populations in several southern states. States like Mississippi and South Carolina caused extreme difficulties and hardships on the already poor lives of the slaves. Leaders in these states, much like Egypt's pharaoh at the time of our text, sought to avoid possible uprisings or revolts.

B. Oppressive Conditions
(Exodus 1:11-14)

Therefore they did set over them taskmasters to afflict them with their burdens. And they built for Pharaoh treasure cities, Pithom and Raamses. But the more they afflicted them, the more they multiplied and grew. And they were grieved because of the children of Israel. And the Egyptians made the children of Israel to serve with rigour: And they made their lives bitter with hard bondage, in morter, and in brick, and in all manner of service in the field: all their service, wherein they made them serve, was with rigour.

Seeking to avoid uprisings, the new king devised what he believed was a shrewd method for diminishing the population. He proclaimed that they be made slaves and be forced into harsh working conditions. In American history, regrettably, African people in this country were already slaves. For the Israelites, however, this state of slavery was a sad, new condition—one that they had feared, but from which had been previously spared as a result of Joseph's past favored relationships with Egyptian royalty.

In this state of slavery, Israelites were forced to build prominent "store" cities for Pharaoh. Their drudgery never ceased, yet the more they were oppressed, the more their fertility rates increased. Some scholars suggest that this continued increase in fertility is consistent with other biblical beliefs that children were divine blessings (note earlier and later lessons where barrenness is seen as a reproach by God). From this point of view, it is clear that God remains on the side of the oppressed. Even in the face of abject slavery, God continued to bless the people with an abundance of offspring, a way of continuing their lineage and heritage. As the people of Israel continued to increase, Pharaoh became increasingly fearful of their potential for revolt. In a state of fear, people often make rash and sometimes harmful decisions. It is here that we see the real threat that Shiphrah and Puah were about to face. It was in this state of mind that the pharaoh sought a different approach to diminish the numbers and strength of the Israelites.

C. Midwives Disobeyed Pharaoh's Edict
(Exodus 1:15-17)

And the king of Egypt spake to the Hebrew midwives, of which the name of the one was Shiphrah, and the name of the other Puah: And he said, When ye do the office of a midwife to the Hebrew women, and see them upon the stools; if it be a son, then ye shall kill him: but if it be a daughter, then she shall live. But the midwives feared God, and did not as the king of Egypt commanded them, but saved the men children alive.

Two women, named Shiphrah and Puah, were Hebrew midwives. That they are named is significant in this context, since many women in the biblical text were identified solely by their relationship to men or their deeds in the context of men. The king of Egypt spoke directly to the women, which established the power of their agency early in the passage. This is significant, as later Shiphrah and Puah would be in a position to exercise this agency. Fortunately, for Shiphrah and Puah, they maintained a skill set that many, including the pharaoh, found exceptionally valuable. As midwives, they were often spoken to directly by men who may have sought their services to rush quickly to the aid of their wives. However, in this case, the king of Egypt was not seeking their services for his personal familial needs. He was seeking to use them for a larger, more sinister political and social purpose. In his directive to Shiphrah and Puah, Pharaoh said (as they performed their jobs as midwives to the Hebrew women) that if the pregnant women bore sons, the midwives should kill them. Girls, however, could live. Pharaoh situated the midwives with the people of Israel by identifying the women they were instructed to serve, whose sons they should kill, as "among their people."

This edict presents an immediate conflict of interest for Shiphrah and Puah. Their job mandated that they deliver life into the world. Further, they were a part of a culture that believed the promise of fertility was a blessing from God. Finally, they were awestruck at the power of God—they feared God. How could they possibly comply with Pharaoh's demand? Equally important for their lives' sakes was their dilemma—how could they *not* comply with Pharaoh's demand? These conflicts of interest for Shiphrah and Puah make some of our worst daily conflicts pale in comparison. These midwives' experience of conflict helps us clearly see the difficulty of choosing among commitments. Their professional commitments were one area of importance in making the decision. Their historically and culturally connected belief systems were other mitigating factors in their decision. Their personal safety was at stake. But these women were God-fearing.

D. Received God's Reward
(Exodus 1:18-21)

And the king of Egypt called for the midwives, and said unto them, Why have ye done this thing, and have saved the men children alive? And the midwives said unto Pharaoh, Because the Hebrew women are not as the Egyptian women; for they are lively, and are delivered ere the midwives come in unto them. Therefore God dealt well with the midwives: and the people multiplied, and waxed very mighty. And it came to pass, because the midwives feared God, that he made them houses.

These major aspects of Shiphrah and Puah's experience give us a guide to some of our conflicting moments of choosing among commitments. We may not find ourselves immediately in harm's way if we fail to meet the demands of a prominent political figure, but we may find ourselves in peril of losing our jobs. If this happens, we may still survive, but may no longer live in the way to which we have grown accustomed. But what would it mean for us to directly contradict all of the above at the same time, in a reckless abandonment of our fear of God?

In Shiphrah and Puah's case, their overriding fear of God's power was the determining factor that helped them make their decision. It would be ideal if the living fear of God's power, which essentially is an acknowledgment of and reverence for God's power, governed our choices. Shiphrah and Puah model for us that the key to effectively choosing the best course of action among competing demands is to have God at the center of the decision-making process.

As a result of their fearing God, Shiphrah and Puah essentially endangered their lives by disobeying Pharaoh's edict. However, their stealthy reply to his query of why the male babies of the Israelites remained alive also protected them from the potential wrath of Pharaoh. They suggested that Hebrew women, compared with Egyptian women, were delivering babies too fast for them to keep up with the delivery times, and the boys were born alive before they could get there.

These two women risked much with their excuse. Yet, their act of civil disobedience is one that can be held up without reproach next to any current expressions of civil disobedience. For Shiphrah and Puah, their perceived benefits far outweighed the associated risks. Their fear of God and appropriate choosing among competing claims on their skills was highly rewarded. They received kindness from God and the people of Israel continued to multiply. Furthermore, as women who had honored God in their choice between competing demands, God gifted them with their own families. This was significant, since women who did not bear children were seen as a reproach. Christians may even now face risky, competing demands for commitment. The possibility of loss often stops individuals short of making the best choice. Shiphrah and Puah illustrate the significance of honoring one's faithfulness and loyalty to God as the appropriate guide for making the right decisions.

III. CONCLUDING REFLECTION

We can conclude from this lesson that making the best decisions involves minds that are focused on what is important. Shiphrah and Puah's experience with Pharaoh reflected their relative status. They were women of notoriety in their field, to the extent that Pharaoh believed they would carry out his plans. His underestimation of them was in his failure to recognize their overarching commitment and faithfulness first to God. Their faithfulness to and fear of God precluded their commitments to their jobs, historical-cultural standards for their behavior, and even the fear for their very lives at Pharaoh's hand.

Shiphrah and Puah illuminate the strength of a stealthy, yet appropriate response to choosing among commitments. They show us that any commitment that seeks to circumvent our recognition of the power of God is suspect. Further, they show that the ultimate, governing decision-making factor when choosing among commitments is in evaluating ones' faithfulness and loyalty to God in light of whatever choices are in front of the person. Choosing among commitments can pose certain risk. Our faithfulness need not be separate and distinct from our vocations. Finally, while we keep God at the center of our decision making, God faithfully rewards our commitments domestically and otherwise.

PRAYER

God, Creator of all, we are grateful. Instruct us in the ways of Your righteousness. Let us be ever equipped for good works in You, exercising our faith, keeping confidence in You. In the face of our challenges, strengthen our failing hearts and hands. Remind us that we have "so great a cloud of witnesses" (as mentioned in Hebrews 12:1) before us. May we be courageous and faith-filled believers. In Jesus' name we pray. Amen.

WORD POWER

Midwife *(yalad [yaw-lad`])*—this means "to bear, to bring forth, beget, gender, travail." **Midwife: a woman assisting at childbirth.**

HOME DAILY BIBLE READINGS
(December 29, 2008–January 4, 2009)

Midwives Serve God

MONDAY, December 29: "Honor Those Who Fear God" (Psalm 15)

TUESDAY, December 30: "Whom Shall I Fear?" (Psalm 27:1-6)

WEDNESDAY, December 31: "Fear No Evil" (Psalm 23)

THURSDAY, January 1: "Delivered from Fear" (Psalm 34:4-14)

FRIDAY, January 2: "The Friendship of the Lord" (Psalm 25:12-21)

SATURDAY, January 3: "Let All Fear the Lord" (Psalm 33:8-18)

SUNDAY, January 4: "Courage in the Face of Threat" (Exodus 1:8-21)

LESSON 6

January 11, 2009

RAHAB HELPS ISRAEL

DEVOTIONAL READING: **Hebrews 11:23-31**
PRINT PASSAGE: **Joshua 2:1-4, 12-14; 6:22-25**

BACKGROUND SCRIPTURE: **Joshua 2; 6:22-25**
KEY VERSES: **Joshua 2:11-12**

Joshua 2:1-4, 12-14; 6:22-25—KJV

AND JOSHUA the son of Nun sent out of Shittim two men to spy secretly, saying, Go view the land, even Jericho. And they went, and came into an harlot's house, named Rahab, and lodged there.

2 And it was told the king of Jericho, saying, Behold, there came men in hither to night of the children of Israel to search out the country.

3 And the king of Jericho sent unto Rahab, saying, Bring forth the men that are come to thee, which are entered into thine house: for they be come to search out all the country.

4 And the woman took the two men, and hid them, and said thus, There came men unto me, but I wist not whence they were:

.....

12 Now therefore, I pray you, swear unto me by the LORD, since I have shewed you kindness, that ye will also shew kindness unto my father's house, and give me a true token:

13 And that ye will save alive my father, and my mother, and my brethren, and my sisters, and all that they have, and deliver our lives from death.

14 And the men answered her, Our life for yours, if ye utter not this our business. And it shall be, when the LORD hath given us the land, that we will deal kindly and truly with thee.

.....

22 But Joshua had said unto the two men that had spied out the country, Go into the harlot's house, and bring out thence the woman, and all that she hath, as ye sware unto her.

23 And the young men that were spies went in, and brought Rahab, and her father, and her mother, and her brethren, and all that she had; and they brought out all her kindred, and left them without the camp of Israel.

Joshua 2:1-4, 12-14; 6:22-25—NRSV

THEN JOSHUA son of Nun sent two men secretly from Shittim as spies, saying, "Go, view the land, especially Jericho." So they went, and entered the house of a prostitute whose name was Rahab, and spent the night there.

2 The king of Jericho was told, "Some Israelites have come here tonight to search out the land."

3 Then the king of Jericho sent orders to Rahab, "Bring out the men who have come to you, who entered your house, for they have come only to search out the whole land."

4 But the woman took the two men and hid them. Then she said, "True, the men came to me, but I did not know where they came from."

.....

12 Now then, since I have dealt kindly with you, swear to me by the LORD that you in turn will deal kindly with my family. Give me a sign of good faith

13 that you will spare my father and mother, my brothers and sisters, and all who belong to them, and deliver our lives from death."

14 The men said to her, "Our life for yours! If you do not tell this business of ours, then we will deal kindly and faithfully with you when the LORD gives us the land."

.....

22 Joshua said to the two men who had spied out the land, "Go into the prostitute's house, and bring the woman out of it and all who belong to her, as you swore to her."

23 So the young men who had been spies went in and brought Rahab out, along with her father, her mother, her brothers, and all who belonged to her—they brought all her kindred out—and set them outside the camp of Israel.

Commitments may create conflicting priorities, require risks, and exact a cost. How does one balance the value of the different sides of a commitment? Rahab willingly faced great personal danger in order to save her family.

24 And they burnt the city with fire, and all that was therein: only the silver, and the gold, and the vessels of brass and of iron, they put into the treasury of the house of the LORD.

25 And Joshua saved Rahab the harlot alive, and her father's household, and all that she had; and she dwelleth in Israel even unto this day; because she hid the messengers, which Joshua sent to spy out Jericho.

24 They burned down the city, and everything in it; only the silver and gold, and the vessels of bronze and iron, they put into the treasury of the house of the LORD.

25 But Rahab the prostitute, with her family and all who belonged to her, Joshua spared. Her family has lived in Israel ever since. For she hid the messengers whom Joshua sent to spy out Jericho.

TOPICAL OUTLINE OF THE LESSON

I. **Introduction**
   A. Challenges
   B. Biblical Background

II. **Exposition and Application of the Scripture**
   A. Rahab's Risk
      (Joshua 2:1)
   B. Spies Spotted
      (Joshua 2:2-4)
   C. Necessary Negotiations
      (Joshua 2:12-14)
   D. Reaping the Rewards
      (Joshua 6:22-25)

III. **Concluding Reflection**

LESSON OBJECTIVES

Upon completion of this lesson, the students are expected to:

1. Know Rahab's story of commitment to protecting her family;
2. Evaluate the risks and costs of Rahab's commitment; and,

3. Consider the challenges of their own commitments to God's service.

POINTS TO BE EMPHASIZED

ADULT/YOUTH
Adult Topic: **Risking One's Life for Good**
Youth Topic: **A Prostitute Becomes Protector**
Adult/Youth Key Verses: **Joshua 2:11-12**
Print Passage: **Joshua 2:1-4, 12-14; 6:22-25**

—Rahab was a prostitute and a woman of faith. In James 2:25-26 and Hebrews 11:31 it is cited Rahab was a person whose faith produced good works.

—The Rahab spoken of in Matthew 1:5 is possibly the same as in the Joshua story. In Matthew, she is spoken of as the mother of Boaz, the ancestor of David and Jesus.

—Joshua made sure that the vows to Rahab were kept when the Israelites successfully conquered the land.

—*Rahab* in Hebrew means "storm and arrogance."

—We can't say how much Rahab and her family understood about the God of the Israelites but they were wise enough to recognize that no other god could compare with the might of Israel's God.

—Using Rahab as God did shows us that God's actions were not confined to Israel and are accessible to people beyond any select group.

CHILDREN
Children Topic: **Committed to Helping Others**
Key Verse: **Joshua 2:12**

Print Passage: Joshua 2:1-4, 8-9, 12-15; 6:22-25

—Rahab agreed to hide the spies and protect their identity.

—The spies promised to protect Rahab and her family when Jericho fell.

—Joshua and the army kept the promise made to Rahab.

—Rahab's family became an important part of the faith community.

I. INTRODUCTION

A. Challenges

Preparing children for school in the morning, maintaining obligations as an employee, and driving on the highway are all forms of some established commitment. Commitments to care for and nurture, to perform job duties, and to drive according to established laws most often reflect minimal risk for all parties involved, but what of those commitments that risk someone's life? The riskier the commitment, the greater the benefit expected for fulfilling the challenge. The challenges of our basic daily commitments rarely involve putting our lives at high risk, but we do sometimes face real loss in a myriad of ways.

The possible losses of relationships, possessions, or social status are but a few of the things we put at risk, especially when committing to God's purpose as a greater good. These potential losses create a need to weigh the consequences of our commitments and the risks they often impose on our lives. Rahab's experience illuminates not only the challenges of risking commitment, but also the possibilities for benefits in risking commitment for a greater good.

B. Biblical Background

The book of Joshua in the Old Testament historical writings is a continuation of the Israelites' expedition. Further, it is set as a "historical" narrative of the Israelite experience not just to recount supposed actual events, but also to give an account of the Israelites' understanding of their experience and how they perceived themselves to be in their relationship with their God. Rahab's experiences with two Israelite spies define the early chapters of the book of Joshua. This story is part of the larger Israelite account of their entry into Canaan, the land God promised to their ancestors. This early account of Israelite experience after the death of Moses lays the foundation for Joshua as a leader. Joshua, as successor to Moses, was critical as prophet and leader to the Israelites as they relocated in Canaan.

Central to the entire book and evidenced early in the text are the themes of obedience and social justice as crucial aspects of this people's covenant relationship with God. Joshua emphasized an establishment of a new social order—violence notwithstanding. Indeed the move into Canaan was nothing short of a military invasion and occupation of another people's territory. The Israelites did this with the belief that it was God's will for them to possess the land.

According to many scholars, Joshua foreshadows the coming Jesus. With many similarities between them, Joshua's ultimate aim seen at the conclusion of the text was also closely aligned with that of Jesus—which was to promote an unyielding indebtedness and faithfulness to God.

II. EXPOSITION AND APPLICATION OF THE SCRIPTURE

A. Rahab's Risk
(Joshua 2:1)

AND JOSHUA the son of Nun sent out of Shittim two men to spy secretly, saying, Go view the land, even Jericho. And they went, and came into an harlot's house, named Rahab, and lodged there.

The prophet Joshua issued a command to two spies to explore the land of Canaan, with a focus on Jericho. The situation that turned risky for Rahab began with someone else's expressed commitment to invade the territory in which she lived. From the start, Rahab personified one of the greatest, yet most off-handed challenges of those who express commitment to God. It happens sometimes that, while we "mind our own business," someone else's expressed "faithfulness" to his or her cause can endanger us. The depth and richness of Rahab's experience of her commitment ran on multiple planes. The two spies that Joshua sent, along with many other Israelites, had already spoken of their obedience to Joshua, stating that whatever he commanded them to do they would do, and that anyone who got in their way would be put to death (see Joshua 1:16-18). Clearly a military operation from the outset, this part of the text sets the stage for the violence to be observed throughout the book of Joshua. Additionally, this passage lays the groundwork for the social dynamic shift that was to occur with the settling of the Israelites in Canaan.

Much speculation is given to the relationship between the spies' purpose and their accommodations at the prostitute's (Rahab's) home. Several scholars suggest that the arrangement and location of Rahab's house made it an ideal location for the spies to stop into quickly on their entrance into Jericho. Others suggest that the spies were there for the business practices in which Rahab engaged. Whatever their rationale, it was at Rahab's house that they stopped and stayed. Rahab's occupation is the source of much disdain in the eyes of conservatives—some condemn her for being a prostitute. What remains clear is that Temple prostitution was a real occupation during this era, and in certain pockets of the world prostitution remains a viable way for women (and men) to earn a living. There were both Temple prostitutes and the more common prostitutes for hire, not unlike some of the prostitution houses with which we are familiar in the twentieth and twenty-first centuries. Rahab was a prostitute of the latter kind. She practiced her trade regularly out of her dwelling space, for a fee. What is significant to how we understand Rahab's commitment is that even in her faithfulness to her profession, she was available for God's purpose.

B. Spies Spotted
(Joshua 2:2-4)

And it was told the king of Jericho, saying, Behold, there came men in hither to night of the children of Israel to search out the country. And the king of Jericho sent unto Rahab, saying, Bring forth the men that are come to thee,

which are entered into thine house: for they be come to search out all the country. And the woman took the two men, and hid them, and said thus, There came men unto me, but I wist not whence they were.

Rahab was not the only one in this lesson text who risked her life. The two spies were greatly at risk, trespassing in someone else's territory to spy them out so that they could occupy their land. The spies' mission and their location were told to the king of Jericho because they too were being spied on while they were "supposed to be" spying. This put their lives at immediate and tremendous risk. The king went so far as to send orders to Rahab, letting her know that he was aware of the spies' purpose and arrival at her home, and demanded that she release them. This is tantamount to someone in our current world harboring a fugitive of the law. What was Rahab to do in this situation? Her business prospects were in peril. Who would want to continue to come to her establishment if the king's spies were hanging around, checking out people's comings and goings?

This fugitive-harboring effort on Rahab's part introduces into the text the seriousness of her element of risk taking. While she did not lie about the spies coming to her home, she did begin a litany of lies thereafter. She declared that she did not know where they went, when in fact she had hidden them on her roof. Rahab undoubtedly was well-known, due to her profession and location, but what was the breadth of her power base? She incurred tremendous risk of her livelihood, her life, and the lives of those in her household.

Her role as the initial power broker in this situation emphasizes that social status and identity are not always commensurate with so-called ideal conceptions of good and who can effect change for good purposes. Rahab,

later described in the New Testament as a woman of faith (see Hebrews 11:31), reminds us that sometimes our most faithful acts require stealthy risk, alongside strategic negotiations. Our modern challenge may be in knowing best when to incorporate this "stealth." Our best aim is to focus on the divine good involved and continue to move forward.

C. Necessary Negotiations (Joshua 2:12-14)

Now therefore, I pray you, swear unto me by the Lord, since I have shewed you kindness, that ye will also shew kindness unto me by father's house, and give me a true token: And that ye will save alive my father, and my mother, and my brethren, and my sisters, and all that they have, and deliver our lives from death. And the men answered her, Our life for yours, if ye utter not this our business. And it shall be, when the Lord hath given us the land, that we will deal kindly and truly with thee.

Rahab recognized the risk that she took and immediately began a negotiation strategy to protect her interests. She told the spies that since she had been good to them, she requested that they return the kindness and protect her family. This was a fair trade-off. Some Christians wrongly assume that they in some capacity owe others, Christians included, some service or goods for free or at best significantly reduced rates—because they are, after all, "good" Christians. As a non-Christian and non-Israelite, Rahab set a stellar example for her time and ours to follow regarding stealthy negotiation strategies. She did not hesitate to ask for what she wanted. Rahab knew what the spies' next move would be and the potential impact it would have on her and her family. She was aware that the spies would return to complete the occupation and kill the inhabitants of Jericho. She sought protection for her life and her families' lives, as well as their possessions. The two spies told her that the deal was their lives for that of hers and her families'. The spies were more than willing to accommodate Rahab. She saved their lives. However, they were shrewd negotiators as well—the deal only counted if she agreed not to disclose any details of their planned activities. They would not allow harm to come to her family, and would honor their commitment to her as soon as they occupied the land.

While Rahab was not an Israelite, she was aware of the power of the Israelites' God (see verses 8-11). This faithfulness to awareness of God's power marked her prominent position in the history of Christianity. Similar to the midwives of the prior lesson, Rahab incurred substantial risk but was in a powerful position to broker a deal for herself and her family, and was willing to do so based on her belief in the power of God.

D. Reaping the Rewards
(Joshua 6:22-25)

But Joshua had said unto the two men that had spied out the country, Go into the harlot's house, and bring out thence the woman, and all that she hath, as ye sware unto her. And the young men that were spies went in, and brought Rahab, and her father, and her mother, and her brethren, and all that she had; and they brought out all her kindred, and left them without the camp of Israel. And they burnt the city with fire, and all that was therein: only the silver, and the gold, and the vessels of brass and of iron, they put into the treasury of the house of the LORD. And Joshua saved Rahab the harlot alive, and her father's household, and all that she had; and she dwelleth in Israel even unto this day; because she hid the messengers, which Joshua sent to spy out Jericho.

Upon the Israelites' occupation of Jericho, Joshua, as leader of the people, reminded the two spies of their commitment to Rahab and told them to do as they had promised.

Sometimes it is incumbent upon leaders to remind other leaders, subordinates, or colleagues to honor their commitments, to be faithful to their roles as leaders. The two spies had Joshua. It is important that our church leaders have "Joshua" types in their lives to help protect the "Rahabs" of our modern social, religious, political, and economic contexts. It is all too easy for a "Rahab" type to slip under the radar after doing some good deed that benefits God's larger purpose. Fortunately for Rahab, she and her family, as a result of her willingness to take a risk for God's good, were rewarded with their lives when everybody around them and many of the people of Jericho were destroyed. The reward was beneficial for Rahab, but we should pause to consider the consequences of destroying other lives in the name of a religious cause.

Key to this lesson is being aware of and knowing when to risk major loss for a greater good. It is difficult and often nearly impossible to get it just right. There are no hard and fast answers about when it is appropriate or best to risk one's life for good. Sometimes the risk is only to our reputations or being laughed at for not joining in on an inappropriate joke. Other times the risk may threaten a career or promotion, but nonetheless require an individual to report a superior engaging in illegal or otherwise improper conduct. What is risked in either of these situations may or may not be outweighed by the greater good for other people involved. Rahab sought not only to save herself, but the people around her as well. Notably, she could not save everybody, just as we sometimes cannot do this. But Rahab could and did make a difference in choosing her loyalties. Taking note of Rahab's experience can benefit us, especially when we are faced with making commitments that may risk our lives.

III. CONCLUDING REFLECTION

We can conclude from this lesson that God has no limit in choosing those who can be used to effect His good purpose. Speculative focus on people's images rather than how God is using them can serve to distract us from the greater good involved. While we consider the possibilities of risking our lives, or anything else, for the greater good, we should maintain a broad view of the world around us. Tunnel vision can prevent us from seeing God's larger work in our lives and in the lives of people around us.

PRAYER

Dear God, we express our gratitude for Your goodness and mercy. We pray that You will strengthen us in our faith, so that we may do what pleases You. Strengthen our stealth in negotiation strategies as we aspire to good, while not doing any harm. We fervently seek Your guidance in the risky areas of commitment of our lives. In Jesus' name we pray. Amen.

WORD POWER

Melt *(macac[ma-ka-k])*—this word is cast in the imperfect tense, which means even before the arrival of the spies, the inhabitants of Jericho were gripped with fear. Mere hearing of the Hebrews macerated the people of Jericho. God sent the fear of the Hebrews ahead so that the people were tormented with excessive fear.

HOME DAILY BIBLE READINGS
(January 5-11, 2009)

Rahab Helps Israel
MONDAY, January 5: "The Courage of Faith" (Joshua 1:10-18)
TUESDAY, January 6: "Rahab—Example of Faith" (Hebrews 11:23-31)
WEDNESDAY, January 7: "Rahab's Declaration" (Joshua 2:8-11)
THURSDAY, January 8: "Rahab's Agreement" (Joshua 2:15-21)
FRIDAY, January 9: "Rahab—Justified by Her Works" (James 2:21-26)
SATURDAY, January 10: "Rahab's Legacy—A King!" (Matthew 1:1-6)
SUNDAY, January 11: "Rahab's Protection" (Joshua 2:1-4, 12-14; 6:22-25)

JOSHUA LEADS ISRAEL

DEVOTIONAL READING: **Psalm 142**
PRINT PASSAGE: **Joshua 3:1-13**

BACKGROUND SCRIPTURE: **Joshua 3**
KEY VERSE: **Joshua 3:7**

Joshua 3:1-13—KJV

AND JOSHUA rose early in the morning; and they removed from Shittim, and came to Jordan, he and all the children of Israel, and lodged there before they passed over.

2 And it came to pass after three days, that the officers went through the host;

3 And they commanded the people, saying, When ye see the ark of the covenant of the LORD your God, and the priests the Levites bearing it, then ye shall remove from your place, and go after it.

4 Yet there shall be a space between you and it, about two thousand cubits by measure: come not near unto it, that ye may know the way by which ye must go: for ye have not passed this way heretofore.

5 And Joshua said unto the people, Sanctify yourselves: for to morrow the LORD will do wonders among you.

6 And Joshua spake unto the priests, saying, Take up the ark of the covenant, and pass over before the people. And they took up the ark of the covenant, and went before the people.

7 And the LORD said unto Joshua, This day will I begin to magnify thee in the sight of all Israel, that they may know that, as I was with Moses, so I will be with thee.

8 And thou shalt command the priests that bear the ark of the covenant, saying, When ye are come to the brink of the water of Jordan, ye shall stand still in Jordan.

9 And Joshua said unto the children of Israel, Come hither, and hear the words of the LORD your God.

10 And Joshua said, Hereby ye shall know that the living God is among you, and that he will without fail drive out from before you the Canaanites, and the Hittites, and the Hivites, and the Perizzites, and the Girgashites, and the Amorites, and the Jebusites.

11 Behold, the ark of the covenant of the Lord of all the earth passeth over before you into Jordan.

Joshua 3:1-13—NRSV

EARLY IN the morning Joshua rose and set out from Shittim with all the Israelites, and they came to the Jordan. They camped there before crossing over.

2 At the end of three days the officers went through the camp

3 and commanded the people, "When you see the ark of the covenant of the LORD your God being carried by the levitical priests, then you shall set out from your place. Follow it,

4 so that you may know the way you should go, for you have not passed this way before. Yet there shall be a space between you and it, a distance of about two thousand cubits; do not come any nearer to it."

5 Then Joshua said to the people, "Sanctify yourselves; for tomorrow the LORD will do wonders among you."

6 To the priests Joshua said, "Take up the ark of the covenant, and pass on in front of the people." So they took up the ark of the covenant and went in front of the people.

7 The LORD said to Joshua, "This day I will begin to exalt you in the sight of all Israel, so that they may know that I will be with you as I was with Moses.

8 You are the one who shall command the priests who bear the ark of the covenant, 'When you come to the edge of the waters of the Jordan, you shall stand still in the Jordan.'"

9 Joshua then said to the Israelites, "Draw near and hear the words of the LORD your God."

10 Joshua said, "By this you shall know that among you is the living God who without fail will drive out from before you the Canaanites, Hittites, Hivites, Perizzites, Girgashites, Amorites, and Jebusites:

11 the ark of the covenant of the Lord of all the earth is going to pass before you into the Jordan.

12 Now therefore take you twelve men out of the tribes of Israel, out of every tribe a man.

13 And it shall come to pass, as soon as the soles of the feet of the priests that bear the ark of the LORD, the Lord of all the earth, shall rest in the waters of Jordan, that the waters of Jordan shall be cut off from the waters that come down from above; and they shall stand upon an heap.

12 So now select twelve men from the tribes of Israel, one from each tribe.

13 When the soles of the feet of the priests who bear the ark of the LORD, the Lord of all the earth, rest in the waters of the Jordan, the waters of the Jordan flowing from above shall be cut off; they shall stand in a single heap."

TOPICAL OUTLINE OF THE LESSON

I. Introduction
  A. Leadership Requires Resources
  B. Biblical Background

II. Exposition and Application of the Scripture
  A. Joshua Instructs the People (Joshua 3:1-4)
  B. The Charge: Sanctify Yourselves (Joshua 3:5-6)
  C. The Lord Magnifies Joshua (Joshua 3:7-9)
  D. Listen and Follow (Joshua 3:10-13)

III. Concluding Reflection

LESSON OBJECTIVES

Upon completion of this lesson, the students are expected to:

1. Review Joshua's commitment to God;

2. Explore issues of their own responsibility and resources for making and keeping commitments; and,

3. Discuss ways to better utilize their resources for making and fulfilling their commitments.

POINTS TO BE EMPHASIZED

ADULT/YOUTH

Adult Topic: Leadership Requires Resources
Youth Topic: Follow the Leader
Adult/Youth Key Verse: Joshua 3:7
Print Passage: Joshua 3:1-13

—Joshua displayed faith by announcing ahead of time what would happen when the priests stepped into the Jordan River.

—When Joshua approached the Jordan River believing that the waters would part, his faith was based not only on God's direct statements to him but also on previous experience (i.e., the parting of the Red Sea).

—Joshua received specific instructions, which helped him to successfully keep his commitment.

—In this story of the crossing of the Jordan, the main role is played by the priests bearing the ark of the covenant containing the Law of Moses (Ten Commandments) and the symbol of the presence of God.

—God in this passage is a living God, not an idea created in the human mind or a principle or force in the world, like gravity.

—God's words and acts represented in the passage serve to validate Joshua's leadership and role in the history of Israel.

CHILDREN
Children Topic: **Following a Committed Leader**
Key Verse: **Joshua 3:7**

Print Passage: **Joshua 3:1-13**
—Joshua was committed to following God's leadership.
—The Hebrew people obeyed God's Word given to Joshua.
—God prepared the people to cross the Jordan and enter into the Promised Land.

I. INTRODUCTION

A. Leadership Requires Resources

Is it wise to make commitments when you are unsure of your level of resources to honor them? Where do such resources originate from? These are critical questions to consider when making commitments that specifically impact only a few people. The questions become even more crucial when leaders, particularly church and religious leaders, make commitments without clear and present resources. Joshua's commitment to leading God's people brought him to the point of receiving God's power as the resource to meet this commitment. This week's lesson will point us toward a deeper understanding of ways to respond to the aforementioned questions. Joshua's relationship with Moses was significant to his having the ability to respond to these questions with finesse and poise that belied his experience. This, we will see, is an internal resource that came as a result of his interaction with experienced and committed leadership. Joshua maintained his ability to connect with the people as he faithfully relied on God's ability to always exceed His ability.

B. Biblical Background

The book of Joshua is a part of a group of books in the Old Testament identified as the historical books. While these texts—Joshua, Judges, 1 and 2 Samuel, 1 and 2 Kings, 1 and 2 Chronicles, Ezra, and Nehemiah—are not literally a concrete historical timeline of events, they do capture some of the signature moments of the times they claim to represent. Scholars do not agree on all chronologically historical aspects of these books, but do agree that these texts craft a historical narrative of the experiences, beliefs, and practices of a particular people—the people of Israel.

This passage in the book of Joshua describes the Israelites' movement into Canaan, with major parallels to their exodus from Egypt. The movement of the Ark of the Covenant before them reminded the people of God's presence and protection as they prepared to cross the Jordan. Similar to the crossing of the Red Sea, God cleared the way by the entry of the priests into the water. Many scholars suggest that this is not an exact historical account of events for the Israelites, but an attempt to capture the idealized version of their entry into the Promised Land and their covenant relationship with God. As in the prior lesson, this passage indicates the Israelites' use of much violence against other people. This is not to be ignored, but should be considered part of the Israelites' understanding of God in their conquering efforts and their faithful relationship with God.

II. EXPOSITION AND APPLICATION OF THE SCRIPTURE

A. Joshua Instructs the People
(Joshua 3:1-4)

AND JOSHUA rose early in the morning; and they removed from Shittim, and came to Jordan, he and all the children of Israel, and lodged there before they passed over. And it came to pass after three days, that the officers went through the host; And they commanded the people, saying, When ye see the ark of the covenant of the LORD your God, and the priests the Levites bearing it, then ye shall remove from your place, and go after it. Yet there shall be a space between you and it, about two thousand cubits by measure: come not near unto it, that ye may know the way by which ye must go: for ye have not passed this way heretofore.

Joshua's work as a leader began early. Before he was ever identified as leader, he *acted* as leader. Many who would be great leaders are waiting on a sanction, a directive, or some other movement to propel them toward their greatness. What if the great leaders of our times waited on political, social, or even economic sanctioning to situate themselves as leaders? Collectively, our lives would be sorely deprived of the rich legacies they leave behind. Joshua's early action of "acting" as a leader without the people's "sanction" that he was their leader was critical to his success. He and the people of Israel left their location and moved forward toward the Promised Land. The leading officers notified the people that upon sight of the Ark of the Covenant, held up by the priests, they should immediately follow. They were told to leave a critical distance between themselves and the ark, for an important reason.

It was believed that, other than the priests, anyone who came close to the ark and touched it would surely die. The ark represented the power and presence of God, a power and presence too great for the common individual to access without the intermediary connection of the priest. Further, they were directed to stay far enough behind so they could continue to see and follow the ark. "Yet there shall be a space between you and it, ... come not near unto it, that ye may know the way by which ye must go: for ye have not passed this way heretofore" (verse 4). They needed to be able to see God giving direction because they were going somewhere they had never been before. This was not a time for them to get ahead of themselves, thinking that they knew the way. This is instructive for us, as we consider what it is to be committed to God through being followers and leaders, knowing that leadership requires resources—and of noteworthy importance, the resource of good direction.

In his leadership, Joshua spoke following the officers, first to the people and then to the priests. This leadership model was directly opposite to the way many leaders operate in our current religio-socio-political context. Many leaders now speak first to the leadership and as a secondary move to the general populace, or body of followers. Joshua's leadership style effectively modeled leadership for the people. Modern leaders who aim to follow and utilize some of the best human resources God has available are wise to emulate this leadership style. Joshua, as a leader, allowed the officers to speak first, and then he spoke. He did not need to be "the first to speak and last heard" to make his position known. He was a leader because he knew how to utilize the resources God had given him.

B. The Charge: Sanctify Yourselves (Joshua 3:5-6)

And Joshua said unto the people, Sanctify yourselves: for to morrow the LORD will do wonders among you. And Joshua spake unto the priests, saying, Take up the ark of the covenant, and pass over before the people. And they took up the ark of the covenant, and went before the people.

Joshua told the people to sanctify themselves because the next day God would do wonders among them. This was a tremendous act of commitment in faith for Joshua to speak this unknown "wonder." How did he know that God was going to do wonders among those people the next day? This would have been a fair question for people preparing to stand in front of a flooding river. Joshua's act helps us see that faith is at the core of all commitment. There is no deeper faith act than for an individual identified as a "leader" to put himself or herself "out there" before the masses of people. Suggesting that God will do something among a large body of people poses a serious risk for modern church leaders. Perhaps this is why so many are silent on massive movements of God in the lives of large groups of people. Perhaps this is why so many church leaders support the Western capitalist individualistic ideals in their messages to their congregants. Joshua's act helps us see that this core faith requirement in commitment is a resource that needs to be replenished in the lives of our leaders. Further, those who would be followers of church leaders also require this faith as core to their commitments to God.

It would be this same critical faith that led the people to follow Joshua's directive, knowing that he was faithfully following God. Their sanctification was an important part of purifying themselves before coming into the presence of God. As a people about to follow the ark (symbolic of God's presence), they needed to be ritually consecrated. This was a commonly understood practice among the people of Israel, and has been exhibited in a variety of ways throughout the Bible. Once the people knew what was expected of them, Joshua then spoke to the priestly leadership, instructing them to carry the ark before the people. The priests followed Joshua's directives. It was no little feat that other significant leaders followed Joshua's instructions. This also pointed to the strength of the resources endowed to Joshua. Joshua's commitment to leading God's people was exemplified in his actions, not his title. Further, we can learn from Joshua the significance of using the resources God has given us. Joshua had been an understudy of Moses. This time of preparation was the central key to his understanding of the resources God had provided. Further, this understudy experience with Moses was itself a rich internal resource upon which Joshua was able to rely heavily. This type of solid mentoring or leadership committed to preparing the next generation is also exemplified in later lessons. Ultimately, Joshua learned what he could and was greatly prepared for the leadership role that would come.

C. The Lord Magnifies Joshua (Joshua 3:7-9)

And the LORD said unto Joshua, This day will I begin to magnify thee in the sight of all Israel, that they may know that, as I was with Moses, so I will be with thee. And thou shalt command the priests that bear the ark of the covenant, saying, When ye are come to the brink of the water of Jordan, ye shall stand still in Jordan. And Joshua said unto the children of Israel, Come hither, and hear the words of the LORD your God.

Joshua's commitment to leading God's people was evidenced in his faith-filled actions. Paradoxically, while he was leading the people of Israel toward greater "promise," Joshua was also taking them directly to a place where their progress would be significantly impeded. Many of us might have turned back when Moses died. The rest of us who "hung in there" might have turned back as soon as we realized we were coming upon "uncrossable" waters. The people of Israel, who were on this journey with Joshua, were not the same complaining folks who started out with Moses. They held on to the rich legacy that had gone before. Those accounts of God's greatness and exploits with their ancestors were a rich and abiding resource. We wisely heed the example of those who continued with Joshua. We need not neglect the rich resource of the overcoming stories of our ancestors. These are our "stones of remembrance."

This was a defining moment for Joshua because up until that time the people were following based solely on Joshua's choice to maintain his personal commitment to lead God's people. Now, according to the report he had received from God, God was going to do something that captured the people's attention so they would know that it was God who led them. Joshua led and they followed, based on Joshua's commitment to God to lead God's people. There were no exploits, other than his commitment and then current actions to lead them. More faith was required of Joshua. Joshua was told by God to tell the priests what to do with the Ark of the Covenant. Joshua's best internal resources were his faith in God's ability, a faithful commitment to continue leading, and an ability to follow instructions. Leaders and faithful followers of all varieties

in religious and faith communities do well to heed Joshua's example. Recognize that the best internal resource to be had as a leader or a follower is an unswerving faith in God's ability.

D. Listen and Follow
(Joshua 3:10-13)

And Joshua said, Hereby ye shall know that the living God is among you, and that he will without fail drive out from before you the Canaanites, and the Hittites, and the Hivites, and the Perizzites, and the Girgashites, and the Amorites, and the Jebusites. Behold, the ark of the covenant of the Lord of all the earth passeth over before you into Jordan. Now therefore take you twelve men out of the tribes of Israel, out of every tribe a man. And it shall come to pass, as soon as the soles of the feet of the priests that bear the ark of the LORD, the Lord of all the earth, shall rest in the waters of Jordan, that the waters of Jordan shall be cut off from the waters that come down from above; and they shall stand upon an heap.

It would prove to be people willing to listen and follow Joshua as Joshua followed God that would allow them to cross the Jordan. Joshua followed God's directive and called the people together to share with them that God would move their enemies out of their path and allow the ark to pass before them through the Jordan. Joshua created the space for the people to exercise their abilities in affecting positive changes in their lives.

It is incumbent upon leaders who have a body of faithful followers to exercise due diligence in creating the space, sacred and secular, for the people of God to effect positive changes in their lives. Joshua told the people of Israel to choose a representative from each of the twelve tribes. This encouraged an act of faith on their part, not just that of the leader. A tremendous difference could be made in the lives of church communities if the people chose significant leaders in the church for themselves, or at least made choices in partnership with the pastor. Giving a good group of followers the space to be individual and community agents in their own faith-filled commitments with God is central to the mark of a powerful leader who recognizes the need for resources in the people of God. Joshua concluded by telling the Israelites that when the priests' feet touched the edge of the water, God would stop the water's flow and cause it to rise up on one side. This final statement of faith was as much a historical reminder of where God had brought them from as a people as it was an indicator of why they should continue to move forward.

III. CONCLUDING REFLECTION

Joshua recognized what he had in resources and utilized them. His richest resource was his faith in God's abilities. At a crucial juncture of leadership and as followers, we must rely on our faith in God as our greatest resource. All successful leaders require their own faith in God, as well as a group of faith-filled believers in God's promise and ability. The full awareness that an impediment does not negate the promise is essential to ongoing leadership resourcefulness. Directions are not always forthcoming, and drawing on our best internal faith resource helps us pace ourselves behind God's directions. This allows us to utilize the best of the external human resources God has placed all around us. These internal and external resources, tangible and intangible, are all well-reinforced by our resourceful use of prior experiences of God's greatness and goodness in our lives.

PRAYER

Dear God, in our weakest hour, when resources to fulfill our commitments to You seem scarce, help us to remember that You are our source, and all that You have given us and continue to give us are our resources. Continue to bless us with Your presence and the powerful remembrance of Your greatness and goodness in our lives. In Jesus' name we pray. Amen.

WORD POWER

Sanctify *(qadash [kaw-dash`])*—this means "to consecrate, sanctify, prepare, dedicate, be hallowed, be holy, be separate."

HOME DAILY BIBLE READINGS
(January 12-18, 2009)

Joshua Leads Israel

MONDAY, January 12: "Military Leader" (Exodus 17:8-16)

TUESDAY, January 13: "Optimistic Spy" (Numbers 14:6-10)

WEDNESDAY, January 14: "Moses's Successor" (Numbers 27:12-23)

THURSDAY, January 15: "Moses's Charge to Joshua" (Deuteronomy 31:1-8)

FRIDAY, January 16: "The Spirit of Wisdom" (Deuteronomy 34:1-9)

SATURDAY, January 17: "The Lord Is with You" (Joshua 1:1-9)

SUNDAY, January 18: "Joshua's Leadership Affirmed" (Joshua 3:1-13)

LESSON 8　　　　　　　　　　　　January 25, 2009

SAMSON'S MOTHER PREPARES FOR HIS BIRTH

DEVOTIONAL READING: **Psalm 91**
PRINT PASSAGE: **Judges 13:1-7, 8-13, 24**

BACKGROUND SCRIPTURE: **Judges 13**
KEY VERSE: **Judges 13:5**

Judges 13:1-7, 8-13, 24—KJV

AND THE children of Israel did evil again in the sight of the LORD; and the LORD delivered them into the hand of the Philistines forty years.

2 And there was a certain man of Zorah, of the family of the Danites, whose name was Manoah; and his wife was barren, and bare not.

3 And the angel of the LORD appeared unto the woman, and said unto her, Behold now, thou art barren, and bearest not: but thou shalt conceive, and bear a son.

4 Now therefore beware, I pray thee, and drink not wine nor strong drink, and eat not any unclean thing:

5 For, lo, thou shalt conceive, and bear a son; and no razor shall come on his head: for the child shall be a Nazarite unto God from the womb: and he shall begin to deliver Israel out of the hand of the Philistines.

6 Then the woman came and told her husband, saying, A man of God came unto me, and his countenance was like the countenance of an angel of God, very terrible: but I asked him not whence he was, neither told he me his name:

7 But he said unto me, Behold, thou shalt conceive, and bear a son.

.....

8 Then Manoah intreated the LORD, and said, O my Lord, let the man of God which thou didst send come again unto us, and teach us what we shall do unto the child that shall be born.

9 And God hearkened to the voice of Manoah; and the angel of God came again unto the woman as she sat in the field: but Manoah her husband was not with her.

10 And the woman made haste, and ran, and shewed her husband, and said unto him, Behold, the man hath appeared unto me, that came unto me the other day.

Judges 13:1-7, 8-13, 24—NRSV

THE ISRAELITES again did what was evil in the sight of the LORD, and the LORD gave them into the hand of the Philistines forty years.

2 There was a certain man of Zorah, of the tribe of the Danites, whose name was Manoah. His wife was barren, having borne no children.

3 And the angel of the LORD appeared to the woman and said to her, "Although you are barren, having borne no children, you shall conceive and bear a son.

4 Now be careful not to drink wine or strong drink, or to eat anything unclean,

5 for you shall conceive and bear a son. No razor is to come on his head, for the boy shall be a nazirite to God from birth. It is he who shall begin to deliver Israel from the hand of the Philistines."

6 Then the woman came and told her husband, "A man of God came to me, and his appearance was like that of an angel of God, most awe-inspiring; I did not ask him where he came from, and he did not tell me his name;

7 but he said to me, 'You shall conceive and bear a son.' "

.....

8 Then Manoah entreated the LORD, and said, "O, LORD, I pray, let the man of God whom you sent come to us again and teach us what we are to do concerning the boy who will be born."

9 God listened to Manoah, and the angel of God came again to the woman as she sat in the field; but her husband Manoah was not with her.

10 So the woman ran quickly and told her husband, "The man who came to me the other day has appeared to me."

UNIFYING LESSON PRINCIPLE

Promise and commitment may arise out of great disappointment. How are people challenged to make new commitments? God sent an angel to prepare Samson's mother for his coming birth.

11 And Manoah arose, and went after his wife, and came to the man, and said unto him, Art thou the man that spakest unto the woman? And he said, I am.
12 And Manoah said, Now let thy words come to pass. How shall we order the child, and how shall we do unto him?
13 And the angel of the Lord said unto Manoah, Of all that I said unto the woman let her beware.

.....

24 And the woman bare a son, and called his name Samson: and the child grew, and the Lord blessed him.

11 Manoah got up and followed his wife, and came to the man and said to him, "Are you the man who spoke to this woman?" And he said, "I am."
12 Then Manoah said, "Now when your words come true, what is to be the boy's rule of life; what is he to do?"
13 The angel of the Lord said to Manoah, "Let the woman give heed to all that I said to her."

.....

24 The woman bore a son, and named him Samson. The boy grew, and the Lord blessed him.

TOPICAL OUTLINE OF THE LESSON

I. **Introduction**
   A. Preparing for Commitment
   B. Biblical Background

II. **Exposition and Application of the Scripture**
   A. Manoah's Wife's Encounter With the Angel (Judges 13:1-7)
   B. Manoah's Prayer Answered (Judges 13:8-10)
   C. The Verbal Exchange (Judges 13:11-13, 24)

III. **Concluding Reflection**

LESSON OBJECTIVES

Upon completion of this lesson, the students are expected to:

1. Examine the circumstances surrounding Samson's birth;
2. Learn to sense God's promise amid disappointments; and,

3. Discuss ways to accept new challenges and to act on them.

POINTS TO BE EMPHASIZED

ADULT/YOUTH

Adult Topic: Preparing for Commitment
Youth Topic: Long Hair Is a Good Thing
Adult/Youth Key Verse: Judges 13:5
Print Passage: Judges 13:1-7, 8-13, 24

—A heavenly being foretold Samson's birth to his parents. Samson shared this distinction with Isaac, John the Baptist, and Jesus.
—To end Israel's punishment, God sought a commitment from Samson's mother. She would have to live in a prescribed manner in order to fulfill her commitment to God.
—Samson's mother would have to help Samson prepare for his commitment.
—Samson's parents questioned the angel in order to know how to fulfill the commitment.
—The nazirite vow, recorded in Numbers 6:1-21, required one to drink no wine, never cut the hair, and abstain from any contact with the dead.

—The vow was intended to be for a limited time (illustrated in Acts 21:20-26), but for Samson it was to be a lifetime commitment.

CHILDREN
Children Topic: Committed Before Birth
Key Verse: Judges 13:5
Print Passage: Judges 13:2-7, 8-13, 24

—Manoah and his wife had no children.
—God promised that Manoah's wife would bear a son.
—Manoah and his wife made particular preparations for the boy's birth.
—Their son, Samson, would lead God's people toward freedom.
—Samson would be a nazirite.

I. INTRODUCTION
A. Preparing for Commitment
Parenting responsibilities are but one of many areas in our lives that we strive to prepare for in our commitments to certain desired outcomes. We prepare for commitments to marriage, being healthy, and obtaining wealth and college degrees. No one attends a major university without some preparatory entrance or placement examination. Most mothers have some level of preparation for the experience of parenting, even if it means engaging in conversation with another mother or a midwife. Any of the significant and deeply held commitments in our lives will require some necessary preparation on the part of the individual, and will from time to time require the individual to help prepare someone else for future commitment. The mother of Samson, had this type of preparatory experience. She prepared not only for her commitment to conceive and bear this son, but also to help rear him according to the promise set forth in the announcement that he would be born. A singular, individual commitment can be taxing, but the unbelievable in our lives often requires of us an unbelievable commitment.

B. Biblical Background
Samson's mother's experience bears striking similarity to announcements of other birth experiences by the angel of the Lord—specifically the births of Isaac, John the Baptist, and Jesus. Manoah's wife's account, as Samson's mother, is described in the book of Judges, a text that combines the stories of different tribes and clans of Israel. Their movement away from the powerful leadership of Moses and Joshua brought new ideas to the people of Israel. They worshiped other gods, provoking God's anger. They went through a continuous period of disobedience toward God, during which God removed their power to withstand their enemies. They were repeatedly defeated as they "did evil again in the sight of the LORD" (Judges 13:1). It was out of these circumstances that "judges," literally military leadership for local tribes, were raised up to lead the people. God expressed pity for the people because of their constant whining and groaning. Yet, after experiencing relief, the Israelites

consistently returned to doing what was considered evil in the sight of God. This ultimately led to God delivering them into the hands of the Philistines.

The Philistines were a people who entered Canaan shortly after the people of Israel. These and other groups were permitted to war against the Israelites, testing the resolve of the generations of Israelites who had no experience of war, to see if they would then obey God's commandments (see Judges 3). But the Israelites continued to disobey God. The lesson text opens at one such juncture.

II. EXPOSITION AND APPLICATION OF THE SCRIPTURE

A. Manoah's Wife's Encounter With the Angel (Judges 13:1-7)

AND THE children of Israel did evil again in the sight of the Lord; and the Lord delivered them into the hand of the Philistines forty years. And there was a certain man of Zorah, of the family of the Danites, whose name was Manoah; and his wife was barren, and bare not. And the angel of the Lord appeared unto the woman, and said unto her, Behold now, thou art barren, and bearest not: but thou shalt conceive, and bear a son. Now therefore beware, I pray thee, and drink not wine nor strong drink, and eat not any unclean thing: For, lo, thou shalt conceive, and bear a son; and no razor shall come on his head: for the child shall be a Nazarite unto God from the womb: and he shall begin to deliver Israel out of the hand of the Philistines. Then the woman came and told her husband, saying, A man of God came unto me, and his countenance was like the countenance of an angel of God, very terrible: but I asked him not whence he was, neither told he me his name: But he said unto me, Behold, thou shalt conceive, and bear a son.

God became weary of the Israelites' failure to obey and made them subject to Philistine rule for forty years. During this period, the wife of Manoah did not have any children; thus, she was considered barren. This emphasis on barrenness is a common theme among women in the Bible, as it was a way, used in that culture, to value women. Manoah's wife was subject to this same scrutiny and associated "valuelessness." Social forces often govern valuations of individuals in society, but we are reminded by Manoah's wife and many other extremely valuable women in the biblical texts that God is indeed the final arbiter of all individual value and does not solely ascribe value to women based on their association with men or their ability to bear children. It is from this perspective that we are introduced to Manoah's wife's experience with the angel of the Lord.

The angel of the Lord directly approached Manoah's wife. This direct point of contact with her illuminates for the reader God's intent to deal specifically with her as a woman. There was no intermediary male, as this was not necessary for God to communicate with her. The angel of the Lord reminded Manoah's wife of her barrenness, and told her that she would nonetheless conceive and have a son. The birthing of male children, specifically, was significant as it indicated a continuation of the heritage of the father. The angel of the Lord gave her instructions according to the tradition of preparation for Nazirites. Nazirites were men who had been set aside for God's purpose by admission of a personal vow to God or the vow of a parent. The latter was the case for Samson. Manoah's wife's commitment to God to live conservatively according to her religious faith was transferred to her son. The regulations for being a Nazirite included not drinking wine or "strong drink," not cutting one's hair, and not coming into contact with dead bodies. Manoah's wife's commitment required that she follow these preparatory regulations, which would later be conveyed to her son.

After being approached with this news, she went to Manoah and shared her experience. She told her husband that the man of God who came to her had an awe-inspiring appearance like an angel of God. She expressed that while she did not ask the angel where he was from and he did not tell her his name, he did tell her that she would conceive and have a child. Manoah's wife's first degree of commitment was one of suspending disbelief. It is a challenge to the faith of many Christians to suspend their disbelief on simple day-to-day matters. The possibility that God could hold them up in traffic and thus cause them to avoid a deadly accident further ahead on the highway is unbelievable to some people. It is a stretch for many to believe that God influences the behavior of people in positions of power. As was told of others in the biblical text, Manoah's wife also received an "unbelievable" visitation foretelling the announcement of a birth she did not, prior to that moment, believe she could experience. The angel of the Lord foretold the birth of her son, Samson.

B. Manoah's Prayer Answered
(Judges 13:8-10)

Then Manoah intreated the LORD, and said, O my Lord, let the man of God which thou didst send come again unto us, and teach us what we shall do unto the child that shall be born. And God hearkened to the voice of Manoah; and the angel of God came again unto the woman as she sat in the field: but Manoah her husband was not with her. And the woman made haste, and ran, and shewed her husband, and said unto him, Behold, the man hath appeared unto me, that came unto me the other day.

Manoah's response to his wife's account seems a spiritually significant request. He implored God to bring back the man of God to them, so that they could learn what they needed to do to rear the child. This account says that God listened to Manoah's request and sent the angel of God directly to his wife again, while she sat in the field without her husband. On a good day, another male's second appearance to his wife might unnerve even the most secure man. It has been suggested by lay persons, clergy, and religious scholars that this type of experience may affect men's response to being actively drawn to the church. Often a man's wife speaks of the (usually) male pastor in awe-inspiring and glowing terms, just as Manoah's wife did about this visiting "angel of the Lord." She described the angel's countenance as "very terrible." Note that *terrible* in this context is not bad. Terrible in this context is more akin to a statement like, "He was awesome…I couldn't take my eyes off him."

Why God chose to send the man of God directly back to Manoah's wife in the absence of her husband is unknown to readers of this text. Yet, this is clearly what transpired, in spite of Manoah's direct request that God send the angel of the Lord back to them. However, her commitment to the process led her to hurriedly go and tell her husband that the man of God who had shown up the day before had returned, albeit only to her. Manoah's response bordered on the humorous, if we allow ourselves to hear it in our modern voices. He followed his wife back into the field and queried this man of God, asking if he was the man that spoke to his wife. The man of God said "I am." Was this an alpha-male ego exchange? Manoah continued the conversation, basically saying to the man of God, "Well, let what you prophesied materialize, then. How are we supposed to rear the child and what are we supposed to do to prepare him?" This line of comments and questioning may sound a little tested to the trained ear. Manoah asked questions that his wife had already answered for him. She had told him that this was the man of God who had previously visited her. She also told him the information the angel of the Lord detailed in their conversation. Nonetheless, the angel of the Lord responded to Manoah, with the instruction that Manoah's wife should follow the rules she had already been given.

C. The Verbal Exchange
(Judges 13:11-13, 24)

And Manoah arose, and went after his wife, and came to the man, and said unto him, Art thou the man that spakest unto the woman? And he said, I am. And Manoah said, Now let thy words come to pass. How shall we order the child, and how shall we do unto him? And the angel of the Lord said unto Manoah, Of all that I said unto the woman let her beware. .... And the woman bare a son, and called his name Samson: and the child grew, and the Lord blessed him.

The verbal exchange between the angel of the Lord and Manoah illustrates that God can and does use anyone to help people understand the weight of their commitments. God is not limited to speaking through designated intermediaries. In our new covenant relationship with God, Christ took care of our "need" for an in-between spokesperson. Our challenge often comes in our unwillingness to receive the instructions for preparation from certain people. Regrettably, in our current era, some men are still challenged to receive the Word of the Lord from a woman. Some women, regrettably, face the same challenge. Churches remain the most segregated institutions on any given Sunday morning in the United States of America. Manoah's wife's exchange with the angel of the Lord and Manoah's subsequent responses illuminate the difficulties we still face as we limit God's voice and guidance to come only through a select group of vessels. It is critical as we commit to all aspects of our Christian experience that we step beyond our limitations and be open to experiencing God's wonders through any channels God chooses.

It remains unclear what Manoah's response was to the angel's final comment to him, but the instruction for preparing Samson was clearly delegated to the mother. However, this likely did not absolve Manoah of his duties as Samson's father. As is the case in current times, women are often the carriers of the spiritual tradition through generations. Historically, the black church is indebted to women in the church for keeping the church alive. While this is historically the case, the black church should not absolve men of their duties and responsibilities for keeping the spiritual traditions of the church and the faith traditions of Christianity alive in both the home and church. Preparation for this commitment, for men and women alike, is sorely lacking and needs strengthening and refining. This requires an untiring commitment to preparation on the part of lay leaders, church leaders, and committed Christians. Manoah's wife exemplified this commitment to preparation.

Nonetheless, as she modeled for us, the commitment to prepare oneself so that one can prepare someone else should govern one's every move and every communication with those most intimately connected with that person. She could not for one moment allow whatever emotional experiences Manoah was having govern her commitment to prepare for the arrival of Samson. Nor could she allow community concerns about how his hair was growing so long—or why he could not eat certain foods—distract her from her commitment to prepare him for his future. These are sterling examples for each of us, as we strive to maintain our preparations for commitment to and within God's service.

III. CONCLUDING REFLECTION

God's promise can and often does emerge in the midst of disappointment, inspiring in us a great commitment. This commitment can manifest as a commitment to preparation for the seemingly unbelievable events that are or will be occurring in our lives. Manoah's wife, in our lesson, modeled for us an unshakable and unbelievable preparation for commitment.

While she encountered the challenges of her times as a "barren" woman, she nonetheless vowed an approach to a way of life that was not popular among her people. In her willingness to vow to this unique way of life, she transferred this way of thinking to her unborn son, Samson. Her encounters with the angel of the Lord were so "unbelievable" that she suspended her disbelief to accept what she was told would occur in her life.

PRAYER

Dear God, we thank You for Your commitment to us. Frequently, we fall short of our commitment to You and Your work in the world, and we are sorry. Help us to be committed even when what we are committing to seems unbelievable. Use us to help prepare somebody else. In Jesus' name we pray. Amen.

WORD POWER

Nazirite *(nazir)*—means "one who is separated." A "Nazirite" usually made a vow voluntarily; however, in the case of Samson (Judges 13:5, 7), his parents dedicated him for life.

HOME DAILY BIBLE READINGS
(January 19-25, 2009)

Samson's Mother Prepares for His Birth

MONDAY, January 19: "Special Vows to the Lord" (Numbers 6:1-8)

TUESDAY, January 20: "Disobeying God" (Judges 2:1-5)

WEDNESDAY, January 21: "A New Generation" (Judges 2:6-10)

THURSDAY, January 22: "Results of Unfaithfulness" (Judges 2:11-17)

FRIDAY, January 23: "Judges Raised Up by God" (Judges 2:18-23)

SATURDAY, January 24: "An Offering to the Lord" (Judges 13:15-23)

SUNDAY, January 25: "The Promise of a Son" (Judges 13:1-13, 24)

LESSON 9 | February 1, 2009

A SHUNAMMITE WOMAN HELPS

DEVOTIONAL READING: **Luke 6:32-36**
PRINT PASSAGE: **2 Kings 4:8-17**

BACKGROUND SCRIPTURE: **2 Kings 4:8-17**
KEY VERSES: **2 Kings 4:9-10**

2 Kings 4:8-17—KJV

8 And it fell on a day, that Elisha passed to Shunem, where was a great woman; and she constrained him to eat bread. And so it was, that as oft as he passed by, he turned in thither to eat bread.

9 And she said unto her husband, Behold now, I perceive that this is an holy man of God, which passeth by us continually.

10 Let us make a little chamber, I pray thee, on the wall; and let us set for him there a bed, and a table, and a stool, and a candlestick: and it shall be, when he cometh to us, that he shall turn in thither.

11 And it fell on a day, that he came thither, and he turned into the chamber, and lay there.

12 And he said to Gehazi his servant, Call this Shunammite. And when he had called her, she stood before him.

13 And he said unto him, Say now unto her, Behold, thou hast been careful for us with all this care; what is to be done for thee? wouldest thou be spoken for to the king, or to the captain of the host? And she answered, I dwell among mine own people.

14 And he said, What then is to be done for her? And Gehazi answered, Verily she hath no child, and her husband is old.

15 And he said, Call her. And when he had called her, she stood in the door.

16 And he said, About this season, according to the time of life, thou shalt embrace a son. And she said, Nay, my lord, thou man of God, do not lie unto thine handmaid.

17 And the woman conceived, and bare a son at that season that Elisha had said unto her, according to the time of life.

2 Kings 4:8-17—NRSV

8 One day Elisha was passing through Shunem, where a wealthy woman lived, who urged him to have a meal. So whenever he passed that way, he would stop there for a meal.

9 She said to her husband, "Look, I am sure that this man who regularly passes our way is a holy man of God.

10 Let us make a small roof chamber with walls, and put there for him a bed, a table, a chair, and a lamp, so that he can stay there whenever he comes to us."

11 One day when he came there, he went up to the chamber and lay down there.

12 He said to his servant Gehazi, "Call the Shunammite woman." When he had called her, she stood before him.

13 He said to him, "Say to her, Since you have taken all this trouble for us, what may be done for you? Would you have a word spoken on your behalf to the king or to the commander of the army?" She answered, "I live among my own people."

14 He said, "What then may be done for her?" Gehazi answered, "Well, she has no son, and her husband is old."

15 He said, "Call her." When he had called her, she stood at the door.

16 He said, "At this season, in due time, you shall embrace a son." She replied, "No, my lord, O man of God; do not deceive your servant."

17 The woman conceived and bore a son at that season, in due time, as Elisha had declared to her.

BIBLE FACT

Paul quoted Jesus who said, "It is more blessed to give than to receive" (Acts 20:35). We should take this injunction to heart and practice it in our daily lives. The Shunammite woman gave all she had and, ultimately, she received more than what she gave.

TOPICAL OUTLINE OF THE LESSON

I. **Introduction**
   A. Commitment Without Reward
   B. Biblical Background

II. **Exposition and Application of the Scripture**
   A. The Shunammite Blesses Elisha (2 Kings 4:8-10)
   B. Elisha Blesses the Shunammite Woman (2 Kings 4:11-13)
   C. Unexpected Reward (2 Kings 4:14-17)

III. **Concluding Reflection**

LESSON OBJECTIVES

Upon completion of this lesson, the students are expected to:

1. Recall the relationship between Elisha and the Shunammite woman;
2. Explore the possibility of commitment without apparent benefits; and,
3. Consider making commitments without thought of personal gain.

POINTS TO BE EMPHASIZED

ADULT/YOUTH

Adult Topic: Commitment Without Reward
Youth Topic: No Strings Attached
Adult Key Verses: 2 Kings 4:9-10
Youth Key Verse: 2 Kings 4:16
Print Passage: 2 Kings 4:8-17

—The Shunammite woman was generous.
—Although her commitment to Elisha had accrued no personal benefit, the Shunammite woman increased her commitment.
—The Shunammite woman made a commitment without an end.
—When the Shunammite woman was asked how her commitment could be rewarded, she indicated this was of no interest to her.
—The Shunammite woman was richly rewarded for her commitment.
—The Shunammite woman's expression of hospitality—with no expectation of a return—to one she considered a "man of God" exemplifies true servanthood.

CHILDREN

Children Topic: Committed to Kindness
Key Verse: 2 Kings 4:10
Print Passage: 2 Kings 4:8-17

—A wealthy woman recognized Elisha as a man of God.
—She convinced her husband that they should prepare a roof room for Elisha.
—As a sign of his gratitude, Elisha promised the woman that she would bear a son.
—Elisha's promise was fulfilled as he predicted.

I. INTRODUCTION

A. Commitment Without Reward

The Shunammite woman in the lesson text served Elisha with eagerness, seemingly not expecting a return, but she nonetheless received the reward of a son. This lesson will help us see the significance of giving without expectation of a returned gift. The Shunammite woman prepared and showed herself to be a "giver." She and her husband prepared a place for the prophet to take rest and refuge on his journeys. This significant act was popular during her era and has historically been a common practice among a variety of cultures. The act of hospitality is in itself a tremendous gift that often serves as a poignant reflection and reminder of God's hospitable nature toward us as God's creation. The gift that keeps on giving is a kindness rewarded by a kindness rewarded. The concept of "paying it forward" is a gift in itself, especially when one knows that the gifting continues.

B. Biblical Background

Second Kings is a continuation of 1 Kings, chronicling the kingdom of Israel from the death of David and the ascension of Solomon as reigning king, forward. These books, now separated, were once a whole text. While a strong political theme runs through the books overall, the primary focus is on the leadership and people's failed compliance with God's laws that leads to religious and moral decay. It ultimately led to the dismantling of Israel as a people and as a nation.

Elisha, a follower of Elijah, was a well-known prophet whose activities were passed down through oral tradition and later written down, as he was said not to have recorded his own text. Elisha performed many miracles, both nationally and abroad, for individuals. The text for this lesson is a part of a larger account of Elisha's miracles. It follows Elisha's first prediction of victory for the Israelites over an enemy (the Moabites), as well as some earlier, less spectacular miracles of Elisha. The company of prophets had earlier identified Elisha as having the spirit of Elijah resting on him, after Elijah had been taken up in the whirlwind and Elisha had parted and crossed the Jericho with Elijah's mantle. The company of prophets was a communal group who lived and traveled together. The wife of a deceased member of this company was the woman whose sons were being taken into slavery to cover a debt. Thus, the experience of the Shunammite's easily recognizing Elisha as a man of God was not uncommon.

II. EXPOSITION AND APPLICATION OF THE SCRIPTURE

A. The Shunammite Blesses Elisha
(2 Kings 4:8-10)

And it fell on a day, that Elisha passed to Shunem, where was a great woman; and she constrained him to eat bread. And so it was, that as oft as he passed by, he turned in thither to eat bread. And she said unto her husband, Behold now, I perceive that this is an holy man of God, which passeth by us continually. Let us make a little chamber, I

pray thee, on the wall; and let us set for him there a bed, and a table, and a stool, and a candlestick: and it shall be, when he cometh to us, that he shall turn in thither.

The text begins with a regular occurrence for Elisha—a journey. A city man, Elisha, unlike Elijah who lived in caves, was a frequent "traveler." As a member of the company of prophets, he was socially acclimated and often found himself around people of considerable influence—for example, the king and military leaders. Elisha was a man acquainted with wealth, and along one of his journeys, he encountered a wealthy woman who was also hospitable. Her hospitality was not uncommon for the times and was a reflection also of her wealth. Her graciousness and open-door hospitable nature is an initial glimpse into her life of commitment.

The Shunammite woman stopped Elisha and invited him to eat with her family. They became regular acquaintances, and each time he passed through her town he knew he had a place to eat. She probably told her husband something like this: "Look now, I can tell this is a prophet, who comes through here regularly. We should fix up a spare space and set up a bed, a table, a stool, and a light for him, so the next time he comes we can invite him to rest for the night." Her recognition of Elisha as a prophet would not have been unusual; it might have been easy to identify him, given some of his earlier recognition among people of notoriety and wealth. So the next time he came, he stayed in the new space built for him, at the Shunammite woman's home, and he rested.

It is important to remember that this was no inconvenience for this woman and her family; they were wealthy people. However, it is equally important to recognize that wealth is not a prerequisite for genuine hospitality. Then

as now, some of our most hospitable actions occur when we assume we have little that is tangible to offer the traveler or wayfarer. This tradition of hospitality is governed by giving the best one has to offer to one's guests, whatever that may be. This stellar treatment of the prophet was not accidental. In fact, it appears to lay the foundation for what would be good treatment of prophets. The people then and for centuries to come believed/will believe in honoring prophets, the ones who spoke in the name of the Lord, with the full awareness that they, whether explicitly requesting or expecting it, would quite likely receive a blessing from God via the prophet.

Our best rewards sometimes come when we least expect them. Sometimes our most appreciated rewards are those we do not expect. These ideas are usually associated with doing something without expecting to gain anything in return. However, it belies an equal, yet often hidden association with the unspoken expectation(s). This can be tricky, especially when people have strong feelings about doing well without wanting anything in return. This lesson helps us see that while the Shunammite woman may not have directly desired anything of Elisha, he, as a prophet, knew this unspoken "rule" within his role. He, as prophet and worker of miracles, was supposed to bless her. It was, indeed, simply part of what he did as a prophet.

His function as a prophet who was supposed to bless the Shunammite woman took nothing away from the sincerity of her generosity. As we consider how hospitable and/or generous we are, the expectation, albeit unspoken, that we will receive something in return should not minimize the authenticity of our generosity. The gift of feeling good about giving is often the reward we expect, yet do not name. It is important as we teach others the value or blessedness of giving that we do not lose sight that the "feel good" effects of giving are often their own reward. Further, knowing where our gifts come from and preparing to give out of our giftedness sets the stage for giving in the concept of "paying it forward."

B. Elisha Blesses the Shunammite Woman (2 Kings 4:11-13)

And it fell on a day, that he came thither, and he turned into the chamber, and lay there. And he said to Gehazi his servant, Call this Shunammite. And when he had called her, she stood before him. And he said unto him, Say now unto her, Behold, thou hast been careful for us with all this care; what is to be done for thee? wouldest thou be spoken for to the king, or to the captain of the host? And she answered, I dwell among mine own people.

Elisha recognized the power of the gift he had been given in this woman's hospitality. She had provided him a space to rest and to recuperate from the journeying life of a prophet. He was able to refuel and recharge himself so that he could continue with God's work. It was out of this mindset that Elisha told his servant to call the Shunammite woman. Elisha then told his servant to ask her, since she had taken such good care of them, what she wanted to have done on her behalf. He asked more specifically whether she wanted him to speak to the king or the military commander for her. Elisha spared nothing in his offer to gift this woman since she had spared nothing in her extended gift of respite to him. His questioning, providing her with a choice, was no small matter.

Elisha, through his servant, raised a significant question, because while Elisha was personally performing miracles that kept God at the forefront of the battle between Israel's God and Baal, the mantle he assumed from Elijah also meant that he assumed a greater commitment to the political issues of the nation of Israel. Elisha had access to the political leaders of the day and would not hesitate to use his connections to the benefit of not just himself but, more importantly, to individual people.

Both Elisha and the Shunammite woman illuminate the value of recognizing what we have to give. While material possessions were not among the things that Elisha offered this woman, he offered her what he considered his best. In some ways, the best he could offer a wealthy woman and her family was access to the king's ear. Her best was a place to rest and regroup, in her wealthy, comfortable home. Giving our best is not about matching what someone else can do, but genuinely reaching inside ourselves for the best we can give materially or intangibly, and giving it from a pure heart. The pure heart dynamic is clear on the side of both Elisha and the Shunammite woman. The Shunammite woman's response is testament to this fact.

The Shunammite woman replied to Elisha, "I dwell among mine own people" (verse 13). Basically, she was saying that she did not need any favors from the king. She and her family were just fine. Elisha then asked what he could do for her. Interestingly, the response came not from the woman, but from Elisha's observant servant, Gehazi.

C. Unexpected Reward (2 Kings 4:14-17)

And he said, What then is to be done for her? And Gehazi answered, Verily she hath no child, and her husband is old. And he said, Call her. And when he had called her, she stood in the door. And he said, About this season,

according to the time of life, thou shalt embrace a son. And she said, Nay, my lord, thou man of God, do not lie unto thine handmaid. And the woman conceived, and bare a son at that season that Elisha had said unto her, according to the time of life.

Gehazi answered Elisha, saying that the woman did not have a child, and her husband was old. This theme, as in prior lessons, emphasized the value society placed on women's ability to bear children. Additionally, the incredibility factor lies in the fact that her husband was old, suggesting that he was no longer able to impregnate her.

At some point, the Shunammite woman moved away, and at Elisha's request was called back into the area. When she stood in the doorway, he told her that in due season she would have a son. Her incredulous response indicated an almost humorous tone. In the vernacular, she might have said "Rev., don't fool me now." What was clear was the truth of what was spoken. The Shunammite woman did conceive and bear a son. The reward that she was given was, indeed, unexpected and more specifically, not requested by her. While she may have known the unspoken rule that when one blessed a prophet, the prophet also blessed oneself, it appears she had no expectation of being gifted with a son. Our unsolicited goodness in the lives of others, with no defined expectation of reward, frequently brings unsolicited goodness back into our lives. The prophet Elisha blessed the Shunammite woman with a gift that by some standards outweighed the value of what she gave. This highlights the importance of giving our best. We often do not know how the recipient of our best may value our gift(s).

The Shunammite woman and Elisha's encounters emphasize that giving to any event or person without apparent desire for personal gain or reward is a noble commitment. We are glad to talk about the gifts given by philanthropists and anonymous donors, and they "never even ask for anything in return." These responses generate a positive flow of communication in our inner circles and larger communities. Yet, even this perception by others of the giver as noble and kindhearted is a reward of sorts. We should not be limited in our hospitality, nor should we refrain from acknowledging that we received something from what we gave. Elisha's and the Shunammite woman's commitment was grounded in an understanding by both the cultural and religious significance of their unspoken expectations of reward. They remind us to examine our cultural and religious understandings of being both givers and receivers. We may be reminded of the hymn that goes "The more you give, the more He gives to you; just keep on giving because it is really true, that you cannot beat God giving, no matter how you try."

III. CONCLUDING REFLECTION

We can conclude from this lesson that unexpected and unspoken rewards can be the fruits of commitment. The Shunammite woman offered space that was designed with Elisha in mind for the prophet to come in and rest and become rejuvenated on his journeys. When we read about the Shunammite's hospitality, this opens up a way for us to view notions of giving and receiving, whether or not we expect rewards. The measure of hospitality the Shunammite woman gave was in direct correlation to what she felt was the best she had to offer. We may take away from her hospitality a valuable lesson to give the best one has to offer. Further, we can see that this may not have been a gift Elisha expected to receive from this particular woman. While as a prophet he might have been inclined to believe that, according to custom, someone would want to offer a resting place for a prophet of God, he had no reasonable expectation that it would be the Shunammite woman.

While she did not directly express an expectation for a gift from the prophet, this lesson illuminated for us the reality of un-spoken expected rewards. It was a common phenomenon that those who took care of the prophet were in some way taken care of by the prophet. This we discovered is not a bad thing. Sometimes our greatest reward is simply in the giving. We intuit from the Shunammite woman's response that her ability to give what she gave in the spirit that she gave it in was reward enough for her. This, we are reminded of is a feel-good reward that is valuable in and of itself. Our giving need not be predicated on receiving a reward, but we should be grateful and glad when we receive one.

PRAYER

Lord, we thank You that You are the gift that keeps on giving. We are grateful for the gift of Your presence in our lives daily. May we be mind-ful to pass this gift forward as Your light shining brightly in our lives. Help us to give without ex-pectations and to receive with grateful spirits that are gift-worthy. In Jesus' name we pray. Amen.

WORD POWER

Blessing *(berakah* [OT:1293])—this means "blessing." The root form of this word is found in northwest and southern Semitic languages. It is used in conjunction with the verb *barak* ("to bless") seventy-one times in the Old Testament. The word appears most frequently in Genesis and Deuteronomy.

HOME DAILY BIBLE READINGS
(January 26–February 1, 2009)

A Shunammite Woman Helps
MONDAY, January 26: "The Call of Elisha" (1 Kings 19:15-21)
TUESDAY, January 27: "The Prophet's Mantle" (2 Kings 2:9-15)
WEDNESDAY, January 28: "Elisha's Prayer for a Child" (2 Kings 4:27-37)
THURSDAY, January 29: "The Death of Elisha" (2 Kings 13:14-20)
FRIDAY, January 30: "Jesus Speaks of Elisha" (Luke 4:23-30)
SATURDAY, January 31: "Welcoming a Prophet" (Luke 6:27-36)
SUNDAY, February 1: "Blessed by Blessing" (2 Kings 4:8-17)

LESSON 10

February 8, 2009

NATHAN CHALLENGES DAVID

DEVOTIONAL READING: **Psalm 51:1-9**
PRINT PASSAGE: **2 Samuel 12:1-7, 13-15**

BACKGROUND SCRIPTURE: **2 Samuel 12:1-15**
KEY VERSES: **2 Samuel 11:27; 12:1**

2 Samuel 12:1-7, 13-15—KJV

AND THE LORD sent Nathan unto David. And he came unto him, and said unto him, There were two men in one city; the one rich, and the other poor.

2 The rich man had exceeding many flocks and herds:

3 But the poor man had nothing, save one little ewe lamb, which he had bought and nourished up: and it grew up together with him, and with his children; it did eat of his own meat, and drank of his own cup, and lay in his bosom, and was unto him as a daughter.

4 And there came a traveller unto the rich man, and he spared to take of his own flock and of his own herd, to dress for the wayfaring man that was come unto him; but took the poor man's lamb, and dressed it for the man that was come to him.

5 And David's anger was greatly kindled against the man; and he said to Nathan, As the LORD liveth, the man that hath done this thing shall surely die:

6 And he shall restore the lamb fourfold, because he did this thing, and because he had no pity.

7 And Nathan said to David, Thou art the man.

. . . . .

13 And David said unto Nathan, I have sinned against the LORD. And Nathan said unto David, The LORD also hath put away thy sin; thou shalt not die.

14 Howbeit, because by this deed thou hast given great occasion to the enemies of the LORD to blaspheme, the child also that is born unto thee shall surely die.

15 And Nathan departed unto his house. And the LORD struck the child that Uriah's wife bare unto David, and it was very sick.

2 Samuel 12:1-7, 13-15—NRSV

AND THE LORD sent Nathan to David. He came to him, and said to him, "There were two men in a certain city, the one rich and the other poor.

2 The rich man had very many flocks and herds;

3 but the poor man had nothing but one little ewe lamb, which he had bought. He brought it up, and it grew up with him and with his children; it used to eat of his meager fare, and drink from his cup, and lie in his bosom, and it was like a daughter to him.

4 Now there came a traveler to the rich man, and he was loath to take one of his own flock or herd to prepare for the wayfarer who had come to him, but he took the poor man's lamb, and prepared that for the guest who had come to him."

5 Then David's anger was greatly kindled against the man. He said to Nathan, "As the LORD lives, the man who has done this deserves to die;

6 he shall restore the lamb fourfold, because he did this thing, and because he had no pity."

7 Nathan said to David, "You are the man!"

. . . . .

13 David said to Nathan, "I have sinned against the LORD." Nathan said to David, "Now the LORD has put away your sin; you shall not die.

14 Nevertheless, because by this deed you have utterly scorned the LORD, the child that is born to you shall die."

15 Then Nathan went to his house. The LORD struck the child that Uriah's wife bore to David, and it became very ill.

BIBLE FACT

Commitments in faithfulness to God can lead some to challenge immoral leadership. Nathan's commitment as a prophet of God led him to challenge King David.

Some commitments we make involve people who have no part in agreeing to the decision. How do we consider how our commitments affect everyone involved? Elisha's commitment to God led him to take on the mantle, and Nathan's commitment to God led him to confront King David.

TOPICAL OUTLINE OF THE LESSON

I. Introduction
A. Challenging Leadership
B. Biblical Background

II. Exposition and Application of the Scripture
A. Nathan Confronts David (2 Samuel 12:1-4)
B. David Passes Judgment on Himself (2 Samuel 12:5-7)
C. David's Contrition and the Child's Death (2 Samuel 12:13-15)

III. Concluding Reflection

LESSON OBJECTIVES

Upon completion of this lesson, the students are expected to:

1. Recall Nathan's commitment to God that results in a confrontation with King David;
2. Explore the effects of commitments they have made without the knowledge and agreement of all parties involved; and,
3. Develop commitments with an awareness of their effects on other people.

POINTS TO BE EMPHASIZED

ADULT/YOUTH
Adult Topic: **Challenging Leadership**
Youth Topic: **A Scandal Exposed**
Adult Key Verses: **2 Samuel 11:27; 12:1**
Youth Key Verse: **2 Samuel 12:13**
Print Passage: **2 Samuel 12:1-7, 13-15**

—Nathan's parable was told in response to David's sin (see 2 Samuel 11).
—David's decision in favor of fourfold restitution is based on the law recorded in Exodus 22:1.
—While David's confession brought him forgiveness, the course of events his choices set in motion remained unchanged. This included the death of David and Bathsheba's first child. For more detail on David's confession, see Psalm 51.
—Nathan's commitment involved hard, unpleasant, and dangerous action.
—David as king was also judge and probably deemed the rich man in Nathan's story as a lawbreaker, hence the "fourfold" restitution (see verse 6).
—Nathan's courage to confront David came from his commitment to God.

CHILDREN
Children Topic: **Blessed to Lead**
Key Verse: **2 Kings 2:9**
Print Passage: **2 Kings 2:6-15**

—Elijah prepared to leave Elisha in charge of his work.
—Elisha asked for a double portion of Elijah's spiritual insight.
—When Elijah and Elisha were separated, Elisha accepted the challenge of succeeding him.
—Other prophets acknowledged Elisha as their leader.

I. INTRODUCTION

A. Challenging Leadership

This lesson will help us see the importance of approaching challenges to leadership with godly wisdom and insight. Noteworthy are the sometimes unfortunate outcomes that can result from challenges to leadership, even when godly wisdom is present. The task of challenging leadership is to give deep and serious consideration to one's approach, as well as the possibilities for a variety of outcomes, not just for the challenger and the one being challenged, but for all parties involved. Nathan's challenging King David led to major outcomes that affected the lives of those associated with David. Avoiding this challenge would have been possible with an unwavering commitment from David to honor God's Law. Highlighted in David's experience is the difficulty many leaders have in maintaining high moral standards and behaviors. Understandably, these behaviors result in consequences that are far-reaching for the challengers, as well as innocent bystanders.

B. Biblical Background

The books of 1 and 2 Samuel, like Kings, were one book—before translation—and then were divided into two books. The second book is a part of a larger body of material in the Old Testament identified as the historical books. While not exactly traceable to particular dates, the writings are indicative of specific periods in Israel's history. They more accurately reflect the specific writer's views and understanding of the relatedness between God and the people of Israel, as descended through Abraham. These writings in 2 Samuel are attributed to the prophet Samuel, although he does not appear in 2 Samuel. This book sets the groundwork for identifying David and Jerusalem as models for future leadership and nations. In 2 Samuel is provided a rich detail into the political and personal quandaries that King David experienced during his reign. A unique focus is also placed on the role of prophets. This specific chapter is a focus on Nathan and David's exchange as Nathan rebuked David for his encounter with Uriah's wife, Bathsheba.

Nathan, one of the prophets during David's reign, was a major consultant on all things concerning God's will for the kingdom of David and his future legacy. Prophets were not endangered for addressing kings' immoral behavior in Israel's monarchist times, because Israelite kings had to be subject to God's Law. Nathan, thus, was in a safe position to challenge David on his actions regarding Bathsheba and Uriah. Nathan presented this challenge as a parable, a commonly used literary tool in the Bible (see the many parables told by Jesus in the New Testament).

II. EXPOSITION AND APPLICATION OF THE SCRIPTURE

A. Nathan Confronts David
(2 Samuel 12:1-4)

AND THE LORD sent Nathan unto David. And he came unto him, and said unto him, There were two men in one city; the one rich, and the other poor. The rich man had exceeding many flocks and herds: But the poor man had nothing, save one little ewe lamb, which he had bought and nourished up: and it grew up together with him, and with his children; it did eat of his own meat, and drank of his own cup, and lay in his bosom, and was unto him as a daughter. And there came a traveller unto the rich man, and he spared to take of his own flock and of his own herd, to dress for the wayfaring man that was come unto him; but took the poor man's lamb, and dressed it for the man that was come to him.

One of the best aspects of this passage is that it starts off with good news. God sent Nathan to David. The act of challenging someone should begin with a well-founded aim. More specifically, challenges to God-appointed leadership should be God-inspired. In this case, the prophet of God was sent to challenge the appointed king of God's people. He went to David and shared the parable of the ewe, which stood for David's recent liaison with Uriah's wife, Bathsheba. The allusion to David's harem of women compared to Uriah's one wife, Bathsheba, set the tone for scolding David regarding the obvious imbalance of power and property between the two men. Surely, he mentally questioned why a man with such great wealth as David's would want to take from one like Uriah, who had so little. David, in a position of authority, was not unfamiliar with being consulted on matters of this kind. Kings commonly judged social and economic matters among the people. David became very angry with the person who would commit this kind of act. Without giving further thought to the possible parallels between his recent sexual activity with Bathsheba and murder of her husband Uriah, David spewed forth his punishment for the offender. This early introduction to the risks of challenging leadership helps us see the immediate danger if the challenge is not God-inspired. The wrong person could thereby be subject to harsh punishment.

B. David Passes Judgment on Himself
(2 Samuel 12:5-7)

And David's anger was greatly kindled against the man; and he said to Nathan, As the LORD liveth, the man that hath done this thing shall surely die: And he shall restore the lamb fourfold, because he did this thing, and because he had no pity. And Nathan said to David, Thou art the man.

The punishment that David issued forth included a fourfold restoration, similar to our modern system of restitution for theft—and the offender would surely die because he did this and was pitiless in his actions. David meant for the offender to suffer and then die. He seemed even to have a soft spot in his heart for the person who had been wronged. Nathan knew all along that he was speaking about David, and let him continue expressing the details of an ideal punishment. Nathan's response is critical to our understanding of challenging leadership to which we are not unfriendly. Nathan was not an enemy of David, so his silence in the face of knowing that David was naming his own punishment was quite telling. As the one sent by God to challenge immoral leadership, Nathan's commitment to following through with the challenge was put to the test when he heard David issuing forth this harsh punishment.

Nathan's commitment to God as a prophet allowed him the courage to confront David this way and maintain his silence. Implicit in his stealthy approach was the awareness that David would not shirk his responsibility to ensure that an appropriate punishment was meted out to the offender. Further, Nathan was well-aware that he would not likely encounter harm from David, since he served as one of David's chief prophetic consultants. Most importantly, what we should be reminded of in this type of leadership challenge is that Nathan remembered he was sent by God for this task. Nathan's decision to challenge David was under-girded by his clarity of intent and mission. This is an important distinction to make between rash, ill-intended motivations for confronting any leader.

C. David's Contrition and the Child's Death (2 Samuel 12:13-15)

And David said unto Nathan, I have sinned against the Lord. And Nathan said unto David, The Lord also hath put away thy sin; thou shalt not die. Howbeit, because by this deed thou hast given great occasion to the enemies of the Lord to blaspheme, the child also that is born unto thee shall surely die. And Nathan departed unto his house. And the Lord struck the child that Uriah's wife bare unto David, and it was very sick.

David responded with deep contrition. This would be our hope for any leader of God's people. Yet we know, as recent and ancient history has shown, that many leaders express no contrition. Rather, some leaders are offended that they have been challenged. They are often disturbed that anyone, whether a fellow leader, colleague, or prophet, or anyone else, would think himself or herself "big" enough to confront the leader on her or his behavior. Many situations in church ministries are reflections

of leadership challenges gone bad. People have been ousted from their significant roles in the church because they challenged the pastor.

Unlike many current leaders, David knew and stated with immediacy that his deepest error as a leader was in failing to honor God's Law. As we consider this lesson, let us pray for the moral fortitude of our church and national leaders. We may not be prophets in the traditional sense, but let us remain firm in our convictions and expectations of high moral standards from our leaders. It is difficult for anyone to admit when he or she is "wrong" in his or her actions. It seems all the more difficult for those in positions of leadership associated with God's work in the world. Fortunately for David, it seemed that his ability to recognize his error and name it worked in his favor. More good news emerged beyond the fact that Nathan was indeed sent by God.

Nathan assured David that all was forgiven and he would not die. However, because of the deeds committed by David, those who were not on the Lord's side now had reason to talk badly about the God of the Israeli nation. This is significant for Christian faith communities. The more morally uncertain Christian behavior is promenaded before society through media moguls, the more ammunition non-Christians have to speak against the "so-called" virtues of the Christian life that no one in their eyes seems to be leading.

Nathan bore the burden of informing David that his punishment would be the death of the child that had been born as a result of his union with Bathsheba. When confronting an immoral leader, the leader may absentmindedly name his or her surface punishment, but there may be other consequences that we, as the challengers, are tasked to name. Fortunately for Nathan, as we have already stated, his position and life were secure. He was not in any real danger of losing his life or position. Nonetheless, he did what any wise "challenger" of such harsh consequences would do: after pronouncing this awful news, Nathan left David's house. Sometimes a greater problem than challenging an immoral leader is getting out of the way once the deed has been done. Often, people get in the way of God's business and start their own. The trustee who tells the pastor that his children's scholarship fund has been eliminated, since the pastor has misappropriated large sums of the church's money, may decide to go on a great crusade to "find" the next pastor. Sometimes in the face of challenges to leadership, the next best move "post-challenge" is to remove oneself from the immediacy of the situation. God will do what God is going to do. Hanging around and trying to gain some false notoriety for "straightening someone out" is a grave danger—one to surely be avoided as was exemplified in Nathan's exit from David's house. As was the case for David, Bathsheba, and their offspring, God did exactly what Nathan declared and Bathsheba and David's child became very ill and later died.

David's contrition overall was moving. Yet, it did not preclude him from experiencing the repercussions of his actions. "I'm sorry" from the mouths of leaders and sometimes just from the mouths of their publicists does not stop the repercussions of their immoral actions. Most telling, in David's experience, is that while on the surface it looked like only David's direct self might be impacted—the possibility that he might die—it was in fact the life of the child who was not spared by God. Bathsheba, at this time, would have been powerless to reject

David's demands. Yet, she too bore the consequences of David's actions. How she must have suffered as a mother. It is very important to weigh the potential consequences that an immoral act or one's challenge of such an act may have on someone other than oneself and the immediate person involved.

The focus may often be put on David, because it is clear that as leader he had a responsibility to uphold God's law, but what about Nathan? Should he, along with those who may find themselves in the position to challenge a leader, also be called into question about their responsibility to consider the consequences of their commitment? The text indicates that God sent Nathan. How many of us in our eagerness to aright someone else's wrong behavior fail to see the potential implications for others involved? Eagerly moving forward in our challenge to immoral leadership, we sometimes overstep needed boundaries ultimately failing to protect those who need the greatest protections.

The foundations of our intent and motivations need to be clear and the consequences seriously considered as we act on our commitments to challenge leadership. What about leaders' families? The Christian community has witnessed many scandals about church leaders engaged in immoral behavior who were challenged for their immorality. While leaders should hold themselves to higher standards and consider the implications of their actions, those who feel compelled to challenge leadership should employ similar considerations. Challenges to leadership are not pleasant events. Nathan's commitment to God reminds us of the difficult and dangerous work of challenging leadership.

III. CONCLUDING REFLECTION

We can conclude from this lesson that challenging a leader's immoral behavior should be grounded in a commitment to God first. Most significantly we should rely on God for our guidance in a leadership challenge. There are significant and immediate risks to an uninspired challenge to leadership. The risks are not only to the relationship, if it is a positive one, but possibly a risk to the life or position of the one presenting the challenge. Nathan's approach was—above all—civil, using a common literary tool in biblical texts: the parable. In David's immediate recognition of the disparity of power and property in the parable, we can glean another significant aspect of challenging immoral leadership—these leaders often mete out their own punishment.

Commitment to truth and the expectation of moral conduct by leaders is often complex and costly to individuals and the larger community. Those who would challenge a leader given to immoral behaviors should consider these costly consequences to the unsuspecting and/or uninvolved "innocent" bystanders. Challenges to leadership are risky and potentially costly to immediately involved and indirectly involved parties. Nathan's commitment to God led him into direct confrontation with the major leader of his day. Commitments to God can include the risky challenging of leadership.

PRAYER

Lord, our world is fraught with the tension of responding to poor Christian leadership. Yet, You are sovereign. Help us to glean wisdom and insight from the critical issues that surround us. Guide us into appropriate actions that challenge the improper behaviors of our leaders. May we forever remain in Your perfect peace. In Jesus' name we pray. Amen.

WORD POWER

Sinned *(Chata`[khaw-taw])* this means "to sin, miss the way or the mark, go wrong, incur guilt, forfeit." When David sinned, he confessed it before the Lord. He was forgiven, and he wrote Psalm 51 to commemorate his experience.

HOME DAILY BIBLE READINGS
(February 2-8, 2009)

Nathan Challenges David

MONDAY, February 2: "Lust and Adultery" (2 Samuel 11:1-5)

TUESDAY, February 3: "An Unsuccessful Cover-up" (2 Samuel 11:6-13)

WEDNESDAY, February 4: "Contrived Murder" (2 Samuel 11:14-21)

THURSDAY, February 5: "An Easy Conscience" (2 Samuel 11:22-27)

FRIDAY, February 6: "A Cry for Forgiveness" (Psalm 51:1-9)

SATURDAY, February 7: "A Broken and Contrite Heart" (Psalm 51:10-19)

SUNDAY, February 8: "You Are the Man!" (2 Samuel 12:1-7, 13-15)

LESSON 11

February 15, 2009

ESTHER RISKS HER LIFE

DEVOTIONAL READING: **Philippians 1:20-30**
PRINT PASSAGE: **Esther 4:1-3, 9-17**

BACKGROUND SCRIPTURE: **Esther 4–5**
KEY VERSE: **Esther 4:16**

Esther 4:1-3, 9-17—KJV

WHEN MORDECAI perceived all that was done, Mordecai rent his clothes, and put on sackcloth with ashes, and went out into the midst of the city, and cried with a loud and a bitter cry;

2 And came even before the king's gate: for none might enter into the king's gate clothed with sackcloth.

3 And in every province, whithersoever the king's commandment and his decree came, there was great mourning among the Jews, and fasting, and weeping, and wailing; and many lay in sackcloth and ashes.

.....

9 And Hatach came and told Esther the words of Mordecai.

10 Again Esther spake unto Hatach, and gave him commandment unto Mordecai;

11 All the king's servants, and the people of the king's provinces, do know, that whosoever, whether man or woman, shall come unto the king into the inner court, who is not called, there is one law of his to put him to death, except such to whom the king shall hold out the golden sceptre, that he may live: but I have not been called to come in unto the king these thirty days.

12 And they told to Mordecai Esther's words.

13 Then Mordecai commanded to answer Esther, Think not with thyself that thou shalt escape in the king's house, more than all the Jews.

14 For if thou altogether holdest thy peace at this time, then shall there enlargement and deliverance arise to the Jews from another place; but thou and thy father's house shall be destroyed: and who knoweth whether thou art come to the kingdom for such a time as this?

15 Then Esther bade them return Mordecai this answer,

Esther 4:1-3, 9-17—NRSV

WHEN MORDECAI learned all that had been done, Mordecai tore his clothes and put on sackcloth and ashes, and went through the city, wailing with a loud and bitter cry;

2 he went up to the entrance of the king's gate, for no one might enter the king's gate clothed with sackcloth.

3 In every province, wherever the king's command and his decree came, there was great mourning among the Jews, with fasting and weeping and lamenting, and most of them lay in sackcloth and ashes.

.....

9 Hathach went and told Esther what Mordecai had said.

10 Then Esther spoke to Hathach and gave him a message for Mordecai, saying,

11 "All the king's servants and the people of the king's provinces know that if any man or woman goes to the king inside the inner court without being called, there is but one law—all alike are to be put to death. Only if the king holds out the golden scepter to someone, may that person live. I myself have not been called to come in to the king for thirty days."

12 When they told Mordecai what Esther had said,

13 Mordecai told them to reply to Esther, "Do not think that in the king's palace you will escape any more than all the other Jews.

14 For if you keep silence at such a time as this, relief and deliverance will rise for the Jews from another quarter, but you and your father's family will perish. Who knows? Perhaps you have come to royal dignity for just such a time as this."

15 Then Esther said in reply to Mordecai,

16 Go, gather together all the Jews that are present in Shushan, and fast ye for me, and neither eat nor drink three days, night or day: I also and my maidens will fast likewise; and so will I go in unto the king, which is not according to the law: and if I perish, I perish.
17 So Mordecai went his way, and did according to all that Esther had commanded him.

16 "Go, gather all the Jews to be found in Susa, and hold a fast on my behalf, and neither eat nor drink for three days, night or day. I and my maids will also fast as you do. After that I will go to the king, though it is against the law; and if I perish, I perish."
17 Mordecai then went away and did everything as Esther had ordered him.

TOPICAL OUTLINE OF THE LESSON

I. **Introduction**
   A. Risky Business
   B. Biblical Background

II. **Exposition and Application of the Scripture**
   A. Mordecai's Lament (Esther 4:1-3)
   B. Esther's Uncommon Courage (Esther 4:9-14)
   C. Esther's Decision (Esther 4:15-17)

III. **Concluding Reflection**

LESSON OBJECTIVES

Upon completion of this lesson, the students are expected to:

1. Explore passages in the book of Esther to identify its messages of commitment, including that of Mordecai;

2. Consider the implications of making commitments without respect to potential personal harm; and,

3. Discuss commitments they have made in spite of personal risk.

POINTS TO BE EMPHASIZED
ADULT/YOUTH

Adult Topic: Risky Commitments
Youth Topic: Risky Business
Adult/Youth Key Verse: Esther 4:16
Print Passage: Esther 4:1-3, 9-17

—Going to the king involved the risk of death for Esther, but keeping silent meant certain death for all Jews, including Esther and her family.

—Fasting was usually accompanied by prayer. Esther recognized the need for spiritual support as she faced her fears.

—Esther was willing to break the law and risk her life for this worthy cause.

—God may have made Esther queen for the purpose of saving the Jews.

—Mordecai's response (verses 13-14) to Esther's thought of personal safety (verses 10-11) suggested that if she kept silent, death would come to all Jews, including her and her family.

—In verse 16, Esther's statement of acceptance of death to save her people, if necessary, shows devotion similar to that of Jesus Christ.

CHILDREN

Children Topic: **Dare to Act**

Key Verse: **Esther 4:16**

Print Passage: **Esther 4:1-2, 9-11, 13, 14-16; 5:1-2**

—Mordecai contacted Queen Esther because all Jews were under a sentence of death.

—Esther feared doing what Mordecai asked because royal law limited her contact with the king.

—Mordecai challenged Esther to save her people and herself.

—Esther fasted and asked others to do the same as she prepared to approach the king.

—When she entered the king's presence, he welcomed her.

I. INTRODUCTION

A. Risky Business

In this week's lesson from the book of Esther we are shown that as a result of various factors that led to the possible demise of an entire race of people, Esther risked her life in an unmatched commitment to her people. Her cunning and prayerful approach won the day for herself and her people. This lesson will help us further examine the risky nature of commitment to God, God's people, and/or God's purpose. While we may not live our days in the swanky luxury of a palace with a ruling leader, it may very well be the case that we find ourselves in some otherwise potentially powerful positions to make a difference for the cause of God. Esther's story will illuminate some possibilities for approaches to making risky yet faith-filled commitments.

B. Biblical Background

The book of Esther is not considered among Bible scholars as a historical text. It is more frequently characterized as creative fiction justifying the Jewish celebration of Purim (the deliverance of Jews from an organized massacre). Some scholars focus on ideas such as the multiple mentioning of the Persian king without even a cursory mention of either God or any of the important Jewish religious practices to validate their claims that this book is not a religiously significant text. However, the implicit message of God's providential action throughout the story is, for others, evidence of its religious importance. More explicit for others in support of this account as a text of religious significance, whether historical or not, is Esther's request of a particular Jewish practice of fasting prior to her presence before the king.

The lead character or protagonist in this biblical account of deliverance is a woman named Esther—also the queen of King Ahasuerus. While women are recognized in the Bible for their wisdom and insightful actions in bearing children, they are usually behind the scenes or in supporting roles with men. Esther's activity is rare because she was in a public-speaking and decision-making role. Vashti, the former queen, while also central to the overall text, was relegated to the more common role women encountered in the biblical text—that of having someone re-tell their experience for them or being refused a voice in any format. Mordecai in this text plays a critically supportive role to his niece Esther. What is clear throughout this short biblical text is that this is not King Ahasuerus's or Mordecai's story—this is Esther's scroll.

II. EXPOSITION AND APPLICATION OF THE SCRIPTURE

A. Mordecai's Lament
(Esther 4:1-3)

WHEN MORDECAI perceived all that was done, Mordecai rent his clothes, and put on sackcloth with ashes, and went out into the midst of the city, and cried with a loud and a bitter cry; And came even before the king's gate: for none might enter into the king's gate clothed with sackcloth. And in every province, whithersoever the king's commandment and his decree came, there was great mourning among the Jews, and fasting, and weeping, and wailing; and many lay in sackcloth and ashes.

In the opening of our lesson passage, Mordecai became aware that the king had issued an edict to massacre all Jews. This led to tremendous grief and mourning among all Jews who knew of it. Mordecai, Esther's uncle, was deeply affected, as were all the Jews who received the news. Lying in sackcloth and ashes was a tradition that identified the depths of a person's grief experience connected to his or her religious commitments. Mordecai's response, however, was more indicative of public protest. He was said to be going out into the streets, even to the extent of going in front of the king's gate expressing his grief with loud cries. Basically, Mordecai was causing a scene, trying to get attention to cause the king to change his mind, but to no avail.

Bad news elicits sad and disheartening responses on many levels. The news of impending death of one person can bring on unmitigated sadness. Imagine being told that all the people in your national, ethnic, or racial background are going to be killed. The imagination does not have to wander too far. A glimpse into the backyards of some of our national neighbors can bring us to this startling reality of so many people. Consider the mass graves in Iraq, Darfur, and Rwanda. Remember Hitler's massive Holocaust and consider the African people's horrific enslavement and slaughter in North America. The deep pain invoked by the thoughts of these cruel actions should illustrate for us the deeply felt emotions of the Jews of Esther's time. These sadly grab our attention, hold us hostage to feelings of hurt, and move us to want to think "happier" thoughts. However, there was no movement to any happier thoughts for Mordecai or any of the Jews of Esther's time. They needed real relief.

The king had issued this edict for the death of all Jews, at Haman's request—further evidence of the king's inability to make sound decisions. Haman, who was offended by Mordecai's refusal to honor or bow to him, decided the best thing to do was to eradicate the Jews. It is from these men's encounter and experience of each other, however, that Esther became the deliverer of the people of Israel.

Our first glimpse into Esther's dilemma is in the midst of Haman and Mordecai's experience. She had already become queen and was in a dynamic position to help her people. In our desire to commit to God's purpose, sometimes our commitment may come at great risk in the middle of someone else's problems. However, our purpose should not be swayed by someone else's mayhem. Esther's function was clearly as a queen. Regardless the encounter of Haman and Mordecai, she remained true to her purpose, not only as a Jewish woman, but also as the queen of Ahasuerus's empire. As is evidenced in the lives of many current political figures, spouses have strong influence on social, economic, and political outcomes. What affected the Jews affected the entire empire, and Esther knew that and accordingly responded. Her wisdom is critical to our understanding of making risky commitments; it starts with knowing one's sphere of influence.

B. Esther's Uncommon Courage (Esther 4:9-14)

And Hatach came and told Esther the words of Mordecai. Again Esther spake unto Hatach, and gave him commandment unto Mordecai; All the king's servants, and the people of the king's provinces, do know, that whosoever, whether man or woman, shall come unto the king into the inner court, who is not called, there is one law of his to put him to death, except such to whom the king shall hold out the golden sceptre, that he may live: but I have not been called to come in unto the king these thirty days. And they told to Mordecai Esther's words. Then Mordecai commanded to answer Esther, Think not with thyself that thou shalt escape in the king's house, more than all the Jews. For if thou altogether holdest thy peace at this time, then shall there enlargement and deliverance arise to the Jews from another place; but thou and thy father's house shall be destroyed: and who knoweth whether thou art come to the kingdom for such a time as this?

Esther utilized her political position to send and gather information. She requested a eunuch to discover what was transpiring with Mordecai that would cause him such grief and to refuse her offer of clothing. It was unnecessary for her to leave her post. Often we are inclined to hop off of our royal seats to "straighten out" the peasant who "got out of line." This figurative expression is used to exemplify the importance of holding one's post and not getting overly, emotionally caught up in difficult situations. Our commitments to God may not only indirectly/directly impact us, but can and often do put us directly in the center of someone else's conflict. It is in these moments that we do wisely to consider the risk of being overly emotional about the exchanges that may arise, and use our resources to the advantage of fulfilling God's purpose.

Hatach (the eunuch) and Mordecai's exchange detailed the events that took place between Mordecai and Haman, the amount of money Haman agreed to pay the king for the destruction of the Jews, as well as a copy of the edict for the Jews' destruction. Mordecai desired Hatach to deliver this news and the copy of the edict to Esther so she could go to the king and make a request of him to spare the lives of her people.

It remains uncertain whether Mordecai felt guilty because his actions inspired this horrific response from Haman. However, Mordecai did, for whatever reason, feel some sense of responsibility to do whatever he could at this point to improve the situation for the Jews. His best recourse was to gather all requisite information and documents to present to Esther to enlist her critical support. Mordecai's expressed commitment shows the importance of avoiding egotistical responses to critical issues.

Esther was made aware of the issues her people faced. She, in turn, made Mordecai aware of the risk she would face attempting to honor his request. It was no secret to anyone that what Mordecai was requesting could have meant her immediate demise. The king had not requested Esther's presence for thirty days.

The rule was that the queen was not allowed to come before the king unless he summoned her. This explicitly meant that unless she was summoned, even though she was queen, she was not to present herself before him. Scholars note that for security reasons, no one could arbitrarily and without notice appear before the king. Equally important was that the king maintained a large harem of which Esther was simply the leader. The best leadership positions often have limitations. Those who would be leaders should consider the limits of a leader's risking "all" for the people. Esther made sure that Mordecai was aware of her risk. Those who are in positions to make a difference through their risky commitments may often feel discomfort when they let others know that they have limitations. Esther's clear communication model for Christians is a solid posture to maintain when one's persuasive political prowess is being demanded for the well-being and, in her case, salvation of others.

Mordecai reminded Esther, not so subtly, that she too was a Jew. He asked whether or not she thought she would escape death if she did nothing. In the same "breath" he told her that if she did nothing, the Jews would be delivered some other way, but that she and her father's family would die. Mordecai's prior statement is often overlooked. Yet, it is clear what he intended. Did this mean he would create some situation for Esther that would lead the king to issue an edict against her and her father's family? If this is questionable for us, imagine what it must have meant to Esther.

C. Esther's Decision
(Esther 4:15-17)

Then Esther bade them return Mordecai this answer, Go, gather together all the Jews that are present in Shushan, and fast ye for me, and neither eat nor drink three days, night or day: I also and my maidens will fast likewise; and so will I go in unto the king, which is not according to the law: and if I perish, I perish. So Mordecai went his way, and did according to all that Esther had commanded him.

Esther's decision to commit to the deliverance of her people may have been inspired by many reasons. Indeed, she was a Jew. She was also a wise woman, who attained her position and status of queen as a result of her wisdom. She recognized the futility of countering Mordecai's distressed threat with her own, even though she was clearly in a position of power to make and honor a threat. Further, she knew the importance of her religious tradition of fasting and prayer. While the text does not directly cite prayer as a part of Esther's request, the Jewish tradition said that fasting was a ritual practice to be combined with prayer. It was this message then that she sent in reply to Mordecai.

She sent word to Mordecai to gather all the Jews together to fast on her behalf for three days. She declared that she and her maids would do the same. This was a significant preparatory move. Esther exhibited unparalleled commitment and wisdom in this moment.

Esther illuminated this important element further as she committed to risking her life. In her concluding statements to Mordecai, she shared that after the three-day fast, she would go before the king—even though the king still had not requested her presence, and going before him was against the law. Finally, she established the depth of her commitment, indicating that if she died, she died. Mordecai proceeded to follow Esther's directives.

Esther's awareness of the strong possibility of her death presents her unwavering strength of commitment. The challenge of modern risky commitments in the name of God and God's people rests in the knowledge that many of us will never be required to risk our lives. Wherein lies the challenge? The challenge is found deeply imbedded in many Christians, especially Christian leaders, to risk anything for God's cause. As many people are suffering and hurting within the four walls of the church, many pastors and preachers remain silent on critical issues affecting their church members' lives. For example, domestic abuse, whether toward males or females, is hardly if ever addressed. A preponderance of evidence shows that this malady affects many more women in our communities than men. Why do clergy avoid this issue? Is there a fear that the men they may be addressing for spousal or partner abuse share the pulpit, or are deacons in the church, administrators, or so forth?

III. CONCLUDING REFLECTION

We can conclude from this lesson that commitment to God is often to the benefit of others at one's own personal risk. Esther's commitment to God's purpose and to her people directly and literally risked her life. Yet, it is as a result of her story that we learn many things about personal risk associated with commitment to God. It is important that we start off in any situation of possible commitment knowing the rules of engagement. It is clear that some rules are made to be broken and some are not. For those rules that are not made to be broken, but nonetheless must be, Esther provided a model of wisdom.

PRAYER

God, our protector and provider of ages past and present, we humbly recognize our deficiencies as we approach Your presence. Yet, we come boldly before You. Ignite in our hearts a greater desire to do what You require in our lives and in the world around us. We ask now for Your wisdom and guidance as we face risky commitments. In Jesus' name we pray. Amen.

WORD POWER

Knoweth (*yada`* [*yaw-dah`*])—this means "to know, learn to know, to perceive and see, to know by experience, to discriminate, distinguish, to recognize, admit, acknowledge, and confess."

HOME DAILY BIBLE READINGS
(February 9-15, 2009)

Esther Risks Her Life
MONDAY, February 9: "The Search for a Queen" (Esther 2:1-11)
TUESDAY, February 10: "A New Queen" (Esther 2:15-18)
WEDNESDAY, February 11: "A Plot Thwarted" (Esther 2:19-23)
THURSDAY, February 12: "An Evil Edict" (Esther 3:7-13)
FRIDAY, February 13: "The Evil Intent Revealed" (Esther 7:1-10)
SATURDAY, February 14: "The People Rescued" (Esther 8:3-8)
SUNDAY, February 15: "If I Perish, I Perish" (Esther 4:1-3, 9-17)

LESSON 12

February 22, 2009

ISAIAH ANSWERS GOD'S CALL

DEVOTIONAL READING: **Revelation 4**
PRINT PASSAGE: **Isaiah 6:1-8**

BACKGROUND SCRIPTURE: **Isaiah 6**
KEY VERSE: **Isaiah 6:8**

Isaiah 6:1-8—KJV

IN THE year that king Uzziah died I saw also the Lord sitting upon a throne, high and lifted up, and his train filled the temple.

2 Above it stood the seraphims: each one had six wings; with twain he covered his face, and with twain he covered his feet, and with twain he did fly.

3 And one cried unto another, and said, Holy, holy, holy, is the LORD of hosts: the whole earth is full of his glory.

4 And the posts of the door moved at the voice of him that cried, and the house was filled with smoke.

5 Then said I, Woe is me! for I am undone; because I am a man of unclean lips, and I dwell in the midst of a people of unclean lips: for mine eyes have seen the King, the LORD of hosts.

6 Then flew one of the seraphims unto me, having a live coal in his hand, which he had taken with the tongs from off the altar:

7 And he laid it upon my mouth, and said, Lo, this hath touched thy lips; and thine iniquity is taken away, and thy sin purged.

8 Also I heard the voice of the Lord, saying, Whom shall I send, and who will go for us? Then said I, Here am I; send me.

Isaiah 6:1-8—NRSV

IN THE year that King Uzziah died, I saw the Lord sitting on a throne, high and lofty; and the hem of his robe filled the temple.

2 Seraphs were in attendance above him; each had six wings: with two they covered their faces, and with two they covered their feet, and with two they flew.

3 And one called to another and said: "Holy, holy, holy is the LORD of hosts; the whole earth is full of his glory."

4 The pivots on the thresholds shook at the voices of those who called, and the house filled with smoke.

5 And I said: "Woe is me! I am lost, for I am a man of unclean lips, and I live among a people of unclean lips; yet my eyes have seen the King, the LORD of hosts!"

6 Then one of the seraphs flew to me, holding a live coal that had been taken from the altar with a pair of tongs.

7 The seraph touched my mouth with it and said: "Now that this has touched your lips, your guilt has departed and your sin is blotted out."

8 Then I heard the voice of the Lord saying, "Whom shall I send, and who will go for us?" And I said, "Here am I; send me!"

BIBLE FACT

Noticing the events around us that God may use to get our attention and being willing to acknowledge where we may need some purifying and/or preparatory work is a good place to start in our commitment to change. Isaiah may have had an advantage in ancient times that perhaps we lack—quiet, stillness, open frame of mind, right setting, and timing.

TOPICAL OUTLINE OF THE LESSON

I. Introduction
A. Isaiah Answers God's Call
B. Biblical Background

II. Exposition and Application of the Scripture
A. Isaiah's Vision (Isaiah 6:1-3)
B. Call Experience (Isaiah 6:4-5)
C. God's Remedy (Isaiah 6:6-7)
D. God Speaks (Isaiah 6:8)

III. Concluding Reflection

LESSON OBJECTIVES

Upon completion of this lesson, the students are expected to:

1. Discover the motivation for Isaiah's commitment;
2. Explore the limits of commitment and identify circumstances in which they might be willing to go beyond these limits; and,
3. Consider moving beyond the present limits of their commitments to God.

POINTS TO BE EMPHASIZED

ADULT/YOUTH
Adult Topic: A Commitment to Change
Youth Topic: Sacrifices for Going Deeper
Adult/Youth Key Verse: Isaiah 6:8
Print Passage: Isaiah 6:1-8

—Isaiah 6 authenticates Isaiah's calling as a prophetic messenger. Isaiah saw the Lord through a divinely imposed vision.
—Isaiah's identification of himself as "a man of unclean lips" (verse 5) is an acknowledgement of his sinfulness.
—God allowed Isaiah freedom of choice by asking rather than telling him to "go."
—Isaiah received forgiveness and sanctification in order to make a commitment to God.
—Isaiah responded affirmatively to God's general call for someone to serve.
—Prophets who spoke for God have, by their humility and devotion to God and God's Word, felt themselves commissioned to proclaim what they have experienced.

CHILDREN
Children Topic: Committed to Speak
Key Verse: Isaiah 6:8
Print Passage: Isaiah 6:1-8

—Isaiah recalled a vision of God he received in the Temple.
—Isaiah acknowledged his sin and received God's forgiveness.
—When God called for someone to deliver a warning to the people, Isaiah accepted the challenge.

I. INTRODUCTION

A. Isaiah Answers God's Call

Old Testament people of commitment and faith stepped out of their comfort zones and gave up their "normal" ways of life to begin anew, according to God's purpose and plan. Some of us find it difficult to simply rearrange our schedule for a different Bible study time, let alone a complete uprooting of our normative standards of existence. Consider Abraham, Lot, Esther, Ruth, and several others who made significant adjustments to their way of life. Abraham went to a place that he was shown while in route. Lot turned and walked away from everything he knew. Esther risked her life for her people. Ruth was faithful to her mother-in-law while others walked away. Now consider yourself. Some may see themselves clearly in their willingness or unwillingness to leave familiar ways of being in the world to literally relocate to a new city or state at God's urging, or walk away from a place of employment to pursue full-time church ministry. We are frequently challenged in our commitment to God to answer a call of distinction to the point of discomfort. Isaiah stands among those who chose to remain committed in spite of the difficulty of the task ahead. This lesson helps us identify how we can commit to change. We are pressed as we consider Isaiah's example to find ways we can identify our shortcomings and then go beyond our comfort zones to fulfill God's call on our lives—whatever that may be. Our call may be to parent, to encourage others, to preach, to exhort, to sing, to pray, or any other purpose that God intends for us to fulfill in our lifetimes. As we review Isaiah's commitment, we are mindful that commitment often requires change.

B. Biblical Background

Isaiah follows in the traditions of the books of the latter prophets. These books include Jeremiah, Ezekiel, and the Twelve (from Hosea to Malachi). Note that the book of Daniel immediately follows Ezekiel but is considered a part of the "writings." The prophets' roles in the prophetic texts are multifaceted. These texts were considered a continuation of the earlier prophetic texts (the former prophets) that focused on the prophets' warning the Israelites of the potential consequences of disobeying God's Law (the Mosaic tradition). Further, they were also believed to predict future occurrences most significantly that involved the fulfillment of God's laws and promises. These prophets, including Isaiah, used great liberty in tone and tenor with their evaluations of their spiritual, social, and political contexts. Many of these views are challenged and debated by biblical and theological scholars.

Biblical and theological scholars do, however, agree in part on the significance of the call narratives to prophetic texts. These narratives tend to follow some common threads. Primarily, there is an emergent and obvious set of unusual conditions that are directly correlative with the call event. Isaiah's "call" experience exemplifies this, as we will observe in further study. While scholars say it is clear that Isaiah did not write all portions of the text, he has nonetheless been a heralded prophet in the Judaic and Christian traditions. Isaiah (a

Hebrew name that means "salvation of God") was a Jerusalem-born prophet; he was married to a woman he called "the prophetess" (Isaiah 8:3), and the father of two or three sons.

II. EXPOSITION AND APPLICATION OF THE SCRIPTURE

A. Isaiah's Vision
(Isaiah 6:1-3)

IN THE year that king Uzziah died I saw also the Lord sitting upon a throne, high and lifted up, and his train filled the temple. Above it stood the seraphims: each one had six wings; with twain he covered his face, and with twain he covered his feet, and with twain he did fly. And one cried unto another, and said, Holy, holy, holy, is the LORD of hosts: the whole earth is full of his glory.

Uzziah reigned in the eighth century B.C. and the year of his death serves as the historical marker for Isaiah's visionary call experience. Isaiah described this occurrence in rich detail. His primary descriptions are of the angels (seraphims), the voice of the Lord, and his direct experience. Some scholars suggest this to be a literal rendering of Isaiah's seeing the Lord directly, while others note it is more likely that he experienced what may have been better described as the "glory" of the Lord. It was believed at the time that no one could directly see God and live. Recall Moses's experience of God as he requested to see the Lord and was told he could only see the back of God's glory. While there have been many portrayals of God for centuries, the picturesque views are highly subjective and governed by the imagination of the creators of the paintings. While Isaiah described seeing the Lord, it is most probable that like the rest of humankind, Isaiah did not literally see the Lord.

Isaiah, after describing the Lord's location, continued in his account to give a description of the angelic host that was present. Isaiah identified these beings as *seraphims*. Scholars describe the "seraphs" or "seraphims" in different ways. Some see them as being akin to "griffin-like" creatures (NRSV). (Classical myth describes them as "a fabled monster, usually having the head and wings of an eagle and the body of a lion" (*Unabridged Webster's Dictionary*). Still others suggest that they were fiery supernatural beings. Regardless of one's view, the beings were likely scary and fierce to look upon, something we might encounter in nightmares. These creatures would hardly resemble the "cherubs" or childlike figures of angels portrayed in our contemporary context. The Victorian angelic image was not what Isaiah had in mind. It is likely these beings would not have been considered attractive. According to our current standards, it is more likely the case that they would be something more akin to gargoyles. These seraphims, or gargoyle-looking creatures, flew around protecting the throne and began to cry out "Holy, holy, holy, is the LORD of hosts; the whole earth is full of his glory" (6:3). Isaiah would continue to use this "holy" description of the Lord throughout the text.

B. Call Experience
(Isaiah 6:4-5)

And the posts of the door moved at the voice of him that cried, and the house was filled with smoke. Then said I, Woe is me! for I am undone; because I am a man of unclean lips, and I dwell in the midst of a people of unclean lips: for mine eyes have seen the King, the LORD of hosts.

Isaiah draws the reader into his space by detailing that the doorposts shook due to the sound of the seraphs crying out, and smoke filled the room. We do not know whether the vision of God was real or imagined. This visionary experience, however, was crucial to any future account Isaiah desired to give to those to whom he would later prophesy, so they would have something to validate that he had indeed been called. This model continues to exist, for better or for worse, in our current social contexts, especially in the black church traditions. Senior clergy persons often query those who announce a call to ministry to share the details of their call experience. Sometimes this is done in the privacy of a pastor's office or in the company of other clergy. This is an aim to establish a valid claim to the call. In some circles, those who have not had an unusual defining call experience (for example: dreams or visions of themselves preaching) are not validated as having authentically been called. Many, who have accepted a call to "the ministry," have given vivid accounts of the Lord speaking to them—and whether real, imagined, or dreamed, we do not know.

For Isaiah, being authenticated in his call would not have been an issue. Isaiah would be in good company with many licensed and ordained clergy persons today. His visionary event was certainly unusual enough to meet these criteria. However, at issue with many is whether or not in the subsequent verses (5-8) these events were a call experience at all. Some suggest that this was nothing more than an intense purifying rite for Isaiah that led him to volunteer his services. Isaiah, in the face of all this "activity," recognized that he was in a holy, reverent situation. He spoke out of this recognition when he declared himself "a man of unclean lips" (verse 5) and a member of a community of people with unclean lips.

It is at this recognition that Isaiah provided for us a critical image worthy of close examination. For any person to truly experience the presence of a holy God is to simultaneously experience his or her own ungodliness (uncleanliness). It is true that we have all sinned and fallen short of the glory of God (see Romans 3:23). It is a much more poignant realization when we are sincerely "before" or "in the presence of" God. Isaiah models for us the importance of recognizing our relative status to God. It is out of this clear recognition of our status that we begin to experience the first movement toward commitment. Our first or primary commitment, as a part of a commitment to change, has to be our recognition for a *need* to change.

C. God's Remedy (Isaiah 6:6-7)

Then flew one of the seraphims unto me, having a live coal in his hand, which he had taken with the tongs from off the altar: And he laid it upon my mouth, and said, Lo, this hath touched thy lips; and thine iniquity is taken away, and thy sin purged.

The seraph remedied this situation for Isaiah. He approached Isaiah with "live" (hot) coals and touched his mouth with them, telling him he was cleansed and that his sins were purged. Essentially, this was the seraph's way of letting Isaiah know that in his recognition was the beginning of his purification or purging of uncleanliness. The hot coals from the altar signified the reality of the seraph's nature (fiery) while also indicating the power of the fiery, purging element of God's presence. Being "cleansed" of our "ungodliness" is not a cool, relaxing, laid-back experience. We often come into the experience of service committing to change and feeling like God has "put some fire up under us." This experience is often felt as a "trial by fire," as we seek to understand how it is our "nature" being changed, sometimes seemingly before our very eyes. This aspect of Isaiah's experience also is promising in our current context, as it shows that God can and does prepare us in whatever ways God chooses and needs. We do not know how Isaiah felt about the hot fiery coals as a literal or dreamlike experience, but the purging, purifying effect is clear.

In keeping with other Hebrew texts, Isaiah's purifying experience represented the Judaic tradition's necessity of being cleansed before approaching God. It was understood in this tradition that one might enter the outer courts of the Temple; select others might then enter the inner courts of the Temple; but only those designated as sacred could enter the Holy of Holies. Isaiah's experience signifies that he was now purified and rightly able to be in the presence of God. This strongly resembles Moses's experience of being in the presence of God and being told to remove his shoes because he was on holy ground. Of course, Moses's experience precedes the building of the Temple, but is emblematic of the import of being in sacred territory. It is only once one recognizes that one is in sacred territory and does whatever is necessary to purify oneself that one can hear from the Lord.

D. God Speaks
(Isaiah 6:8)

Also I heard the voice of the Lord, saying, Whom shall I send, and who will go for us? Then said I, Here am I; send me.

Once Isaiah's purifying ritual was experienced, he then heard God speak. Prior to this Isaiah was recounting the words of the seraphim. Isaiah said that he "heard the voice of the Lord, saying, Whom shall I send, and who will go for us?" (verse 8). Many scholars note that there is no explicit greeting or acknowledgment of Isaiah as the intended recipient and/or respondent to this query. While scholars may hotly debate the issue, what remains clear in biblical history is that Isaiah did what he believed to be the work of the Lord, to God's glory. How we reflect upon this notion of *call* will likely come out of our own experiences and belief systems. Some faith traditions believe strongly that people can volunteer to "go" on God's behalf, while others believe that only certain avenues of "going" for God should be pursued voluntarily, suggesting that others require a direct call from God. Whether voluntary or directly called, what remained most salient was Isaiah's prior recognition of his need to be "changed" or purified by God to do this "going."

The text does not indicate that Isaiah sought out additional clarification before saying "yes" to the Lord. This well-elucidated "yes" to the Lord brought to the fore the importance of having a strong clarity of purpose to the Lord when committing to change for the work of the Lord. While continued study would reveal the nature and challenge of Isaiah's assignment, his clarity of purpose before being assigned the details of the task was compelling.

Isaiah's commitment to change was expressed in his receptivity to acknowledging and purifying his shortcomings to volunteer himself for God's task, in spite of the absence of assignment details. This can inspire us to respond to our inner sense of calling without hesitation. Like many in the Old Testament, Isaiah was not privileged to get every detail of his forthcoming assignments. Waiting on the next move of God is also a major part of the commitment to change. It is a much more subtle internal change. This internal change allows us to "notice." Isaiah may have simply been in a good place to notice God's movement around him. It was in the year that King Uzziah died that Isaiah saw the Lord. Grief over the loss of someone significant to our experience often puts us in a place of noticing everything from our own mortality to God's sovereignty and holiness. It is not likely that Isaiah was exempt from this human process.

III. CONCLUDING REFLECTION

We can conclude from this lesson that commitment to the Lord requires change. This type of change often moves us from a place of comfortable and recognizable familiar territory into the unknown or unfamiliar. This is well-seen in Isaiah's account of seeing the Lord in the year that King Uzziah died. The common life that Isaiah may have known up to that point was forever and completely disrupted. He was immediately faced with a challenge to fear death or to accept the experience. His acceptance of the experience allows us the privilege to read the text identified as his prophetic message.

Whether we go forth voluntarily or by some extreme direct "call" from God, it is salient that we go forth with an unshakable commitment to change. Considering Isaiah's experience should help us in our reliance on God to give us instruction as we go forward—faith-filled in our commitment to change in giving service to God.

PRAYER

Gracious and almighty God, we thank You that You speak to us. Hear our humble prayer as we seek in faith to commit to Your works. Reveal in our lives the spaces and places that require the burning fire of Your Spirit to invoke real change in us. Let us be willing to sacrifice as we are called to be representatives of You in the world. In Jesus' name we pray. Amen.

WORD POWER

Holy *(qadesh or qadash)* this means: "to be holy; to sanctify; pure; clean and free from defilement." In our text, the heavenly hosts were adoring and ascribing holiness to God.

HOME DAILY BIBLE READINGS
(February 16-22, 2009)

Isaiah Answers God's Call

MONDAY, February 16: "An Emerald Rainbow" (Revelation 4:1-6a)

TUESDAY, February 17: "Holy, Holy, Holy" (Revelation 4:6b-11)

WEDNESDAY, February 18: "A Call to Leave" (Genesis 12:1-5)

THURSDAY, February 19: "A Call to Stay" (Genesis 26:1-5)

FRIDAY, February 20: "A Call to Deliver" (Judges 6:11-23)

SATURDAY, February 21: "An Answer for Uncertainty" (Judges 6:36-40)

SUNDAY, February 22: "Here Am I, Send Me!" (Isaiah 6:1-8)

New Creation in Christ

GENERAL INTRODUCTION

Studies this quarter are explorations of the creative nature of Christ as it affects human life and the implications of His life for the world in which we live. The first unit is drawn from Ezekiel and the second and third units come from the New Testament.

Unit I, *The Promise of New Life,* is a look at five well-known passages from the book of Ezekiel. The first three lessons are examinations of new life as it was promised to Israel in exile. In lessons 4 and 5 we look to the future God promised—as it would be fulfilled many generations later in Jesus Christ.

Unit II, *The Path to New Life,* is developed from three passages in Luke and one in Acts. Lessons 6 and 7 are examinations of the suffering and death of Jesus and His triumph over death on the first Easter Sunday. Lesson 8 is a continued look at the last resurrection appearance of Jesus in the book of Luke. Lesson 9 finds Peter in Lydda and Joppa bringing new life to others in the name and power of Christ.

Unit III, *The Way of New Life,* is an exploration of the book of Ephesians through five concepts in that letter: church as family, life, revelation, home life, and equipping ourselves for Christian living.

Note: For children, Unit I follows the selected passages from the book of Ezekiel. For Unit II, the chosen passage for lesson 6 tells the story of Jesus' arrival in Jerusalem for the last time. In Unit III, lessons 10-12 are based on texts from the book of 1 John.

LESSON 1   March 1, 2009

A NEW SPIRIT

DEVOTIONAL READING: **2 Corinthians 3:1-11**
PRINT PASSAGE: **Ezekiel 11:14-21**

BACKGROUND SCRIPTURE: **Ezekiel 11:14-21**
KEY VERSE: **Ezekiel 11:19**

Ezekiel 11:14-21—KJV

14 Again the word of the LORD came unto me, saying,

15 Son of man, thy brethren, even thy brethren, the men of thy kindred, and all the house of Israel wholly, are they unto whom the inhabitants of Jerusalem have said, Get you far from the LORD: unto us is this land given in possession.

16 Therefore say, Thus saith the Lord GOD; Although I have cast them far off among the heathen, and although I have scattered them among the countries, yet will I be to them as a little sanctuary in the countries where they shall come.

17 Therefore say, Thus saith the Lord GOD; I will even gather you from the people, and assemble you out of the countries where ye have been scattered, and I will give you the land of Israel.

18 And they shall come thither, and they shall take away all the detestable things thereof and all the abominations thereof from thence.

19 And I will give them one heart, and I will put a new spirit within you; and I will take the stony heart out of their flesh, and will give them an heart of flesh:

20 That they may walk in my statutes, and keep mine ordinances, and do them: and they shall be my people, and I will be their God.

21 But as for them whose heart walketh after the heart of their detestable things and their abominations, I will recompense their way upon their own heads, saith the Lord GOD.

Ezekiel 11:14-21—NRSV

14 Then the word of the LORD came to me:

15 Mortal, your kinsfolk, your own kin, your fellow exiles, the whole house of Israel, all of them, are those of whom the inhabitants of Jerusalem have said, "They have gone far from the LORD; to us this land is given for a possession."

16 Therefore say: Thus says the Lord GOD: Though I removed them far away among the nations, and though I scattered them among the countries, yet I have been a sanctuary to them for a little while in the countries where they have gone.

17 Therefore say: Thus says the Lord GOD: I will gather you from the peoples, and assemble you out of the countries where you have been scattered, and I will give you the land of Israel.

18 When they come there, they will remove from it all its detestable things and all its abominations.

19 I will give them one heart, and put a new spirit within them; I will remove the heart of stone from their flesh and give them a heart of flesh,

20 so that they may follow my statutes and keep my ordinances and obey them. Then they shall be my people, and I will be their God.

21 But as for those whose heart goes after their detestable things and their abominations, I will bring their deeds upon their own heads, says the Lord GOD.

BIBLE FACT

God cannot dwell in an unholy place. It is against His very nature to reside where sin abides. God and sin are like oil and water—the two cannot mix. This was the revelation that God gave to Ezekiel when He revealed the desecrated Temple.

The frustrations of life, especially problems of our own making, may entice us to give up hope for change. Is everything truly lost because we must reap the rewards of our own folly? "Absolutely not," claimed the prophet—for the God who never abandons us promises to give us a fresh start by providing a new heart and spirit.

TOPICAL OUTLINE OF THE LESSON

I. Introduction
   A. Tests
   B. Biblical Background

II. Exposition and Application of the Scripture
   A. The Need for Judgment (Ezekiel 11:14-16)
   B. The Promise of Restoration (Ezekiel 11:17-21)

III. Concluding Reflection

LESSON OBJECTIVES

Upon completion of this lesson, the students will know that:

1. Even though the children of Israel were scattered, God still took care of them by being a sanctuary for them;
2. Ultimately God restored Israel to her original relationship with Him;
3. Eventually God would grant a new heart to Israel; and,
4. God would never abandon Christians to a hopeless situation.

POINTS TO BE EMPHASIZED

ADULT/YOUTH
Adult Topic: A New Spirit of Hope
Youth Topic: Beyond Consequences
Adult/Youth Key Verse: Ezekiel 11:19
Print Passage: Ezekiel 11:14-21

—The new heart and spirit (verse 19) would be the result of God's grace and the response of the exiles: God would gather the people (verse 17), and in response, the people would observe God's commandments, willingly removing that which had caused them to sin (verse 18).
—The hope of a new heart and spirit was not merely human wish fulfillment, a reflection of Ezekiel's deepest longings and desires; it was an integral part of God's own assurance to those living in exile.
—Ezekiel prophesied to the exiled Jews in captivity in Babylon.
—To these, Ezekiel promised that God was with them in this strange and distant land as their sanctuary and that God would restore them to their homeland.
—A heart renewed by the Holy Spirit is best fit to obey God and walk in God's ways.

CHILDREN
Children Topic: A New Start
Key Verse: Ezekiel 11:19
Print Passage: Ezekiel 11:14-21

—God is always faithful to the promises He has made.
—God is a refuge for us.
—We can receive renewed hearts and spirits from God.
—When we follow God's will, we show that we belong to God.

I. INTRODUCTION

A. Tests

A popular worship song boasts, "Our trials come to only make us strong." But if you took a poll among Christians around the world, and asked them how they would prefer to learn life's lessons, they would unanimously proclaim that they would prefer to learn an easier way. That is because spiritual growth can be painful.

Consider the testimony of the famous Christian singer, Larnell Harris. During a grueling musical tour, his voice became so strained that he could no longer make a sound. His doctor warned him that if he intended to continue his career as a singer, he would have to take a year off from singing, and even speaking, and allow his vocal cords time to heal. Larnell is proud to admit that he learned more about God during that year of silence, than in all his years of musical study at Western Kentucky University.

Another case in point: steel is the strongest metal in existence and it is not easily manufactured. It is an alloy or mixture of iron and small amounts of carbon and other materials; so exact is the recipe for steel that it is measured in microscopic portions. During the manufacturing process, steel undergoes a slow-cooking operation. As it cooks, it becomes carbonized. This carbonization is what makes steel the strongest metal in existence. But even after it is cooked, it is still not approved for use. It must then go through more than thirty-five tests before it is certified to carry the label of *steel*.

That is the way our Christian lives unfold. Through test after test, God exacts the characteristics or traits that He will need for our own individual assignments. And in the process, we become hardened in our determination to hold fast to our faith. Each test proves God's ability to save us, sustain us, and shape us into tools of His choosing. Life's hardest lessons can only be learned through "tests" of our faith.

B. Biblical Background

In Hebrew, *Ezekiel* means "God strengthens." The purpose of prophecy was to strengthen God's chosen people by forewarning them of the ramifications of their sins.

Ezekiel gave a detailed account of God's denunciation of disobedient Judah and Israel, and the impending ruin of their holy city, Jerusalem. His prophecies seem to be dated around the time of King Jehoiachin (598 B.C.) because thirteen of Ezekiel's prophecies are dated precisely to the day, month, and year of his exile to Babylon. When the prophet Ezekiel was sent into exile in Babylon, in the fifth year of King Jehoiachin's exile, to decry the wickedness of God's people and to call for their repentance, his message was not initially received as one of hope. This is a book of deep symbolism and unique visions that reveal the prophet's intimate knowledge of coming events.

During the exile of the Jews from their homeland, Ezekiel acted as the Lord's watchman. *Watchman* was the term used for the soldiers who stood on the outer wall of the city and cried aloud when an enemy approached. As God's watchman, Ezekiel was called to cry aloud when the enemy called *sin* began to overtake his people. His account of the ramifications or punishments for their disobedience is so vivid that it makes the reader shudder. In chapters 8-11, Ezekiel is raptured in the spirit to Jerusalem where he saw all kinds of loathsome idolatry being practiced in the Temple courts. While he watched the desecration in the Holy of Holies (see 8:4), he witnessed as God's divine glory left the Temple and the holy city. His vision is meant to symbolize God's abandonment of His disobedient people.

Abandonment by God is the ultimate punishment. But God never leaves His people without hope. From the beginning of Creation, God made provision to rescue man from his own destruction. At this point in Israel and Judah's sinful rebellion, Ezekiel was sent into exile with them, to call for their repentance and restoration. While this restoration is projected far into the future, it serves to sustain God's chosen people through their period of exile. Ezekiel carries with him the promise that God can change the stoniest of hearts and gather His scattered chosen people to Him once again.

II. EXPOSITION AND APPLICATION OF THE SCRIPTURE

A. The Need for Judgment
(Ezekiel 11:14-16)

Again the word of the Lord came unto me, saying, Son of man, thy brethren, even thy brethren, the men of thy kindred, and all the house of Israel wholly, are they unto whom the inhabitants of Jerusalem have said, Get you far from the Lord: unto us is this land given in possession. Therefore say, Thus saith the Lord God; Although I have cast them far off among the heathen, and although I have scattered them among the countries, yet will I be to them as a little sanctuary in the countries where they shall come.

The elders of Israel felt secure in Jerusalem. They took for granted that the holy city would be their home forever and that God would shelter and protect them in spite of their disobedience. Similarly, we are, by our own carnal natures, prone to become too comfortable with God. That is just what happened to the Israelites. Their familiarity with God led them to take His forgiveness for granted. It must have been quite a shock to hear the message delivered by Ezekiel that God would drive Israel out of their comfort zone and give them over to foreign control. Hearing that God would allow the destruction of the holy city of Jerusalem and permit the captivity of the Israelites was a message that we can be sure most of the hearers rejected. The Israelites must have been sure that God would never destroy the very place where He resided.

The Israelites had entered into a dangerous comfort zone. As the chosen people, they had become complacent about their worship and their faith. They were resting in the knowledge that they had been set apart by God to be His ambassadors, and they had become convinced in their own spirit that God would never break His covenant relationship with them.

As Christians, there is danger in becoming self-righteous about our own faith. The apostle Paul warned that we must never sin simply because we know that we will be forgiven. Paul said, "What shall we say then? Shall we continue in sin, that grace may abound? God forbid. How shall we, that are dead to sin, live any longer therein?" (Romans 6:1-2). This was the lesson that God's chosen people, and we today, needed to learn. God's forgiveness—grace and mercy—is not a tool to be used as a safety net by sinners.

Though Ezekiel delivered the message, he was frightened by the idea of the complete annihilation of God's chosen people, and he pleaded with God for mercy (see 9:8). He reacted the same way Abraham did when God told him that He would destroy Sodom and Gomorrah. He was shocked and dismayed. It was then that God gave Ezekiel a twofold response. He first comforted Ezekiel with the knowledge that a remnant of Israel would not be destroyed. God always preserves a remnant to carry His plan of salvation forward. The second part of God's response was to show Ezekiel the need for judgment on Jerusalem. God pointed out that Jerusalem's morality had become distorted. The Israelites in Jerusalem thought that those already in exile (Judah) were the ones who were far away from the Lord. They were counting on the fact that their right to the land given them by God was secure, since it was still in their possession.

Possession, it is said, is nine-tenths of the law, but not according to God's divine order. Humankind often develops a sense of false security as long as they are in possession of what they want. The elders of the city had forgotten that when God gave them the Promised Land, He also threatened to remove them from it for disobedience (see Deuteronomy 28:36, 64-68). So instead of telling the people to heed Ezekiel's warning, they encouraged the Jerusalemites to forget the prophet's predictions of the coming Babylonian invasion.

God promised Ezekiel that He would spare a remnant (see Ezekiel 6:8; 12:16) but it would not include the arrogant, haughty, self-righteous leaders of Jerusalem. These would be part of the generation in exile that would fade away.

B. The Promise of Restoration (Ezekiel 11:17-21)

Therefore say, Thus saith the Lord GOD; I will even gather you from the people, and assemble you out of the countries where ye have been scattered, and I will give you the land of Israel. And they shall come thither, and they shall take away all the detestable things thereof and all the abominations thereof from thence. And I will give them one heart, and I will put a new spirit within you; and I will take the stony heart out of their flesh, and will give them an heart of flesh: That they may walk in my statutes, and keep mine ordinances, and do them: and they shall be my people, and I will be their God. But as for them whose heart walketh after the heart of their detestable things and their abominations, I will recompense their way upon their own heads, saith the Lord GOD.

The covenant between God and Israel was a redemptive and restorative one. In other words, Ezekiel's vision pointed to a brighter future for God's chosen people. But this restoration of which Ezekiel spoke was not the one that took place immediately after the Israelites' return from Babylonian captivity. This prophecy of a new national restoration and gathering of Israel pointed to a time very far into the future, at the beginning of the Millennium (see 36:24-38). In spite of the fact that Ezekiel spoke of a millennial restoration, the exiled Jews eventually found great comfort in his message.

This millennial return to the Promised Land would be accompanied by a spiritual renewal, as referenced by verse 19, when God said, "I will give them one (undivided) heart, and I will put a new spirit within you." We see here that not only would the land be purged of idolatry, but the people would be purged as well.

God's promise through Ezekiel refers to the indwelling of the Holy Spirit in Israel. It is important to note that until this point, the Holy Spirit dwelled only in select individuals who were temporarily enabled by God for specific tasks. (For example, Sampson was given strength to tear down the Temple and its false worship, and destroy his adversaries.) But in Ezekiel's proclaimed New Millennium, the Holy Spirit would dwell in all believing Israelites (see 36:26-27). The prophet Joel predicted this same outpouring of the Holy Spirit, saying in Joel 2:28: "And it shall come to pass afterward, that I will pour out my spirit upon all flesh; and your sons and your daughters shall prophesy, your old men shall dream dreams, your young men shall see visions."

This prophecy promise refers to the new covenant inauguration that would begin with the death of Jesus Christ (see Matthew 26:28; Mark 14:24) and fully culminate in the national gathering of Israel once again to their Promised Land.

We can only imagine the pain of this vision experience for Ezekiel, who loved his people and desired so greatly that they would repent and once again be one with God. In the vision, God gave Ezekiel the assurance he needed—that Israel would one day be obedient and keep God's laws (verses 20-21). God promised that Israel's new revived spirit would produce righteous actions that would reflect their renewed relationship with Him. This was the assurance Ezekiel was longing for—that Israel would become God's people once again, and He would be their God.

III. CONCLUDING REFLECTION

God is warning us today, just as He did the Israelites, that disobedience can and will draw us away from His presence and His protection. Disobedience is not as hard to fall into as some might think. It is easy to slide ever so slowly to the left in our commitment to Christ, when we permit outside influences to color or influence our worship and alter our interpretation of the covenant.

Many Christians have started the Christian race, but because they took their "blinders" off, they cast off the tunnel vision that would have kept them focused on Christ, and instead permitted themselves a more panoramic view of the world through their own eyes. The result was that their faith produced a watered-down religion that ultimately separated them from their covenant relationship. The end result of this is always a *form* of religion, without faith.

Today, more than ever, we face the threat of a "New Age Movement" of faith that combines Eastern religion with occult mysticism. This threat actually began in the Garden of Eden when Satan enticed Eve with the promise that her eyes would be opened if she ate of the forbidden fruit. Christians face a similar enticement with astrology, "900 numbers" that promise mystics who will read our futures, and motivational speakers who are paid a high price to attract us with their mode of success via pre-packaged selling points and mass marketing. As their followers grow in number, it is apparent that humankind is always in search of new meaning and consequently susceptible to its influence.

It would be sad, but somehow understandable, if these followers did not include Christians who have somehow mistaken this "New

Age" philosophy for truth. There is a growing number of Christians who continue to fall for the lies that Satan has been perpetrating since the Garden of Eden.

With so much at stake and so many misconceptions that go with this "New Age" philosophy, it is imperative that today's twenty-first-century Christians do not lose sight of who we are, and whose we are. We must not become like the Israelites who slowly and steadily moved away from the one true and living God as their *personal* God. The task is not an easy one because our pathway is very narrow, but we are given the responsibility of sharing the truth with all of the world's deceived people. As the old hymn writer said, we must carry the narrowly defined albeit precise message that, "My hope is built on nothing less, than Jesus' blood and righteousness" (from the hymn, "My Faith Is Built on Nothing Less," *Baptist Standard Hymnal*, p. 286).

If we are called to preserve our new covenant faith heritage received through our Lord and Savior Jesus Christ, we must be careful to protect it from outside influences that would alter its original content and meaning. This is our duty as Christians and faithful followers of God. How do we accomplish this duty? We do it by studying the Word diligently and conscientiously, practicing it ever so faithfully, and spreading it wholeheartedly and enthusiastically.

PRAYER

Heavenly Father, we thank You for Your messengers who delivered to Your children a word of hope. Today, we are thankful for the everlasting hope that comes through Your Son, Jesus Christ. In Jesus' name we pray. Amen.

WORD POWER

Hope *(elpis)*—this means "favorable and confident expectation" (contrast the Septuagint in Isaiah 28:19, "an evil hope"). It has to do with the unseen and the future (see Romans 8:24-25). *Hope* describes: (a) "the happy anticipation of good" (Titus 1:2; 1 Peter 1:21); (b) "the ground upon which *hope* is based" (Acts 16:19; Colossians 1:27); "Christ in you, the *hope* of glory"; and (c) "the object upon which the *hope* is fixed" (1 Timothy 1:1).

HOME DAILY BIBLE READINGS
(February 23–March 1, 2009)

A New Spirit
    MONDAY, February 23: "Evil Hearts" (Genesis 6:1-8)
    TUESDAY, February 24: "Willing Hearts" (Exodus 25:1-9)
    WEDNESDAY, February 25: "Defiant Hearts" (Deuteronomy 2:26-30)
    THURSDAY, February 26: "Obedient Hearts" (Deuteronomy 5:28-33)
    FRIDAY, February 27: "Proud Hearts" (Deuteronomy 8:11-19)
    SATURDAY, February 28: "Loving Hearts" (Deuteronomy 10:12-21)
    SUNDAY, March 1: "One Heart, a New Spirit" (Ezekiel 11:14-21)

NEW LEADERSHIP

DEVOTIONAL READING: **John 10:11-18**
PRINT PASSAGE: **Ezekiel 34:23-31**

BACKGROUND SCRIPTURE: **Ezekiel 34**
KEY VERSE: **Ezekiel 34:31**

Ezekiel 34:23-31—KJV

23 And I will set up one shepherd over them, and he shall feed them, even my servant David; he shall feed them, and he shall be their shepherd.

24 And I the LORD will be their God, and my servant David a prince among them; I the LORD have spoken it.

25 And I will make with them a covenant of peace, and will cause the evil beasts to cease out of the land: and they shall dwell safely in the wilderness, and sleep in the woods.

26 And I will make them and the places round about my hill a blessing; and I will cause the shower to come down in his season; there shall be showers of blessing.

27 And the tree of the field shall yield her fruit, and the earth shall yield her increase, and they shall be safe in their land, and shall know that I am the LORD, when I have broken the bands of their yoke, and delivered them out of the hand of those that served themselves of them.

28 And they shall no more be a prey to the heathen, neither shall the beast of the land devour them; but they shall dwell safely, and none shall make them afraid.

29 And I will raise up for them a plant of renown, and they shall be no more consumed with hunger in the land, neither bear the shame of the heathen any more.

30 Thus shall they know that I the LORD their God am with them, and that they, even the house of Israel, are my people, saith the Lord GOD.

31 And ye my flock, the flock of my pasture, are men, and I am your God, saith the Lord GOD.

Ezekiel 34:23-31—NRSV

23 I will set up over them one shepherd, my servant David, and he shall feed them: he shall feed them and be their shepherd.

24 And I, the LORD, will be their God, and my servant David shall be prince among them; I, the LORD, have spoken.

25 I will make with them a covenant of peace and banish wild animals from the land, so that they may live in the wild and sleep in the woods securely.

26 I will make them and the region around my hill a blessing; and I will send down the showers in their season; they shall be showers of blessing.

27 The trees of the field shall yield their fruit, and the earth shall yield its increase. They shall be secure on their soil; and they shall know that I am the LORD, when I break the bars of their yoke, and save them from the hands of those who enslaved them.

28 They shall no more be plunder for the nations, nor shall the animals of the land devour them; they shall live in safety, and no one shall make them afraid.

29 I will provide for them a splendid vegetation so that they shall no more be consumed with hunger in the land, and no longer suffer the insults of the nations.

30 They shall know that I, the LORD their God, am with them, and that they, the house of Israel, are my people, says the Lord GOD.

31 You are my sheep, the sheep of my pasture and I am your God, says the Lord GOD.

BIBLE FACT

Ezekiel's prophecy that God would restore Israel was not fulfilled when Israel returned to her land after the Babylonian Captivity. This prophecy refers to a future event, which will be fulfilled in the New Millennium.

UNIFYING LESSON PRINCIPLE

Sometimes people become very disappointed with leaders who are self-serving and disconnected from their constituents. What remedy can be found when such a person is in a leadership position? Ezekiel told us that God will provide new servant-leaders who care tenderly for their flock, just as God the Good Shepherd does.

TOPICAL OUTLINE OF THE LESSON

I. Introduction
   A. Leadership
   B. Biblical Background

II. Exposition and Application of the Scripture
   A. The Lord's Intention (Ezekiel 34:23-24)
   B. A Covenant of Peace (Ezekiel 34:25-31)

III. Concluding Reflection

LESSON OBJECTIVES

Upon completion of this lesson, the students will know that:

1. It can be very disappointing when leaders are self-serving and disconnected from their constituents;
2. A remedy can be found when such a person is in a leadership position; and,
3. God will provide new servant-leaders who care tenderly for their flock, just as He does.

POINTS TO BE EMPHASIZED

ADULT/YOUTH

Adult Topic: The Importance of Servant-Leaders
Youth Topic: Lead by Serving
Adult/Youth Key Verse: Ezekiel 34:31
Print Passage: Ezekiel 34:23-31

—The servant-leader in this passage helps bring about the blessings of peace, abundance, and the absence of fear.
—The traits of the human shepherd-leader in this passage reflect the characteristics of God.
—God will establish a new and better leadership of God's people, who had been mistreated by previous leaders.
—God will rule out of the lineage of David.
—This new leader will not be an independent king of the old and failed theocracy, but a prince through whom God will rule directly.
—God cares for His people both spiritually and physically.

CHILDREN

Children Topic: A Leader Is Chosen
Key Verse: Ezekiel 34:23
Print Passage: Ezekiel 34:23-31

—God chose many people to be shepherds to God's people in the manner of David.
—God expected Israel to follow the new leader because God had chosen him.
—Those who follow God receive blessings.
—The example of a shepherd and sheep provides a picture of God's care for His people.
—God promised to deliver, provide for, and be present with Israel.

I. INTRODUCTION

A. Leadership

There has been so much written about effective leadership. Effective leaders must be able to assess their market, focus on the customer, provide quality service, inspire teamwork, and arouse commitment. All these factors are vitally important for the success of any venture. Most of these leadership characteristics can be applied to the church as well. Church leaders must be able to earmark their "target group" for evangelism; they must be able to focus all the energies of every ministry on reaching the lost; they must inspire excellence, teamwork, and commitment in every member—if the vision for their church is to be fulfilled.

Jesus Christ was a leader with a clear vision. His primary purpose was the glorification of His heavenly Father. He lived and taught what He believed. Today we call this lifestyle *evangelism.* A clear mission serves as a compass to point us in the right direction. Our mission keeps us focused on what is important. It serves as a filter for new ideas, and as an evaluation tool for our ministries. But there was more to His leadership than mission—there was character. Mission is what we do; character is how and why we do it. Character is the motivation behind the work. It lends credibility to our purpose, so that our mission actually affects the lives of those we lead. Character also proves the seriousness of our commitment.

Integrity and maturity are two character traits vital to the heart of a leader. Without them, a leader has no credibility. If a leader has no credibility, he or she forfeits the right to lead. Integrity is being honest with others and yourself. It means that your "yes" is *yes*, and your "no" is *no*. Maturity balances courage with sensitivity and helps the leader to make wise decisions.

Ezekiel's prophecy concerning the leaders of Israel points out one more critical factor of leadership: diligence. If God's people are neglected or suffering, then the leader's qualifications to lead are definitely called into question. A clear mission, consistent character, and capability are all essential for a leader of God's people, and should produce favorable results.

B. Biblical Background

In our text, God gave the shepherds or leaders of Israel a performance review, and it was not a favorable one. The spiritual leaders were spending most of their energies feeding themselves rather than feeding their flock (see Ezekiel 34:2-8). As a result, the people were scattered because of these cruel and indifferent shepherds. The only way God's people would be rescued and restored would be through God's direct intervention. God would have to intervene personally on Israel's behalf.

God's first action would be to restore Israel to her land. Their years in captivity would eventually come to an end. God would do what the false shepherds had failed to do: tend

His flock. He would seek them out, bring them back, and strengthen His lost sheep. This was a tall order for a nation who had been captured and taken far from their homeland by King Nebuchadnezzar and his marauding armies.

The nation of Israel was no longer acting like God's chosen people because the leaders of Israel had lost sight of the fact that they were serving for the good of the Kingdom and for those around them. Trust and respect, two vital traits of an effective leader, were sorely lacking in Israel. Those who were entrusted with preserving the covenant relationship between God and Israel were committing all manner of abominations that invalidated their ministry and their mission.

II. EXPOSITION AND APPLICATION OF THE SCRIPTURE

A. The Lord's Intention
(Ezekiel 34:23-24)

And I will set up one shepherd over them, and he shall feed them, even my servant David; he shall feed them, and he shall be their shepherd. And I the Lord will be their God, and my servant David a prince among them; I the Lord have spoken it.

The first word "And" is a connective word, meaning that the previous paragraph and the current one are dealing with the same issue. The shepherds of the people were corrupt, and the spiritual life of the people was at its lowest ebb. This was a great reason God was assuming the responsibility of choosing the right shepherd with a right heart. In order to see the reason for this section, Ezekiel 34:7, 8, 10 reads: "Therefore... because my flock became a prey, and my flock became meat to every beast of the field... Behold, I am against the shepherds; and I will require my flock at their hand... for I will deliver my flock from their mouth, that they may not be meat for them."

The words "I will" mean that God would henceforth not trust the shepherds of Israel because of the wickedness in their hearts. The one shepherd would be by divine appointment, alluding to the declaration of God to David (see 2 Samuel 7:12). *One shepherd* literally meant one of His kind. "My servant David" referred to David's greater Son, the Messiah—the only true shepherd of God (Jesus Christ)—who took the pain of the entire world upon Himself.

In our contemporary world, we are witnessing a lot of sad news regarding shepherds of God's people. Charles Spurgeon said there are "ministers sailing in false colors." Unfortunately, many sheep are grazing in dangerous fields. The sheep are unsuspecting of the hearts of their ministers. The desire to become rich at all costs without regard to God's standard has gripped the hearts of many people. There are books on self-help: *How to Become Rich, You Can Have All You Want,* and *God Is No Tyrant,* to mention a few. The titles of these books are inviting, but their insides are full of poison. Many sheep are racing from one conference to the other in order to get the latest Bible prophecy that will change their lives. The current situation is not different from Ezekiel's time—it may even be worse. In the midst of this chaos, the voice of God says, "I will set up one shepherd."

This one shepherd is Jesus Christ, and we must look to Him for peace and serenity. God promised to separate these false teachers from their flocks and put an end to their wicked practices. He promised He would rescue the oppressed and judge the aggressors.

This beautiful message portrays the fate of the present shepherds, the work of the new shepherd, and the future of the sheep.

B. A Covenant of Peace
(Ezekiel 34:25-31)

And I will make with them a covenant of peace, and will cause the evil beasts to cease out of the land: and they shall dwell safely in the wilderness, and sleep in the woods. And I will make them and the places round about my hill a blessing; and I will cause the shower to come down in his season; there shall be showers of blessing. And the tree of the field shall yield her fruit, and the earth shall yield her increase, and they shall be safe in their land, and shall know that I am the Lord, when I have broken the bands of their yoke, and delivered them out of the hand of those that served themselves of them. And they shall no more be a prey to the heathen, neither shall the beast of the land devour them; but they shall dwell safely, and none shall make them afraid. And I will raise up for them a plant of renown, and they shall be no more consumed with hunger in the land, neither bear the shame of the heathen any more. Thus shall they know that I the Lord their God am with them, and that they, even the house of Israel, are my people, saith the Lord God. And ye my flock, the flock of my pasture, are men, and I am your God, saith the Lord God.

What will be the result of God's care and protection for His people? The result will be *peace*. Israel would finally experience the peace that they had always longed for. The uncertainties of famine and drought would be replaced with peace, tranquility, and prosperity.

This prophecy was difficult for the Jews to embrace while they were in captivity, for several reasons. First, while the Jews were taken from their homeland and subjected to a caste system of government (a system that relegates certain people to the lower echelons of society), they were still completely free to settle and live their lives as they pleased. This is documented in many business records of Jewish households found in Nippur, located on the Chebar canal. Many of the Jews became so settled in their adopted land that they refused to leave it at the end of the Exile period. Even to this day, the majority of the Hebrew descendants still live outside of Israel. The Jews in exile in Babylon became comfortable with their new lifestyle, and quickly began to adapt to its demands. This weakened their response to Ezekiel's prophecy of restoration and promise of peace.

This "covenant of peace" paints a picture of life's blessings for Israel in the New Millennium. Israel would be permanently established in her homeland with David as her shepherd. God restored Israel because of her unique relationship to Him. They were the sheep of His pasture, and He was their God.

Peace has a great price. Nations use the threat of weaponry and strong armies to ensure their peace, and are often forced to exercise that threat with war to protect the peace that they enjoy. Humanity's peace is transitory because it is based on our own strengths and weaknesses. But God's peace, the peace that He promised to Israel, is everlasting. This peace of which Ezekiel prophesied seemed far removed to the Israelites while they were in captivity. After all, how could there be any sense of peace when they were possessed by another nation? And even today, in this century, with all of the warring between nations in the Middle East, it can seem just as far removed to those of us who pray for Israel's peace. Many nations attempted to orchestrate a peace treaty between Israel and those who threatened her borders. It would seem that such a peace had to prevail before the fulfillment of Ezekiel's prophecy—that the people of Israel who were scattered to many nations would return to their homeland in peace.

As Christians, it is important for us to understand that real peace hinges on what happens inside us, not around us. While we are all tempted to believe the lie that our contentment or our happiness hinges on our ability to control what is going on around us, the truth is that Christ introduced a greater concept of peace. It is a peace that surpasses all understanding. According to Paul (in Philippians 4:19), this kind of peace comes from trusting that God will supply all of our needs according to His riches in glory. Our peace—the kind of peace that sustains us when everything around us is falling apart—keeps us content, even when the world is in turmoil.

The question always arises: "Why is America so interested in Israel and its peace?" We live in a nation founded on Judeo-Christian principles. Christianity is rooted in biblical Judaism, and there is a dynamic relationship that binds root and branch together. It begins with Isaiah 53, which is an illumination of the primacy or dominance of the Messiah's redemptive ministry way before it flowed into the pages of the New Testament. In other words, we are permanently bound together, because we understand that Jesus Christ is the fulfillment of their prophecy, and we are obligated by faith to share that revelation with God's chosen people.

We know that the covenant God formed with Israel is still valid because we still await the fulfillment of Ezekiel's prophecy of the great restoration of Israel. Until all prophecy is fulfilled, God's covenant relationship with His chosen people remains intact.

III. CONCLUDING REFLECTION

Israel's prominence in today's global affairs points toward the fulfillment of the New Millennium prophecies. The wheels are in motion for God to usher in His restoration of Israel and His judgment for those who would desire her destruction. Christian nations have aligned themselves with Israel and promised to protect her, while enemies of Israel vow to annihilate her. We can easily see that the world stage is being set for this final showdown between God and Satan.

Christians are challenged to watch world leaders closely as leaders emerge on the world stage who may be ushered in by God to advance God's plan for Israel and all humankind. Jesus gave us the prescription for sound "shepherd leadership." If we use Christ's prescription for good leadership, we will readily recognize when good leaders arrive on the world scene. As the Good Shepherd, Jesus modeled His approach by laying down His life for His sheep (see John 10:11-17). He put all on the line for His own sheep. His death and resurrection guaranteed the security, safety, and sufficient supply, if we would believe in Him. These are the same "gifts" that good leaders provide for their followers. They do all in their power to provide security, safety, and a sufficient supply of all the necessities to sustain life.

Those who hold leadership positions in their churches should ask the tough question: "How well am I providing for those who follow me?" God grants leadership positions for a purpose. They are temporary gifts from God to be held in trust during the leader's brief time of service. When leaders find themselves holding on to their positions like possessions—or worse, when they crave the power that the position affords—it is time for God to take the position away and remove those persons from office. Leaders should always hold their positions with a light touch, ever mindful that whatever opportunities they have to serve God are gifts *from* God. We are all under-shepherds of the Great Shepherd, and we are called to manage rather than to own.

Here are some penetrating questions for the teacher to ask participants:

1. What does it mean to have a leader with a servant heart?

2. How do we discern a leader with a servant heart?

3. Why did the leaders of God's people fail to care for the flock of God?

4. Should our church leaders, particularly pastors, receive theological education?

5. What do we need to do to retain servant leaders in our churches?

PRAYER

Heavenly Father, strengthen our characters so that we can carry out the mission You have called us to do. Help us to be effective leaders as we seek to guide Your sheep. In Jesus' name we pray. Amen.

WORD POWER

To Shepherd *(ra`ah)*—means "to pasture, shepherd." *Ra`ah* represents what a shepherd allows domestic animals to do when they feed on grasses in the fields. *Ra`ah* can also represent the entire job of a shepherd. Used metaphorically, this verb represents a leader's or a ruler's relationship to his or her people. The verb is used figuratively, in the sense "to provide with nourishment" or "to enliven."

HOME DAILY BIBLE READINGS
(March 2-8, 2009)

New Leadership

MONDAY, March 2: "A Begotten Son" (Psalm 2:4-11)

TUESDAY, March 3: "The Good Shepherd" (John 10:11-18)

WEDNESDAY, March 4: "Trusting in the Lord" (Psalm 21:1-7)

THURSDAY, March 5: "An Enduring Throne" (Psalm 45:1-7)

FRIDAY, March 6: "A Righteous King" (Psalm 72:1-7)

SATURDAY, March 7: "An Exalted King" (Psalm 110)

SUNDAY, March 8: "You Are My Sheep" (Ezekiel 34:23-31)

GOD'S PEOPLE RESTORED AGAIN

DEVOTIONAL READING: **Psalm 25:11-22**
PRINT PASSAGE: **Ezekiel 36:22-32**

BACKGROUND SCRIPTURE: **Ezekiel 36:22-32**
KEY VERSE: **Ezekiel 36:23**

Ezekiel 36:22-32—KJV

22 Therefore say unto the house of Israel, Thus saith the Lord GOD; I do not this for your sakes, O house of Israel, but for mine holy name's sake, which ye have profaned among the heathen, whither ye went.
23 And I will sanctify my great name, which was profaned among the heathen, which ye have profaned in the midst of them; and the heathen shall know that I am the LORD, saith the Lord GOD, when I shall be sanctified in you before their eyes.
24 For I will take you from among the heathen, and gather you out of all countries, and will bring you into your own land.
25 Then will I sprinkle clean water upon you, and ye shall be clean: from all your filthiness, and from all your idols, will I cleanse you.
26 A new heart also will I give you, and a new spirit will I put within you: and I will take away the stony heart out of your flesh, and I will give you an heart of flesh.
27 And I will put my spirit within you, and cause you to walk in my statutes, and ye shall keep my judgments, and do them.
28 And ye shall dwell in the land that I gave to your fathers; and ye shall be my people, and I will be your God.
29 I will also save you from all your uncleannesses: and I will call for the corn, and will increase it, and lay no famine upon you.
30 And I will multiply the fruit of the tree, and the increase of the field, that ye shall receive no more reproach of famine among the heathen.
31 Then shall ye remember your own evil ways, and your doings that were not good, and shall lothe yourselves in your own sight for your iniquities and for your abominations.
32 Not for your sakes do I this, saith the Lord GOD, be it known unto you: be ashamed and confounded for your own ways, O house of Israel.

Ezekiel 36:22-32—NRSV

22 Therefore say to the house of Israel, Thus says the Lord GOD: It is not for your sake, O house of Israel, that I am about to act, but for the sake of my holy name, which you have profaned among the nations to which you came.
23 I will sanctify my great name, which has been profaned among the nations, and which you have profaned among them; and the nations shall know that I am the LORD, says the Lord GOD, when through you I display my holiness before their eyes.
24 I will take you from the nations, and gather you from all the countries, and bring you into your own land.
25 I will sprinkle clean water upon you, and you shall be clean from all your uncleannesses, and from all your idols I will cleanse you.
26 A new heart I will give you, and a new spirit I will put within you; and I will remove from your body the heart of stone and give you a heart of flesh.
27 I will put my spirit within you, and make you follow my statutes and be careful to observe my ordinances.
28 Then you shall live in the land that I gave to your ancestors; and you shall be my people, and I will be your God.
29 I will save you from all your uncleannesses, and I will summon the grain and make it abundant and lay no famine upon you.
30 I will make the fruit of the tree and the produce of the field abundant, so that you may never again suffer the disgrace of famine among the nations.
31 Then you shall remember your evil ways, and your dealings that were not good; and you shall loathe yourselves for your iniquities and your abominable deeds.
32 It is not for your sake that I will act, says the Lord GOD; let that be known to you. Be ashamed and dismayed for your ways, O house of Israel.

UNIFYING LESSON PRINCIPLE

Although the fruits of action are often visible, the reasons for an action taken at a particular time and in a certain place are more difficult to discern. What motivates actions? According to Ezekiel, God's promise to restore Israel was not motivated by Israel itself, but rather for the sake of God's holy name.

TOPICAL OUTLINE OF THE LESSON

I. Introduction
   A. Representing Christ
   B. Biblical Background

II. Exposition and Application of the Scripture
   A. Redeeming a Heart of Stone
      (Ezekiel 36:22-26a)
   B. Creating a Heart of Flesh
      (Ezekiel 36:26b-27)
   C. Healing a Nation
      (Ezekiel 36:28-32)

III. Concluding Reflection

LESSON OBJECTIVES

Upon completion of this lesson, the students will know that:

1. Even though the Israelites had polluted God's name among the heathen, yet He would vindicate His holy name;
2. God's mercy would prevail by giving them a new heart; and,
3. If we truly repent of our sins, God will pardon us unreservedly.

POINTS TO BE EMPHASIZED

ADULT/YOUTH
Adult Topic: Restoring Human Lives
Youth Topic: Undeserved U-Turn
Adult Key Verse: Ezekiel 36:23
Youth Key Verse: Ezekiel 36:27
Print Passage: Ezekiel 36:22-32

—God's action to restore the Lord's holy name would benefit the house of Israel materially and spiritually.

—The people's return to the land, at God's initiative, would result in their repentance—as God's holiness and their past sinfulness were revealed.

—As the covenant was renewed in the restored land to which the house of Israel would return, the new heart and spirit God would grant the people would enable them to obey Him.

—Israel was rescued and restored by God, not because Israel is deserving, but because of God's purposes.

—Therefore, God restored undeserving Israel as an instrument to make the nations know God's power, sovereignty, justice, and care as manifested in the regeneration of Israel and restoration of their land.

—God's great power was manifested in two ways: (a) the regeneration of the people Israel; and (b) the restoration of the land of Israel.

CHILDREN
Children Topic: A New Relationship
Key Verse: Ezekiel 36:23
Print Passage: Ezekiel 36:22-32

—God's holiness is displayed by the things He does.

—God wants a relationship with us.

—God provides opportunities for us to be obedient.

—God offers cleansing for our disobedience.

—In the work God did through Israel, others saw God's holiness.

I. INTRODUCTION

A. Representing Christ

Christianity's growth rate is directly tied to the effectiveness of our witness. Many people today have grown cynical about religion. We need to be careful about the way we present the Gospel to others, so that our message is straightforward and credible. We must be careful not to fall into what Paul described as the desire to use flattering words or compromise our credibility (see 1 Thessalonians 2:5). The key to Christianity's integrity is the realization that God Himself has entrusted us with His message. We must therefore carefully consider the ways in which we present Christ to people around us.

Our methods and our motives must never conflict with the message God has given us. At Athens, Paul addressed the Greeks in three different settings (the synagogue, the tribunal, and the marketplace) with three different approaches. He customized his presentation for maximum reception. He was willing to take his message of salvation into every arena and beyond the confines of personal experience.

Since our habits speak louder than our words, our lifestyles are our greatest witness for Christ. If we live selfishly, preferring to lavish ourselves with life's rewards instead of sharing our blessings with others, we send mixed signals to those with whom we share the love of Christ. If we hold grudges against our enemies, we send those same mixed signals. We must be willing and prepared to represent Christ and His values in every aspect of our lives, both at home and in the workplace. The consistency of our lifestyles will draw others with far greater magnetism and influence than our words.

Christians live in a "fishbowl" existence. God wants us to take seriously the privilege of representing Christ in our community and workplace. We are the method by which God makes His name known to the nations and people of the world. Aside from the direct witness of Scripture and the life and work of Jesus Christ Himself, God's primary method is through the use of men and women who have dedicated themselves to Him and want to live as He commands. We are that light of the world, about whom Christ spoke in Matthew 5:14-16. Our good works light the way for the unbeliever to find his way to Jesus Christ and salvation. This means that God's very reputation is at stake when it comes to how we conduct our lives.

B. Biblical Background

Ezekiel was called to be a prophet in the fifth year of his captivity (see Ezekiel 1:1-2). His ministry lasted twenty-two years. We know little about his personal life, other than the fact that he was married. He was a powerful preacher who possessed a deeply introspective and religious nature, using allegory, vivid figures, and symbolic actions to send the clear message that "the hand of the Lord was upon me" (see 1:3; 3:14, 22). Ezekiel felt compelled to communicate the message given to him by God, and he carried that message directly to his Jewish brethren in exile. When Jerusalem was finally destroyed some ten years after he arrived in Babylon, Ezekiel entered into the sufferings of his people. On the day that the final siege of Jerusalem began, his wife died suddenly. God did not allow Ezekiel to go through the customary period of mourning the death of his wife, perhaps because God wanted him to be an example of the greater sorrow coming upon the nation of Israel. Regardless, much of the people of Israel resented Ezekiel's prophecies because they held out little hope for the immediate future of the Israelites.

Israel's duty was to preserve God's reputation. God made a covenant with them to be His people (see Ezekiel 20:5-6). They were chosen to introduce monotheism to a world bent on serving idol gods. They accepted their covenant duty, but they reneged on their commitment—not once but three times—

before they even got to the Promised Land. Instead of serving the Lord, they turned back to the idols that they had learned to worship in Egypt. And each time the Lord threatened His fury on them for disobedience, He spared them from annihilation for one reason only: God wanted the rest of the world to know who He was. If Israel had been completely destroyed, the pagan nations of the world would have lost the only witness they had to the one true and living God.

The negative reaction Ezekiel received from his peers did not discourage or deter him. And eventually his message was received, because the Exile experience became a time of purging for Judah. It was during this purging that Ezekiel's message emerged as one of promise—that God would bring His people back to their land, send the Son of David to reign over them, and give them a new heart.

II. EXPOSITION AND APPLICATION OF THE SCRIPTURE

A. Redeeming a Heart of Stone
(Ezekiel 36:22-26a)

Therefore say unto the house of Israel, Thus saith the Lord God; I do not this for your sakes, O house of Israel, but for mine holy name's sake, which ye have profaned among the heathen, whither ye went. And I will sanctify my great name, which was profaned among the heathen, which ye have profaned in the midst of them; and the heathen shall know that I am the Lord, saith the Lord God, when I shall be sanctified in you before their eyes. For I will take you from among the heathen, and gather you out of all countries, and will bring you into your own land. Then will I sprinkle clean water upon you, and ye shall be clean: from all your filthiness, and from all your idols, will I cleanse you. A new heart also will I give you, and a new spirit will I put within you.

Ezekiel's message was a tough pill to swallow for God's chosen people. He told the Israelites that they had angered God by committing the

ultimate sin of misrepresenting their Lord to the heathen world. Other nations viewed the sovereign God through the actions of Israel, and she had besmirched His holy name. Israel never considered that her actions would sever her relationship with God. But sin does just that—it severs humanity from God. Adam severed his perfect relationship with God when he disobeyed in the Garden of Eden. From that time forward, it was God's mercy alone that sustained man's connection with Him.

Israel's adulterous relationship with idol gods was enough reason for God to divorce Himself from them. They no longer deserved to be His bride. However, God said He would vindicate and manifest His holy name in opposition to the pagan reproaches of it, which was brought on by the Jews' waywardness.

It was for this reason that mercy pleaded Israel's case. Regardless of their unworthiness, God told them through His prophet Ezekiel that He would restore Israel, not for her sake, but for His name's sake. Restoration was imperative because God's character was at stake. Just as Christ did not wait for our worthiness in order to save us, God did not wait to fill the void left by Israel's sin. He simply filled the void with grace and mercy. A remnant of Israel had to be saved. Instead of destruction and permanent separation, the lineage of David was prophesied to usher in the Messiah when the fruit of grace and mercy were ripe with promise.

God promised that if Israel would repent, there would be no limit to the blessings of her new relationship with Him. Again, Israel did nothing to deserve restoration. God was simply being the merciful sovereign Master that He is. Ezekiel revealed the means by which God would show His holiness. First, He would restore the nation physically. He would gather her from all the countries of the world and bring her back into her own land.

However, Israel's restoration would be more than physical. God promised, "Then will I sprinkle clean water upon you, and ye shall be clean: from all your filthiness, and from all your idols, will I cleanse you" (Ezekiel 36:25). The sprinkling of water did not refer to baptism. Since Israel's sin was like the ceremonial impurity of menstruation (see 36:17), her cleansing was compared to the ceremonial act of purification. The "sprinkling of water" was symbolic of Israel being purified from her sin. God would then impart a *new spirit*, and replace Israel's heart of stone with a heart of flesh.

B. Creating a Heart of Flesh (Ezekiel 36:26b-27)

And I will take away the stony heart out of your flesh, and I will give you an heart of flesh. And I will put my spirit within you, and cause you to walk in my statutes, and ye shall keep my judgments, and do them.

In this selection, there are many phrases we need to pay attention to: three times God, through His prophet, said, "I will." Each of these phrases has a complement, which is a promise. When God said "I will," He meant business. When we human beings say "I will," we are often quick to run away from keeping our promise, because of circumstances which are beyond our control. But when God says "I will" there are no circumstances which will cause Him to go back on His promise. That being said, in the first "I will" statement, God said that He would "take away the stony heart...." A "stony heart" is not receptive to the promptings of the Holy Spirit, but God promised His people that He would do this. Even though there are Jews whose hearts are still not receptive to God's Word, God will ultimately give them hearts of flesh (receptive hearts). God will cause them to serve Him.

A *stone* is a solid, almost impenetrable substance. A stone's properties make it impossible for it to absorb anything. Instead, it repels whatever it comes in contact with. But soft, pliable flesh is penetrable. This was the obvious analogy of God's message to Israel. He would remove their impenetrable heart of stone and replace it with a penetrable heart of flesh. This Old Testament positive implanting of a new nature in Israel was a prerequisite to the new nature that all believers receive who repent and accept Christ as their Lord and Savior. Implanting God's spirit within a believer produces a new relationship with God. When we are released from the penalty of sin, we see the full measure of God's mercy and grace toward us, and we realize that we do not deserve this favor. Just as the blackness of Israel's past actions contrasted so starkly with the light of God's grace, we who are baptized into the body of Christ and experience salvation instantly see the stark contrast of our sinful past against the purity of a new life in Christ. This Holy Spirit baptism magnifies another truth. It is the truth that salvation cannot be earned.

C. Healing a Nation
(Ezekiel 36:28-32)

And ye shall dwell in the land that I gave to your fathers; and ye shall be my people, and I will be your God. I will also save you from all your uncleannesses: and I will call for the corn, and will increase it, and lay no famine upon you. And I will multiply the fruit of the tree, and the increase of the field, that ye shall receive no more reproach of famine among the heathen. Then shall ye remember your own evil ways, and your doings that were not good, and shall lothe yourselves in your own sight for your iniquities and for your abominations. Not for your sakes do I this, saith the Lord GOD, be it known unto you: be ashamed and confounded for your own ways, O house of Israel.

Forgiveness promotes healing. This was the lesson God wanted Israel to learn. He wanted the Israelites to understand that while sin could not completely destroy their relationship with Him ("But where sin abounded, grace did much more abound"—Romans 5:20), it was surely damaging their testimony to the world and destroying their fellowship.

We do not have a license to sin. God's abundant grace should spur us to obedience. When we do sin, repentance brings quick reconciliation to the sinful heart. God's forgiveness then becomes a living testimony of His grace and mercy.

God's forgiveness did not mean that Israel would not suffer consequences for her long-standing disobedience. There is a cause-and-effect relationship at work in our lives, despite the forgiveness of God. While we may be forgiven for our sinful actions, we may still have to suffer the consequences of those actions. This does not spell out a conflict between forgiveness and consequences. At the moment of trusting Christ as our Savior, forgiveness and consequences are on a parallel course to accomplish an essential part of God's plan for all believers. We learn both by God's forgiveness and by the consequences for our sinful actions. While it is true that we can pay a high price for our mistakes ("He that soweth to his flesh shall of the flesh reap corruption"—Galatians 6:8), we must not focus on the negative. Instead, we must celebrate the positive side of God's valuable principle ("He that soweth to the Spirit shall of the Spirit reap life everlasting" —Galatians 6:8).

Ezekiel prophesied of a time when Israel's healing would be complete. The consequences for their sinful actions would give way to the healing of the nation. The healing would be complete when Israel realized the full implications of her sin and began to loathe her own past. The timing of this healing of Israel, which the Scriptures paint as a visible blessing, would be tied to their ultimate acceptance of Christ as Messiah.

III. CONCLUDING REFLECTION

As Christians, we must always be keenly aware of whom we represent. Our actions are often the only Bible non-believers will ever experience. Their perception of God may rest solely in our ability to live Christlike lives in their presence.

Consider all the times in your life when God's mercy and compassion preceded your own feelings of remorse and repentance. These are the greatest demonstrations of our Father's love for us. God offers a lifeline of hope to everyone because He desires that humans would fulfill their destiny as God's own people. But there is a limit to God's patience. When we do seek forgiveness, we are moving forward toward spiritual good health. God can then entrust us with the awesome responsibility of correctly portraying His character to the world, so that our Christlike attitude will draw the unsaved to His Son Jesus Christ.

In light of Israel's history, believers today need to be careful about our reputations as Christians. We must ask ourselves the tough questions: "Are my actions worthy of the Lord I claim to serve? Are people attracted to God or repelled by my conduct? Is God honored by the things that I do and say?"

If Israel had repented of her adulterous faith, God would have forgiven her and healed her land (see 2 Chronicles 7:14). God offers that same hope for all sinners today. Humility, prayer, the rejection of sin, and the worship of God are the keys that open heaven's heart and allow mercy to begin the healing process.

PRAYER

Heavenly Father, help us to light the way for the unbeliever to find his or her way to Jesus Christ and salvation. In Jesus' name we pray. Amen.

WORD POWER

Restoration *(apokatastasis*—from "apo")—this means "back, again"; *kathistemi,* "to set in order," is used in Acts 3:21—(RV): "restoration"; *Restoration*—in the papyri it is used for "a temple cell of a goddess"; a "repair" of a public way; the "restoration" of estates to rightful owners; and a "balancing" of accounts.

HOME DAILY BIBLE READINGS
(March 9-15, 2009)

God's People Restored Again
MONDAY, March 9: "Restored with God's Help" (Psalm 60:1-5, 11-12)
TUESDAY, March 10: "Restored to Be Saved" (Psalm 80:1-7)
WEDNESDAY, March 11: "Restored to Our Salvation" (Psalm 85:1-9)
THURSDAY, March 12: "Restored to God" (Lamentations 5:15-21)
FRIDAY, March 13: "Restored Through Repentance" (Jeremiah 31:7-9, 16-20)
SATURDAY, March 14: "Restored to Service" (Jeremiah 15:15-21)
SUNDAY, March 15: "For the Sake of God's Name" (Ezekiel 36:22-32)

PROPHESYING NEW LIFE

DEVOTIONAL READING: **Romans 6:1-14**
PRINT PASSAGE: **Ezekiel 37:1-14**

BACKGROUND SCRIPTURE: **Ezekiel 37**
KEY VERSE: **Ezekiel 37:6**

Ezekiel 37:1-14—KJV

THE HAND of the LORD was upon me, and carried me out in the spirit of the LORD, and set me down in the midst of the valley which was full of bones,

2 And caused me to pass by them round about: and, behold, there were very many in the open valley; and, lo, they were very dry.

3 And he said unto me, Son of man, can these bones live? And I answered, O Lord GOD, thou knowest.

4 Again he said unto me, Prophesy upon these bones, and say unto them, O ye dry bones, hear the word of the LORD.

5 Thus saith the Lord GOD unto these bones; Behold, I will cause breath to enter into you, and ye shall live:

6 And I will lay sinews upon you, and will bring up flesh upon you, and cover you with skin, and put breath in you, and ye shall live; and ye shall know that I am the LORD.

7 So I prophesied as I was commanded: and as I prophesied, there was a noise, and behold a shaking, and the bones came together, bone to his bone.

8 And when I beheld, lo, the sinews and the flesh came up upon them, and the skin covered them above: but there was no breath in them.

9 Then said he unto me, Prophesy unto the wind, prophesy, son of man, and say to the wind, Thus saith the Lord GOD; Come from the four winds, O breath, and breathe upon these slain, that they may live.

10 So I prophesied as he commanded me, and the breath came into them, and they lived, and stood up upon their feet, an exceeding great army.

11 Then he said unto me, Son of man, these bones are the whole house of Israel: behold, they say, Our bones are dried, and our hope is lost: we are cut off for our parts.

12 Therefore prophesy and say unto them, Thus saith the Lord GOD; Behold, O my people, I will open your graves, and cause you to come up out of your graves, and bring you into the land of Israel.

Ezekiel 37:1-14—NRSV

THE HAND of the LORD came upon me, and he brought me out by the spirit of the LORD and set me down in the middle of a valley; it was full of bones.

2 He led me all around them; there were very many lying in the valley, and they were very dry.

3 He said to me, "Mortal, can these bones live?" I answered, "O Lord GOD, you know."

4 Then he said to me, "Prophesy to these bones, and say to them: O dry bones, hear the word of the LORD.

5 Thus says the Lord GOD to these bones: I will cause breath to enter you, and you shall live.

6 I will lay sinews on you, and will cause flesh to come upon you, and cover you with skin, and put breath in you, and you shall live; and you shall know that I am the LORD."

7 So I prophesied as I had been commanded; and as I prophesied, suddenly there was a noise, a rattling, and the bones came together, bone to its bone.

8 I looked, and there were sinews on them, and flesh had come upon them, and skin had covered them; but there was no breath in them.

9 Then he said to me, "Prophesy to the breath, prophesy, mortal, and say to the breath: Thus says the Lord GOD: Come from the four winds, O breath, and breathe upon these slain, that they may live."

10 I prophesied as he commanded me, and the breath came into them, and they lived, and stood on their feet, a vast multitude.

11 Then he said to me, "Mortal, these bones are the whole house of Israel. They say, 'Our bones are dried up, and our hope is lost; we are cut off completely.'

12 Therefore prophesy, and say to them, Thus says the Lord GOD: I am going to open your graves, and bring you up from your graves, O my people; and I will bring you back to the land of Israel.

UNIFYING LESSON PRINCIPLE

Sometimes situations seem so overwhelming that we fall into despair. Where can we find hope? Ezekiel's prophecy of the valley of dry bones vividly illustrates how God enlivens people and fills them with the breath of life and hope.

13 And ye shall know that I am the LORD, when I have opened your graves, O my people, and brought you up out of your graves,
14 And shall put my spirit in you, and ye shall live, and I shall place you in your own land: then shall ye know that I the LORD have spoken it, and performed it, saith the LORD.

13 And you shall know that I am the LORD, when I open your graves, and bring you up from your graves, O my people.
14 I will put my spirit within you, and you shall live, and I will place you on your own soil; then you shall know that I, the LORD, have spoken and will act, says the LORD."

TOPICAL OUTLINE OF THE LESSON

I. Introduction
A. Newness of Life
B. Biblical Background

II. Exposition and Application of the Scripture
A. God's "Dry Bones" Promise (Ezekiel 37:1-6)
B. Ezekiel's "Dry Bones" Participation (Ezekiel 37:7-13)
C. God's Spirit Gives Power (Ezekiel 37:14)

III. Concluding Reflection

LESSON OBJECTIVES

Upon completion of this lesson, the students will know that:

1. These are some situations in life that seem so overwhelming that we fall into despair;
2. We can find hope in God; and,
3. God enlivens people and fills them with the breath of life and hope.

POINTS TO BE EMPHASIZED

ADULT/YOUTH
Adult Topic: Renewal of Life
Youth Topic: Vitality for Victims!
Adult/Youth Key Verse: Ezekiel 37:6
Print Passage: Ezekiel 37:1-14

—After several years in exile and the destruction of Jerusalem, the house of Israel had abandoned hope.
—In the dead, dry bones, Ezekiel is shown a symbol of the house of Israel.
—In this passage, the word *spirit* (*rúah* in Hebrew) refers to: (1) the Spirit of the Lord (verse 1); (2) the life-giving breath of the Lord (verses 5, 6, 10); and (3) the four "winds" of heaven (in its plural form, verse 9).
—Ezekiel's prophecy depicts a people that will rise from the dead to become a living community that will obediently live by the things of God that bring and preserve true life.
—Life comes to these dry bones, not just when they are covered with flesh, but when they are given the breath of life from God.
—The new life for Judah would be so radical that it would be very apparent that such new life could only be from God.

CHILDREN
Children Topic: Another Chance
Key Verse: Ezekiel 37:14
Print Passage: Ezekiel 37:1-14

—God showed the prophet what being separated from God looked like.

—God's actions through the prophet demonstrated that God can do the impossible.

—Obedience to God results in people's lives taking on new meaning and hope.

—God provides hope, gives new life, and reveals His power.

I. INTRODUCTION

A. Newness of Life

Regeneration is "the act of rebirth." It has as its basic idea "to be born again" or "to be restored." It is the spiritual change that is wrought in the hearts of humankind by an act of God in which a person's inherently sinful nature is changed so that he or she can respond to God in faith. Christ impregnates humanity with a portion of God's Spirit, and a new *seed* sprouts. The Bible calls this *newness of life*. Though the word *regeneration* is used only twice—and only in the New Testament—it is appropriate to consider its definition in light of Ezekiel's prophecies to Israel.

The need for regeneration comes out of the nature of humanity's sinfulness. As long as a person is living in sin, he or she cannot believe in God. Sin keeps humans from standing in the presence of God. To get a person to believe in a Supreme Being, God must initiate a change by which his or her soul is released from the bondage of his or her own will to sin.

Regeneration, then, is the natural by-product of a new life in Christ. Like a seed whose outer shell has been watered and fed, this new life has no choice but to burst forth and blossom.

B. Biblical Background

This chapter of Ezekiel is a vivid illustration of the promises of the previous chapter. God had just announced that Israel would be restored to her land under the leadership of David her king. But since the purging of Israel was not yet complete, this promise seemed far off. Israel was dead as a nation—deprived of her land, her king, and her Temple. She had been divided and scattered for so long that unifying her seemed impossible. If the Israelites were going to make it through the spiritually dry period of their exile, they needed a sign. That sign was Ezekiel's promise that God, acting in love through His mercy, would release them from the bondage of separation and restore them to Himself.

We can be sure that God's promise to fully restore Israel has not yet been fulfilled. Despite the speculative hope of many, the return of many Israelis to Israel, Palestine, and the Gaza Strip is not the fulfillment of this prophecy. It will only be fulfilled when God gathers all believing Israelites to the land of their forefathers (see Jeremiah 31:33, 33:14-16), when Christ returns to establish His kingdom (see Matthew 24:30-31).

II. EXPOSITION AND APPLICATION OF THE SCRIPTURE

A. God's "Dry Bones" Promise
(Ezekiel 37:1-6)

THE HAND of the LORD was upon me, and carried me out in the spirit of the LORD, and set me down in the midst of the valley which was full of bones, And caused me to pass by them round about: and, behold, there were very many in the open valley; and, lo, they were very dry. And he said unto me, Son of man, can these bones live? And I answered, O Lord GOD, thou knowest. Again he said unto me, Prophesy upon these bones, and say unto them, O ye dry bones, hear the word of the LORD. Thus saith the Lord GOD unto these bones; Behold, I will cause breath to enter into you, and ye shall live: And I will lay sinews upon you, and will bring up flesh upon you, and cover you with skin, and put breath in you, and ye shall live; and ye shall know that I am the LORD.

Ezekiel's "dry bones" experience pictorially describes the broken relationship between God and His chosen people. The valley of dry bones represented the hopeless plight, not only of Israel and Judah, but also of sinful humanity. Israel and Judah had breached their covenant agreement with their Creator, just as Adam had done in the Garden of Eden. Here is the comparison: until the Jews were released from the penalty for their adulterous religious practices, they would remain dead as a nation; and until humanity is released from their sin, they too are spiritually dead, and cannot exercise freedom. Only God has the power to release Israel from the penalty for disobedience, and only God has the power to release people from sin. The Lord promised to revive and regenerate Israel and Judah under a new covenant. He also promised to regenerate the spirit of humanity through the immediate agency of the Holy Spirit operative in humans (see Colossians 2:13), which originates in people new lives in Christ.

But this new life is not merely a new state that arises out of forgiveness of sins. Ezekiel's fast-forward vision took him beyond the Old Testament to witness the restorative power of God through Jesus Christ. For the Jews, and for humankind, regeneration is the positive implantation of Christ's righteousness in all humankind, by which people are: 1) *quickened* ("As the Father raiseth up the dead, and quickeneth them; even so the Son quickeneth whom he will"—John 5:21); 2) *begotten* ("Whosoever believeth that Jesus is the Christ is born of God: and every one that loveth him that begat loveth him also that is begotten of him"—1 John 5:1); 3) *made new creations* ("Therefore if any man be in Christ, he is a new creature: old things are passed away; behold, all things are become new"—2 Corinthians 5:17); and 4) *given new lives* ("Therefore we are buried with him by baptism into death: that like as Christ was raised up from the dead by the glory of the Father, even so we also should walk in newness of life"—Romans 6:4).

Most Israelites may have doubted God's promise of restoration. Their condition at that time conflicted with the possibility of their restoration. So God, through Ezekiel, stressed the fact of His sovereign power and ability to carry out this remarkable promise. God made it clear to His prophet that their fulfillment depended on Him, not on circumstances. Just as the people in their dead state of sin could do nothing to redeem themselves, Israel and Judah could do nothing to initiate their own restoration.

Notice that in the vision, the bones were very dry, bleached by the desert's hot sun. Ezekiel was not looking at dead bodies; he was looking at *parts* of dead bodies. God asked Ezekiel a strange question—whether there was potential for life in those lifeless bones. Of course, Ezekiel knew that humanly speaking, that was impossible, so he said, "O Sovereign Lord, you alone know" (see Ezekiel 37). His guarded response demonstrated his belief that God alone could accomplish such a feat.

Regeneration gives humans new minds, changed wills, and renewed natures. If it is real, it is irrevocable because it alters a person's governing disposition, and restores him to a right relationship with God through Christ.

B. Ezekiel's "Dry Bones" Participation (Ezekiel 37:7-13)

So I prophesied as I was commanded: and as I prophesied, there was a noise, and behold a shaking, and the bones came together, bone to his bone. And when I beheld, lo, the sinews and the flesh came up upon them, and the skin covered them above: but there was no breath in them. Then said he unto me, Prophesy unto the wind, prophesy, son of man, and say to the wind, Thus saith the Lord God; Come from the four winds, O breath, and breathe upon these slain, that they may live. So I prophesied as he commanded me, and the breath came into them, and they lived, and stood up upon their feet, an exceeding great army. Then he said unto me, Son of man, these bones are the whole house of Israel: behold, they say, Our bones are dried, and our hope is lost: we are cut off for our parts. Therefore prophesy and say unto them, Thus saith the Lord God; Behold, O my people, I will open your graves, and cause you to come up out of your graves, and bring you into the land of Israel. And ye shall know that I am the Lord, when I have opened your graves, O my people, and brought you up out of your graves.

God then directed Ezekiel to prophesy to the dry bones. The content of his message was that God would blow His breath of life into these lifeless bones. The word *breath* could also be translated as *wind* or *spirit*. Possibly, God had in mind Genesis 2:7, when He created Adam and blew the breath of life into his nostrils.

Whether God was referring to the wind, the breath, or the Holy Spirit is not certain. But what is certain is the end result. As Ezekiel preached, God instilled new life into the old, dry, bleached bones. The bones developed skin, came together, and stood up.

What did this vision tell Ezekiel about the state of his nation? The nation of Israel was in captivity. They were dead as a nation. Like unburied corpses, they were pining away in Babylon, and there was no end in sight to their captivity. The Scripture states that they were "cut off." Israel felt that their national hopes had been destroyed and there was no hope of resurrection. But the revival of the dry bones told the rest of the story. It was the sign God gave of Israel's impending restoration. Ezekiel's vision showed that Israel's new life depended on God's power, not outward influence. God promised to renew them not only physically, but also spiritually. The breath of life was a symbol of the Holy Spirit of Israel's New Covenant (see Ezekiel 36:24-28).

This recorded vision was not just to encourage Israel. It is difficult for *all* of humankind to accept the possibility of complete restoration. Though our New Testament covenant with Christ offers absolute redemption through His blood, thousands approach the altar of God with their minds doubting His ability to fix their brokenness. But if their confession and their desire to be made whole are real, they soon find themselves quickened by the "breath" of God's Spirit within them. It cannot be emphasized enough that new life depends not on outward circumstances, but on God alone.

C. God's Spirit Gives Power (Ezekiel 37:14)

And shall put my spirit in you, and ye shall live, and I shall

place you in your own land: then shall ye know that I the Lord have spoken it, and performed it, saith the Lord.

No matter how much we think we can motivate ourselves back to wellness, the truth is that only God can truly regenerate and restore a broken spirit by His Spirit. In regeneration, the soul is both passive and active. It is passive while it is in bondage to sin. But it becomes active when it is released. The regenerating work of the Holy Spirit is not motivated by a prior submission of the soul. That would be like putting the cart before the horse. It is the act of releasing the soul from sin (which can only be accomplished by God's power) that causes the soul to turn toward God in fellowship. The souls of all humans remain dead until God breathes His breath of life into them.

The Holy Spirit empowers in many ways. He dwells with us ("Even the Spirit of truth; whom the world cannot receive, because it seeth him not, neither knoweth him: but ye know him; for he dwelleth with you, and shall be in you"—John 14:17); He empowers us to bear witness ("But this cometh to pass, that the word might be fulfilled that is written in their law, They hated me without a cause"—John 15:25); He convinces us of sin ("And when he is come, he will reprove the world of sin, and of righteousness, and of judgment"—John 16:8); He teaches God's teaching and brings it to our remembrance ("But the Comforter, which is the Holy Ghost, whom the Father will send in my name, he shall teach you all things, and bring all things to your remembrance, whatsoever I have said unto you"—John 14:26); and He calls ministers ("Ye call me Master and Lord: and ye say well; for so I am"—John 13:13). He also sends out workers ("Jesus knowing that the Father had given all things into his hands, and that he was come

from God, and went to God"—John 13:3). He forbids certain actions ("Nevertheless I tell you the truth; It is expedient for you that I go away: for if I go not away, the Comforter will not come unto you; but if I depart, I will send him unto you"—John 16:7), and intercedes on our behalf ("Likewise the Spirit also helpeth our infirmities: for we know not what we should pray for as we ought: but the Spirit itself maketh intercession for us with groanings which cannot be uttered"—Romans 8:26). The Holy Spirit can be lied to and tempted (Acts 5:3-4, 9), resisted (Acts 7:51), grieved (Ephesians 4:30), outraged (Hebrews 10:29, RSV), and blasphemed against (Matthew 12:31). This brief description of the Holy Spirit reinforces God's ability to completely possess a person who desires to be possessed.

God promised the Israelites that when their restoration was complete, they would know, by the aid of the Holy Spirit, that their regeneration and restoration as a nation were solely at the hand of God. It is important for us, as Christians, to understand the magnitude of God's Holy Spirit power as it relates to our New Testament Covenant. Though the Holy Spirit was placed upon certain people in the Old Testament for specific purposes, it was Jesus who first released its power on the New Testament believer. On the evening of the Resurrection, Jesus breathed on His disciples and told them to "Receive ye the Holy Ghost." But this was a provisional release, meant to enable the disciples to persevere in prayer until the Day of Pentecost.

At Pentecost, a new phase of God's revelation to humanity began. It was as new as the day the Word became flesh and dwelt among us. But this time, the Word would not dwell among us, but in us. This New

Testament Spirit would one day be released upon a repented and restored Israel.

III. CONCLUDING REFLECTION

Renewed spirits are a powerful witness for Christ. That is why a repentant sinner often brings more new converts into the church than those who have been in church all their lives. The experience of regeneration or renewal inspires those who witness it to be a part of the experience. All of us can recall the miraculous transformation of some sinner who was received into the body of Christ. When we experience such a powerful conversion, the entire body of Christ is energized by the transformation and experiences a renewal of faith as well.

When we witness the fall of a saint into a life of sin, there should be a gentle and deliberate effort by the church to restore that individual to a right relationship with God, even if it takes longer than we hoped it would. Every soul is worth saving. God desires that none should perish. His regenerative Holy Spirit seeks to save every person from the vilest of sins. Seasoned Christians know that our sovereign God can breathe life into the most hopeless of situations because He breathed life into us.

PRAYER

Heavenly Father, thank You for helping us to understand that no man can earn salvation or prepare himself to receive it. Thank You for helping us to see that salvation is a free gift that we can either accept or reject. In Jesus' name we pray. Amen.

WORD POWER

Transform *(hapak)*—"to turn, overturn, change, transform, and turn back." In its simplest meaning, *hapak* expresses the turning from one side to another, such as "turning" one's back.

HOME DAILY BIBLE READINGS
(March 16-22, 2009)

Prophesying New Life
MONDAY, March 16: "God Will Do Something New" (Isaiah 43:14-21)
TUESDAY, March 17: "A New Strength" (Isaiah 40:25-31)
WEDNESDAY, March 18: "A New Covenant" (Luke 22:14-23)
THURSDAY, March 19: "A New Creation" (2 Corinthians 5:16-21)
FRIDAY, March 20: "New Mercies Every Day" (Lamentations 3:19-31)
SATURDAY, March 21: "A New Song" (Psalm 40:1-5)
SUNDAY, March 22: "You Shall Live!" (Ezekiel 37:1-14)

ENVISIONING NEW LIFE

DEVOTIONAL READING: **John 4:7-15**
PRINT PASSAGE: **Ezekiel 47:1-12**

BACKGROUND SCRIPTURE: **Ezekiel 47:1-12**
KEY VERSE: **Ezekiel 47:9**

Ezekiel 47:1-12—KJV

AFTERWARD HE brought me again unto the door of the house; and, behold, waters issued out from under the threshold of the house eastward: for the forefront of the house stood toward the east, and the waters came down from under from the right side of the house, at the south side of the altar.

2 Then brought he me out of the way of the gate northward, and led me about the way without unto the utter gate by the way that looketh eastward; and, behold, there ran out waters on the right side.

3 And when the man that had the line in his hand went forth eastward, he measured a thousand cubits, and he brought me through the waters; the waters were to the ankles.

4 Again he measured a thousand, and brought me through the waters; the waters were to the knees. Again he measured a thousand, and brought me through; the waters were to the loins.

5 Afterward he measured a thousand; and it was a river that I could not pass over: for the waters were risen, waters to swim in, a river that could not be passed over.

6 And he said unto me, Son of man, hast thou seen this? Then he brought me, and caused me to return to the brink of the river.

7 Now when I had returned, behold, at the bank of the river were very many trees on the one side and on the other.

8 Then said he unto me, These waters issue out toward the east country, and go down into the desert, and go into the sea: which being brought forth into the sea, the waters shall be healed.

9 And it shall come to pass, that every thing that liveth, which moveth, whithersoever the rivers shall come, shall live: and there shall be a very great multitude of fish, because these waters shall come thither: for they shall be healed; and every thing shall live whither the river cometh.

10 And it shall come to pass, that the fishers shall stand upon it from En-gedi even unto En-eglaim; they shall be a place to spread forth nets; their fish shall be according to their kinds, as the fish of the great sea, exceeding many.

Ezekiel 47:1-12—NRSV

THEN HE brought me back to the entrance of the temple; there, water was flowing from below the threshold of the temple toward the east (for the temple faced east); and the water was flowing down from below the south end of the threshold of the temple, south of the altar.

2 Then he brought me out by way of the north gate, and led me around on the outside to the outer gate that faces toward the east; and the water was coming out on the south side.

3 Going on eastward with a cord in his hand, the man measured one thousand cubits, and then led me through the water; and it was ankle-deep.

4 Again he measured one thousand, and led me through the water; and it was knee-deep. Again he measured one thousand, and led me through the water; and it was up to the waist.

5 Again he measured one thousand, and it was a river that I could not cross, for the water had risen; it was deep enough to swim in, a river that could not be crossed.

6 He said to me, "Mortal, have you seen this?" Then he led me back along the bank of the river.

7 As I came back, I saw on the bank of the river a great many trees on the one side and on the other.

8 He said to me, "This water flows toward the eastern region and goes down into the Arabah; and when it enters the sea, the sea of stagnant waters, the water will become fresh.

9 Wherever the river goes, every living creature that swarms will live, and there will be very many fish, once these waters reach there. It will become fresh; and everything will live where the river goes.

10 People will stand fishing beside the sea from En-gedi to En-eglaim; it will be a place for the spreading of nets; its fish will be of a great many kinds, like the fish of the Great Sea.

UNIFYING LESSON PRINCIPLE

Humankind depends on the water that covers the vast areas of earth's landscape. What impact do these bodies of water have on humanity and all creation? In a vision, Ezekiel saw a sacred river that flowed freely from God's throne, sustaining life.

11 But the miry places thereof and the marishes thereof shall not be healed; they shall be given to salt.

12 And by the river upon the bank thereof, on this side and on that side, shall grow all trees for meat, whose leaf shall not fade, neither shall the fruit thereof be consumed: it shall bring forth new fruit according to his months, because their waters they issued out of the sanctuary: and the fruit thereof shall be for meat, and the leaf thereof for medicine.

11 But its swamps and marshes will not become fresh; they are to be left for salt.

12 On the banks, on both sides of the river, there will grow all kinds of trees for food. Their leaves will not wither nor their fruit fail, but they will bear fresh fruit every month, because the water for them flows from the sanctuary. Their fruit will be for food, and their leaves for healing."

TOPICAL OUTLINE OF THE LESSON

I. Introduction
   A. Brokenness
   B. Biblical Background

II. Exposition and Application of the Scripture
   A. God's Life-Giving Power and Presence (Ezekiel 47:1-6)
   B. God's Healing and Provision (Ezekiel 47:7-12)

III. Concluding Reflection

LESSON OBJECTIVES

Upon completion of this lesson, the students will know that:

1. Humanity depends on the bodies of water that cover the vast areas of earth;

2. These sources of water have an impact on humanity and all creation; and,

3. There is a sacred river that flows freely from God's throne, sustaining life.

POINTS TO BE EMPHASIZED

ADULT/YOUTH

Adult Topic: Spiritual Fruitfulness and Healing

Youth Topic: Water Power!

Adult/Youth Key Verse: Ezekiel 47:9

Print Passage: Ezekiel 47:1-12

—Ezekiel observes a life-giving river that is bordered by trees that produce fruit with nourishing food and leaves that can be used for healing.

—The river, whose source is the throne of God, bestows life wherever it flows and to whatever it touches.

—The stream starts as a trickle, but without tributaries builds into a deep, wide, and rushing river from God, unable to be crossed.

—The life-giving God has a presence and work beyond the Temple compound.

—The life-giving God will abundantly provide for the needs of God's people.

CHILDREN

Children Topic: Water Power!

Key Verse: Ezekiel 47:12

Print Passage: Ezekiel 47:1-9, 12

—God has different ways of getting messages to us, as evidenced in Ezekiel's vision of water.

—God illustrated the act of renewal through the flow of water.

—Ezekiel's vision brought hope for renewed life of the people.

—This renewal included provisions for food and healing.

I. INTRODUCTION

A. Brokenness

The term *restore* is an interesting one. In the Greek, it means "to set a broken bone back in place." If you have ever had a broken bone set, you know how painful and unpleasant it can be. But the resetting of the bone has to take place if the bone is going to grow properly. Without the proper resetting, the brokenness will always be present.

There is always an element of pain with restoration. As the bone knits itself back to wholeness, the fracture fights the natural process until it finally gives in. When a Christian is broken by sin, his or her carnal nature will fight against the need for mending. This is where the edification of the body becomes so critical. It is the duty of the body of Christ to mend a fallen brother or sister until he or she is whole again.

Broken bones are always stronger after the mending. The experience of brokenness causes the bone to generate new strength against a possible future break. It is the same with Christians. Each time a Christian falls into sin and is successfully retrieved from the grips of Satan, he is more prepared for the next attack. The process of falling (a popular song says, "We fall down, but we get up.") may seem like a handicap to the church, whose benchmarks are often set too high for the new Christian to achieve. But the actual process of "setting the brokenness" of a struggling Christian is designed not only to strengthen the fallen, but the witnessing congregation as well.

It is our duty to instill in novice or new Christians the importance of a healthy relationship with God that strengthens our spiritual bones against adversity and attack. Like a soldier being prepared for battle, the church edifies the body in preparation for the world's attacks. When the soldier returns to us wounded, we repair the wound with the Word of God, and send the soldier back out onto the battlefield with new and improved equipment. No matter how awful or disappointing the breach, God is able to mend.

B. Biblical Background

Like all of Ezekiel's visions, this one focuses on the glory and character of God. It was Ezekiel's prophetic commission to a hardened and obstinate people to keep God's character always before the people while they were in captivity, and to keep God's name from being profaned. The nation of Israel had not experienced a spiritual revival since Josiah revived Judah in 622 B.C. The years that followed were marked by unholy alignments with the Assyrians and the Egyptians, which eventually led to the overthrow of Judah, and finally Israel.

Caught in the throes of disobedience and rebellion against their Old Testament covenant relationship, Israel is a perfect example of what happens when one loses sight of God's true character and one's special mission to reflect God's character to the rest of the world.

The greatest promise of God is His desire to restore the broken. Israel's relationship with God was shattered. They had lost their homeland and the Temple where they worshiped. But worse, they had severed their connection with their Creator. Perhaps the greatest part of Israel's restoration would one day be the resurrection of the Temple in Jerusalem, the place where they could rekindle the covenant relationship.

An angelic guide led Ezekiel through the wonderful vision of this promise fulfilled. The vision included specific details about the size of the Temple, its surrounding grounds, the duties of the priests, and much more. The purpose of these vivid details was to demonstrate the power of God to restore Israel completely—their Temple, their worship, and their land.

II. EXPOSITION AND APPLICATION OF THE SCRIPTURE

A. God's Life-Giving Power and Presence (Ezekiel 47:1-6)

AFTERWARD HE brought me again unto the door of the house; and, behold, waters issued out from under the threshold of the house eastward: for the forefront of the house stood toward the east, and the waters came down from under from the right side of the house, at the south side of the altar. Then brought he me out of the way of the gate northward, and led me about the way without unto the utter gate by the way that looketh eastward; and, behold, there ran out waters on the right side. And when the man that had the line in his hand went forth eastward, he measured a thousand cubits, and he brought me through the waters; the waters were to the ankles. Again he measured a thousand, and brought me through the waters; the waters were to the knees. Again he measured a thousand, and brought me through; the waters were to the loins. Afterward he measured a thousand; and it was a river that I could not pass over: for the waters were risen, waters to swim in, a river that could not be passed over. And he said unto me, Son of man, hast thou seen this? Then he brought me, and caused me to return to the brink of the river.

Many Bible readers have erroneously suggested that the life-giving river in Ezekiel's vision refers only to the symbolism of God's blessings that flow from His presence. While symbolism plays an important role in the book of Ezekiel, the vision of the restoration of Israel in chapter 47 was meant to be taken literally.

The benefits of a river existence are apparent to the farmer. Until humankind's modern irrigation techniques were developed, no farm could survive without a water source. The river provides the farmer with an endless source of life-giving water that will sustain him and his crops. Its banks overflow with new growth and seasonal sustenance. This is the focus of Ezekiel's river vision. God's power and presence are exemplified in the river's ability to restore a barren and destitute land. The prophet Joel mentioned this same river (Joel 3:18), and Zechariah spoke of it after Israel returned from Babylonian captivity (Zechariah 14:8). This prophecy would take place in the Millennium, and the river would be an ever-present reminder of God's presence and blessing of Israel.

God's river city is spoken of in Psalm 46:4-7. "There is a river, the streams whereof shall make glad the city of God, the holy place of the tabernacles of the most High. God is in the midst of her; she shall not be moved: God shall help her, and that right early. The heathen raged, the kingdoms were moved: he uttered his voice, the earth melted. The LORD of hosts is with us; the God of Jacob is our refuge." Defense and deliverance are the stuff that people shout about. Victories cause our souls to well up with songs of celebration. Psalm 46 is such a song. It was most probably written to celebrate Israel's victory over the Assyrians, when they came down "like a wolf on the fold" and Sennacherib and all his army were swept into swift destruction by the blast of the breath of God's nostrils. Consider this river by which the psalmist says this city is planted. It is a symbol of great joy and truth. Its significance is derived from the geographical peculiarity of Jerusalem. Of all the great cities, Jerusalem alone had no broad river. One little perennial stream or rill of living water was all it had. But Siloam, as it was called, was mightier and more blessed for God's city dwellers than the Euphrates, Nile, and Tigris combined. Standing by that stream, one can envision the psalmist looking over the plain eastward and remembering the mighty forces that came against them, symbolized by the breadth, depth, and swiftness of the great river upon which Nineveh sat like a queen. Then he considers the little tiny thread of living water that flows past the base of the rock upon which the Temple is perched. It seems small and inconspicuous—nothing compared to the dash of the waves and rise of the floods of those mighty secular empires. But still, "There is a river, the streams whereof shall make glad the city of God." The psalmist knew that these waters would never fail. This tiny river would one day be the great river that fed Israel's restored nation.

While this prophecy brought great comfort to Israel, it should do the same for the twenty-first-century Christian because it demonstrates God's presence in the life of His people. This river, which will overpower the forces of nature and turn a desert wasteland into an Eden, will be a visual display of God's threefold character: 1) His omnipresence [God is everywhere, always!] ("For the LORD will not forsake his people for his great name's sake: because it hath pleased the LORD to make you his people"— 1 Samuel 12:22); 2) His omnipotence [God is all-powerful] ("And Jesus came and spake unto

them, saying, All power is given unto me in heaven and in earth"—Matthew 28:18); and 3) His omniscience [God is all-knowing] ("I am Alpha and Omega, the beginning and the ending, saith the Lord, which is, and which was, and which is to come, the Almighty"— Revelation 1:8).

B. God's Healing and Provision (Ezekiel 47:7-12)

Now when I had returned, behold, at the bank of the river were very many trees on the one side and on the other. Then said he unto me, These waters issue out toward the east country, and go down into the desert, and go into the sea: which being brought forth into the sea, the waters shall be healed. And it shall come to pass, that every thing that liveth, which moveth, whithersoever the rivers shall come, shall live: and there shall be a very great multitude of fish, because these waters shall come thither: for they shall be healed; and every thing shall live whither the river cometh. And it shall come to pass, that the fishers shall stand upon it from En-gedi even unto En-eglaim; they shall be a place to spread forth nets; their fish shall be according to their kinds, as the fish of the great sea, exceeding many. But the miry places thereof and the marishes thereof shall not be healed; they shall be given to salt. And by the river upon the bank thereof, on this side and on that side, shall grow all trees for meat, whose leaf shall not fade, neither shall the fruit thereof be consumed: it shall bring forth new fruit according to his months, because their waters they issued out of the sanctuary: and the fruit thereof shall be for meat, and the leaf thereof for medicine.

Notice that where the river flows, everything will live. Fishermen will crowd the shores to catch all manner of fish from this miraculous source of supply. The trees on the riverbanks will produce an abundance of fruit year-round.

This prophecy paints the picture of a completely revived and restored nation. This complete restoration of Israel will be a great end-time miracle, as Israel is brought back to her former state, and to spiritual health. God's redemption and restoration represent a complete makeover. But this should come as no surprise because God's healing and provision are *always* complete. God's very character will not permit Him to leave humankind wanting and destitute, without hope.

If we are to believe in Ezekiel's prophetic promise of a nation blooming in the desert, we must first accept a strong belief in miracles. Belief in miracles is indispensable to our understanding of the living God, and to our trust in His ability to save our souls. Miracles provide us with a special exhibition of God's supernatural power. What is a miracle? *Webster* defines a *miracle* as "an event or effect in the physical world deviating from the known laws of nature, or transcending our knowledge of these laws; an extraordinary anomalous or abnormal event brought about by super-human agency." Biblically speaking, a *miracle* is defined as a "work wrought by a divine power for a divine purpose by means beyond the reach of humankind." The general idea is that it is something wonderful or unusual. It can be an event, an experience, or a discovery—so strange as to awaken in humanity the feeling of awe.

Bible miracles often display the reversal of nature's own course, as in this promise for Israel. Scientists make the argument that the laws of nature are self-existent and uncaused, and that there cannot be any deviation from them. But if these laws were designed by a Supreme Will, surely this Will has the power to introduce a new agency into them. God created nature, and He therefore has the power to control it and reverse its previously assigned patterns.

The Bible not only exalts God above nature, but it also brings Him into direct relation to nature, so that everything is filled by Him. God dwells in nature as the omnipresent, as well as the omnipotent, God. He is the life of all that lives—the Spirit of all spirits. As He is all in all, so is all in Him. He transcends nature (see Psalm 90:2); He is immanent in nature (see Ephesians 1:11); He continually exercises His power before our blinded eyes. Nature has therefore been referred to as "God's Braille for a blind humanity."

If, as Christians, we can take the whole Bible in our hands and say without fear or hesitation that we hold the revealed Word of God handed down, without essential loss, from generation to generation throughout the centuries—if we accept the Bible as God's pure and unadulterated Word—then we can trust God to fulfill this promise to Israel because the Bible has already recorded countless historical examples of God's miraculous power. His very work of grace and salvation is a miracle, for it requires the exercise of a supernatural power who can heal and cast out demons, and restore a person to his or her original, perfect form.

Restoration is the visible evidence of God's miraculous presence in the life of a believer. There are six steps to a person's restoration: 1) the person must be led to recognize his or her failure; 2) the person must acknowledge responsibility for his or her sin; 3) the person must be led to repent; 4) the person must understand the necessity of restitution; 5) the person who is caught in sin must be led to receive the message God wants to teach him or her through his or her failure; and 6) the person must be led to respond to God's chastisement with gratitude. The spirit in which we restore a fallen brother or sister is of vital importance to the body of Christ. We must avoid spiritual bandages that only cover up the problem. Real restoration is often a long and painful process and must be done with a spirit of humility and love.

III. CONCLUDING REFLECTION

Biblical miracles were designed to symbolize the spiritual blessings that God is able and willing to bestow upon our needy hearts. They have a twofold value, in that they are both physical and spiritual. God used miracles to authenticate Christ's divine mission, and Jesus used those miracles as evidence that He was *from* God. For the New Testament believer, Christ's expulsion of demons symbolizes His power over the spirit world of evil; the healing of the lepers illustrates the removal of sin's loathsome defilement; and the raising of the dead demonstrates Christ's power to raise those who are dead in sin.

Israel can look forward to a newly restored nation of plenty, fed by a life-giving river. But to the New Covenant believer, Christ is our "River" from which flows the life-giving source of our redemption. We are replenished daily by His grace, His mercy, and His Holy Spirit.

Christ's blood, which has flowed for centuries and will continue to flow as the only source for redemption and restoration, is the fountain that turns our sinful lives' wasteland into places of promise and hope of eternal life.

PRAYER

Heavenly Father, thank You for restoring us to a right relationship with You after we have sinned and fallen. In Jesus' name we pray. Amen.

WORD POWER

To Heal *(rapa', "to heal")*—this word is common to both ancient and modern Hebrew. To *heal* may be described as "restoring to normal," an act which God typically performs. Some of the uses of *rapa'* express the "healing" of the nation; such "healing" not only involves God's grace and forgiveness, but also the nation's repentance.

HOME DAILY BIBLE READINGS
(March 23-29, 2009)

Envisioning New Life

MONDAY, **March 23: "Wash Yourselves" (Isaiah 1:12-17)**
TUESDAY, **March 24: "The Water of Rebirth" (Titus 3:1-7)**
WEDNESDAY, **March 25: "Like Showers and Spring Rains" (Hosea 6:1-6)**
THURSDAY, **March 26: "Planted by Streams of Water" (Psalm 1)**
FRIDAY, **March 27: "Give Me Living Water" (John 4:7-15)**
SATURDAY, **March 28: "The Water of Life" (Revelation 22:12-17)**
SUNDAY, **March 29: "Water from the Sanctuary" (Ezekiel 47:1-12)**

SUFFERING UNTO DEATH

DEVOTIONAL READING: **1 Corinthians 15:1-11**   BACKGROUND SCRIPTURE: **Luke 23:32-46**
PRINT PASSAGE: **Luke 23:32-46**   KEY VERSE: **Luke 23:46**

Luke 23:32-46—KJV

32 And there were also two other, malefactors, led with him to be put to death.

33 And when they were come to the place, which is called Calvary, there they crucified him, and the malefactors, one on the right hand, and the other on the left.

34 Then said Jesus, Father, forgive them; for they know not what they do. And they parted his raiment, and cast lots.

35 And the people stood beholding. And the rulers also with them derided him, saying, He saved others; let him save himself, if he be Christ, the chosen of God.

36 And the soldiers also mocked him, coming to him, and offering him vinegar,

37 And saying, If thou be the king of the Jews, save thyself.

38 And a superscription also was written over him in letters of Greek, and Latin, and Hebrew, THIS IS THE KING OF THE JEWS.

39 And one of the malefactors which were hanged railed on him, saying, If thou be Christ, save thyself and us.

40 But the other answering rebuked him, saying, Dost not thou fear God, seeing thou art in the same condemnation?

41 And we indeed justly; for we receive the due reward of our deeds: but this man hath done nothing amiss.

42 And he said unto Jesus, Lord, remember me when thou comest into thy kingdom.

43 And Jesus said unto him, Verily I say unto thee, To day shalt thou be with me in paradise.

44 And it was about the sixth hour, and there was a darkness over all the earth until the ninth hour.

45 And the sun was darkened, and the veil of the temple was rent in the midst.

46 And when Jesus had cried with a loud voice, he said, Father, into thy hands I commend my spirit: and having said thus, he gave up the ghost.

Luke 23:32-46—NRSV

32 Two others also, who were criminals, were led away to be put to death with him.

33 When they came to the place that is called The Skull, they crucified Jesus there with the criminals, one on his right and one on his left.

34 Then Jesus said, "Father, forgive them; for they do not know what they are doing." And they cast lots to divide his clothing.

35 And the people stood by, watching; but the leaders scoffed at him, saying, "He saved others; let him save himself if he is the Messiah of God, his chosen one!"

36 The soldiers also mocked him, coming up and offering him sour wine,

37 and saying, "If you are the King of the Jews, save yourself!"

38 There was also an inscription over him, "This is the King of the Jews."

39 One of the criminals who were hanged there kept deriding him and saying, "Are you not the Messiah? Save yourself and us!"

40 But the other rebuked him, saying, "Do you not fear God, since you are under the same sentence of condemnation?

41 And we indeed have been condemned justly, for we are getting what we deserve for our deeds, but this man has done nothing wrong."

42 Then he said, "Jesus, remember me when you come into your kingdom."

43 He replied, "Truly I tell you, today you will be with me in Paradise."

44 It was now about noon, and darkness came over the whole land until three in the afternoon,

45 while the sun's light failed; and the curtain of the temple was torn in two.

46 Then Jesus, crying with a loud voice, said, "Father, into your hands I commend my spirit." Having said this, he breathed his last.

TOPICAL OUTLINE OF THE LESSON

I. **Introduction**
   A. Facing Death
   B. Biblical Background

II. **Exposition and Application of the Scripture**
   A. Numbered with the Sinners (Luke 23:32-33)
   B. Praying for the Sinner (Luke 23:34)
   C. Mocked by the Sinner (Luke 23:35-37)
   D. Misunderstood by the Sinner (Luke 23:38-46)

III. **Concluding Reflection**

LESSON OBJECTIVES

Upon completion of this lesson, the students will know that:

1. A range of emotions, from suffering to joy, can accompany the death event;
2. We can face death with trust in God; and,
3. Jesus' trust in God led Jesus through to triumph and sustained Him in suffering.

POINTS TO BE EMPHASIZED

ADULT/YOUTH

Adult Topic: **Facing Death**
Youth Topic: **Suffering to Save**
Adult/Youth Key Verse: **Luke 23:46**
Print Passage: **Luke 23:32-46**

—The book of Luke is the only gospel that offers the prayer of Jesus from the cross: "Father, forgive them; for they do not know what they are doing" (see verse 34).
—The book of Luke is the only one of the gospels that speaks of the penitent thief on the cross. Even while facing death, this seemingly hopeless man is given hope through Jesus.
—The tearing of the curtain that separated the holy place from the Holy of Holies suggests at least two possible interpretations: (1) the death of Jesus provided access to God; or (2) the splitting of the curtain indicated God had exited the Temple. Jesus' death signified judgment on Israel.
—Jesus' confidence in God was demonstrated by His commending Himself into God's care at His death.
—Jesus' final moments before death teach us about what a relationship with God can mean to individual persons as they face death.
—Three hours of darkness signified the apparent victory of evil, but the torn Temple curtain showed that Christ's victory opened direct access to God.

CHILDREN

Children Topic: **On to Jerusalem**
Key Verse: **Luke 19:38**
Print Passage: **Luke 19:28-38**

—Jesus gave the disciples instructions to prepare for His entry into Jerusalem.
—The disciples obeyed Jesus' instructions and delivered the colt Jesus would use.
—Jesus' triumphant entry into Jerusalem is called Palm Sunday because of the use of palm branches as a sign of victory.
—The people along the route to Jerusalem praised God and

shouted to express joy for the deeds of power they had observed Jesus perform.

—The people recognized Jesus as the King who came in the name of the Lord.

I. INTRODUCTION

A. Facing Death

How should a believer view death? Daniel described *death* in terms of "those who sleep," which is actually a metaphor for a temporary condition. Those who sleep are expected to wake up from sleep and go on to an eternal state—"some to everlasting life, some to shame and everlasting contempt" (Daniel 12:2). The Old Testament writers expressed this same view that death is not the end of existence. Some describe it euphemistically as a reunion with one's ancestors (see Genesis 15:15). Others refer to it in a way that shows they expected to meet God when they died (see Psalm 17:15). In Ephesians 5:14, the apostle Paul used similar language to describe the sleep of death. The bottom line is that death does not have the final say. We are invited into eternal life with God through the provision of Jesus Christ, who Himself died and came back to life and enabled us to escape condemnation and death.

B. Biblical Background

The name *Luke* is most likely abbreviated. It was a common practice, as it is today, to shorten long names (*Demetrius* was known as Demas; *Apollonias* was known as Apollos). The legend that Luke was one of the seventy sent out by Jesus is pure conjecture, as is the belief that Luke was one of the Greeks who came to Philip for an introduction to Jesus, or the companion of Cleopas on the walk to Emmaus. Most theologians agree that Luke was not an eyewitness to the ministry of Jesus. In Acts, Paul set Luke apart from "those of the circumcision"; therefore, Luke likely was not a Jew. Luke may not have been from Antioch, but we do know that he had family connections there.

Luke was a physician, so he was well-acquainted with death. In Colossians 4:14 it is suggested that he was also a Gentile and a proselyte, or early Christian recruiter. As an educated and cultured man, Luke wrote in the sophisticated tradition of the Hellenistic historians, with polished language. For this reason, Luke gave us some of the most powerful descriptive writing in the New Testament. It is clear that, as a physician, Luke would have been deeply moved by the power of Christ to overcome death.

Luke's writings were targeted to the educated Greeks, to sway them to Christianity. He wrote to Theophilus to inform him about the truthfulness of the Gospel as it was told to him by Paul and other witnesses. Many of the incidents and accounts are peculiar to Luke's gospel, including Christ's prayer on the cross and the story of the penitent thief, which is the subject of today's lesson.

II. EXPOSITION AND APPLICATION OF THE SCRIPTURE

A. Numbered with the Sinners
(Luke 23:32-33)

And there were also two others, malefactors, led with him to be put to death. And when they were come to the place, which is called Calvary, there they crucified him, and the malefactors, one on the right hand, and the other on the left.

It is not indicated in the Bible why Christ was crucified between two thieves. The day could have been set aside for executions. Or maybe the Jewish leaders pressed Pilate to execute Jesus with other criminals, to add weight to their position that He was no more than a mere man, an imposter who deserved to die just as other criminals. Or it may have been just the simple reasoning that it was cheaper to execute three at once. Whatever the reason, the fact that the Son of God was executed right along with other criminals adds to the shame and reproach He bore, even though it was a necessary fulfillment of prophesy. As prophesied by Isaiah (53:12), Jesus was "numbered with the transgressors; and he bare the sin of many...."

The Crucifixion itself was the most horrible of deaths. Besides the pain of having stakes driven into the body, there was the additional pain of the weight of the body pulling on those open wounds. The scorching sun and unquenchable thirst added to the agony. For Jesus, there were also the multiple open wounds from the scourging he had just received, and the piercing thorns of a mocking crown.

The Crucifixion took place on a hill called Golgotha, which means "the skull." It was probably called this because it was known as a place that was inhabited by the bones of dead people. We get the word *Calvary* from the Latin word with the same meaning—*Calvaria*. It is described in ancient documents as an ugly place, and a terrible place to die.

Everything about the Crucifixion symbolized death, and it was here that Jesus became the substitute sacrifice for all sin, deliberately and purposefully, and was crucified at the hand of His Father, God. God Himself, by His own predetermined plan, ordained that His Son Jesus Christ would *deliberately* die for the sins of the world.

One of the holiest of days in the Jewish faith was the Day of Atonement. On this day, "the goat for Azazel (scapegoat)" was taken away into the wilderness. The act of sending the goat out of the camp was a symbolic action for sending sin out from among God's people. The idea was that this innocent goat known as the scapegoat (and from which we get our present definition of a "scapegoat") would bear all Israel's guilt upon it, and then be sent away, the goat bearing "upon him all their iniquities unto a land not inhabited" (Leviticus 16:22). We see here the great symbolism in Christ being marched out beyond the walls of Jerusalem, to a far hillside, carrying with Him the sins not only of His persecutors, but the sins of the world—and becoming the final "scapegoat" for all humankind.

B. Praying for the Sinner
(Luke 23:34)

Then said Jesus, Father, forgive them; for they know not what they do. And they parted his raiment, and cast lots.

Despite the Old Testament prayers for vengeance (for example: Jeremiah 17:18), while dying on the cross, Jesus prayed that

God would forgive His persecutors. This was a breach from the expectation of those who witnessed His crucifixion. It was expected that Jesus would say, "May my death atone for all my sins." But instead, Jesus confessed the sins of His persecutors who had falsely convicted Him, who under rabbinical law were liable for His penalty before God.

Jesus publicly forgave His enemies, painting a picture of love and forgiveness right to the very end of His earthly ministry. This act of forgiveness made Jesus the perfect Mediator. His prayer supported the prophetic claims that the Messiah would come for this very purpose—to stand as Mediator between God and sinful humanity.

Christ prayed for God to forgive those who were crucifying Him. No one was excluded from His request for forgiveness—not the Sanhedrin Council, nor Pilate, nor the angry mob that followed Him to Calvary. Jesus made it clear that the very purpose for His coming was to make provision for forgiveness of sin—all sin. The men who crucified Jesus did not know what they were doing, because they failed to recognize Him for who He really was—the Savior of the world.

Christ's prayer on the cross of Calvary proclaimed that God would hold no sin against any person, if that person would personally trust His Son. If God forgave the men who killed His only Son, God will forgive any person for any sin—if that person will just ask in the name of Jesus Christ.

Christians are charged to follow Christ's example and pray for others daily. Whether friend or foe, our desire for them should be the same—that God would draw them to Him and, by His Spirit, prepare them to receive the message of salvation. Our prayer then should be, "Lord, use me to carry Your message!"

C. Mocked by the Sinner
(Luke 23:35-37)

And the people stood beholding. And the rulers also with them derided him, saying, He saved others; let him save himself, if he be Christ, the chosen of God. And the soldiers also mocked him, coming to him, and offering him vinegar, And saying, If thou be the king of the Jews, save thyself.

It was the custom for soldiers to gamble for the clothing of crucified criminals. Jesus' coat was valuable for two reasons: 1) it was woven from one seamless thread, just like the garments worn by the High Priests; and 2) it was worn by the most famous Man in the known world. The prophets foretold that men would gamble for Christ's coat (see Psalm 22:18). That He forfeited His coat is no sacrifice at all when one considers that He also gave His life. But losing His coat is symbolic of allowing the last of His mortality to be stripped off, so that He might abolish death, and bring life and immortality to light.

Having completely misunderstood God's promise of a Messiah, the people and the religionists mocked Jesus at His crucifixion. The soldiers joined in on the mockery. It was evident at the Cross that position or profession did not make a person. Men (and women) are capable of shameful behavior regardless of their stations in life. We falsely believe that persons' stations in life somehow make them respectable. But all persons "have sinned, and come short of the glory of God" (Romans 3:23).

Jesus was offered some type of drugged wine at the beginning of His crucifixion, but He refused it (verse 36). Just before His death, John recorded that the soldiers offered Jesus vinegar as a further form of mockery (see John 19:29).

The sign that was placed on the cross, "This is the King of the Jews," was intended to mock not only Jesus but the Jewish authorities as well, and to criticize (censure) Jesus' claim of messiahship. But people's intentions are always superseded by God's Will. God used the declaration nailed on the cross by adversaries to proclaim Christ's deity and honor to the whole world. And in the end, the world came to realize that it was not the crucifixion that killed Jesus, but His humility and His love for humankind.

D. Misunderstood by the Sinner
(Luke 23:38-46)

And a superscription also was written over him in letters of Greek, and Latin, and Hebrew, THIS IS THE KING OF THE JEWS. And one of the malefactors which were hanged railed on him, saying, If thou be Christ, save thyself and us. But the other answering rebuked him, saying, Dost not thou fear God, seeing thou art in the same condemnation? And we indeed justly; for we receive the due reward of our deeds: but this man hath done nothing amiss. And he said unto Jesus, Lord, remember me when thou comest into thy kingdom. And Jesus said unto him, Verily I say unto thee, To day shalt thou be with me in paradise. And it was about the sixth hour, and there was a darkness over all the earth until the ninth hour. And the sun was darkened, and the veil of the temple was rent in the midst. And when Jesus had cried with a loud voice, he said, Father, into thy hands I commend my spirit: and having said thus, he gave up the ghost.

The account of the two thieves crucified with Jesus is a story of the contrast between repentance and hardness of heart. One criminal mocked the very thought that Jesus was the Christ, while the other demonstrated the steps to salvation: 1) he feared God (verse 40); 2) he declared Jesus to be righteous (verse 41); and 3) he asked Jesus to remember him (verse 42). The repentant thief recognized that Jesus was all the hope he had of overcoming death.

In contrast, the unrepentant thief could not accept Christ's messiahship. His heart was hardened by sin. This is the same unrepentant hardness of heart we often encounter in our daily witness. There will always be some men and women who refuse to accept Jesus as their Christ, regardless of our efforts to unravel the truth of the Gospel before them.

The question often arises, and should be addressed here: "Do we go to heaven immediately upon death, or must we wait for the millennial resurrection, when Christ comes to reclaim His church, and "the dead in Christ shall rise"? (see 1 Thessalonians 4:16). Humans are composed of minds, bodies, and souls. The mind and the body belong to the world, but the soul belongs to God. At the death of a believer, the soul (which cannot be contained in a grave) is swept into heaven's presence. When Christ returns to rapture His church, the dead in Christ will be bodily resurrected to rejoin the soul. This is what is referred to as the "Rapture." Some faiths make the weak argument that the soul does not go to heaven, but waits in some "holding pattern" until Christ returns. But proof of this fallacy is found in the testimony of Christ Himself, who proclaimed to the dying and repentant thief, "Today thou shalt be with me in paradise!"

The repentant thief had no need to fear death, while the unrepentant thief had no choice but to fear death. One accepted eternal life as the consequence of his confession, while the other received eternal separation from God as the consequence of his unbelief.

III. CONCLUDING REFLECTION

There are a great number of biblical writers who affirm God's power over death.

- In the story which tells of Adam and Eve's sin the Garden of Eden, death was ushered into the world by disobedience. Then a later record by Moses reveals God's curse, which included a word of hope. God promised that the *tempter* who brought sin and death into the world would eventually be conquered (see Genesis 3:14-15).
- Isaiah promised that God would swallow up death forever and wipe away all tears (see Isaiah 25:8). This was of course accomplished with the resurrection of Christ, who conquered death, hell, and the grave for every believer.
- As Jeremiah lamented the tragic death of the holy city Jerusalem, he sounded a bright note of hope by reminding his listeners of God's mercies, which are "new every morning" (Lamentations 3:23). He reminded us that we have hope in God because salvation is of the Lord (see Lamentations 3:22-27).
- Paul echoed Hosea's words when he rhetorically asked, "O death, where is thy sting? O grave, where is thy victory?" (1 Corinthians 15:55). Then Paul added, "Thanks be to God, which giveth us the victory through our Lord Jesus Christ" (1 Corinthians 15:57).
- John foresaw the end of death in his vision of a new heaven and a new earth (see Revelation 21:1, 4).

Because Christ offers everlasting life in His presence to those who believe in Him (see John 11:25-26), Christians everywhere can rejoice at the funerals of fellow believers. Even as we grieve the loss of our loved ones, we also rest in the hope that we will be reunited with them in heaven.

PRAYER

Heavenly Father, thank You for dying on the cross, so that we who believe in You might have eternal life. In Jesus' name we pray. Amen.

WORD POWER

Death, Death-Stroke *(thanatos)*—meaning "death," is used in the Scriptures for: (a) the separation of the soul (the spiritual part of man) from the body (the material part)—the latter ceasing to function and turning to dust; and (b) the separation of humans from God; (Adam figuratively died on the day he disobeyed God).

HOME DAILY BIBLE READINGS
(March 30–April 5, 2009)

Suffering unto Death

MONDAY, March 30: "The Message of the Cross" (1 Corinthians 1:18-25)
TUESDAY, March 31: "The Suffering Servant" (Isaiah 53:1-9)
WEDNESDAY, April 1: "A Ransom for Many" (Mark 10:32-44)
THURSDAY, April 2: "A Sacrifice of Atonement" (Romans 3:21-26)
FRIDAY, April 3: "A Single Sacrifice for Sin" (Hebrews 10:10-18)
SATURDAY, April 4: "Bought with a Price" (1 Corinthians 6:12-20)
SUNDAY, April 5: "The Death of Jesus" (Luke 23:32-46)

LESSON 7   April 12, 2009 (Easter)

RESURRECTED UNTO NEW LIFE

DEVOTIONAL READING: **1 Corinthians 15:12-26**   BACKGROUND SCRIPTURE: **Luke 24:1-12**
PRINT PASSAGE: **Luke 24:1-12**   KEY VERSE: **Luke 24:5**

Luke 24:1-12—KJV

NOW UPON the first day of the week, very early in the morning, they came unto the sepulchre, bringing the spices which they had prepared, and certain others with them.

2 And they found the stone rolled away from the sepulchre.

3 And they entered in, and found not the body of the Lord Jesus.

4 And it came to pass, as they were much perplexed thereabout, behold, two men stood by them in shining garments:

5 And as they were afraid, and bowed down their faces to the earth, they said unto them, Why seek ye the living among the dead?

6 He is not here, but is risen: remember how he spake unto you when he was yet in Galilee,

7 Saying, The Son of man must be delivered into the hands of sinful men, and be crucified, and the third day rise again.

8 And they remembered his words,

9 And returned from the sepulchre, and told all these things unto the eleven, and to all the rest.

10 It was Mary Magdalene, and Joanna, and Mary the mother of James, and other women that were with them, which told these things unto the apostles.

11 And their words seemed to them as idle tales, and they believed them not.

12 Then arose Peter, and ran unto the sepulchre; and stooping down, he beheld the linen clothes laid by themselves, and departed, wondering in himself at that which was come to pass.

Luke 24:1-12—NRSV

BUT ON the first day of the week, at early dawn, they came to the tomb, taking the spices that they had prepared.

2 They found the stone rolled away from the tomb,

3 but when they went in, they did not find the body.

4 While they were perplexed about this, suddenly two men in dazzling clothes stood beside them.

5 The women were terrified and bowed their faces to the ground, but the men said to them, "Why do you look for the living among the dead? He is not here, but has risen.

6 Remember how he told you, while he was still in Galilee,

7 that the Son of Man must be handed over to sinners, and be crucified, and on the third day rise again."

8 Then they remembered his words,

9 and returning from the tomb, they told all this to the eleven and to all the rest.

10 Now it was Mary Magdalene, Joanna, Mary the mother of James, and the other women with them who told this to the apostles.

11 But these words seemed to them an idle tale, and they did not believe them.

12 But Peter got up and ran to the tomb; stooping and looking in, he saw the linen cloths by themselves; then he went home, amazed at what had happened.

BIBLE FACT
A new life in Christ carries with it the responsibility to demonstrate the fruits of our "new life" experience.

TOPICAL OUTLINE OF THE LESSON

I. Introduction
   A. Accept or Reject
   B. Biblical Background

II. Exposition and Application of the Scripture
   A. The Witnesses (Luke 24:1-3)
   B. The Message from Two Angels (Luke 24:4-8)
   C. The Unbelief of Peter and the Apostles (Luke 24:9-12)

III. Concluding Reflection

LESSON OBJECTIVES

Upon completion of this lesson, the students will know that:

1. Death seems final to many people;
2. Luke's record of Easter morning assures us that new, resurrected life is possible; and,
3. Jesus rose from the dead.

POINTS TO BE EMPHASIZED

ADULT/YOUTH

Adult Topic: **Implications of New Life**
Youth Topic: **Live Again!**
Adult Key Verse: **Luke 24:5**
Youth Key Verses: **Luke 24:6-7**
Print Passage: **Luke 24:1-12**

—Christ's followers did not anticipate a sequel to the Crucifixion; the women went to the tomb with spices, expecting to encounter a lifeless body.

—That the women in the story did not expect a resurrected Jesus is evident in the bewilderment they experienced at seeing the stone rolled away from the tomb's entrance and the absence of Jesus' body.

—According to the passage, two messengers mildly rebuked the women for seeking "the living among the dead"; the implication was that the women should have remembered Jesus' previous words about His crucifixion and His resurrection on the third day (see verse 8).

—After the Sabbath rest, the women came to Jesus' tomb with the spices to prepare Jesus' body for burial.

—Luke plainly pointed out that the appearances of the risen Christ—not the empty tomb, nor Jesus' prediction, nor the women's report of the angels' message—are the basis for the disciples' belief in the resurrection of Jesus.

CHILDREN

Children Topic: **Jesus Lives!**
Key Verse: **Luke 24:5**
Print Passage: **Luke 24:1-12**

—The women were perplexed when they went to the tomb and found it empty.

—The prophecy that Jesus would be raised from the dead was fulfilled.

—Upon the discovery of Jesus' resurrection, the women told the eleven disciples.

—The disciples found it hard to believe the women's report.

—Peter had to see the tomb for himself.

I. INTRODUCTION

A. Accept or Reject

Regardless of what the manufacturers of beauty creams and vitamins promise, no one can stop the aging process that leads to the ultimate death of this mortal body. Immortality comes—not from bottles or jars, but from God alone. God promises that those who put their trust in Jesus Christ have the hope of eternal life through Him.

Many people are hesitant to believe in eternal life. They find matters of faith foreboding and even frightening. To them, religion seems like nothing but judgment and condemnation. But the truth is that Jesus came not to condemn, but to save. His primary purpose was to offer life to dying people, inviting them to experience forgiveness, healing, and hope. "Come," He says to those who are thirsty, "Whoever will, let him take the water of life freely" (see John 7:37-38; Revelation 22:17). Centuries before, Isaiah foretold this very invitation (see Isaiah 55:1, 3). This is a powerful invitation because the same Jesus who extends it has the power to withdraw it from those who reject Him and continue to live lives of rebellion against Him. Just as Jesus has the power to welcome us into His kingdom, He also has the authority to command us to depart—saying that He never knew us. It is by grace that He chooses to offer eternal life to every person. It is ours to accept or reject.

Every person is required by God to make a decision about Christ. Once a person has been evangelized—given the opportunity to hear the gospel—there is no option to delay a decision. Those who think they are waiting—who continue in sin, and use the excuse that they are not ready—have already made their decision, and it is one of rejection. There are only two choices we can make: "Yes, I believe" and "No, I do not believe."

The completeness of the biblical account of the life of Christ, and the empowerment of the Church of Jesus Christ to "Go ye therefore and teach all nations…" gives us all the necessary tools to infiltrate the deepest recesses of the world with God's salvation message.

B. Biblical Background

The classic introduction to the gospel of Luke supports the idea that he was a man of culture and education. His *Greek* has a literary flavor that is comparable to Paul's writings.

Writers compiling a work usually start with one main source and weave in secondary material from another source or sources. It is important to note that Luke began with Mark as his main source, but he used many eyewitnesses who were still alive at the time of his historical writing.

Historical accounts were written so that people would know the truth. Their purpose was to provide exact information while the witnesses to an event were still alive and able to establish firsthand or eyewitness documentation. It was proper for a good historian to check the data that came to him, and then to keep the content of his account precise, so that it could fit on a standard scroll. Both of the books Luke and Acts, written by Luke, were of this caliber.

Men of wealth and position sponsored historical writings. The book of Luke was sponsored by Theophilus. Luke referred to Theophilus as "Most excellent," which could literally mark him as a member of a high class in Roman society, but he may also have used the title as a mere courtesy. In either case, Theophilus's desire for verification was reasonable, in light of the many competing claims to religious truth in the Roman Empire.

II. EXPOSITION AND APPLICATION OF THE SCRIPTURE

A. The Witnesses
(Luke 24:1-3)

NOW UPON the first day of the week, very early in the morning, they came unto the sepulchre, bringing the spices which they had prepared, and certain others with them. And they found the stone rolled away from the sepulchre. And they entered in, and found not the body of the Lord Jesus.

Luke clearly stated that Jesus arose "Upon the first day of the week, very early in the morning." This was significant to the early Christian believers, who broke away from the Sabbath worship and began to worship on Sunday, the day of the resurrection of their Lord (see Acts 20:7; 1 Corinthians 16:2). There are no commandments or exhortations in the New Testament that require the keeping of the Sabbath Day. Rather, the early church gathered on the first day of the week in celebration and remembrance of the Resurrection. This is evident throughout the book of Acts (see Acts 20:7 and also 1 Corinthians 16:2). Acts 20:7 is the clearest verse in the New Testament which indicates that Sunday was the normal meeting day of the apostolic church.

The women at the tomb were actual witnesses of Jesus' *death and burial*. They knew He was dead, and where He had been laid. They had followed along behind the procession to the tomb (see Matthew 27:55-56, 61; Mark 15:40-41, 47; Luke 23:55-56) so there was no question that Jesus had died and was buried. These women had purchased spices and had come to anoint Jesus' body, which had been hastily buried because of the encroaching Sabbath. Both Marys were religionists or "good Jews" who followed the strict letter of the Jewish law in the observance of the Sabbath, so the anointing of Jesus' body for burial had to be put off until Sunday.

When they arrived at the tomb, it is important to note that the stone had been rolled away—not to aid Jesus in His escape from the grave, but to allow the witnesses to see that the tomb was empty. The empty tomb is the greatest testament we have to the resurrection of Jesus Christ. It changed the death of Christ from a secret to be hoarded into a story to be heralded. This was not the first resurrection the men and women of that day had experienced. Remember that there are several resurrections noted in the Bible, in both the Old and the New Testaments. But in each of those resurrections, the person eventually returned to the grave. Christ's resurrection was unique. Christ died, was resurrected, and ascended. He never went back into a grave.

There have been several theories posed to discount the validity of the Christ's deity. One theory is that Jesus did not die on the cross, but merely fainted. They believe that the cool, damp environment of the tomb revived Him. But there are several problems with this theory from both a biblical and a practical viewpoint. First, there are the witnesses. It is stated in the Bible that He was dead. The angels said He was dead. Even the Pharisees who wanted the tomb sealed believed that He was dead. Add to that the fact that the fainting theory does not understand the horror of crucifixion. Even the soldiers who started to break Jesus' legs determined that He was already dead. Finally, how could someone who endured the pain of crucifixion push away the huge stone that sealed the door?

Another theory holds that the body was stolen. If this was true, there were only two groups who could have stolen it—Jesus' friends or His enemies. Many of Christ's friends were martyred for the cause of Christ. Would they have sacrificed their lives for a lie? As for the enemies, they did strike a deal with the soldiers standing guard at the tomb. If the soldiers had stolen the body, wouldn't they have been pressured (or threatened) to produce the body when news of the Resurrection began to spread like wildfire?

The best proofs we have of the Resurrection are the eyewitnesses. Christ appeared to Mary Magdalene (John 20:11-18), the other woman (Matthew 28:1-10), Peter (1 Corinthians 15:5), the two on the road to Emmaus (Luke 24:13-27), ten of the disciples (John 20:19-24), eleven disciples (8 days later), John 20:26-29), seven disciples (John 21:1-23), five hundred followers (1 Corinthians 15:6), James (1 Corinthians 15:7), all the disciples at the Ascension (Acts 1:3-11), Paul (1 Corinthians 15:8), and finally the apostle John (Revelation 1:9-18).

B. The Message from Two Angels (Luke 24:4-8)

And it came to pass, as they were much perplexed thereabout, behold, two men stood by them in shining garments. And as they were afraid, and bowed down their faces to the earth, they said unto them, Why seek ye the living among the dead? He is not here, but is risen: remember how he spake unto you when he was yet in Galilee, Saying, The Son of man must be delivered into the hands of sinful men, and be crucified, and the third day rise again. And they remembered his words.

One of the most fascinating aspects of the story of the empty tomb is the presence of the two angels.

Every reference to angels in the Bible is incidental to some other topic, and so God never really informs us about their nature. When they are mentioned, it is always to inform us further about God, what He does, and how He does it. Even so, their mention permits us to glean certain information about their existence: 1) angels are inclusive in Scripture, being mentioned 326 times; 2) angels are mentioned throughout at least thirty-four of the sixty-six books of the Bible, which establishes their importance; and 3) as the Creator of all things (see Colossians 1:16), Jesus often referred to the angels.

Angels are ministering spirits, sent out to render service for the sake of those who will inherit salvation (see Hebrews 1:14). They were created by God to serve Him, and as such, they should never be worshiped. The Hebrew word for "angel" is *malach;* in Greek it is *angelos*—and both mean "messenger." These celestial beings,

God's heavenly host (*host* means "army"), are dispatched by God at His will. They are created spiritual beings, and not the spirits of departed or glorified human beings (see Psalm 148). God uses them to perform distinct functions, such as the delivery of the important message at the empty tomb of Jesus Christ. In addition to the Resurrection, they are also further proof of the existence of eternal life.

C. The Unbelief of Peter and the Apostles (Luke 24:9-12)

And returned from the sepulchre, and told all these things unto the eleven, and to all the rest. It was Mary Magdalene, and Joanna, and Mary the mother of James, and other women that were with them, which told these things unto the apostles. And their words seemed to them as idle tales, and they believed them not. Then arose Peter, and ran unto the sepulchre; and stooping down, he beheld the linen clothes laid by themselves, and departed, wondering in himself at that which was come to pass.

When the women ran to tell of their joy at finding the tomb empty, we are struck by the immediate unbelief of the disciples. The men treated the news from the women as an idle tale, and they did not believe the account. They were gripped with skeptical, unbelieving spirits. Though Jesus had spent many months drilling them about His impending death and resurrection, the disciples still did not understand the implications of the empty tomb.

Peter, the Rock, was the one who responded with action. He rushed to the tomb to confirm what he had just heard. He took John with him to the tomb, but it was John, not Peter, who first understood the significance of what they found (see John 20:1-10). Peter left the tomb still wondering what had happened.

Deniers of the miraculous are like the poor: they are always with us. Bible miracles are stated as facts, and by faith we accept them. If we reject the miracles, particularly those of Christ and His disciples, as being the imaginative concoctions of New Testament writers, then we attribute these eyewitnesses of the supernatural as misrepresentation or fraud.

It is important to remember that Gospel miracles were wrought in the presence of enemies, and as such, they were subjected to the stiffest scrutiny. Even so, they emerged as being among those things most surely believed by the apostles.

The evidence of our faith would be seriously damaged if the miracles were set aside. Without the miracles, we would lose the positive evidence we now possess of our Lord's saving power.

Peter later believed in the Resurrection because he saw Jesus, not once but several times before the Ascension. In his early years, Peter became an aggressive evangelist. His unbridled zeal for his Savior set him up for embarrassment and even shame before the Cross, yet the same man gave us one of the most succinct statements on the topic of evangelism to be found anywhere in the Scriptures. No doubt Peter struggled, as we all do, with what our part in evangelism is and what God's part is. What we must remember is that Christ is in control. He is our consuming passion, and we can trust Him to show us when, where, and how to share His Gospel message.

We believe, by faith, in the Gospel message as passed down by Peter and all the eyewitnesses. But we also believe by faith, as a result of our own miraculous transforming experiences of salvation.

III. CONCLUDING REFLECTION

The discovery of the empty tomb was the greatest discovery in human history. Yet, the great tragedy is that most people either are not aware that Jesus arose or do not believe that He arose. Everyone has to discover that fact for himself or herself.

We find in this story of the Resurrection that it can be quite dangerous not to accept God's Word at face value because not accepting it can lead to certain unbelief. Unbelief will pull a person away from God's truth, as was the case at one time with Peter.

It is this truth upon which all of our Christian faith is built, and it is this truth, as told by angels, that guarantees our right to live eternally with our Savior.

The crux of this lesson is for every Christian to be resurrected to a new life. Many church members have celebrated resurrection services many times, yet their lives have not truly demonstrated real change. Paul, in his epistle to the Galatians, said, "I am crucified with Christ: nevertheless I live; yet not I, but Christ liveth in me: and the life which I now live in the flesh I live by the faith of the Son of God, who loved me, and gave himself for me" (Galatians 2:20). If we are not able to declare what Paul did, we have yet to possess resurrected lives.

PRAYER

Heavenly Father, we believe that You are the Son of God and that You were raised from the dead on the third day. We pray today for those who do not believe, hoping that they too will find You and have eternal life. In Jesus' name we pray. Amen.

WORD POWER

Resurrection *(anastasis)*—denotes "a raising up," or "rising" (*ana*—"up," and *histemi*— "to cause to stand"), of "resurrection" from the dead, of Christ as the author of "resurrection," of those who are Christ's at His *parousia* (coming).

HOME DAILY BIBLE READINGS
(April 6-12, 2009)

Resurrected unto New Life
MONDAY, April 6: "God Raised Him from the Dead" (Acts 13:26-33)
TUESDAY, April 7: "God's Power for Us" (Ephesians 1:15-23)
WEDNESDAY, April 8: "First Fruits of the Dead" (1 Corinthians 15:12-26)
THURSDAY, April 9: "Buried and Raised with Christ" (Colossians 2:6-15)
FRIDAY, April 10: "Walk in Newness of Life" (Romans 6:3-11)
SATURDAY, April 11: "Seek the Things Above" (Colossians 3:1-11)
SUNDAY, April 12: "Christ Has Risen" (Luke 24:1-12)

WITNESSES TO NEW LIFE

DEVOTIONAL READING: **Acts 2:22-32**
PRINT PASSAGE: **Luke 24:44-53**

BACKGROUND SCRIPTURE: **Luke 24:36-53**
KEY VERSES: **Luke 24:48-49**

Luke 24:44-53—KJV

44 And he said unto them, These are the words which I spake unto you, while I was yet with you, that all things must be fulfilled, which were written in the law of Moses, and in the prophets, and in the psalms, concerning me.

45 Then opened he their understanding, that they might understand the scriptures,

46 And said unto them, Thus it is written, and thus it behoved Christ to suffer, and to rise from the dead the third day:

47 And that repentance and remission of sins should be preached in his name among all nations, beginning at Jerusalem.

48 And ye are witnesses of these things.

49 And, behold, I send the promise of my Father upon you: but tarry ye in the city of Jerusalem, until ye be endued with power from on high.

50 And he led them out as far as to Bethany, and he lifted up his hands, and blessed them.

51 And it came to pass, while he blessed them, he was parted from them, and carried up into heaven.

52 And they worshipped him, and returned to Jerusalem with great joy:

53 And were continually in the temple, praising and blessing God. Amen.

Luke 24:44-53—NRSV

44 Then he said to them, "These are my words that I spoke to you while I was still with you—that everything written about me in the law of Moses, the prophets, and the psalms must be fulfilled."

45 Then he opened their minds to understand the scriptures,

46 and he said to them, "Thus it is written, that the Messiah is to suffer and to rise from the dead on the third day,

47 and that repentance and forgiveness of sins is to be proclaimed in his name to all nations, beginning from Jerusalem.

48 You are witnesses of these things.

49 And see, I am sending upon you what my Father promised; so stay here in the city until you have been clothed with power from on high."

50 Then he led them out as far as Bethany, and, lifting up his hands, he blessed them.

51 While he was blessing them, he withdrew from them and was carried up into heaven.

52 And they worshiped him, and returned to Jerusalem with great joy;

53 and they were continually in the temple blessing God.

BIBLE FACT

Believers have the same weaponry given to those early disciples. The Holy Spirit empowers us to be bold witnesses in spite of opposition and rejection. Our power source is God Himself, and He alone can give power to our evangelism outreach.

TOPICAL OUTLINE
OF THE LESSON

I. **Introduction**
   A. Evangelizing Christians
   B. Biblical Background

II. **Exposition and Application of the Scripture**
   A. Prophecy Fulfilled (Luke 24:44-49)
   B. Jesus' Last Appearance (Luke 24:50-53)

III. **Concluding Reflection**

LESSON OBJECTIVES

Upon completion of this lesson, the students will know that:

1. Resurrection was not a figment of imagination of the disciples;
2. Jesus appeared to several of His disciples after He had resurrected;
3. Jesus' ascension was a historical fact as recorded in the Bible; and,
4. Evangelism is a command which Christians must carry out.

POINTS TO BE EMPHASIZED
ADULT/YOUTH

Adult Topic: **Good News Is for Sharing**
Youth Topic: **Power from on High**
Adult/Youth Key Verses: **Luke 24:48-49**
Print Passage: **Luke 24:44-53**

—The disciples needed concrete and intellectual evidence to convince them of the reality of the Resurrection.

—Jesus' resurrected body displays both spiritual and human characteristics.

—Jesus patiently helped the disciples connect His life, death, and resurrection with the witness of Old Testament writings.

—After hearing Jesus' explanation of the Scriptures, the disciples were expected to proclaim the Good News and minister in Jesus' name to all peoples.

—The mood of sadness overwhelmed the disciples after the Crucifixion, but with the Ascension their mood was changed to joy.

—This Scripture is set in the seven weeks between the Resurrection and Pentecost.

—Jesus appeared to His disciples and explained to them through the Old Testament Scriptures that He was the Messiah (Christ), the one sent by God the Father to save the people.

CHILDREN

Children Topic: **Jesus Shows Up!**
Key Verse: **Luke 24:36**
Print Passage: **Luke 24:36-46**

—The disciples were terrified and amazed when Jesus appeared in their midst.

—Jesus helped the disciples distinguish between an illusion and a reality by showing them His wounds.

—Jesus reminded the disciples of the prophecy regarding the Messiah and affirmed that they were witnesses to the fulfillment of the prophecy.

—As further evidence of His bodily resurrection, Jesus asked for, received, and ate food.

I. INTRODUCTION

A. Evangelizing Christians

Evangelism makes many Christians nervous. If we would confess our fears, most would admit that they fear their witnessing will be ineffective or, worse, rejected. Witnessing is an art, and a mystery because it involves connecting one's faith with other people's experience in a way that they can understand it; it means being willing to cooperate with God and partner with Him to reach another soul with the message of salvation.

The difficulty comes when we try so hard that we fail to leave the results in God's hands. We are a society that responds to instant results. Unfortunately, there is no such thing as instant or "microwave" evangelism. The seeds we plant today may not even sprout in our lifetimes. But God has empowered us with His Word to sow a great harvest, and He will not hold us accountable for seeds that do not sprout. As long as we are obedient and sincere in our witness, we are fulfilling our duty as evangelizing Christians. We are called to share the Word of God with others, but it is God who orchestrates events in people's lives so they will turn toward Him.

B. Biblical Background

The ascension of Jesus Christ was a powerful event, full of significance to every Christian. In biblical times, it was not difficult for Luke to convince others that the Ascension was real. Both Jewish and Greek readers could relate to the idea of the ascension of a great hero to heaven. The Greeks believed that Hercules ascended to heaven, and the Jews believed that Moses and Elijah ascended as well. But the difficulty in Luke's witness was the fact that Jesus ascended to sit at the right hand of God. This meant that the people would have to accept the truth that Jesus reigned as God's agent or intercessor (see Psalm 110:1).

Though the societal climate was treacherous enough in the last days of Christ, afterwards hatred for Christ's followers was magnified many times over. The government, fearful of a revolution, sought to stem the tide of new converts following the Ascension, and the Jewish hierarchy heartily concurred. Yet, the disciples remained fearless in the face of their enemies. They knew that the multitudes were ready to welcome the Good News. The harvest was ready for reaping, but the laborers were few. Jesus had passed the mantle of soul-saving responsibility to His carefully chosen followers.

The idea of passing one's calling to another was not new. Moses had passed on his work to Joshua, Elijah to Elisha, and rabbis and philosophers to their disciples. The model of succession created by these familiar narratives described the passing on of a teacher's call. Jesus' ascension immediately after the Great Commission of Acts 1:8 leaves all believers as His successors, and each of us is responsible for the job of world evangelization, until His return in the same glorified body.

II. EXPOSITION AND APPLICATION OF THE SCRIPTURE

A. Prophecy Fulfilled
(Luke 24:44-49)

And he said unto them, These are the words which I spake unto you, while I was yet with you, that all things must be fulfilled, which were written in the law of Moses, and in the prophets, and in the psalms, concerning me. Then opened he their understanding, that they might understand the scriptures, And said unto them, Thus it is written, and thus it behoved Christ to suffer, and to rise from the dead the third day: And that repentance and remission of sins should be preached in his name among all nations, beginning at Jerusalem. And ye are witnesses of these things. And, behold, I send the promise of my Father upon you: but tarry ye in the city of Jerusalem, until ye be endued with power from on high.

Since His resurrection, this was the first time that Jesus appeared to His disciples all at once. There were two purposes for Jesus' appearance. The first was to prove without question that He had risen from the dead. There is nothing like an eyewitness to prove facts. The second purpose was to point out to the disciples that all Scriptures concerning the coming Messiah had been fulfilled.

Jesus had already appeared four times prior to this moment. He appeared to Mary Magdalene (see John 20:14), to the women visiting the tomb (see Matthew 28:1; Mark 16:1), to two who were walking on the road to Emmaus (see Luke 24:15), and to Simon Peter (see Luke 24:34). Word of His appearing had spread quickly, and the apostles and disciples rushed to the place where Jesus had told them to meet Him. We can be sure there was electricity in the air as each of them began to grasp what was about to happen. Any sadness they felt over the loss of their great Teacher was now replaced with great anticipation.

Many Bible students ask the question, "How did the Lord's resurrected body differ from His earthly body?" We can draw some conclusions by comparing Christ's resurrected body to the glorified body promised to believers. Christ's resurrected body was His body, but it was radically changed. It had the appearance of a physical body, but it was not bound by the properties of the physical world. It bore the marks of His physical body (see John 20:20) and the disciples could recognize Him upon close examination, but unlike His earthly body, Jesus could now travel and appear anyplace at will. His glorified body was unhampered by space and time (see Luke 24:36; John 20:19). The new properties of this glorified body somehow made Him difficult to identify. Mary Magdalene thought He was the gardener (see John 20:15). The two travelers on the road to Emmaus thought He was a traveler (see Luke 24:31). The disciples who were fishing did not recognize Him standing on the seashore (see John 21:4). But in each of these instances, upon closer examination, Jesus became recognizable.

"There is a natural body, and there is a spiritual body"—according to 1 Corinthians 15:44. "The spiritual body is a perfected body, no longer subject to pain, tears, death, or sorrow. It was sown in corruption, but it is raised as incorrupt—sown in weakness but raised in power. Jesus stood before them with all power, ready to commission His army."

Jesus' first words to the crowd were "Peace be unto you." Though this was the regular greeting used by the Jews in that day, at that moment it took on new significance. Jesus was bestowing a peace on them that only He could bestow as their risen Savior (see Ephesians

2:13-14). The impact of Christ's resurrection was now fully manifested in the fact that Jesus now stood before them. There must have been mixed reactions to His sudden appearing. Fear, doubt, indifference, and complete acceptance stood before Jesus in one massive gathering, as Jesus unfolded the proof that He was not a spirit, a vision, nor a hallucination. He was the risen Lord, standing before them bodily. It was different in the mere fact that His glorified body was no longer subject to the limitation and frailties of the physical universe and its laws—but He was Jesus, their Christ, standing before them in the flesh.

The second statement Jesus made was to point out that all Scriptures had been fulfilled concerning His messiahship. Notice that Christ gave the three divisions of the Old Testament—the law, the prophets, and the psalms—as evidence that the whole Old Testament prophesied of His coming and His gift of salvation. In other words, He opened their eyes to understanding. His appearing should not have been a surprise to the disciples because He had foretold of this event and forewarned His followers (see Luke 18:31-34). He had told them that He must suffer and arise (see Luke 18:31-34). He had told them that repentance and forgiveness must be preached (see Matthew 26:28). And He had told them that the Holy Spirit must be given (see John 14:15-26). In other words, the believer had to be equipped for witnessing. Jesus had to open His disciples' spiritual eyes so that they could understand (see 1 Corinthians 2:14).

B. Jesus' Last Appearance
(Luke 24:50-53)

And he led them out as far as to Bethany, and he lifted up his hands, and blessed them. And it came to pass, while he blessed them, he was parted from them, and carried up into heaven. And they worshipped him, and returned to Jerusalem with great joy: And were continually in the temple, praising and blessing God. Amen.

Luke closed his gospel with the ascension of Christ, and began Acts with the ascension of Christ. The Ascension is said to be the final chapter and consummation of Christ's journey on earth. But the Ascension also opened the Lord's heavenly ministry—Christ's mission of intercession for the world, and His mission of bearing witness through the lives of His followers. Therefore, the Ascension is the last chapter in Christ's earthly ministry and the first chapter in His life as our risen Lord. At the point of His ascension, Christ became the propitiation "for the sins of the whole world" (1 John 2:2).

The disciples' response to the ascension of Jesus was threefold. First, the Ascension made them worshipful. They now knew beyond a shadow of a doubt that Jesus was the true Messiah, the Son of God. He was now due all of their adoration and praise. Second, the disciples were filled with joy and rejoicing because Christ was now exalted and sitting at the right hand of God, and they knew that He would be with them forever. Nothing would ever separate them from Him again. And third, the church was now the focus of God's presence and worship, and the center for teaching. It would be the gathering place for all who desired to be instructed in the Scriptures.

Jesus could not ascend before carefully unfolding the prophetic fulfillment of His mission. He challenged the disciples to remember the prophecies of His coming, taught by the rabbis from the books of Law and Prophecy and the Psalms. They had to fully understand that His appearance was all the proof they needed now of the complete fulfillment of God's promise.

But Jesus' primary purpose was to equip the believer for witnessing and, by His ascension, to release the power of the Holy Spirit upon His followers. What is this power that Jesus released upon His followers, past and present?

John the Baptist was the first to introduce this idea of a person possessing a power greater than his own. In all probability, the people had no idea what it meant to be baptized by the Holy Spirit. They may have had ideas, but nobody knew exactly what he meant. Jesus did not speak of the baptism of the Holy Spirit until He prepared to ascend into heaven. In these verses of Luke, Jesus equated the Holy Spirit with "the promise of the Father," and more importantly (in Acts 1:4) that "which ye have heard of Me." Jesus was referring to a conversation with His disciples just before His arrest, when He promised to send the Holy Spirit after He departed (see John 14:16-17). In that conversation, Jesus said that He would ask the Father to send the Spirit and that the Father would do it. Jesus made a promise on behalf of His Father, which was the same as the Father promising the Holy Spirit.

No ministry of the Holy Spirit has been more misunderstood than the baptism of the Holy Spirit. But the Bible is clear and consistent in its explanation of the baptism of the Spirit, and there is no need for confusion. Nowhere in the Bible does it support the idea of two levels of believers—those who have received the Spirit and those who have not. In fact, this way of thinking opposes everything the Bible teaches about spiritual gifts and the body of Christ. First Corinthians 12:13 is a guide to teach that every believer has been baptized by the Holy Spirit. Baptism symbolizes our identification with the body of Christ. It happens at the moment of salvation. If you trust Christ as your Savior, you have the baptism of the Holy Spirit.

Some people think you can receive the Holy Spirit through the laying on of hands, and they point to a delay between salvation and the baptism of the Spirit found in Acts 8:16-17. They use this Scripture to support the idea that baptism comes with the laying on of hands. But if that were true, Philip could have accomplished it on his own, without the help of Peter and John. There is another explanation for the delay in the baptism of the Spirit on these early converts. Philip was in Samaritan territory. The Jews despised the Samaritans. If the Samaritans had received the Holy Spirit automatically, there would have been uproar in the Jewish community. This delay allowed the apostles to lay their hands on the Samaritans and, in so doing, put their stamp of approval on the whole Samaritan missionary movement, which united the early church.

III. CONCLUDING REFLECTION

Unbelievers respond to the Resurrection in five ways: 1) they are terrified and troubled by the Resurrection, because it means they must obey and serve Christ. If He is the living Lord, then it means man is His subject; 2) they question the truth of the Resurrection. The idea that a person could arise from the dead is beyond their acceptance; 3) they ignore the Resurrection and count it as meaningless; 4) they react to the Resurrection with anywhere from mild opposition to the persecution of any who bear witness to the Resurrection; and 5) they respond to the Resurrection, accepting Jesus Christ as their Savior and Lord. We should not anticipate an unbeliever's response, nor attempt to shape our Gospel message to make it more palatable to those who oppose it. God has equipped us for any battle. The greatest of all tragedies is that there are those who, despite irrefutable evidence, refuse to believe in the resurrection of Jesus Christ. Centuries have come and gone, and thousands upon thousands of witnesses have carried the first story of the Resurrection forward into many generations, as told by eyewitnesses. Not "one jot or tittle" has been altered in the telling of the story. Despite the authenticity of the account, millions have chosen to discount its accuracy and legitimacy. However, those of us who are empowered by the Holy Spirit will never let this deter us from the task of being witnesses for Jesus Christ.

As Christians, we have a duty to tell the story and to spread the Good News about the resurrection of Jesus. The wisest advice concerning evangelism came from Peter, whose exhortation was, "Always be prepared to give an answer to everyone who asks you to give the reason for the hope that you have" (1 Peter 3:15, NIV). We must be ready at all times to explain the newness of life that we so freely demonstrate.

PRAYER

Heavenly Father, continue to put a burden on our hearts for those who are lost without You. In Jesus' name we pray. Amen.

WORD POWER

Witness: 1) *martus* or *martur* ("martyr," one who bears "witness" by his death); it denotes "one who can or does aver what he has seen or heard or knows"; it is used of God, of Christ, of those who "witness" for Christ by their death; 2) *marturia* ("testimony, a bearing witness") is translated "witness"; and 3) *marturion* ("testimony or witness as borne, a declaration of facts") is translated "witness."

HOME DAILY BIBLE READINGS
(April 13-19, 2009)

Witnesses to New Life
  MONDAY, April 13: "Women at the Tomb" (Matthew 28:6-10)
  TUESDAY, April 14: "Mary Magdalene" (John 20:11-18)
  WEDNESDAY, April 15: "On the Road to Emmaus" (Luke 24:13-23, 28-31)
  THURSDAY, April 16: "Thomas" (John 20:24-29)
  FRIDAY, April 17: "Seven Disciples" (John 21:1-14)
  SATURDAY, April 18: "Witnesses of the Resurrection" (1 Corinthians 15:1-8)
  SUNDAY, April 19: "You Are Witnesses" (Luke 24:44-53)

LESSON 9   April 26, 2009

BRINGING NEW LIFE TO THOSE IN NEED

DEVOTIONAL READING: **John 14:8-14**   BACKGROUND SCRIPTURE: **Acts 9:32-43**
PRINT PASSAGE: **Acts 9:32-43**   KEY VERSE: **Acts 9:38**

Acts 9:32-43—KJV

32 And it came to pass, as Peter passed throughout all quarters, he came down also to the saints which dwelt at Lydda.

33 And there he found a certain man named Aeneas, which had kept his bed eight years, and was sick of the palsy.

34 And Peter said unto him, Aeneas, Jesus Christ maketh thee whole: arise, and make thy bed. And he arose immediately.

35 And all that dwelt at Lydda and Saron saw him, and turned to the Lord.

36 Now there was at Joppa a certain disciple named Tabitha, which by interpretation is called Dorcas: this woman was full of good works and almsdeeds which she did.

37 And it came to pass in those days, that she was sick, and died: whom when they had washed, they laid her in an upper chamber.

38 And forasmuch as Lydda was nigh to Joppa, and the disciples had heard that Peter was there, they sent unto him two men, desiring him that he would not delay to come to them.

39 Then Peter arose and went with them. When he was come, they brought him into the upper chamber: and all the widows stood by him weeping, and shewing the coats and garments which Dorcas made, while she was with them.

40 But Peter put them all forth, and kneeled down, and prayed; and turning him to the body said, Tabitha, arise. And she opened her eyes: and when she saw Peter, she sat up.

41 And he gave her his hand, and lifted her up, and when he had called the saints and widows, presented her alive.

42 And it was known throughout all Joppa; and many believed in the Lord.

43 And it came to pass, that he tarried many days in Joppa with one Simon a tanner.

Acts 9:32-43—NRSV

32 Now as Peter went here and there among all the believers, he came down also to the saints living in Lydda.

33 There he found a man named Aeneas, who had been bedridden for eight years, for he was paralyzed.

34 Peter said to him, "Aeneas, Jesus Christ heals you; get up and make your bed!" And immediately he got up.

35 And all the residents of Lydda and Sharon saw him and turned to the Lord.

36 Now in Joppa there was a disciple whose name was Tabitha, which in Greek is Dorcas. She was devoted to good works and acts of charity.

37 At that time she became ill and died. When they had washed her, they laid her in a room upstairs.

38 Since Lydda was near Joppa, the disciples, who heard that Peter was there, sent two men to him with the request, "Please come to us without delay."

39 So Peter got up and went with them; and when he arrived, they took him to the room upstairs. All the widows stood beside him, weeping and showing tunics and other clothing that Dorcas had made while she was with them.

40 Peter put all of them outside, and then he knelt down and prayed. He turned to the body and said, "Tabitha, get up." Then she opened her eyes, and seeing Peter, she sat up.

41 He gave her his hand and helped her up. Then calling the saints and widows, he showed her to be alive.

42 This became known throughout Joppa, and many believed in the Lord.

43 Meanwhile he stayed in Joppa for some time with a certain Simon, a tanner.

UNIFYING LESSON PRINCIPLE

Various sources of physical and spiritual assistance clamor for the world's attention. To what do we turn for help in times of physical illness and death? Through the power of Christ, Peter was able to heal Aeneas and raise Tabitha from the dead.

TOPICAL OUTLINE OF THE LESSON

I. **Introduction**
   A. Word of Mouth
   B. Biblical Background

II. **Exposition and Application of the Scripture**
   A. Dedication to Duty (Acts 9:32-33)
   B. Deliverance from Sickness (Acts 9:34-35)
   C. Power over Death (Acts 9:36-43)

III. **Concluding Reflection**

LESSON OBJECTIVES

Upon completion of this lesson, the students will know that:

1. It was through the power of Christ that Peter was able to raise Tabitha from the dead and heal Aeneas; and,
2. Christians will be able to feel the power of Christ's presence in times of need.

POINTS TO BE EMPHASIZED
ADULT/YOUTH

Adult Topic: **Seeking Help in Times of Need**
Youth Topic: **Power to Live**
Adult Key Verse: **Acts 9:38**
Youth Key Verse: **Acts 9:40**
Print Passage: **Acts 9:32-43**

—Peter's healing of Aeneas was similar to his earlier miracle, but his raising of Tabitha was unprecedented among the apostles.
—Peter demonstrated that the holistic ministry of Jesus continues in the new community of faith.
—News of miracles led many to faith in Jesus Christ.
—Dorcas was a woman of good works who had helped many widows by giving them clothing she had made.
—Peter continued the healing ministry of Jesus.
—These healings were manifestations of the power of God and God's love for God's people.

CHILDREN

Children Topic: **Seeking Help in Times of Need**
Key Verse: **Acts 9:40**
Print Passage: **Acts 9:36-43**

—Believers in Joppa called on Peter to come in response to their need.
—In Jesus' name, Peter brought new life to Tabitha.
—People believed in Jesus after hearing about the healing of Tabitha.
—The Gospel was being spread beyond Jerusalem.

I. INTRODUCTION

A. Word of Mouth

The message of repentance and salvation through Jesus Christ is the message that has been ringing through countless generations—the message that we are compelled to carry to the world. And the one prerequisite for the successful spread of the Gospel is our own faithfulness to duty.

God reaches the lost by what most would refer to as "the old-fashioned way": by word of mouth. The reason for this is simple: there will never be a more powerful medium for the sharing of the Gospel than a great verbal testimony in the flesh. God uses the personal challenges in our lives to strengthen our testimony and perfect our witness. Our own life experiences become the well from which we draw the words that will change lives.

Consider the milestones in your life that were achieved with the help of the Lord. These are your tools of witnessing. They define who you are in Christ, and they have prepared you to help others who struggle with their own trials. The purpose of every challenge in life is to make us stronger and more confident in our belief.

B. Biblical Background

Peter was dedicated to the Lord's mission. Jesus had chosen Peter to be the leader among the Jews, and it was his duty to reach out to the Jewish converts throughout the known world. By this time, the Jews were scattered all over Palestine because of extreme persecution (see Acts 8:1-4). Peter's task was to set out on an evangelistic mission to strengthen new converts and to preach Christ to all who would listen.

Peter did not confine himself to one area. He traveled throughout Judea, Galilee, and Samaria (see Acts 8:4, 14, 25), preaching the Gospel message to the lost, as he edified the new believers. He even willingly sacrificed his own comfort, leaving his family and friends behind, to fulfill his duty as a disciple of Jesus Christ.

Originally called Simon, a very common Jewish name in the New Testament, Peter was the son of Jona. He had a younger brother named Andrew, who first brought Peter to Jesus (see John 1:40-42). His native town was Bethsaida, on the western coast of the Sea of Galilee. He was brought up on the shores of the Sea of Galilee as a fisherman. His father died when Peter was young, so he and his brother were brought up under the care of Zebedee and his wife Salome (see Matthew 27:56; Mark 15:40; 16:1). Peter spent his boyhood years in constant fellowship with Andrew, James, and John, and enjoyed all the advantages of religious training. Peter would have been well-acquainted with the great prophecies regarding the coming of the Messiah, even if he did not receive formal training under any of the rabbis of his day. When Peter appeared before the Sanhedrin, he looked like an "unlearned" man (Acts 4:13).

The Galileans had a reputation for independence and energy. Peter was no exception. His energy often became turbulent. He was more frank and transparent than his Jewish brethren to the south. In all respects—in bluntness, impetuosity, headiness, and simplicity—Peter was a genuine Galilean. The Galileans had a distinct accent, and their pronunciations were considered harsh in Judea. His accent betrayed him as a follower of Christ when he stood within the judgment hall (see Mark 14:70). It betrayed his own nationality and that of those with him on the day of Pentecost (Acts 2:7). Peter was married (Matthew 8:14) and in all probability, his wife accompanied him on his missionary journeys (1 Corinthians 9:5).

Peter displayed great commitment as *the Rock*. That is the duty of every believer to witness and share Christ wherever we are, no matter what gifts or talents we may have received of God. The *testimonial* seeds we scatter at random will one day produce a great harvest.

II. EXPOSITION AND APPLICATION OF THE SCRIPTURE

A. Dedication to Duty
(Acts 9:32-33)

And it came to pass, as Peter passed throughout all quarters, he came down also to the saints which dwelt at Lydda. And there he found a certain man named Aeneas, which had kept his bed eight years, and was sick of the palsy.

Peter went to Lydda, where the Scriptures state *saints* lived. Lydda was a city ripe for the truth of the Gospel of Jesus Christ. Peter was chosen to go to this important commercial district, thirty miles northwest of Jerusalem and ten miles south of Joppa. The city was ready to receive word of the Messiah because it was a place where many Jews had gone to live following the end of Babylonian captivity. Lydda was on the caravan route to Egypt, so it was a great place to *spread* the Gospel. Merchants who passed through the city would carry news of the Messiah to parts north and south of Jerusalem.

Peter came across Aeneas, a man paralyzed and bedridden for eight years, and whose condition was critical because he could not care for himself. Jewish law taught that suffering was the direct result of sin. If a person was sick from birth, it was believed that he was being punished for the sins of his parents (see John 9:2). A person who suffered severe illness was treated as an outcast. But when Peter saw the hopelessness and despair that surrounded the paralytic man, he was moved with compassion.

Sickness comes in many forms. It is not always a medical condition. Christians are called to minister to all manner of sickness. The sickness of sin, which manifests itself in many ways, can sometimes threaten to create distance between family members. It is often easier to turn our backs on those who offend God than to persist in our witness to them. But Christ taught us that the quickest way to save a soul is to love the person into the Kingdom. We as Christians should never abandon someone who is suffering because we are angry or disapproving of his or her lifestyle. Christ has the right to call into question the legitimacy of any Christian who is not moved with compassion toward those who are caught in the throes of sin. The Holy Spirit will guide our response to sin and give us the power to be effective witnesses to the lost. Though we may not see visible results immediately, we must trust

God at His Word, who said, "So then neither is he that planteth any thing, neither he that watereth; but God that giveth the increase" (1 Corinthians 3:7).

B. Deliverance from Sickness
(Acts 9:34-35)

And Peter said unto him, Aeneas, Jesus Christ maketh thee whole: arise, and make thy bed. And he arose immediately. And all that dwelt at Lydda and Saron saw him, and turned to the Lord.

The entire populations of Lydda and Saron were watching Peter when he entered the city and healed the paralytic man. They were a "prepared people," ready to receive the Gospel, and they were awestruck by Peter's demonstration of the power of Christ. What primed Lydda's citizens to receive Peter's message? There were two things: 1) they knew that God had promised a Messiah; and 2) they knew that they needed a Savior. We need only seek out people who are just like the citizens of Lydda and Saron, people who have been prepared by God to receive the Good News.

Jesus designated Peter as the starting point from which Christ would build His church. As Christ's *rock*, Peter was the charter member of the church. But Jesus never made reference to any architectural plans or a specific denomination. He appointed Peter to simply begin the outflow of churches that would dot the landscape and spread through many generations. Peter's faithfulness to evangelism duty ensured that the Gospel would spread beyond his small group of apostles.

The church is made up of those who have placed their belief, like Peter, in the person of Jesus Christ. It has always been the work of the church to bring others to belief in Christ and to experience a personal relationship with Him. Those who believed in Christ became His church and took on the responsibility that comes with belief, which is a commitment to continue the world that Christ began. Peter's fulfillment of his Christian duty in the cities of Lydda and Saron planted seeds of faith that produced many new converts, and proved to those who witnessed the healings that the apostles were the church—not the building called the Temple.

The church is not a building; it is the people. A denomination defines a particular group or belief system that focuses on certain theological interpretations, but it does not define the universal church of Jesus Christ. The *church* is defined as "baptized believers in Jesus Christ." And our duty to spread the Good News includes trusting the power of God to exercise the truth of the Gospel. Had Peter not trusted God's power to heal, his ministry would have fallen flat, and the "rock" would have turned out to be nothing more than a pebble.

Many have questioned why there are not more miraculous healings today. But aren't there? Two thousand years after the Resurrection, sophisticated society has now decided to believe more in luck and odds than in God's divine intervention. Science explains away cures in such a way that God receives no credit at all for healing. Christians pray for their own pre-defined results, and they become disillusioned when God's plan differs from theirs. There is an atmosphere of disbelief in the church that causes would-be "Peters" to hesitate to pray for divine healing.

God does not always respond to our desires, and He frequently allows circumstances to manifest that we wish He would not. Theologically, we call this *sovereignty*. Inherent in our faith is the scriptural truth that God is in control. This includes the events He directs and the circumstances He allows, according to His will (see Psalm 50:1; 115:3).

God often chooses to veil the ways in which He exercises His rights. Therefore, our requests will not always coincide with God's response. Peter understood this as it applied to suffering: "So then, those who suffer according to God's will should commit themselves to their faithful Creator and continue to do good" (1 Peter 4:19, NIV).

Christians have a tendency to doubt God's sovereignty in tumultuous times. But when we doubt, we are actually presuming to comprehend more than God does. We might think that God's miraculous intervention would produce an affirmation of His authority, but in reply to the rich man, Jesus said, "If they do not listen to Moses and the Prophets, they will not be convinced even if someone rises from the dead" (Luke 16:31, NIV). The Bible records Peter's (and the other apostles') successes in healing, but for every success there had to have been countless failures—yet, that did not deter him from continuing to evangelize His world. We must learn to embrace the sufficiency of God's grace in all circumstances. It is imperative that the God of the mountaintop also be the God of the valley. The apostle Paul asked three times to be healed of his "thorn in the flesh," but God's response was, "My grace is sufficient for you, for my power is made perfect in weakness" (2 Corinthians 12:9, NIV). The sufficiency of God's grace is found in that we can endure suffering just as Jesus endured the Cross!

C. Power over Death
(Acts 9:36-43)

Now there was at Joppa a certain disciple named Tabitha, which by interpretation is called Dorcas: this woman was full of good works and alms deeds which she did. And it came to pass in those days, that she was sick, and died: whom when they had washed, they laid her in an upper chamber. And forasmuch as Lydda was nigh to Joppa, and the disciples had heard that Peter was there, they sent unto him two men, desiring him that he would not delay to come to them. Then Peter arose and went with them. When he was come, they brought him into the upper chamber: and all the widows stood by him weeping, and shewing the coats and garments which Dorcas made, while she was with them. But Peter put them all forth, and kneeled down, and prayed; and turning him to the body said, Tabitha, arise. And she opened her eyes: and when she saw Peter, she sat up. And he gave her his hand, and lifted her up, and when he had called the saints and widows, presented her alive. And it was known throughout all Joppa; and many believed in the Lord. And it came to pass, that he tarried many days in Joppa with one Simon a tanner.

Peter's fame must have spread quickly. No one could perform the miraculous deeds Peter performed without being noticed. When word arrived in Joppa that Peter had raised a paralytic man from his bed of affliction, two disciples from Joppa compelled him to come to the rescue of a dead woman.

There was no doubt in Peter's mind that a deceased body could be raised from the dead. He had seen Christ perform this miracle more than once, including raising His own body from death to life. Peter was that *rock* on whom Jesus was counting to be a willing vessel through which the Holy Spirit could channel all of His power.

These miracles performed by Peter and those performed by the other disciples immediately following the resurrection of Jesus Christ were the indisputable signals that the kingdom of God had arrived on earth. Today, our culture challenges the credibility of miracles.

Humankind is capable of accomplishing many physical feats once thought to be impossible (flying, curing leprosy, x-rays, surgery). For this reason, unbelievers (and even some proclaimed believers) attempt to rationalize the stories of miracles in the Bible: "Maybe Jesus was a physician"; "Maybe Peter only *appeared* to heal, and somehow duped the onlookers"; "Maybe the miracles never occurred, but were simply the embellished stories of disciples eager to spread the news of Christ's power." The mind that cannot fully accept humanity's limitations versus God's power will continue to be troubled by disbelief. It will dismiss the stories of miracles in the Scriptures as fables, or explain them away as mere *flukes in nature.*

III. CONCLUDING REFLECTION

The amazing power that God has placed within us, by the aid of the Holy Spirit, all too often goes untested because we put limitations on our faith. But the Holy Spirit has the same power to use us as the conduit through which it performs miracles even today. Though the miracles of the Scriptures seem to have been clustered around certain periods in the life of God's people (Israel's early history; the prophetic ministries of Elijah and Elisha; Jesus' earthly life; the early church), this should not cause us to question or put limits on God's power in the present age.

PRAYER

Heavenly Father, those around us who are struggling and distressed are ready to receive the Good News of a Savior who can change their circumstances. Help us to carry Your message to them. In Jesus' name we pray. Amen.

WORD POWER

Miracle—it is used to denote works of a supernatural origin and character, such as could not be produced by natural agents and means. It is translated "miracles" in the RV and KJV; 2) *semeion:* "a sign, mark, token" (akin to *semaino,* "to give a sign"; *sema,* "a sign") is used to describe miracles and wonders as signs of divine authority; it is translated "miracles" in the RV and KJV.

HOME DAILY BIBLE READINGS
(April 20-26, 2009)

Bringing New Life to Those in Need

MONDAY, April 20: "Father Is Glorified" (John 14:8-14)
TUESDAY, April 21: "The Promise of Healing" (Isaiah 57:14-21)
WEDNESDAY, April 22: "O Lord, Heal Me" (Psalm 6)
THURSDAY, April 23: "Heal My Sin" (Psalm 41)
FRIDAY, April 24: "Return and Be Healed" (Jeremiah 3:19-23)
SATURDAY, April 25: "Joy Comes with the Morning" (Psalm 30:1-5)
SUNDAY, April 26: "God Healing Through Peter" (Acts 9:32-43)

NEW FAMILY IN CHRIST

DEVOTIONAL READING: **Exodus 19:1-8**
PRINT PASSAGE: **Ephesians 1:3-14**

BACKGROUND SCRIPTURE: **Ephesians 1:3-14**
KEY VERSE: **Ephesians 1:5**

Ephesians 1:3-14—KJV

3 Blessed be the God and Father of our Lord Jesus Christ, who hath blessed us with all spiritual blessings in heavenly places in Christ:

4 According as he hath chosen us in him before the foundation of the world, that we should be holy and without blame before him in love:

5 Having predestinated us unto the adoption of children by Jesus Christ to himself, according to the good pleasure of his will,

6 To the praise of the glory of his grace, wherein he hath made us accepted in the beloved.

7 In whom we have redemption through his blood, the forgiveness of sins, according to the riches of his grace;

8 Wherein he hath abounded toward us in all wisdom and prudence;

9 Having made known unto us the mystery of his will, according to his good pleasure which he hath purposed in himself:

10 That in the dispensation of the fulness of times he might gather together in one all things in Christ, both which are in heaven, and which are on earth; even in him:

11 In whom also we have obtained an inheritance, being predestinated according to the purpose of him who worketh all things after the counsel of his own will:

12 That we should be to the praise of his glory, who first trusted in Christ.

13 In whom ye also trusted, after that ye heard the word of truth, the gospel of your salvation: in whom also after that ye believed, ye were sealed with that holy Spirit of promise,

14 Which is the earnest of our inheritance until the redemption of the purchased possession, unto the praise of his glory.

Ephesians 1:3-14—NRSV

3 Blessed be the God and Father of our Lord Jesus Christ, who has blessed us in Christ with every spiritual blessing in the heavenly places,

4 just as he chose us in Christ before the foundation of the world to be holy and blameless before him in love.

5 He destined us for adoption as his children through Jesus Christ, according to the good pleasure of his will,

6 to the praise of his glorious grace that he freely bestowed on us in the Beloved.

7 In him we have redemption through his blood, the forgiveness of our trespasses, according to the riches of his grace

8 that he lavished on us. With all wisdom and insight

9 he has made known to us the mystery of his will, according to his good pleasure that he set forth in Christ,

10 as a plan for the fullness of time, to gather up all things in him, things in heaven and things on earth.

11 In Christ we have also obtained an inheritance, having been destined according to the purpose of him who accomplishes all things according to his counsel and will,

12 so that we, who were the first to set our hope on Christ, might live for the praise of his glory.

13 In him you also, when you had heard the word of truth, the gospel of your salvation, and had believed in him, were marked with the seal of the promised Holy Spirit;

14 this is the pledge of our inheritance toward redemption as God's own people, to the praise of his glory.

Family life offers opportunities for rewards and challenges, for close ties and for estranged relationships. How do we see ourselves within the context of our families? In letters to first-century churches, Paul and John celebrated and gave thanks for those whom God had adopted into a new family in Christ.

TOPICAL OUTLINE OF THE LESSON

I. **Introduction**
   A. Inheritance
   B. Biblical Background

II. **Exposition and Application of the Scripture**
   A. Heavenly Blessings (Ephesians 1:3)
   B. Holy, Adopted, and Forgiven (Ephesians 1:4-10)
   C. Sealed with His Spirit (Ephesians 1:11-14)

III. **Concluding Reflection**

LESSON OBJECTIVES

Upon completion of this lesson, the students will know that:

1. As Christians, we are admonished to recognize and appreciate our blessings and responsibilities as God's children; and,

2. As God's children, we are challenged to live harmoniously with each other.

POINTS TO BE EMPHASIZED

ADULT/YOUTH

Adult Topic: **The Spiritual Family**
Youth Topic: **Sealed by the Holy Spirit**
Adult/Youth Key Verse: **Ephesians 1:5**
Print Passage: **Ephesians 1:3-14**

—God's lavish grace is mediated to believers through Jesus Christ.
—Jesus Christ is the way for mortals to access the blessings of godly living.
—The "seal" and "pledge" of the Holy Spirit is evidence that believers will experience the fullness of salvation.
—In this Scripture, Paul used the image of adoption into a family to describe the community of believers.
—God chose Christians to be God's children through God the Son.
—God gives Christians forgiveness and grace, and God reveals His purposes through God the Son.

CHILDREN

Children Topic: **Love One Another**
Key Verse: **1 John 3:11**
Print Passage: **1 John 3:1-3, 11, 23-24**

—God has given us such love that we are children of God right now.
—Whatever we might become in the future, we know we will be like God.
—God's message has always been clear: love one another.
—If we obey God's commands to believe in Christ and to love one another, then God will be with us and we will be with God.
—God has assured us through the Holy Spirit that we will be united with God.

I. INTRODUCTION

A. Inheritance

Adoption is the process by which people take a child who was not born to them and raise him or her as a member of their family. An adopted child has the same legal rights as any other member of the family. He or she has full access to the parents' inheritance.

As Christians, we are the adopted sons and daughters of almighty God, who loved us enough to provide the means by which we could be adopted into His family. Once we have become God's own, we have the same rights as any other member of the body of Christ. While the laws of some states require a child to live in the home of his or her adoptive parents for a certain length of time before the adoption becomes final, with God, the adoption is final the moment we confess our sins and accept His beloved Son. From that moment on, no man-made court of law can disinherit us from our Father's will.

This lesson reveals the wealth of our inheritance in Jesus Christ, and assures us that we are God's own.

B. Biblical Background

Paul considered his calling to serve Jesus Christ a great privilege. He acknowledged Jesus Christ as the very Son of God Himself, the Supreme Lord of the universe, who rules and reigns as God almighty. The word *apostle* (*apostolos*) means "one called and sent forth on a very special mission." Paul's mission was to be a messenger. The word *apostle* has both a narrow and a broad usage in the New Testament. In the narrow sense, it refers to the twelve apostles and to Paul as an apostle. The apostles were men who had either seen or been companions of the Lord Jesus, or who had been eyewitnesses of the resurrected Lord. In the broader sense, it refers to men who preached the Gospel—men like Barnabas, Silas, Titus, and others.

Jesus Christ called Paul to proclaim the glorious message of salvation to the world. The point Paul made is that Jesus needed messengers who would take the glorious news of salvation to the world. Today, thousands of years have passed and the entire world still has not been reached with the glorious news of Jesus Christ, God's very own Son. There are still large pockets of people who have not yet been evangelized. For this reason, if God calls a person to mission work abroad, that person must answer the call and go, or one day face a terrible day of accountability.

It was important for Paul to acknowledge to the Ephesians that he did not choose his work; God did the choosing. He needed to make it clear to them that His ministry was not chosen because it was a profitable profession to enter into, or because some friends thought he would make a good preacher. He was a minister because God had called him to be a minister (see Matthew 12:50). This preemptive statement let the Ephesians know that what he was about to share with them was of the utmost importance because it came directly from God.

II. EXPOSITION AND APPLICATION OF THE SCRIPTURE

A. Heavenly Blessings
(Ephesians 1:3)

Blessed be the God and Father of our Lord Jesus Christ, who hath blessed us with all spiritual blessings in heavenly places in Christ.

Of all the verses in the Bible, this is one of the most significant because it deals with God's eternal plan for the world. It has always been God's plan to pour out great blessings on humankind. Throughout biblical history God has used two methods to bless people. Before Christ, God blessed humankind materially. He promised Abraham and Israel a land *flowing with milk and honey*. But Israel misused its blessings, and instead of sharing them with other nations, they hoarded them and claimed superiority over the other nations of the earth. However, since the resurrection of Jesus, God deals with humans through spiritual blessings.

Spiritual blessings have far more significance than material blessings. Consider that while a person may be depressed, oppressed, and feeling down, if he or she has received the blessing of the Holy Spirit upon his or her life, that person is able to conquer his or her emotions and live victoriously in spite of the circumstances. God's greatest blessing allows humans to control their own lives without being subject to the physical or emotional. They are the blessings of the inner person—immortal blessings—and they are *only* found in Jesus Christ.

The topic of predestination immediately raises many questions in the life of a believer. Many wrongly assume that predestination implies that the details of every converted life are pre-packaged and prepared according to God's plan. If that were the case, humankind would not continue to sin after their conversion.

But if we take the revealed Word of God as our guide, we accept the doctrine of predestination with all its mysteriousness as meaning that God is in control.

Rightly understood, predestination always relates to the gift of salvation. It means that we acknowledge God in all His sovereignty, that salvation is entirely of His grace, and that He desires that all should be saved, both Jews and Gentiles. Since every person should serve God, the gift of salvation should deepen our humility and elevate our confidence in God's power. God's foreknowledge is God's knowledge of His own eternal purpose, which is to save humanity from destruction.

B. Holy, Adopted, and Forgiven
(Ephesians 1:4-10)

According as he hath chosen us in him before the foundation of the world, that we should be holy and without blame before him in love: Having predestinated us unto the adoption of children by Jesus Christ to himself, according to the good pleasure of his will, To the praise of the glory of his grace, wherein he hath made us accepted in the beloved. In whom we have redemption through his blood, the forgiveness of sins, according to the riches of his grace; Wherein he hath abounded toward us in all wisdom and prudence; Having made known unto us the mystery of his will, according to his good pleasure which he hath purposed in himself: That in the dispensation of the fulness of times he might gather together in one all things in Christ, both which are in heaven, and which are on earth; even in him.

Our very first blessing from heaven is *holiness*. God showers this blessing upon those who are crucified with Christ and resurrected anew. His blessing of holiness allows us never to be separated from God again. Sin no longer has power over us. The word *holy* means "to be set apart and consecrated to God." In the original

Greek, the words *holy* and *saint* are the same (Greek: *hagious;* see Ephesians 1:1). We are also blessed to be "blameless" (Philippians 2:15), which means "to be free from sin." Together, holiness and blamelessness mean that we are chosen to be perfect representations of Jesus Christ, through His shed blood on Calvary.

God's next heavenly blessings are *adoption* and *predestination*. God preordained that we would be adopted into His family through the shed blood of Jesus Christ. Our adoption is a privilege in which we should take great pleasure. The believer can rest assured that God has predestined him or her to be delivered from the suffering and struggles of this world. God's purpose for adopting us is that we might live forever, to the praise and glory of His grace.

The third heavenly blessing is *redemption*. God has delivered us, or set us free by paying a ransom for us. We were powerless to free ourselves from sin because humankind was under the power and influence of Satan, who had blinded our eyes to God's Word. Humankind needed to be liberated; therefore, God redeemed humanity by the blood of Jesus Christ (see 1 Corinthians 6:20).

The fourth blessings are *wisdom* and *prudence*. God gives His wisdom only to those who honor Him and His Son, Jesus. The word *wisdom* means "knowing the truth," and *prudence* means "knowing how to use the truth." These practical heavenly blessings help us to cope with the challenges of day-to-day living. Wisdom and prudence are the gifts that temper our approach to evangelism. They put us on a solid footing and allow us to know when and how to witness.

The fifth blessing is *the mystery of God's will*. In the Bible, a mystery is not something mysterious and hard to understand. It is a truth that has heretofore been locked up until God is ready to reveal it to humankind (see 1 Corinthians 2:7). God's will is to gather together all things in a spirit of peace under the authority and glorification of Jesus Christ; He moves His plan forward until the whole of His purpose and plan is revealed.

C. Sealed with His Spirit (Ephesians 1:11-14)

In whom also we have obtained an inheritance, being predestinated according to the purpose of him who worketh all things after the counsel of his own will: That we should be to the praise of his glory, who first trusted in Christ. In whom ye also trusted, after that ye heard the word of truth, the gospel of your salvation: in whom also after that ye believed, ye were sealed with that holy Spirit of promise, Which is the earnest of our inheritance until the redemption of the purchased possession, unto the praise of his glory.

The sixth of the blessings mentioned previously is *inheritance*. When we hear the word *inheritance*, we instantly picture some material object of great value, whether it is jewelry, real estate, or money. That is because these are the things we value most. If we were asked to name our most cherished possession, we might boast of a diamond wedding ring, a luxury automobile, a dream home, a boat, or any such valuables that men and women accumulate in their lifetimes. But there is an inheritance that has far more value than anything our earthly monetary system can produce. The greatest inheritance of all is knowing that we possess God, and better still, that He possesses us. Our inheritance as believers in Jesus is the promise of life in an eternal state of being. Notice that we do not inherit God: God inherits us. When we repent and accept Christ as Lord and Savior, God chooses us. We are made His inheritance and given the glorious privilege of existing forever with Him. Humankind is God's most cherished possession.

The seventh blessing is the greatest blessing of all—the Holy Spirit. It is the indwelling of God Himself within us. The mere fact that God would permit Himself to take up residence in sinful humanity is assurance enough of our own salvation. As believers, we know that we are God's cherished possessions, redeemed by the Holy Spirit, who now lives within us. But what is the full implication of the Holy Spirit living within us? A true Christian life is one that is personally conducted by the Holy Spirit at every turn. In other words, we do not possess the Spirit; the Spirit possesses us. We no longer have to shoulder the care, worry, and anxiety as to the decisions we must make in life. The Holy Spirit undertakes that responsibility for us. We are not governed by a long set of rules on the outside of us, but by a living and ever-present Spirit within us.

We have a Father who loves us as no earthly father could, who longs to have His children realize that they belong to Him. And when we look up into His face with hearts which the Holy Spirit has filled, and we call Him *Abba, Father*, there is no language that can describe the joy of God.

III. CONCLUDING REFLECTION

Can you feel the wonder of it all—that God would offer His only begotten Son, that we might be redeemed, and make way for the Spirit of the living God to dwell in us? God's heavenly gifts do nothing less than prepare us for all that life throws at us and make us rise to new heights of spiritual awareness of God and His awesome presence.

PRAYER

Heavenly Father, there is no greater privilege than to have a personal relationship with Your Son, Jesus Christ. So today we surrender our lives completely to Christ. In Jesus' name we pray. Amen.

WORD POWER

Adoption (*huiothesia*)—from *huios*, "a son," and "thesis, "a placing," akin to *tithemi*, "to place," it signifies the place and condition of a son given to one to whom it does not naturally belong. The word is used by the apostle Paul only.

HOME DAILY BIBLE READINGS
(April 27–May 3, 2009)

New Family in Christ
MONDAY, April 27: "A Priestly Kingdom" (Exodus 19:1-8)
TUESDAY, April 28: "An Inheritance Promised" (Galatians 3:15-18)
WEDNESDAY, April 29: "Children of God Through Faith" (Galatians 3:23-29)
THURSDAY, April 30: "Adoption as God's Children" (Galatians 4:1-7)
FRIDAY, May 1: "Inheriting Eternal Life" (Matthew 19:23-30)
SATURDAY, May 2: "Guided by the Spirit" (Galatians 5:16-25)
SUNDAY, May 3: "God's Own People" (Ephesians 1:3-14)

NEW LIFE IN CHRIST

DEVOTIONAL READING: **Psalm 86:1-13**　　　　BACKGROUND SCRIPTURE: **Ephesians 2:1-10**
PRINT PASSAGE: **Ephesians 2:1-10**　　　　　　KEY VERSE: **Ephesians 2:8**

Ephesians 2:1-10—KJV

AND YOU hath he quickened, who were dead in trespasses and sins;

2 Wherein in time past ye walked according to the course of this world, according to the prince of the power of the air, the spirit that now worketh in the children of disobedience:

3 Among whom also we all had our conversation in times past in the lusts of our flesh, fulfilling the desires of the flesh and of the mind; and were by nature the children of wrath, even as others.

4 But God, who is rich in mercy, for his great love wherewith he loved us,

5 Even when we were dead in sins, hath quickened us together with Christ, (by grace ye are saved;)

6 And hath raised us up together, and made us sit together in heavenly places in Christ Jesus:

7 That in the ages to come he might shew the exceeding riches of his grace in his kindness toward us through Christ Jesus.

8 For by grace are ye saved through faith; and that not of yourselves: it is the gift of God:

9 Not of works, lest any man should boast.

10 For we are his workmanship, created in Christ Jesus unto good works, which God hath before ordained that we should walk in them.

Ephesians 2:1-10—NRSV

YOU WERE dead through the trespasses and sins

2 in which you once lived, following the course of this world, following the ruler of the power of the air, the spirit that is now at work among those who are disobedient.

3 All of us once lived among them in the passions of our flesh, following the desires of flesh and senses, and we were by nature children of wrath, like everyone else.

4 But God, who is rich in mercy, out of the great love with which he loved us

5 even when we were dead through our trespasses, made us alive together with Christ—by grace you have been saved—

6 and raised us up with him and seated us with him in the heavenly places in Christ Jesus,

7 so that in the ages to come he might show the immeasurable riches of his grace in kindness toward us in Christ Jesus.

8 For by grace you have been saved through faith, and this is not your own doing; it is the gift of God—

9 not the result of works, so that no one may boast.

10 For we are what he has made us, created in Christ Jesus for good works, which God prepared beforehand to be our way of life.

BIBLE FACT

In the incredibly sinful world of the first century, Paul called Christians to a life that was observably different from the pagans. He made it clear that Christians are not to imitate the life of the unsaved people all around them.

UNIFYING LESSON PRINCIPLE

Before we invest our time, our money, or ourselves, we want to be certain that our outlay will repay us well. How do we know that a potential investment will yield a good return? Both Paul and John claim that when we by faith invest our lives in Christ, we receive new life—the unparalleled benefit of God's love.

TOPICAL OUTLINE OF THE LESSON

I. Introduction
A. A Changed Person
B. Biblical Background

II. Exposition and Application of the Scripture
A. Life Without Christ (Ephesians 2:1-3)
B. The Work of God's Mercy (Ephesians 2:4-7)
C. The Work of God's Grace (Ephesians 2:8-10)

III. Concluding Reflection

LESSON OBJECTIVES

Upon completion of this lesson, the students will know that:

1. A potential investment will yield a good return; hence, both Paul and John claimed that when we (by faith) invest our lives in Christ, we receive new life—the unparalleled benefit of God's love; and,

2. In response to receiving new life, Christians are admonished to recognize and appreciate the significance of our relationship with God through Christ.

POINTS TO BE EMPHASIZED

ADULT/YOUTH
Adult Topic: Receiving Benefits
Youth Topic: Fringe Benefits
Adult Key Verse: Ephesians 2:8
Youth Key Verses: Ephesians 2:4-5
Print Passage: Ephesians 2:1-10

—In Ephesians 2:3 it is declared that humans actively rebel against God.
—Paul recognized that the grace of God is able to transform sinners.
—God loves all humans in spite of their sin and invites them to commit themselves to the new way of life in Jesus Christ.
—Salvation is a gift of God. It cannot be earned or achieved through human effort.
—By grace, Christians are saved through faith, are empowered to do good works in Christ, and receive the gift of eternal life with God.

CHILDREN
Children Topic: Living in Love
Key Verse: 1 John 4:16
Print Passage: Ephesians 2:8-10; 1 John 4:7-16

—Grace is a gift that comes to us freely from God, not because of anything we do.
—God's love for us is shown by God's sending Jesus so that we might live through God.
—In response to God's love in Christ, we are told to love one another and thus live a new kind of life in which God lives in us and we live in God.
—This new relationship with God through Christ is what we are created for by God, and it is to be our way of life.

I. INTRODUCTION

A. A Changed Person

What was life like for you before you came to know Christ? Can you remember? Have you ever thought about what God thought of you before you were converted? What were you like? There are three obstacles in the life of an unbeliever—death, sin, and disobedience. Together they become the magnet that pulls a person away from his or her only hope of rescue. And ultimately, the unbeliever faces the worst pain of all: God's wrath.

Unsaved men and women live life as dying men and women. They are like the inmates in the movie "Dead Man Walking." Each morning they awaken to the cold reality that life for them is soon to end. Death, for them, is more than just the end of life. It is eternal separation from God. God never intended for humans to live in such abhorrent, sinful conditions. God's ecclesiastical plan is that the soul would live out its earthly life in an obedient body and one day be released back to heaven to spend eternity with God.

B. Biblical Background

Paul's letter to the church in Ephesus is an important instructional document for any church in its formative stage. For the Ephesians, it was the tool needed to combat the blatant sin and idol worship that surrounded them. Ephesus was a busy commercial city and the home of those who worshiped the goddess Diana, the goddess of nature. Since Ephesus was the capitol of Asia Minor, "Diana" of Ephesus became the goddess whom all of Asia and the world worshiped. Ephesus was primarily colonized by Greeks from Athens. In the time of the Romans it bore the title of "the first and greatest metropolis of Asia." In addition to the temple of Diana, Ephesus was known for its theatre—the largest in the world. It was capable of seating 50,000 spectators. Like most ancient theatres, it was open to the sky. In this arena, the Greeks staged fights between wild beasts and men.

Imagine the difficulty the early Christians had trying to serve Christ in the midst of this heathen experience. Many Jewish converts took up residence in Ephesus immediately following Pentecost, to sow the seeds of the Gospel of Jesus Christ (Acts 2:9; 6:9). Paul visited this city for the first time at the close of his second missionary journey, when he was returning from Greece to Syria. He stayed only for a short time, but left Aquila and Priscilla behind to carry on the work of spreading the Gospel. He later returned to Ephesus for a period of three years, and his mission there was so successful that "all they which dwelt in Asia heard the word of the Lord Jesus, both Jews and Greeks" (Acts 19:10).

Paul's objective in his letter to the Christians in Ephesus was to set forth the foundation and the course for Christ's church. He wrote to the church of Ephesus as an example of how the universal church of Jesus Christ must operate. It is important to note that the word *church* is always used in the singular, never the plural form, because it denotes *one body* of baptized believers.

II. EXPOSITION AND APPLICATION OF THE SCRIPTURE

A. Life Without Christ
(Ephesians 2:1-3)

AND YOU hath he quickened, who were dead in trespasses and sins; Wherein in time past ye walked according to the course of this world, according to the prince of the power of the air, the spirit that now worketh in the children of disobedience: Among whom also we all had our conversation in times past in the lusts of our flesh, fulfilling the desires of the flesh and of the mind; and were by nature the children of wrath, even as others.

In the first chapter of Ephesians, Paul took us to the heart of the Gospel, which is new life in Christ. At this point, we are aware of the great gulf that exists between the exalted Christ and defeated humankind. We see the great contrast between the glory of the risen Lord and the tragedy of broken people. So in chapter two, Paul began bluntly by saying, "As for you, you were dead in your transgressions and sins" (verse 1, NIV). The acclaimed theologian Warren Wiersbe put it this way: "The unbeliever is not sick, he is dead! Lost sinners are dead, and the only difference between one sinner and another is the state of their decay. The lost derelict on skid row may be more decayed outwardly than the unsaved society leader, but both are dead in sin, and one corpse cannot be more dead than another."

Paul offered four characteristics of the unsaved person: verse 1—the sinner is *dead* (supporting Scripture: Colossians 2:13); verse 2—the sinner is *disobedient* (supporting Scripture: Romans 8:7); and verse 3—the sinner is *depraved* (supporting Scripture: Matthew 15:19) and *doomed* (supporting Scripture: Romans 6:23).

But sinners seldom see themselves as being in any immediate danger. They may dislike or even detest some of their own habits, but their feeling is that their choices in life are theirs to make. They acknowledge their responsibility to care for the mind and the body, but few admit the existence of the soul. It is the soul, therefore, that goes neglected and unattended. Yet it is the soul that is the most important of humanity's framework. The world would be swarming with new converts if it were easy to make humankind see the futility of their thinking.

Before conversion, persons live lives of sin. Their sins separate them from God and put them on the path to eternal death. The definition of *sin* is "missing the mark." Remember that Paul said that a man who is determined to follow Jesus will "press toward the mark for the prize of the high calling of God in Christ Jesus" (Philippians 3:14). People must press toward Jesus, or they will miss the mark and live lives of sin.

B. The Work of God's Mercy
(Ephesians 2:4-7)

But God, who is rich in mercy, for his great love wherewith he loved us, Even when we were dead in sins, hath quickened us together with Christ, (by grace ye are saved;) And hath raised us up together, and made us sit together in heavenly places in Christ Jesus: That in the ages to come he might shew the exceeding riches of his grace in his kindness toward us through Christ Jesus.

The most profound word in this study of Ephesians 2:1-10 is found in verse 4. It is the word *but*. Notice the exciting progression of thought in verses 3 and 4: We "were by nature the children of wrath, even as others. But God…." Humanity is doomed to destruction—*but*! Humanity is dead in their sins—*but* God is rich in mercy! God has interrupted the doom of death and judgment and replaced it with His mercy.

Consider the many ways that God has interrupted your own life. What means did God use to bring you to repentance? If we were each to rewrite these verses of Ephesians in light of our own personal experience with God, there is no doubt that the words would leap off the page at us.

Mercy is a distinctive Bible word characterizing God as revealed to human beings. In the Old Testament it is most often translated as *kindness*. But in the New Testament, it is translated as *bowels*, meaning a deep compassion or pity. Mercy is compassion for the miserable. Its very target is misery. By the atoning sacrifice of Christ a way is opened for the exercise of mercy towards the sons of men, in harmony with the demands of truth and righteousness. It is affirmed in verses 4-7 that as believers, we have been quickened or "made alive" with Christ—we have been raised from the dead; we have been invited to sit in heavenly places, and all of this is to show us the depth of God's mercy. God's very nature would not allow Him to act as humans act: distant, disinterested, unconcerned, and vengeful. His merciful nature is full of compassion, affection, and kindness. God desires to "succor" or tenderly draw us to Him. Thus, He quickens or regenerates us, and makes us alive through the salvation of Jesus Christ.

C. The Work of God's Grace
(Ephesians 2:8-10)

For by grace are ye saved through faith; and that not of yourselves: it is the gift of God: Not of works, lest any man should boast. For we are his workmanship, created in Christ Jesus unto good works, which God hath before ordained that we should walk in them.

When William Tyndale worked to translate the Bible into English, he searched and searched for a word that would encompass the meaning of the Hebrew word for "grace"—*chesed*. Unable to find the right word, he created a word of his own—*loving-kindness*. The word stuck, and the literate world began to interpret grace as "loving-kindness." But the Greek word for "grace" is *charis* or *gift*. Though the word *grace* is attributed to Jesus only twice in the New Testament—once in the gospel of Luke and once in the gospel of John—we clearly see that Jesus overwhelmingly understood and taught the concept of grace.

"We are God's workmanship" is the major affirmation. The word *workmanship* is not the same as that translated *works*. The word *workmanship* means that we are God's finished products; we are created by God for a special purpose—therefore, we are extremely valuable to God.

Salvation is the sole work of God. Those who find some self-satisfaction in their own acts of repentance have missed the whole meaning of a true relationship with Christ. Humanity cannot save themselves. Paul stated it clearly: We are saved by God's grace. Salvation is not something we accomplish; rather, it is something that God grants. We can cooperate by obedience and faith, but salvation is always a gift of God—"Not of works, lest any man should boast" (Ephesians 2:9). We are saved by the act of God, and God alone (see Romans 3:23-24).

People can never earn, win, or merit salvation. All they can do is accept the fact of the free offer of salvation coming from God through Jesus Christ (see Romans 11:6). Once we accept God's plan of salvation, God transforms us into "new" beings. We become His workmanship. This is the act of GRACE—**G**od's **R**iches **A**t **C**hrist's **E**xpense.

Grace is one of the attributes that is unique to God. Man follows the formula that "a person gets what he or she deserves," but God grants us unmerited and undeserved favor. In return, every Christian has the opportunity to help others according to their talents, skills, and abilities God has made available to them. God's grace is shared without measure to all; His spiritual gifts are distributed to specific individuals for specific purposes. Each Christian has the backing of God's resources to perform the specific task the Lord has assigned him or her to do. The purpose of the gifts and the grace of God are clear. Every believer is equipped that we might know that we do not earn our way to God, but we, by His grace, are called to serve. God's grace imparts salvation and teaches us, by the aid of the Holy Spirit, God's will and His ways—that "we should walk in them."

that you do not deserve. Grace and mercy are generally found in the same wrapped package.

The benefits of God's grace and mercy are often held in abeyance by the heart that refuses to repent. The "shower" of grace, this inexplicable gift of God, is turned on through faith in Christ. When we believe that Christ died for our sins, God opens up the heavens and showers down His grace and mercy. Salvation has been wrapped up as a gift, but it is not ours to open until we confess Jesus Christ as Lord and Savior.

Like Paul, we must be consumed with the Gospel of grace. He was willing to die for it, but he was also willing to live for it—not for the Law of God or the righteousness of God, but for the grace of God.

III. CONCLUDING REFLECTION

"Grace" and "mercy" are kissing cousins. *Mercy* is the gift of not receiving punishment that you deserve. *Grace* is receiving a gift

PRAYER

Heavenly Father, we thank You for loving us so much that You were willing to send Your only Son to die for us. In Jesus' name we pray. Amen.

WORD POWER

Quicken: 1) *zoopoieo* means "to make alive"; 2) *zoogoneo* means "to endue with life, produce alive, preserve alive"; 3) *suzoopoieo* or *sunzoopoieo* means "to quicken together with, make alive with" (sun, "with" and No. 1), used in Ephesians 2:5; Colossians 2:13—of the spiritual life with Christ, imparted to believers at their conversion.

HOME DAILY BIBLE READINGS
(May 4-10, 2009)

New Life in Christ

MONDAY, May 4: "Full of Grace and Truth" (John 1:14-18)
TUESDAY, May 5: "Wait for the Gracious Lord" (Isaiah 30:15-21)
WEDNESDAY, May 6: "No Good Withheld" (Psalm 84:8-12)
THURSDAY, May 7: "The Throne of Grace" (Hebrews 4:14–5:10)
FRIDAY, May 8: "Set Your Hope on Grace" (1 Peter 1:10-16)
SATURDAY, May 9: "The Blessing of Grace" (Numbers 6:22-27)
SUNDAY, May 10: "Saved by Grace Through Faith" (Ephesians 2:1-10)

LESSON 12   May 17, 2009

NEW REVELATION IN CHRIST

DEVOTIONAL READING: **Isaiah 40:1-11**
PRINT PASSAGE: **Ephesians 3:1-13**

BACKGROUND SCRIPTURE: **Ephesians 3:1-13**
KEY VERSES: **Ephesians 3:8-9**

Ephesians 3:1-13—KJV

FOR THIS cause I Paul, the prisoner of Jesus Christ for you Gentiles,

2 If ye have heard of the dispensation of the grace of God which is given me to you-ward:

3 How that by revelation he made known unto me the mystery; (as I wrote afore in few words,

4 Whereby, when ye read, ye may understand my knowledge in the mystery of Christ)

5 Which in other ages was not made known unto the sons of men, as it is now revealed unto his holy apostles and prophets by the Spirit;

6 That the Gentiles should be fellowheirs, and of the same body, and partakers of his promise in Christ by the gospel:

7 Whereof I was made a minister, according to the gift of the grace of God given unto me by the effectual working of his power.

8 Unto me, who am less than the least of all saints, is this grace given, that I should preach among the Gentiles the unsearchable riches of Christ;

9 And to make all men see what is the fellowship of the mystery, which from the beginning of the world hath been hid in God, who created all things by Jesus Christ:

10 To the intent that now unto the principalities and powers in heavenly places might be known by the church the manifold wisdom of God,

11 According to the eternal purpose which he purposed in Christ Jesus our Lord:

12 In whom we have boldness and access with confidence by the faith of him.

13 Wherefore I desire that ye faint not at my tribulations for you, which is your glory.

Ephesians 3:1-13—NRSV

THIS IS the reason that I Paul am a prisoner for Christ Jesus for the sake of you Gentiles—

2 for surely you have already heard of the commission of God's grace that was given me for you,

3 and how the mystery was made known to me by revelation, as I wrote above in a few words,

4 a reading of which will enable you to perceive my understanding of the mystery of Christ.

5 In former generations this mystery was not made known to humankind, as it has now been revealed to his holy apostles and prophets by the Spirit:

6 that is, the Gentiles have become fellow heirs, members of the same body, and sharers in the promise in Christ Jesus through the gospel.

7 Of this gospel I have become a servant according to the gift of God's grace that was given me by the working of his power.

8 Although I am the very least of all the saints, this grace was given to me to bring to the Gentiles the news of the boundless riches of Christ,

9 and to make everyone see what is the plan of the mystery hidden for ages in God who created all things;

10 so that through the church the wisdom of God in its rich variety might now be made known to the rulers and authorities in the heavenly places.

11 This was in accordance with the eternal purpose that he has carried out in Christ Jesus our Lord,

12 in whom we have access to God in boldness and confidence through faith in him.

13 I pray therefore that you may not lose heart over my sufferings for you; they are your glory.

TOPICAL OUTLINE OF THE LESSON

I. Introduction
   A. Effective Witnesses
   B. Biblical Background

II. Exposition and Application of the Scripture
   A. The Mystery Gives Us Purpose (Ephesians 3:1-5)
   B. The Mystery Grants Us Favor (Ephesians 3:6)
   C. The Effects of the Revelation (Ephesians 3:7-13)

III. Concluding Reflection

LESSON OBJECTIVES

Upon completion of this lesson, the students will know that:

1. In and through Jesus Christ the mystery of God is made known;
2. Paul was a chosen vessel to uncover the mystery that the gentiles are included in the salvation plan; and,
3. Christians are put in position to demonstrate the power of God over principalities and powers.

POINTS TO BE EMPHASIZED

ADULT/YOUTH

Adult Topic: **Come One and All**
Youth Topic: **A Detective Story**
Adult/Youth Key Verses: **Ephesians 3:8-9**
Print Passage: **Ephesians 3:1-13**

—Paul affirms the doctrine of revelation.
—Paul's commission to bring the message of salvation to the Gentiles came to him by divine revelation.
—The mystery now revealed is that Gentiles may receive God's grace.
—Paul describes the equality of Jews and Gentiles as "fellow heirs, members of the same body, and sharers in the promise in Christ Jesus" (verse 6) [emphasis added].
—The mandate of the church is to share the good news with all people. No group is excluded.
—The Gospel is a mystery, in that it is revealed by God and not deciphered by human wisdom.

CHILDREN

Children Topic: **Life Forever**
Key Verse: **1 John 5:12**
Print Passage: **1 John 5:1-5, 11-12**

—We are God's children if we believe that Jesus is the Messiah (Christ).
—As God's children, we love God and obey God's commandments.
—When we obey God's commandments and believe Jesus is God's Son, we can overcome temptations.
—God's gift of eternal life comes only through God's Son; this is God's testimony.
—Those who believe in Jesus as the Son of God will possess a victorious faith.

I. INTRODUCTION

A. Effective Witnesses

How effective is your witness? Effective witnessing is propelled by the presence of the Holy Spirit in the life of the witness. Simply put, others will listen to what we have to say about Christ, if we are living lives that reflect Christ. Christians who harbor prejudice, bitterness, hatred, hurt, and anger cannot possibly represent Christ effectively.

Negative emotions promote division, and division is one of the greatest problems confronting the world today. It is the most serious problem confronting God because as long as humankind is separated from one another, there is no hope of people ever being reconciled to God.

How does God deal with the terrible division in our world? God's timeless plan is to create a new body of people—people who will love Him and each other completely. Once we accept God's plan and allow the Holy Spirit to remove the stumbling blocks from our personalities, Christ's church will experience an explosive growth movement.

B. Biblical Background

At the outset of this third chapter, Paul identified himself as a prisoner. He had been arrested in Jerusalem and was now awaiting trial in Rome. Yet, in spite of his circumstances, Paul did not believe that he was representing a lost cause. He wanted everyone to know that he was "the prisoner of Jesus Christ for you Gentiles" (Ephesians 3:1).

Until the death and resurrection of Jesus Christ, the Jewish faith was the only way to have a relationship with the one true and living God. God's covenant relationship with Israel was a two-sided contract, similar to a standard contract. But in the Bible, a covenant involves much more than a simple agreement. A contract has an ending date, but a covenant is a permanent agreement. God's covenant with Israel was especially significant because it established a special relationship between God and His chosen people.

The Israelites could not keep God's perfect Law, so God promised a new covenant through the prophet Jeremiah. Under the new covenant, God would write His Law directly on human hearts. This new covenant was one-sided in its initiative; it was motivated by love, grace, and the desire for God to restore His family. Based on the new covenant, God offers forgiveness of sins and eternal life to all who respond and put their faith in His Son Jesus Christ.

Paul's mission was to the Gentiles, who were not part of the covenant. What follows in chapter three is Paul's prayer for the Gentile converts. He prefaced his prayer with the recognition that he was a prisoner for their sakes. This led him to expand on the central theme of the Ephesians letter—the grace of God as it had been shown toward the Gentiles. In Ephesians 3:2-13 is formed a parenthesis in which Paul discussed the uniqueness of his ministry to them (the prayer actually begins at verse 14). In this interlude before his prayer, Paul affirmed his commission to serve the Gentiles.

II. EXPOSITION AND APPLICATION OF THE SCRIPTURE

A. The Mystery Gives Us Purpose
(Ephesians 3:1-5)

FOR THIS cause I Paul, the prisoner of Jesus Christ for you Gentiles, If ye have heard of the dispensation of the grace of God which is given me to you-ward: How that by revelation he made known unto me the mystery; (as I wrote afore in few words, Whereby, when ye read, ye may understand my knowledge in the mystery of Christ) Which in other ages was not made known unto the sons of men, as it is now revealed unto his holy apostles and prophets by the Spirit.

There was no doubt in the apostle's mind that his field of service was the Gentile world. Because of his ministerial commission, Paul helped Christianity break the barriers of race and tradition, and sent the Gospel message out to reach people of all nations.

Paul's great emphasis of his calling by God could have been motivated by the knowledge that he did not have the unanimous support of the Jewish converts. Regardless of their hesitation in supporting him, Paul was confident that his task was "the stewardship of God's grace."

How did Paul view his qualification for the big assignment God had given him? For the answer, we have to take a quick look forward at verse 8. Paul clearly stated that (from a carnal assessment) he was the least qualified for the job, and certainly the least worthy of such a calling. After all, Paul had been a Christian killer, and had captured many Christians who were sentenced to death. But still, with all his negative history, Paul was confident that he was obeying God's call to ministry. God equips those He calls with the talent and means to complete the task.

As the people read Paul's epistle about the mystery of Christ, it struck a familiar chord. The people were acquainted with the mystery religions that were common in the first-century Roman world. These religions claimed to have special knowledge about God that could be revealed only to those who had been initiated into the cult. Paul wrote that Christianity too has its mystery. "The mystery of Christ," however, was dramatically different.

God's redemptive plan for mankind is a mystery to the finite mind. Theologians refer to His redemptive plan as *the mystery of Christ.* So what exactly is the mystery? It is certainly not a mystery that God would send a Messiah to save His chosen people of Israel. Neither was it a mystery that Gentiles would be saved, for Isaiah 42:6 reads, "I the LORD have called thee in righteousness, and will hold thine hand, and will keep thee, and give thee for a covenant of the people, for a light of the Gentiles." God even revealed through His prophets that the Messiah would be a suffering servant (see Isaiah 53). So what is the great mystery?

What was hidden in the secret counsels of the Almighty was the plan that an entirely new creation, made up of a diverse assortment of people including both Jews and Gentiles, possessing incredible spiritual riches (see Ephesians 3:8), would come into existence. This new creation is described as being in a living, organic union with the resurrected and glorified Jesus Christ. This mystery union is called "the body of Christ," the "Bride of Christ," or "the Church." Unlike any union known to humanity, this is a living, breathing *organism,* with the Lord Jesus as its Head. Ephesians 5:23b reads, "Christ is the head of the church: and he is the saviour of the body."

B. The Mystery Grants Us Favor
(Ephesians 3:6)

That the Gentiles should be fellowheirs, and of the same body, and partakers of his promise in Christ by the gospel.

Until the Resurrection, no person could receive salvation except through the Jewish religion. The Jews had favor with God by way of their covenant relationship with Him. But afterwards, with the death and resurrection of Jesus Christ, all people of the earth could approach God and receive salvation. All barriers to salvation were removed.

This new supernatural union, created by God through Christ and fueled by His Holy Spirit, opened the door for members to enter this "body" by the supernatural act of baptism (in Greek, *baptizo* means "to immerse"). This sacrament of baptism causes each member to become one with Christ. Galatians 3:27 reads, "For as many of you as have been baptized into Christ have put on Christ."

Baptism is not a ceremony, but a work of the Holy Spirit. First Corinthians 12:13 reads, "For by one Spirit are we all baptized into one body, whether we be Jews or Gentiles, whether we be bond or free; and have been all made to drink into one Spirit."

The placing of a believer into the body is what is meant by the phrase "in Christ." The mystery of God's redemptive plan is revealed each time a believer is baptized into this exalted position as a child of God. A genuine baptism is a glorious, life-transforming experience. The Lord Jesus Christ then takes up permanent residence in the Christian the moment that he or she trusts the Savior—as it is stated in Colossians 1:27, "To whom God would make known what is the riches of the glory of this mystery among the Gentiles; which is Christ in you, the hope of glory." It is an awesome union: Christ in the believer, and the believer in Christ.

C. The Effects of the Revelation
(Ephesians 3:7-13)

Whereof I was made a minister, according to the gift of the grace of God given unto me by the effectual working of his power. Unto me, who am less than the least of all saints, is this grace given, that I should preach among the Gentiles the unsearchable riches of Christ; And to make all men see what is the fellowship of the mystery, which from the beginning of the world hath been hid in God, who created all things by Jesus Christ: To the intent that now unto the principalities and powers in heavenly places might be known by the church the manifold wisdom of God, According to the eternal purpose which he purposed in Christ Jesus our Lord: In whom we have boldness and access with confidence by the faith of him. Wherefore I desire that ye faint not at my tribulations for you, which is your glory.

The mystery of Christ profoundly affected Paul. Paul's greatest glory was God's call and God's work. He saw the dignity of the ministry, the dignity of being especially chosen by God. God did not have to persuade Paul to be a minister. No one had to persuade Him to teach (see Ephesians 4:1), to sing (Ephesians 5:19), to speak for God (Ephesians 4:17), to visit (2 Corinthians 13:1f), to administer the affairs of the church (1 Corinthians 7:1f), or to give his money (2 Corinthians 8:1f; 2 Corinthians 9:1f). As a believer in Jesus Christ, Paul did not have to be coerced. He saw his service as a great privilege.

Paul recognized that his call to be a minister and a preacher was a free gift of God's grace. There was no merit, no worth, and no value within Paul that caused God to choose him as a minister and as a preacher. Paul may have simply exclaimed, "What a privilege! What a responsibility! The less of the least called of God to minister and to preach!" (see verse 8).

One of life's toughest questions—"Why do good people suffer?"—is answered in these verses. Paul was aware that his imprisonment might discourage the Ephesians. In verses 1 and 13, we are given a clue to his thinking. The term *your glory* means "your good" or "your benefit." Paul accepted that his suffering was for the Gentiles' benefit. This was his opportunity to let his life be an example of the sacrificial nature of Jesus Christ.

If Paul had allowed discouragement or financial influence to squash his ministry, the Gospel of Jesus Christ might never have filtered into the Gentile world. God requires sacrifice from all of His followers. The intensity of our sacrifice is directly related to the depth of our faith. We know that God will only require of us what we are able to endure. But often, Christians shirk their assigned duties and allow worldly distractions to take center stage in their lives. Consider how many ministries suffer, especially in the area of missions, because those who are called are not willing to inconvenience themselves for the sake of the Gospel.

In verse 10, Paul spoke of the principalities and powers in heavenly places. Who are they? And how are they involved in the ministry of Jesus Christ? A well-known theologian, Willard Taylor, wrote, "Doubtless these angels of God who rule the spheres have an interest in the scheme of man's redemption" (see 1 Peter 1:12). Angels stand in stark amazement at what God is doing in the church. They are amazed at the power of God to transform the lives of sinners. And they are amazed at what believers are able to accomplish in His name.

Finally, we are reminded by Paul that Christ's power within us gives us boldness and confidence to witness for Him. There is tangible evidence of the presence of the Holy Spirit in the life of believers that is manifested in the way we act and interact with unbelievers, to draw them to Christ. We may not always be privileged to see the end result of our witness, but we should not permit that to discourage us. We witness with boldness and with the confidence that God, and God alone, orchestrates the end result.

First Corinthians 3:7 reads: "So then neither is he that planteth any thing, neither he that watereth; but God that giveth the increase."

III. CONCLUDING REFLECTION

What effect has the mystery of Christ had on you since your baptism? As Paul was willing to suffer for the church, so we too should be willing to suffer, if our baptism "in Christ" is genuine. The glory of our future with Christ should cause us to realize that any suffering is worth the reward. And no reward we receive in this life can compare to the reward of eternal life.

In this twenty-first century, the church of Jesus Christ cannot afford to faint. There are still many areas of the world that the Gospel message has not reached. The Lord is looking for faithful followers who will hear the call and, like Paul, be willing to confess, "I am crucified with Christ: nevertheless I live; yet not I, but Christ liveth in me: and the life which I now live in the flesh I live by the faith of the Son of God, who loved me, and gave himself for me" (Galatians 2:20).

There are many areas of the world where Christians are persecuted for their proselytizing.

- A Christian congregation in Malaysia is suing their local government over the destruction of their church on June 4, 2007.
- On January 30, 2008, a Christian pastor in Pakistan was murdered for his efforts to evangelize Muslims.
- On January 30, 2008, in the Yunan Province of China, police officials severely beat members of a local Christian congregation and burned all the Bibles in the church.
- On February 1, 2008, a court in Cairo, Egypt ruled against a Muslim being permitted to convert to Christianity.

- Jordan has begun to expel Christians in an effort to legitimize their country as a Muslim nation.

But no amount of persecution will stop the spread of the Gospel by those who are truly called. Our union with Christ is worth the price of whatever suffering we are called to bear, even our martyrdom.

PRAYER

Heavenly Father, we humbly bow before You, asking that You forgive us of our sins. Help us to put You first in our lives daily. In Jesus' name we pray. Amen.

WORD POWER

Mystery (*musterion*)—means primarily that which is known to the *mustes*, "the initiated" (from *mueo*, "to initiate into the mysteries"); cf. Philippians 4:12 (RSV): *mueomai*, "I have learned the secret." In the New Testament it denotes, not the mysterious, but that which, being outside the range of unassisted natural apprehension, can be made known only by divine revelation, and is made known in a manner and at a time appointed by God, and to only those who are illumined by His Spirit.

HOME DAILY BIBLE READINGS
(May 11-17, 2009)

New Revelation in Christ
- MONDAY, May 11: "God's Dominion over All" (Job 12:13-25)
- TUESDAY, May 12: "Secrets of the Kingdom" (Matthew 13:10-17)
- WEDNESDAY, May 13: "God Reveals Mysteries" (Daniel 2:25-30)
- THURSDAY, May 14: "God's Secret Revealed" (Amos 3:1-8)
- FRIDAY, May 15: "The Son Reveals the Father" (Matthew 11:25-30)
- SATURDAY, May 16: "Stewards of God's Mysteries" (1 Corinthians 4:1-5)
- SUNDAY, May 17: "Sharing the Promise in Christ" (Ephesians 3:1-13)

LESSON 13   May 24, 2009

NEW LIFE IN THE HOME

DEVOTIONAL READING: **1 Corinthians 1:4-17**
PRINT PASSAGE: **Ephesians 5:21-33; 6:1-4**

BACKGROUND SCRIPTURE: **Ephesians 5:1–6:4**
KEY VERSE: **Ephesians 5:21**

Ephesians 5:21-33; 6:1-4—KJV

21 Submitting yourselves one to another in the fear of God.

22 Wives, submit yourselves unto your own husbands, as unto the Lord.

23 For the husband is the head of the wife, even as Christ is the head of the church: and he is the saviour of the body.

24 Therefore as the church is subject unto Christ, so let the wives be to their own husbands in every thing.

25 Husbands, love your wives, even as Christ also loved the church, and gave himself for it;

26 That he might sanctify and cleanse it with the washing of water by the word,

27 That he might present it to himself a glorious church, not having spot, or wrinkle, or any such thing; but that it should be holy and without blemish.

28 So ought men to love their wives as their own bodies. He that loveth his wife loveth himself.

29 For no man ever yet hated his own flesh; but nourisheth and cherisheth it, even as the Lord the church:

30 For we are members of his body, of his flesh, and of his bones.

31 For this cause shall a man leave his father and mother, and shall be joined unto his wife, and they two shall be one flesh.

32 This is a great mystery: but I speak concerning Christ and the church.

33 Nevertheless let every one of you in particular so love his wife even as himself; and the wife see that she reverence her husband.

.....

CHILDREN, OBEY your parents in the Lord: for this is right.

2 Honour thy father and mother; which is the first commandment with promise;

3 That it may be well with thee, and thou mayest live long on the earth.

Ephesians 5:21-33; 6:1-4—NRSV

21 Be subject to one another out of reverence for Christ.

22 Wives, be subject to your husbands as you are to the Lord.

23 For the husband is the head of the wife just as Christ is the head of the church, the body of which he is the Savior.

24 Just as the church is subject to Christ, so also wives ought to be, in everything, to their husbands.

25 Husbands, love your wives, just as Christ loved the church and gave himself up for her,

26 in order to make her holy by cleansing her with the washing of water by the word,

27 so as to present the church to himself in splendor, without a spot or wrinkle or anything of the kind—yes, so that she may be holy and without blemish.

28 In the same way, husbands should love their wives as they do their own bodies. He who loves his wife loves himself.

29 For no one ever hates his own body, but he nourishes and tenderly cares for it, just as Christ does for the church,

30 because we are members of his body.

31 "For this reason a man will leave his father and mother and be joined to his wife, and the two will become one flesh."

32 This is a great mystery, and I am applying it to Christ and the church.

33 Each of you, however, should love his wife as himself, and a wife should respect her husband.

.....

CHILDREN, OBEY your parents in the Lord, for this is right.

2 "Honor your father and mother"—this is the first commandment with a promise:

3 "so that it may be well with you and you may live long on the earth."

Family life is often disrupted by internal conflict. How can families learn to live together in harmony? In Ephesians, Paul urged believers to serve one another in the home in the name and Spirit of Christ.

4 And, ye fathers, provoke not your children to wrath: but bring them up in the nurture and admonition of the Lord.

4 And, fathers, do not provoke your children to anger, but bring them up in the discipline and instruction of the Lord.

TOPICAL OUTLINE OF THE LESSON

I. **Introduction**
   A. Family
   B. Biblical Background

II. **Exposition and Application of the Scripture**
   A. The Key Called "Submission" (Ephesians 5:21-24)
   B. The Key Called "Love" (Ephesians 5:25-33)
   C. The Key Called "Obedience" (Ephesians 6:1-4)

III. **Concluding Reflection**

LESSON OBJECTIVES

Upon completion of this lesson, the students will know that:

1. As Christians, we are admonished to learn to be subject to others in the family; and,
2. Through the power of Christ we are empowered to work toward healing conflict and to live together in harmony.

POINTS TO BE EMPHASIZED

ADULT/YOUTH

Adult Topic: **Harmony at Home**
Youth Topic: **Fortifying Families**
Adult/Youth Key Verse: **Ephesians 5:21**
Print Passage: **Ephesians 5:21–6:4**

—The relationship of Christ and the church informs the husband-wife relationship even as the husband-wife relationship helps us understand the relationship between Christ and the church.
—Paul warned husbands that their role of head of the family is one of sacrificial responsibility more than of privilege.
—Children are addressed directly by the apostle, suggesting children were present with the adults in first-century Christian worship experiences.
—Fathers are singled out for special responsibility in parenting children.
—Parents are commanded to watch their parenting so that they "bring [their children] up in the discipline and instruction of the Lord" (verse 4, NRSV).
—Paul told how wives are to be subject to their husbands and told husbands how to love their wives in a spirit of mutuality.

CHILDREN

Children Topic: **Live in Love at Home**
Key Verse: **Ephesians 5:1**
Print Passage: **Ephesians 5:1; 6:1-4**

—We should, like children, imitate God in our actions and live in love together.
—Children should obey their parents.
—Children should honor their parents.
—Parents should, without provoking their children to anger, raise their children in the teachings and discipline of God.

I. INTRODUCTION

A. Family

Ancient society placed great value and emphasis on one's faithfulness to blood relatives. Jesus pushed His followers even further beyond the normal confines of familial relationships and challenged them to accept God's new definition of *family*—a family that had no blood-relation barriers. This new family included anyone who did the will of God (see Matthew 12:48-50). Jesus was introducing them to this new concept of family because He was preparing them for the new union that would take place between Christ and the church.

Our twenty-first-century society is painfully discovering that there is no substitute for a solidly established home life. When parents are absent, negligent or abusive, children do not learn to cope with life in a healthy way. In Proverbs 4:3-4 we are told that we are to teach our children wisdom. Parents are to add their insight and knowledge to a child's own experiences so that the next generation heads in the right direction. According to God's plan, both parents are to be involved in their family's growing and maturing process. Fathers are admonished to take the lead, and be sources of sound guidance. Mothers are given the responsibility of nurturing and care of the children in accordance with God's Word (see Proverbs 1:8; 4:1; 6:20). But according to Proverbs 4:3-4, grandparents also play a vital role, incorporating their own parenting skills with their children. This demonstrates that the care of the family is a generational process.

Conflict seems almost inevitable within families. Family members can always find something to disagree about. In fact, the bitterest of fights usually take place between people who claim that they married for love. It is hard to understand how people who are so familiar with each other could suddenly find themselves so far apart. One reason is that regardless of how intense our love and commitment are toward each other, families are still unions of sinners (see 1 John 1:8, 10). Despite the tensions that exist from time to time, even in Christian families, God's original design for the family will never be destroyed. No governmental adaptations to sinners' demands will ever modify God's purpose and plan for His family.

B. Biblical Background

In the beginning, God instituted the family when He created Adam and Eve, and joined them together as one flesh. Sin and rebellion brought havoc into their relationship, and into all subsequent families. In their own family, Adam and Eve soon experienced violence when Cain killed Abel.

But even in a fallen world of sin, God desires His best for the family structure. The Bible holds out great hope for the restoration of marriage. It is encouragement to parents to raise children in an environment of truth and integrity (see Deuteronomy 6:2-9). It offers a touching illustration of aid to a family devastated by death and the prospect of poverty (Ruth 1-4). It shows a family destroyed by senseless evil, but restored twofold by a faithful God (see Job). It affirms the beauty of sexual love within the confines of marriage, in terms of passion, fidelity, and integrity (see Song of Solomon). It encourages the restoration of broken relationships, which parallels the relationship God has with us (see Hosea 1:2–2:23). And it offers guidelines for marriage in terms of mutual submission, loyalty, love, and discipline for children that do not alienate them, as we see in Ephesians 5:21–6:4.

The most important duty of the family is to preserve the truth of the Word of God, and to teach scriptural truth to the succeeding generations. One of the most effective ways to teach these truths is through song. The Hebrew people were keenly aware of this; thus they composed many songs that were sung during religious celebrations. One such song is Psalms 113–118. These six songs were sung during the Passover celebration. Each of the psalms commemorated an aspect of their escape from bondage, and for this reason they became known as the *Hallel*, which means "praise." These songs were probably sung by Jesus and His disciples at the Last Supper in the upper room (see Matthew 26:30; Mark 14:26).

Family life is a generational process to which God calls us. That is why Paul devoted so much of the book of Ephesians to issues relating to family. He addressed married couples in 5:22-33; he addressed children in 6:1-3; and he addressed fathers in 6:4. Through his teaching, we see that every member of the family has his or her own distinct interactive role. We also learn that the nurturing of the family unit is a lifetime calling, from honeymoon to childrearing to empty nest. Marriages are meant to last.

II. EXPOSITION AND APPLICATION OF THE SCRIPTURE

A. The Key Called "Submission"
(Ephesians 5:21-24)

Submitting yourselves one to another in the fear of God. Wives, submit yourselves unto your own husbands, as unto the Lord. For the husband is the head of the wife, even as Christ is the head of the church: and he is the saviour of the body. Therefore as the church is subject unto Christ, so let the wives be to their own husbands in every thing.

Submission is an unpopular word because it is most often viewed as a negative. The world teaches us that we should covet *control* and *power* because those who are in leadership are the ones who determine our ultimate direction.

We are taught that the success of any venture rests almost entirely on sound leadership.

But consider what happened at Mount Sinai to the ultimate leader—God Himself—who experienced disappointment when His mission went awry (see Genesis 19–20). While God called Moses to the top of Mount Sinai to impart His wisdom and give the Israelites the foundational rules for their new faith, the Israelites were in the valley succumbing to the temptation of idol worship. We learn from this biblical account of Moses and the Ten Commandments that authority is a two-way street. There can be no leaders without followers. Superior authority is ineffective without subordinate acceptance. Those who *submit* are actually doing their part to contribute to the success of a mission. God's disappointment at Mount Sinai could have been abated if the young Hebrew nation had been willing to submit to authority.

Submission plays a vital role within the family unit. It allows the family to move itself forward as a cohesive unit toward one set of goals. When Christian family members develop a lifestyle of submissiveness, they demonstrate the godly humility that every Christian ought to possess. This humility must be evident in all members of the family so that submission becomes an easy duty for all. Family members, especially the head of the household, will attract support when they submit to God and His plan for their lives and the lives of those in their families.

This role of submission applies not only to our familial relationships, but also to the family of God, the church. Christ forms a new family out of all believers. Having experienced the same gift from God—forgiveness and hope—we are now brothers and sisters in Christ. As members of the family of God, we are charged to submit to our leaders as they submit to Christ. Submission allows the precepts of God to be established within God's family. Submission and obedience are also the fuel for the work of the church. Without these Christlike expressions, the work of Kingdom building would never move forward or accomplish its goals.

Our biological families and our church family are mutually dependent upon each other. Each needs the other in order to function in a godly and effective way. When one breaks down the other needs to offer support and assistance.

B. The Key Called "Love"
(Ephesians 5:25-33)

Husbands, love your wives, even as Christ also loved the church, and gave himself for it; That he might sanctify and cleanse it with the washing of water by the word, That he might present it to himself a glorious church, not having spot, or wrinkle, or any such thing; but that it should be holy and without blemish. So ought men to love their wives as their own bodies. He that loveth his wife loveth himself. For no man ever yet hated his own flesh; but nourisheth and cherisheth it, even as the Lord the church: For we are members of his body, of his flesh, and of his bones. For this cause shall a man leave his father and mother, and shall be joined unto his wife, and they two shall be one flesh. This is a great mystery: but I speak concerning Christ and the church. Nevertheless let every one of you in particular so love his wife even as himself; and the wife see that she reverence her husband.

The Bible exalts genuine love. But how do we know love is genuine? Popular culture teaches of *love* in terms of sexuality, passion, and blind devotion. But if we use that as our measuring rod, we reduce love to nothing more than an uncontrollable attraction toward another person that comes and goes without any conscious effort on our part. This kind of love only seeks its own gain, and it walks away when its demands are unsatisfied.

Real love—the kind of love that the Bible teaches about—pursues a radically different path. The Greeks called this type of love *agape*; it is a biblical love that requires us to commit to others for *their* benefit, regardless of the response, because it is selfless and sacrificial in nature. We see the perfect example of this in the way that God loved Israel. Though Israel was an adulterous nation, God continued to love her.

The Bible invites us to exalt genuine love through our unselfish devotion to each other. First Corinthians 13, called the "love chapter," is a challenge to every Christian to take love beyond the "talk" phase to the "walk" phase. We are challenged to love as God intended—with commitment, sacrifice, and service as our love expressions. This is the kind of love that benefits both the giver and the receiver.

The greatest opportunity for love's expression in the family relationship is through prayer. Yet, it is the most neglected of all duties. Parents should have an open line of communication with God. Husbands and wives should pray together often, and not just at the dinner table. Children need to hear their parents' petitions to God. They need to hear what their parents' hopes and desires are for their future, and the future of the family. This is how parents teach their children to connect with God. There are many examples in the Bible of people who prayed for their families. Abraham's servant prayed for help to find a wife for Isaac; Isaac prayed about Rebekah's barrenness; Hannah prayed for a son; David prayed that God would spare his life, and many more.

"The family that prays together stays together" is an old cliché that started in a religious advertising campaign many years ago. No greater truth about the family has ever been spoken. When family members show no hesitation in exposing to each other the importance of their relationship with God, they are taking a giant leap forward in building a close family unit that operates under the guidance of the Holy Spirit.

C. The Key Called "Obedience"

(Ephesians 6:1-4)

CHILDREN, OBEY your parents in the Lord: for this is right. Honour thy father and mother; which is the first commandment with promise; That it may be well with thee, and thou mayest live long on the earth. And, ye fathers, provoke not your children to wrath: but bring them up in the nurture and admonition of the Lord.

The English word *obey* comes from the Latin word meaning "to hear." A frustrated parent asked her child, "Why didn't you come when I called you?" The child responded, "I didn't hear you until the third time!" From this humorous example, we discover that obedience involves a conscious choice that begins with listening.

There are clear benefits from listening to and obeying God's voice. It is promised in Psalm 119:2 that if we will obey the Word of God and seek the Lord with our whole hearts, blessings will abound—from avoiding sin and pursuing godliness (Psalm 119, verses 3,11,12, 36, 133) to gaining wisdom and guidance for daily living (verses 24, 66, 105, 130, 176). But a person must first know how to listen to God. Christians become good listeners when they study God's Word and become familiar with His value system, then allow obedience to trigger their positive responses.

There are also clear benefits from listening to and obeying parents and spouses. Of course, obedience is easier when the married couple is equally yoked and living a Christlike life. But marriage to an unbeliever is no excuse for disobedience (or divorce). Those who are unequally yoked are still commanded to fulfill God's role for them in the family unit (see 1 Corinthians 7:13-15). Married couples who obey are giving their spouses the greatest gift of encouragement and support that one person can give to another. First Corinthians 7:16 is a reminder to us that our submission and our obedience are the means by which we are witnesses to faith in Christ. The display of these attributes gives us the opportunity to save our lost spouses.

As the head of the house, the father needs to know that he has the full support of a family that trusts his judgment as he follows God's plan. As the husband honors the wife, so the wife ought to honor her husband. We can see that God's plan for the family is founded upon mutual cooperation and teamwork.

Children who obey are wisely acknowledging that their God-given parents are building for them a solid foundation of wisdom for their future. Obedience will also provide them with a concrete reference when they are later exposed to the influence of teachers, coaches, and peers who will attempt to impose new or different values upon them.

III. CONCLUDING REFLECTION

The family *bond* extends far beyond our blood relations, to a bond that includes those who share our faith in Jesus Christ. By centering on the Lord, this *family* finds a great measure of fulfillment and reward. Family life can be satisfying and secure when we build our homes and our churches on a godly foundation.

Though we may still experience the struggles of human relationships, and even the pain of broken families, we can still have hope that God's healing and love will ultimately win out. It is stated in Revelation 21:4 that He will "wipe away all tears." God is able to repair any breach in familial relationships when His love is combined with submissive hearts that have learned to obey His Word.

PRAYER

Heavenly Father, we thank You for those we call "family." In Jesus' name we pray. Amen.

WORD POWER

Family *(patria)*—means primarily "an ancestry, lineage" and signifies in the New Testament "a family or tribe" but is narrower than *phule* ("a tribe"), as it is used of the "family" of David.

HOME DAILY BIBLE READINGS
(May 18-24, 2009)

New Life in the Home

MONDAY, May 18: "Trained by God's Grace" (Titus 2:1-13)
TUESDAY, May 19: "Partnership in Marriage" (Genesis 2:18-25)
WEDNESDAY, May 20: "Interpreting Traditions" (Exodus 12:21-28)
THURSDAY, May 21: "Parental Advice" (Proverbs 4:1-9)
FRIDAY, May 22: "Spiritual Guidance for Families" (Colossians 3:12-24)
SATURDAY, May 23: "Providing for Family Members" (1 Timothy 5:1-8)
SUNDAY, May 24: "Christian Family Relationships" (Ephesians 5:21–6:4)

LESSON 14   May 31, 2009

EQUIPPED FOR NEW LIFE

DEVOTIONAL READING: **Luke 11:14-23**
PRINT PASSAGE: **Ephesians 6:10-18**

BACKGROUND SCRIPTURE: **Ephesians 6:10-18**
KEY VERSE: **Ephesians 6:13**

Ephesians 6:10-18—KJV

10 Finally, my brethren, be strong in the Lord, and in the power of his might.

11 Put on the whole armour of God, that ye may be able to stand against the wiles of the devil.

12 For we wrestle not against flesh and blood, but against principalities, against powers, against the rulers of the darkness of this world, against spiritual wickedness in high places.

13 Wherefore take unto you the whole armour of God, that ye may be able to withstand in the evil day, and having done all, to stand.

14 Stand therefore, having your loins girt about with truth, and having on the breastplate of righteousness;

15 And your feet shod with the preparation of the gospel of peace;

16 Above all, taking the shield of faith, wherewith ye shall be able to quench all the fiery darts of the wicked.

17 And take the helmet of salvation, and the sword of the Spirit, which is the word of God:

18 Praying always with all prayer and supplication in the Spirit, and watching thereunto with all perseverance and supplication for all saints.

Ephesians 6:10-18—NRSV

10 Finally, be strong in the Lord and in the strength of his power.

11 Put on the whole armor of God, so that you may be able to stand against the wiles of the devil.

12 For our struggle is not against enemies of blood and flesh, but against the rulers, against the authorities, against the cosmic powers of this present darkness, against the spiritual forces of evil in the heavenly places.

13 Therefore take up the whole armor of God, so that you may be able to withstand on that evil day, and having done everything, to stand firm.

14 Stand therefore, and fasten the belt of truth around your waist, and put on the breastplate of righteousness.

15 As shoes for your feet put on whatever will make you ready to proclaim the gospel of peace.

16 With all of these, take the shield of faith, with which you will be able to quench all the flaming arrows of the evil one.

17 Take the helmet of salvation, and the sword of the Spirit, which is the word of God.

18 Pray in the Spirit at all times in every prayer and supplication. To that end keep alert and always persevere in supplication for all the saints.

BIBLE FACT

Sharing your wisdom, experience, and counsel with other believers helps them to grow in areas where they might have remained weak.

UNIFYING LESSON PRINCIPLE

Life is challenging because competing voices beckon us to follow different paths. How can we stand firm in the face of opposition to what we believe? Paul taught that God arms us to fight spiritual battles.

TOPICAL OUTLINE OF THE LESSON

I. Introduction
   A. Under Attack
   B. Biblical Background

II. Exposition and Application of the Scripture
   A. The Devil and His Strategies (Ephesians 6:10-12)
   B. The Soldier's Duty and Armor (Ephesians 6:13-17)
   C. God's Supernatural Provision: Prayer (Ephesians 6:18)

III. Concluding Reflection

LESSON OBJECTIVES

Upon completion of this lesson, the students will know that:

1. Through the power of Jesus Christ we can stand firm in the face of opposition to what we believe;
2. As Christians, we are encouraged to fight spiritual battles as they arise; and,
3. With the "armor of God" we are equipped for life as Christians.

POINTS TO BE EMPHASIZED

ADULT/YOUTH

Adult Topic: Armed for Battle
Youth Topic: Stand Firm in God's Armor
Adult/Youth Key Verse: Ephesians 6:13
Print Passage: Ephesians 6:10-18

—Christians face an active adversary intent on destroying their relationship with God.
—The Gospel provides all of the needed defenses against the spiritual forces that seek to destroy believers and the body of Christ.
—While defensive forces dominate this passage, believers are expected to be on the offensive with the proclamation of the Gospel of peace and the sharing of the Word of God.
—Prayer is a vital part of being able to stand firm in the spiritual battles of life.
—Paul exhorted us to be strong for God and to draw on God's strength.
—Paul pointed out that Christian struggles are not against human enemies, but against spiritual forces of evil.

CHILDREN

Children Topic: Protected by God!
Key Verse: Ephesians 6:11
Print Passage: Ephesians 6:10-18

—Christians are encouraged to be strong in the strength and power of God.
—We are to arm ourselves in every way to withstand the powers of evil and opposition in the world.
—Christians are to be ready to proclaim the Gospel of peace.
—We are to pray constantly to God and keep alert at all times.

I. INTRODUCTION

A. Under Attack

Did you know that speaking the truth and living with integrity are not always rewarded in our world? As mirror reflections of Christ, we should expect that our visible obedience to Him would cause the non-believer great anxiety. It should come as no surprise, then, that we become convenient targets for hostility when our integrity exposes the duplicity and deception of others.

Faith attacks are not a new phenomenon. Men and women have been attacked because of their faith since religion was introduced into our humane society. Christians today must avoid the mistake of taking these faith attacks personally. When our walks with Christ expose the sins of others, those whose sins are exposed feel compelled to fight back. A sense of guilt and fear of judgment motivates them to attack—not *our* character, but the very character of *God Himself.* Any counterattack on their part is merely their way of crying out for redemption.

It is through these attacks on our faith that we are given the greatest opportunity to witness. Our visible response to the unsaved world will serve as the catalyst to draw men and women to God.

Christians who are under attack must be reminded, then, that this battle has been waged since Adam and Eve fell from grace in the Garden of Eden. It is not a new battle, and it is not our battle. This war is by nature a spiritual one. It is a battle between God and the forces of evil.

B. Biblical Background

Metaphorical or figurative expression was and still is a popular method for teaching. A *metaphor* is "an implied comparison between two different things." Jesus used this method of teaching, along with parables, to unravel the mystery surrounding faith in God.

In this metaphor, the apostle Paul compared the Christian life to a battlefield. Battles were a common phenomenon in biblical history. Israel's history was littered with battles in which Jews were both the conquerors and the conquered. The battle between Pharaoh and the Hebrew nation, which ended at the Red Sea, was the first of many battles the Israelites encountered. So they understood the metaphorical reference to the pains of battle and the need for preparation.

As we read Paul's letters, we instantly understand the parallel between military and spiritual battles. Both require armor and special training; both require the stamina or strength to face the enemy.

We often view our persecution as our own unique circumstance. But Jesus and Paul wanted all Christians to know that our trials and tribulations are commonplace and to be expected. Expectation triggers preparation.

Preparation is the focus of these verses of Scripture. Being caught off-guard leaves a person unable to adequately respond. Training is the underpinning that keeps a believer functioning at peak capacity as a soldier for Jesus Christ.

II. EXPOSITION AND APPLICATION OF THE SCRIPTURE

A. The Devil and His Strategies (Ephesians 6:10-12)

Finally, my brethren, be strong in the Lord, and in the power of his might. Put on the whole armour of God, that ye may be able to stand against the wiles of the devil. For we wrestle not against flesh and blood, but against principalities, against powers, against the rulers of the darkness of this world, against spiritual wickedness in high places.

Paul began with a charge to the soldier who is called to battle. The charge is specific to the soldier, not the world, because it is the soldier who needs to heed his warning if he is to successfully oppose his enemy, Satan. The soldier who does not heed the "call" will certainly cave in to temptation and sin.

The charge to the believer is twofold. First, the believer must be strong in the Lord. The word *strong* (Greek: *endunamoo*) means "powerful." This is an internal strength that Paul was referring to. But where does that strength come from? It is God's power and strength, not the soldier's own power and strength. It comes from the Lord's power and the Lord's might. The believer must possess God's sovereign and unlimited power (*kratos*)—"the power that has dominion over all." And he or she must possess the Lord's might (*ischuos*)—"the ability to use force wisely." All this is necessary in order to conquer his or her indomitable foe. The soldier cannot win this battle using his or her own limited resources.

Satan uses cunning tactics to remove God's armor from His soldiers. He will convince a believer that the abilities he or she possesses are self-made—that he or she can face life's challenges alone. And when Satan is successful in *undressing* a believer (removing his or her armor), he leaves that believer vulnerable to attack. Christians need God's armor to fight spiritual battles. If Christians could fight without the aid of God's Spirit, Jesus would never have said: "Lo, I am with you always, even unto the end of the world" (Matthew 28:20b).

God's power and might prepare the soldier from within. But the believer must also be prepared from without. His or her external armor is as essential as his or her internal armor (the details of that armor are covered later). Still, no amount of armor is effective unless the believer has the "heart" to fight. We cannot wage war against sin and temptation unless we do it under God's power (see Colossians 1:11; 2 Timothy 1:7).

The word *wiles* means "deceit, craftiness, and trickery." These are the tactics that Satan uses to discourage and trap the believer. Satan's strategy is to cause the believer to miss: 1) the joy of an abundant life, 2) the experience of living under God's providential care, and 3) the certainty of a redeemed future.

B. The Soldier's Duty and Armor (Ephesians 6:13-17)

Wherefore take unto you the whole armour of God, that ye may be able to withstand in the evil day, and having done all, to stand. Stand therefore, having your loins girt about with truth, and having on the breastplate of righteousness; And your feet shod with the preparation of the gospel of peace; Above all, taking the shield of faith,

wherewith ye shall be able to quench all the fiery darts of the wicked. And take the helmet of salvation, and the sword of the Spirit, which is the word of God.

Notice that Paul again stressed the need to take the *whole* armor of God. This evil day that Paul was attempting to prepare us for is the onslaught of evil in the world today. He referred to the barrage of temptations that every believer is called to withstand (see Romans 13:12). It is stated in 2 Corinthians 10:4 that we cannot use carnal weapons to confront these enemies. We must use God's weaponry to pull down these strongholds. And to be successful, believers must put on the whole armor. One piece left off will court disaster.

One of the essential pieces of armor is the *belt of truth* ("girt about with truth"). Paul used this familiar reference to the practice of *girding one's loins*. In those days, men wore belts fashioned from wool or leather to hold their robes closed. When a man prepared for active work, the rear hem of his robe was lifted forward through the legs to his waist, and tucked into his belt. This exposed and freed his legs for movement. When the Israelites left Egypt, they girded their loins in order to hurry and handle their heavy loads. Elijah ran before Ahab with girded loins. The ideal wife of Proverbs 31 girds up her loins to work beside her servants. Paul's metaphor, then, shows us the importance of being ready for mental action in our Christian lives.

The next piece of armor is the *breastplate of righteousness*. The breastplate covered the soldier's body from the neck to the thighs. It was used to protect the most vital of all organs—the heart. Paul was pointing out that the heart was the most vital of a Christian's organs because it was at the heart that people made the decision to follow Christ. The believer's heart is focused on Christ and His righteousness, and that focus must be protected. Righteousness is the Christian soldier's breastplate. When a person is saved, God imputes the righteousness of Jesus Christ to him or her. Righteousness keeps the heart from ever being wounded and losing its focus.

Even the *feet* must be covered with *armor*. Paul said in verse 15 that our "feet [should be] shod with the preparation of the gospel of peace." In Jesus' time, wearing sandals was a sign of readiness. Roman sandals were made with nails that gripped the ground when they walked. The Christian's sandals are a sign that he or she is ready to accept his or her marching orders and to bear witness to the Gospel.

The *shield of faith* offers a more complete picture of a well-prepared believer (verse 16). The shield referred to here is not the small one we see in most history books, but rather, it is the body shield that was used by Roman soldiers—a great oblong shield—that protected soldiers from the shoulders to the knees. In battle, it was common practice for the enemy to dip his arrows in tar or some other combustible substance and light them with fire. These "fiery darts" were difficult to avoid. Thus, the Roman army outfitted themselves with large shields capable of protecting themselves from this type of attack. Paul was warning Christians that Satan uses "fiery darts" to shake Christians from their spiritual foundations. He uses darts like depression, sickness, marital troubles, doubt, lust, greed, and more to attack the believer.

The *head* is the mind of the believer—the core from which the person is empowered to wage war. His or her thinking ability is the most important factor in determining victory. Therefore, the head had to be protected with a helmet. For the Christian, his or her helmet was and is salvation. Unless a person has been saved, his or her mind cannot be protected. The mind of an unsaved person is focused on the world, but the mind of a saved one is focused on Christ (see Romans 8:6).

The idea of the *breastplate of righteousness* and the *helmet of salvation* comes originally from Isaiah 59:17. But in Isaiah, the intention was to attack, and the breastplate and helmet were worn by the Lord as He went forward as vindicator and deliverer. The righteousness in Isaiah refers to vindication, and the helmet to deliverance. But here in Ephesians, Paul offered them for our defense. God is covering us with His righteousness and surrounding us with His salvation, or His power to deliver. The joy is in knowing that we have the same protection that God Himself has!

The *sword of the Spirit* assures the believer that the Word of God is alive and active within him or her. The soldier's sword was used for both defense and offense to ward off the enemy. Christians use the Word of God in the same manner, to spread the Gospel and to defend its cause (see Hebrews 4:12).

Notice that no part of the soldier, while in war facing evil head-on, is left unprotected. The painted picture is one of a soldier in readiness—able to bear full witness of the Gospel. Wherever his feet take him, he is able to stand firm under the weight of any conflict.

With his armor, the believer is called to defend God, but he is also called to share the wisdom of God with other believers (see Matthew 28:19; Acts 5:42). Our weapons of warfare are also for the training of others. Seasoned soldiers are expected to impart the wisdom of their years of training to novice believers, so that the future generation of soldiers will be as strong or stronger. Paul said, in 2 Timothy 2:2: "And the things that thou hast heard of me among many witnesses, the same commit thou to faithful men, who shall be able to teach others also."

C. God's Supernatural Provision: Prayer (Ephesians 6:18)

Praying always with all prayer and supplication in the Spirit, and watching thereunto with all perseverance and supplication for all saints.

The believer's armor must be combined with prayer, that spiritual assault weapon that equally confounds the enemy. Notice that Paul's admonition to pray is twofold. They were charged to pray for all the people of God, and for Paul and his ministry. Their prayer would have been for the spiritual well-being of the people of God and the furtherance of God's kingdom through His ministers.

The picture is one of a believer entering conflict fully prepared and armed with great confidence and courage, which can only come from a spirit of prayer. He or she has maintained a constant unbroken consciousness of God's presence and care. This readiness infuses him or her with the confidence, assurance, and courage the person needs for battle.

Note that Christ's view of prayer and the scriptural view of prayer are not as a means to obtain personal favors or even guidance, but as a means of furthering the kingdom and the kingly rule of God. In fact, Jesus said that personal prayer for material things merely demonstrates that we doubt God will provide all we need (see Matthew 6:8).

Matthew described this readiness in this manner: "Ask, and it shall be given you; seek, and ye shall find; knock, and it shall be opened unto you" (Matthew 7:7). First Thessalonians 5:17 reads: "Pray without ceasing." The idea is not for the believer to spend all of his or her time in prayer. What is required is a constant attitude of dependence upon God. It is not a formal set of prayers, but a relationship to God's Spirit.

There is no time for lethargy or sluggishness in our prayer attitudes. Instead, the believer should be in a constant and unselfish state of communication with God. Believers know that they are not alone in battle, and that the outcome will be determined by the collective efforts of thousands who stand with them, praying with the same boldness and confidence they possess. The supernatural power of that collective prayer will put the enemy to flight and capture souls for the Gospel.

III. CONCLUDING REFLECTION

Jesus taught that there would inevitably be attacks from the unsaved (see Luke 17:1). But God's spiritual armor provides the believer with the ability to respond to attacks with resolute faith, prayer, and measured resistance. Their purpose is to remove all obstacles to the growth of God's kingdom on earth (see 2 Corinthians 10:4).

Though in the natural world it is difficult not to react negatively to criticism of our faith in the spiritual world, God has granted us His very own power to resist our adversaries. We learn not to escalate attacks, but rather to use all the spiritual resources God provides to resist and persist, knowing that God will eventually reward us for our perseverance.

PRAYER

Heavenly Father, thank You for allowing us to be soldiers in Your army. Give us strength as we fight Your battles. In Jesus' name we pray. Amen.

WORD POWER

Soldier— 1) *stratiotes*, meaning "a soldier," is used in the natural sense and metaphorically of one who endures hardship in the cause of Christ; 2) *strateuma*, meaning "an army," is used to denote "a company of soldiers"; 3) *sustratiotes*, "a fellow-soldier," is used metaphorically to denote fellowship in Christian service.

HOME DAILY BIBLE READINGS

(May 25-31, 2009)

Equipped for New Life

MONDAY, May 25: "Truth" (Psalm 25:1-5)

TUESDAY, May 26: "Righteousness" (Proverbs 11:1-10)

WEDNESDAY, May 27: "The Good News of Peace" (Isaiah 52:7-12)

THURSDAY, May 28: "Faith" (Hebrews 10:35–11:3)

FRIDAY, May 29: "Salvation" (Isaiah 12:1-6)

SATURDAY, May 30: "The Word of God" (Psalm 119:105-112)

SUNDAY, May 31: "The Whole Armor of God" (Ephesians 6:10-18)

Call Sealed with Promise

GENERAL INTRODUCTION

The study this quarter begins with the theme of God's call of a covenant community as reflected in the Old Testament Books of the Law, specifically Exodus, Leviticus, Numbers, and Deuteronomy. The call of God to live in covenant community today is emphasized through these lessons.

Unit I, *Called Out of Egypt,* is coverage of four lessons. It is concerned with God's call to Moses, the responses of Moses and Aaron, Pharaoh's refusal of God's call, and God's call to the people to leave Egypt.

Unit II, *Called to Be God's People,* has four lessons—the first of which is an exploration of how God's call led to the establishment of a new covenant; the other three lessons are focused on the people's response to that call in celebration and worship, in commitment to special service, and in establishing the ideal of jubilee.

Unit III, *Called to Choose Life,* is a reflection on God's ongoing call to obedience and in which it is outlined what actions demonstrate faithfulness and rebelliousness. Five Old Testament lessons are illustrations of how God remains faithful to His promise—whether or not we choose to obey. However, God's faithfulness has different consequences for those who choose life than for those who choose to reject life.

LESSON 1   June 7, 2009

GOD CALLS MOSES

DEVOTIONAL READING: **Hebrews 3:1-13**
PRINT PASSAGE: **Exodus 3:1-12**

BACKGROUND SCRIPTURE: **Exodus 2:23–3:12**
KEY VERSE: **Exodus 3:10**

Exodus 3:1-12—KJV

NOW MOSES kept the flock of Jethro his father in law, the priest of Midian: and he led the flock to the backside of the desert, and came to the mountain of God, even to Horeb.

2 And the angel of the LORD appeared unto him in a flame of fire out of the midst of a bush: and he looked, and, behold, the bush burned with fire, and the bush was not consumed.

3 And Moses said, I will now turn aside, and see this great sight, why the bush is not burnt.

4 And when the LORD saw that he turned aside to see, God called unto him out of the midst of the bush, and said, Moses, Moses. And he said, Here am I.

5 And he said, Draw not nigh hither: put off thy shoes from off thy feet, for the place whereon thou standest is holy ground.

6 Moreover he said, I am the God of thy father, the God of Abraham, the God of Isaac, and the God of Jacob. And Moses hid his face; for he was afraid to look upon God.

7 And the LORD said, I have surely seen the affliction of my people which are in Egypt, and have heard their cry by reason of their taskmasters; for I know their sorrows;

8 And I am come down to deliver them out of the hand of the Egyptians, and to bring them up out of that land unto a good land and a large, unto a land flowing with milk and honey; unto the place of the Canaanites, and the Hittites, and the Amorites, and the Perizzites, and the Hivites, and the Jebusites.

9 Now therefore, behold, the cry of the children of Israel is come unto me: and I have also seen the oppression wherewith the Egyptians oppress them.

10 Come now therefore, and I will send thee unto Pharaoh, that thou mayest bring forth my people the children of Israel out of Egypt.

11 And Moses said unto God, Who am I, that I should go unto Pharaoh, and that I should bring forth the children of Israel out of Egypt?

Exodus 3:1-12—NRSV

MOSES WAS keeping the flock of his father-in-law Jethro, the priest of Midian; he led his flock beyond the wilderness, and came to Horeb, the mountain of God.

2 There the angel of the LORD appeared to him in a flame of fire out of a bush; he looked, and the bush was blazing, yet it was not consumed.

3 Then Moses said, "I must turn aside and look at this great sight, and see why the bush is not burned up."

4 When the LORD saw that he had turned aside to see, God called to him out of the bush, "Moses, Moses!" And he said, "Here I am."

5 Then he said, "Come no closer! Remove the sandals from your feet, for the place on which you are standing is holy ground."

6 He said further, "I am the God of your father, the God of Abraham, the God of Isaac, and the God of Jacob." And Moses hid his face, for he was afraid to look at God.

7 Then the LORD said, "I have observed the misery of my people who are in Egypt; I have heard their cry on account of their taskmasters. Indeed, I know their sufferings,

8 and I have come down to deliver them from the Egyptians, and to bring them up out of that land to a good and broad land, a land flowing with milk and honey, to the country of the Canaanites, the Hittites, the Amorites, the Perizzites, the Hivites, and the Jebusites.

9 The cry of the Israelites has now come to me; I have also seen how the Egyptians oppress them.

10 So come, I will send you to Pharaoh to bring my people, the Israelites, out of Egypt."

11 But Moses said to God, "Who am I that I should go to Pharaoh, and bring the Israelites out of Egypt?"

12 And he said, Certainly I will be with thee; and this shall be a token unto thee, that I have sent thee: When thou hast brought forth the people out of Egypt, ye shall serve God upon this mountain.

12 He said, "I will be with you; and this shall be the sign for you that it is I who sent you: when you have brought the people out of Egypt, you shall worship God on this mountain."

TOPICAL OUTLINE OF THE LESSON

I. **Introduction**
   A. Ministry Calling
   B. Biblical Background

II. **Exposition and Application of the Scripture**
   A. The Type of Man God Calls (Exodus 3:1-3)
   B. The Call of God Himself (Exodus 3:4-6)
   C. The Reason for the Call (Exodus 3:7-8)
   D. The Response to the Call (Exodus 3:9-12)

III. **Concluding Reflection**

LESSON OBJECTIVES

Upon completion of this lesson, the students will know that:

1. God is still calling people to discharge duties for Him;
2. Obedience to His call is the primary duty of the one called; and,
3. God can use any situation to draw our attention to Him if only we are sensitive.

POINTS TO BE EMPHASIZED

ADULT/YOUTH

Adult Topic: Hearing Requires Listening!
Youth Topic: Burning Questions
Adult Key Verse: Exodus 3:10
Youth Key Verses: Exodus 3:11-12
Print Passage: Exodus 3:1-12

—The passage shows that God's call can come in unexpected ways.
—God responds to human suffering and crises encountered by God's people by calling humans to participate in human redemption.
—God's call involved a two-way interaction between God and Moses.
—Moses is the pivotal human figure of the Old Testament.
—God is responsive to human suffering.
—This story is the transition between forty years of wilderness and forty years of leadership.

CHILDREN

Children Topic: Standing on Holy Ground
Key Verse: Exodus 3:10
Print Passage: Exodus 3:1-12

—While Moses was living the life of a shepherd, he was drawn to a bush that was on fire but not being consumed.
—God spoke from the burning bush.
—God revealed His concern for the suffering of the Israelites enslaved in Egypt.
—God commissioned Moses to free God's chosen people from slavery and lead them to a "good and broad land" (verse 8).
—Moses questioned his ability to carry out God's commission.

I. INTRODUCTION

A. Ministry Calling

From the moment of conversion, there is a calling on every Christian's life. Each of us is given gifts and talents that are to be used for the purpose of furthering the kingdom of God on earth. Though each of the spiritual gifts granted by God is unique in its own right, they all work together harmoniously toward the same goal (see Ephesians 4:11-13). Through these gifts, God provides for us in a way that only a supreme God can.

The Spirit-filled life is interdependent; we not only depend upon the Holy Spirit, but we also depend upon each other. Just as the different parts of our bodies work to carry out the will of the brain, so the members of Christ's church carry out the will of the Father. God assigns the appropriate gifts and talents to complete each calling, to ensure the success of His work.

Yet, much of the world still suffers. Much of that suffering can be directly attributed to our refusal to answer God's call, both individually and collectively. Who among us has not made some excuse at one time or another as to why we cannot go somewhere nor do something for God? Even Moses made excuses. When we refuse to answer God's call, we are robbing the body of Christ and forcing others to carry our loads. The truth is that nobody can utilize your gift as well as you can. Failure to take our gifts and use them is a betrayal of God. The outcome is that we become dysfunctional, dead weight that is out of step with the will of God.

B. Biblical Background

The book of Exodus is the second of the first five books of the Old Testament known as the Pentateuch, or the Books of Law. The word *Exodus* means "departure." The book of Exodus is the story of the Jews' departure from Egypt, and it is indeed a record of the "calling out" of God's chosen people. It begins with the account of the birth of God's people as His people, and burns with the conviction that God is vitally present among His people.

Though the theme of the book of Exodus is that God comes to His people and rescues and guides them, it also reveals the depth to which God imparts His gift of power to deal with our day-to-day experiences and our command to serve Him. Whom God calls, He also equips. As we study the call of Moses, we are reminded that each of us is called to a particular purpose—to serve in this present age—and each of us is given the gifts and talents necessary to complete our assigned tasks. As the book of Exodus demonstrates, if there is any lack, it is only in obedience.

In our text, Moses has left the privileged court of Pharaoh and taken up residence in the land of Midian, where Jethro was a priest. Moses eventually became a herdsman under Jethro. It is interesting to note that Moses dwelled in Midian for forty years before God called him to Mount Horeb, and gave him the assignment of deliverer of God's people. This is the same length of time that the Israelites wandered in the wilderness before finally arriving in the Promised Land.

II. EXPOSITION AND APPLICATION OF THE SCRIPTURE

A. The Type of Man God Calls
(Exodus 3:1-3)

NOW MOSES kept the flock of Jethro his father in law, the priest of Midian: and he led the flock to the backside of the desert, and came to the mountain of God, even to Horeb. And the angel of the LORD appeared unto him in a flame of fire out of the midst of a bush: and he looked, and, behold, the bush burned with fire, and the bush was not consumed. And Moses said, I will now turn aside, and see this great sight, why the bush is not burnt.

Moses is an example of the type of person God calls to serve Him. The fact that he was a shepherd suggests that he had a heart that could shepherd God's people. Shepherds were assigned the task of feeding and watering the sheep, guiding and protecting them, and seeking and saving those who became separated or lost. It was also the shepherd's duty to keep the sheep separated from the goats. In each of these duties, we can see the parallel between shepherding sheep and shepherding God's people.

It took a very special heart to be a shepherd. The shepherd had to be tough and tender, hard and compassionate, disciplined and soft. He also had to spend a great deal of time alone with God. In biblical times, shepherds became men of great devotion and prayer.

Moses spent forty years perfecting his craft and drawing nearer to God, and when he was ready, God called him to receive his instruction.

God's call never comes to a particular profession—it comes to a particular heart. God looks for the heroic heart, a heart that is willing to tackle a heroic task. In the case of Moses, God was seeking to call a man who knew how to be tough but tender, hard but compassionate, disciplined but soft—a man who would use his time wisely to draw near to God, a man who would be willing to feed and guide God's people. "I will give you pastors according to mine heart, which shall feed you with knowledge and understanding" (Jeremiah 3:15).

Moses demonstrated other qualities desired to be a deliverer. He was hardworking and industrious, not lazy and slothful. We see this in his willingness to tend Jethro's flock on the *far* side of the desert. Then we see in the second verse that Moses was also a man of faith, who believed the miracles of God and the "impossible" acts of God. When he saw the burning bush, he did not turn away. Moses became curious about the strange phenomenon (the bush was burning but was not consumed). If he had turned away, he would have missed the blessing of God and the call of God upon his life. Instead, he chose to draw closer. We are reminded that we too must seek to draw closer to God and to desire deeper spiritual experiences. God may use any means to get our attention for His service.

B. The Call of God Himself
(Exodus 3:4-6)

And when the LORD saw that he turned aside to see, God called unto him out of the midst of the bush, and said, Moses, Moses. And he said, Here am I. And he said, Draw not nigh hither: put off thy shoes from off thy feet, for the place whereon thou standest is holy ground. Moreover he said, I am the God of thy father, the God of Abraham, the God of Isaac, and the God of Jacob. And Moses hid his face; for he was afraid to look upon God.

God's call to Moses is an example of exactly what happens when God calls a person, and outlines each of the factors pertaining to that call. In verse 4, we see that first God calls a *seeking* individual. Moses was seeking the meaning of the burning bush when God called him. Note carefully that: in verse 2, an angel of God appeared; in verse 3, Moses turned; and in verse 4, God spoke. Those three steps are important in Moses's response. If Moses had ignored the burning bush and concluded that it was not worth his investigation, God likely would not have called him. That is because God was in need of a man who had a desire to seek truth and understanding. We meet God when we are sensitive to Him. God requires a heart that is open to receive His message and His purpose.

Second, God's call was of a personal nature. God called Moses by his name. And just as He knew Moses, He knows each of us by our names. A classic example of this is how Jesus called Paul to the ministry (found in Acts 9:4): "He fell to the earth, and heard a voice saying unto him, Saul, Saul, why persecutest thou me?" When God calls, we must be prepared to respond in a positive fashion—like Abraham (see Genesis 22:1), Samuel (see 1 Samuel 3:4), Isaiah (see Isaiah 6:8), and Paul (see Acts 9:6), who all said, "Here I am!"

Third, God's call is a holy one. God Himself is holy and He will call people who have become holy through Jesus Christ. We know this because God ordered Moses to stop in his tracks and remove his shoes because the ground on which he stood was holy. It was not the ground itself that was holy; it was the presence of God that made it holy. In commanding Moses to remove his shoes, God was teaching Moses the meaning of holiness. *To be holy* means "to be separated and distinctly different from other people." God is holy because He is our supreme Lord and the Ruler of the universe. He is not a chummy friend or a grandfather-type who lets us act any way we wish and gives us anything we want—or "the man upstairs," as He is so often irreverently called. God is holy; therefore, to stand in His presence, one must be reverent, submissive, and respectful.

Finally, God's call comes from the only one who can deliver on His promises. Moses learned from this personal encounter with God that God is real—that He actually exists. Before this encounter, Moses knew only of the stories of Abraham, Isaac, and Jacob, and God's faithfulness to them. Now Moses, too, would understand and know the mind of God, through his own personal encounter with God.

C. The Reason for the Call
(Exodus 3:7-8)

And the LORD said, I have surely seen the affliction of my people which are in Egypt, and have heard their cry by reason of their taskmasters; for I know their sorrows; And I am come down to deliver them out of the hand of the Egyptians, and to bring them up out of that land unto a good land and a large, unto a land flowing with milk and honey; unto the place of the Canaanites, and the Hittites,

and the Amorites, and the Perizzites, and the Hivites, and the Jebusites.

There were three reasons why God called Moses to be God's deliverer for the Israelites. First, there was the fact that God was deeply concerned about the affliction and suffering of His people. It is stated in verse 7 that God *saw* their affliction and misery at the hand of their taskmasters. God saw the state of hopelessness that they were in. From this verse, we receive the assurance that God sees our own suffering and shares our deepest sorrows. Peter knew this when he said, "Casting all your care upon him; for he careth for you" (1 Peter 5:7).

Second, God came down to deliver His people. He came to do the work of redemption—to save His people, and to deliver them from bondage. This lets us know that God is able to deliver any person from any type of bondage—physical, emotional, or spiritual (see 2 Samuel 22:2; Psalm 91:3; Jeremiah 1:8).

Third, God wanted to give the Promised Land to His people. The Promised Land of Canaan was a type of the promise of heaven. God had told Abraham: "Get thee out of thy country, and from thy kindred, and from thy father's house, unto a land that I will shew thee" (Genesis 12:1). It was now time for God to lead His people to that land of promise—time for them to be separated from the world and inherit a land "flowing with milk and honey." This lets us know that God not only redeems us *from* something, He redeems us *to* something. He redeems us from Satan and the world, and redeems us Himself, so that we may inherit eternal life.

D. The Response to the Call
(Exodus 3:9-12)

Now therefore, behold, the cry of the children of Israel is come unto me: and I have also seen the oppression wherewith the Egyptians oppress them. Come now therefore, and I will send thee unto Pharaoh, that thou mayest bring forth my people the children of Israel out of Egypt. And Moses said unto God, Who am I, that I should go unto Pharaoh, and that I should bring forth the children of Israel out of Egypt? And he said, Certainly I will be with thee; and this shall be a token unto thee, that I have sent thee: When thou hast brought forth the people out of Egypt, ye shall serve God upon this mountain.

God expected two responses from Moses. They are the same two responses He expects from every person who is called to serve Him. Moses was to "lay hold" of God's vision, and become God's messenger.

In verse 9, God repeats His affirmation that He sees and hears the cries of His people. Why did He repeat Himself? God wanted Moses to know that the Israelites' suffering had deeply touched His heart, and He wanted it to touch Moses's heart just as deeply. God needed an individual whose heart was broken by compassion—one who could grasp the great vision God had for His people.

Then, God wanted a man who was willing to put his life on the line for His people. Moses was not merely being appointed as God's spokesman; he was being anointed as God's deliverer. Only God has the power to commission a person to represent Him and fulfill His call to service.

Moses's initial response was one of doubt. He doubted that he could convince Pharaoh to release the Hebrews from bondage. Moses was assessing his ability through human eyes. Our finite minds can never fully comprehend the infinite possibilities we can achieve through the power of God. That is where faith comes in. We must learn, like Moses, to trust that God can do what we cannot.

III. CONCLUDING REFLECTION

If the church of Jesus Christ is handicapped in the twenty-first century it is due, in large part, to the lack of exercise of the gifts granted her by the Holy Spirit. Though we see this deficiency manifested most in the area of missions (the cry for missionaries can be heard from every denomination), it is not the only area lacking within the body of Christ. There is a great need for administrative gifts, teaching gifts, and healing and evangelical gifts right here at home.

If the twenty-first-century church is to make a substantial impact on the global world, it will require every Christian, young and old, to discover and exercise the gifts and talents bestowed upon us by God. For some, this means we will have to realign our thinking and rearrange our schedules to make time for God.

Moses used excuses to question God's choice of him as a deliverer. What are we using as an excuse to bow out of the church's evangelistic enterprise? Is it the pursuit of a career? Is it the raising of children? Is it our workload? Or is it some other perceived handicap? When we conjure up excuses for relieving ourselves of duty to Christ, we endanger the souls who would otherwise be saved by our witness.

Much has happened to change the landscape of our lives in this twenty-first century. Peace is no longer something we take for granted. We can see the hand of God moving upon the church of Jesus Christ and we can hear God's call for soldiers who will catch His vision and hasten to share the Good News around the world. God will use those who heed His call, to "deliver us from evil" and to prepare us to receive His promises.

PRAYER

Father in heaven, help us to hear when You call us. Help us to correctly discern Your voice, so that we can achieve the goal for which You have called us. In Jesus' name we pray. Amen.

WORD POWER

Send (Hebrew: *Shalack [shaw-lak]*)—means "to send away" or "out on a mission." There are other Hebrew words for *send*, which carry the idea of "expulsion from" or "sent away to work as a slave." But in the Key Verse, God sent Moses away on a mission to Pharaoh. The "sending away" is with a backing of the authority of the One who sent him.

HOME DAILY BIBLE READINGS
(June 1-7, 2009)

God Calls Moses

MONDAY, June 1: "Moses's Birth" (Exodus 2:1-10)
TUESDAY, June 2: "Moses Flees" (Exodus 2:11-22)
WEDNESDAY, June 3: "Moses's Purpose Misunderstood" (Acts 7:23-29)
THURSDAY, June 4: "Moses's Call" (Acts 7:30-34)
FRIDAY, June 5: "Moses's Death Foretold" (Deuteronomy 32:48-52)
SATURDAY, June 6: "Moses's Uniqueness" (Deuteronomy 34)
SUNDAY, June 7: "Come, I Will Send You" (Exodus 3:1-12)

LESSON 2   June 14, 2009

MOSES AND AARON RESPOND

DEVOTIONAL READING: **Proverbs 1:20-33**
PRINT PASSAGE: **Exodus 4:10-16, 27-31**

BACKGROUND SCRIPTURE: **Exodus 4:10-16, 27-31**
KEY VERSE: **Exodus 4:30**

Exodus 4:10-16, 27-31—KJV

10 And Moses said unto the LORD, O my Lord, I am not eloquent, neither heretofore, nor since thou hast spoken unto thy servant: but I am slow of speech, and of a slow tongue.

11 And the LORD said unto him, Who hath made man's mouth? or who maketh the dumb, or deaf, or the seeing, or the blind? have not I the LORD?

12 Now therefore go, and I will be with thy mouth, and teach thee what thou shalt say.

13 And he said, O my Lord, send, I pray thee, by the hand of him whom thou wilt send.

14 And the anger of the LORD was kindled against Moses, and he said, Is not Aaron the Levite thy brother? I know that he can speak well. And also, behold, he cometh forth to meet thee: and when he seeth thee, he will be glad in his heart.

15 And thou shalt speak unto him, and put words in his mouth: and I will be with thy mouth, and with his mouth, and will teach you what ye shall do.

16 And he shall be thy spokesman unto the people: and he shall be, even he shall be to thee instead of a mouth, and thou shalt be to him instead of God.

.....

27 And the LORD said to Aaron, Go into the wilderness to meet Moses. And he went, and met him in the mount of God, and kissed him.

28 And Moses told Aaron all the words of the LORD who had sent him, and all the signs which he had commanded him.

29 And Moses and Aaron went and gathered together all the elders of the children of Israel:

30 And Aaron spake all the words which the LORD had spoken unto Moses, and did the signs in the sight of the people.

31 And the people believed: and when they heard that the LORD had visited the children of Israel, and that he had looked upon their affliction, then they bowed their heads and worshipped.

Exodus 4:10-16, 27-31—NRSV

10 But Moses said to the LORD, "O my Lord, I have never been eloquent, neither in the past nor even now that you have spoken to your servant; but I am slow of speech and slow of tongue."

11 Then the LORD said to him, "Who gives speech to mortals? Who makes them mute or deaf, seeing or blind? Is it not I, the LORD?

12 Now go, and I will be with your mouth and teach you what you are to speak."

13 But he said, "O my Lord, please send someone else."

14 Then the anger of the LORD was kindled against Moses and he said, "What of your brother Aaron the Levite? I know that he can speak fluently; even now he is coming out to meet you, and when he sees you his heart will be glad.

15 You shall speak to him and put the words in his mouth; and I will be with your mouth and with his mouth, and will teach you what you shall do.

16 He indeed shall speak for you to the people; he shall serve as a mouth for you, and you shall serve as God for him."

.....

27 The LORD said to Aaron, "Go into the wilderness to meet Moses." So he went; and he met him at the mountain of God and kissed him.

28 Moses told Aaron all the words of the LORD with which he had sent him, and all the signs with which he had charged him.

29 Then Moses and Aaron went and assembled all the elders of the Israelites.

30 Aaron spoke all the words that the LORD had spoken to Moses, and performed the signs in the sight of the people.

31 The people believed; and when they heard that the LORD had given heed to the Israelites and that he had seen their misery, they bowed down and worshiped.

UNIFYING LESSON PRINCIPLE

Because some persons believe they are not adequate for a task, they are fearful of and resistant to accepting it. How can people who are afraid be encouraged to do the work assigned them? Moses resisted God's call, but then he accepted aid from his brother Aaron, according to God's command.

TOPICAL OUTLINE OF THE LESSON

I. Introduction
A. Excuses
B. Biblical Background

II. Exposition and Application of the Scripture
A. A Reluctant Prophet (Exodus 4:10-13)
B. God's Response to Reluctance (Exodus 4:14-16)
C. The Impact of Obedience (Exodus 4:27-31)

III. Concluding Reflection

LESSON OBJECTIVES

Upon completion of this lesson, the students will know that:

1. When we accept the responsibility to work for God, He takes charge to help us through;
2. Our reluctance is part of a lack of full trust in God; and,
3. God will move in the heart of the people to accomplish His task.

POINTS TO BE EMPHASIZED

ADULT/YOUTH

Adult Topic: **Accepting Responsibility**
Youth Topic: **Who, Me?**
Adult Key Verse: **Exodus 4:30**
Youth Key Verse: **Exodus 4:10**
Print Passage: **Exodus 4:10-16, 27-31**

—Moses understood the very real, life-threatening risks of God's call to liberate the people of Israel from Egypt.
—Moses was reminded that God is the one who creates, who has power, and who is always present.
—God is the source of the "speech" that would transform and liberate Israel.
—Even though God became angry at Moses's reluctance, God offered help through Aaron.
—Aaron accepted God's call to meet Moses in the wilderness.
—Moses's inadequacies were a problem to Moses but not to God.

CHILDREN

Children Topic: **Answering God's Call**
Key Verse: **Exodus 4:15**
Print Passage: **Exodus 4:10-16, 27-31**

—Moses offered an excuse he thought would change God's mind about selecting him for a very challenging task.
—God reminded Moses who God is.
—God selected Aaron to assist Moses and equipped them for the task.
—Moses told Aaron what God had assigned him to do.
—Moses and Aaron met with the elders of the Israelites and shared God's plan with them.
—The people believed what they heard, bowed down, and worshiped God.

I. INTRODUCTION

A. Excuses

To begin with, don't we just hate it when people make excuses? Husbands make excuses, wives make excuses, and children make excuses. In churches, we see similar trends when church members make excuses for not working in the church. Excuses mean that somebody is trying to avoid responsibility. On the surface the excuses seem reasonable to the human mind, but a closer examination reveals a lack of understanding of who God really is.

Did you know that no one is a spiritual island? Our personal spiritual progress and the progress of the entire church of Jesus Christ hinges on our willingness to work together. It is impossible to walk in the Spirit without functioning in the body of Christ. We were never designed to work that way. If we are spirit-filled and spirit-controlled, we are naturally drawn to working with others toward the common goal—and that is exalting the name of the Lord. We look for ways to become involved and to advance the course of Christ, which is to spread the Gospel throughout the world. Spirit-filled men and women jump at the chance to carry their fair share of the load.

B. Biblical Background

Moses, Aaron, and Miriam were siblings, the children of Amram and Jochebed. Miriam was the oldest child, while Aaron was the oldest son, and Moses was the last born. Aaron was three years older than Moses, and Miriam was approximately twelve years older than Moses (see Exodus 7:7). The two male children were referred to as Levites; they were Levites on both their father's and their mother's sides. Aaron was obviously born before Pharaoh's edict that all Hebrew male infants were to be murdered; thus, he escaped death by little more than one year.

As the firstborn male child, Aaron would be the priest of the household and inherit all the rights of the firstborn male child. The first mention of Aaron in the Scriptures appears in our text today when, in answer to Moses's objection that he did not have the eloquence needed to perform God's mission, God said, "Is not Aaron the Levite thy brother?" (Exodus 4:14). The birth of the Levite tribe of priests to Israel can be traced back to this moment in biblical history, when God appointed Aaron as the spokesman for Israel. The fact that God referred to Aaron as "the Levite" implies most probably that Aaron had already taken a leadership role in the tribe.

After forty years of separation, the Lord directed Aaron to "Go into the wilderness to meet Moses" (Exodus 4:27). He met Moses in the "mount of God" where the flaming bush had been revealed. When it comes to age, God has no preference. Moses was the youngest, and He used him. In terms of eloquence Moses was a stammerer, and yet God did not look at that; He used him anyway.

II. EXPOSITION AND APPLICATION OF THE SCRIPTURE

A. A Reluctant Prophet
(Exodus 4:10-13)

And Moses said unto the Lord, O my Lord, I am not eloquent, neither heretofore, nor since thou hast spoken unto thy servant: but I am slow of speech, and of a slow tongue. And the Lord said unto him, Who hath made man's mouth? or who maketh the dumb, or deaf, or the seeing, or the blind? have not I the Lord? Now therefore go, and I will be with thy mouth, and teach thee what thou shalt say. And he said, O my Lord, send, I pray thee, by the hand of him whom thou wilt send.

This chapter and the previous one mark the beginning of the emancipation of the Israelites from the clutches of Pharaoh. The people of God, who were well-cared for when Joseph was in power, were in deep depression at the time of our text. A new Pharaoh who did not know Joseph had come to the position of power. He became a real thorn in the flesh for the Israelites. Therefore, they cried to God for deliverance. God heard their cry and went to meet Moses in the wilderness near Mount Horeb. Moses gave several excuses to God for his unwillingness to answer the call to lead His people out of bondage, but his last two excuses moved God to anger. We do not often reflect on our ability to anger God. We would rather think of our disobedience as mere disappointments to God. But God can become angered by our disobedience, and He sometimes takes action against us for our insubordination.

Moses's first three excuses were that he thought: 1) he was incapable and unqualified. Moses wanted God to take him off the hook because he was not eloquent, and thought that his inability to verbalize as others did would be a good excuse for him; 2) the people would be skeptical of God's ability to help them; and 3) the people would not believe him. It is revealed through these first three excuses (Exodus 3:11–4:9) that Moses fought with bold honesty against God's call upon his life. As a shepherd, Moses was simply expressing his humility and fear. How could a simple man who spent the last forty years as a herdsman effectively challenge the most powerful government on earth? God responded to Moses's fears with His assurance that He would provide Moses with the inner strength and guidance he needed. Even so, Moses came up with yet another excuse.

The fourth excuse revealed a weak faith. Moses complained that he was not eloquent enough in speech to be a spokesman for God. There is also evidence to suggest that Moses may have been tongue-tied, or that he stuttered (see Exodus 6:12, 30). Moses implied that if he could not stand and speak with ease in God's presence, how would he be able to speak to Pharaoh? He was slow of speech, and he would probably embarrass himself and God. God's answer reveals what we often forget—that God created us and gave us life. If He can create life, He can certainly loosen a stammering tongue!

Like Moses, we often assume that leadership roles require someone who is silver-tongued and smooth-talking, someone who speaks with ease and without nervousness. Political successes and corporate giants have been born out of a leader's strong command of language. But the converse is also true: God also blesses the spiritual work of the common laborer and the uneducated person. The limitations we perceive in our lives should lead us to humble ourselves before the Lord so that He can demonstrate His power in and through us.

When God calls us to any task, He knows our weaknesses ahead of time. If the work He calls us to do involves some of our weak areas, then we can trust that He will provide the words, strength, support, and abilities we need. We must remember that before we came into this world, God made all the provisions we would need. Therefore, we should regard His asking us to work for Him as an honor, and we must accept it with humble spirits.

B. God's Response to Reluctance (Exodus 4:14-16)

And the anger of the Lord was kindled against Moses, and he said, Is not Aaron the Levite thy brother? I know that he can speak well. And also, behold, he cometh forth to meet thee: and when he seeth thee, he will be glad in his heart. And thou shalt speak unto him, and put words in his mouth: and I will be with thy mouth, and with his mouth, and will teach you what ye shall do. And he shall be thy spokesman unto the people: and he shall be, even he shall be to thee instead of a mouth, and thou shalt be to him instead of God.

It was Moses's fourth excuse that kindled God's anger against him. Moses wanted God to send someone else to do the job. He refused to be God's messenger and bring deliverance to Israel. He was rejecting God's call to go to work for Him. What was God's response? God silenced Moses and laid out His plan. God would still be merciful toward Moses, but He meant business! He ordered Moses to go and proclaim the glorious deliverance that was coming. There would be no more arguments or excuses.

God finally agreed to let Aaron speak for Moses. Moses's feelings of inadequacy were so strong that he could not even trust God's ability to deliver the Israelites from their bondage. God gave Moses four assurances: 1) that He would give Moses a helper, his brother Aaron, to be the spokesman (4:14); 2) that Aaron was already on his way to visit Moses, and would rejoice at the opportunity to serve the Lord (4:14); 3) that Moses was to share God's Word with Aaron freely (4:15); and 4) that Aaron was to be Moses's mouth, literally! (4:16). Aaron would be the spokesman to the people, and Moses would be as God to Aaron. In other words, God would speak through Moses to Aaron.

In our own lives, when we face difficult or frightening circumstances, we must be willing to let God help us. There is nothing beyond the control of the almighty God. We know God is omnipotent (all-powerful), but we often deny that claim when life becomes unpleasant.

The story of Moses teaches us that rejecting God's call is serious business. Moses could have been the spokesman that God intended. He would not have been the first leader whose stutter miraculously disappeared when he "ascended to his pulpit." But his weak faith forced God to replace Moses in a significant area—that of being God's spokesman and messenger to the people. Moses, the Levite, lost the great privilege of being God's spokesman, but God did not leave His work undone. God always finishes what He starts.

God's plan was not thwarted by Moses's disobedience. Aaron, also a Levite, became the first of the Levite priests when, soon after Israel was set free, Aaron and his sons—of the tribe of Levi—became God's messengers, mediators, and ministers to the house of Israel.

C. The Impact of Obedience (Exodus 4:27-31)

And the Lord said to Aaron, Go into the wilderness to meet Moses. And he went, and met him in the mount of

God, and kissed him. And Moses told Aaron all the words of the LORD who had sent him, and all the signs which he had commanded him. And Moses and Aaron went and gathered together all the elders of the children of Israel: And Aaron spake all the words which the LORD had spoken unto Moses, and did the signs in the sight of the people. And the people believed: and when they heard that the LORD had visited the children of Israel, and that he had looked upon their affliction, then they bowed their heads and worshipped.

Our disobedience never thwarts God's plans; it places them in a subordinate position. While God was dealing with Moses's disobedience, He was simultaneously working on Aaron's heart, preparing him to serve at Moses's side. Though they had been separated for a long time, Aaron responded positively to the Lord's command to search for his brother Moses in the wilderness. He left the land of Goshen and struck out in a Holy Spirit-led direction. Imagine the shock and the shame Moses felt when, following his refusal to accept God's call, God told Moses that He had chosen Aaron, Moses's brother, to be His spokesman, and Aaron suddenly appeared after forty years.

The reunion between the brothers must have been a wonderful time. Then when Moses shared God's plan with Aaron, to Moses's surprise, Aaron embraced the plan without hesitation. Aaron was the perfect example of the obedience God had expected of Moses.

When the two brothers gathered together the elders of Israel, Aaron shared what God had told Moses. Aaron was evidently a man of influence among the Israelites, and his message was well-received. He was able to convey God's divine commission of Moses with such persuasive power that the people "believed … bowed their heads and worshipped" (Exodus 4:31).

The essence of this section is the responses of the Israelites to Aaron and Moses. They believed, contrary to the expectation of Moses. They also worshiped God when they saw the signs. The signs led them to know that truly God had sent Moses and Aaron to go before Pharaoh to demand their release.

If we do not obey and surrender to God's call, He cannot direct our lives. To direct our lives in spite of our disobedience would be to give license to rebellion and sin. Like Moses, we must learn that obedience truly is better than sacrifice, and if we are to be God's ambassadors, we must place no limitations on our service and commitment.

III. CONCLUDING REFLECTION

The question has been asked by many Christians: "How do I know that I am serving God in the right capacity?" When people serve within the context of their spiritual gifts, they seem to perform their duties effortlessly. They show little signs of stress, and they do not get tired easily. In fact, they emerge from each season of service with more excitement than when they began, and they are generally ready for another assignment. They realize that it is God who is working through them.

On the other hand, if they take on a job for which they are *not* gifted, the position may become quite stressful. They may end up wishing they had not gotten involved. A Sunday school teacher who dreads the teaching hour and would rather be doing something else for God is not helping to advance Christ's kingdom. Others may think they are not committed, but nothing would be further from the truth. It is not a matter of commitment; it is a matter of giftedness.

When Christians discover their niche in the Kingdom-building process, they enjoy exercising their gifts. They look forward to the responsibilities assigned to them, and their commitment motivates others around them. It does not matter what one's talents are as long as he or she is using them to move the kingdom of God forward. When we minister to others through our gifts, we are tapping into the inexhaustible energy and motivation of God. We are doing what we have been called and equipped to do. And the bonus is that we experience an extra measure of energy, joy, productivity, and success.

The awareness of our limitations should help us to depend on God to deliver His messages through us. Paul helped to explain that God has chosen weak things to confound mighty ones, so that God can take His glory.

We must bear in mind that no matter how plausible our excuses are God will still have His way through us. God is longsuffering. Many older preachers who blazed the trail of evangelism had limited education. Some had never received formal schooling, yet their work is still with us today.

PRAYER

Father in heaven, help us to respond to You when You call us for Your service. Help us to understand that Your call is an honor and You will supply our needs to do the job to Your satisfaction. In Jesus' name we pray. Amen.

WORD POWER

Sign (Hebrew: *Owth [oth]*)—"a distinguishing, miraculous mark" and "a remembrance sign." The sign performed by Aaron in the presence of Pharaoh was real. Pharaoh's magicians performed their own signs, but they were foiled. The preceding definitions help us to know that the signs of Aaron had distinguishing marks; they were miraculous; and they served as a remembrance to the potent power of God as opposed to the impotent power of Pharaoh.

HOME DAILY BIBLE READINGS
(June 8-14, 2009)

Moses and Aaron Respond
MONDAY, June 8: "The God Who Calls" (Exodus 3:13-18a)
TUESDAY, June 9: "The God Who Equips" (Exodus 4:1-9)
WEDNESDAY, June 10: "The God Who Sends Back" (Exodus 4:18-23)
THURSDAY, June 11: "Do Not Be Afraid" (Zechariah 8:11-17)
FRIDAY, June 12: "God Will Help You" (Isaiah 41:8-13)
SATURDAY, June 13: "Refusing God's Call" (Proverbs 1:20-33)
SUNDAY, June 14: "A Team of Two" (Exodus 4:10-16, 27-31)

LESSON 3   June 21, 2009

PHARAOH IGNORES GOD'S CALL

DEVOTIONAL READING: **Psalm 10:1-14**   BACKGROUND SCRIPTURE: **Exodus 5:1–6:1**
PRINT PASSAGE: **Exodus 5:1-9, 22-23; 6:1**   KEY VERSE: **Exodus 5:1**

Exodus 5:1-9, 22-23; 6:1—KJV

AND AFTERWARD Moses and Aaron went in, and told Pharaoh, Thus saith the LORD God of Israel, Let my people go, that they may hold a feast unto me in the wilderness.

2 And Pharaoh said, Who is the LORD, that I should obey his voice to let Israel go? I know not the LORD, neither will I let Israel go.

3 And they said, The God of the Hebrews hath met with us: let us go, we pray thee, three days' journey into the desert, and sacrifice unto the LORD our God; lest he fall upon us with pestilence, or with the sword.

4 And the king of Egypt said unto them, Wherefore do ye, Moses and Aaron, let the people from their works? get you unto your burdens.

5 And Pharaoh said, Behold, the people of the land now are many, and ye make them rest from their burdens.

6 And Pharaoh commanded the same day the taskmasters of the people, and their officers, saying,

7 Ye shall no more give the people straw to make brick, as heretofore: let them go and gather straw for themselves.

8 And the tale of the bricks, which they did make heretofore, ye shall lay upon them; ye shall not diminish ought thereof: for they be idle; therefore they cry, saying, Let us go and sacrifice to our God.

9 Let there more work be laid upon the men, that they may labour therein; and let them not regard vain words.

.....

22 And Moses returned unto the LORD, and said, Lord, wherefore hast thou so evil entreated this people? why is it that thou hast sent me?

23 For since I came to Pharaoh to speak in thy name, he hath done evil to this people; neither hast thou delivered thy people at all.

Exodus 5:1-9, 22-23; 6:1—NRSV

AFTERWARD MOSES and Aaron went to Pharaoh and said, "Thus says the LORD, the God of Israel, 'Let my people go, so that they may celebrate a festival to me in the wilderness.'"

2 But Pharaoh said, "Who is the LORD, that I should heed him and let Israel go? I do not know the LORD, and I will not let Israel go."

3 Then they said, "The God of the Hebrews has revealed himself to us; let us go a three days' journey into the wilderness to sacrifice to the LORD our God, or he will fall upon us with pestilence or sword."

4 But the king of Egypt said to them, "Moses and Aaron, why are you taking the people away from their work? Get to your labors!"

5 Pharaoh continued, "Now they are more numerous than the people of the land and yet you want them to stop working!"

6 That same day Pharaoh commanded the taskmasters of the people, as well as their supervisors,

7 "You shall no longer give the people straw to make bricks, as before; let them go and gather straw for themselves.

8 But you shall require of them the same quantity of bricks as they have made previously; do not diminish it, for they are lazy; that is why they cry, 'Let us go and offer sacrifice to our God.'

9 Let heavier work be laid on them; then they will labor at it and pay no attention to deceptive words."

.....

22 Then Moses turned again to the LORD and said, "O LORD, why have you mistreated this people? Why did you ever send me?

23 Since I first came to Pharaoh to speak in your name, he has mistreated this people, and you have done nothing at all to deliver your people."

Some people fail to recognize true authority and power, erroneously believing that the authority and power rest within themselves. What brings us to recognize a higher authority? When Pharaoh refused to obey God's command to release the Israelites from slavery in Egypt, God promised to force obedience with a mighty hand.

.....

THEN THE LORD said unto Moses, Now shalt thou see what I will do to Pharaoh: for with a strong hand shall he let them go, and with a strong hand shall he drive them out of his land.

.....

THEN THE LORD said to Moses, "Now you shall see what I will do to Pharaoh: Indeed, by a mighty hand he will let them go; by a mighty hand he will drive them out of his land."

TOPICAL OUTLINE OF THE LESSON

I. Introduction
   A. Authority and Submission
   B. Biblical Background

II. Exposition and Application of the Scripture
   A. Opposing God's Will (Exodus 5:1-9)
   B. Doubting God's Power (Exodus 5:22-23)
   C. Receiving God's Assurance (Exodus 6:1)

III. Concluding Reflection

LESSON OBJECTIVES

Upon completion of this lesson, the students will know that:

1. Nothing can stop God from accomplishing His purposes;
2. The best we can do is to be still and see God in action; and,
3. We are empowered to go to the next level in accomplishing our purposes in life.

POINTS TO BE EMPHASIZED

ADULT/YOUTH

Adult Topic: Recognizing True Authority
Youth Topic: Who Do You Think You're Talking To?
Adult Key Verse: Exodus 5:1
Youth Key Verse: Exodus 5:2
Print Passage: Exodus 5:1-9, 22-23; 6:1

—Pharaoh refused to recognize the authority of Yahweh when he said, "I do not know the LORD, and I will not let Israel go" (verse 2). The word *know* includes the ideas of "being familiar with" and "accepting authority."
—This Scripture set the stage for the drama of the authority of God versus the authority of Pharaoh.
—Moses accused God of doing nothing to liberate the people.
—God had the last word: "Now you shall see what I will do to Pharaoh" (6:1, NRSV). God acted through Pharaoh, even as he resisted God's authority.
—Pharaoh reflects a leader who not only ignores a people's plight but also is vindictive when his authority is challenged.
—The condition of the Israelites should be viewed in light of Exodus 1:8, NRSV: "Now a new king arose over Egypt who did not know Joseph."

CHILDREN

Children Topic: Bricks Without Straw
Key Verse: Exodus 5:2
Print Passage: Exodus 5:1-9, 22-23; 6:1

—God sent a message to Pharaoh, through Moses and Aaron, to let the people of Israel go.
—Pharaoh asked who God was, that he should listen to Moses and Aaron.

—Pharaoh wanted to keep his workforce producing, so he refused to let the Israelites go to make sacrifices to God.

—Pharaoh ordered the taskmasters and supervisors to stop supplying the straw to make bricks, but he required the same output.

—Pharaoh's resistance caused Moses to wonder why God had chosen him to lead the people.

—God told Moses that he would see God's mighty hand change Pharaoh's mind.

I. INTRODUCTION

A. Authority and Submission

We do not eagerly acknowledge authority over us. We are born with an innate and natural desire to be in complete control of ourselves, to command our surroundings, and to answer to no one. Even children, early in life, begin to defy parental authority. Students from elementary-age to college-age are anti-authority. Looking at this issue critically, rejection of authority is part of our sinful natures because it reflects our pride and self-centeredness. Rejection of authority, if not checked early in life, may lead to rejection of God's authority later on.

Salvation and submission are inseparable. We cannot have one without the other. Salvation is the gift God grants the repentant and submissive heart. When we submit to God, we allow Him to have authority over our lives. We no longer desire to run our lives without godly authority, but instead, we acknowledge that there is a greater force behind all that we are and do. Paul, in his epistle to the Galatians, said, "I am crucified with Christ: nevertheless I live; yet not I…" (Galatians 2:20). A Christian lives in daily consciousness of God's presence.

Many people are just plain stubborn when it comes to submission to authority. They are hardheaded and stubborn about what they want. God calls this a "heart problem." These people simply refuse to allow Him into their hearts to take control over their lives and circumstances.

Pharaoh is probably the best illustration in the Bible of a person with a hard heart. He was exposed to the truth over and over again, yet he refused to respond accordingly. We are told in Exodus 4:21 that God engineered Pharaoh's hard heart—"I will harden his heart, that he shall not let the people go." God repeatedly presented Pharaoh with the truth of who He was, yet despite the overwhelming evidence presented, Pharaoh simply would not let the Israelites go. He refused to accept any of God's warnings; even when faced with undeniable evidence that he was wrong, Pharaoh still would not give in.

In the story of Pharaoh, God gives us a blueprint for what happens when a person refuses to accept and bend his or her will to God's will.

B. Biblical Background

"Pharaoh" was the official title given to all Egyptian kings. The name literally means "the great house." At the time of the Exodus, the ruling pharaoh was a ruthless and evil leader who ordered the Israelites to be reduced to the status of slaves. Pharaoh was familiar with many gods, but he had never heard about the God of Israel. As far as Pharaoh was concerned, there could be no other gods like his own god. The gods of Egypt were under his control. How could slaves under him talk about their God? It was unthinkable to him.

Bondage was not new in Egypt. If a person was not self-supporting, he or she became a bondservant to someone who would care for him or her in exchange for their services. Bond service was a part of the ancient societal structure before Moses was born, and was even in existence among the Hebrews. But the practice took on evil proportions when the Israelites, who were encamped in the northeastern section of Egypt known as Goshen, became slaves under a new pharaoh. Under Pharaoh's rule, they were subjected to his complete control, and the system of bond service suffered evil deterioration.

Under Pharaoh's class system, the Hebrews became mere slaves. They were denied "citizenship" in Egypt, but were considered chattel or possessions. Pharaoh misused his authority and made the oppression of God's people the law of the land.

When the Israelites were finally freed from Egypt, Moses regulated the laws governing bond service, thereby mitigating its evil and restricting its duration. "Man stealing" became a capital crime (see Deuteronomy 24:7). The Mosaic Law jealously guarded human life and liberty as sacred. Masters were required to treat Hebrew servants as *hired* servants, showing them the courtesy one would afford a brother, and liberally compensating them for their service (see Leviticus 25:39-41; Deuteronomy 15:12-18). No Israelite was required to serve his or her master for more than six years (see Exodus 21:2). And in the seventh (or Jubilee) year, every Hebrew had the right to claim freedom for themselves and their families, and reclaim their land. In this way, the Israelites were able to keep the oppression of the rich in check. Even in war, the Israelites were not permitted to take their conquered enemies into bondage (see 2 Chronicles 28:8-15).

All of these Mosaic Law restrictions were aimed at eradicating the evil and oppression of slavery.

II. EXPOSITION AND APPLICATION OF THE SCRIPTURE

A. Opposing God's Will
(Exodus 5:1-9)

AND AFTERWARD Moses and Aaron went in, and told Pharaoh, Thus saith the Lᴏʀᴅ God of Israel, Let my people go, that they may hold a feast unto me in the wilderness. And Pharaoh said, Who is the Lᴏʀᴅ, that I should obey his voice to let Israel go? I know not the Lᴏʀᴅ, neither will I let Israel go. And they said, The God of the Hebrews hath met with us: let us go, we pray thee, three days' journey into the desert, and sacrifice unto the Lᴏʀᴅ our God; lest he fall upon us with pestilence, or with the sword. And the king of Egypt said unto them, Wherefore do ye, Moses and Aaron, let the people from their works? get you unto your burdens. And Pharaoh said, Behold, the people of the land now are many, and ye make them rest from their burdens. And Pharaoh commanded the same day the taskmasters of the people, and their officers, saying, Ye shall no more give the people straw to make brick, as heretofore: let them go and gather straw for themselves. And the tale of the bricks, which they did make heretofore, ye shall lay upon them; ye shall not diminish ought thereof: for they be idle; therefore they cry, saying, Let us go and sacrifice to our God. Let there more work be laid upon the men, that they may labour therein; and let them not regard vain words.

In this section, we will first focus on four important phrases, namely: "Thus saith the Lord," "Let my people go," "Who is the Lord?" and, "I know not the Lord."

Moses and Aaron went into the presence of Pharaoh to demand the release of the Hebrews. It was a simple demand—"Let my people go." The word *let* is a very important word. This word was a simple entreatment. It appealed to the heart of Pharaoh, but he refused to obey. Following this request was, "My people." "My" is a possessive pronoun, meaning that the Hebrews were not ordinary people, as Pharaoh thought. They were the possession of the Lord, and no earthly power would be able to suppress them.

The second phrase is, "Who is the Lord?" Pharaoh had been seen as a god by his own people. He could not think of any greater power than himself; hence, he posed a question, "Who is the Lord?" Once Pharaoh asked this question, the logical conclusion followed, "I know not the Lord." Pharaoh was right—he did not know the Lord because he believed in the gods of the Egyptians, who he thought were subject to him. The priests of the Egyptian gods were his servants; they could not say anything against the will of Pharaoh. However, Pharaoh could have allowed for the possibility of the existence of a more powerful God, but he was a proud king and would not do this.

Pharaoh knew that the economy of his country would suffer a serious setback if the Hebrews were released; after all, they were working without pay.

To appreciate the magnitude of the calling placed upon Moses and Aaron, we must consider the scene within the royal palace and court of Egypt. The great king Pharaoh, most likely the most powerful man on earth, found himself confronted by Moses, a simple shepherd, and Aaron, a slave. The elders of Israel probably accompanied Moses and Aaron, for God had told Moses to take them with him (see Exodus 3:18). Pharaoh would have willingly granted an interview to the elders of the Hebrew nation, thinking that some official business needed to be discussed. But there was no preparation for what he was about to hear—a demand that he free God's people so they could make a religious pilgrimage to worship and serve God in the wilderness.

There were five reasons why Pharaoh did not take Moses's demands seriously. First, Pharaoh did not know God. He thought God had no authority over his life. His response was immediate and terse. He would not let the Israelites go.

Second, he saw Moses and Aaron simply as men who were disturbing the peace and doing nothing more than hindering the work of the slaves. We have to remember that the work produced by Israel was enormous because the people had grown to an estimated two million plus in population.

Third, Pharaoh was malicious, hard-hearted, and ruthless. We see this is his order to remove the supply of straw the Israelites used to make their quota of bricks. The slaves were forced to scatter all over Egypt, separated from their families, in order to locate sufficient straw for their work.

Fourth, Pharaoh considered the message from God to be a lie. He was no different from those today who discount the Word that comes through God's messengers and preachers.

And finally, Pharaoh prided himself on the misuse of his authority. As far as he was concerned, there was none greater than Pharaoh. One of the greatest problems within our society today is the misuse of authority and power—whether it is the authority of a king or president or the authority of a supervisor. God is clear that those in authority must not misuse their power.

The phrase "Who is the Lord?" (verse 2) reveals Pharaoh's arrogance. As far he was concerned, there was no other authority besides him. He saw himself as a god. He certainly felt no need to cave in to the demand of some other unknown god. Unfortunately, Pharaoh had not encountered the true God of Israel; this is the reason he responded with arrogance "I will not let thee go" just as God had predicted in Exodus 3:19; 4:21-23. Note that Pharaoh had not yet hardened his heart, something not stated until Exodus 7:13.

As we come to verse 3 of our text, we see that the boldness of Moses and Aaron was replaced with panic. Pharaoh became angry and said in verse 4, "Wherefore do ye, Moses and Aaron, let the people from their works?" Then he issued a strong command: "Get you unto your burdens."

When we are called by God to deliver messages to His people, like Moses and Aaron, we need to persist. When others reject our message we should not be discouraged. We must keep telling it because God is behind us.

B. Doubting God's Power
(Exodus 5:22-23)

And Moses returned unto the Lord, and said, Lord, wherefore hast thou so evil entreated this people? why is it that thou hast sent me? For since I came to Pharaoh to speak in thy name, he hath done evil to this people; neither hast thou delivered thy people at all.

Moses and Aaron were anxious to hear Pharaoh's decision regarding the release of the people, so they went to meet Israel's representatives, hoping to hear a favorable response (see Exodus 5:21). What happened next must have

shocked Moses. Instead of bringing Moses and Aaron good news, the representatives bitterly blamed Moses and Aaron for the brutal and savage abuse Pharaoh was now heaping upon them.

As painful as it was, as a true minister of God, Moses stood fast and listened to their complaints. The representatives angrily accused Moses of being at fault for their added suffering at the hand of Pharaoh. They bewailed their new fears that Pharaoh might take up the sword and kill them at any moment.

It disturbed Moses to have his people so viciously attack him. As their leader, he must have been crushed. He did what any spiritual leader would do in such a situation—he got alone with God and cried out to Him in prayer (see Exodus 5:22). He asked, "Why is it that thou hast sent me?" Moses initially was reluctant in taking the assignment to meet Pharaoh. He questioned his own call to the ministry and blamed himself for having brought such trouble upon his people. Faced with his own despair, Moses cried out to God, "Neither hast thou delivered thy people at all" (Exodus 5:23).

The demand of Moses for a release of the Israelites failed. Pharaoh increased their labor. Moses was devastated, seeing that his people were experiencing deep anguish with no end in sight. Moses expected quick action from God and fewer problems, but the reverse happened. Pharaoh intensified his oppressive rule. Moses then did what all people do—he voiced his disappointment to God.

We should remember that when trouble looms and there seems to be no hope, God is still on the throne. Enduring suffering builds our character. In James 1:2-4, we are encouraged to be happy when difficulties come our way. Problems develop patience and character by teaching us to trust God to do what will glorify His name.

C. Receiving God's Assurance
(Exodus 6:1)

THEN THE Lord said unto Moses, Now shalt thou see what I will do to Pharaoh: for with a strong hand shall he let them go, and with a strong hand shall he drive them out of his land.

The phrase "Now shalt thou see" was the welcoming message that Moses needed to hear from God. It was designed to bolster Moses's courage. Up until now nothing had happened because God had not acted. "With a strong hand" was another way of telling Moses that Pharaoh would put up resistance. The economy of Egypt would suffer a serious hemorrhage if the slaves were allowed to go. God had to release His people with a strong hand, or else Pharaoh would not believe in the God of Israel.

If we learn nothing else from the story of Moses, we learn that God sees our dilemmas, feels our despair, and answers our prayers. He felt Moses's despair and sent immediate personal encouragement. First, God reinforced what He had already promised on Mount Horeb—during the flaming bush experience— that He would raise His mighty hand against Pharaoh and force Pharaoh to free the people. This promise bore repeating because Moses was still full of doubt. Moses needed to be reassured of God's promise time and again—that God would force the terrible enslaver to free the people of God.

If we read further, we find that God reminded Moses of who He is—Jehovah, Yahweh. By this assertion, God was reminding Moses that the very name *Jehovah* meant "Savior," "Deliverer," and "Redeemer." The Lord wanted Moses to understand that he and the nation of Israel would be the catalysts for spreading the name of God across the pages of human history. God's name as LORD would be fulfilled in the redemption and release of Israel from slavery to freedom (see Exodus 6:2-3).

We learn from the story of Moses that, though circumstances may seem bleak, we must trust that the Lord can deliver us by His mighty hand. God has the power to deliver us from all of our enemies, seen and unseen, in both the physical and the spiritual realms.

III. CONCLUDING REFLECTION

All of us have experienced the stubborn desire to have things *our way*, even when our way is not God's way. Wise Christians learn from the experience. Those who refuse to ultimately submit to God's will are in danger of following in Pharaoh's footsteps.

All of us want things the way *we* want them. We are more comfortable when things are going *our way*. The tension arises when we discover that what we want is not what God wants. And if we refuse to respond to God, time and time again, our self-centeredness will corrode our hearts, and nothing will be able to melt our hardness.

Speaking of the Romans' rejection of Christ, the apostle Paul wrote, "They glorified him not as God, neither were thankful; but became vain in their imaginations, and their foolish heart was darkened" (Romans 1:21). It is dangerous to reject the truth because there will come a time when God will allow us to have our way. Paul warned that God will give us reprobate minds (see Romans 1:28). In other words, God will eventually let us have our way—and we will soon find out that our way is not as appealing as it seems.

To avoid the pitfalls created by self-centeredness, we must learn to recognize the warning signs of a hard-hearted lifestyle. Hard-hearted persons will lack concern for spiritual things, and show insensitivity to God's work. Hard-hearted persons will ignore the testimony of other people, and even ignore undeniable evidence of God's will for their lives. Hard-hearted persons will recognize sin, but refuse to deal with it because they are full of pride. They may eventually acknowledge their sins, but they may attempt to make deals with God so that they are not plagued by the consequences of sin.

Humankind can bargain in that manner, and rationalize and promise all we want, but the story of Pharaoh reminds us that unless we come to an accurate understanding of God's will for our lives, and then submit to His will, we will experience a miserable failure.

We must also recognize that God is sovereign, meaning that He is in control of the entire universe. He has not yielded His position of authority to mundane power. The experiences we face in life may go contrary to our understanding of who God is, but He is in full control. At His time He will deliver with His strong hand.

PRAYER

Heavenly Father, give to us hearts of flesh that will recognize Your sovereignty in all spheres of existence. Help us to know that, no matter what our circumstances are, You are in control. In Jesus' name we pray. Amen.

WORD POWER

Know (*yada [ya-dah]*)—means "to perceive," "to acquire knowledge," or "to be acquainted." In Exodus 5:2, the word *know (yada)* is preceded by a negative *(not)*. Pharaoh declared, "I know not." This meant that he had no subconscious knowledge of God, or he had no heart knowledge of God. The statement is also cast in the perfect tense, which means that his lack of knowledge of God was a completed action. He had no regard for God and he wished not to acknowledge Him or be acquainted with Him.

HOME DAILY BIBLE READINGS
(June 15-21, 2009)

Pharaoh Ignores God's Call

MONDAY, June 15: "Making Bricks Without Straw" (Exodus 5:10-21)
TUESDAY, June 16: "The Voice of the Lord" (Psalm 29)
WEDNESDAY, June 17: "Return to God and Heed Him" (Deuteronomy 4:25-31)
THURSDAY, June 18: "God's Plan to Strengthen" (Zechariah 10:6-12)
FRIDAY, June 19: "The Lord's Deliverance" (Psalm 18:13-19)
SATURDAY, June 20: "All Nations Shall Worship God" (Zechariah 14:12-19)
SUNDAY, June 21: "Moses's Complaint" (Exodus 5:1-9, 22-23; 6:1)

LESSON 4   June 28, 2009

GOD CALLS THE PEOPLE OUT OF EGYPT

DEVOTIONAL READING: **Exodus 15:1-13**
PRINT PASSAGE: **Exodus 14:15-25, 30**

BACKGROUND SCRIPTURE: **Exodus 13:17–14:30**
KEY VERSE: **Exodus 14:30**

Exodus 14:15-25, 30—KJV

15 And the LORD said unto Moses, Wherefore criest thou unto me? speak unto the children of Israel, that they go forward:

16 But lift thou up thy rod, and stretch out thine hand over the sea, and divide it: and the children of Israel shall go on dry ground through the midst of the sea.

17 And I, behold, I will harden the hearts of the Egyptians, and they shall follow them: and I will get me honour upon Pharaoh, and upon all his host, upon his chariots, and upon his horsemen.

18 And the Egyptians shall know that I am the LORD, when I have gotten me honour upon Pharaoh, upon his chariots, and upon his horsemen.

19 And the angel of God, which went before the camp of Israel, removed and went behind them; and the pillar of the cloud went from before their face, and stood behind them:

20 And it came between the camp of the Egyptians and the camp of Israel; and it was a cloud and darkness to them, but it gave light by night to these: so that the one came not near the other all the night.

21 And Moses stretched out his hand over the sea; and the LORD caused the sea to go back by a strong east wind all that night, and made the sea dry land, and the waters were divided.

22 And the children of Israel went into the midst of the sea upon the dry ground: and the waters were a wall unto them on their right hand, and on their left.

23 And the Egyptians pursued, and went in after them to the midst of the sea, even all Pharaoh's horses, his chariots, and his horsemen.

24 And it came to pass, that in the morning watch the LORD looked unto the host of the Egyptians through the pillar of fire and of the cloud, and troubled the host of the Egyptians,

25 And took off their chariot wheels, that they drave them heavily: so that the Egyptians said, Let us flee from the face of Israel; for the LORD fighteth for them against the Egyptians.

Exodus 14:15-25, 30—NRSV

15 Then the LORD said to Moses, "Why do you cry out to me? Tell the Israelites to go forward.

16 But you lift up your staff, and stretch out your hand over the sea and divide it, that the Israelites may go into the sea on dry ground.

17 Then I will harden the hearts of the Egyptians so that they will go in after them; and so I will gain glory for myself over Pharaoh and all his army, his chariots, and his chariot drivers.

18 And the Egyptians shall know that I am the LORD, when I have gained glory for myself over Pharaoh, his chariots, and his chariot drivers."

19 The angel of God who was going before the Israelite army moved and went behind them; and the pillar of cloud moved from in front of them and took its place behind them.

20 It came between the army of Egypt and the army of Israel. And so the cloud was there with the darkness, and it lit up the night; one did not come near the other all night.

21 Then Moses stretched out his hand over the sea. The LORD drove the sea back by a strong east wind all night, and turned the sea into dry land; and the waters were divided.

22 The Israelites went into the sea on dry ground, the waters forming a wall for them on their right and on their left.

23 The Egyptians pursued, and went into the sea after them, all of Pharaoh's horses, chariots, and chariot drivers.

24 At the morning watch the LORD in the pillar of fire and cloud looked down upon the Egyptian army, and threw the Egyptian army into panic.

25 He clogged their chariot wheels so that they turned with difficulty. The Egyptians said, "Let us flee from the Israelites, for the LORD is fighting for them against Egypt."

.....

30 Thus the LORD saved Israel that day out of the hand of the Egyptians; and Israel saw the Egyptians dead upon the sea shore.

.....

30 Thus the LORD saved Israel that day from the Egyptians; and Israel saw the Egyptians dead on the seashore.

TOPICAL OUTLINE OF THE LESSON

I. Introduction
A. Fear and Its Antidote
B. Biblical Background

II. Exposition and Application of the Scripture
A. God's Great Promise and Purpose (Exodus 14:15-18)
B. The Great Deliverance (Exodus 14:19-25)
C. God's Salvation to His People (Exodus 14:30)

III. Concluding Reflection

LESSON OBJECTIVES

Upon completion of this lesson, the students will know that:

1. Regardless of earthly opposition the counsel of God will stand;
2. Natural phenomenon cannot thwart the plan of God; and,
3. Fear disappears in the presence of God.

POINTS TO BE EMPHASIZED

ADULT/YOUTH

Adult Topic: **Finding and Giving Protection**

Youth Topic: **Protection in the Wilderness**

Adult Key Verse: **Exodus 14:30**

Youth Key Verse: **Exodus 13:21**

Print Passage: **Exodus 14:15-25, 30**

—When Pharaoh let the people go, God led the way.

—The central drama of Exodus 14 is the triumph of the power of God over the power of Egypt and Pharaoh.

—The approach of Egypt's armies in the wilderness caused great fear and loss of faith in the people of Israel. They did not trust God's protection.

—God illuminated true power when He told Moses, "And the Egyptians shall know that I am the Lord, when I have gained glory for myself over Pharaoh, his chariots, and his chariot drivers" (verse 18, NRSV).

—God's will for liberation and freedom was revealed when the people, led and protected by God, crossed the waters.

—God's protection of the Israelite community was amazingly comprehensive—from God's revelation to Moses, to the angelic presence, to the pillar of cloud, and to God's defeat of Pharaoh's army.

—Despite God's demonstrated acts of deliverance, Moses and the Israelites continued to need reassurance of God's protection.

CHILDREN

Children Topic: **Protected and Delivered!**

Key Verse: **Exodus 14:13**

Print Passage: **Exodus 14:10-14, 21-23, 26-29**

—Pharaoh sent his army to pursue the freed Israelites.

—The Israelites were terrified when they saw the Egyptian army behind them.

—Moses assured the Israelites that God would protect them.

—Moses followed God's instructions to part the sea and make a dry pathway for God's people.

—As Pharaoh's army followed the Israelites onto the path through the sea, God caused the sea to close.

—The Israelites escaped into the wilderness, but Pharaoh's army was destroyed in the sea.

I. INTRODUCTION

A. Fear and Its Antidote

There are different types of fear: fear of tomorrow, fear of human beings, fear of health problems, fear of financial problems, fear of darkness, and fear of God. In our text, Moses was confronted with two types of fear: fear of human beings (Pharaoh), and fear of God. "The fear of the LORD is the beginning of wisdom; A good understanding have all those who do His commandments" (Psalm 111:10, NKJV). Fear and doubt are like a two-sided coin, walking hand-in-hand. What causes us to doubt God's power? For the Israelites, it was hundreds of years of slavery and oppression. Though they were doctrinally taught that God would be their deliverer, their inability to see beyond their bleak circumstances took its toll on their faith as a people. Oppression, whether it is fueled by slavery or some other condition, can weigh down our worship and fuel the same kind of disbelief and skepticism that caused the Israelites to doubt God's power and presence among them.

We must realize that weak faith can lead to fear. We can become oppressed by our own fear. The question arises: "Why should we be free of fear?" Is it because God does not like fearful people? Is it because fear is synonymous with a lack of faith and is therefore sinful? Is it because fear serves no useful function in our lives? Though these are provocative questions, the fact is that fear is a mystery with many faces that we do not fully understand.

Though there are many motivating facts for fear, we can all agree that fear immobilizes, torments, and paralyzes its object. The Lord knows that as humans we will experience fear, but He also wants us to know that fear is nothing more than a "warning system" to alert us to potential danger and to teach us to depend more on Him. Just as pain is necessary to the body to warn us of disease and damage, so fear warns us to trust in God. When we allow our fear to point us toward God, He takes control of our lives and works through us to resolve our unpleasant circumstances.

As God called His people out of slavery, the clarion call today again is that God is calling each of us from every form of bondage to the freedom in Jesus Christ. The death of His Son on the cross is the unmistakable love of God for humanity. The sins of the world were nailed to the Cross. If we come to Him, He will in no wise cast us out. The resurrection and ascension of Jesus are assurances that even death cannot hold us in bondage.

B. Biblical Background

The Exodus is the event that terminated the Israelites' sojourn in Egypt and the commencement of the trip to the Promised Land. *Exodus* comes from the Latin Vulgate through the Greek Septuagint; the word *Exodus* in both languages means "departure," "going," or "way out." In many commercial buildings there are signs that read *exit*—meaning "the way out." The word *exit* has its root in *exodus*. The Hebrews' long enslavement, which had begun when the family of Jacob (Israel) had voluntarily entered Egypt during a time of severe famine in Canaan, was now coming to an end. The land of Goshen in the northeastern section of Egypt was given to them by a sympathetic pharaoh who knew Joseph. Goshen was not a large area, encompassing only about 900 square miles, but because of irrigation, it was considered some of the best land in Egypt. Archaeologists believe that it was this fertile land that enticed at least two pharaohs to build their great cities in Goshen. It was this attraction that led to the worst years of Israelite enslavement and became the catalyst for God's intervention and their ultimate exodus (exit).

Through the mercies of God, the Israelites were left to themselves for most of the 400 years they were in Egypt. They increased dramatically, to the consternation of the pharaoh in today's Scriptures. The time came when Pharaoh felt threatened by the Israelites and put them to forced labor. There were several cities built by the great pharaohs of Egypt; however, Pithom and Raamses were built as "store" or "treasure" cities by the Hebrews (see Exodus 1:11). These two cities bear proof of Exodus 5:7-13. In excavating them, it was found that three types of bricks were used to build these cities. The bases of the buildings were made with bricks of straw. The next layer bore bricks containing stubble and bits of straw, and the third layer was devoid of straw.

Archaeology then bears proof that Goshen held bitter memories for the enslaved Israelites. Yet fear of their oppressors caused them to tolerate rather than challenge their bitter state of slavery for many years until God sent Moses. Now, with their release from captivity, they were leaving Egypt to venture into the unknown.

II. EXPOSITION AND APPLICATION OF THE SCRIPTURE

A. God's Great Promise and Purpose
(Exodus 14:15-18)

And the Lord said unto Moses, Wherefore criest thou unto me? speak unto the children of Israel, that they go forward: But lift thou up thy rod, and stretch out thine hand over the sea, and divide it: and the children of Israel shall go on dry ground through the midst of the sea. And I, behold, I will harden the hearts of the Egyptians, and they shall follow them: and I will get me honour upon Pharaoh, and upon all his host, upon his chariots, and upon his horsemen. And the Egyptians shall know that I am the Lord, when I have gotten me honour upon Pharaoh, upon his chariots, and upon his horsemen.

There are some important verbs in this section that arrest our attention: *criest, speak, stretch,* and *harden,* to mention a few of them. The word *criest* indicates that Moses did not cry to God one time when he saw the Red Sea; rather, it was a continuous cry. This is the reason why God commanded him to "speak." In other words, the word was in Moses's mouth, and all he needed to do was to speak instead of cry. Another command was given to Moses—stretch. Moses had all he needed to move forward, but the Red Sea was too mighty for him to command. As children of God, the devil always plays on our ignorance of what is available to us. He fills us with forgetfulness and fear.

Finally, God told Moses, "I will harden the hearts of the Egyptians." The expression "And they shall know" was to let Pharaoh and his people come to know that there was the God of heaven, Who ruled and rules in the affairs of the world. We see from this section that God was (and is) able to lift up and bring down. The choice was clear—the Egyptians had been under the delusion that Pharaoh was a god, and for that reason God proved Himself in unforgettable phenomena. Even though we are children of God, through the redemption God Himself made available, we must be constantly sensitive to His presence.

The Israelites left Egypt full of fear and trepidation. Fear would have been a natural emotion for people who had so long been hopeless and helpless. It was no wonder that when they saw the armies of Pharaoh coming over the horizon, they were frightened. They were a defenseless people about to be attacked by the mightiest army on earth. There appeared to be no way of deliverance, and they were gripped with a deep, intense despair.

Yes, fear was natural in their circumstances. But what was unnatural was their condemnation of God's leader and their inability to trust in him as God's ambassador for freedom. In a very short time, perhaps days, they had forgotten God's mighty arm of salvation and deliverance. Their rejection of Moses revealed a shallow, weak faith. It was clear that they were not trusting God to deliver them. Their memories were short-lived.

Consider what God had already done for them. The Lord had just demonstrated His mighty power in launching the ten plagues of judgment upon Egypt. All the Israelites had witnessed God's mighty power firsthand. God then delivered the Israelites from enslavement in Egypt and promised to take them into the Promised Land of Canaan.

The moment called for a strong faith in God's promise and in His mighty arm that had already been proven time and time again. But the Israelites' faith was sorely lacking. Despite God's demonstration of His power, fear still convinced them that there was no possible way they could be saved from so great an enemy as Pharaoh's army.

Moses himself was in despair when he saw the Red Sea ahead of him. The command to Moses was unequivocal—to tell the children of Israel to go forward, not backward (verse 15). The matching order was to go forward. God's Word was and is clear. We are not to allow fear to control us. No matter how serious the circumstance, or how terrifying the problem, as believers, we are not to be overtaken by fear and faithlessness.

With the people standing on the shores of the Red Sea, Moses lifted his rod in obedience to God's command, the sea was parted, and the Israelites escaped their enemies on dry ground. God not only divided the Red Sea to keep His promise that He would deliver His people from their enemies, but He also did this to gain glory through the demonstration of His justice and judgment, and to show the Egyptians that He was the only God of deliverance and salvation.

The phrase "The Egyptians shall know that I am the Lord" points to the almightiness of God. Pharaoh hitherto had been playing games with the people of God. Each time he saw a plague, he would send for Moses and Aaron to tell them to go; then he would change his mind. But this final crossing of the Red Sea was undeniable. Moses's rod was the same celebrated rod of God that Moses had used in bringing forth many of the plagues against the Egyptians (see Exodus 4:20).

B. The Great Deliverance
(Exodus 14:19-25)

And the angel of God, which went before the camp of Israel, removed and went behind them; and the pillar of the cloud went from before their face, and stood behind them: And it came between the camp of the Egyptians and the camp of Israel; and it was a cloud and darkness to them, but it gave light by night to these: so that the one came not near the other all the night. And Moses stretched out his hand over the sea; and the Lord caused the sea to go back by a strong east wind all that night, and made the sea dry land, and the waters were divided. And the children of Israel went into the midst of the sea upon the dry ground: and the waters were a wall unto them on their right hand, and on their left. And the Egyptians pursued, and went in after them to the midst of the sea, even all Pharaoh's horses, his chariots, and his horsemen. And it came to pass, that in the morning watch the Lord looked unto the host of the Egyptians through the pillar of fire and of the cloud, and troubled the host of the Egyptians, And took off their chariot wheels, that they drave them heavily: so that the Egyptians said, Let us flee from the face of Israel; for the Lord fighteth for them against the Egyptians.

What happened next was a spectacular display of God's mighty power. The angel of God moved from the front to the rear of the Israelites, to stand between Israel and Pharaoh's army. The Lord made a fire wall between the children of Israel and Pharaoh's army. There was darkness in front of Pharaoh's army and light in front of the children of God. In addition, a pillar of cloud moved to the rear of the Israelites and hung between them and their enemy. This pillar of cloud took on the miraculous properties of being a wall of darkness to the Egyptians and a wall of light to the Israelites throughout the night's journey across the Red Sea. This meant that the Egyptians lost sight of the teeming tens of thousands of Israelites in the pitch darkness, while the same cloud lit the way for the massive number of escaping Hebrews while they pressed their way across the sea to the other side. The angel of God and the pillar of cloud cooperated to protect and lead the Israelites. The pillar of cloud was later strongly associated with the Lord Himself (see Exodus 33:9-11).

While God's almighty power was demonstrated when Moses stretched out his hand over the sea, this escape provision was further proof that God was with the Hebrew nation. We should note that the Scriptures state that God divided the sea. The word *divided* (*baqa*) is a word used for splitting rocks and wood or for splitting asunder the earth with a violent earthquake. The Lord actually split the sea asunder and made a valley or passageway through the sea wide enough to accommodate the people of God to pass through in one night. And the Scripture reads that they were able to accomplish it (see Exodus 14:24; Psalm 78:13) and arrive on the other side very early in the morning watch. A "watch" was the fourth part of the time from sunset to sunrise. They arrived on the other side of the Red Sea between 3:00 a.m. and 6:00 a.m.

Every eye must have been fastened upon the unbelievable, surging, massive walls of water that had divided and made a half-mile passage through the sea. And all night, as they marched, they witnessed the miraculous power and mighty deliverance of God.

In verse 21, there was no way of escape, but the Lord miraculously opened up the Red Sea. Sometimes, we find ourselves caught in a problem and see no way out. We must not panic; God can open up a way.

C. God's Salvation to His People
(Exodus 14:30)

Thus the Lord saved Israel that day out of the hand of the Egyptians; and Israel saw the Egyptians dead upon the sea shore.

God saved Israel from the ancient Egyptians, but He did not just bring them *through* something, He brought them *to* something. God never acts without purpose. The Israelites had just experienced a mighty miracle which was designed to address their fear, reinforcing the power and presence of God among His chosen people. It was also designed to prepare them for the enormous responsibility of spreading monotheism (the belief in one God) to a heathen world.

The Exodus had now been accomplished. The enemy lay dead upon the seashore. God had liberated the Israelites by a miraculous demonstration of His supremacy and authority over human power and nature. And the Israelites now placed their trust in God and His chosen leaders, Moses and Aaron. They were now ready to follow God and His servant Moses into the Promised Land and fulfill their destiny as God's chosen people.

Above all else, God wants us to believe in and trust in Him. He performed miracles for the Israelites for the same reason that He intervenes in our own lives in miraculous ways: to build up our faith in Him, and to prove His undying love for us. As the prophet recorded in Isaiah 43:10, "Ye are my witnesses, saith the Lord, and my servant whom I have chosen: that ye may know and believe me, and understand that I am he: before me there was no God formed, neither shall there be after me."

III. CONCLUDING REFLECTION

In Exodus 14:15, the Lord told Moses to stop praying to Him regarding moving forward. Moses had to move forward. Prayer must have a vital place in our lives, but there is also a time for action. Sometimes, we pray expecting God to guide us, but in actuality our prayer is nothing more than an excuse to postpone the project. This is the reason why God told Moses to move forward.

Has God told you to move forward? Are you still praying and seeking His guidance? You may not receive any more directives from the Lord. At a point Satan may come and seize the occasion to substitute his own guidance. Second Corinthians 11:14 reads, "And no marvel; for Satan himself is transformed into an angel of light."

There is ample evidence to show that the high demands and stresses of modern life are taking their toll on and distorting our fear warning systems. Natural brain tranquilizers—produced within the brain to keep us at peace when there is no real threat or to enable us to act constructively when in danger—are being depleted by our overworked brains. The result is a high incidence of incapacitating, purposeless anxiety disorders. This dilemma causes us to lose productivity at an alarming rate, not just in the workplace, but in the church as well. Consider the many ministries that have gone unfulfilled because of fear!

The word *fear* is mentioned 411 times in the Bible. Psalm 118:6 serves as an encouragement to us to keep our focus on God, saying, "The LORD is on my side; I will not fear: what can man do unto me?" And what does Jesus say about fear and anxiety? In John 16:33b, Jesus gives us this encouragement: "In the world ye shall have tribulation: but be of good cheer; I have overcome the world."

God is sovereign and in control of our lives, even during challenging times. We are called to overcome our fear by stepping out in faith and allowing God to transform our situations by His power.

There comes a time when God hears the cry of each and every one of us. The problem is that we are not sensitive to His voice. Egypt was a land of oppression for the children of God. They cried and God heard. "And it came to pass...and the children of Israel sighed by reason of the bondage, and they cried, and their cry came up unto God by reason of the bondage" (Exodus 2:23).

Today, God is still calling His people "out of Egypt." Each of us knows our "Egypt," and we can cry to God for deliverance; He will not ignore our cry.

PRAYER

Father, we are grateful for Your deliverance from the evil one. We ask that You help us to continue living in the consciousness of Your presence. In Jesus' name we pray. Amen.

WORD POWER

Save (*Yasha [ya-shah]*)—means "to save," "to be saved," "to be delivered from trouble," or "to give victory." In the Key Verse, we are told that "the Lord saved." The grammatical structure reveals that the action was done by God. Moses stretched forth his rod, but at the point of stretching, the Lord Himself was the one who did the parting of the sea for His people. The Lord delivered them from two troubles: the sea and Pharaoh's army.

HOME DAILY BIBLE READINGS
(June 22-28, 2009)

God Calls the People Out of Egypt

MONDAY, June 22: "Led to Freedom by God" (Exodus 13:17-22)

TUESDAY, June 23: "Pursued by the Enemy" (Exodus 14:1-9)

WEDNESDAY, June 24: "Overtaken by Fear" (Exodus 14:10-14)

THURSDAY, June 25: "God Is Our Refuge" (Psalm 46)

FRIDAY, June 26: "Trust in the Lord" (Proverbs 3:3-10)

SATURDAY, June 27: "Celebrating Deliverance" (Exodus 15:1-13)

SUNDAY, June 28: "Saved from the Enemy" (Exodus 14:15-25, 30)

LESSON 5   July 5, 2009

GOD CALLS PEOPLE TO COVENANT

DEVOTIONAL READING: **Matthew 22:34-40**
PRINT PASSAGE: **Deuteronomy 5:1-9, 11-13, 16-21**

BACKGROUND SCRIPTURE: **Deuteronomy 5:1-27**
KEY VERSE: **Deuteronomy 5:1**

Deuteronomy 5:1-9, 11-13, 16-21—KJV

AND MOSES called all Israel, and said unto them, Hear, O Israel, the statutes and judgments which I speak in your ears this day, that ye may learn them, and keep, and do them.

2 The LORD our God made a covenant with us in Horeb.

3 The LORD made not this covenant with our fathers, but with us, even us, who are all of us here alive this day.

4 The LORD talked with you face to face in the mount out of the midst of the fire,

5 (I stood between the LORD and you at that time, to shew you the word of the LORD: for ye were afraid by reason of the fire, and went not up into the mount;) saying,

6 I am the LORD thy God, which brought thee out of the land of Egypt, from the house of bondage.

7 Thou shalt have none other gods before me.

8 Thou shalt not make thee any graven image, or any likeness of any thing that is in heaven above, or that is in the earth beneath, or that is in the waters beneath the earth:

9 Thou shalt not bow down thyself unto them, nor serve them.

…..

11 Thou shalt not take the name of the LORD thy God in vain: for the LORD will not hold him guiltless that taketh his name in vain.

12 Keep the sabbath day to sanctify it, as the LORD thy God hath commanded thee.

13 Six days thou shalt labour, and do all thy work.

…..

16 Honour thy father and thy mother, as the LORD thy God hath commanded thee; that thy days may be prolonged, and that it may go well with thee, in the land which the LORD thy God giveth thee.

17 Thou shalt not kill.

18 Neither shalt thou commit adultery.

19 Neither shalt thou steal.

Deuteronomy 5:1-9, 11-13, 16-21—NRSV

MOSES CONVENED all Israel, and said to them: Hear, O Israel, the statutes and ordinances that I am addressing to you today; you shall learn them and observe them diligently.

2 The LORD our God made a covenant with us at Horeb.

3 Not with our ancestors did the LORD make this covenant, but with us, who are all of us here alive today.

4 The LORD spoke with you face to face at the mountain, out of the fire.

5 (At that time I was standing between the LORD and you to declare to you the words of the LORD; for you were afraid because of the fire and did not go up the mountain.) And he said:

6 I am the LORD your God, who brought you out of the land of Egypt, out of the house of slavery;

7 you shall have no other gods before me.

8 You shall not make for yourself an idol, whether in the form of anything that is in heaven above, or that is on the earth beneath, or that is in the water under the earth.

9 You shall not bow down to them or worship them.

…..

11 You shall not make wrongful use of the name of the LORD your God, for the LORD will not acquit anyone who misuses his name.

12 Observe the sabbath day and keep it holy, as the LORD your God commanded you.

13 Six days you shall labor and do all your work.

…..

16 Honor your father and your mother, as the LORD your God commanded you, so that your days may be long and that it may go well with you in the land that the LORD your God is giving you.

17 You shall not murder.

18 Neither shall you commit adultery.

19 Neither shall you steal.

UNIFYING LESSON PRINCIPLE

People make agreements to give structure and rules for their life together. What regulations are necessary to enjoy mutually beneficial lives? God set forth ten rules of conduct governing behavior, property, relationships, and worship.

20 Neither shalt thou bear false witness against thy neighbour.
21 Neither shalt thou desire thy neighbour's wife, neither shalt thou covet thy neighbour's house, his field, or his manservant, or his maidservant, his ox, or his ass, or any thing that is thy neighbour's.

20 Neither shall you bear false witness against your neighbor.
21 Neither shall you covet your neighbor's wife. Neither shall you desire your neighbor's house, or field, or male or female slave, or ox, or donkey, or anything that belongs to your neighbor.

TOPICAL OUTLINE OF THE LESSON

I. **Introduction**
   A. The Importance of Laws
   B. Biblical Background

II. **Exposition and Application of the Scripture**
   A. The Covenant—The Heart of the Law
      (Deuteronomy 5:1-5)
   B. Our Duty to God
      (Deuteronomy 5:6-9, 11-13)
   C. The Human Beings' Duty to Human Beings
      (Deuteronomy 5:16-21)

III. **Concluding Reflection**

LESSON OBJECTIVES

Upon completion of this lesson, the students will know that:

1. The commandments were given to foster a strong relationship between God and His people; and,
2. Obeying the commandments of God is not optional—it is required.

POINTS TO BE EMPHASIZED

ADULT/YOUTH

Adult Topic: **Accepting Rules for Living**
Youth Topic: **Called to Covenant**
Adult Key Verse: **Deuteronomy 5:1**
Youth Key Verse: **Deuteronomy 5:3**
Print Passage: **Deuteronomy 5:1-9, 11-13, 16-21**

—God gave the Decalogue, or Ten Commandments, directly to the people at Mount Horeb (see 4:40-44; 5:22-24).
—The Decalogue begins by recognizing God as the source of salvation and the source of the Law.
—The Decalogue offers fundamental principles of human behavior that will create a just and merciful community.
—Faithfulness to the covenant involves faithfulness to God along with respect for and just treatment of other members of the community.
—By giving divine commandments, God communicated His desire for all creation to have God's best.
—God expects followers to live a certain way and bases their safety and prosperity on their obedience.

CHILDREN

Children Topic: **Rules to Live By**
Key Verse: **Deuteronomy 5:1**
Print Passage: **Deuteronomy 5:1-2, 6-8, 11-13, 16-21**

—Moses reminded the people of the covenant God made with them at Mount Horeb.
—Moses called the people to renew their commitment by obeying the commandments God set down.
—The people were not to forget that God alone had delivered them from slavery and they owed allegiance to God alone.

—Moses recited the Ten Commandments in the people's hearing—four commandments concerning their relationship with God, and six concerning their relationship with people.

I. INTRODUCTION

A. The Importance of Laws

Laws are a necessary part of maintaining safe communities. As the set of enforced rules under which a society is governed, laws promote the safety and welfare of our neighborhoods and ourselves. No society could exist if people were permitted to do as they pleased, without regard for the rights of others. The law is established rules that outline a person's rights and obligations and that set forth the penalties for those who do not adhere to the law.

When nations attempt to rule without God, they risk creating laws that are unjust. This is why the laws of human beings are often changed. Human laws must be frequently scrutinized for fairness, and altered to reflect society's enlightened attitudes.

While some laws are changed through civil disobedience (consider the many unjust laws that were eradicated by the Civil Rights Movement), in general, we expect everyone to adhere to the rules and regulations of our society. Without such obedience, our communities would dissolve into chaos.

In our lesson, we will study the laws of God, given to Moses for the children of Israel to follow. Unlike human laws, these laws are timeless and eternal. They represent the perfect will of God. They are the meat of His covenant relationship with Israel, and they are with us still today. Surviving thousands of years in their unchanged form, no one has ever been able to prove the need to reverse or alter their content.

B. Biblical Background

The Ten Commandments, or the Decalogue, is a summary of God's absolute and indisputable moral laws. The moral law is the revealed will of God about human conduct, binding on all human beings to the end of time. These commandments were first given in their written form to the people of Israel when they encamped in Sinai after they came out of Egypt. They were written by the finger of God on two tablets of stone. The first tablets were broken by Moses when he brought them down from Mount Sinai (see Exodus 32:19) and threw them on the ground. At the command of God, Moses took two other tablets into the mount, and God wrote on them "the words that were in the first tables" (Exodus 34:1). Afterwards, the Ten Commandments were placed in the Ark of the Covenant (see Deuteronomy 10:5).

The tablets are referred to as "the covenant" in biblical history (see Deuteronomy 4:13). The subsequent history and location of the ark and its contents are unknown. Many have speculated that when the Babylonians conquered Israel, the Levite priests may have anticipated the need to hide the Ark of the Covenant (see 2 Chronicles 36:18). Others are of the opinion that the tablets were destroyed when the Temple was burned. Archeologists and religionists of the Jewish faith have been searching for the lost ark for centuries.

The tablets containing the Ten Commandments were considered Israel's most precious possessions, and as such they were retained in a box (the Ark of the Covenant), made of acacia wood. The lid of the box was called the "mercy seat" and was regarded as the most important feature in the holiest place (see Leviticus 16:2). On top of it was the meeting place between God and humankind.

Though the precious ark and its contents have been lost, when Jesus was crucified for the sins of the world He became the true "mercy seat" (see Psalm 85:10), and the meeting place between the holy God and guilty human beings.

II. EXPOSITION AND APPLICATION OF THE SCRIPTURE

A. The Covenant—The Heart of the Law (Deuteronomy 5:1-5)

AND MOSES called all Israel, and said unto them, Hear, O Israel, the statutes and judgments which I speak in your ears this day, that ye may learn them, and keep, and do them. The Lord our God made a covenant with us in Horeb. The Lord made not this covenant with our fathers, but with us, even us, who are all of us here alive this day. The Lord talked with you face to face in the mount out of the midst of the fire, (I stood between the Lord and you at that time, to shew you the word of the Lord: for ye were afraid by reason of the fire, and went not up into the mount;) saying.

As we study this section of our lesson, let us again call attention to the Key Verse. Even though the topic for today is "God Calls People to Covenant," there were important things that preceded the covenant. In verse 1, Moses used three words before reading the covenant, which were: "learn," "keep," and "do." These three words call for action. The Israelites would have to put their will to work. It is not how great a document is, but whether we are willing to obey the revealed truth. We cannot pick and choose what we will obey and dismiss what seems irrelevant to us. This is the reason why Moses said "learn," "keep," and do."

Moses did a lot of exposition in the book of Deuteronomy. Unlike the commandments in the book of Exodus, here Moses was explaining the covenant of God in more detail. When the Israelites heard, they must keep. "To keep" means to make the revealed truth a personal treasure. It would enable them to pass the truth on to the next generation. Hypocrisy creeps in when we hear commands and we fail to carry them out, but still force them on others. Hence, Moses told the people, "Do them." We also read in the letter of James, "Be doers of the word." Only the doer is blessed.

If we too want to experience the presence of God in our lives in a positive way, we must learn how to hear, keep, and do. When we are obedient, our children will see this in us, and they too will benefit from our actions.

Moses called the Israelites together to stress obedience to God's Law. Everyone was commanded to hear what God had to say. No person was too important to be above God's command. The people were to first hear the laws—to pay careful attention and listen with rapt attention. Second, they were to learn the laws—to grasp the meaning of the laws and memorize them. The laws were to be cultivated within them like a crop of seed, and take root in them, so that they would be well-informed and knowledgeable about the ways of God. And third, they were to observe or follow the laws, and to be completely obedient to the laws and carry them out to the fullest extent.

When the laws of God are mentioned, most people picture the Ten Commandments. Perhaps this is because the Ten Commandments are at the very heart of God's Law and the basis and foundation of life, which tells people exactly how God wants them to live.

Moses sought to drive the point home—that the Ten Commandments must be learned and followed. But before he outlined the terms of the covenant and the nature of the relationship, Moses had to first establish the parties involved in the covenant. The parties to the covenant were God and humankind, everyone who was alive and standing before Moses. God did not make this covenant (found in 5:1-6) with the fathers of Israel—Abraham, Isaac, and Jacob. Rather, God made the covenant with the Israelites who had been freed from Egyptian slavery and who were to follow God into the Promised Land.

In one word, God told His people what He expected of them: obedience. He had saved and delivered them; now He expected them to follow the laws and to keep His covenant. God wanted them to know that the source of the covenant was God Himself (verse 4). Human beings did not dream up the Ten Commandments or the covenant of the Law. God gave the Ten Commandments—face-to-face, word for word. There would be no excuse

for disobedience because the commandments came from God Himself.

The mediator for the covenant was Moses. In this sense, Moses was a type of Christ—an intercessor, and a picture of the coming Messiah who would stand as the ultimate mediator between God and human beings.

B. Our Duty to God (Deuteronomy 5:6-9, 11-13)

I am the LORD thy God, which brought thee out of the land of Egypt, from the house of bondage. Thou shalt have none other gods before me. Thou shalt not make thee any graven image, or any likeness of any thing that is in heaven above, or that is in the earth beneath, or that is in the waters beneath the earth: Thou shalt not bow down thyself unto them, nor serve them. . . . . . Thou shalt not take the name of the LORD thy God in vain: for the LORD will not hold him guiltless that taketh his name in vain. Keep the sabbath day to sanctify it, as the LORD thy God hath commanded thee. Six days thou shalt labour, and do all thy work.

God reminded the Israelites that He was the one who brought them out of the house of bondage, and only He knew everything about them. God's laws were based upon their needs (and that of all humankind), because only God knows what human beings need to live fulfilled and orderly lives.

Beginning with verse 7, God begins to outline humankind's duty to Him as their creator. This is the beginning of God's moral Law. The world offers varying opinions about morality, and we see the results in the tragedy of sin and evil sweeping throughout the world. At times, sin and evil seem crushing and overpowering. There can be only one solution for a world that has gone berserk. It is a plan that was intended to guide humankind down through the centuries: it is a plan that will work as well now as it worked in ancient times. There is no generation gap when it comes to the Ten Commandments. What was declared to be wrong in biblical times is still wrong today.

Embodied in these verses are four commandments relating to humanity's relationship with God. The first and second commandments require that we worship neither other gods nor idols. In these commandments, God is declaring that He alone is supreme, and we should have no other gods before Him. The words *before me* (*al-paanaaya*) mean literally "before my face," "against my face," "in hostility toward me," "in my presence," and "in my sight." But human beings have become caught up in the worship of other gods in this twenty-first century. We worship our own ability to achieve, the power of science, money and materialism, and even nature, placing more importance on these things than on God. We prefer to put God in a box labeled "heaven" and leave Him there until we need Him.

The third and fourth commandments deal with misuse of God's name. God charged us to guard against misusing His name. Taking the Lord's name in vain means using God's name in thoughtless and insincere ways. Why is this sin? Because God is our salvation; He is the one who brought us out of sin and rescued us from eternal hell. He is the one who has given us eternal life. How could we ever misuse His name?

We are charged to keep the Sabbath day holy. The word *keep* means "to observe," "to attend to," or "to build a hedge around." God warns that nothing should get in the way of our worship of Him, one day of the week. Resting once a week is absolutely essential. Why? Because it not only continually renews our relationship with and our concentration on God, it also helps to rejuvenate our own bodies

as well. No human being can work seven days a week without eventually being prematurely worn out. The human body requires a time of refreshing. When we worship the Lord one day a week, we set aside time to refresh ourselves, both physically and spiritually, at God's mercy seat. A favorite hymn, "Come, Ye Disconsolate," highlights this great need for rest, saying, "Come to the mercy seat, fervently kneel; Here bring your wounded hearts, here tell your anguish, Earth has no sorrow that Heav'n cannot heal" (#196, *BSH*).

C. The Human Beings' Duty to Human Beings (Deuteronomy 5:16-21)

Honour thy father and thy mother, as the Lord thy God hath commanded thee; that thy days may be prolonged, and that it may go well with thee, in the land which the Lord thy God giveth thee. Thou shalt not kill. Neither shalt thou commit adultery. Neither shalt thou steal. Neither shalt thou bear false witness against thy neighbour. Neither shalt thou desire thy neighbour's wife, neither shalt thou covet thy neighbour's house, his field, or his manservant, or his maidservant, his ox, or his ass, or any thing that is thy neighbour's.

In the list of the Ten Commandments, our duty to God is followed by our duty to each other. We can see that evil is sweeping the world today. The breakdown in the family (divorce and adultery), the disregard for human life (abortion, drive-by shootings, capital punishment), and the rise in theft and covetousness (materialism) all point to a lawless society that is on the fast track toward complete chaos. God counteracts these terrible evils in a very simple way, using very simple words in the last six of the Ten Commandments.

We are to honor our parents. The Hebrew word *honor* (*kabad* or *kabed*) means "to respect" or "hold in high esteem." God wants us not only to respect our parents, but to listen to their instructions and obey them. This fifth commandment establishes the importance of the family unit as the basic unit and foundation of society. If honor and respect control the behavior of the family, it will help to control the behavior of our communities and society. In Ephesians 6:1-3, long life is promised to those who obey this commandment.

The sixth commandment has raised much controversy today. While most of us readily agree that murder is wrong, it is in our definition of *murder* that we part company. Capital punishment and abortion are the topics on the front lines of disagreement. The Hebrew word for *kill* (*ratsach*) means "premeditated, in a violent unjust manner." This makes it difficult if not impossible to defend premeditated acts of abortion. God says that murder is wrong because He alone gives life, and He alone can take it away.

Adultery is so prevalent in our society today that the seventh commandment may be the most ignored of the ten. Acts of premarital sex and multiple sexual partners even after marriage that were once seen only in the movies have become so commonplace that many family units are in danger of destruction. Why is this commandment so important? If a person will not be faithful and loyal to his or her family, how can that person be trusted to be loyal to his or her church, nation, society, and to God? It is far easier to be loyal to what we can physically see, such as one's family, than to what is only a concept, such as a nation, society, or civilization. Immorality strikes at the very foundation of society and causes suffering, guilt, secrecy, and unfaithfulness. Immorality and adultery teach that behavior such as selfishness, unfaithfulness, distrust, disloyalty, secrecy, and irresponsibility are acceptable. God gave us

this commandment against adultery to preserve our lives and bring the great qualities of peace, love, and trust to our lives.

Stealing has become so commonplace today that a thief who does not assault or kill his victim is referred to as a *common thief.* Thievery, robbery, and swindling have reached epidemic proportions, further contributing to the lawlessness within our world. Stealing takes on many forms, including government misuse of funds and employer theft (a case in point was the ENRON debacle). We see unfair wages, dishonest athletes (steroid use), tax fraud (no matter how small the amount), extravagant and indulgent lifestyles that disregard desperate needs in the world, and misuse of earth's wealth and resources. Stealing shows disrespect for property and for human life. The thief may appear to go undetected, but a thief always loses his or her reputation, integrity, and character before God.

Lying, or bearing false witness, threatens society's foundation. Nothing can survive for long when it is filled with lies, whether it be families, friendships, businesses, schools, churches, communities, or even governments. Any organization will collapse in the wake of mistrust and broken, severed relationships. *Bearing false witness* means far more than just lying against someone under oath. It encompasses all lying (see Hosea 4:2). We tend to forget that the source of lies is Satan. He was the first ever to lie, and he is called the father of lies. Those who lie follow in his footsteps and are called "children of the devil" (see John 8:44).

The Hebrew word for *covet* (`avah*) means "to be desirous," "thirst for," or "lust after." The word *covet* can apply to both the good and the bad. In the tenth commandment, God forbids the latter. There is a great difference between *covetousness* and *coveting*. The Bible encourages us to covet those things that will promote love, joy, and peace—the perfect gifts from God. But *covetousness* is an inward sin of the heart and mind that manifests itself in sinful outward action. Before a person commits sin, the sin is first *conceived* within the heart. It is that inward sin that manifests itself in outward action.

III. CONCLUDING REFLECTION

Human beings have never disputed the need for laws, but we have disputed who should make the laws. In a democracy, the majority ideally establishes the law. But even in a democracy, judicial review (the Supreme Court) often overturns the will of the majority.

Our laws may have to change, but God's Law never changes. That which was perfect from the beginning never needs changing! If justice is the moral standard that applies to all human conduct, then God is the only one capable of establishing perfect justice.

PRAYER

Our Father in heaven, we are grateful for Your love and the laws You gave to us. Help us to obey them for our sakes, that we may have peace with You and our neighbors. In Jesus' name we pray. Amen.

WORD POWER

Hear (*shama [sha-maw]*)—is a command (imperative). It means "to hear intelligently with a view to carrying out what is commanded" or "stated with full obedience." It is one thing to listen to instructions from the Lord, but it is quite another thing to walk in obedience. In this text, the Israelites were instructed to hear and obey. Disobedience to God's laws will cause unexpected consequences.

HOME DAILY BIBLE READINGS
(June 29–July 5, 2009)

God Calls People to Covenant

MONDAY, June 29: "A Covenant by Sacrifice" (Psalm 50:1-6)
TUESDAY, June 30: "Listening to the Prophet" (Acts 3:17-25)
WEDNESDAY, July 1: "A Covenant of Obedience" (Psalm 132:11-18)
THURSDAY, July 2: "Mediator of a Better Covenant" (Hebrews 8:6-12)
FRIDAY, July 3: "A Covenant of Mercy" (Romans 11:25-32)
SATURDAY, July 4: "The Greatest Commandment" (Matthew 22:34-40)
SUNDAY, July 5: "God Makes a Covenant" (Deuteronomy 5:1-9, 11-13, 16-21)

GOD CALLS PEOPLE TO REMEMBER

DEVOTIONAL READING: **1 Corinthians 5:1-8**
PRINT PASSAGE: **Deuteronomy 16:1-8** *11:19*

BACKGROUND SCRIPTURE: **Deuteronomy 16:1-8**
KEY VERSE: **Deuteronomy 16:1**

Deuteronomy 16:1-8—KJV

OBSERVE THE month of Abib, and keep the passover unto the LORD thy God: for in the month of Abib the LORD thy God brought thee forth out of Egypt by night.

2 Thou shalt therefore sacrifice the passover unto the LORD thy God, of the flock and the herd, in the place which the LORD shall choose to place his name there.

3 Thou shalt eat no leavened bread with it; seven days shalt thou eat unleavened bread therewith, even the bread of affliction; for thou camest forth out of the land of Egypt in haste: that thou mayest remember the day when thou camest forth out of the land of Egypt all the days of thy life.

4 And there shall be no leavened bread seen with thee in all thy coast seven days; neither shall there any thing of the flesh, which thou sacrificedst the first day at even, remain all night until the morning.

5 Thou mayest not sacrifice the passover within any of thy gates, which the LORD thy God giveth thee:

6 But at the place which the LORD thy God shall choose to place his name in, there thou shalt sacrifice the passover at even, at the going down of the sun, at the season that thou camest forth out of Egypt.

7 And thou shalt roast and eat it in the place which the LORD thy God shall choose: and thou shalt turn in the morning, and go unto thy tents.

8 Six days thou shalt eat unleavened bread: and on the seventh day shall be a solemn assembly to the LORD thy God: thou shalt do no work therein.

Deuteronomy 16:1-8—NRSV

OBSERVE THE month of Abib by keeping the passover to the LORD your God, for in the month of Abib the LORD your God brought you out of Egypt by night.

2 You shall offer the passover sacrifice for the LORD your God, from the flock and the herd, at the place that the LORD will choose as a dwelling for his name.

3 You must not eat with it anything leavened. For seven days you shall eat unleavened bread with it—the bread of affliction—because you came out of the land of Egypt in great haste, so that all the days of your life you may remember the day of your departure from the land of Egypt.

4 No leaven shall be seen with you in all your territory for seven days; and none of the meat of what you slaughter on the evening of the first day shall remain until morning.

5 You are not permitted to offer the passover sacrifice within any of your towns that the LORD your God is giving you.

6 But at the place that the LORD your God will choose as a dwelling for his name, only there shall you offer the passover sacrifice, in the evening at sunset, the time of day when you departed from Egypt.

7 You shall cook it and eat it at the place that the LORD your God will choose; the next morning you may go back to your tents.

8 For six days you shall continue to eat unleavened bread, and on the seventh day there shall be a solemn assembly for the LORD your God, when you shall do no work.

BIBLE FACT

There are many rules and regulations in the Bible, particularly in the Old Testament. The key to doing God's will rests in remembering His words, which involves reading and meditating daily on God's Word. If we fail to remember and meditate, the enemy will continue to rob us of our peace of mind.

UNIFYING LESSON PRINCIPLE

Individual persons and communities regularly remember and celebrate great occasions with thanksgiving. How do we commemorate significant events in our lives? God commanded the Israelites to remember their deprivation by eating only unleavened bread and simple meat at sundown.

TOPICAL OUTLINE OF THE LESSON

I. Introduction
   A. Christian Family Reunion
   B. Biblical Background

II. Exposition and Application of the Scripture
   A. A Celebration of Deliverance (Deuteronomy 16:1-2)
   B. The Bread of Affliction (Deuteronomy 16:3-4)
   C. The Purpose of the Pilgrimage (Deuteronomy 16:5-8)

III. Concluding Reflection

LESSON OBJECTIVES

Upon completion of this lesson, the students will know that:

1. It is important to keep records of important landmarks in our lives;
2. The Israelites celebrated Passover as a remembrance of God's mighty act; and,
3. Celebration of important Christian events helps the coming generations to know that God is actively involved in the world.

POINTS TO BE EMPHASIZED

ADULT/YOUTH

Adult Topic: Remembering and Celebrating
Youth Topic: Called to Remember and Celebrate
Adult/Youth Key Verse: Deuteronomy 16:1
Print Passage: Deuteronomy 16:1-8

—The celebration of Passover ties together the past and present and unifies the people with a common heritage and memory.
—Over time, the sacrifice of an animal at Passover moved from separate family dwellings (see 12:1-13, 21-23) to a sacrifice at the central sanctuary (16:6-8).
—The celebration of the Passover was closely linked to the early spring "month" (more accurately, "new moon") of Abib.
—*Passover* is an act of remembering and celebrating God's rescue of Israel from slavery and bondage in Egypt to freedom.
—This annual event—one of the most important in Jewish faith practice—is designed to keep God and God's redemptive acts in the minds of the people of God.

CHILDREN

Children Topic: An Event to Celebrate
Key Verse: Deuteronomy 16:1
Print Passage: Deuteronomy 16:1-8

—Moses instructed the people about the rituals to commemorate the first Passover.
—The Passover celebration would reenact certain aspects of the Exodus.
—The celebration would include a gathering of the people to worship God.
—The Passover was to be observed according to detailed regulations.

I. INTRODUCTION

A. Christian Family Reunion

Family reunions are extremely popular. Families set aside this time to come together in the time-honored tradition of celebrating their oneness and the importance of keeping their history as a family.

There are time-honored celebrations in the family of God that accomplish that same purpose. Christian celebrations such as Communion and Easter reinforce our bond with Jesus Christ as members of His family. They demonstrate the importance of our common faith experience and remind us that Christ is the Head of our families, on whom we depend for our very existence. They also teach us the value of our faith history and provide a way to pass our faith to the next generation.

B. Biblical Background

The Passover, or Pesach, celebrates the memory of God's saving actions of liberation from slavery in Egypt. When God warned of the death angel that was coming to claim the lives of all the firstborn, He instructed the Israelites to spread sacrificial blood over the door frames of their homes using hyssop, a plant that is associated with purification. When the death angel came, he passed over the houses of the Israelites, hence the familiar statement, "When I see the blood, I will pass over you" (Exodus 12:13). This final plague upon Egypt was the one that finally convinced Pharaoh to let the Israelites go. God commemorated this event in their lives with this celebration called the Passover—because that night, the death angel *passed over.*

In biblical times, the Passover celebration began with a special sacrifice offered in the Temple by the chief priests (see Numbers 28 and 29). This sacrifice was called the *chagigah* (see Deuteronomy 16:2; 2 Chronicles 35:7-9). It is commanded in Deuteronomy 16:7 that the Israelites roast and eat the animal sacrifice. Today, when the Jews celebrate the Passover, they place a roasted egg on the *seder* plate as a reminder of the chagigah.

Passover was celebrated by Jesus just before His crucifixion. According to the books of Matthew, Mark, and Luke, Jesus shared the Passover meal, or *seder,* with His disciples on that Thursday evening. The most important preparation for the Passover *seder* was the provision of a lamb to be sacrificed by the head of the household. As the group leader on that Thursday evening, that task would have fallen to Jesus. Could we perhaps consider the possibility that Jesus presented Himself to His disciples that evening as the sacrificial Lamb of God who was shortly to offer Himself on the cross as a redemptive sacrifice? (See Luke 22:15.) The disciples did not understand the implications of this symbolism at the time, but it became clear afterwards. This was why Paul later described Jesus as the Passover Lamb (see 1 Corinthians 5:7).

II. EXPOSITION AND APPLICATION OF THE SCRIPTURE

A. A Celebration of Deliverance
(Deuteronomy 16:1-2)

OBSERVE THE month of Abib, and keep the passover unto the Lord thy God: for in the month of Abib the Lord thy God brought thee forth out of Egypt by night. Thou shalt therefore sacrifice the passover unto the Lord thy God, of the flock and the herd, in the place which the Lord shall choose to place his name there.

Specifically, the Passover was observed on the fourteenth of Abib or Nisan, which correspond to our March-April (see Exodus 12:1-28), but no mention of that is made here. Nor are the other feasts specifically dated. Moses did not state the obvious. This is a further indication of Mosaic authorship. A later writer would probably have felt it necessary to date the events more specifically. "Observe the month" may signify all the different religious days in it, thus the opening of the new moon day on the first of Abib, the setting aside of the lamb or kids on the tenth, and the weekly Sabbaths. It also included the Passover itself, with the feast of the unleavened bread and its special Sabbaths on the opening and closing days. The whole month was seen as important because it was the month of deliverance, and Moses wanted it to be well-remembered.

The Passover night, with the lamb or kid having been slain toward evening, was itself a feast of remembrance. It was in the night that they partook of the lamb, along with the bitter herbs and unleavened bread. During this time they would go through the question-and-answer ritual connected with the Passover (see Exodus 12:26-27). It was a reminder of how God had brought them out of Egypt by night. This could have been in the same fashion that the West African griots, or storytellers, would recount the history of their tribes.

The *pilgrimage law* in ancient Israel required the Jews to make an annual pilgrimage to their central worship center. No matter how far away the Israelite lived—on the west coast of the sea or in the east on the other side of the Jordan, or the farthest border of the north or south—they were to make this pilgrimage three times a year to the central worship center. Though it was a difficult law to keep, the Jews were determined to follow God's command to remember His blessings of freedom, salvation, and guidance. We trace the establishment of this law back to our text, when the Lord commanded Moses and the Israelites to annually remember the Passover.

The Passover, instituted by God through Moses, celebrates the most wonderful event in Israel's history. Moses commanded the Israelites to remember the great deliverance of God from Egypt through the sacrifice of the lamb. Though they did not yet know, the Passover lamb was a symbol of Christ, the Lamb of God. In the gospel of John we read, "Behold the Lamb of God, which taketh away the sin of the world" (John 1:29). Up to this point, the greatest event in Israel's history had been its miraculous deliverance from Egyptian slavery. The mere mention of the Passover was bound to remind the Israelites of God's execution of the firstborn son of every Egyptian family, and how the Israelites had escaped the death angel by putting the blood of a lamb on their doorposts. They escaped the wrath of God by believing in Him and trusting the blood of the sacrificial substitute, the blood of the Passover lamb.

On that very night when God's terrifying judgment fell, the Egyptians were humbled by God's mighty power, and they freed the Israelites from 400 years of enslavement.

It is important to remember that the substitute sacrifice is a symbol of Christ, the Passover Lamb who was sacrificed for us. There was only one place where the sacrifice offering could be made: the place chosen by God Himself. God alone determined where and how He was to be approached. There was only one *place* appointed by Him and only one *way* appointed by Him. This was a picture that pointed to Jesus Christ, the only way and place that a person could ever become acceptable to God.

B. The Bread of Affliction
(Deuteronomy 16:3-4)

Thou shalt eat no leavened bread with it; seven days shalt thou eat unleavened bread therewith, even the bread of affliction; for thou camest forth out of the land of Egypt in haste: that thou mayest remember the day when thou camest forth out of the land of Egypt all the days of thy life. And there shall be no leavened bread seen with thee in all thy coast seven days; neither shall there any thing of the flesh, which thou sacrificedst the first day at even, remain all night until the morning.

Deuteronomy 16:3a reads, "Thou shalt eat no leavened bread with it." *With it*, that is, with the sacrifice of the Passover, the Israelites were to eat no leavened bread; they were to eat unleavened bread for seven days.

Unleavened bread, or bread made without yeast, was bread eaten in haste just prior to the Israelites' exodus from Egypt (see Exodus 12). The Israelites were commanded to eat this unleavened bread at the Feast of the Passover for seven days. Called "the bread of affliction," it is still a symbol of the urgency with which the Israelites left Egypt on their march to the Promised Land.

Passover, also called "The Feast of Unleavened Bread," coincides with the April barley harvest in the month of Abib, which is the beginning of the harvest season. Like the unleavened bread, eating the first fruits of the harvest before fermentation symbolizes a new beginning. The Hebrews were also not permitted to let sacrificial meat remain until morning (see Deuteronomy 16:4). This meant that the entire sacrifice had to be consumed before retiring for the evening. This practice was a symbol that pointed to Jesus Christ as the ultimate and complete sacrifice for the sins of humankind.

Besides the actual memorial, there was much symbolism beyond that which has been mentioned. Yeast was a symbol of corruption and sin, which was why it was excluded from grain offerings. The removal of all leaven from the whole country was therefore a symbol of the need for the Israelites to be free from corruption. Even those who could not come to the feast had to observe the prohibition of the leaven.

During the celebration, the Hebrews were to make sure that no yeast was in their possession for seven days. Today, Jewish mothers spend several days cleaning their homes in preparation for the Jewish seder, to ensure that no breadcrumbs remain in the home for the holiday celebration.

It is very possible that the feast of unleavened bread was already an ancient feast, probably in that case going back to the patriarchs, for they would unquestionably have celebrated religious feasts at important times of the year as all their neighbors did. This was both to celebrate the lambing and to celebrate the harvests of various kinds—and once established, these would have carried on through the centuries in the old way, even though the move to Egypt resulted in different seasons. People did not easily relinquish old customs which were treasured and passed on from one generation to another. The full moon feast of Abib was probably one such celebration. Whether the same was true of the Passover is debatable. All indications seem to suggest that it was probably a new addition to an old feast because of the night of deliverance.

C. The Purpose of the Pilgrimage (Deuteronomy 16:5-8)

Thou mayest not sacrifice the passover within any of thy gates, which the Lord thy God giveth thee: But at the place which the Lord thy God shall choose to place his name in, there thou shalt sacrifice the passover at even, at the going down of the sun, at the season that thou camest forth out of Egypt. And thou shalt roast and eat it in the place which the Lord thy God shall choose: and thou shalt turn in the morning, and go unto thy tents. Six days thou shalt eat unleavened bread: and on the seventh day shall be a solemn assembly to the Lord thy God: thou shalt do no work therein.

Moses and the Israelites were charged never to celebrate the Passover in any place other than the place where God's name was honored. As the great Creator and Savior of humankind, God alone had the right to determine where and how people could approach Him. For the Israelites in the wilderness, the tabernacle was God's dwelling place where sacrifices were offered. The sacrifice was to be made in the evening on the anniversary of the Israelites' deliverance from Egypt. The animal was to be roasted and eaten only at the place chosen by God: the sanctuary.

This emphasizes His sovereignty in the arrangement. He was their Lord; they were His subjects. He had chosen this place to dwell in and for the Israelites to come with their sacrifices. It would appear from this that the Passover was celebrated in the open air—the men and the households sitting together among so many other households on the holy ground around the tabernacle, the place chosen by God. In the strictest sense of Jewish tradition, only the men were required to gather at the feasts, but they would regularly bring some or most of their households along with them, as is made clear in Deuteronomy 12:18. The sacrifice was to be roasted (*bashal*). The verb here simply means "cooked" but can mean either "roasted" or "boiled." However, it is declared in Exodus 12:8-9 that it should be roasted, and when the verb refers to *boiling*, "with water" is normally added. Compare 2 Chronicles 35:13a, where the verb means "cooked" and "with fire" is added, while in Numbers 11:8 and 2 Samuel 13:8 it refers to "cooking cakes." Only the Levite priests were permitted to eat of the sacrificial meat offered in the Temple.

For six days unleavened bread had to be eaten, and the final day of the seven was to be a solemn Sabbath, a day for public rites and the religious festival, on which no work was to be done. Of course on that day also unleavened bread was to be eaten (compare with verse 4). If all leaven had been removed from within their borders as previously asserted, there would have been no alternative.

The Passover celebration is a symbol of Jesus Christ, our Passover Lamb, who was sacrificed for us. Jesus Christ is the perfect fulfillment of the Old Testament Passover Lamb that was slain on behalf of God's people. Through the blood of Jesus Christ, a person escapes the judgment of God. God accepts the blood of the substitute sacrifice as full payment for the sins committed by people (see Isaiah 53:4).

III. CONCLUDING REFLECTION

Celebrating the Feast of Unleavened Bread paints a clear picture for the believer of the urgency for the believer to be freed from the world and its enslavement to sin and death. We are called to be set free from the oppressions and pollutions of this world, from all the sin and evil, immorality, lawlessness, and corruption. We are to be set free and liberated to live for God, and to follow Him in our march toward the promised land of heaven.

The preservation of our religious celebrations is critical to the continuation of the faith legacy we pass from generation to generation. It is not enough to celebrate; we must teach our children the true meaning behind each celebration. The force that drives our nation's economy has infiltrated God's holiest of celebrations, Easter and Christmas, and has attempted to reduce them to nothing more than profit-making ventures. Economists agree that it is the consumer who drives the demand for goods and services. If this is the case, Christians have been a party, in more than a marginal fashion, to taking the focus of our celebrations off God and putting it on profits.

God expects Christians to adhere to our holy traditions, protect our holidays as *holy days,* and prevent secularism from destroying their purpose and significance.

PRAYER

Father in heaven, we are grateful for Your kindness and the many important things You have done for us. Help us not to forget the death, resurrection, and ascension of Your Son. Help us to keep looking for His second coming. In Jesus' name we pray. Amen.

WORD POWER

Observe (*shamar*)—means to "keep," "guard," "observe," "give heed," or "pay attention to." The Hebrews were told to strictly observe the Passover feast throughout all generations. They were to tend to it as a farmer tends to his garden, lest weeds overtake it. The reason for its lasting observation is so that no one can say that the last plague which killed all the firstborn in Egypt was a figment of the human imagination.

HOME DAILY BIBLE READINGS
(July 6-12, 2009)

God Calls People to Remember
MONDAY, July 6: "Remember and Rejoice" (Ecclesiastes 11:7–12:1)
TUESDAY, July 7: "Remember the Lord's Deeds" (Psalm 77:3-15)
WEDNESDAY, July 8: "Remember and Give Thanks" (Psalm 105:1-11)
THURSDAY, July 9: "Keeping the Covenant" (2 Kings 23:1-3, 21-23)
FRIDAY, July 10: "Preparing for the Passover" (Luke 22:7-13)
SATURDAY, July 11: "Christ, Our Paschal Lamb" (1 Corinthians 5:1-8)
SUNDAY, July 12: "The Passover Observance" (Deuteronomy 16:1-8)

GOD CALLS PEOPLE TO SPECIAL SERVICE

DEVOTIONAL READING: **Romans 11:33–12:2**
PRINT PASSAGE: **Leviticus 8:1-13**

BACKGROUND SCRIPTURE: **Leviticus 8:1-13**
KEY VERSE: **Leviticus 8:12**

Leviticus 8:1-13—KJV

AND THE LORD spake unto Moses, saying,

2 Take Aaron and his sons with him, and the garments, and the anointing oil, and a bullock for the sin offering, and two rams, and a basket of unleavened bread;

3 And gather thou all the congregation together unto the door of the tabernacle of the congregation.

4 And Moses did as the LORD commanded him; and the assembly was gathered together unto the door of the tabernacle of the congregation.

5 And Moses said unto the congregation, This is the thing which the LORD commanded to be done.

6 And Moses brought Aaron and his sons, and washed them with water.

7 And he put upon him the coat, and girded him with the girdle, and clothed him with the robe, and put the ephod upon him, and he girded him with the curious girdle of the ephod, and bound it unto him therewith.

8 And he put the breastplate upon him: also he put in the breastplate the Urim and the Thummim.

9 And he put the mitre upon his head; also upon the mitre, even upon his forefront, did he put the golden plate, the holy crown; as the LORD commanded Moses.

10 And Moses took the anointing oil, and anointed the tabernacle and all that was therein, and sanctified them.

11 And he sprinkled thereof upon the altar seven times, and anointed the altar and all his vessels, both the laver and his foot, to sanctify them.

12 And he poured of the anointing oil upon Aaron's head, and anointed him, to sanctify him.

13 And Moses brought Aaron's sons, and put coats upon them, and girded them with girdles, and put bonnets upon them; as the LORD commanded Moses.

Leviticus 8:1-13—NRSV

THE LORD spoke to Moses, saying:

2 Take Aaron and his sons with him, the vestments, the anointing oil, the bull of sin offering, the two rams, and the basket of unleavened bread;

3 and assemble the whole congregation at the entrance of the tent of meeting.

4 And Moses did as the LORD commanded him. When the congregation was assembled at the entrance of the tent of meeting,

5 Moses said to the congregation, "This is what the LORD has commanded to be done."

6 Then Moses brought Aaron and his sons forward, and washed them with water.

7 He put the tunic on him, fastened the sash around him, clothed him with the robe, and put the ephod on him. He then put the decorated band of the ephod around him, tying the ephod to him with it.

8 He placed the breastpiece on him, and in the breastpiece he put the Urim and the Thummim.

9 And he set the turban on his head, and on the turban, in front, he set the golden ornament, the holy crown, as the LORD commanded Moses.

10 Then Moses took the anointing oil and anointed the tabernacle and all that was in it, and consecrated them.

11 He sprinkled some of it on the altar seven times, and anointed the altar and all its utensils, and the basin and its base, to consecrate them.

12 He poured some of the anointing oil on Aaron's head and anointed him, to consecrate him.

13 And Moses brought forward Aaron's sons, and clothed them with tunics, and fastened sashes around them, and tied headdresses on them, as the LORD commanded Moses.

UNIFYING LESSON PRINCIPLE

Some persons in a community are set aside for special service to the community. How do we discern, acknowledge, and affirm those people chosen for special service? God commanded that Aaron and his sons be recognized by consecrating them with water and holy garments.

TOPICAL OUTLINE OF THE LESSON

I. Introduction
   A. Call to Ministry
   B. Biblical Background

II. Exposition and Application of the Scripture
   A. Aaron and His Sons Ordained (Leviticus 8:1-5)
   B. The Spiritual Cleansing (Leviticus 8:6-9)
   C. The Anointing (Leviticus 8:10-13)

III. Concluding Reflection

LESSON OBJECTIVES

Upon completion of this lesson, the students will know that:

1. Aaron and his sons were recognized and ordained;
2. Recognizing people for special events is not out of order in God's house; and,
3. Recognizing people for special positions is an added responsibility.

POINTS TO BE EMPHASIZED

ADULT/YOUTH

Adult Topic: Commissioning for Service
Youth Topic: Called by God to Special Service
Adult/Youth Key Verse: Leviticus 8:12
Print Passage: Leviticus 8:1-13

—Appointment to the high priesthood was based on the call of God, and it was celebrated with the rites of ordination.
—Leviticus 8 is a historical narrative of Israel establishing an ordained priesthood to function as intercessors and mediators, as Moses was commanded to do in Exodus 29.
—Ordination is not a private right, but a public vesting of authority for service.
—The service of consecration reflects and affirms the understanding that the lineage of the priesthood begins with Aaron.
—Two roles of religious leadership are evident in the passage: the prophetic role of Moses, and the priestly role of Aaron.
—Vestments and other symbols of the authority of priesthood are bestowed on Aaron.

CHILDREN

Children Topic: Called to Serve
Key Verse: Leviticus 8:12
Print Passage: Leviticus 8:1-13

—The congregation was assembled to recognize the call of God on Aaron and his sons for special service.
—Aaron and his sons wore clothes that were specific to their task and symbolic of their role.
—Moses anointed Aaron for the task.
—Moses performed the ceremony before the people as the Lord commanded.

I. INTRODUCTION

A. Call to Ministry

Why do people enter the ministry? Some enter the ministry because they like the idea of serving and ministering to people. Others like the professionalism of the ministry and the opportunity for leadership within the community that the ministry offers. Others like the opportunity for speaking and teaching on a regular basis. They may feel that they have the *talent* for such appointments. Some are attracted to the prestige, image, and respect usually shown a minister.

There are many reasons why a person might choose to serve in the ministry. But there is only one legitimate reason: the call and ordination of God. No person should ever serve in the ministry unless he has been called and ordained by God to serve. Since it is God who calls and ordains, this is the only legitimate reason for the church to ordain a person to serve God's people.

The writer of Hebrews said, "No man taketh this honour unto himself, but he that is called of God, as was Aaron" (Hebrews 5:4). It must be noted and emphasized that at the time of the writing of this epistle (Hebrews), the Romans selected the high priest in Jerusalem. However, in the Old Testament, God chose Aaron and his descendants for the office of the high priest. Jesus Christ, like Aaron, was chosen and called by God.

B. Biblical Background

Ordination is "the act by which a person is set aside for service to God." It is God who calls, and God who ordains. Ordination is essential if a person is to serve God, and no one should ever try to serve in the ministry unless one has been called and ordained by God.

As in this ordination of Aaron to the priesthood office, sacrificial blood and oil were used to anoint the priests. The use of sacrificial blood to sprinkle the people was unusual and occurs in only one other place in the Scriptures (see Exodus 24:8). The blood was significant because it marked the beginning of two things: 1) in Exodus, it marked a new beginning between God and the Israelite nation, one of complete obedience to God's will by them; and 2) in our text today, it marked the beginning of the royal priesthood—those who would act as Old Testament mediators between God and human beings, and assume the great responsibility for the preservation of their faith relationship with God.

A special bond was established through this symbolic act of ordination, which marked the person as God's own. In this ceremony, a person was called, set apart, and consecrated to the service of God, by God. Since the ministry belongs to God, only He has the right to decide who will serve in ministry, and no one can serve God effectively unless one is called and ordained by God.

II. EXPOSITION AND APPLICATION OF THE SCRIPTURE

A. Aaron and His Sons Ordained
(Leviticus 8:1-5)

AND THE LORD spake unto Moses, saying, Take Aaron and his sons with him, and the garments, and the anointing oil, and a bullock for the sin offering, and two rams, and a basket of unleavened bread; And gather thou all the congregation together unto the door of the tabernacle of the congregation. And Moses did as the LORD commanded him; and the assembly was gathered together unto the door of the tabernacle of the congregation. And Moses said unto the congregation, This is the thing which the LORD commanded to be done.

Aaron and his sons had been called and appointed by God to the priesthood, to be ministers of God to His people. The significance of the ceremony was to demonstrate that calling before the people. This special calling had to be performed in such a way that the priests' ordination would make a lasting impression on them and would permanently bond them to their special duties as God's ambassadors. The ceremony also had to make a lasting impression on the people, so that the people would hold Aaron and his sons in high regard, with the respect due their position as spiritual leaders. The ordination was so important that all the people needed to witness to it (verse 3).

Before ordination can take place, a person has to be called to serve the people of God. We notice in our lesson that God's call came through His mediator, Moses, who was a symbol of Christ. Those who are called under the New Covenant relationship are called through Christ Himself.

Being ordained to the priesthood or ministry is of critical importance to God. A person is to be ordained only if he or she has been called of God and willingly submits to that call. This is dramatically pictured in the ordination of Aaron and his sons to the priesthood of Israel. Two calls were issued: there was the call to the priests (ministers) to prepare for the ordination; and there was the call to the people to assemble and gather for the ordination service. The elders would have joined Moses and the priests at the entrance of the Tabernacle and all the people would have stood at the entrances to their tents (see Exodus 33:8).

While up to this point and even beyond the people constantly complained about Moses, he was, in the final analysis, the one whom they trusted implicitly. And while Aaron had been with him throughout their various adventures in Egypt, it was Moses whom they had always looked on as the prime figure and symbol of godly leadership. It was he who had divided the Red Sea. It was he who had been with God on the Mount, who had brought the people the Law, and who had previously acted as priest when it was necessary to do so. It was he whom they had seen go into the old tent of meeting to meet with the Lord. It was he who had organized the making and the erection of the tabernacle in the wilderness. They might well have asked at this point, prior to Aaron and his sons' ordination, why Aaron should now supplant Moses. Others might simply have looked on all of this as Mosaic nepotism. So Moses wanted them to be sure that they were aware of the truth—that Aaron was appointed by none other than God to be their high priest. So then, once again we see Moses as the intermediary between God and the people, hearing the voice of God on their behalf.

Notice that everyone was obedient and did exactly what God commanded. This further highlights the fact that we are to follow whom

God sets apart for service. Our Baptist church polity and autonomy permit us to choose our own spiritual leaders, but we must be careful not to search in the wrong place using man-made criteria for our selection process. We must remember that it is God who appoints. For this reason, every church must approach the pastoral selection process with much prayer and waiting on God.

B. The Spiritual Cleansing
(Leviticus 8:6-9)

And Moses brought Aaron and his sons, and washed them with water. And he put upon him the coat, and girded him with the girdle, and clothed him with the robe, and put the ephod upon him, and he girded him with the curious girdle of the ephod, and bound it unto him therewith. And he put the breastplate upon him: also he put in the breastplate the Urim and the Thummim. And he put the mitre upon his head; also upon the mitre, even upon his forefront, did he put the golden plate, the holy crown; as the LORD commanded Moses.

Moses, God's mediator, took the men to be ordained and washed them in water. *Washing in water* was a symbol for Aaron and his sons to be spiritually and morally cleansed. Moses, God's mediator, did the washing and the cleansing. No person can cleanse himself or herself, spiritually, from sin. Only God's Mediator can wash and cleanse a person spiritually.

So the first act of Moses with Aaron and his sons was to wash them with water. This was a ceremonial washing and indicated the preliminary removal, from Aaron and his sons, of the taint of earthiness. They were to be made outwardly as free of earthly taint as they were when they came into the world (that is, once they had been washed after birth). No earthly stains of life should remain on them. They were coming into the presence of the Holy One, the One who was not of this earth. Therefore nothing earthly should now cling to them.

Likewise, no person today can be spiritually cleansed unless he or she is first washed by our Mediator, Jesus Christ. Our spiritual cleansing takes place when we repent of our sins and are ceremonially washed in the blood of the Lamb, through the act of baptism. As Aaron and his sons were set apart for the priesthood, we are then set apart for discipleship (see Psalm 51:2, 7; Acts 22:16; 1 John 1:7).

Notice that the washing and cleansing with water took place just before Aaron and his sons received their priestly robes. The act of putting on holy clothing symbolizes the putting on of the righteousness of God. No one can put on righteousness, unless one is first cleansed of all sin. The call to minister before God and to the people of God is a holy calling. We must not rush to do anything until we are sure of God's leadership.

As with all ceremonial acts, there is great importance placed on the clothing worn for the priesthood or ministry. The high priest symbolized the High Priesthood of Jesus Christ, and the clothing symbolized the righteousness of Jesus. A person must be covered with the righteousness of Jesus in order to be acceptable to God. The purpose of the special clothing worn by the high priest was to declare two truths: 1) that the high priest was set apart and different from the people, because his demeanor pointed to the righteousness of Jesus Christ and His perfection; and 2) that the high priest was holy, set apart to God, and must be respected and honored as the Mediator between human beings and God.

The high priest was clothed with an ephod, or special tunic. It was a long coat-like garment that covered the whole body, and it symbolized the putting on of God's righteousness. The multicolored sash of fine linen was symbolic of the truth of God's

Word, and was comparable to the belt of truth which every believer is commanded to put on (referred to in Ephesians 6:14). Just as the belt held a garment together, so the truth of the Word of God holds every believer. It enlightens and wraps together everything in the believer's spiritual wardrobe.

The robe symbolized the intercessory ministry of the high priest. It was an ornately embroidered robe trimmed with gold bells (see Exodus 28:33). Tucked in the hem of this garment were two onyx stones with the names of Israel's twelve tribes engraved on them, six names on each stone. The stones symbolized that the priest carried the names of God's people before the Lord as their mediator and intercessor. The Urim and Thummim were two stones carried in a breastplate pouch worn close to the heart, which symbolized that the high priest carried the names of God's people upon his heart, and continually represented them before the Lord. The high priest was also clothed with a turban, which symbolized that the mind and thoughts of the priest must be subjected to God and His righteousness—and the medallion attached to its front, with the words "HOLINESS TO THE LORD" written upon it, symbolized that the high priest bore the guilt for the shortcomings of the people.

As with the ceremony itself, the symbolism in the robe demonstrated that no person should be ordained unless one had been completely clothed in the righteousness of Jesus Christ, and demonstrated that one would walk in that righteousness and bring dignity and honor to the ministry of God.

In like manner was Christ also arrayed in His priestly robes through His exemplary life, girded with truth, and He wore the "ephod" as one who was spoken to directly from God. On the Mount of Transfiguration, the beauty of His garments, so hidden on earth, was revealed (see Matthew 17:2; Mark 9:3; Luke 9:29), and He was appointed God's High Priest so that He could offer up Himself as a sacrifice for sin.

C. The Anointing
(Leviticus 8:10-13)

And Moses took the anointing oil, and anointed the tabernacle and all that was therein, and sanctified them. And he sprinkled thereof upon the altar seven times, and anointed the altar and all his vessels, both the laver and his foot, to sanctify them. And he poured of the anointing oil upon Aaron's head, and anointed him, to sanctify him. And Moses brought Aaron's sons, and put coats upon them, and girded them with girdles, and put bonnets upon them; as the Lord commanded Moses.

"The anointing" is perhaps the most common phrase in modern Christianity. Christian writers have published books and articles on this important subject in an effort to shed some light on its significance and meaning. Throughout the Scriptures, both people and places were anointed with oil if they were to be consecrated to God.

Oil is a symbol of consecration and of the Holy Spirit, who anoints a person for service—and with it: 1) Moses anointed the tabernacle and its furnishings because the tabernacle was consecrated and set apart for the service of God; 2) he anointed the altar seven times because the altar was where the atoning sacrifice was offered, the place where the full and complete payment or ransom for sin was made; it provided a perfect redemption for human beings. Throughout the Bible, the number *seven* symbolizes the idea of completion, fullness, and perfection. The altar was anointed seven times to symbolize that a complete, full, and perfect sacrifice was being made for the Hebrews' reconciliation and redemption; 3) Moses anointed Aaron's head to symbolize that Aaron was being consecrated to God and His service; and 4) Moses anointed and clothed the other priests to symbolize that they too were being set apart for the service of God.

While Aaron's sons were set apart or ordained as priests, they were not anointed. Only the high priest was anointed. A person being ordained to the ministry must be anointed by the Spirit of God, and be called by God and led to the point of dedication and consecration to God. The person must be totally dedicated to the service of God through the presence and power of the Holy Spirit.

III. CONCLUDING REFLECTION

Ministry is undertaken with fear and trembling because true ministers know that they are ill-equipped for the task unless they surrender wholly and completely to God and His Holy Spirit. If great oratory skills were the requirement, the world would be flooded with men and women ready to superficially impress us with their prowess. If a compassionate heart was the requirement, many an unsaved philanthropist could claim that he or she has done a great work for the Lord.

God chooses and uses whom He sees fit to meet the varied ministry needs of His numerous and diverse creation. The foremost and essential ingredient for ministry's calling is a saved heart, filled by God's grace, open to God's will, and endowed with God's calling to a specific spiritual leadership purpose.

PRAYER

Father, help us to fulfill our calling in life. Help us to constantly ask for fresh empowerment to do our work, that at the end only Your name may be exalted. In Jesus' name we pray. Amen.

WORD POWER

Pour (*yatsaq*)—means "to empty out," "to empty out self," or "to flow out." Moses poured the anointing oil in his hand on Aaron's head. The anointing with oil at this point was an acknowledgement that all fitness for his office and all the power with which he would rightly fulfill his duties came from the Lord. We too have access to the Holy Spirit and we must continue to ask for fresh pouring out of the Holy Spirit to discharge the ministerial calling.

HOME DAILY BIBLE READINGS
(July 13-19, 2009)

God Calls People to Special Service
MONDAY, July 13: "We Are God's" (Psalm 100)
TUESDAY, July 14: "Sanctify the Congregation" (Joel 2:12-16)
WEDNESDAY, July 15: "The Ministry of Generosity" (2 Corinthians 9:6-12)
THURSDAY, July 16: "Doing the Father's Will" (Matthew 21:28-32)
FRIDAY, July 17: "Present Your Bodies" (Romans 11:33–12:2)
SATURDAY, July 18: "The Example Christ Left" (Romans 15:1-6)
SUNDAY, July 19: "Consecrated for Service" (Leviticus 8:1-13)

LESSON 8   July 26, 2009

GOD CALLS PEOPLE TO JUBILEE

DEVOTIONAL READING: **Matthew 18:21-35**
PRINT PASSAGE: **Leviticus 25:8-21, 23-24**

BACKGROUND SCRIPTURE: **Leviticus 25:8-24**
KEY VERSE: **Leviticus 25:10**

Leviticus 25:8-21, 23-24—KJV

8 And thou shalt number seven sabbaths of years unto thee, seven times seven years; and the space of the seven sabbaths of years shall be unto thee forty and nine years.

9 Then shalt thou cause the trumpet of the jubile to sound on the tenth day of the seventh month, in the day of atonement shall ye make the trumpet sound throughout all your land.

10 And ye shall hallow the fiftieth year, and proclaim liberty throughout all the land unto all the inhabitants thereof: it shall be a jubile unto you; and ye shall return every man unto his possession, and ye shall return every man unto his family.

11 A jubile shall that fiftieth year be unto you: ye shall not sow, neither reap that which groweth of itself in it, nor gather the grapes in it of thy vine undressed.

12 For it is the jubile; it shall be holy unto you: ye shall eat the increase thereof out of the field.

13 In the year of this jubile ye shall return every man unto his possession.

14 And if thou sell ought unto thy neighbour, or buyest ought of thy neighbour's hand, ye shall not oppress one another:

15 According to the number of years after the jubile thou shalt buy of thy neighbour, and according unto the number of years of the fruits he shall sell unto thee:

16 According to the multitude of years thou shalt increase the price thereof, and according to the fewness of years thou shalt diminish the price of it: for according to the number of the years of the fruits doth he sell unto thee.

17 Ye shall not therefore oppress one another; but thou shalt fear thy God: for I am the LORD your God.

18 Wherefore ye shall do my statutes, and keep my judgments, and do them; and ye shall dwell in the land in safety.

19 And the land shall yield her fruit, and ye shall eat your fill, and dwell therein in safety.

Leviticus 25:8-21, 23-24—NRSV

8 You shall count off seven weeks of years, seven times seven years, so that the period of seven weeks of years gives forty-nine years.

9 Then you shall have the trumpet sounded loud; on the tenth day of the seventh month—on the day of atonement—you shall have the trumpet sounded throughout all your land.

10 And you shall hallow the fiftieth year and you shall proclaim liberty throughout the land to all its inhabitants. It shall be a jubilee for you: you shall return, every one of you, to your property and every one of you to your family.

11 That fiftieth year shall be a jubilee for you: you shall not sow, or reap the aftergrowth, or harvest the unpruned vines.

12 For it is a jubilee; it shall be holy to you: you shall eat only what the field itself produces.

13 In this year of jubilee you shall return, every one of you, to your property.

14 When you make a sale to your neighbor or buy from your neighbor, you shall not cheat one another.

15 When you buy from your neighbor, you shall pay only for the number of years since the jubilee; the seller shall charge you only for the remaining crop years.

16 If the years are more, you shall increase the price, and if the years are fewer, you shall diminish the price; for it is a certain number of harvests that are being sold to you.

17 You shall not cheat one another, but you shall fear your God; for I am the LORD your God.

18 You shall observe my statutes and faithfully keep my ordinances, so that you may live on the land securely.

19 The land will yield its fruit, and you will eat your fill and live on it securely.

The accumulation of property in the hands of a very few people means that some are wealthy while others have no chance to escape poverty. How can communities care for the poor in just ways? God gave laws for the just redistribution of wealth to provide for the poor and, thereby, to honor God, who provides all.

20 And if ye shall say, What shall we eat the seventh year? behold, we shall not sow, nor gather in our increase:
21 Then I will command my blessing upon you in the sixth year, and it shall bring forth fruit for three years.

.....

23 The land shall not be sold for ever: for the land is mine; for ye are strangers and sojourners with me.
24 And in all the land of your possession ye shall grant a redemption for the land.

20 Should you ask, "What shall we eat in the seventh year, if we may not sow or gather in our crop?"
21 I will order my blessing for you in the sixth year, so that it will yield a crop for three years.

.....

23 The land shall not be sold in perpetuity, for the land is mine; with me you are but aliens and tenants.
24 Throughout the land that you hold, you shall provide for the redemption of the land.

TOPICAL OUTLINE OF THE LESSON

I. Introduction
  A. Humanity's Avarice
  B. Biblical Background

II. Exposition and Application of the Scripture
  A. Jubilee's Meaning
     (Leviticus 25:8-12)
  B. Jubilee's Requirements and Rewards
     (Leviticus 25:13-21)
  C. The Law Guarding the Land
     (Leviticus 25:23-24)

III. Concluding Reflection

LESSON OBJECTIVES

Upon completion of this lesson, the students will know that:

1. Accumulation of property by the privileged class leads to continuous poverty in the world today;
2. The Year of Jubilee was ordered by God for redistribution of wealth;

3. The Israelites, for greediness' sake, did not observe it as it was ordered; and,
4. Greed has become an idol in the world in which we live.

POINTS TO BE EMPHASIZED
ADULT/YOUTH

Adult Topic: Spreading the Wealth
Youth Topic: Called to Be Just
Adult Key Verse: Leviticus 25:10
Youth Key Verse: Leviticus 25:17
Print Passage: Leviticus 25:8-21, 23-24

—The concept of jubilee replaced land ownership with the principle of land stewardship.
—The sabbatical year (Leviticus 25:1-7) is similar in scope to the Sabbath every week (Exodus 23:10-12).
—Obedience to jubilee laws was rewarded with peace and plentiful crops (verses 18-19).
—Sabbatical years gave rest to the poor; jubilee promised them a new start.
—In this passage, the jubilee code assumes that the land ultimately belongs to God; it cannot be sold in perpetuity.
—Every seventh year is a Sabbath year: this was the land's Sabbath; everything is to lie fallow (to rest).
—Every fiftieth year was the jubilee year: all debts were forgiven, all land was returned, and all Hebrew slaves were freed.

Children Topic: A Neighbor to Help

Key Verses: Deuteronomy 15:4-5

Print Passage: Exodus 23:10-12; Deuteronomy 15:1-11

—Laws governing the sabbatical year were made to help feed the poor.

—Laws governing the sabbatical year required canceling debts.

—Moses encouraged the people to be generous in giving to the needy neighbor, to go beyond help given on the seventh year.

—Giving liberally honors God and brings God's blessing.

I. INTRODUCTION

A. Humanity's Avarice

As humorous as it may seem, the Disney folks got it right when they released a movie called "The Lion King," whose central theme was that we are all connected in the circle of life. Every aspect of nature is somehow connected to the next, to create a perfect balance in which all nature thrives. The only glitch in the ecosystem is in human beings.

Human beings were not created to possess creation, but to care for it. Along with the responsibility to care for nature, we were also charged to care for each other. We are to nurture and cultivate our co-existence in such a way that we adhere to the sharing principles of our generous heavenly Father.

Unfortunately, human beings have a "Nimrod" mentality, which sometimes makes them think that they possess intellects superior to God's. Consequently, our civil liberties and laws often conflict with God and His principles. These conflicts have led to turmoil and the complete disruption of God's laws governing creation.

Human beings have spent centuries in pursuit of freedom, but God wants us to know that true freedom has a price. We will never be free until we understand that the true cost of freedom is obedience to God. God owns everything, but we have yet to grasp this truth, and for that reason we continue to want more of everything.

B. Biblical Background

Numbers are important in the Bible. The number *seven* is often referred to as God's number because it represents renewal or completeness. Here are some examples: God created the world in six days, and on the seventh day He rested (see Genesis 2:2); Noah was instructed to put seven of each clean animal into the Ark (see Genesis 7:2); Jacob worked seven years for Leah, and another seven years for Rachel (see Genesis 29:18-28); and in his vision on the Isle of Patmos, John saw seven stars and seven golden candlesticks (see Revelation 1:12, 16). In each of these instances, we can see that the number *seven* represents completeness.

Under the Jewish law, the Sabbatical year (see Leviticus 25:2-7) was to be a year when the land was to lie untilled and undisturbed. This seventh year gave the land a chance to replenish itself, an astonishing fact when we consider that it was long before farmers realized the wisdom of crop rotation to preserve and replenish the soil. But this was not the focus of God's Sabbatical year plan—it was simply a by-product of obedience. God used the Sabbatical year to teach His people to trust and depend on Him. In that seventh year, the Israelites had to completely depend upon God for sustenance. Covetousness was then and still is the driving force behind economics. The ban on farming heightened the importance of God's command not to covet (see Exodus 20:17). In the seventh year, the Israelites were forced to share their resources.

Biblical history records that the Israelites failed to keep the Sabbatical year during the 490-year period, and as a result, God's judgment fell on them, and they were conquered and taken into captivity by the Babylonians (see 2 Chronicles 36:21).

Beyond the Sabbatical year, God established a Year of Jubilee—the fiftieth year. Following seven cycles of the Sabbatical year, there was a great celebration called the Jubilee. The Year of Jubilee was a celebration of liberty, freedom, and redemption.

II. EXPOSITION AND APPLICATION OF THE SCRIPTURE

A. Jubilee's Meaning
(Leviticus 25:8-12)

And thou shalt number seven sabbaths of years unto thee, seven times seven years; and the space of the seven sabbaths of years shall be unto thee forty and nine years. Then shalt thou cause the trumpet of the jubile to sound on the tenth day of the seventh month, in the day of atonement shall ye make the trumpet sound throughout all your land. And ye shall hallow the fiftieth year, and proclaim liberty throughout all the land unto all the inhabitants thereof: it shall be a jubile unto you; and ye shall return every man unto his possession, and ye shall return every man unto his family. A jubile shall that fiftieth year be unto you: ye shall not sow, neither reap that which groweth of itself in it, nor gather the grapes in it of thy vine undressed. For it is the jubile; it shall be holy unto you: ye shall eat the increase thereof out of the field.

The word *Jubilee* comes from Hebrew *yobel,* which means "to be jubilant" and "to exult." The word also means "a ram's horn or trumpet." The Jubilee year was apparently announced by various horn blowers stationed within each city and tribe throughout the land. At the blowing of the horns, every person returned to his original promised and deeded land. Every debt was paid, both public and private—the slate was wiped clean, and all was new.

In the Year of Jubilee, everyone and everything was to be set free. It was a common practice to mortgage one's land or sell oneself into slavery to pay off a debt. But in the Year of Jubilee, all mortgaged land was returned to its original owner. Financial obligations were written off after a debtor's earnest six-year attempt to satisfy the debt—not as a bad debt to be hung over a person's head for ten years, as in our present bankruptcy system, but completely erased. The fiftieth year was a special year in which to proclaim liberty throughout all the land (verse 10). All obligations and enslavements due to debt were to be wiped out. But as with the Sabbatical year, the Israelites did not always obey the laws governing the Year of Jubilee (see Jeremiah 34:13-16).

The year of grand release might well never have been put fully into practice throughout the whole of Israel, as it required full ownership of all the land, and some tribes found difficulty in possessing the land (see Judges 1:27-36). But we cannot discount the fact that it might well have been put into practice in the early days in the parts which were securely taken. It was certainly expected that it would be (see Numbers 36:4). The early enthusiasm would suggest that it would be applied in the early days in those areas were it could be applied, the areas which were securely subjugated. This would be, for example, in the days of the elders who outlived Joshua (see Joshua 2:7), and even beyond in some form. We may even surmise that it was the monarchy with its ways that finally brought it to an end.

The Jubilee year is a symbol of what happens to a person who accepts Jesus Christ. When we accept Christ, we are reconciled to God and inherit the hope of the promised land of heaven. On that day of salvation, every sinner is absolved of sin's debt; the debt is cancelled, and the believer is set free.

Certainly Ezekiel saw the future in terms of it, and stressed that the true Prince to come would not break this law and trust people out of the land of their inheritance. "Thus saith the Lord GOD; If the prince give a gift unto any of his sons, the inheritance thereof shall be his sons'; it shall be their possession by inheritance. But if he give a gift of his inheritance to one of his servants, then it shall be his to the year of liberty; after it shall return to the prince: but his inheritance shall be his sons' for them. Moreover the prince shall not take of the people's inheritance by oppression, to thrust them out of their possession; but he shall give his sons inheritance out of his own possession: that my people be not scattered every man from his possession" (Ezekiel 46:16-18).

The trumpet announcing the Year of Jubilee was blown on the Day of Atonement (verse 9). On the Day of Atonement, a sacrifice for sin had to be made to God before a person was set free. Each person had to offer God an unblemished sacrifice, to be killed on the altar as a symbol of his or her repentance.

It was like the sabbatical years in that the land was to be left fallow, and in it no sowing, reaping, or organized gathering of grapes was to take place. Instead all that was in the fields and the vineyards would be open for anyone who wanted it. All could gather to their hearts' content, for the produce that year was God's.

Verse 12 reads, "For it is the jubile." Because it was the Jubilee, all that the ground yielded spontaneously during that year might be eaten. It was a free-for-all year. No people were at liberty to hoard or create a private reserve. Jubilee was a year of grand release of one form or another, with the releasing of property, bondsmen, and debts, and a period when men reverted to living off the land without labor. It was to be very special to the Israelites. It may have indicated a time of the flowing forward of God's purposes.

But humankind had a guilty and polluted conscience, which could not be cleansed by sacrificial offerings in the Temple. Even the ritual of the Day of Atonement offered only temporary relief. Only through the sacrificial blood of Jesus Christ were we permanently reconciled to God and set free from the penalty of sin, once and for all (see 1 Peter 2:24). The "once and for all" sacrifice of Jesus Christ results in permanent cleansing that empowers us to enter into the presence of God.

The Jewish Day of Atonement became our Easter, when through Christ's death and resurrection, we were saved from sin's penalty. We celebrate, not with sacrifice, but with humble thanksgiving for the gift of salvation.

It must be noted that even though we have been released from sin through the death and resurrection of Jesus Christ, sin is still running amuck. Oppression is a common practice among Christians. Laborers are being exploited. All around us we see how Christian investors are cheating their clients on a grand scale. Truly we are released, but we are in bondage to human beings.

B. Jubilee's Requirements and Rewards (Leviticus 25:13-21)

In the year of this jubile ye shall return every man unto his possession. And if thou sell ought unto thy neighbour, or buyest ought of thy neighbour's hand, ye shall not oppress one another: According to the number of years after the jubile thou shalt buy of thy neighbour, and according unto the number of years of the fruits he shall sell unto thee: According to the multitude of years thou shalt increase the price thereof, and according to the fewness of years thou shalt diminish the price of it: for according to the number of the years of the fruits doth he sell unto thee. Ye shall not therefore oppress one another; but thou shalt fear thy God: for I am the LORD your God. Wherefore ye shall do my statutes, and keep my judgments, and do them; and ye shall dwell in the land in safety. And the land shall yield her fruit, and ye shall eat your fill, and dwell therein in safety. And if ye shall say, What shall we eat the seventh year? behold, we shall not sow, nor gather in our increase: Then I will command my blessing upon you in the sixth year, and it shall bring forth fruit for three years.

The Year of Jubilee was a year of release from all kinds of debt. The poor were to be released from servitude and enjoy debt cancellation. The land of the poor was to be returned to them so that they could have new beginnings. It was meant to be a year of sharing. The bottom line in the Year of Jubilee was release from burden. The rich were expected to share with the poor. But unfortunately, there is no indication in the Bible that the Year of Jubilee was ever carried out. If the people of God had followed this practice faithfully, they would have been a society without permanent poverty.

Communal sharing is a foreign concept in America. Our free-enterprise system challenges each of us to fend for ourselves, and to covet as much as we can acquire in our lifetime. The idea of communal sharing can only work when people have strong ties to each other through a common interest, which is a strong vertical relationship with the Lord Jesus Christ.

In the case of the Israelites, that common interest was God. Israel, like the early church, was a community of people united in worship of the true and living God. In times of revival, the majority of Israel's citizens would have been God-fearing men and women who were earnest in obeying God's Law. The Year of Jubilee required a degree of sharing that goes against our sinful nature. Today's self-seeking population probably would not tolerate Israel's land reforms and rules governing debt resolution. Though these laws would be difficult to duplicate in our day, they can teach us the importance of curbing the tendency to allow wealth to be controlled by the few.

Communal sharing is successful as long as those in the commune share a common bond. When Israel became co-mingled with other nations, her God-given civil legislation deteriorated, and her faith was watered down by heathen influence. As Christians, we are called by God to be generous in our giving, and responsible for those among us (widows and orphans) who cannot support themselves. But our faith is watered down by civil legislation that protects every human's right to keep what belongs to him or her.

While good government should deal effectively with problems of poverty, Christians should be willing to go beyond the call of citizenship in our willingness to share our bounty with others.

C. The Law Guarding the Land
(Leviticus 25:23-24)

The land shall not be sold for ever: for the land is mine; for ye are strangers and sojourners with me. And in all the land of your possession ye shall grant a redemption for the land.

The success of any law depends upon obedience. The success of God's special blessing upon Israel was contingent upon their willingness to obey God's laws. If Israel obeyed the sabbatical and Jubilee requirements, God promised to provide ample rain, hold back pestilence, and cause their nation to flourish. This was His promise. They were to keep His statutes and His ordinances as laid down through Moses; and He in turn would ensure that the land yielded its fruit, and that they could eat to their satisfaction. It was doubly stressed that if they did these things they would dwell in safety.

But we serve a jealous God, who warned Israel, as a condition of their covenant relationship with Him, to worship no other gods. Unfortunately, despite the warnings of the prophets, Israel turned toward other gods, and God brought leanness to their land until they learned to honor the Sabbath rest (see 2 Chronicles 36:21).

What does the Year of Jubilee mean to the church of Jesus Christ in the twenty-first century? It is a concept. It reminds us that God's purposes go forward to a specific goal, a time when all will be restored and all God's people will receive the blessings that God has for them, when all will be put right. Whatever the future

holds, we need not fear, for one day we will come to the glorious Year of Jubilee—the year of restoration, the year of liberty. Daniel described it in Daniel 9:24. It is a reminder of the glorious heavenly future, a future of permanence of blessings that nothing can take away.

III. CONCLUDING REFLECTION

The Year of Jubilee revealed the love of God for all humanity, and various classes of people. It was intended to prevent accumulation of land in the hands of a few people. It was to help the underprivileged out of destitution. God did not create an inferior class to perpetually be under the hand of the privileged few—hence, the Year of Jubilee.

Jubilee guaranteed personal liberty. The fiftieth year was to be a time when liberty would be proclaimed to all the inhabitants of a country. Both the privileged and the underprivileged were protected. God knew that if wealth continued to accumulate in the hands of the few, there could be an underclass, which could eventually lead to chaos. The Year of Jubilee was a time when restitution was practiced. It was a time of fixing the price of real property (see Leviticus 25:15; compare with verses 25-28). The sad thing about it was that the Hebrews failed to practice Jubilee, and this landed them in exile (see Jeremiah 34:13-16).

In our modern society, we have (by our wickedness) created a permanent underclass. At the time of this writing, many are ready to have their homes foreclosed on, many are jobless, and the price of gas is rising beyond the reach of the underclass we have created. Instead of bailing out the poor, the Federal Reserve Bank is bailing out the financial institutions. We have laid aside the wisdom of God in pursuing our personal ambitions. It may seem that God is unconcerned about this open wickedness, but at the right time He will mete out His judgment on the wicked.

God provides us with freedom that has parameters and boundaries. To some, freedom that has boundaries may seem like an oxymoron. We interpret freedom as the ability to do whatever we want.

God does not arbitrarily make up rules for us to follow. Instead, His rules flow from His perfect character, and His concern for us. They provide a source of protection for us. For every one of God's rules, there is a principle that comes from the nature of God. God is the perfect definition of love, and He will never ask us to do something just for the sake of putting another rule on the books. God's motivation is always our well-being.

The lesson today is that we can never be truly free outside of a relationship with God. We must learn to obey God and trust Him for our livelihoods. If we seek Him first, He promises to give us the necessities of life. Jesus still calls today, "Come unto me, all ye that labour and are heavy laden, and I will give you rest" (Matthew 11:28).

PRAYER

Father, we have yet to obey You as we ought. The Hebrews disobeyed, and they paid for their disobedience. Help us to obey You in all matters of our relationship with You. In Jesus' name we pray. Amen.

WORD POWER

Proclaim (Hebrew: *qara [ka-ra]*)—means to "cry out," "call out," or "proclaim." This word is found in the Key Verse, and it is cast in the perfect tense, which means the action which is announced has already been completed. The slaves from all corners of the Hebrew lands had to be notified that the Year of Jubilee had arrived. They were to come out of their servitude and reclaim their lives and enjoy peace and the abundance of God.

HOME DAILY BIBLE READINGS
(July 20-26, 2009)

God Calls People to Jubilee
MONDAY, July 20: "Jesus' Vision of Ministry" (Luke 4:14-19)
TUESDAY, July 21: "Forgiveness and Mercy" (Matthew 18:21-35)
WEDNESDAY, July 22: "Compassion and Mercy" (Luke 10:25-37)
THURSDAY, July 23: "Compassion for the Helpless" (Matthew 9:35-38)
FRIDAY, July 24: "Compassion for the Bereaved" (Luke 7:11-17)
SATURDAY, July 25: "Ministry to the Needy" (Matthew 25:31-40)
SUNDAY, July 26: "The Year of Jubilee" (Leviticus 25:8-21, 23-24)

LESSON 9

PEOPLE GRUMBLE

DEVOTIONAL READING: **Psalm 142**
PRINT PASSAGE: **Numbers 11:1-6, 10-15**

BACKGROUND SCRIPTURE: **Numbers 11**
KEY VERSES: **Numbers 11:4-6**

Numbers 11:1-6, 10-15—KJV

AND WHEN the people complained, it displeased the LORD: and the LORD heard it; and his anger was kindled; and the fire of the LORD burnt among them, and consumed them that were in the uttermost parts of the camp.

2 And the people cried unto Moses; and when Moses prayed unto the LORD, the fire was quenched.

3 And he called the name of the place Taberah: because the fire of the LORD burnt among them.

4 And the mixt multitude that was among them fell a lusting: and the children of Israel also wept again, and said, Who shall give us flesh to eat?

5 We remember the fish, which we did eat in Egypt freely; the cucumbers, and the melons, and the leeks, and the onions, and the garlick:

6 But now our soul is dried away: there is nothing at all, beside this manna, before our eyes.

…..

10 Then Moses heard the people weep throughout their families, every man in the door of his tent: and the anger of the LORD was kindled greatly; Moses also was displeased.

11 And Moses said unto the LORD, Wherefore hast thou afflicted thy servant? and wherefore have I not found favour in thy sight, that thou layest the burden of all this people upon me?

12 Have I conceived all this people? have I begotten them, that thou shouldest say unto me, Carry them in thy bosom, as a nursing father beareth the sucking child, unto the land which thou swarest unto their fathers?

13 Whence should I have flesh to give unto all this people? for they weep unto me, saying, Give us flesh, that we may eat.

14 I am not able to bear all this people alone, because it is too heavy for me.

15 And if thou deal thus with me, kill me, I pray thee, out of hand, if I have found favour in thy sight; and let me not see my wretchedness.

Numbers 11:1-6, 10-15—NRSV

NOW WHEN the people complained in the hearing of the LORD about their misfortunes, the LORD heard it and his anger was kindled. Then the fire of the LORD burned against them, and consumed some outlying parts of the camp.

2 But the people cried out to Moses; and Moses prayed to the LORD, and the fire abated.

3 So that place was called Taberah, because the fire of the LORD burned against them.

4 The rabble among them had a strong craving; and the Israelites also wept again, and said, "If only we had meat to eat!

5 We remember the fish we used to eat in Egypt for nothing, the cucumbers, the melons, the leeks, the onions, and the garlic;

6 but now our strength is dried up, and there is nothing at all but this manna to look at."

…..

10 Moses heard the people weeping throughout their families, all at the entrances of their tents. Then the LORD became very angry, and Moses was displeased.

11 So Moses said to the LORD, "Why have you treated your servant so badly? Why have I not found favor in your sight, that you lay the burden of all this people on me?

12 Did I conceive all this people? Did I give birth to them, that you should say to me, 'Carry them in your bosom, as a nurse carries a sucking child,' to the land that you promised on oath to their ancestors?

13 Where am I to get meat to give to all this people? For they come weeping to me and say, 'Give us meat to eat!'

14 I am not able to carry all this people alone, for they are too heavy for me.

15 If this is the way you are going to treat me, put me to death at once—if I have found favor in your sight—and do not let me see my misery."

TOPICAL OUTLINE OF THE LESSON

I. Introduction
A. Human Nature—Grumbling
B. Biblical Background

II. Exposition and Application of the Scripture
A. Dealing with Hardships (Numbers 11:1-3)
B. Moving Forward, but Looking Back (Numbers 11:4-6)
C. The Burden of Leadership (Numbers 11:10-15)

III. Concluding Reflection

LESSON OBJECTIVES

Upon completion of this lesson, the students will know that:

1. Leaders have their weaknesses as well;
2. Human beings forget the blessings of God during difficult times; and,
3. We should always remember that God cares for us, in spite of who we are.

POINTS TO BE EMPHASIZED

ADULT/YOUTH

Adult Topic: Complaints and Cravings
Youth Topic: Can't Get No Satisfaction!
Adult/Youth Key Verses: Numbers 11:4-6
Print Passage: Numbers 11:1-6, 10-15

—Unlike previous cases of complaining (Exodus 16:2-3), this complaint had no external cause; thus, it was considered to be rebellious.
—The "fire of the Lord" is a sign of God's presence (Exodus 3:2) and of God's judgment (Numbers 16:35).
—When the people cried to Moses (Numbers 11:2), he assumed the role of intercessor and prayed to God.
—Unlike in Exodus 16, the peoples' complaint is not a lack of food, but their disgust with manna; thus, it was a rejection of God's providence.
—The liberated but wandering people begin to complain that they were better off when they were enslaved in Egypt.
—The people named foods that they had eaten in Egypt, but they seemed to have forgotten that they did so as slaves.

CHILDREN

Children Topic: People Forget to Be Thankful
Key Verse: Psalm 103:2
Print Passage: Numbers 11:4-14, 16-18

—Some of the people complained because they had a craving for food other than manna.
—The people compared the variety of diet they had in Egypt to the sameness of the manna in the desert.
—They forgot that manna was a special provision of God to them.

—In the face of their difficulties, the Israelites forgot how God had already blessed them.

—God provided Moses with elders to help bear the burden of the people.

—Although the people's complaint angered the Lord, God gave the people meat.

I. INTRODUCTION

A. Human Nature—Grumbling

With the journey of the Israelites beginning again after their stay in Sinai, the grumbling of the people started all over again (see Exodus 16:1-12; 17:1-3). The way was unquestionably difficult, to say the least. The sun was beaming down on them incessantly; the wilderness was characteristically dry, and the desert road was definitely not suitable for such a large group of travelers. Given the way that many people react to adversity, it was not long before murmuring and grumbling raised their ugly heads. As so often happens, the Israelites' eyes were not on God, but on the uncomfortable conditions that they experienced along the journey. As they struggled through the sweltering and oppressive heat with no real end in sight, they began to feel sorry for themselves, and to think that deliverance was not all it was cracked up to be. In the midst of their troubles, God brought home a powerful message which contrasted with their desire for earthly gratification and His willingness to provide the Spirit for both comfort and guidance.

We are often frustrated when life does not go as planned. We even go so far as to blame God when bad things happen to us. But bad things do happen to God's people. Jesus affirmed that when He said, "In the world ye shall have tribulation" (John 16:33).

It is not what happens to us, but how we react to what happens that defines who we are. Two people may experience the same circumstances in life; one may fall apart at the seams and end up destitute and destroyed, while the other may be inspired by the challenge, and overcome all odds.

As believers, God wants us to know that our strength to overcome comes from Him. It is His gift to every believer. The Word is filled with examples of men and women who overcame great obstacles by tapping into the power of a perfect relationship with the Lord. Samson tore down a building with his bare hands—using God's power; Daniel defeated lions—using God's power; Paul escaped from prison—through God's power. In each instance, these men were victorious over great odds because they trusted in God.

B. Biblical Background

Rebellion was the enemy of the Israelites. A study of their wilderness journey from Egypt to the Promised Land reveals that, had it not been for their continual mutiny against God, they could have spared themselves a great deal of heartache.

This time the complaint focused on their diet: manna—a plant-like substance that fell from heaven daily. There was little available to eat in the desert plains of Paran. The nearest Hebrew word for "wilderness"—*midhbar*—suggests that it was a place that was only good for driving cattle. No crops could flourish among the rocks and sand, and the area it encompassed was known as *tsiyyah*—the land of drought. There were numerous demonstrations of God's goodness, from the sweetening of the bitter waters at Marah to the provision of the manna and quail buffets in Paran. But the Israelites were never able to fully trust God in spite of His faithfulness to them. Consequently, their wilderness journey, which would have taken approximately forty days, lasted for forty years.

II. EXPOSITION AND APPLICATION OF THE SCRIPTURE

A. Dealing with Hardships
(Numbers 11:1-3)

AND WHEN the people complained, it displeased the Lord: and the Lord heard it; and his anger was kindled; and the fire of the Lord burnt among them, and consumed them that were in the uttermost parts of the camp. And the people cried unto Moses; and when Moses prayed unto the Lord, the fire was quenched. And he called the name of the place Taberah: because the fire of the Lord burnt among them.

The Israelites were complaining and murmuring about the hardships of the wilderness. They had been encamped at the base of Mount Sinai for eleven months awaiting God's instruction, and now they were just three days into their journey to the Promised Land when they began to grumble about the hardships. Some began to say that if God had chosen their pathway, He would have made it easier. They were so gripped by a spirit of dissatisfaction that they developed a critical demeanor and pressed Moses for a resolution. It did not matter that the Lord Himself had provided a heavenly substance called *manna* to sustain them on their journey. This was not the life they had envisioned when they left Egypt. Their new challenges seemed to be just as hard as the taskmaster's whip. And they blamed God.

We seldom see God as capable of anger toward us, but He is. When His anger is kindled, He takes action directed not just at reprimand or chastisement, but to demonstrate His power and bring us back into alignment with His will. When the Lord heard the grumbling from the Israelites, He ignited a fire on the outskirts of their camp. The Israelites immediately cried out to Moses for help. The Lord heard their prayer and extinguished the fire. Moses named the place *Taberah*, which means "burning," and he marked it as a place of awful judgment and a warning for the future: God judges those who complain and murmur against Him because of hardships.

Complaining about hardship is a sign of carnality and spiritual immaturity. Carnal hearts are incapable of riding out a storm with God because they focus only on the physical. Immature believers very quickly lose sight of their faith's directives when presented with challenges. This was the sin of Israel. Time and again they failed to trust God to sustain them and bring them through their storms.

When we complain, we reveal our unbelief and our lack of trust in God's power to work the situation out and resolve the hardship. If we truly trust God, we will pray to Him when hardships come, and ask for His help. When the Israelites faced hardship, they grumbled, not just against God, but against their leadership. Trusting hearts never complain against God or His servants (see Philippians 2:14).

We may see this as an act of grace. By acting quickly the people had been made to think so that they would be more careful in the future. As we have learned, in the past they had a tendency to grumble, so this was not the first time. God had to deal with their behavior since the journey from Sinai began.

B. Moving Forward, but Looking Back (Numbers 11:4-6)

And the mixt multitude that was among them fell a lusting: and the children of Israel also wept again, and said, Who shall give us flesh to eat? We remember the fish, which we did eat in Egypt freely; the cucumbers, and the melons, and the leeks, and the onions, and the garlick: But now our soul is dried away: there is nothing at all, beside this manna, before our eyes.

The Israelites complained and grumbled about the food God had provided for them. Throughout the Old Testament, the imagery of eating signifies the presence and promises of God. During the entire wilderness journey, God rained down manna on the Israelites every day (see Exodus 16). As the Israelites gathered the manna each morning and ate it, it reminded them of God's presence among them. But the promise of "a land flowing with milk and honey" was always foremost in their minds, and it came to symbolize the richness of what lay ahead for them. Because they could almost "taste" that promise, it was not long before they expressed their discontent with the manna.

In the midst of difficulty, it is natural to reflect on a time of peace and contentment. But we should never permit our nostalgic reflections to turn into an obsession with the past. The Israelites became so weighed down by their own discontent that they began to live in the past and to desire to return to their old ways. The phrase "This manna" (verse 6) is one of contempt—an attitude that would peak years later (see 21:5).

There is always a troublesome minority among all people. In the Israelites' case these were the ones who started the complaints and stirred up the people, so that dissatisfaction soon spread and clearly deeply upset a people already traumatized by the conditions under which they were traveling. It had caught them unprepared, even though God had tried to prepare them. The stronger were undermining the weaker. We must all be careful when we begin to murmur that we do not undermine the faith of others in the congregation. Those of us who are strong, the Bible says, should bear the burdens of those who are weak (see Romans 15:1), not undermine them and cause a spirit of confusion within the church.

But the Israelite malcontents could not have succeeded if Israel had been looking to God; in essence they simply lost sight of God and the things of the Spirit. While the Israelites mentioned "Who shall give us flesh to eat?" they were thinking more about a change of diet, as their list of the pleasures of Egypt brought out. In their list they did not actually mention meat, but fish and vegetables. The manna was regarded by the Israelites as monotonous, something that caused the inner being to be dried up. What they really wanted was something different from manna. It is true that they could have eaten their cattle and sheep, but they were reluctant to do that when they were not actually starving. Those animals were necessary for the future. A different diet was not essential. They had the manna to keep them alive. But what they wanted were delicacies and a change of diet. It is interesting to note their contemptuous dismissal of "this manna" (verse 6). When they had been starving, they had delighted in it. Now God had in His providence seen fit to keep their stomachs full, and they still were not satisfied. They were lacking, as many do, in appreciation and gratitude: the enjoyment of food had become more important to them than appreciating what God had given them.

This is a classic struggle of the flesh against the spirit. Had their hearts been set on and satisfied with God, the Israelites would have rejoiced to receive the manna from His hands. They would have been full of joy continually. But greed for delicious food was so strong that they wept.

Bible students have often asked the question, "How could the Israelites have become discontent so quickly, after witnessing God's great power just a few short days previously at Taberah?" We are left shocked, and wondering how people could be so earthly minded and unbelieving, given their various encounters with God.

Lust and covetousness are usually stirred within from some outside influence. The Israelites' complaining was stirred up by outsiders—non-Israelites who had joined in the great Exodus from Egypt (verse 4). They were the ones who lusted for the provisions of Egypt. And they soon convinced the Israelites of the need to give up a desert life with God for the multiplicity of Egypt's storehouse. The fact that the Israelites were so easily influenced by the mixed multitude should point to our own need to keep ourselves separated from worldly influences.

C. The Burden of Leadership
(Numbers 11:10-15)

Then Moses heard the people weep throughout their families, every man in the door of his tent: and the anger of the LORD was kindled greatly; Moses also was displeased. And Moses said unto the LORD, Wherefore hast thou afflicted thy servant? and wherefore have I not found favour in thy sight, that thou layest the burden of all this people upon me? Have I conceived all this people? have I begotten them, that thou shouldest say unto me, Carry them in thy bosom, as a nursing father beareth the sucking child, unto the land which thou swarest unto their fathers? Whence should I have flesh to give unto all this people? for they weep unto me, saying, Give us flesh, that we may eat. I am not able to bear all this people alone, because it is too heavy for me. And if thou deal thus with me, kill me, I pray thee, out of hand, if I have found favour in thy sight; and let me not see my wretchedness.

The Israelites' spirit of discontent is seen most vividly in their reference to "this manna" in verse 6. The bitter sarcasm of their complaint implied that they had lost their appetite for God! As slaves, they had known nothing but horror, yet now they were willing to relinquish their freedom for food.

Manna was not some tasteless cardboard substance. It was like coriander, a small spicy seed from the carrot family. It was gathered and crushed, then cooked into cakes. But no matter how tasty it was, they were not satisfied. The grumbling spread like fire throughout the camp, and the complaints grew to a crescendo in Moses's ears.

To what do leaders turn when their followers become unhappy? If they are God-ordained, they turn to the Lord. By his prayer to God, we see that Moses was greatly affected by the crushing unhappiness of the people. His own feeling of discouragement caused him to make some false assumptions that: 1) God had somehow orchestrated the trouble; 2) God was displeased with him; and 3) God had deliberately placed this burden on him. We learn from Moses's complaining that leaders are not immune to mumbling and murmuring.

When a burden is too heavy, a leader takes it to God, often in desperation. Moses's burden was so great that he wanted to die right there on the spot. But if we read further in the chapter, we find that God answered Moses's prayer and relieved the pressure by instructing him to appoint seventy men to aid in administration. The enormous weight of the ministry was lifted. When God's leaders call, He answers.

Moses was instructed by God to select seventy elders of Israel, men whom he knew to be true and reliable elders, to become officers over the Israelites. He was to bring them to the Tent of Meeting so that they might stand there with Moses before God as those who would be Moses's assistants. They were to be endued with gifts in order to perform the supervisory tasks that up to this time had been borne by Moses alone.

III. CONCLUDING REFLECTION

As mature Christians, we must learn to differentiate between what we want and what we really need. It is affirmed in Psalm 46:1 that "God is our refuge and strength, a very present help in trouble." But that statement remains mere words unless each believer puts his or her faith to the test and learns to trust God.

Discontentment is a lack of faith in God's love and concern for us. When we express discontent, we are suggesting that God has somehow lost control, or that He does not care. The apostle Paul had a resolute faith that allowed him to say, "I can do all things through Christ which strengtheneth me" (Philippians 4:13) and "My God shall supply all your need according to his riches in glory by Christ Jesus" (Philippians 4:19). Like Paul, we must learn to trust God completely, in spite of our circumstances and surroundings.

PRAYER

Father, we are thankful for Your love. We are sorry for looking back over our lives and failing to realize that the best is ahead of us. Help us to continue to lean on You. In Jesus' name we pray. Amen.

WORD POWER

Remember (Hebrew: *Zakar [za-kar]*)—is "to remember," "to recall," and "to bring to the conscious level." The action (to remember) is in the perfect tense, which means that the Israelites had thought it out and reached a final conclusion: their lives in Egypt were far better than what they were experiencing at the time of the writing of this text.

HOME DAILY BIBLE READINGS
(July 6–August 2, 2009)

People Grumble

MONDAY, July 27: "Give Heed to My Cry" (Psalm 142)
TUESDAY, July 28: "A Test of Obedience" (Exodus 16:1-12)
WEDNESDAY, July 29: "Living Bread" (John 6:41-51)
THURSDAY, July 30: "Complaining and Turning Back" (John 6:60-68)
FRIDAY, July 31: "An Example to Instruct Us" (1 Corinthians 10:1-11)
SATURDAY, August 1: "Faith, Love, and Mercy" (Jude 1:14-23)
SUNDAY, August 2: "Complaining About Hardships" (Numbers 11:1-6, 10-15)

LESSON 10   August 9, 2009

PEOPLE REBEL

DEVOTIONAL READING: **Psalm 78:5-17**
PRINT PASSAGE: **Numbers 14:1-12**

BACKGROUND SCRIPTURE: **Numbers 14:1-25**
KEY VERSE: **Numbers 14:3**

Numbers 14:1-12—KJV

AND ALL the congregation lifted up their voice, and cried; and the people wept that night.

2 And all the children of Israel murmured against Moses and against Aaron: and the whole congregation said unto them, Would God that we had died in the land of Egypt! or would God we had died in this wilderness!

3 And wherefore hath the LORD brought us unto this land, to fall by the sword, that our wives and our children should be a prey? were it not better for us to return into Egypt?

4 And they said one to another, Let us make a captain, and let us return into Egypt.

5 Then Moses and Aaron fell on their faces before all the assembly of the congregation of the children of Israel.

6 And Joshua the son of Nun, and Caleb the son of Jephunneh, which were of them that searched the land, rent their clothes:

7 And they spake unto all the company of the children of Israel, saying, The land, which we passed through to search it, is an exceeding good land.

8 If the LORD delight in us, then he will bring us into this land, and give it us; a land which floweth with milk and honey.

9 Only rebel not ye against the LORD, neither fear ye the people of the land; for they are bread for us: their defence is departed from them, and the LORD is with us: fear them not.

10 But all the congregation bade stone them with stones. And the glory of the LORD appeared in the tabernacle of the congregation before all the children of Israel.

11 And the LORD said unto Moses, How long will this people provoke me? and how long will it be ere they believe me, for all the signs which I have shewed among them?

12 I will smite them with the pestilence, and disinherit them, and will make of thee a greater nation and mightier than they.

Numbers 14:1-12—NRSV

THEN ALL the congregation raised a loud cry, and the people wept that night.

2 And all the Israelites complained against Moses and Aaron; the whole congregation said to them, "Would that we had died in the land of Egypt! Or would that we had died in this wilderness!

3 Why is the LORD bringing us into this land to fall by the sword? Our wives and our little ones will become booty; would it not be better for us to go back to Egypt?"

4 So they said to one another, "Let us choose a captain, and go back to Egypt."

5 Then Moses and Aaron fell on their faces before all the assembly of the congregation of the Israelites.

6 And Joshua son of Nun and Caleb son of Jephunneh, who were among those who had spied out the land, tore their clothes

7 and said to all the congregation of the Israelites, "The land that we went through as spies is an exceedingly good land.

8 If the LORD is pleased with us, he will bring us into this land and give it to us, a land that flows with milk and honey.

9 Only, do not rebel against the LORD; and do not fear the people of the land, for they are no more than bread for us; their protection is removed from them, and the LORD is with us; do not fear them."

10 But the whole congregation threatened to stone them. Then the glory of the LORD appeared at the tent of meeting to all the Israelites.

11 And the LORD said to Moses, "How long will this people despise me? And how long will they refuse to believe in me, in spite of all the signs that I have done among them?

12 I will strike them with pestilence and disinherit them, and I will make of you a nation greater and mightier than they."

UNIFYING LESSON PRINCIPLE

When dissatisfaction grows great, people may rebel against their leaders and benefactors. What leads people to rebel against leadership and authority? The deprivation of the Israelites and the threats of destruction at the hand of others led the Israelites to seek new leadership and a return to Egypt.

TOPICAL OUTLINE OF THE LESSON

I. **Introduction**
   A. Thorough Repentance
   B. Biblical Background

II. **Exposition and Application of the Scripture**
   A. Israel's Fatal Mistake (Numbers 14:1-5)
   B. Joshua and Caleb's Plea for Courage (Numbers 14:6-9)
   C. God's Anger and Moses's Plea (Numbers 14:10-12)

III. **Concluding Reflection**

LESSON OBJECTIVES

Upon completion of this lesson, the students will know that:

1. Dissatisfaction is the root of rebellion;
2. Rebellion incurs God's anger; and,
3. God is always ready to receive those who truly repent and turn to Him.

POINTS TO BE EMPHASIZED

ADULT/YOUTH

Adult Topic: Dissatisfaction Leads to Rebellion
Youth Topic: Let's Rebel!
Adult Key Verse: Numbers 14:3
Youth Key Verses: Numbers 14:3-4
Print Passage: Numbers 14:1-12

—People accuse God of evil motives in bringing them into the wilderness.
—The complaint leveled against God (verse 3) became the judgment of God on the people (see verses 28-45).
—Going "back to Egypt" is equivalent to rebellion against God.
—Joshua and Caleb saw Canaan as an opportunity for success, and the ten spies saw it as a threat of annihilation.
—In this text, the Israelites' complaining was, in fact, rebellion against God.
—In rebellion, the people wanted to choose their own leader over Moses—whom God had chosen.

CHILDREN

Children Topic: The People Won't Go
Key Verses: Numbers 14:3-4
Print Passage: Numbers 14:1-10, 19-20

—The Israelites thought a return to slavery in Egypt would be better than facing possible death in the Promised Land.
—Joshua and Caleb tried to persuade them that the odds were in their favor with God on their side.
—The people's fear led to rebellion, inability to see reason, and even hostility against those who tried to change their minds.
—Moses interceded for the people with a plea to God for forgiveness for their rebellion.

I. INTRODUCTION

A. Thorough Repentance

Charles Spurgeon wrote: "Repentance is not a thing of days and weeks…to be got over as fast as possible. No, it is the grace of a lifetime, like faith itself." *Repentance* is perpetual or ongoing. A true believer's repentance never reaches the point of completion. It is the act of taking full responsibility for one's sins—past, present, and future. We can perhaps understand it better in light of David's confession: "I acknowledged my sin unto thee, and mine iniquity have I not hid" (Psalm 32:5a). David did not make excuses for his sin or complain to God that he was "only human." He never accused Bathsheba of provoking his sin, nor did he ever mention her name in his confession. David understood that he alone committed the sin. He owned up to his sin.

We learn from this biblical account that there is a limit to God's patience. If we continue to taint our faith relationships with disobedience and unrepentant hearts, God will cancel the blessings He has in store for us. Thorough repentance and a plea for a right spirit within should be the goal of all Christians.

B. Biblical Background

A spirit of negativism can destroy a person, or even a nation. It certainly destroyed the Israelites, who began a forty-year journey with the hope of reaching the Promised Land. Nine times God had forgiven them for their discontent, doubt, and dissatisfaction; yet they continued to display unrepentant hearts.

In the preceding chapter, Moses sent twelve men on a spy mission to survey the land promised by God and assess its inhabitants. The result was that ten came back with a negative report, and two came back with a positive report.

The deeply rooted negative attitude of the ten spies spread quickly throughout the Israelite camp, and led to rebellion and a rejection of the truth brought by the remaining two spies, Caleb and Joshua. Galatians 5:9 reads: "A little leaven leaveneth the whole lump." The negative attitude of the ten spies had a quick effect on the entire congregation. The fundamental problem with Israel was their negative, defeatist, fearful, unbelieving attitude. And the result was tragic: they rebelled against God and His servant Moses.

II. EXPOSITION AND APPLICATION OF THE SCRIPTURE

A. Israel's Fatal Mistake
(Numbers 14:1-5)

AND ALL the congregation lifted up their voice, and cried; and the people wept that night. And all the children of Israel murmured against Moses and against Aaron: and the whole congregation said unto them, Would God that we had died in the land of Egypt! or would God we had died in this wilderness! And wherefore hath the LORD brought us unto this land, to fall by the sword, that our wives and our children should be a prey? were it not better for us to

return into Egypt? And they said one to another, Let us make a captain, and let us return into Egypt. Then Moses and Aaron fell on their faces before all the assembly of the congregation of the children of Israel.

Before we launch into the exposition of this passage, we should examine a few phrases from the entire text in order to shed light on the lesson. Verse 1 reads: "And all the congregation lifted up their voice." Why did this involve the entire congregation? The evil report brought by the ten spies took little time to spread. It was like an aggressive cancer which claims its victim in a very short time. The people had forgotten what God had done just a short time before, when the firstborn of all the Egyptians died, including domestic animals. No community was spared among the Egyptians when the death angel visited Egypt. A little disappointment in our lives can easily lead to the forgetfulness of God's goodness if we choose to not pay attention to His interventions in our lives.

The Israelites were forgetful to the point of saying, "Would God we had died in this wilderness!" Did they really want to die? They looked for instant death by saying "this wilderness"; in other words, they were not ready to depart from their present location. Death was preferable to God's intervention. They knew it was God who brought them this far, but now they were unable to provide for their needs. We too have ways by which we deny the presence of God. How many times have we forgotten to say a simple "Thank You" for what we have received? Many who have been in leadership roles have laid down their arms because it seemed things were not going the way they expected.

Following the negative reports of the ten spies, the people wept all night. They described the land as evil, even though God had told them it was "flowing with milk and honey." Such a report showed contempt for God. It brought out doubt and negative reactions from the people. The people had lost hope in their dreams about better lives ahead. They grumbled against Moses and Aaron, and believed they would be better off going back to Egypt. The worst they did was to think that God would bring them to a place where they would all die—men, women, and children.

A negative attitude is often the result of our refusal to face the truth. In the case of the Israelites, their grumbling was born out of their refusal to trust the truth of God's promises, in spite of how things looked. The scriptural record places great emphasis on the people's unbelief as being the root cause of the rebellion. Notice that it states "all the people," "all the Israelites," and "the whole assembly" was guilty of this great skepticism. Not a single person was willing to trust God and believe that He could lead them into the Promised Land.

Discontent leads to dissatisfaction. The first two things we lose when we become dissatisfied are peace and joy. But the Bible teaches us that peace and joy are two of the fruits of the Holy Spirit. If we lose our peace and joy when our circumstances turn sour, the peace and joy we previously experienced were not fruits of the Spirit to begin with—they were just the fruits of circumstance.

Real contentment hinges on what is happening *inside* us rather than around us. As long as we blame our circumstances for our lack of contentment, we are missing the opportunity to find real peace. When circumstances rob us of our peace, as they did the Israelites, we must take responsibility and admit that we are looking to what we cannot control to provide us with our contentment.

The nation of Israel's peace and joy were tied to the comforts of living, rather than the knowledge that God was their rich benefactor whom they could trust to supply all their needs. And so they railed against Moses and Aaron, and accused the Lord of forsaking their families. They threatened to choose a new leader who would lead them back to Egypt. They were completely forgetful of God's power. And the more they complained, the greater the crescendo in Moses's ears.

Moses and Aaron did the only thing they could do—they fell on their faces before the people, cried out to the Lord, and asked for deliverance through God's power and intervention.

B. Joshua and Caleb's Plea for Courage (Numbers 14:6-9)

And Joshua the son of Nun, and Caleb the son of Jephunneh, which were of them that searched the land, rent their clothes: And they spake unto all the company of the children of Israel, saying, The land, which we passed through to search it, is an exceeding good land. If the Lord delight in us, then he will bring us into this land, and give it us; a land which floweth with milk and honey. Only rebel not ye against the Lord, neither fear ye the people of the land; for they are bread for us: their defence is departed from them, and the Lord is with us: fear them not.

Joshua and Caleb's response contrasted remarkably with the foolish terror of the people. In ritualistic fashion, they "rent" or tore their clothes as a symbol of mourning. They too wept, but for the sins of the people, and declared two truths before the grumbling Israelites: 1) the Lord would lead His people into the Promised Land if they would obey Him; and 2) the people must not be afraid of the inhabitants of the land.

Joshua and Caleb were the perfect examples of having peace and joy from within. They knew that God, their perfect heavenly Father, knew exactly what this young nation needed, and would not fail to provide for that need. Still, it took great courage to stand before an entire nation, look into their angry faces, and declare this truth. The crowd was so very out of control that they threatened to stone Joshua and Caleb. So they pleaded with them not to rebel against God nor to fear the people of the land. Against God the people of the land would have no defense; their defense was removed. Their protective shadow was gone. Rather than the land eating up its inhabitants, they would be eaten up by the Israelites. Defeating them would be as easy as eating bread.

This parallel of killing people by eating bread is found elsewhere in the Scriptures. The psalmist spoke of those "who eat up my people as they eat bread" (Psalm 14:4), and Micah described the unjust rulers of Israel as those "Who hate the good, and love the evil...Who also eat the flesh of my people" (Micah 3:2, 3). Thus, we see that "eating flesh" or "eating people" signified killing them or doing them great harm. In the same way, Joshua and Caleb saw the task of defeating the people in Canaan as being as simple as eating bread when they had God's power with them.

Let us ponder on these two wise men—Joshua and Caleb. They encouraged people to act on God's promise and move ahead into the Promised Land. The people violently refused their advice and were ready to stone them. Do not be irrational to reject advice you do not like. Take time to ponder it carefully, comparing it to the revealed truth in the Word of God. The advice may be from God. Never allow your emotions to attach themselves to your *wants*, or your complaining could end up sounding like that of the Israelites.

C. God's Anger and Moses's Plea
(Numbers 14:10-12)

But all the congregation bade stone them with stones. And the glory of the Lᴏʀᴅ appeared in the tabernacle of the congregation before all the children of Israel. And the Lᴏʀᴅ said unto Moses, How long will this people provoke me? and how long will it be ere they believe me, for all the signs which I have shewed among them? I will smite them with the pestilence, and disinherit them, and will make of thee a greater nation and mightier than they.

The words of Joshua and Caleb stirred up two reactions—one from the people, and the other from God. The congregation wanted to stone their leaders, and there was a sudden appearance of God's glory to save His faithful leaders. God can only take so much rebellion before we force Him to act. His anger was so greatly kindled against Israel that His glory burst forth in the tabernacle. The Lord had been provoked.

In order for God to become angry, He first had to *care for* His ambassadors. Caring always precedes confrontation. Parents become angry when their children are disobedient because they care about their children's welfare and well-being. There is a limit to how much disobedience they will tolerate before they take disciplinary action. It is the same with our relationship with God. He cares about the impact of our disobedience. He wants to teach us His ways, so that we will not suffer the ramifications or consequences of our ways. Just as parents (who have had to administer tough love) will admit, there is a limit to how much rebellion God will tolerate.

Have you ever thought about what provokes God's anger? We get angry over the simplest of things—a traffic jam, a car that will not start, a child who's late for dinner, the cancellation of our favorite TV program, or an unkind word. But God's anger is never so superficial. God's anger is rooted in righteousness; it is always justified.

God is angered by chronic disobedience and rebellion. He may be loving and forgiving, but there is a limit to His tolerance! Just as submission paves the way to blessings, disobedience leads to destruction. God will withdraw His hand of protection from those who rebel against His will.

God threatened to destroy the Israelites with a plague and to create a new race of people who would obey Him. But Moses pleaded with God on behalf of the people, saying that the world would learn of their disobedience and God's own reputation and character would be at stake. Moses feared that the Canaanites, who had already heard of the Israelites' great deliverance from Egypt, would question the power and promises of God to His people if God now destroyed Israel. Then Moses reminded God that He was loving and forgiving; that was the part of Moses's intercessory prayer that changed God's plan. God would not destroy Israel; He would forgive them.

III. CONCLUDING REFLECTION

One of the reference points used in directing travelers through London is the Charing Cross. The cross is near the center of the city, and is used as a navigational tool for people who are confused by the streets.

A little girl was lost in the great city of London. A policeman found her, and between her sobs and cries she explained that she did not know her way back home. She did not know her address, or her last name, or her phone number. But when the policeman asked her what she did know, her face lit up. "I know the cross! Show me the cross and I will know which way I have to turn to get home."

The Cross must be the turning point in our lives, if we are to follow our God-ordained paths. If we provoke God with continual disobedience, we will miss the opportunity to experience the fullness of what He has planned for us. Our Promised Land is directly tied to our submission to God's will and our reverence to Him as the Lord of our lives.

Rebellion is as old as the first man created by God. As a matter of fact, rebellion started from heaven. Satan saw himself as a powerful and beautiful angel and he rebelled against God, but God would and will not tolerate rebellion. The prophet Ezekiel said of Satan, the first rebel, "Thou hast been in Eden the garden of God...Thou art the anointed cherub ...Thine heart was lifted up because of thy beauty...Thou hast defiled thy sanctuaries by the multitude of thine iniquities... therefore will I bring forth a fire... it shall devour thee... thou shalt be a terror, and never shalt thou be any more" (Ezekiel 28:13, 14, 17, 18, 19).

Each of us should be careful of having a rebellious spirit. Once we sense it in our lives or in our children, we must stand up against it.

PRAYER

Father in heaven, help us to realize that even though the cloud over us is thick, yet Your hands are able to pull it back. Help us to enjoy our deliverance from the evil one and help us to be faithful to You. In Jesus' name we pray. Amen.

WORD POWER

Return (Hebrew: *shuwb [shub]*)—is "to return," or "turn back." This word is loaded with meaning. It is an action of the will to return to serve a lesser god. The Hebrews, in essence, were rebelling against their God. They were ready to apostatize, or renounce, their faith. The God who emancipated them from the clutches of Pharaoh had become *Deus absconditus* ("the hidden, or unknown, God").

HOME DAILY BIBLE READINGS
(August 3-9, 2009)

People Rebel

MONDAY, August 3: "Rebelling Against God" (Psalm 78:5-17)

TUESDAY, August 4: "Reaping the Whirlwind" (Hosea 8:1-10)

WEDNESDAY, August 5: "An Offering for Transgression?" (Micah 6:1-8)

THURSDAY, August 6: "Mourning for Our Rebellion" (Lamentations 1:16-21)

FRIDAY, August 7: "Return to the Lord" (Lamentations 3:39-50)

SATURDAY, August 8: "A Compassionate God" (Micah 7:14-20)

SUNDAY, August 9: "Go Back to Egypt?" (Numbers 14:1-12)

LESSON 11   August 16, 2009

MOSES DISOBEYS

DEVOTIONAL READING: **Psalm 95**
PRINT PASSAGE: **Numbers 20:1-13**

BACKGROUND SCRIPTURE: **Numbers 20:1-13**
KEY VERSE: **Numbers 20:12**

Numbers 20:1-13—KJV

THEN CAME the children of Israel, even the whole congregation, into the desert of Zin in the first month: and the people abode in Kadesh; and Miriam died there, and was buried there.
2 And there was no water for the congregation: and they gathered themselves together against Moses and against Aaron.
3 And the people chode with Moses, and spake, saying, Would God that we had died when our brethren died before the LORD!
4 And why have ye brought up the congregation of the LORD into this wilderness, that we and our cattle should die there?
5 And wherefore have ye made us to come up out of Egypt, to bring us in unto this evil place? it is no place of seed, or of figs, or of vines, or of pomegranates; neither is there any water to drink.
6 And Moses and Aaron went from the presence of the assembly unto the door of the tabernacle of the congregation, and they fell upon their faces: and the glory of the LORD appeared unto them.
7 And the LORD spake unto Moses, saying,
8 Take the rod, and gather thou the assembly together, thou, and Aaron thy brother, and speak ye unto the rock before their eyes; and it shall give forth his water, and thou shalt bring forth to them water out of the rock: so thou shalt give the congregation and their beasts drink.
9 And Moses took the rod from before the LORD, as he commanded him.
10 And Moses and Aaron gathered the congregation together before the rock, and he said unto them, Hear now, ye rebels; must we fetch you water out of this rock?
11 And Moses lifted up his hand, and with his rod he smote the rock twice: and the water came out abundantly, and the congregation drank, and their beasts also.

Numbers 20:1-13—NRSV

THE ISRAELITES, the whole congregation, came into the wilderness of Zin in the first month, and the people stayed in Kadesh. Miriam died there, and was buried there.
2 Now there was no water for the congregation; so they gathered together against Moses and against Aaron.
3 The people quarreled with Moses and said, "Would that we had died when our kindred died before the LORD!
4 Why have you brought the assembly of the LORD into this wilderness for us and our livestock to die here?
5 Why have you brought us up out of Egypt, to bring us to this wretched place? It is no place for grain, or figs, or vines, or pomegranates; and there is no water to drink."
6 Then Moses and Aaron went away from the assembly to the entrance of the tent of meeting; they fell on their faces, and the glory of the LORD appeared to them.
7 The LORD spoke to Moses, saying:
8 Take the staff, and assemble the congregation, you and your brother Aaron, and command the rock before their eyes to yield its water. Thus you shall bring water out of the rock for them; thus you shall provide drink for the congregation and their livestock.
9 So Moses took the staff from before the LORD, as he had commanded him.
10 Moses and Aaron gathered the assembly together before the rock, and he said to them, "Listen, you rebels, shall we bring water for you out of this rock?"
11 Then Moses lifted up his hand and struck the rock twice with his staff; water came out abundantly, and the congregation and their livestock drank.

UNIFYING LESSON PRINCIPLE

Even great leaders may fail to heed higher authority. Why do people disregard authority? Moses disobeyed God because he did not trust God to provide for the people.

12 And the LORD spake unto Moses and Aaron, Because ye believed me not, to sanctify me in the eyes of the children of Israel, therefore ye shall not bring this congregation into the land which I have given them.

13 This is the water of Meribah; because the children of Israel strove with the LORD, and he was sanctified in them.

12 But the LORD said to Moses and Aaron, "Because you did not trust in me, to show my holiness before the eyes of the Israelites, therefore you shall not bring this assembly into the land that I have given them."

13 These are the waters of Meribah, where the people of Israel quarreled with the LORD, and by which he showed his holiness.

TOPICAL OUTLINE
OF THE LESSON

I. **Introduction**
   A. Challenge of Leadership
   B. Biblical Background

II. **Exposition and Application of the Scripture**
   A. Miriam's Death in Zin (Numbers 20:1)
   B. The Sin of the People (Numbers 20:2-5)
   C. The Disobedience to God's Directive (Numbers 20:6-13)

III. **Concluding Reflection**

LESSON OBJECTIVES

Upon completion of this lesson, the students will know that:

1. Leaders are accountable to God for their overt and covert actions;

2. Spiritual leaders must guard their inward and outward thoughts and behaviors; and,

3. Disobedience to God's directives leads to unfulfilled missions in life.

POINTS TO BE EMPHASIZED
ADULT/YOUTH

Adult Topic: Disregarding the Directive
Youth Topic: Less than Your Best
Adult/Youth Key Verse: Numbers 20:12
Print Passage: Numbers 20:1-13

—Moses's failure to follow God's directive denied his and Aaron's entrance into the Promised Land.

—Partial obedience (compare verse 8 with verses 9-11) is the same as disobedience.

—Despite the care God had provided, the people continued to grumble over each new problem that arose, doubting God's care.

—Following God's directions, Moses and Aaron obtained water for the people and flocks in a miraculous way—but one for which Moses and Aaron did not give God the credit and glory.

—The Lord told Moses and Aaron that because of their lack of trust and their failure to show God's holiness to the people, Moses and Aaron would not lead the people into the Promised Land.

—Although the indictment against Moses is somewhat unclear, Moses appeared to accept it.

CHILDREN

Children Topic: Failure to Trust
Key Verse: Numbers 20:12
Print Passage: Numbers 20:1-13

—When the Israelites failed to find water, they continued

their habit of complaining.

— Moses and Aaron asked for God's help in locating water.

— God gave Moses detailed instructions for getting water.

— Moses and Aaron obeyed the first part of the Lord's instructions, but then they took matters into their own hands.

— Moses and Aaron did not trust God to provide water.

— Moses and Aaron found there would be serious consequences for their disobedience.

I. INTRODUCTION

A. Challenge of Leadership

Our last few lessons have dealt with the disobedience of Israel, and the resulting punishments. Disobedience never produces a positive result. But disobedience among leaders has far greater implications than with the laity.

The story is told of a man found guilty of kidnapping, who accepted Jesus Christ while in prison. Several years later, on the day of his release, he was handed a letter by another prisoner. It said, "When I came into this jail I despised all preachers, hated the Bible and everything it represented. I went to the Bible class and worship services because there wasn't anything else to do. When I saw you at the same services, I thought, there's a man who's taking the same Gospel road to early parole that I'm taking. But I watched you for five years. You didn't know it, but I watched you in the yard, and when you were working in the shop. I watched you when you played, and I watched you when you prayed. And now I am a Christian. The Savior who saved you has saved me. You never made a single slip." The released man bowed his head and thanked God that he never slipped!

If each of us is called to a special purpose, then spiritual leaders have an even greater responsibility. The continuance of our faith legacy rests on their shoulders. When leaders set a wrong example for their followers, they run the risk of generations being cursed by their error. Therefore, spiritual leadership should never be entered into lightly, but soberly and reverently, understanding the full responsibility of its call. Spiritual leaders should never be motivated by a desire for power or position. In the life of a spiritual leader, that place is reserved for God, and God alone.

B. Biblical Background

By the fortieth year of Israel's wandering in the wilderness, most of the first generation of Israelites were already deceased. Camped in and around Kadesh, on the southern border of the Promised Land of Canaan, they served out the remaining years of their forty-year sentence imposed by God—one year for each day that their tribal representatives had spent spying Canaan's land—until the entire rebellious generation died. The wilderness of Zin was another place where the Israelites lodged their complaints against God. The *King James Version* uses an archaic English word—*chode*. The word carries the idea of speaking irreverently and without regard to age and position of authority. Such words were indirectly spoken to God.

The Israelites' stay in Kadesh Barnea may have lasted as long as several months. During that period, they had plenty of time to reflect on their disobedience, and many were probably humbled by God's vivid rebuke of the nation of Israel.

II. EXPOSITION AND APPLICATION OF THE SCRIPTURE

A. Miriam's Death in Zin
(Numbers 20:1)

THEN CAME the children of Israel, even the whole congregation, into the desert of Zin in the first month: and the people abode in Kadesh; and Miriam died there, and was buried there.

The glorious day of entering the Promised Land was around the corner. Many of the Israelites who left Egypt had died, but Moses, Caleb, Joshua, and Miriam were still alive until this point. Miriam was a leader among the congregation of Israel (see Micah 6:4). It was Miriam who led the women in praise to God when their feet touched dry land on the eastern shore of the Red Sea. But her leadership was tainted by her attempt to secure authority for herself and her brother when she accused Moses before God (see Numbers 12:1-2). It was this rebellion against God and His appointed minister, Moses, which prevented Miriam from entering into the Promised Land.

Our study begins with the sadness of Miriam's death, and her burial in the desert of Zin. In the first month the people arrived in the wilderness of Zin in the Negev. This was probably the first month of the fortieth year after leaving Egypt. But the emphasis here is on the month in which it occurred. "The first month" would be very special to early readers of the text, in that it was the anniversary of the Passover. It should have reinvigorated the people and encouraged their hopes of deliverance, but instead of the joyous celebrations and hope that there should have been, we find sorrow in its place. As the people settled down in the area of Kadesh, Miriam the prophetess died.

There are at least two reasons for the mention of this sad event. The first was because her death was linked with the shortage of water. There was both a physical drought as well as a spiritual drought. This suggests what a terrible blow this was to the people. In spite of her failings and shortcomings, Miriam had been a provider of spiritual sustenance to the people, and they recognized that her death would bring them a spiritual drought along with the physical drought caused by the lack of water. The second was that Miriam's death brought home God's warning that the generation of which she was a member was doomed to die in the wilderness.

When the people of God are at their lowest, God always meets them with greater blessings, but in this case it would be a mixed blessing, for at Meribah Aaron and Moses would disqualify themselves from entry into the Promised Land. This would lead to the death of Aaron and to more gloom.

The enemies of life conquered Miriam, instead of her conquering them. She had given in to the grumblings of the people, and actually rebelled against God herself. Consequently, she never inherited the promise that God had for her. We learn from Miriam that grumbling and unbelief will keep us out of our own Promised Land (see Hebrews 3:12-13).

B. The Sin of the People
(Numbers 20:2-5)

And there was no water for the congregation: and they gathered themselves together against Moses and against Aaron. And the people chode with Moses, and spake, saying, Would God that we had died when our brethren died before the LORD! And why have ye brought up the congregation of the LORD into this wilderness, that we and our cattle should die there? And wherefore have ye made us to come up out of Egypt, to bring us in unto this evil place? it is no place of seed, or of figs, or of vines, or of pomegranates; neither is there any water to drink.

We will first look at the word *chode*. This word was in the imperfect tense, which carries the idea of an action preliminary to its completion. The Hebrews would do anything to vent their anger. Because this word was in the imperfect tense, its use might have signified that the people were inclined to kill Moses and Aaron. Their complaints were about their future, which was guaranteed by God, but it was not unfolding the way they expected. The condition leading to the fulfillment of the land of milk and honey was unbearable to them. They were complaining about their food and water, and were afraid that their children might die in the wilderness. When they were pressing hard on Moses and Aaron, the two ran into the tabernacle for protection and petitioned the Lord.

While they bowed on their faces, the glory of the Lord descended on them. Moses was instructed to speak to the rock to get water. We do not know the pressure on Moses at this point in time, but he hit the rock twice inside of speaking to it. The anger of the Lord was kindled against Moses. Some Bible interpreters have surmised that the Rock that Moses hit was Jesus (see 1 Corinthians 10:4). There is no definitive interpretation of this, but it is worth studying.

When the people gathered to argue with Moses over their lack of water, it was far more serious than their previous grumblings. Lost in translation from Hebrew to English is the seriousness of the matter. The Israelites presented the equivalent of a legal complaint or lawsuit against Moses and Aaron. It could also be described as a legal quarrel or strife, similar to the one between Abraham and Lot in Genesis 13. In any event, they were not only accusing God of failing them, they were also challenging Moses's ability to lead. They blamed Moses for bringing them into the wilderness with their valuable livestock, only to face death from extreme thirst.

Once again we see the rebellion of the people in this section. They sent their leaders to make their feelings known to Moses. They "chode" with Moses, and their cry expressed the wish that they had not survived to have to face up to such thirst. They rather wished that they had died when their fellow tribesmen had died before God. Judgment would have been better than this, they incorrectly reasoned. Their thoughts were seemingly still on the ground that had swallowed up Dathan and Abiram (see Numbers 16). It would have been better for them, they reasoned, if they too had died. However, it was equally possible that they were referring to those who had died throughout the period in the wilderness as having died before God because as they viewed this, it was His specific judgment on them.

The question they could not answer was "Why?" The only reason for their still being alive, it appeared, was that they had been brought to this wilderness to die, along with their herds and flocks. They despaired. Note their accusation. They claimed to be "the congregation of the LORD" (verse 4), and yet they had no trust in God to provide. They were simply using the idea in order to put Moses and Aaron in the wrong. They were trying to make plain the greatness of Moses and Aaron's failure as leaders. How could they bring "the congregation of the LORD" to such a place? Did Moses and Aaron not realize that they were to be seen as completely to blame for the Israelites' predicament and for letting down God's holy people? It was they who had brought "the congregation of the LORD" into the wilderness to die, when they could have been worshiping God back in Egypt. They reasoned that Moses and Aaron would be held responsible before God.

Such was their hypocrisy. Yet, it was not only an accusation against the leadership of Moses—it was an unspoken, backhanded accusation against God Himself. Moses had told them that they were His people, that they were "the congregation of the LORD," but now, they thought, even He had brought them to die a miserable death there in the wilderness.

What they should have realized was that if they were "the congregation of the LORD" their disappointment would only be for a moment. If they would but look to Him in confident trust they would be doubly blessed—first by the joy of trusting Him even in darkness, and then by the equal joy of receiving blessings and experiencing God's awesome power when the water came out of the rock.

Sin can damage our faith to the point that we question our very salvation. It was clear that the Israelites felt abandoned in the wilderness. Their sin had brought upon them a feeling of estrangement and isolation from God.

The irony of their tribal demands is seen in their wish that they had died in Egypt with their fallen ancestors. And God gave them just what they wanted because not one of them lived to enter into Canaan. These people were not able to accept the fact that they brought their problems upon themselves, so they blamed Moses for their condition. Quite often our troubles result from our own disobedience or lack of faith. We cannot blame God for our sins. Until we face this reality, we will have little peace and no spiritual growth.

C. The Disobedience to God's Directive (Numbers 20:6-13)

And Moses and Aaron went from the presence of the assembly unto the door of the tabernacle of the congregation, and they fell upon their faces: and the glory of the LORD appeared unto them. And the LORD spake unto Moses, saying, Take the rod, and gather thou the assembly together, thou, and Aaron thy brother, and speak ye unto the rock before their eyes; and it shall give forth his water, and thou shalt bring forth to them water out of the rock: so thou shalt give the congregation and their beasts drink. And Moses took the rod from before the LORD, as he commanded him. And Moses and Aaron gathered the congregation together before the rock, and he said unto them, Hear now, ye rebels; must we fetch you water out of this rock? And Moses lifted up his hand, and with his rod he smote the rock twice: and the water came out abundantly, and the congregation drank, and their beasts also. And the LORD spake unto Moses and Aaron, Because ye believed me not, to sanctify me in the eyes of the children of Israel, therefore ye shall not bring this congregation into the land which I have given them. This is the water of Meribah; because the children of Israel strove with the LORD, and he was sanctified in them.

The action Moses and Aaron took was to leave the assembly and approach the door of the tabernacle. That is always a good place to go in the time of crisis, and there they fell on their faces "and the glory of the LORD appeared unto them" (verse 6). God had not deserted them. He was still the same as ever. He did not and does not change; it is humankind that changes.

The Lord's instructions to Moses were clear: he was to take his staff and gather the people together; he was then to speak to the rock that God identified as being the source of water that would keep them alive. To the New Testament Christian, this rock was Jesus Christ (see 1 Corinthians 10:4).

God made a unique promise to Moses when He promised that water would flow miraculously from the rock. Moses's response was immediate and obedient. He took the staff from the tabernacle and gathered the people as God had commanded. That was when the tragedy occurred. Moses committed three gross errors of disobedience. First, he spoke to the people and not to the rock (verse 10). Second, he did not give God the full credit and honor, but instead put himself on a level with God, suggesting that it was he and God who were going to provide them with water. He failed to honor God as the only one who could supply humanity's need for *living water,* and instead exalted himself. He accepted some of the credit for the miracle that was about to happen. Third, Moses struck the rock not once, but twice. This was a clear demonstration that he was completely controlled by his anger and frustration.

The Lord responded immediately. His love required that the water gush forth. But His justice required that He chastise Moses and Aaron. For this reason, Moses named the location *Meribah*—"the place of strife."

We learn two important lessons from this event in biblical history. First, we learn that God will not share His glory with anyone (see Psalm 29:2). Second, we learn that God never allows His people to continue in sin without correcting them. To permit sin without fear of chastisement would be to encourage its destructive behavior (see Hebrews 12:5-6). There is a vast difference between a passion for excellence and a passion for power. The desire for excellence is a gift from God. It is characterized by respect for quality and a yearning to use God's gifts in a way that pleases Him. The desire for power is a craving for that which glorifies self. The quest for excellence is a mark of maturity. The quest for power is childish. Moses's act of disobedience must have broken God's heart. In that fleeting moment, Moses lost sight of the truth that only God could meet the needs of humanity. It was a childish moment that cost Moses his right to inherit the Promised Land.

III. CONCLUDING REFLECTION

Some may think that God's punishment was too harsh. We have no trouble envisioning God as loving and forgiving, yet we struggle with the thought that God is capable of anger and punishment. But the sin committed by Moses was a serious one. As God's chosen leader, Moses stole God's title of Provider, even if only for a moment. When we put "title" ahead of obedience, we risk losing our blessing. Moses broke the first of the Ten Commandments God had entrusted to his care: "Thou shalt have no other gods before me!" In that instance, Moses made himself a god.

In Numbers 20:6, Moses and Aaron went before the tabernacle door for refuge against the increasing fury and agitation of the people. This action tells us to always remember that God is truly our refuge and strength, a very present help at all times.

A thousand years from now, the titles we have pursued and attained in this life will matter little in contrast to whose children we are. This is the difference between doing our best to glorify self and doing our best to glorify God! For this Moses was prevented from entering into the Promised Land. We may conclude that God's punishment of Moses was too harsh. Looking at the story critically, it was the people who pushed Moses to react the way he did. But Moses could have restrained himself from his unguarded speech. He was, after all, the leader of and model for the people. We too must be extra careful. We are under a different dispensation, but we are serving the same God.

Moses was an exemplary leader. He labored to bring his people out of the land of Egypt. Numbers 12:3 reads, "Now the man Moses was very meek, above all the men which were upon the face of the earth." God described Moses as being meek above all men, but Moses's life took a different turn when he disobeyed God and struck the rock instead of touching it. Because of this, God did not allow him to enter the Promised Land.

Leaders must be very careful of how they react, even when followers push them to the wall. They must still be calm and ask for the help of the Holy Spirit in the midst of the highest provocations. Every child of God must seek immediate help from the Holy Spirit when he or she is disturbed.

PRAYER

O God, our Father, help us to recognize our limitations when we use Your name. Help us to hallow Your name all the time. In Jesus' name we pray. Amen.

WORD POWER

Sanctify (Hebrew: *qadash [ka-dash]*)—means "to be set apart," "to be consecrated," or "to be hallowed." Since the beginning, God's name must be referenced and hallowed. God's name must not be used casually or carelessly. Moses, even though he was pushed to equalize himself with God, had to hallow His name. Isaiah 42:8 reads: "I am the Lord: that is my name: and my glory will I not give to another."

HOME DAILY BIBLE READINGS
(August 10-16, 2009)

Moses Disobeys

MONDAY, August 10: "Rebelled Against the Command" (Numbers 20:22-29)

TUESDAY, August 11: "Tested at Meribah" (Psalm 81:1-10)

WEDNESDAY, August 12: "Do Not Harden Your Hearts" (Psalm 95)

THURSDAY, August 13: "Trust in the Lord" (Jeremiah 17:5-10)

FRIDAY, August 14: "The Foundation of Faith" (Matthew 16:13-18)

SATURDAY, August 15: "Water for the Thirsty" (Revelation 21:1-7)

SUNDAY, August 16: "Because Moses Did Not Trust" (Numbers 20:1-13)

GOD CALLS FOR OBEDIENCE

DEVOTIONAL READING: **Proverbs 2:1-11**
PRINT PASSAGE: **Deuteronomy 6:1-9, 20-24**

BACKGROUND SCRIPTURE: **Deuteronomy 6**
KEY VERSES: **Deuteronomy 6:4-6**

Deuteronomy 6:1-9, 20-24—KJV

NOW THESE are the commandments, the statutes, and the judgments, which the LORD your God commanded to teach you, that ye might do them in the land whither ye go to possess it:

2 That thou mightest fear the LORD thy God, to keep all his statutes and his commandments, which I command thee, thou, and thy son, and thy son's son, all the days of thy life; and that thy days may be prolonged.

3 Hear therefore, O Israel, and observe to do it; that it may be well with thee, and that ye may increase mightily, as the LORD God of thy fathers hath promised thee, in the land that floweth with milk and honey.

4 Hear, O Israel: The LORD our God is one LORD:

5 And thou shalt love the LORD thy God with all thine heart, and with all thy soul, and with all thy might.

6 And these words, which I command thee this day, shall be in thine heart:

7 And thou shalt teach them diligently unto thy children, and shalt talk of them when thou sittest in thine house, and when thou walkest by the way, and when thou liest down, and when thou risest up.

8 And thou shalt bind them for a sign upon thine hand, and they shall be as frontlets between thine eyes.

9 And thou shalt write them upon the posts of thy house, and on thy gates.

.....

20 And when thy son asketh thee in time to come, saying, What mean the testimonies, and the statutes, and the judgments, which the LORD our God hath commanded you?

21 Then thou shalt say unto thy son, We were Pharaoh's bondmen in Egypt; and the LORD brought us out of Egypt with a mighty hand:

22 And the LORD shewed signs and wonders, great and sore, upon Egypt, upon Pharaoh, and upon all his household, before our eyes:

Deuteronomy 6:1-9, 20-24—NRSV

NOW THIS is the commandment—the statutes and the ordinances—that the LORD your God charged me to teach you to observe in the land that you are about to cross into and occupy,

2 so that you and your children and your children's children may fear the LORD your God all the days of your life, and keep all his decrees and his commandments that I am commanding you, so that your days may be long.

3 Hear therefore, O Israel, and observe them diligently, so that it may go well with you, and so that you may multiply greatly in a land flowing with milk and honey, as the LORD, the God of your ancestors, has promised you.

4 Hear, O Israel: The LORD is our God, the LORD alone.

5 You shall love the LORD your God with all your heart, and with all your soul, and with all your might.

6 Keep these words that I am commanding you today in your heart.

7 Recite them to your children and talk about them when you are at home and when you are away, when you lie down and when you rise.

8 Bind them as a sign on your hand, fix them as an emblem on your forehead,

9 and write them on the doorposts of your house and on your gates.

.....

20 When your children ask you in time to come, "What is the meaning of the decrees and the statutes and the ordinances that the LORD our God has commanded you?"

21 then you shall say to your children, "We were Pharaoh's slaves in Egypt, but the LORD brought us out of Egypt with a mighty hand.

22 The LORD displayed before our eyes great and awesome signs and wonders against Egypt, against Pharaoh and all his household.

UNIFYING LESSON PRINCIPLE

When people obey laws, they expect that life will be good. Why do people care at all about laws and try to follow them? Deuteronomy states that God gives laws for our benefit.

23 And he brought us out from thence, that he might bring us in, to give us the land which he sware unto our fathers.
24 And the LORD commanded us to do all these statutes, to fear the LORD our God, for our good always, that he might preserve us alive, as it is at this day.

23 He brought us out from there in order to bring us in, to give us the land that he promised on oath to our ancestors.
24 Then the LORD commanded us to observe all these statutes, to fear the LORD our God, for our lasting good, so as to keep us alive, as is now the case.

TOPICAL OUTLINE OF THE LESSON

I. Introduction
  A. Languid Christianity
  B. Biblical Background

II. Exposition and Application of the Scripture
  A. The Greatest Commandment (Deuteronomy 6:1-5)
  B. Obedience as Duty (Deuteronomy 6:6-9)
  C. Our Duty to Our Children (Deuteronomy 6:20-24)

III. Concluding Reflection

LESSON OBJECTIVES

Upon completion of this lesson, the students will know that:

1. Parents are responsible for teaching their children the ways of God;
2. A positive response to God's laws is indicative of our love for Him; and,
3. God reserves blessings for those who follow Him with their hearts.

POINTS TO BE EMPHASIZED

ADULT/YOUTH

Adult Topic: Obeying the Commands
Youth Topic: The Bottom Line
Adult/Youth Key Verses: Deuteronomy 6:4-6
Print Passage: Deuteronomy 6:1-9, 20-24

—"Fear the LORD" (verse 2) is equivalent to trust and respect.
—"The LORD is one" is a declaration that this God is unique, which in turn is an answer to Exodus 15:11. The name of "the LORD" (YHWH) used in this text identified a specific God to whom the nation of Israel was committed in a world that recognized multiple gods.
—The Shema is a summary of the Ten Commandments (see Deuteronomy 5:6-21.)
—Before we can love God (verse 5), we have to hear or listen to God (verse 4).
—Naming the various places at which the commandments of God are to be placed (verses 6-9) essentially means the commands are to become so familiar to us they become "second nature"—we see them everywhere.
—Guidance essential for living is given to God's people as they prepare to enter into the Promised Land.
—The heart of the Law is total love for God with one's whole being and the covenant community's recognition that God had saved and protected it.

CHILDREN

Children Topic: The Bottom Line
Key Verse: Deuteronomy 6:5

Print Passage: Deuteronomy 6:1-9, 20-24

—God gave commands for people's benefit.

—The people were responsible for teaching these laws to their children.

—The first and primary law is that God alone is God and the only Being worthy of our total allegiance.

—The people were also to tell their children the story of their deliverance from slavery in Egypt.

—God's commands are good and are meant for people's lasting benefit.

I. INTRODUCTION

A. Languid Christianity

Does your life write God's message out loud? There was a young lady who, as valedictorian of her class, wanted to testify about Christ. Her principal gave her a flat-out "No!" Only the threat of a lawsuit changed his mind. Then she was asked to "tone it down a bit" and re-write her speech. She said, "No." The speech was given exactly as she had planned. It is clear from this story that Christians are under attack. The girl could have quoted Confucius, Shirley MacClaine, or Buddha, but not God. Others have free speech, but Christians do not.

The sad truth is that this attack on Christianity has impacted the Christian ethic. Christians today are more into tolerance than truth. We are too accommodating because we do not want to offend people. We are often even ashamed to tell the truth. Truth has been sold out for popularity and acceptance. Preachers are encouraged to "tone it down" and not be so "negative." The church has lost its zeal and aggressiveness and begun to act passive and defeated. The early church was militant about its message, but we are trying to be righteous without being Christlike. The world is not listening to the church because the church is talking the world's language. A. W. Tozer said, "Christianity has been watered down that if its solution were poison it will hurt no one."

We have been charged to carry the message of Jesus Christ to the world. Everything about that message is offensive to the world because God's truth is offensive. God's message was just as offensive to the disobedient in biblical times as it is today. Sinners never want to confront their sins. But just as Moses was ordered to teach God's laws to a new generation of Israelites, the church is charged to teach Christ to every future generation whether they like it or not!

B. Biblical Background

To the secular world, the Ten Commandments are a set of biblical rules that state the basic religious and moral ideals of Judaism and Christianity. But to the believer, they are the foundation of life for all human beings. They tell us exactly how to live. God, the creator of life, knows exactly how life should be lived. The Ten Commandments were entrusted to Moses, because God wants us to learn how to live full and victorious lives. But obedience is the key to every law's application. If we obey God's laws, we will experience the fullness of life and conquer all the enemies who oppose life.

The commandments teach all generations to fear the Lord. The Hebrew definition for *fear* is "to honor the Lord," "to give Him reverence," "to respect His justice," and "to accept His judgment." This is the definition of true worship. When we fear God, we surrender our lives to serve God and obey His commands. God gave Moses the Ten Commandments so that the people would learn to fear Him.

The commandments prolong life. One who obeys God will suffer far less guilt, pressure, and tension—emotions that drain life from us. Wisdom, then, is the acceptance of God's Law as the source of abundant life.

God promised the Israelites abundant life if they would obey these ten rules of His covenant relationship with them. Two hundred years after the resurrection of Jesus Christ, Christians taught that God had stamped the commandments on the conscience of every human being. In A.D. 400, every Christian was required to memorize the Ten Commandments, and by A.D. 800, these ten laws had become a central part of all Christian education. In the 1200s, leading Christian scholars regarded these laws as principles of a universal natural law that governed human conduct.

Today, though there is a concerted effort in America to replace God's justice with our interpretation of law, God's plan for our abundant lives still remains: "O that there were such an heart in them, that they would fear me, and keep all my commandments always, that it might be well with them, and with their children for ever!" (Deuteronomy 5:29).

II. EXPOSITION AND APPLICATION OF THE SCRIPTURE

A. The Greatest Commandment
(Deuteronomy 6:1-5)

NOW THESE are the commandments, the statutes, and the judgments, which the LORD your God commanded to teach you, that ye might do them in the land whither ye go to possess it: That thou mightest fear the LORD thy God, to keep all his statutes and his commandments, which I command thee, thou, and thy son, and thy son's son, all the days of thy life; and that thy days may be prolonged. Hear therefore, O Israel, and observe to do it; that it may be well with thee, and that ye may increase mightily, as the LORD God of thy fathers hath promised thee, in the land that floweth with milk and honey. Hear, O Israel: The LORD our God is one LORD: And thou shalt love the LORD thy God with all thine heart, and with all thy soul, and with all thy might.

The first verse of this section of our lesson text reveals important instructions. There are three words which will illuminate our understanding: "commandment," "statute," and "judgment." The word *commandment* could mean "precept," "principle," or general rule of action. God's intention for His people is to enjoy life, but there are certain simple principles that must be adhered to. The word *statute* is a prescribed task. It is akin to the first word, but with a slight difference. In order to follow a simple order, one must understand it in bits. The last word is *judgment,* which involves acts of deciding a case. God gave these three words in order that the Hebrew society would operate under a theocracy, a society that was ruled strictly by God's laws.

The new land had its code of conduct, and unless the people followed these instructions, they would not enjoy the peace and presence of God in the new land.

Following God's charge to Moses to teach the Israelites to obey His commandments, God reinforced the greatest of the commandments which simply states, "Thou shalt love the LORD thy God with all thine heart, and with all thy soul, and with all thy might" (verse 5); Jesus Christ affirmed this truth in Matthew 22:37-38, when He condensed all of God's laws into just two simple sentences. His answer opened the eyes of many who saw God's laws as a complex quagmire of Pharisaic interpretation that was impossible to keep. This simplification of our obedience was designed by Jesus to point us to the truth of God as our sovereign creator. Notice that from this great commandment we learn that God is Lord of all. We are not to believe that there is one God for the Jews and another God for the Gentiles. There is only one God who created the universe and only one God who is the God of all humankind—"In him we live, and move, and have our being" (Acts 17:28). God does not play favorites or show partiality to make it difficult for us to be saved. He treats us equally. "There is one God, and one mediator between God and men, the man Christ Jesus" (1 Timothy 2:5).

This commandment also points out that there is a personal relationship between God and all believers. That relationship establishes Him as the one true and living God and we as His people. The relationship is a daily experience—not some distant, far-removed ideal. We are as close to God as our hearts permit us to be because love and sensitivity to His presence is the key that unlocks the door to our relationship with Him.

God placed great emphasis on how we are to love Him. He categorized it in three ways. We are to love Him with all our hearts, all our souls, and all our strength. The *heart* is the seat of our affection and devotion. When we love God with all our hearts, we focus our affections on Him and love Him supremely. The *soul* refers to our consciousness. It is the essence of who we are, and it distinguishes us from all other creatures in God's creation. We are living souls (see Genesis 2:7); therefore, God commands us to love Him with all of our being. The word *might* means "full strength, to the point of exhaustion." In other words, God wants us to focus our complete energy on worshiping Him.

B. Obedience as Duty
(Deuteronomy 6:6-9)

And these words, which I command thee this day, shall be in thine heart: And thou shalt teach them diligently unto thy children, and shalt talk of them when thou sittest in thine house, and when thou walkest by the way, and when thou liest down, and when thou risest up. And thou shalt bind them for a sign upon thine hand, and they shall be as frontlets between thine eyes. And thou shalt write them upon the posts of thy house, and on thy gates.

With belief comes duty. No one can believe in God without also desiring to serve Him. As believers, we cherish God's laws and cradle them in our hearts. Our faith is a total commitment to God and His commands (see Deuteronomy 11:18).

Our internal commitment to God produces outward evidence of our faith. It is our outward demonstration of belief in God. The best way to spiritually educate our children and the community around us is to live godly lives in their presence. It is not enough to teach facts and principles for the sake of passing on information. We must be living examples of the application of those facts and principles. When others see the commandments lived before their very eyes, they too will make them part of their lives. This is the valuable principle Moses was instructed to teach the Israelites: the most valuable possession one has to pass on to one's children is one's faith legacy. If we learn the commandments and live the commandments, we will be powerful examples of God's life-giving principles (see John 20:31).

The believer's duty is not only to learn the commandments and live them in his or her home, but also to use the commandments as strong public testimony. When an Israelite was out in public, he was required to bind the commandments on his hands and forehead. His arm and headgear (called frontlets) were worn as symbols of his commitment to God. In the home, the Israelites wrote God's laws on their doorposts and on their gates (see Deuteronomy 11:18-20). The Jews still practice this tradition today by attaching a *mezuzah,* which contains two passages of Scripture, in a metal or glass case, to the right doorpost of every entrance to their homes.

God was teaching the Israelites and us that the home is to be the center for witnessing about the truth of His commandments. Our homes are to be known as righteous homes, where God's truth is lived openly and outwardly.

C. Our Duty to Our Children
(Deuteronomy 6:20-24)

And when thy son asketh thee in time to come, saying, What mean the testimonies, and the statutes, and the judgments, which the LORD our God hath commanded you? Then thou shalt say unto thy son, We were Pharaoh's bondmen in Egypt; and the LORD brought us out of Egypt with a mighty hand: And the LORD shewed signs and wonders, great and sore, upon Egypt, upon Pharaoh, and upon all his household, before our eyes: And he brought us out from thence, that he might bring us in, to give us the land which he sware unto our fathers. And the LORD commanded us to do all these statutes, to fear the LORD our God, for our good always, that he might preserve us alive, as it is at this day.

Moses was charged by God to teach the truth of salvation and the commandments to children. Teaching the truth to children is one of the primary duties of Christian parents. If we were diligent to honor God with our obedience, our Sunday schools would be running over with children. Our children are naturally inquisitive about God and His laws, and parents have a duty to study and live those principles in the presence of their children.

When Israelite children asked their parents about the truth of God's deliverance from Egypt, their parents were expected to be prepared to explain it in detail. Their great deliverance story was the heart of their faith because it was historical proof of God's covenant relationship with Israel.

Our covenant relationship with God is historically recorded in the New Testament, with the birth, death, and resurrection of our Lord Jesus Christ. Christian parents should be able to articulate the details of our "great deliverance" from sin, and add our own personal testimonies of God's mercy toward us.

But explaining salvation is not enough. The Israelite parents had to teach the truth of God's commandments to their children—that if they obeyed God, they would be counted righteous before God. The word *righteousness* means "to cleanse oneself" or "to make righteous." The children were to be taught that righteousness meant living lives that were noble and good (see Deuteronomy 31:13; Proverbs 22:6).

Like the Israelites, we too are charged to teach our children not just the importance of *knowing* God, but of *obeying* God. Peter confessed that he knew Jesus as the Son of God.

But Jesus let Peter know that his confession was not enough. Faith must compel a believer to action. Jesus therefore told Peter, "Feed my sheep!"

III. CONCLUDING REFLECTION

Since the coming of Jesus Christ, righteousness is no longer attained by the works of the Law. No person can keep the Law perfectly. Our New Testament covenant tells us that God accepts a person only when he or she comes through the righteousness of Christ. A person must approach God through Jesus Christ in order to be accepted by God. Once God accepts a person, that person must then seek to obey God and to fulfill His commandments. That fulfillment includes spreading the Gospel message, not just among our children, but also throughout the world.

Obedience is a heart attitude which is very difficult to cultivate, but it is required if we are truly born again. The children of God in the Old Testament were warned against disobeying God. Severe consequences were stipulated for any violation of God's commandments. Yet, they still sinned. But they did not escape the consequences of their actions.

Even though we are under grace, we cannot flagrantly disobey God and expect a pat on the back. Hebrews 10:26-27 reads, "For if we sin wilfully after that we have received the knowledge of the truth, there remaineth no more sacrifice for sins, But a certain fearful looking for of judgment."

PRAYER

Father in heaven, help us to realize that the strength to love You comes from You. We ask that You grant us the strength to love You with all our might and to teach the truth of Your Word to our children. In Jesus' name we pray. Amen.

WORD POWER

Might (Hebrew: *m@'od [meh-ode]*)—*might* represents "the outgoings and energies of all the vital powers." It also means "to love unreservedly and entirely" or "to love God out of pure hearts." *To love with might* indicates that there may be other competing gods, but that one must consciously disregard them and put God on the throne.

HOME DAILY BIBLE READINGS
(August 17-23, 2009)

God Calls for Obedience

MONDAY, August 17: "Rewards of Obedience" (Leviticus 26:3-13)

TUESDAY, August 18: "Penalties of Disobedience" (Leviticus 26:14-26)

WEDNESDAY, August 19: "Consequences of Disobedience" (1 Samuel 15:17-26)

THURSDAY, August 20: "Disobeying the Son" (John 3:31-36)

FRIDAY, August 21: "Listening and Obeying" (Psalm 81:11-16)

SATURDAY, August 22: "Treasure God's Commands" (Proverbs 2:1-11)

SUNDAY, August 23: "Diligently Observing God's Law" (Deuteronomy 6:1-9, 20-24)

LESSON 13   August 30, 2009

GOD CALLS FOR DECISION

DEVOTIONAL READING: **Joshua 24:14-24**
PRINT PASSAGE: **Deuteronomy 30:1-10**

27-14-

BACKGROUND SCRIPTURE: **Deuteronomy 30**
KEY VERSE: **Deuteronomy 30:6**

Deuteronomy 30:1-10—KJV

AND IT shall come to pass, when all these things are come upon thee, the blessing and the curse, which I have set before thee, and thou shalt call them to mind among all the nations, whither the LORD thy God hath driven thee,

2 And shalt return unto the LORD thy God, and shalt obey his voice according to all that I command thee this day, thou and thy children, with all thine heart, and with all thy soul;

3 That then the LORD thy God will turn thy captivity, and have compassion upon thee, and will return and gather thee from all the nations, whither the LORD thy God hath scattered thee.

4 If any of thine be driven out unto the outmost parts of heaven, from thence will the LORD thy God gather thee, and from thence will he fetch thee:

5 And the LORD thy God will bring thee into the land which thy fathers possessed, and thou shalt possess it; and he will do thee good, and multiply thee above thy fathers.

6 And the LORD thy God will circumcise thine heart, and the heart of thy seed, to love the LORD thy God with all thine heart, and with all thy soul, that thou mayest live.

7 And the LORD thy God will put all these curses upon thine enemies, and on them that hate thee, which persecuted thee.

8 And thou shalt return and obey the voice of the LORD, and do all his commandments which I command thee this day.

9 And the LORD thy God will make thee plenteous in every work of thine hand, in the fruit of thy body, and in the fruit of thy cattle, and in the fruit of thy land, for good: for the LORD will again rejoice over thee for good, as he rejoiced over thy fathers:

10 If thou shalt hearken unto the voice of the LORD thy God, to keep his commandments and his statutes which are written in this book of the law, and if thou turn unto the LORD thy God with all thine heart, and with all thy soul.

Deuteronomy 30:1-10—NRSV

WHEN ALL these things have happened to you, the blessings and the curses that I have set before you, if you call them to mind among all the nations where the LORD your God has driven you,

2 and return to the LORD your God, and you and your children obey him with all your heart and with all your soul, just as I am commanding you today,

3 then the LORD your God will restore your fortunes and have compassion on you, gathering you again from all the peoples among whom the LORD your God has scattered you.

4 Even if you are exiled to the ends of the world, from there the LORD your God will gather you, and from there he will bring you back.

5 The LORD your God will bring you into the land that your ancestors possessed, and you will possess it; he will make you more prosperous and numerous than your ancestors.

6 Moreover, the LORD your God will circumcise your heart and the heart of your descendants, so that you will love the LORD your God with all your heart and with all your soul, in order that you may live.

7 The LORD your God will put all these curses on your enemies and on the adversaries who took advantage of you.

8 Then you shall again obey the LORD, observing all his commandments that I am commanding you today,

9 and the LORD your God will make you abundantly prosperous in all your undertakings, in the fruit of your body, in the fruit of your livestock, and in the fruit of your soil. For the LORD will again take delight in prospering you, just as he delighted in prospering your ancestors,

10 when you obey the LORD your God by observing his commandments and decrees that are written in this book of the law, because you turn to the LORD your God with all your heart and with all your soul.

People want to experience a satisfying life, to attain joy and prosperity. How do we get what we want out of life? Moses claimed that God wants us to love God so much that we want nothing more than to obey Him.

TOPICAL OUTLINE OF THE LESSON

I. **Introduction**
  A. Decision and Consequences
  B. Biblical Background

II. **Exposition and Application of the Scripture**
  A. The Covenant's Conditions (Deuteronomy 30:1-2)
  B. The Covenant's Restoration (Deuteronomy 30:3-10)

III. **Concluding Reflection**

LESSON OBJECTIVES

Upon completion of this lesson, the students will know that:

1. Remembering God's Word and acting on it leads to spiritual and physical liberation;
2. God is aware that our enemies will try to do evil, but He will prevent them; and,
3. Consciousness of God's presence in our lives leads to obeying His promptings.

POINTS TO BE EMPHASIZED

ADULT/YOUTH

Adult Topic: The Promise of Life
Youth Topic: Choose Love and Live
Adult Key Verse: Deuteronomy 30:6
Youth Key Verses: Deuteronomy 30:9-10
Print Passage: Deuteronomy 30:1-10

—This is part of a covenant renewal ceremony held in the plains of Moab.
—This passage is parallel to Deuteronomy 4:25-31.
—Recalling what God has done gives assurance of God's compassion and protection for the future.
—Loving and obeying God will not guarantee freedom from difficulties and tough times, but it will assure God's presence in those times and, ultimately, God's blessing and prosperity.
—As God has prospered those who have committed to loving obedience in the past, so God will prosper those who now commit themselves to God in loving obedience.
—This passage is part of Moses's last words to Israel—a kind of "last will and testament."
—God's deepest desire, as expressed here, is to have a people who will lovingly obey Him.

CHILDREN

Children Topic: Choose Life
Key Verses: Deuteronomy 30:19-20
Print Passage: Deuteronomy 29:2-3; 30:15-16, 19-20; 31:1-3

—Moses called on the people to remember God's great deeds on their behalf.
—Loving and obeying God brings life and God's blessing.
—Moses showed the people their options—death or life.
—Moses called on the people to choose life.
—The people's decision would affect their future and that of their children's.
—Moses reminded the people that God would go before them into the land.

I. INTRODUCTION

A. Decision and Consequences

Christians are sometimes confronted by decisions that are difficult—decisions that involve personal challenges, marital problems, employment issues, or even national or world issues. We are often guilty of making decisions without prayerful consultation with God, and our hasty decisions have resulted in painful consequences.

All decisions and actions have consequences. But the good news is that for the believer, even when the consequences are painful, God is still working. God promises forgiveness for the repentant believer who desires to begin again. That is the *alpha* of the Gospel, and we begin again, not with tears, but with joy. The sins and blunders of the past remind us not to go back again. There will be flashbacks, but we must consciously move forward. "Where sin abounded, grace did much more abound" (Romans 5:20). Our restoration then becomes the gracious work of God.

B. Biblical Background

This chapter begins by recognizing that both the blessings and the curses described in Deuteronomy 28 will finally have their effects. Moses was fully aware that God had not permanently given to His earthly people hearts to know, eyes to see, and ears to hear (see Deuteronomy 29:4). It was He Himself who had declared that they were a stiff-necked people (see Deuteronomy 9:6) and needed to be circumcised at heart (see Deuteronomy 10:16). He had certainly experienced enough in the wilderness to know how unreliable the people were. He therefore had to reluctantly recognize that God had given these warnings because He knew that they would necessarily be fulfilled. Their decisions to disobey God had made judgment inevitable. Through judgment Israel would have to learn their lesson.

God is able to see into the future, and for this reason He was able to predict the terrible apostasy of the Israelites. God chose to give Israel a "heads up" to its impending dilemma by revealing His punishment beforehand through Moses. Would the Israelites have been more obedient if they had known that their ten instances of national rebellion would send them into exile for seventy years? Probably not! Consider the fact that the Bible has been predicting the final punishment for our sinful natures for more than two millennia, yet we still refuse to repent and obey God.

II. EXPOSITION AND APPLICATION OF THE SCRIPTURE

A. The Covenant's Conditions
(Deuteronomy 30:1-2)

AND IT shall come to pass, when all these things are come upon thee, the blessing and the curse, which I have set before thee, and thou shalt call them to mind among all the nations, whither the LORD thy God hath driven thee, And shalt return unto the LORD thy God, and shalt obey his voice according to all that I command thee this day, thou and thy children, with all thine heart, and with all thy soul.

Aware from the long experience of the truth about the people he was dealing with, Moses informed them that he was aware that in the future they would experience both the blessing and the curse as described in Deuteronomy 28. He expected that for a time they would keep God's covenant and as a result would experience blessings. The blessings would come on them due to their obedience. But then as time went by, he was sadly confident that the faithfulness of many of them would lapse, and then they would begin to experience curses, until finally God had to drive them out of the land.

But when that happened they were to call to mind, when they were "among all the nations" (verse 1) to which God had driven them, all that God had said through him related to the blessings and the curses. Note the emphasis on "all the nations." No particular place is named. This is not a prophecy, except for the fact that it is a declaration that the curses were to be taken seriously and would inevitably be carried into effect. This reference to both blessings and curses takes us directly back to Deuteronomy 28.

The covenant's conditions are clearly spelled out. Moses had just preached to the Israelites about the complete forsaking of their commitment to God. He had warned them

that the day was coming when they would turn toward idolatry and false worship, and as a result, judgment would fall upon them. Moses had warned that a foreign nation would conquer the Israelites, enslave them, and remove them from their homeland (see Deuteronomy 28:36).

Here, Moses was predicting a day of restoration when God's people would fulfill the conditions of their covenant relationship and be redeemed. To a nation that was facing exile, the promise of restoration brought a sense of comfort. The likely question was, "What must we do to be redeemed?" God's disciplining of Israel would end when she returned to Him with all her heart.

Moses gave them the clear answer. The people would have to first sense the sincere need for repentance. As a nation, they would have to recall their disobedience and the curses that followed. They would also one day have to recall the many blessings that God bestowed upon them. And by meditating and reflecting upon those blessings and curses, only then would they begin to sense their great need for repentance.

In order to experience a sense of remorse for our sins, we must first acknowledge them. The problem with the Israelites, as with most sinners, was their refusal to admit that they had sinned. Tragically, Moses was telling the Israelites that they would one day understand their need for repentance, but only after they were enslaved by the world and had suffered a broken heart. We call that "hitting rock bottom." When you hit rock bottom, your hypocrisy melts away and exposes your false worship. Only then can you experience true remorse that will compel you to turn from sin and return to a right relationship with God.

B. The Covenant's Restoration
(Deuteronomy 30:3-10)

That then the Lord thy God will turn thy captivity, and have compassion upon thee, and will return and gather thee from all the nations, whither the Lord thy God hath scattered thee. If any of thine be driven out unto the outmost parts of heaven, from thence will the Lord thy God gather thee, and from thence will he fetch thee: And the Lord thy God will bring thee into the land which thy fathers possessed, and thou shalt possess it; and he will do thee good, and multiply thee above thy fathers. And the Lord thy God will circumcise thine heart, and the heart of thy seed, to love the Lord thy God with all thine heart, and with all thy soul, that thou mayest live. And the Lord thy God will put all these curses upon thine enemies, and on them that hate thee, which persecuted thee. And thou shalt return and obey the voice of the Lord, and do all his commandments which I command thee this day. And the Lord thy God will make thee plenteous in every work of thine hand, in the fruit of thy body, and in the fruit of thy cattle, and in the fruit of thy land, for good: for the Lord will again rejoice over thee for good, as he rejoiced over thy fathers: If thou shalt hearken unto the voice of the Lord thy God, to keep his commandments and his statutes which are written in this book of the law, and if thou turn unto the Lord thy God with all thine heart, and with all thy soul.

The promise of the covenant is threefold: restoration, forgiveness, and acceptance. The Lord promised that once Israel demonstrated a truly repentant heart, He would restore them as a nation, forgive their sins, and accept them once again as His chosen people.

When that time came, God would have compassion on them. He would reverse their situation. As He had brought them from Egypt, so would He bring them from all the people among whom He had scattered them, and restore them to the land which would now welcome them again because they were responding to the covenant from their hearts. What is stressed and emphasized here is the fact that the Lord would know exactly where His people were. He was/is not just a local God. He is God of the whole earth.

We must remember here that the purpose of the land was that the kingly rule of God would be built up in it. But once that kingly rule was seen as available because its nature was heavenly, the land became redundant. In the end the land was superseded by its greater spiritual reality, and today that kingly rule is centered on another land—the heavenly realm. The earthly land then becomes of no importance. All things are now centered on the kingly rule of God and on the King, Jesus Christ—and on our future with Him in the new heaven and the new earth (see 2 Peter 3:13; Revelation 21:1). If some of the Jews are to have a part in it, and they probably are, it can only be by becoming Christians. But the land is no longer the goal.

It must be noted here that a welcome within the covenant was always available, right from the start, to any who chose to follow God and come on His terms. Indeed, from the beginning Israel was inclusive of many who were not strictly descended from the patriarchs. These included the servants and slaves of the households, the mixed multitude of Exodus 12:38 and many who subsequently united with Israel in the covenant witnessed to by names such as that of Uriah the Hittite.

The mixed multitude was added to by the proselytes who joined themselves to Israel in the post-Old Testament days. The Christian church of new Israel is made up of both Jews and Gentiles; it was simply following the same pattern as seen in the Old Testament. There can be no other Israel in biblical terms than the one composed of those who are in Christ—the believing Israel (see Romans 9:6; 11:17, 23). There cannot be two Israels. If the rejected Israel is to become the believing Israel, it will be by response to Christ and a uniting with His people, who are now the true Israel.

This is the same restoration promise that God extends to each of us. Only God can recognize true repentance, and when He sees it, He is there with open arms to receive sinners, restore them, forgive them, and accept them into the family of God.

Consider the great compassion that God demonstrated toward the Israelites. He promised to bring together all the people of Israel, no matter how far away they had been scattered, and restore them to their Promised Land. He promised that they would once again prosper and multiply. He promised to chisel away their stubborn hearts (verse 6) so that they could understand the full meaning of love and worship of Him. And He would transfer their curse to their enemies! He promised all of this in spite of their many years of rebellion and disobedience.

This new people would be established because of what God would do, because of His work in their hearts (see Philippians 2:13). The idea behind this way of describing it (circumcising the heart) is taken from Deuteronomy 10:16. The thought is of a transformed heart which is turned to righteousness, either by the cutting away of sin and disobedience, as the foreskin is cut away in circumcision, or through the shedding of blood of the covenant, as the blood is spilled in circumcision (compare Genesis 17). But while in 10:16 they were to circumcise their own hearts, (although the thought was always there that it was with God's assistance), here it is God who is to circumcise their hearts. The circumcision of the heart was done by God, working in sovereign power, transforming the Israelites' lives and putting love for Him in their hearts so that they could fulfill their life purposes. This sovereign act of God once again demonstrated His mercy toward His people. We, modern Christians, are enjoying the mercy of God through the accomplished work of Christ on Calvary.

As always the thought behind living is not only that of being alive, but living abundant and fruitful lives—lives of joy and well-being and blessing (what Jesus spoke of as eternal life)—life under the kingly rule of God (see John 10:10).

God's blessings are innumerable, but they are conditional. To be blessed by God, we must first recognize that He is sovereign and supreme in the universe. We must then accept Him as our crucified and resurrected Savior. And finally, we must regard Him as our Father. Ideally, our fathers are the ones in our lives who provide and protect. This is what God did for Israel, and this is what God does for us. He provides for our needs (see Matthew 6:25-34). He protects us from harm (see Psalm 139:5). He has adopted us (see Ephesians 1:5) and He has given us His name (see 1 John 3:1). He has proven Himself to be a faithful Father. It is up to us to trust Him as His children.

Israel would eventually learn to trust God as their Provider, and be returned from exile. But Moses had to lay out the conditions for that restoration—obey God, and repent. First John 1:9 serves as a reminder to us that these same conditions apply to us today: "If we confess our sins, he is faithful and just to forgive us our sins, and to cleanse us from all unrighteousness."

The remnant of Israel who did return to God were few in number. They did eventually prosper and enjoy the covenant blessings that the Lord had promised to them. They experienced the abundance of God, they were fruitful in bearing many children, and their cattle and crops were abundant. This promise in fact has mainly continued to this day for those who are the church, the true Israel. God blesses their births, God blesses their work, and God blesses their productivity. Indeed, one of the church's great problems has always been that those who became Christians tended to prosper, and this then led to complacency and forgetting God. This is not, however, to doubt that there are many Christians who are poor, but God has a way by which He blesses everyone.

III. CONCLUDING REFLECTION

The renewal or rededication of a person's life involves two things: repentance and obedience to the Lord. No matter how terrible the sin we have committed, God will forgive us and restore us. But we must sense the need for repentance and actually repent. Then obedience, which is a by-product of true repentance, will be the outward sign that our hearts and souls now belong to God.

God has indescribable love for us as His children. God wants to forgive us and bring us back to Himself, too. The irony of this is that some people will not learn this until their world has crashed in around them.

PRAYER

Father in heaven, help us to be obedient to Your instructions that it may go well with us and our children. Remove the veil from our hearts so that we can seek You with pure hearts. In Jesus' name we pray. Amen.

WORD POWER

Circumcise (Hebrew: *muwl [moo- ool]*)—means to "cut off," "circumcise," or "remove impure things." In the Key Verse, "to circumcise" carries a deeper meaning. It means "to remove impure things from the mind, to purge by all means all residue of sin and profane things."

HOME DAILY BIBLE READINGS
(August 24-30, 2009)

God Calls for Decision

MONDAY, August 24: "Observe God's Laws" (Psalm 105:37-45)

TUESDAY, August 25: "Obey Christ's Commands" (Matthew 28:16-20)

WEDNESDAY, August 26: "A Gracious and Merciful God" (Nehemiah 9:16-20)

THURSDAY, August 27: "A Pledge of Obedience" (Joshua 24:14-24)

FRIDAY, August 28: "To Love God Is to Obey" (1 John 5:1-5)

SATURDAY, August 29: "I Love You, O Lord" (Psalm 18:1-6)

SUNDAY, August 30: "Return to the Lord" (Deuteronomy 30:1-10)